A GAZETTEER OF FRANCE • CLEMENT CRUTT[

Publisher's Note

The book descriptions we ask booksellers to display prominently warn that this is an historic book with numerous typos or missing text; it is not indexed or illustrated.

The book was created using optical character recognition software. The software is 99 percent accurate if the book is in good condition. However, we do understand that even one percent can be an annoying number of typos! And sometimes all or part of a page may be missing from our copy of the book. Or the paper may be so discolored from age that it is difficult to read. We apologize and gratefully acknowledge Google's assistance.

After we re-typeset and design a book, the page numbers change so the old index and table of contents no longer work. Therefore, we often remove them.

Our books sell so few copies that you would have to pay hundreds of dollars to cover the cost of our proof reading and fixing the typos, missing text and index. Instead we usually let our customers download a free copy of the original typo-free scanned book. Simply enter the barcode number from the back cover of the paperback in the Free Book form at www.general-books.net. You may also qualify for a free trial membership in our book club to download up to four books for free. Simply enter the barcode number from the back cover onto the membership form on our home page. The book club entitles you to select from more than a million books at no additional charge. Simply enter the title or subject onto the search form to find the books.

If you have any questions, could you please be so kind as to consult our Frequently Asked Questions page at www.general-books.net/faqs.cfm? You are also welcome to contact us there. General Books LLC™, Memphis, USA, 2012.

NEW J E *Я?.* FY COLLEGE ¿.IbR.-kKY л

GAZETTEER

O F FRANCE, *C0KÎA1KIKG* CITY, TOWN, AND VILLAGE, IN THAT EXTENSIVE COUNTRY,

Shewing the Diftances of the Cities and great Towns from PARIS-.

And at the End of the fmall Towns and Villages noting the Post» Ornees through which Letters, &c. are conveyed to each.

With a dejeriftive Accnnt tf EVERY COUNTRY; BOUNDARIES, EXTENT, AND NATURAL PRODUCE»

Including the chief Harbours, Bays, Rivers, Canals, Forefts, Mine«, Hills, Vales, and Medicinal Springs.

The Whole including above Forty Tboufand Places,

Illuftrated with a Mar, divided into Departmsnts.

I N T H RE E VOLUMES. VOL. ЦТ.

LONDON:

Printed for G. G. J. and J. ROBINSON, Pater-nofler-Rew.   M,DCC,XCHL

JESTIPRE, a village of Flan-ladois, in the election of Condom, *f.* irs, in the diocefe of Ypres, and *Condom.* QU *Quemmexy,* a village of Picardy, irr the diocefe of Noyon. *p. Noycn Quenne,* a river of Niyernois.

Quemcie, a village of FrancheComté, in the bailiwick, of VefouL *p. Vejoui.*
Quenoirville, a village of Normandy, in the eleftion of Caudebec. *p. Caudebec.*
Queraudy, a village of Bretagne, in the diocefe and receipt of Treguier. *p. Guingamp. Quercy, le,* a province in the government of Guienne, bordered on the eaft by Rouerguc and Auvergne, on the fouth by upper Languedoc, on the weft by Périgord, and Agénois, and on the north by Limofin ¡ it contains two bifhopricks Cahors and Montauban: the air is good and the land fertile. Cahors is the capital. *Querenam,,* a place of Flanders, in the generality of Maubeugc. *p. Valencicnnes. Querfuntun, Quergloff, Quergriß, & Quergriß-Mtelou,* villages of Bretagne, in the diocefc and receipt of Quimper. *p. Quimper. Querien,* a village of Bretagne, in the diocefc and receipt of Quimper. *p. Quimptrle. Quenen-pres-Quimperle',* a village of Bretagne, in the diocefe and receipt ef Quimper. *p. Rofporden. Querieux,* a village of Picardy, in the eleftion of Doulens. *p. Corbie. Querigut,* or *Guerigut,* a fmall town of Donnezan, in the receipt of Foix. *p. Mont-Louis. Querity,* a village of Bretagne, in the diocefe and receipt of S. Bricux. *p. S. Brieux.* ¿¿*verle,* a convent, in the diocefe of Quimper, in Bretagne, *p. Quimper. Querlouan,* a village of Bretagne, in the diocefe and receipt of S. Polde-Léon. *p. Morlaix. Quermarie-Sulard,* a village of Bretagne,-in the diocefe and receipt of Treguier. *p. Guingamp. Queme',* a pariih of Normandy, in the diocefc of Coûtances./. *Coûtâmes. Qirthou,* a market town of Nor» mandy, in the election of Valognes. *p, Valognes. Suaigny,* aparilhof Burgundy, in the diocefe and bailiwick of Dijon. *p. Dijon.* ¡¡¡*uettnille,* a town of Normandy, in the election of Pont-Audemer. *f. Pont-Audtmer. Sjinuu-villers,* a town of Picardy, in the diocefe and election of Amiens. *p. Amiens. Sueue-itAjajJ'e,* a village bf Poitou, in the election of Niort, *p. Niort.* ¿*lueue-dc-MouШ,* a village of Champagne, in the diocefe and election of Langres. *p. Langres. Sfuène-en-Biie, la,* a village of the Ifle of France, in the diocefe and election of Paris, in the road from Paris to Angers; 7 leagues from Verfaillcs, 8 from Dreux', 10 from Séve, and 13 from Paris. *Bureau de pofie. Sfaevcr,* a village of Bretagne, in the diocefç and receipt of S. *M»o.p. Diñan.' Quevillm,* or S *Martin-de-Sluevillon,* a village of Normandy, in the diocefe and election of Rouen.. *Rouen. Qucvilly,* a fmall town of Normandy, m the diocefe and election of Rouen. *Rouen. Queulbe, la,* a town of Auvergne, in the diocefe and election of Clermont, *p. Clermont. Sluiurecoun,* a village of Normandy, 111 the election

of Ncufchûtcl. *p. Ñeufcbatel. Sueremont*, a village of Normandy, in the election of Arques, *p. Diefpe. Querevilte*, a viilageof Normairdy,. in the election of Pont-de-PArche *p. Pont-de-ΓAnbe. Quereville-la-Mtlon*, a village of Normandy, in the diocefe and election of Rouen, *p. Rouen. Queujfey-Us-Grancey*, a village of Champijjnc, in the diocefe and election of Langres. *p. Langres. Sjteutrey*, a village of FrancheComté, in the bailiwick of Gray. *Gray. ¿¡ueuvri, la*, a village ef Orleân» . *Racbieufe-de-Vaugrenan, la, л* villige of Burgundy, in the bailiwick of Auxonne. *p. Challón. Raconay*, a place of Burgondy,.in the diocefe and bailiwick of Challón. *f. Challón. Racju'mgbem*, a village of Artois, in the bailiwick of Aire. *p. S. Omer. Radion & Chaffendu*, a village of Franche-Comté, in the bailiwick of Veíoul. *p. Lure. Rademont*, a place of Brie, in the diocefe and eleflion ofMeaux. *p-Lify. Radenac*, a village of Bretagne, in the diocefe and receipt of Vannes, *p. Pontivi. Radepont&le HameUde-Bonnemarre*, a village of Normandy, in the diocefe and election of Rouen.*p. Ecouy. Raderßeitn*, a place of Alface, in the bailiwick of Thann, *p. Rouffach. Radeval*, a village of Normandy in the eleflion of Andely. *p. Gaillon. Radicaßel*, a village of Normandy, in the election. of Caudebec. *p, Lillebonne. Radingbem*, a village of Artois, in the bailiwick of S. Pol./. *Aire. Radinguiben*, a fmalltown of Flanders, in the fubdeligation of Lille. . *tille. Radon*, a village of Normandy, in the eleflion of Alencon./). *Alençm. Radonmlliers*, a village of Champagne, in the eleflion of Bar-furAube. *p. Vandeurvrt. Raffe*, a priory of Champagne, in Ihe dioceie of Tonnerre, *p. Tonnerre. Raffetot*, a village of Normandy, in the eleflion of Caudebec. *p. Lillebonne. Rageaurt*, a village of Champagne, in the eleflion of Joinville. *p. Join-mille. Ragny.* I. A place of Burgundy, in the bailiwick of Avalon, *p. Avelon.* a. A place of Burgundy, in the diocefe and bailiwick of Challón, *p. Challón. Ragny-le-Cbâteau*, a place of Burgundy, in the bailiwick of Challón. *f. Auxonne. Ragußt*, a village of Provence, in the diocefe and viguery of Riez. *p. Barjols. Rahay*, a village of Maine, in the eleflion of Chàtcau-du-Loir./. *Mondoubleau. Rahon.* I. A village of Franche. . Comté, in the bailiwick of Dole. *p. Dole.* 2. A village of Franche-Comté, in the bailiwick of Baume.. *Baume. Rajajp, la,я* village of Forez, inthc eleflion of Montbrifon./». *Aiontbrifon. Raillanne*, See *Reillanne. Raillencourt.* See 6. *Olle. Raillicourt*, a village of Champagne, in the eleflion of Rethel. *p. Retbel. Rahnbertot*, a village of Normandy» in the eleflion of Montivilliers. *p. Harßeur.*
Äaba»i,avil!ageofFranche-Comté, in the bailiwick of Dole. *p. Dole. Ramcbeval*,avillageof Picardy, in the eleflion of Doulens. *p. Douler.s. Raincourt*, a village of FrancheComté, in the bailiwick of Vcfoul. *p. Yc/oul.-.*
Raineval. I. A village of Picardy, in the eleflion of Mondidicr. *p. Mondier,* 2. A village of Picardy, in the diocefe and eleflion of Laon. *p. Loon. Raneville.* i. A village of Picardyj in the eleflion of Doulens. *p.Douleni,* 2. A village of Champagne, in the diocefe and eleflion of Rheims, *p. Rheims. Rainey, le,* or *Lhny-le-Cbdteau*, a village of the Ifle of France, in the diocefe and eleflion of Paris, *p. Bondf. Rainfremlle*, a village of Normandy, in the eleflion of Arques.. *Dieppe, Rainfart*, a village of Flanders, in the government of Maubeuge. *fx. Maubeuge. Raitrval.* See *Raingeval. Rain-villier*, a village of Picardy, in the diocefe and eleflion of Beauvais. *p. Beauvais. Ran.* See *Ret». Raijmos*, a villnge of Flanders, in the diocefe of Cambr ay. *p. Valendenms. Rmffac.* I. A village of Roucrgue, in the eleflion of Milhaud. /. *Milbaud,* i. A village of upper Langue» 1 doc, in the dioceie and receipt of Car caffonne. *p. Carcaffbnne. Jз/»оиге*,a place of Franche-Comté, in the bailiwick of Orgelet, *p. LomU'Saatàcr; Raivon*, a village of Limofin, in the dioccfe and generality oi Limoges. *p. Limoges. Ra'uc*, a village of Angoumois, in the dioccfe and election of Angoal&rhe. *p. Villefagnan. Raixe.* See *Refe. Ravzeu*, a village of Beauce, in the election of Orleans, *p. Chartres. Ralleu*, a place of Rouffiillon,
in the viguery of Conflans. *p. Villefrancbt-de-Conßans. Ramaffe*, a village of Breflê, in the bailiwick of Bourg, *p. Bourgen-BreJfè. Ramatuelle*, a village of Provence, in the viguery of Draguignan. *p. Eraguignan. Rambaud*, a village of Dauphiny, in the dioccfe and election of Gap. *p. Gap. Rambefeaurt*, a village of Champagne, in the election of Vitry. *p. Vitry.* jRWü¿ft,aplaceof Franche-Comté, in the bailiwick of Lons-le-Saunier. *p. Lons-le-Saunier. Rambluxin*, a place of Merlin, in the dioccfe and receipt of Verdun, *p. Verdun. Rambouillet.* I. A market town of Beauce, in the dioccfe and election of Chartres, in the road from Paris to Chartres, 5 leagues from Maintenon, 9 from Chartres; 7 from Verfailles, 10 from Séve, and 13 from Pari«. *Sureau Je poße.* 2. A château in the neighbourhood of Paris, fo called.
Rambure, a town of Picardy, in the dioccfe and election of Amiens. *p. Abbeville. Ramburelles*, a village of Picardy, m the dioctfeandelection of Amiens. *p. Ameni.. Rame*, a village of Dauphiny, in the receipt of Briançon. *p. Embrun. Rameau*, a place of Champagne, in the election of Jonnerre. *p. Chablis. Ramecourt*, a place of Artois, ia Ihe bailiwick of S. Pol. *p. Лги. Ramée, la.* See *Vinay. Ramejan*, a place of lower Languedoc, in the dioccfe and receipt of Béliers, *p. Be'xurs. Ramerfmatt*, a place of Alface, in the bailiwick of Thann./». *Rcuffacb. Rameru*, a town of Champagne, in the dioccfe and election of Troyes. *p. Arch. Ramicowt*, a village of Picardy, in the clectionofS. Quentin./. *S.Sjuentiit. Ramier*, awood of Io54arpcnrs,ia the jurifdiction of the Ifle of Jourdain. *Ramillards, les*, a village of Nivernois, in the election of Gannat. *p. Cannât. RamilTiet.* I. A village of Flanders, in the diocefe of Cambray. *p. Cambray.* 2. A village in the province of Brabant, above 4 leagues from Namur, memorable by a victory obtained by the Duke of Malborough over the French army in 170S. *Ramilly-les-VaudcK*, a village of Champagne, in the diocefe and election of Troyes. *p. Troyes. Ramillu.* See *Ramiltics. Ramons*, a place of Beam, in the receipt of Orthez. *p.*

Ortbez. Ramon-ville, a village of upper Languedoc, in the dioccfe and receipt of Touloufe. *p. Touloufe. Ramoru.* See *Rameru. Ramoulens,* a village of Armagnac, in the diocefe and election of Auch. *p. Aucti. Ramovhi,* a village of Orléannoîs, in the election of Pithiviers. *p. Pitbiviers. Ramoufies,* a village of Flanders, in the government of *Avefnes. pAvef/ies. Rampan,* a village of Normandy, in the election of S. Lo. *p. S. Lo. Rampieu,* a village of Périgord, in the diocefe and election of Sarlat. *p. Sarlat. RampiHcn,a* village of Brie, in the election of Rozoy. *p. Nanga.. Rampant,* a village of Mcflîn, in the dioccfe and receipt of Verdun. /V *Verdun. Rampoux,* a village of Quercy, ip the diocefe and election of Cahors. *p. Cahors. Ranafe',* a town of Anjou, in the diocefeand election ofAngers.jb.-¿i»¿erí *Ranbures.* See *Rambure. Ranbhiffm,* a place of Meflin, in the diocefe and receipt of Verdun, *p. Verdun. Rancay,* a fief of Berry, in theparifh of Nierne. *Ranee, la,* a river of Bretagne, which empties itfelf into the fea near S. Malo. *Raneé,* I. A place of Bretagne, in the diocefeand receipt of Rennes, *p. Semes,* 2. Aplace of Domhes.in the thatellany of Ligneu. *p. Villefranche.*
Äa»ce/iay,aplaceof Franche-Comté, in the diocefe and bailiwick of Befan£on. *p, Bejançon. Rancermes Cbarmoy,* a village ef Flanders, in the diocefe of Cambray, *p. Cbarlentont. Ranees,* a village of Champagne, in the diocefe and election of Troyes./. *Vttry. Ranchat,* a village of Beaujolois, in the election of Villefranche. *p. Fille' franche. Rancbecourt,* a place of Artois, in the diocefe and bailiwick of Arras. *p. Arras. Ranchen,* a village of Normandy, in the election of Caudebec. *p. Catsdebic. Rancbot,* a village of FrancheComté, in the bailiwick of Dole. *p. Vole. Rancby,* a village of Normandy, in the diocefe and election of Bayeux. *p. Bayeux. Rancogne,* a fmall town of Angcumois, in the diocefe and election of Angoulême. *p. la Rochefoucault. Rançon.* Ï. A town ofLimofin, in the diocefe and election of Limoges. 4 *p. Bellac.* 2. A fmall rjver f Normandy, that falls into the Seine, at Caudebec. 3. A wood of 1190 arpents in the jurifdiction of Gueret.

Rancours, a village of Picardy, in the election of Péronne. *p. Perenne.* (Umcurel, a village of Dauphiny, in the diocefe and election of Va» lence. *p. Valence. Rancy iä Molaife,* a village of Burgundy, in the bailiwick of S. Laurent, *p. Macon. Rancy-les-Viltars,* a village of Burgundy, in the bailiwick of Challón, *p. Louans. Randans,* a town of Auvergne, in the election of Riom. *p. Riem. Randes, les,* a village of FrancheComté, in the bailiwick of Dole. *p. Dole. RandevMlers,* a village of FrancbeComté, in the bailiwick of Baume. *p. Baume. Randeynes,* a village of Rouergue, in the diocefe and election of Rhodez. *p. Rhoden. Randon* Ê? *Rochebelot,* a village of lower Languedoc, in the diocefe and receipt of Mende. *p. Mende. Randonay,* a village of Perche, in the election of Mortagne. *p. Γ Aigle. Rendue,* a village of Alface, in the bailiwick of Ville, *p. Scheiefiat. Ranée,* a place of Bretagne, in the diocefe and receipt of Nantes, *p. Vitre'. Ranfeugere,* a village of Normandy, in the diocefe and election of Rouen, *p. Rouen. Rangée £wr/,*avillage of Champagne, in the diocefe and election of Langrcs. *p. Langres. Rangen & Mittelkurtos,* places of Alface, in the diocefe of Strafburg. *p. Slrafiurg. Rangmal,* or *Raima!,* an abby in the diocefe of Toul. *p. Tail. Rans & les Randes,* a village of Franche-Comté, in the bailiwick of Dole. *p. Dole. Ranjannes,* or £ *§juentin-de-Ranfan nés,* a village of Saintonije, in the election of Saintes, *p. S, Clbardeaux. Rat/art.* I. A village of Artois, in the diocefe and bailiwick of Arras, *p. Arras.* 2. A place of Picardy, in the election of Doulens. *p. Doulens. Ranfinniere,* a village of Champagne, in the election of Langres. *p. Langres.* Ёлмu1щ a convent in the faux. bourg of *Auxtm.p. Auxerrt. Rantigny,* a village of Picardy, in the eleflion of Clermont.*p. Clermont. Ronton,* a town of Tourainc, in the diocefe of Angers, *p. Lovdun. Rantziviller,* a village of Alface, in the bailiwick of Landfer./. *Altcbircb. Ranville,* a village of Normandy, in the eleflion of Caen. *p. Trouard. Ranzev*elle, a place of FrancheComté, in the bailiwick of Vefoul. *p. Vefoul. Rafee', let,* a beautiful feat in the quarter of S. Antoine, Paris. *Rafi/ly,* a village of Normandy, in the election of Falaife. *p. Falaife. Rapolfflein,* or *Ribauiere,* a town of Alface, fituated near the river Stenbach, about 3 leagues from Colmar. *p. Colmar. Rappentzvitler,* a village of Alface, în the bailiwick of Ferrette, *p. Hinhaue. Rapjecourt,* a village of Champagne, in the eleflion of Ste. Manéhould. *p. Sie. Mane'hould. Rapfy,* a fmall town of Artois, in the bailiwick of Hefdin, *p. Hefdin. Raray,* a village of Picardy, in the diocefe and elect ion of Scnlis./. *Senlis. Rara,* See 5. Pierremotit. *Rat-de-Blanquet,* a narrow ftrair of the fea, between Aldernay and Cape la Hogue. *Refit.* See *Razese. Raßguierit,* a village of Upper Languedoc, in the diocefe and receipt of Alet. *p. Limoux. Raine,* a town of Normandy, in the eleflion of Falaife. *p. Argentan. Rafincs,* a village of Poitou, in the eleflion of Richelieu, *p. Richelieu. Rafieh,* a village of Quercy, in the the diocefe and eleflion of Cahors. *p. Cabort. Rafleau, le,* a village of Venaiffin, in the judicature of Carpentras. *p. Avignon. Ratayrens,* a place of Languedoc, in the diocefe and receipt of Alby. *p. Alby. Raleen, le,* л village of Marche, in the eleflion of Guerer. *p. Gueref. Rattnelle,* a village of Burgundy, in the diocefe and bailiwick of Challón, *p. Challón. Ratier,* a place of Franche-Comté, in the bailiwick of Dole. *p. Dole. Raiieres,* a village of Dauphiny, in the eleflion of Romans, *p. Tain. Raiten* 65? *Nantet,* a village of Dauphiny, in the diocefe and election of Grenoble, *p. Grenoble. RatimUle',* a village of Normandy, in the diocefe and eleflion of Rouen. *p. le Bolebard. Ratonneau,* one of three i Hands, about a league for Marfeilles. *Ratte,* a parifh of Burgundy, in the bailiwick of Challón, *p. Louant. Raixrveiller,* a place of Alface, in the bailiwick of Thann, *p. Rouffaib. Ravaux.* i. A village of Ñiver» nois, in the eleflion of Charité-furLoire, *p. la Charit/, z.* A priory in the diocefe of Angoulême. *p. It Rocbefoucault. Raucoulet,* a place of Upper Languedoc, in the diocefe and receipt of Alby. *p. Alby. Raucour,* a village of FrancheComté, in the bailiwick of Gray. *p. Gray. Raucourt.* 1. A fmall town of Champagne, in the receipt of Sedan, *p. Sedan,* a. A village of Meffin, in the diocefe and receipt of Metz. *p. Metx.* 3. A place of Picardy, in the diocefe and eleflion of Laon. *p S. Quentin.* 4. A place of Flanders in the government of Qucfnoy. *p. le Quefmy. Rarveau,* a village of Nivernois, in the eleflion of Charité, *p. la Charité. Ravel,* a village of Dauphiny, in the eleflion of Montelimart. *p. Montelimart. Ravenel,* a town of Picardy, ir» the eleflion of Mondidier. *p. S. Jufl. Rauenne-Fontawe,* .a village of Champagne, in the diocefe and election of Langres. *p. Langret.* Ra-venouville, a village of Normandy, in the eleflion of Caientaov, *Carentan. Rcrviiſstrgbe,* a village of Flankers, in the cúocefe of S. Omer.' *p. Gravelines. Ravie'res,* a town of Champagne, $n the election of Tonnerre, about 2 leagues from Argenteuil. *p. Tonnerre. Ramgné,* a town of Maine, in the diocefe and eleflion of Mans./. *Preztn-Pail.* RavilloUs, a place of FrancheComté, in the diocefe and bailiwick of S. Claude, *p. S. Claude. Rauften,* a town of Auvergne, in the eleflion of Aurillaq. *p. Aurillac. Ranrah,* a priory in the diocefe of Meaux. *Rauſsmillc,* aparifh of Normandy, in the diocefe of Coûtances. *p. Coûtâmes. Raumlle-la-Bigot, & Rauvlle-larlact,* fmall towns of Normandy, in the eleftion of Valognes. *p. ValogЖX. Rauxbemlourg,* a château in the diocefe of Strafburg. *p. Haguenau. Rauxier,* a foreft of 17СЮ arpents, in the generality of Montaubau. *Raiman, a* fmall town of Bajadois, in the election of Condom, *p. Coffalon. Rataangues,* a village of Armagac, in the diocefe and eleflion of Auch. *p. Aucb. Ray.* 1, A fmall town of Normandy, in the election of Verncuil. *f. Vtmeuil.* 2. A fmall town of franche-Comté, in the bailiwick of Cray. *p. Gray.* 3. A village of Artois, in the bailiwick of Hefdin. . *Befdm. RayKJfon,* a wood of 80 arpents, in the jurifdiftion of Gueret in Marche. *Raymont,* a village of Bourbonnais, in the diocefe of Bourges, *p. Bourges. Rays,* a village of Normandy, in the eleftion of Carenten. *p. Canutan. Rayffac,* » place of Upper Languedoc, in the diocefe and receipt of Mircpoix. *p. Mirepoix. Raxat,* a fmall town of Périgord, in the diocefe and eleflion of Périgueux, *p. Bergerac. Razat a"Emit, & Razat-de-Sauſsgnac,* towns of Périgord, in the diocefe and eleflion of Sarlat. *p. Sarlat. Raxe,* a village of Franche-Comté, in the bailiwick of Vefoul. . *Ycfoul. Razengues,* a village of Armagnac, in the diocefe and eleflion of Auch. *p. Aucb. Razez.* i. A country of Languedoc, of which Liinoux is the capital. 2. A fmall town of Limofin, in the diocefe and eleflion of Limoges. *Bureau de poſse. Re',* or *Rb/,* an ifland in the bay of Bifcay, about 3 leagues westward of Rochelle; it contains 6 pariihe» and 4 forts; its chief productions arc wine and fait. *Real.* i. A village of Rouffillon, in the viguery of Conflans. *p. Vdlefrancbe-de-Conſsans.* 2. An abby in the diocefe of Poitiers, *p. Cbauny.* 3. A judicature dependant on the fénéchaufsée of Riom. *p. Riom. Real, la,* a town of Rouffillon, in the diocefe and viguery of Perpignan. *p. Perpignan. Reale, la,* an abby in the diocefe of Perpignan, *p. Perpignan: Re'alcamp,* a village of Normandy, in the eleflion of Eu. *p. Anmale. Réaîmont,* a town of Upper Languedoc, in the diocefe and receipt of Alby. *p. Caſsres. Re'alon,* a place of Dauphiny, in the diocefe and eleflion of Gap. *p. Gap. Re'ahÀlle,* a town of Quercy, on the rjver Aveyrou, about z leagues from Montauban. *p. Muniaubau. Rc'au,* a village of Gâtinois, in the eleflion of Melun, *p. Mehm. Reau,* or *la Reaux,* an abby in the diocefe of Poitiers, *p. Poitiers. Re'aule.* See *Rale. Reaumont,* a village of DaupVny, in the eleflion of Romans, *p. Rattans. Reaumur,* a town of Poitou, in the eleflion of Fontenay. *p, Pouffange. Rcaut,* a village of Condomois, in the diocefe ind election of Condom. *p. Condom. Reauville,* a village of Provence, in the diocefe of Die. *p. le Buis. Reauvis,* a village of Berry, in the eleflion of Châtre, *p. la Chatre. Reaux,* a town of Saintonge, in the diocefe and eleflion of Saintes. *p. Jomsac. Rebais,* or *Rebels,* a town of Brie, in the diocefe of Meaux, and election of Coulomiers; about 3 leagues from Coulomiers, 6 from Creffy, and 7 from Meaux. *Bureau de poſse. Rebec,* a place of Agénois, in the diocefe and eleflion of Agen. *p. Agen. Rebel.* See *Revel. Rebenacq,* a village of Beam, in the receipt of Pau. *p. Oleron. Reberques,* a village of Picardy, in the generality of Amiens, *p. Montreuil. Reberv'dler,* a village of Normandy, in the eleflion of Verneuil. *p. Verneuil.. Rebefques* Êf *Choquel,* a village of Artois, in the bailiwick of Aire. *p. Aire. Rebetos.* I. A village of Normandy, in the diocefe and eleflion of Rouen, *p. Rouen,* a. See *Rebais.* .*Rebique,* a village of Upper Languedoc, in the diocefe and receipt of Touloufe. *p. Touloufe. Rebmrcin,* a village of Berry, in the eleflion of Iffoudun. *p. Vatan. Rebourguil,* a village or Rouergue, in the eleflion of Milhaud. *p. S. Affrique. Rebourfe,* a village of Niverneis, in the eleflion of Charité-fur-Loire. *p. la Chante'. Rebrechien,* a town of Orléannois, in the diocefe and generality of Orléans, *p. Orleans. Rebreviette,* a village of Artois, in the bailiwick of S. Pol. *p. Doutent. Rebreuves-fur-Cauche,* a village of Artois, in the bailiwick of S. Pol.*p. Doulens. Rebreu: is,* a village of Artois, in the diocefe and bailiwick of Arras. *p. Arras. Rebuùns, Its,* a place of Burgundy, in the generality of Dijon, *p. BarJur-Sàne. Recamadour.* See *Roquemadour. Recanoz,* a village of FrancheComté, in the bailiwick of Poligny. *p. Lons-le-Saunier. Recey-fur-Omfe,* a village of Burgundy, in the bailiwick of Challón. *p. Challón. Recbaſsjere, la.* See *Communailles. Recbcray & Adromay,* a village of Meffin, in the diocefe and receipt of Metz, *p. Met». Recbcfy,* a village of Alface, in th« bailiwick of Dolle. *p. Alfcbircb. Recbicourt-la-Pet'tie,* Êf *Rechicourtlc-Cbâteau,* villages of Merlin, in the diocefe and receipt of Metz. *p. Chrmont-en-Argonne. Rechotte,* a place of Alface, in the bailiwick of Beftort. *p. Beffort. Reclame & Baugy,* a parifh of Burgundy, in the diocefe and bailiwick of Autun. *p. Autun. Reclainwlle,* a village of Beauce, in the diocefe and eleflion of Chartres, *p. Chartres. Reclancourt,* a place of Champagne, in the eleftion of Chaumout. *p. Chaumont.* Recline. Sec *Reclame.* Reclenne. See *Villfrs.* Rcclingbcm, a village of Artois, in the bailiwick of Aire, *pi Aire.* Recloje, a village of Gitinois, in the eleftion of Nemoura. *p. Fontainebleau.* Reclus, le, a village of Champagne, in the diocefe and eleftion of Troyes, *p. Sezanne.* Reclus, le, Sf *la Prrinery*, a village of Forez, in the eleftion of S. Etica, ne. *p. S. Etienne.* Recologne, a village of FrancheComté, m the diocefe and bailiwick of Befancon. *p. Lure.* Rtcohgnesles-Gray, a place of Franche-Comté, in the bailiwick, of Gray, *p. Gray.* Rccoubel, a village of Dauphiny, in the election of Montelimart. *p. Die.* Rkduus, a village of Lower Languedoc, in the diocefe and receipt of Mende. *p. Marvejols.* Recourfe, a river of Burgundy, that falls into the Loire. Recourt. I. A village of Champagne, in the diocefe and election of Langrcs. *p. Langres.* 1. A village cf Meifin, in the diocefe and receipt cf Verdun, *p. Verdun.* 3. A place cf Artois, in the diocefe and bailivick of Arras, *p. Arras.* Recourt, le. See *Ltxay, Cuctery.* Recouvrance. 1. A village of Champagne, in the diocefe and election of Kheims. *p. Retbel.* 2. A place of Alface, in the bailiwick of Delle, *p. S'f'rt.* Recoux, le, a village of Lower Languedoc, in.the diocefe and receipt of Mende. *p. Mende.* Recaues c£f *Vroland*, a village of Artois, in the diocefe and bailiwick cf S. Orner, *p. Montreuil.* Recruttet, a forcft on the frontiers of Lorraine and Meflin. Reculais, a village of Dauphiny, in the election of Romans. *Romans.* Reculas, a village of Dauphiny, in the diocefe and election of Grenoble. *p. Grenoble.* Recullc, le, a village of Normandy, in the election of Vire, *p. Vire.* Recurt, a village of Armagnac, in the election of Rivière-Verdun, *p. Caflelnau-de-Mtdoc.* Recy, a village of Champagne, in the diocefe and election of Chalons. /. *Cbálom.* Rcdcne', a village of Bretagne, in the diocefe and receipt of Vannes, *p. £$uimperle'.* Riderdorff, a village of Alface, in the bailiwick of Ferrette. *p. Huningue.* Rcdejan, a village of Lower Ladjutdoc, in the diocefe and receipt of Nîmes, *p. Beaucaire'.* Redon, a town of Bretagne, fitu-ated on the Vilaine, in the diocefe and receipt of Vannes; about 3 leagues from Rieux, 5 from Rochefort, 23 from Rennes, and 15 from Vannes. Bureau de pofie. Redondem, a forcft of 44 arpents, in the jurifdiction of Gueret in Marche.

Redorte, la, a place of Upper Languedoc, in the diocefe and receipt of Mirepoix. *p. Narbonne.* Redours, les, a village of Poitou, in theelection of Fontenay. *p. Fonttnay le-Comte.* Reacurtier, a village of Dauphiny, in the election of Montelimart. *p. Montelimart.* Rcfrancbe, a village of FrancheComté, in the bailiwick of Ornans. *p. Bejancon.* Refuge, or *le Refuge*, a convent in the diocefe of Cambray. Regalle, a village of Gafcony, in the diocefe and election of Comminges. *p. Montrejeau.* Regat, a fmall town of Upper Lan» guedoc, in the diocefe and receipt of Mirepoix. *p. Mirepoix.* Regenart, a village of Maine, in the election of Laval. . *Laval.* Reges, a village of Champagne, in the diocefe and election of Tfoycs. *p. Arcis-fur-Aube.* Regbade, a village of Auvergne, in the election of Brioude. *p. Brioude,* Regie, la, a convent in Limofin. Regliade, a village of Auvergne, in the election of Brioude. *p. Brioude.* Regijheim, a village of Alface, in the bailiwick of Bollveiller. *p. Rouf. ficb.* Regmalard. See *Remalard.* Rignaunillc, a village of Artois, in the bailiwick of Hcfdin. *p. Hefdin,* Regncv'ille. I. A village of Normandy, in the diocefe and election of of Coûtanccs. *p. Coûtances.* 2. A village of Normandy, in the election of Valognes. *p. Valognes.* 3. A village of Meflin, in the diocefe and: receipt of Verdun, *p. Verdun,* Recency, a village of FrancheComté, in the bailiwick of Vefoul. *p. Vefoul.* RegnUr-l'Eduje, a village of Picàrdy, in the election of Doulenj. *p. jOoulens.* Regny. I. A town of Forez, in the election of Roanne, *p. Roanne,* 2. A village of Berry, in the diocefe and election of Bourges, *p. Bourges.* 3. A village of Berry, in the election of S. Amand. *S. Amand.* 4. A village of Picardy, in the election of Guife. *p. Guife.* 5. A pariih of Burgundy, in the bailiwick of Charolks. *p. Dijon.* Regues, a village of Lower Languedoc, in the diocefe and receipt of Alais, *p. Aim.* Seguigny, a village of Bretagne, in the diocefe and receipt of Vannes. /. *Vannes.* Regujfe, a village of Provence, in the viguery of Barjols. *p. Barjo/s.* Recberray, a village of Meflin, in the bailiwick of Vic. *p. Vic.* Rebeu, le, a village of Bretagne, in the diocefe and receipt of Rennes, *p. JUnnes.* Rebon &Пиtoм, a place of Meflin, jn the diocefe and receipt of Metz. *p. Longwy.* Rejaumcnt. 1. A village of Armagnac, in the election of Lomagne. *p. Caßelnau-de-Magnac.* 2. A forelt of 300 arpents, in the generality of Montauban. Reiciemceyer, or *Reicbenveyler*, a town of Alface, near Keyfcrfberg. *p. Colmar.* Reichsfelden, a village of Alface, in the diocefe of Strafburg. *p. Molfhe'm.* Reich//,offen. See *Rei/boffen.* Riigadc, a village of Limofin, in the diocefe and election of Tulles, *p. Tulles.* Reig/ife, a village of Picardy, in the election of Péronne. *p. Péronne.* Reignac, or *le Fan*, a village of Touraine, in the election of Loches. *p. Loches.* Relgnat, a village of Auvergne, in the diocefe and elelion of Clermont, *p. Clermont.* R/ignat-jur-Champcix, a village of Auvergne, in the diocefe and election of Clermont, *p. Clermont.* Reigne'. See *Souligné.* Rtltiac is *Treignac*, a village of Limofin, in the diocefe and election of Tulles, *p. Tulles.* Rcillac-Xaintrle, a town in the diocefe and election of Tulles. . *Tulles.* Reillanne, an ancient city of Provence, fituated on the fide of a hill, near the fmall river Largue, about 1 leagues from Manofque and Forcalquier, 4 from Apt, and 9 from Aix. *p. Forcalquier.* Rúllannet!, a fmall town of Dauphiny, with a château, *p. Aft.* Reillans, a place of Franche-Comté, in the bailiwick of Baume, *p. Baume.* Ríilly, a figniory of Normandy, in the election of Gifors. *p. Cbaumont.* Reimbacb, a place of Alface, in the bailiwick of Thann, *p. Rouffacb.* Reimbacb (ä Kircbberg, a village of Alface, in the bailiwick of Beffort. *p. Beffort.* Reitr.erfheim, a village of Alface, in the bailiwick of Landfer. *p. Huni»* Reimerfweiller, a place of Alface, in the bailiwick of Hatten, *p. FortLouis.* Reims. See *Rheims.* Reims-le-Brûlé, a village of Champagne, in the election of Vitry. *p. Vitry.* ReinetMle, I. A place of Champagne, in the diocefe and election of Chalons, *p. Rheims.* 2. See *Herpont. Reingeldoiff,* a place of Alface, in the bailiwick of Hagucnau./. *Haguenau. Rtinhards-Munflcr,* a place of Alface, in the bailiwick of Weftoffcn» *p. Saverne. Reiningben,* a village of Alface, in the diocefe of Bale. *p. Rouffacb. Reinnecourt,* a village of Picardy, in the election of Péronne. *p. Clermont.* ... *JRe'iperJweiUr,* a town of Alfacev *Reitcbsfeldten.* See *Rricbsftldtn. Reifhwog& Griefenbeim,* a village of Alface, in the bailiwick of Fleckenftein. *p. Straßurg. Rcifhiffen,* a town of Alface, in the bailiwick of Obcrbronne. *p. Haguenau. Reifebulleiller,* a village of Alface, in the dioccfe of Straiburg. *p. Straffarg. ReittbweUler,* a village of Alface, in the bailiwick of Bouxvillier. *p. Saverne. Reix,* a village of Marche, in the eleftion of Buurganeuf. *p. Gueret. Mans,* a village of FrancheComté, in the bailiwick of Lons-leSaunier. *p. Lons-leSaunier. Rt. 'ay, le,* a priory in the dioccfe of Tours, *p. lours. Relecq,* or *Reßes,* an abby in the dioccfe of S. Pol-de-Léon. *p.Morlaix. Reliae.* 1, A town of Auvergne, in the election of Brioudc. *p. Brioude.* a. A village of Quercy, in the election of Figeac. *p. Figeac. Reliaguet,* a village of Quercy, in the eleftion of Figeac. *p. Cat in. Relique..* See *Relecq. Rtllis,* a pari(h of Touraine. *Rey,* a village of Artois, in the bailiwick of Aire. *p. Aire. Remalard,* a village of Perche, in the dioccfe of Séez, and eleftion of Mortagne: 4 leagues from Bellêmc, 5 from Châteauneuf, 11 from Bonneftable, iS from Mans, 15 from Chartres, and 35 from Paris. *Bureau de foße. Retnaucourt.* 1. A village of Picardy, in the eleftion of S. Quentin, *p. S. ¿juenlin.* a. A village of Champagne, in the dioccfe and eleftion of Rheims, *p. Rheims. Remaudiere,!a,3* village of Bretagne, in the diocefe and receipt of Nantes. *f. Nantes. Remaugii,* a village of Picardy, in the eleftion of Mondi Jicr. *p. Mmd.dicr. Remauville,* a village of Gâtinois, in the eleftion of Nemours *ft 1ftKtuis, RcmiervUler,* a town of Meflin,jn the diocefe of Toui. *p. LunevilU. Remereuil,* a village of Poitou, in the eleftion of Cluitclleraut. *p. CbJtelleraut. Re-*

menil. See *Remefml. Rtmerangle,* a village of Picardv, in the eleftion of Clermon t. *p. S. Jifl. Remereville,* a town of Meffin, in the dioccfe of Toul. *p. Vic. Remefcourt,* a place of Picardy, in the eleition of Clermont, *p. Clermont. Remefml,* a village of Picardy, in the eleftion of Doulens. *¿. Doulens. Remc%htyt* a place of Mefiin, in the diocefe and receipt of Meta, *p Meta. Remiccart,* a village of Champagne, in the eleftion of Ste. Manehould. *p. Ste. Manébould. Remieneourt. 1.* A village of Picardy, in the diocefe and eleftion of Amiens, *p. Amiens.* 2. A village of Picardy, in the eleftion of Mondidier. *p. Cbagny. Remigny,* a village of Burgundy, in the diocefe and bailiwick of Challón, *p. Challen. Remilly.* I. A fmall town of Normandy, in the dioccfe and eleftion of Coûtances. *p. Coûtâmes.* a. A village of Burgundy, in the diocefe and bailiwick of Dijon, *p. Dijon.* 3. A village of Champagne, in the diocefe and eleftion of Rheims, *p Manieres.* 4. A village of Burgundy, in the diocefe and receipt of Arnay-le-Duc. *p. Dijon.* 5. A village of Meflin, in the diocefe and receipt of Metz, *p. Metz.* 6. A parifli of Nivernoit compofed of fcveral hamlets, in the diocefe and eleftion of Nevers. *f. blovers. Remilly, les,* a fmall town on the frontiers of Champagne, in the generality of Metz. *p. Moufon. Remilly-le-Comte,* a village of Artois, in the bailiwick of Aire. *p. Aire. Remlniae,* a village of Bretagne, in the dioccfe and receipt of S. Malo. *f. Malo. Remirtconrt.* See *Amiefentainik Remiremont,* a town of Lorraine, 3 leagues from Plombières. *Remcnd,* a village of Berry, in the áiocefe and election of Bourges, *p. Bourges. Remcndans,* a village of FrancheComté, in the bailiwick of Baume, *f. C/er-vaJ. Remonte.* Sec *Ba'tron. Remonvaux,* a priory of Burgundy, in the diocefe of Langrcs. *Remomrd'.e,* a village of Champagne, in the election of Ste. Manéhould *p. Stenay. Ranorentin.* See *Romorant'tn. Remouillé,* a town of Poitou, in the elect:un of Mauleon./». *Montaigne. Removlim,* a town of lower Languedoc, on the Gardon, in the diocefe and receipt of Uzés, 6 leagues from Tarafcon, 26 from

Aix, 6 from Avignon, 4 from Nîmes, 59 from Lyons, and 174Í from Paris. *Bureau de poße. Remcu ay,* a village of FrancheComté, in the bailiwick of Pontarlier. *p. Pontariier. Rempnac,* a village of Marche, in the election of Bourganeuf. *p Bourganevf. Remuée, ¿a,* a village of Normandy, in the election of Montivilliers. *p. ?, Romain. Remungol,* a village of Bretagne, in the diocefe and receipt of Vannes, *p. Vanna. Remufat,* a village of Provence, in the diocefe of Die. /. *le Buh, Remy.* i. A town of Picardy, in the election of Clermont, *p. Compiegne.z.* A village of Picardy, in the diocefe and election of Laon. *p. la Fere.* 3. A village of Artois, in the diocefe and bailiwick of Arras, *p. JT-ras. Remyesne,* a fmall town of lower Languedoc, in the diocefe and receipt of Mende. *p. Mende. Rt nac,* a village of Bretagne, in tlie diocefe and receipt of Vannes, *p. Redon, Renaifon,* a town of Forer, in the election of Roanne, *p. Roanne. Bcnatwurt,* a village of Franche
Comté, in the bailiwick of Grav..
Cray.
Renaudierc, la, я town of Anjou, in the diocefe and election of Angers. *p. singers. Renen,* i. A village of Beauce, in the election of Châtcaudun. *p. Vendóme, z.* A village of Beauce, in the"" election of Chateaudun.. *Cbáttaudun. Renaze,* a town of Anjou, in the diocefe and election of Angers, *p. singers. Rencennes & Cbarmy,* a village of Flanders, in the receipt of Charlcmont. *p. G'net. Rencbettes,* a village of FrancheComté, in the diocefe and bailiwick of S. Claude, *p. S. Claude. Rtncbon,* villageofNormandy,in the election of Caudebec.. *Caudebec. Renccugne,* a village of Angoumois, in the diocefe and election of Angoulêmc. *p. Angoulême. Rendam 6» la Salle,* a village of Forez, in the election of Montbr. fon. *p. Mc ithrijm. Rendam.* See *Randans. Rendeuille,* a plrce of Normandy, in the diocefe of Coûtances. *p. Cmtanas. Rendue, la.* Sec *Neu-vlle. Rendus, Us,* a village of Normandy, in the election of Eu. *p. En. Rent' ®"Efpieres,* a town of Maine, In the diocefe and election of Mans. *p. Frefnay. Renedales,*

a place of FrancheComté, in the bailiwick of Ornans. *p. Befancom. Rene/,* a village of Champagne, in the election of Chaumont.. *Joinmlle.* Renelle, a fmall river of Normandy which brtes itfclf in the Seine at Rouen.

Rencmefn'il, a place of Normandy, in the election of Caën. *p. Cain. Renepml,* a village of Champagne, in the election of B»r-iur-Aube. /. *Bar-Jur-Aube.* Renefve, a village of Burgundy, in the diocefe and bailiwick of Dijon. *p. Auxontre.* Rineville, a village of upper Lan. 1 guedoc, in the diocefe and receipt of' Mircpoix. *p. Mirepoix.* . *Rcngcardi,* a village of Saintonge, in the diocefe and election of Saintes. *p. Sa nta. Rinlief,* a village of Flanders, in the government of Maubcuge. *p. Maubcuge.* Renne, a place of Franche-Comté, in the bailiwick of Salins, *p. Salins.* Renne-Moulm, a place in the diocefe and election of Paris, *p. Villepreux.* Rennet. T. An ancient city the capital of Bretagne, fituated on the Vilaine; the fee of a bilhop, with a government, &c. belidcs the cathedral it has 8 parifh churches, a magnificent college, &c. i6Jcagucs from S. Malo, 28 from Nantes, 112 from ßourdeaux,2i from Lamballe,26 frum S. Brieux, 33 from Guingamp, 48 from Morlaix, 60 from Breft, 27 from,Mayenne, 4.1 from Alenon, 19 from Laval, 55 from Tours, 39 from Caen, 29 from Sablé, and 88 from Paris. Sureau de prße.-z.A town of Maine, in the diocefe and election of Mans. *p. Mayenne.* 3. A village of upper Languedoc, in the diocefe and receipt of Akt. *p. Limiux.* Renoj or 5. *Viclor-de-Reno, Rena,* or *S Marc-de-Reno,* towns of Perche, in the diocefe of Séez, and election of Mortagne. *p. Mortagne.* Reno, a forcft of 1807 arpents, in the jurifdiflion of Bellefme, in Normandy. *Renouard, le,* afmall town of Normandy, in the election of Argentan. *p. Argentan.* Rehlecbaux, a place of FrancheComté, in the bailiwick of Ornans. *p. Bejancon. Rcntvij,* a village of the Ifle of France, in the diocefe and election of Paris, *p. Lagny.* Renty, a town of Artois, fituated on the Ал, about 4 leagues from S. Omer, 5 from Aire, and 12 from Arras, *p. S. Oner.* Renville, a village of Angoumois, in the eleition of Cognac, *p. Cognac, Renunfo* a village of Gafcony, *m* the receipt of Marfan, *p. Mwit-dcMarfan. Rcvcy,'* a fmall town of Champagne, in the diocefe and election of Rheims, *p. Rheims.* R/ole la, or *Re'olle, la,* a town of Bazadois, on the Garonne, in the road from Bourdeaux, to Touloufc, i8£ leagues from Bourdeaux,9 from Tonreims, 19 from Agen, 38 from Montauban, and 50 from Touloufe. *Bureau depeße.* Reome, or *Ie Moutier-S.-jfcaa.* See *Moutier-S.-yean,* Reotie, la. See *Mont-Olivet.* Reorte, la, a fmalltown of Poitou in the election of Fontcnay. *p. Fcrttenay.* Reortbe, la, or *S,-Mars-la-Reotbe3* a fmall town of Poitou, in the election of Thouars. *p. Tbouars.* Reoule, or *Reaule, la.* See *Reble,* Repaire, la, a place of Marche, in the election of Gueret. *p. Gueret.* Repara, la, a village of Dauphiny, in the election of Montelimart,-/. *Montelimart.* Reparjac, a village of Angoumoi, in the election of Cognac, *p. Cognac.* Repas, a village Burgundy, in the diocefe and bailiwick, of Autun. *p% Autun.* Repas, le, a place of Normandy, in the election of Falaifc. *p. Fa/aife.* Repe', or *la Repe',* a village of Burgundy, in the bailiwick of Arnay-'leDuc. *p. Dijon.* Repent 'tgny, a village of Normandy, in the election of Pontl'Eveqne. *p. Pont-PE-veque.* Repertzweiiler, aplace of Alface, in the diocefe of Straiburg. *p. Strafburg,* Repes, a mineral fpring near Vcfoul, in Franche-Co m té. Reploagc, a i'mall town of BreíTe, in the bailiwick of Bourg, *p. Mâcon,* Repos, le, a village of Normandy, in the election of Argentan, *p. Argentan.* Repas, le, & Malmagr'w. я village.of Franc hc-Coxnté, in tUeiai-jiwiclt fï-ons-le-Ssunier./». Lons-h-Saunier. *Rcpofcur,* a place of Burgundy, »n the bailiwick of Avalon, *p. Aval'"* Requel, a town of-Anjou, in the election of Flèche, *p. Foultcurte..* Reques, a village of Boulonnois.in the generality of Amiens, *p. Montrât':!. Rcjukourt,i* figniory of Normandy, in the eleflion of Giffors. *p. Giffirs.* Requifla, a village of Rouergue, in the diocefe and eleflion of Rhodez. *p. Rbadex.* Rerieu, i place of Dombcs, in the chatcliany *oiTxwom. p. Villefrancke.* Ren e, a fmall river of Orléannois, which falls into the Saudre a league above Romorantin. *Rtfe,* a fmall river of Berry, which runs into the Saudre at Romorantin. *Reße-la-Grandt,* a village of Franche-Comté, in the diocefe and bailiwick of Gray. *p. Gray Reße-S.-Marün,-A* place of FrancheComté, in the bailiwick of Gray. *p. pray.* Reßgny & Train, a village of Picardy, in the diocefe and election of Laon. *p. Laon. Rejr.el,* a confiderable trail of land in the eleflion of Clermont. *Refnieres-cn-Tieracbe,* a village of Flanders, in the government, of Landrecy. *p. Landrecy.* Refiuze, a fmall river of Breffe, which loffcs itfelf in the Saône. *Refpaitlc,* a village of Armagnac, in the eleflion of Altarac. *p. Mirande.* Rejpoede, a fmall town of Flanders, in the fubdeligation of Bergues. *f. Jiergues. Rejj'art, le,* a place of Franche'Comté, in the bailiwick of Poligny. *f. Salins.* Rej/in,a village of Champagne, in the eleflion of Rethcl. *p. Reibe/.* Reß'm-le-Long, a village of Picardy, in the diocefe and eleflion of Soiffons. *p. Soiflins.* Reßbm. i. A town of Picardy, in the eleflion of Mondidier. *p. Mьniidier.* 2. A village of Normandy, in the eleflion of Chaumont. *p. Claumcnt.* ReJfort'de-CSte, le, a town of Anjou, in the eleflion of Château-Gont.er. *p.Cbátcau-Gonticr. RefJart-de-Nogent, le,* a place of Normandy, in the eleflion of Argentan, *p. Argentan. Reßirt-d'Aveze, le,* Rejfort-Gátineau, le, £f Reßbrt-S.-Cafme, le, places of Perche, in the eleflion of Mortagne. *p. Mortagnc. RtJJùintiS, les,* a village of Normandy, in the eleflion of Verneuil. *p. Verneuil.* Reß.ud & S Cbrißafbe, a fmall town of Saintonge, in the diocefe arid eleflion of Saintes, *p. Saintes. Rßis.* See *Reiecj.* Reßigne, a town of Aniou, in the eleflion of Sauniur./i. *lei Trois Valets.* Riflinelieres, a place of lower Languedoc, in the diocefe and receipt of Montpellier, *p. Sommieres. Rijlonval,* a village-of Normandy, in the eleflion of Neufchâtcl. *p. Aumale.* Reßouil, a village of Limofin, in the diocefe and eleflion of Limoges. *p. Limoges. Rcteaumlle,* a place of Picardy, in the diocefe and eleflion of Amiens. *p. Amiens.* Reterre, a fmall town of Auvergne, in the eleflion of Combrailles. *p Cbambon.* *Rctbel,* an ancient city of Champagne, fituated on a mountain near the Aifne, in the diocefe of Rheims, and generality of Châlons, the feat of a bailiwick, eleflion, &c. it lies in the road from Paris to Sedan, 9 leagues from Rheims, 13 from Jonchcry, 9 from Mecieres, 22 from Soiffons, 12 from Sedan, 18 from Stenay, 22 from Montmedy, 40 from Liege, and 46 from Paris. *Bureau de poße. Retbelds, It,* a country of Champagne, in the environs of Rethcl, which is the capital, it contains mines; of iron and coal, and produces, paffurage and great plenty of wood. *RclbeuV,* a village of Picardy, in the election of Crêpy. *p. Crepy. RetbojvUle,* a village of Normandv, in the election of Valogncs. *p. Va logHCS. Retby,* a village of Picardy, in the generality of Amiens, *p. Boulogne. Rellin,* a village of Bretagne, in the diocefe and receipt of Rennes, *fü Rennes. Retonde,* a village of Picardy, in the dîoccfe and election of Soiffons. *p. Compie'gne. Retonfey,* a place of Mcflin, in the diocefe and receipt of Metz. *p. Max. Retonv lier,* a village of Picardy, in the election of Péronne. *p. iVtbnne.* Retourhur, a villageof Vivarais, in the diocefe and receipt of Viviers, *p. Vwiers.* Retournée, a town of lower Languedoc, in the diocefe and receipt of Puy. *p. Marvejols.* Retournelon. See *Fßerr.ay.* Retours, *les,* a pillage of Normandy, in the election of Falaife. *p. Falaife.* Rettlel, a place of Merlin, in the diocefe and receipt of *Metz.p. Мaя, Reiz,* or *Raïs,* a country of Bretagne, fouth of the Loire. Machecou is the chief place. *Réveillon.* I. A fmall town of Normandy, in the election of Verreuil. *p. Enjilles, 2.* A village of Perche, in the election of Mottagne. *p. Mortagne.* 3. A village of Normandy in the election of Argentan. *p. Troarn.* 4 A village of Brie, in the election of Sezanne, *p. la Fcrte' Gaucher.* Revel. I. A town of upper Languedoc, fituated i 11 Lauraguais near the Mountain Noire, in the diocefe of Lavaur, about *2* leagues from S. Papoul. *p.Caßelneandary. 2.* A village of Dauphiny, in the diocefe and election of Grenoble, *p. Grenoble.* 3. A village of Dauphiny, in the diocefe and

election 01 Vienne, *p. la CoSteS.-Andri.* 4. A place in the valley of Bitelonnctte in the diocefe of Em brun. *p. Embrun* Revellc, a village of Burgundy, *iff* the diocefe and bailiwick of Dijon. *p. Dijon.* Revelles, a fmall town of Picardy, in the diocefe and elect ion of Amiens. *p. Ameins.* Reven, a village of lower Languedoc, in the diocefe and receipt of. Alais *p. le Vigan.* Reventin, a village of Dauphiny, in the diocefe and election of Vienne. *p. tienne.* Rcvtrcourt, a village of Normandy, in the election of Verncuil. *p. Brefilles.* Rivermont, 3 fmall country of Brefle, between the jurifdiction of Coligny, and of Pont d'Ain. *Revery & Crcuz:,* places of Picar» dy, in the election of Doulens. *p. Doutent. Reveje,* a village of Dauphiny, in the election of Montelimart. *p. Montdimart. Reveß, le.* J. A village of Province, in the diocefe andviguery of Toluou./. *Toulon. 1.* A village of Provence; in the viguery of Draguignan. *p. Draguignan. Reveß-di-Bion,* a place of Dauphiny, in thetliocefe of Sifteron. *p. Apt.* Reveß*dc-Brmße,* a village of Provence, in the viguery of Forcalquier. *p. Forcalquier.* Retigny. i. A town of Touraine, in the election of Amboife.. *p. Amboife.* 2. A village of Biurbonnois, in the election of Montluçon. *p. Montluçon.* 3. A village of FrancheComté, in the bailiwick of Omans. *p. Befaneon.* 4. A parifh of Nivcrnois, in the diocefe and el.ction of Ncvers. *p. Nevers.* Riviers, a village of Normandy, in the election of Caen. *p. Caen.* Revigny, a village of Franche» Comté, in the bailiwick of Lons-leSaunier. *p. Lons-le-Saunier,* Reuil. I. A village of Champagne, in the election of Epernay. *p. F.per-. nay.* X. A village of Normandy, ia the cleilion of Verncuil. *p. VernaM* g. A village of Brie, in the diocefe and election of Meäux. *p. la FerteJout-Jouare.* 4. A place of Picardy, in the election of Clermont./. *Beau ЧНЛ5.* Reville. I. A fmall town of Normandy, in the election of Valognes. *p. Vaiognts.* 2. A village of Mefiin, in the diocefe and receipt of Metz. *p. Sedan.* 3. A village of Normandy, in the election of Bernay. *p. MontreuM-V Argdle.* Rcvilley, a place of Burgundy, in the bailiwick, of Beaunc. *p. Beaune.* Revi/

lion, a place of Burgundy, in the bailiwick ofSaulicu. *p. Dijon.* Revillotf. i. A village of Picardy, in the diocefe aud election of Laon. *p. Fifincs.* 2. A place of Burgundy, in the bailiwick of Arnayie-Duc. *p. Dijon.* 3. See *Cbamussy* Reuilly. i.,A town ot Berry, iituated on the river Arnon, about 6 leagues from Bourges, *p. Iffbudun.* 2. A place of Burgundy, in the baiI i wick of Beaune-*p, Beaune.* 3. A chateau near Paris, *p. Bonny.* Rei.it'*IySauiàgny,* a town of Brie, in the elc£tion of Château-Thierry. *p. Cbâteau-Tbierry.* Revittj a town fituatcd on the river Mcnfe, a little below CharleviUe. *p. Rocroy.* Reule-de-Saubeßre, *la,* an abby in the town of Pau in Beam. Radiée, r. A village of Burgundy, in the bailiwick of Nuits, *p. Ñutts.* 2. A village of Burgundy, in the bailiwick of Beaune. *p. Beaune* 3. Aplace in the parilh of Vergy, in the diocefe of Autun in Burgundy, *p. Cbalfon.* Reumonty a village of Flanders, in the generality of Lille, *p. Cam/ray.* Revona%, a village of BreíTc, in Ггrc bailiwick of Bourg, *p. Bourg tn Breje.* Reaves, a village of Brie, in the election, of Sezanne, *p. Scixartne,* Reuville, a village of Normandy, in tifc election of Arques, *p. Terцz'Me. RtwCj* a village of Normandy, in from Landrecy, 3§ from Cam-Villefranche, 24 from Cahors, 21 bray, 67 from Calais, 14 frorh from Mende, ai from S. Flour, 16 Lanoy, 30 from Mariemburg,30 from from Alby, and 136J from Paris.

Verdun, 69 from Vefoul, 45 from *Bureau de poße.*

Metz, 43 from Chaumont, 114 from Rhone, or *Rbojne,* a large.and one

Lyons, ill from Geneva, 31 from of the molt rapid rivers in Europe;

Bar-le-Duc, 52 from Nancy, 88 from it rifes in the mountain of Fourche, Stralburg, and 38 from Paris. *Bu*-one of the Alps in Switzerland, then *reau de foße.* running through the country of Va *Rbemois,* a fmall country in the lais and the lake of Geneva, paffei environs of Rheims, which is the that city and joins the Saône, at *Rbcu, le,* a place of Eretagne, in cöurfe till it falls into the Mediter the diocefe and receipt of Rennes, *p.* ranean, weftward of Marfeilles, paff *Rinnes.* ing by Orange, Avignon, Aries, &c.

Rbien, a place of Franche-Comté, *Rboni,* a fmall river of Lower in the diocefe and bailiwick of S. Languedoc that falls into the Viftre. *Rbimpochxeli',* a place of Alface,in land in the cleftion of Chaumont. the bailiwick of Rouffach. *p. Rouf-Rhcfnc.* See *Rbine. fach. Rbcfnel, le,* a priory in the diocefe *Rhin,* or *Rhein, le,* a very large river of Beauvais. which rifes in the country of the *Rbuc.* See *Rue.*

Grifons in Switzerland, it foon af-*Rbuh,* an ifland or peninfula on ter forms a lake called Confiance; the coaft of Bretagne, in the diocefe and from thence it paffes by the of Vannes.

cities Confiance, Schaffaufen, and *Ria,* a village of Rouergue, in the

Bafil, direflly north, and divides viguery of Confions, *p. Villeframbe*

Suabia from Alface, then running *de-* *Conßans.* through the Palantine, and receiving *Riaille',* a village of Bretagne, in the Neckar, the Maine, and Mofelle, the diocefe and receipt of Nantes, *p.* it continues its courfe by Mcntz, *jincenis,*

Coblentz, and Cologn; after which *Riancey,* a village of Champagne, arriving at Skenkihchans, in the in the diocefe and eleftion of Troyes.

Netherlands, it divides into feverál *p. Troyes.* channels, the two largeft of which *Riait,* a town of Berry, in the d:c« are named the Lech and the Waal, cefe and elcilion of Bourges. *p.* which running through the United *Bourges.*

Provenccs, difcharge themfelves into *Riar.s,* a town of Provence, in the the fea below Rotterdam: the an-» diocefe and viguery of Aix. *pi Bar* cient channel is choaked up. It gives *jols.* . name to two circles of Germany, the' *Riant,* a village of Bretagne, in the

Upper and Lower Rhine. diocefe and receipt of Vannes, *p. Rhin, le,* a fmaty river that falls *Rennes.* into the Loire near Roanne. *Riaucourt,* a village of Champagne, -*Rb'inau,* a town of Alface, in the in the diocefe and election of Chalons, bailiwick of Benfeld. *p. Benfeld. p. Chalons. Rhodts,* ar ancient and handfome *RiaviUt.* See *Vmhcuille,* city of Rouergue, of which it is the *Riaule.*

See *Re'ole.* capital; the fee of a biihop, fuff'ragan *Ribagnac,* a fmall town of Peri of Alby, the chief place of an.elecgord, in the diocefe and ckcTion of tion, &c. about 12 leagues from Sarlat. *f. Birgiret.* capital.

Claude, *p. S. Claude.* , *Ribagnat,* a place of Marche, in the election of Gueret. *p. Cueret. Ribaucourt.* I. A village of Champagne, in the. eleâion of Chaumont. *f Ligny.* 2. A village of Picardy, in the eleäion of Doulcns. *p. Dotdetis. Ribaudas,* the name of one of the ifles of Hieres,on the coaft of Provence. *Ribaupiere.* See *Raporßein. RièaudoTi,* or *Ribaudan,* one of the Hieres near Ribaudas. *Rlbaute.* I. A village of Lower Languedoc, in the diocefe and receipt of Alais, *p. Alan.* 2. A village of Lower Languedoc, in the diocefe and receipt of Narbonne. *p. Narbonne.* 3. A place of Lower Languedoc, in the diocefe and receipt of Béziers. *p. Ré%ers. RibauiUU.* I. A village of Alface, the chief place of a bailiwick, in the diocefe of Bale. *p. Colmar,* a. A. village of Picardy, in the deition of Guife. *p. Gi,ife. RibauviHier,* a town of Alface, the chief place of an ancient Comté, in the diocefe of Bâie. *p. Colmar Ribay.* See *Rubay. Ribecairt.* 1. A village of Picardy, in the diocefe and election of Noyon. *p. Noyon.* 2. A village of Flanders, in the diocefe and fubdelegation of Cambray. *p. Cambrúy. Rtbcment,* a village cf Picardy, in the election of Doulens. *p. Corb'u. Ribgmont,* or *Riblemont,* a town of Picardy, ne:,r the river of Oife, about 4 leagues from S. Quentin, *p. S. Suintm. Riltnne,* a village of Lower Languedoc, in the diocefe and receipt of Mende. *p. Marvejoh. Ribtrpri,* a village cf Normandy, in the election of Ncufchâtel. *p. Neuftbáte!. Riba,* a village of Lower Langue. doc in the diocefe and receipt of Viviers, *p. ¡es Vans. Ribes, les, л* village of Lower Languedoc, in the diocefe and receipt of Lodeve. *p. Lodt-ve. Ribeuf,* a figniory of Normandy, ia the election of Arques. *Dkpfe.* tou, bu'ilt by Cardinal Richelieu in 1537, with a château and park 4 leagues in circumference, in the diocefe of Poitiers, and generality of Tours, about 9 leagues from Poitiers, and 10 from Tours. *Bureau de foße. . Ribemottt.* I. A fmall town of Normandy, in the election of Eu. *p. Aumak.* 2. A village of Marche, in the cleftion of Gueret. *p. Gueret.* j. A place of Limofia, in the diocefe and election of Limoges. *RkhemcntjOV S. Georges de Riebetnonl,* a village of Saintonge, in the diocefe and eleftion of Saintes, *p. Cognac. Richement Èf Vipinviïle,* a village Oí Meffin, in the diocefe and receipt óf Metz. *p. Tbionville. Ricberencbes,* a village of Venaiffin, in the judicature of *Vzirezs. p.Paireas. Riebet,* a village of Gafcogne, in the eleftion of Landes./. *S. Sever. Ricbeval& Habiten,* places of Meffin, in the diocefe and receipt of Metz. *p. Sarbourg. Ricbeville,* a village of Normandy, in the election of Gifors. *p. le Tillé. Ricbflett,* a village of Alface, in the bailiwick of Wantzcnau.J.6Vnj/ W£. *Ricbtol%bem,* a place of Alface, in the bailiwick of Marckolfheim, *p. &rajburg. Ricbweir,* a fmall town of Alface, in the diocefe of Bale. *p. Colmar. Ricourt,* a villageof Armagnac, in the cleftion of Altarac. *p. Mirande. Ricquehour,* a village of Picardy, in theelcftion of Mondidier..Comfiig«. *Ridcauville,* a village of Normandy, in the eleftion of Valogncs.f.A'*ilogms. Rk'.* I. An ifland on the coall of Poitou, with two parilhes of the fame name. *p. S. Gilles.* 2. A village of Normandy, in the eleftion of Argentan, *p. Argenten. R'tec,* a village of Bretagne, in the diocefe and receipt of Quinrper. *p. Quimpcrlc. Riedcßeimt,* a village of Alface, in the bailiwick of Altkirch.. *Altkireb. Ritdjeltx,* a village of Alface j in the bailiwick of Oberbronn- . л *Wißembourg. Riei-les-Eaux,* a village of Bur gundy, in the diocefe and generality of Dijon, *p. Cbátillon. Ricncourt,* a village of Picardy, in the diocefe and cleftion of Ameins. *p. Amiens. Riencourt-les-Bapaume & Rienceurtles-Hendencowt,* villages of Artois, in the bailiwick of Bapaume. *p.Bapaume. Rieftacb,* or, *Repe,* a village of Alface,in the bailiwick of Than. *p. Rouffad,. Ricfpacb)* a villageof Alface, in the bailiwick, of Ferrctte. *p. Huningue. Rietbeintj* a place of Alface, in the bailiwick of Bouxviller. *p. Saverne, RicUf* or *S. Laurent-du-RicU)* a place of Normandy, in the dioceie and eleftion of Bayeux. *f. Ißgr.y, Rjeucerze,* a village of Gafcony, in the diocefe and election of Comminges. *p.Montreje.m, RieucroSy* a village of Upper Languedoc, in the diocefe and receipt of Mirepoix. *p. MirepoIx. Rieufct,* a village of Lower Languedoc, in the diocefe and receipt of Viviers, *p. Viviers. RieulaSj* a village of Gafcony, in the diocefe and election of Comminges *p. Lombez. Riei/majout* a villageof Upper Languedoc, in the diocefe and receipt of Touloufc. *p. Touloufe. Ricumet,* a town of Armagnac, in the. election of Rivière-Verdun. *f. S amatan. RieujJ'ee'j* a village of Lower Languedoc, in the diocefe and receipt of S. Pons. *p. Bexten, Rieutordf om S-FcliX'de-Ricutordz.* villageof Upper Lauguedoc, in the diocefe and receipt of Mirepoix. *f.. Mirepoix, Rieutordfi* village of Lower Languedoc, in the diocefe and receipt of Mende *p. Marvejols. Rieux,* I. A town of Upper Languedoc, in the generality, of Toulonfe. *p. Touhuft.* a. A town of Lower Languedoc, in the diocefe *stni* receipt of Narbonne. *p. Narhme.* J. A v.Ilage of Rouffillon, in the diocefe and viguery of Perpignan, *p. Perpignan.* 4. A village of Flanders, in the fubdelegation of Bouchain. *p. Scucbain.* 5. A village of Picardy, in the diocefe and election of Senlis. *p. &n!is.* 6. A village of Normandy, in the election of Eu. *p. Eu.* 7. A village of Brie, in the election of Sezanne, *p. Sezanne.* 8. A village of Bretagne, in the diocefe and receipt of Vannes, *p. Reden. Riiux-en-Val,* a place of Upper Languedoc, in the diocefe and receipt of Carcaflonne. *p. CarcajJ'onne. Rieuxpeyroux,* a priory in the generality of Montauban. *Riez,* an ancient city of Provence, in the generality of Aix, and viguery of Mouftiers, fituated in a very fertile plain about 16 leagues from Aix, 8 from Manofque, 9 from Digne, 7 trom Barjollcs, 10 from Brignolles, II from Draguignan, 17 from Fréjus, 24 from Antibes, 10 from Forcalquier, 18 from Aubagnes and 21 from Marfeille. *Bureau de f ojie. Rie'ze,s* fmall river of Guitnne.that runs into the Garonne near Savcrdan. *Ria &val,* or *Rlmial,* an abby in the diocefe

of Tool. *p. Tew/. Rißay,* a village cf Fop-Z, in the election of Montbrifon. *p.Mantbrijm.* Rigades, a place of Gafcony, in the d o cfc ar.d election of Comminge», *p. Montrejecu. Rigai da,* a village of Rouffillon, in the viguery of Conflans. *p. J'illij"ramhe-de-Conßam. Rign.ic.i.* A town of Saintongc, in the diocefe and election of Saintes. *p. Saintes, z.* A fmall town of Guien. ne, in the diocefe and election of Bourdcaux. *p. Bmrdeaux.* 3. A village of Rouergue, in the diocefe and election of Rhodcz. *p. Rbodez.* 4 A village of Condomois, in the diocefe and election of Condom./). *Condom. Rigne'.* i. A vill ge of Poitou, in the election of Thouars./). *Cbauvigny.* a. A figniory of Anjou, in the election of Rangé, *p. Bauge'.*
Vol. III.

ît has paflcd Pont-Audemer.
Rille, i. A town »f Anjou, in the election of Bauge. *p. Bauge'.* 2. A pariih of Touraine, near Amboife. *p. ¿imboife. Rulçf,* or *Relay,* an abby in the diocefe of Rennes.*Remes. Rillieu,* a village of Brefle, in the bailiwick of Bourg, *p. Bnurg-enBrefe. Rilly.* i. A town of Touraine, in the election of Amboife. *p. Amboife.* 2. A village of Touraine, in the election of Chinon. *p. Cbinon.* 3. See *&e. Sire. Rilly-aux-Oyts,* a village of Champagne, in the election of Rethel. *p. Reib el. Ril/y-la-Monîagrte,* a fmall town of Champagne, in the diocefe and election of Rheims, *p. Rbiems. Rimarein,* a village of Marche, in the election of Gueret. Д *Gueret. Rimaucourt. 1.* A town of Champagne, in the diocefe of Lan gres, and election of Chaumont. *p. Cbaumont.* 2. See *la Chapelle.* Rimbault, a village of Poitou, in the election of Niort, *p. Niort,. Rimbir Csf S.-Pe'-Brocas,* a village of Gaf ony, in the diocefe of Aire. *p. Mont-deMarfan. Rimbercourt-Grifolle,* a village of Picardy, in the diocefe and election of Noyon. *p. Ncyon.* Rimbcual, a'village of Artois, in the diocefe and bailiwick of S. Omer, *p.* 5. *Omer. Rimeux* É2? *Affctival, pUces* of Artois, in the diocefe and bailiwick of Aire./ *Aire.* Remogne, a village of r'hampngne, in the diocefe and election of Rheims. *p. Rocrsy. Riman/,* a place of Burgundy, in the dio-

cefe and b-iliwick of Challón. *p. Cballon.* Rimond, or *S.-Benût-de-Rimond,* a village of Dauphiny, in the election f Montelimart./. *Die. Rinr.ndtix,* a village of Marche, in the election of Gueret. *p. Gueret.* Rimns, a village of Bwadois, in, the election of Condom. *Touloufe.* Rmonty a fmall town of Uppr Languedoc, in the diocefe and receipt of *Bjpux. p. Touloufe. R mouj* a place of Bretagne, in the diocefe and receipt of Rennes. *Fougères. ' Rincourt,* a priory in the diocefe of Beauvais. /». *Beawvais.* Ringendorffy a village of Alface, in the bailiwick of Bomtviller. *p. Cc/mar.* Rinsy or 5. *Vncent-de-Rniy* a fmall town of Beaujolois, in the diocefe of Lyons, *p. VUlefranche. R'mvM.* See *RicxvaL* Rinxenty a place of Picardy, in the generality of Amiens, *p. Boulogne. Riocauty* a village of Agénois, in the diocefe and election of Agen. *p. Agen. Riúcourty* a village of Champagne, in the election of Chaumont. *p. Cbaumont.* » Rioly Ief a village of Upper Languedoc, in the diocefe and receipt of Alby.i. *Alby.* Riots, a fmall town of Lower Languedoc, in the diocefe and receipt of S. Pons. *p. Bexten.* Rionty a city of Auvergne, in the-diocefe of Clermont, the feat of an election &c. 3 leagues from Clermont, 5 from Gannat, 19 from Moulins, and 90 from Paris. *Bureau de peße. Riom-des-Montagnes,* a town of Auvergne, in the diocefe and election of S. Fl«ur. *p. Clermont.* Rionet, a convent in Carcaflbne. *Rwnet 6? Mer/an,* a village of Guienne, in the diocefe and election of Bourdeaux. *p. Bourdeaux. Rkns.* i. A town of Guienne, about 3 leagues from Bourdeaux. *p. Cadillac.* 2. A village of Dauphiny, in the election of Montelimart. *p Villenevve-de-Berg. Riotcr-en-Faye & Rtotor-en-Joyeufe,* villages of Forez, in the diocefe of Lyons, and election of S. Etienne. *p. S. Etienne.* Riouy a fmall i Hand near Marfeille. *Uten & Morfon,* a village of Anou9 in the election of Saumur. *p. Saumur. Riounoguis,* a place of RTillon, in the diocefe and viguery of Perpignan, *p. Perpignan.* RiouJJc. i. A village of Bourbonno'is, in the election of Moulins, *p. Tfevers.* 2. A village in the dtoceie and-.lection of Nevers. *p.*

Nevtrs. Ri ux, a town of Saintonge, in the diocefe and election of Saintes, *p. S. Cozem. Rjoux-Martbiiatovm* of Saintonge, in the diocefe and election of Sa. ntes. *£. Saintes. Rieb & Mllaudon,* a village of Franche-Comté, in the bailiwick of Vefoul. *p. Vejml. Rlperbré,* a village of Normandy, in the election of Neufchâtel. *p. JSleufcbatel. Rifont,* a village of Champagne, in the diocefe and electron of Rheum. *JUbcims. Rippes, lesy* a p'ace of Breffe, in the baltiwick of Bourg, *p. Bourg-enB₂ɸ. Ris,* a town of Bourbonnois, near the Allier, in the election of Gannat. *p. S. Gtrand. Ris, & la Borde,* a village of the ifle of France, in the diocefe and tketion of Paris. *Bureau deptße. Rife, la,* a fmall river of Foix, that îofes itfelf in the Ariégc. *Rífele,* a town of Armagnac, in the diocefe and election of Auch. *p. Mont-de-Marjan. Rifnel,* a fmall town of Champagne, in the diocefe of Toul. *p. Tout. Rifyttebourg,* a village of Artois, in the bailiwick of 5. Pol. *p. Beibune. R'iffac,* a village of Rouergue, in the election of Milhaud. *p. Mi/baud. Ritovi/le,* a parifh of Normandv, in the diocefe of Coûtances. *p. Couiancet. Rittemlurg,* a villrge of Alface, in the diocefe of Straftmrg. *p. &'uezrnc. &itterJhoffeny* a village of Alface, in the bailiwick of Hatten, *p. Wifjembourg. Rivarannes,* a town of Toura'mej in the election of Chinon. *p, Cbinon. Rtvarermes,* a village of Berry, itk the election of Blanc, *p. Argentan. Rivas,* a village of Porer, in the election of Mnntbrifon. *p. S. Etienne. R'rvau, le, Mculino, л* wood of 196 arpents, in the jurisdiction of Autun. *Rivtcourt,* a village of Picardy, in the election of Compiégne. *p. Verberie. Rive.eger,* a fmall town of Forefc, in the election of S. Etienne, *p. S. Etienne. Rivery & Creufe,* places of Picardy, in the election of Doulens *p. DouLns. Rites,* a village of Dauphiny, in theelection of Romans, *p. Màrans» Rives & le Truel,* a village of Rouerguc, in the election of Milhaudv *p. IMhhaud. Rii-efahes,* a town of RoufTillon, celebrated for its wine about 3 leagues from Perpignan, *p. Perpignan. Rivet,* an abby in the diocefe of Bazas, *p. Bataas. Riveyroles,* a place of Lower Languedoc, in the diocefe and receipt of Puy. *p. h Buy. Rivière,* i. A country of Gafconv, making part of Armagnac, fituated along the Garonne: one part called Rivière-Verdun, from Verdun the capital, forms an elation, the feat of which is at Grenade. 2b A village of Gafcony, in the election of Landes. *p. Dax.* 3. A village of Armagnac, m the diocefe and election of Auch. *p. siucb.* 4. A village of FrancheComté, in the bailiwick of Pontarlier. *p. Pcntarlier.* 5, A vilbge of Alface, in the bailiwick of Beftort. *p.. Btjfort* 6. A fmall parilh of Touraine. *p. ClAnon. Rivière, la.* I. A village of Guienne, in the diocefe and election oi' Bourdeaux. *¿. L'ibourne.* 2. A village of Dauphiny, in the diocefe and e'.çn. tion of Valence, *p. Valence.* 3. A village of Foix, in the diocefe ot Panicrs. *p. Foix,* 4. A place of Normandy, in the election of Andcly. *p. Ccitlon,* 5. See *S. Julien. Riviere, la Grande,* a fmall town of Franche-Comté, in the dioccfe and bailiwick of S. Claude, *p. S. Claude. Rivière & IJfac curt,* places of Champagne, in the receipt of Mou-' fon./. *Moufon. Rivicre-de-Corpst la.* See *Sie. Sauine. Rivicre-en-ГAdrien, la.* a vilage ot Forez, in the election of Montbrifon. *p. Montbrifon. Reviere-Furent, la,* a village of Bugey, in the bailiwick of Bclley./. *Collonac. Rtv'ùre-le-Cbateleufe, la,& Afonia/,* a village of Burgundy, in the bailiwick of Avalon.*p. Avalon. Rivicre-tres-S. Sever y la,* a village of Gafcony, in the election of Landes. *p. S. Sever. Riviere-Verdun,* an election of Armagnac. See *Rivière,* 1. *Rivieres.* 1. A fmall town of Angoumois, in the diocefe and cjectinnof Angoulêmc *p. la Rocbefoucault.* 2. A village of Poitou, in the election of Richelieu, *p. Richelieu.* 3. A vilJage of Artois, in the diocefe and bailiwick of Arras, *p. Arras. Rivieres, les. t.* A place of Champagne, in the election of Vitrv. *p. Vkry.* 2. A fmall diftrift of Coôtantin, near the fea oppofite the Ifle of Guernfcy, where much white fait is made. 3. See *Efltrnay. R'tvièrcs-d" Aurecy, les,* a village of 'Forez, in the election of Montbrifon. *f. Montbrifon. Rivières-devant & derrière,* a fmall town of Franche-Comté, in the Hlocefeand bailiwick of S.Claude, *p. & Claude. Riviires-étQrpra.* See *Debate. Rivicresle-Bois,* a village of Champagne, in the diocefe and election of Langres. *p. Sangres. r Rivicrti-lcs-Foffex,* a fmall town of Champagne, in the diuc'fe and election of Langres. *p. SeUn¿ey. Rivures-Ncrt,* a village of Gafcony, in the diocefe and election of Comminges. *p. Touloufe. Ri'jb.'e,* a village of Normandy, in the election of Caudebcc. *p. Valltmont. Rivirie,* a village of Forez, in the election of S. Etienne, *p. S. Etienne. RivoirCf la.* i. A village of Valromcy, in the dioccfe of Belley. *p. Belley.* 2. A place of Franche-Comté, in the diocefe and bailiwick of S. Claude, *p. S. Claude. Rtvollct,* a village of Beaujolois, in the diocefe of Lyons, *p. Villefrancbe. Rivoure,* a village of Champagne, in the dioccfe of Troyes. *p. Troyes. Riupeyrons,* a village of Beam, in the receipt of Morias, *p. Pau. Rix.* I. A place of Nivernois, in the election of Clamccy. *p. Clameey.* 2. A place of Franche-Comté, in the bailiwick of Salins, *p. Salins. Rixbe'tm,* a village of Alface, in the bailiwick of Landfer. *p. Huningue. Rixoufe,* a village of FrancheComté, in the dioccfe and bailiwick of S. Claude, *p. S. Claude. Rizauccurt,* a village of Champagne, in the bailiwick of Bar-furAube. *p. Bar-furAube, Rizoui,* a village of Dauphiny, in the diocefe and election of *Gap. p. Cap. Ro,* a place of Roufiillon, in the viguery of Cerdagne. *p. Mont-Louis, Roanne,* or *Rouanne,* an ancient town of Forcz, in the diocefe and generality of Lyons, iiruated on the Loire, which becomes here navigable for barges. It is the feat of a bailiwick, election, &c. 24 leagues from Moulins, 20 from Lyons, 27 from Vienne, 46 from Valence, and 95- from Paris. *Bureau de peße. Roanness,* or *Roannois,* a fmall country of Forez, in the environs of Roanne., which is the capital. *Roaïx,* a figniory of Venaiífin *p. Avignon. R'.becy* a fmall river of NormandVi which falls into the Seine n«r Rouen. *Robegue,* or *Robeqne,* the name of a maiquifate in the bailiwick,' of Lilliers. *Robebomme,* a village of Normandy, in the election of Caen *p. Tnuard. Rcbeiffiet-le-Grandj & Robernecie-Pitity* villages of Flanders,' in the fubdelegation of Merville. *p. Betbune. Roberfat,* a figniory in Fbnders. *p. Betbune. Robert-Magny,* a village of Champagne, in the election of loinville.*p. Roberto?,* a village of Normandy, in the election of Caudebcc./. *Cany. Retine, ¿a,* or *Rotreux,* a village of Province, in the diocefe and viguery of Digne, *p. Digne. Robincaux,* a place of Gàtinois, in the diocefe and election of Sens. *p. Sens Roblón,* i. A village of Provence, in the viguery of Caftellane, *p. Caftellane.* 2. A fmallriver ofDauplvny, that runs into the Rhône, a little below Montelimart. 3. See *Roubun. Rob/ins, ¡es.* See *S. Marui. Robclfe.* See *Roulkbolfe. Roc-des-Rouges,* a village of Quercy, in the election of Cahots, *p. Figea c. Rícadet,* a village of Agéneis, in the diocefe and election of Agen. *p. Agen. Rocfiie/le.* See *Ranal/y. Roccafort,* a village of Provence, in the viguery of S. Paul./f. *¿Entibes. Rece',* a village of Beauce, in the election of Vendôme, *p. Vendôme. Rccbe. l.* A village of Forez, in the election of Montbrifon. *p. M'.ntbiifon.* 2. A village of Champagne, in the election of Vitry. *p. S. Difier.* 3. A village of Dauphi'ny, in the election of Vienne, *p. Vienne.* 4. A village of Franche-Comté, in the bailiwick of Befancon. *p. Cierva/.* 5. See *Hommes-dc-la-Roche. Rocbe,la.* I. A village of Limofin, in the élection of Tulles, *p. 4'uiles.* %. A village of Tourainc, in the election of Chinon. *p. Cbinon.* 3. A village of Auvergne, in the election of *Rocbe-Cbouart,* a town of Poitou, built on a mountain, near the river Vienne, in the diocefc of Poitiers, and election of Confolans; about 16 leagues from Angoulêmc, and 25 from Poitiers. *Bureau de poße. Reche-Concnек,* a village of Orleannois, in the election of Beaugency. *p. Beavgcncy. Rocbe-Courbon,* a fmall town of Touraine, in the diocefe and election of Tours, *p. Tours. Roche-Cultrut,* or *la Rocbe-Cultrat,* a viih'ge of Champagne, in the election of Chaumont. *p. Cbaumont. Rocbe-d'Agout,* a village of Bourbonnois, in the diocefe of Gannat. *p. Riom. Rocbe-de-Glun, la,* & *Roche Montferner,la,* villages of Dauphiny, in the diocefc and election of Valence. *f.*

Valence. Rocbe-Je-Menon, fa, a village of Poitou, in the election of Châtellerauit. *p. Preuilly. Roche-de-Nonan, la,* a village of Normandy, in trie election of Argentan, *p. Argentan. Rarbe-Derïeu, la,* a i#own of Bretagne, about 2 leagues from Treguier. *f. Guingamp. Rocbe-des-Arnauds, la,* a village of Dauphiny, in the diocefc and election of Gap. *p. Gap. Rocbe-des-Bords,* a village of Poit*oxij* in the diocefe and election of Poitiers, *p. Cbaunay. Rocbe-Dcnnai, la,* a fmall town of Auvergne, in the diocefe and election of Clermont, *p. Clermont. Rocbe-tFOr, la.* See *Gcraife. Roebe-dtt-Bacbas, la, Rocke en Reynier, la,* villages of Lower Languedoc, in the diocefe and receipt of Puy. *p. le Piy. Rocbe-Emau,* a place of Touraine, near Chinon. *p. Chinen. Rocbe-en-Brny, la,* a village of Burgundy, in the diocefe and bailiwick of Sercur-en-Auxois. *p. SauVteu. Roc be-Fernere,* a chatcllany in the generality of Poitiers. rion of Rochelle; 7 leagues from Rochelle, 10 from Saintes, 42 from Nantes, 42 from Bourdeaux, 16 from Cognac, 26from Angoulême, frci Limoges, 16 from Niort, 35 from Poitiers, and 122 from Paris. *Bureau de Paßt.* 2. A town of Forez, on the river Lignon, in the election of Roanne, *p. Montlrijon.* 3. A town of Auvergne, in the diocefc and election of Clermont, *p. Clermont.* 4. A town of Beauce, with a beautiful château, about 11 leagues from Paris, in the election of Dourlan. 5. A village of Franche-Comté, in the bailiwick, of Dole. *p. Dole.* 6. A village of Bretagne, in the diocefeand receipt of Vannes, *p. Rcd.n.* 7-A village of Dauphiny, in the election of Montclimart. *p. Montelimart.* 8. A village of Lower Languedoc, in the diocefe and receipt of Uzés. *p. Uze's.* 9. A villr.gc of Champagne, in the election of Chaumont. *p. Chaumonr.* 10. A village of Lyonnoisjin the diocefe and eleftion of Lyons, *p. Lyon.* II. See *Sournac. Rochefort,* or *S. Antoine-de-Rochefort,* a tovrW of Maine, in thè diocefe and election of Mans. *p. le Mens. Rocbefort,* or *Ste. Croix de Rocbcfcrt,* a town of Anjou, in the diocefe and election of Angers. *p. Angers. Rocbefort & St. Michel,* a fmall town of Picardy, in the

ekctton of Guife. *p. Gv'tfe. Rocbefort (S Sarf.n,* a vilbge of Dauphiny, in the diocefe and election of Valence, *p. Vienne. Rtcbtf'jrt-U-Cbùtcau,* a village of Lower Languedoc, in the diocefe and' receipt of Puy. *p it Puy. Rocbefort-S. Haond,* a place in the diocefe and receipt of Puy. *p: le Puy. Rocbefort-fur-Brenon,* a parilh of Burgundy, in the bailiwick of Châtillon, *p. Cháulhn. Roucbefoucautt la,otRoche-Fouca ud la,* a town of Angoumois, fituated on the Tardoirc, in the diocefe and election of Angoulême, in the road from Limoges to Saintes; 19 leagues from Limoges, 5 from Angoulême, 15 from Cognac, 21 from Saintes, 4e from Bourdeaux, and 116 from Paris. *Bureau de'pofle. Rcсbegiron,* a village of Provence, in the viguery of Forcalquicr.*p. For. ealqiiier. Rochegondes,* a village of Auvergne, in the diocefe and elcâion of S. Flour, *p. S. Flour. Rockigudc.* I. A village of Lower Languedoc, in the diocefe and receipt of Uzés. *p. Usee's.* 2. A fmall town, one part of which is in Venaifiin, and the other in Dauphiny, *p. Orange. Rocbejan,* a village of FrancheComté, in the bailiwick of Pontarlier. *p. Pontarlier. Rocbeijrane,* a village of Dauphiny, in the election of Montelimart. *p. Montclimart. Rocbelamoliere,* avillage of Forez,in the election of S. Etienne.. *S. Etienne. Rochelle, la,* a large, ftrong, and celebrated fea-port of Aunis, the fee of a bifhop, the feat of an admiralty, election, &c. fituated in the bav of Bifcay, oppofite the Ifle of Re, 7 leagues from Rochcfort, 35 from Nantes, 16 from Niort,. 3Ягот, Poitiers, 17 from Saintes, 45 from Bourdeaux, and 105 from Paris. *Bureau de poße.* 2. A village *of* Normandy, in the dnccfe. fid election of Avranrhcs. *p. Avranchc:-.* 3. A village of Frnr.chc-Comté, in the bailiwick of Vefoul. *p. Vejoul. Ro.bemantru,* a village of Bretagne, in thediocefe and receipt of Nantes. *p. Ancenis. Rocbemaure 6? Meyffe,* a fmall town of Lower Languedoc, in the diocefe and receipt of Viviers, *p.. Montclimart. Rocbemoflt, la,* a village of Auvergne, in the election of Comhrailles. *p. Montlucon. Rvcbemoitt-Ferrier, la,* a village of Dauphiny, in the diocefe and election of Valence, *p. Valence. Rocbefaute,* a fmall town of Vivarais, in the diocefe and receipt f Viviers, *p. Viviers, Rocbepotj la,* a village of Burgundy, in the bailiwick, of Beaunc. *p. M taunt. Rocher, fe,* a fmall town of Norinandy, in the election of Mortain. *Rocberaud.* See *Roullst. Rocberey la-,* a village of Dauphiny, in the election of Urenuble. *P. Grenoble. Rochery,* a village of Alface, in the bailiwick of Deile. *p. Huningue. Rocbes.* i. A village of Champagne, in the diocefe and election of Lanares, *p. Langres.* 2. A village of Marche, in the election of Gueret. *p. Gueret.* 3. A place of Champagne, in the diocefe and election of Rheims. *p. Rheims. Roches, hi,* a village of Beauce, in *thet. WÙ'iorioï'Vcndôme.p.Cbâteauiiun. Rocbes Primary, les,* a village of Poitou, in the diocefe and election of JPoitieis. *p. Cbinon. Rjcbefawve,* See *Rocbe-Sawve. licchejnard, la.* See *Rcche-Atnard. Rccbette,* a village of Dauphiny/ in the election of Montelimart. *p. le Buy. t?oJ¿et:e,la.* 1. A village of Anpiumms, in the diocefe and election of AngoUlêmc. *p. Ar.gQuléme.* 2. A viÜagj of Li moña, in the diocefe and cleft i jn pf Limoges, *p. Limoges,* 3. A village of Dauphiny, in the diocefe and election of Grenoble, *p. C⊰ф.* 4. A village of Dauphiny, in the diocefe and ckction of Valence. *p. Valence,* 5. A place of Burgundy, in the bailiwick of Amay-le-Duc. *p. Dijon. Rocbette, ¡a & S. Maurice,* a village of Burgundy, in the bailiwick of Mâcon. *p. Tournus. Rochette-de-Cbauon,* a village of Provence, in the v guery of Guillaume, *p. Cafteilane. Rotbtte-Lkre X, la,* a village of Marche, in the election of Gueret. *p. Auiujln. Rochort iil'er,* a place of MeiTin, in the diocefe and receipt of Metz. *p. Métz. Rocby-Cojidé,* a village of Picard, in the diocefe and election of Beau vais. *p. Bcauimis. Rockettbüujen,* a fmall village of Alface, in the bailiwick of Landfer. *p. Humrgue Roclancouri,* a village of Arts, in the diocefe and bailiwick of Arras. *p. Arras. Rocíes,* i. A village of lower Languedoc, in the receipt of Viviers, *p Villenewve-de-Btrg.* 2. A village of Bourbonnois, in the election ofMontluçon. *p. Mcntluçon.* 3.A village of lower Languedoc, in the diocefe and receipt of Mende. *p. Langogne.* 4. A village of upper Languedoc, in the diocefe and receipt of Mirepoix. *p. Mirepoix. Rocologne,* a place of FrancheComté, in the bailiwick of VefouL *p. Vejoul. Recourt,* a village of Picardy, in the diocefe and election of Soiflons, *p. Soiff'ons. Ruourt-en-LeaU)* aplace of Artois, in the bailiwick of S. Pol. *pArras. Rocq,* a place of Flanders, in the government of Maubeuge. *p. Maù beugh Rccroy,* or *Rocrois,* a ftrong town of Champagne, on the frontiers of Hainaut, in the diocefe of Rheims, and generality of Chalons, 9 leagues from Givet, 24 from Laon, 6 from Chimay, 13 from Avefnes, 17 from Landrecy, 20 from Quefnoy, 2,7 from Valenciennes, 4.0 from Lille, 7 from Mecieres, T2 from Sedan, 29 from Stenay, 31 from Verdun, 41 from Ste. Manéhcjuld, 35 from Rheims, 41Í from Chalons, 29 from Liege, 17 from Maubeiue, 21 from Möns, 33 from Bruffds, 46 from Metz, 5 from Manembouvg, and-57 from Paris. *Bureau depcß. Roddon,* a village of Bcauce, in the election of Vendórríe. *p. Vindim. Rodde* village of Rouergue, in the diocefe and election of Rhodes, *p. Rhodes, Rodel'nghen,* a village of PiçarJy, ia the l'overcinty of *&iàic$. f. Ardi'tu Hedem,* a vill?ge of Mefiin, in'the diocefe and receipt of Metz. *p. Sarhuis, Rodemarcker,* a village of Meflin, in the diocefe and receipt of Metz. *p. Met. Roderen.* i. A village of Alface, in the bailiwick of Thann. *p.Rouffacb,* a. A village of Alface, in the bailiwick of Ribauville. *p. B effort. Rode%.* I. A village of Rouíullon, in the viguery of Conflans. *p. Perpignan* 2. See *Rbodex. Rbodome,* a village of upper Languedoc, in the diocefe and receipt of Alet. *p. Limoux, Rodon,* a village of Beauce, in the election of Châteaudun. *p. Vendôme. Rce'y U,* a town of Anjou, in the flection of Chateau-G on tier. *p. Chateau Gontier. Roeux,* a village of Artois, in the diocefe and bailiwick of Arras, *p. ¿b-ras. Rceux Êf Lourcbes,* a village of Flanders, in the fubdelegation of-Bouchain. *p. Bouc bain, Roffe%* a village of Champagne, in the election ofTonnerre. *p.Tomterre, Rojfiat)* a fmail town of Auvergne, in the diocefe and election of S. Flour. *p. S. Flour. RogericcfUr,* a village of Picardy, in the diocefe and election of Laon. *p. Laon, RogeriAllej* a village of Normandy, in the election of Montivillicjs. *p Harßeur. Roglaion.* See *Se-vre. Rognac,* a village of Provence, in 4hc diocefe and viguery of Aix. *p. le JVtartigues. Rcgnains,* a town of Beaujolois, in the ele&ton of Vi lief ranche, *p. Villefranche, Rognât,* a village of Franche Comté, in the diocefe and bailiwick of S. Claude, *p. S. Claude. Rognes,* i. A village oflowcy Languedoc, jn the diccefc and receipt of Alais, *p. Sumefne.* 2. See *Rougnes. Rognkourt.* See *Boulleaux. Hognis,* a village of Picardy, in the diocefe and election of Laon. *p» Marie. Rognonas,* a place of Provence, in the viguery of Tarafcon. *p. Avignon Rogny,* a village of Gatinois, .in the election of Montargis. *p. CbШhn-fur-Low. Rogón.* See *Rougon. Rogyy* a village of Picardy, in the diocefe and election of Amiens, *p. Breteu'd. Robaire,* a village of Normandy, in the election of Verneuil. *p. VirneuxL Roban.* I. A town of Bretagne, oи the Aoufte, about ю leagues from Vannes, *p. Pont'ny.* 2. A place of Rouflillon, in the viguery of Cerdagne. *p. Perpignan. Robr,* a place of Alface, in tlx bailiwick of Kokerlberg. *p. Strafburg. Robrtveilkr,* a village of Alface, in the bailiwick of OrfFendorff. *p. Strafbourg. Rcie.* See *Roye. Roiffe'j* a village of Poitou, in" the election of Loudun. *p. Lcudun» RoiHecourty* a village of Artois, in the bailiwick of S. Pol. *p. Arras. Roilly,* a village of Burgundy, in the bailiwick of Semur. *p Semur. Roimelf'a* village of upper Languedoc, in the diocefe and receipt of Alby. *p. Alby. Roin,* a town of Auvergne, near Maringucs. *p. Riom. Rcinvi/le.* i. A village of Beauce, in the diocefe and election of Chartres, *p. Chartres. %.* A vilbge of Beauce, in the election of Dourdnn *p. Dourdan. Roin-vilTier,* a village cf Gâtinoîs, in the election of Etampes. *p. Etampes. Rcifely* a village of Picardy, in tb election of Peronne. *p. Ptronne. Reifes,* i. A pbee of Mcflin, in the diocefe and receipt of Toul. *p. Toù/.* 2. A parilh of Champagne, in the bailiwick of Chaumont.

jf. *Chaumont.* Roiffac, See *Geanfac* Roißard, a village of Dauphiny, in the diocefe and eleition of Grenoble. *p. Grenoble.* Roijjay, a village of Poitou, in the election of Loudun. *p. Loudun.* Roißat, a place of Breffe, in the bailiwick of Bourg, *p. Bourg-enBrejje.* Roffi. I. A town in the Ifle of France, in the diocefe and election of Paris, *p. Lagny.* 2. A village of Champagne, in the diocefe and election of Rheims, *p. Rubel.* Roiffy-en-Brie, a village in the Ifle of France, in the diocefe and election of Paris, *p. Dammart'm.* Roitiers, a village of Dauphiny, in the election of Montelimart. *p. Montttlmart.* Raize', a town of Maine, in the diocefe and election of Mans. *p. MaJhorne.* Roizille, a village of Normandy, in the election of Argentan, *p. Argentan.* Rolands, Us trcis, a village of Franche-Comté, in the bailiwick of Baume, *p. Bourne.* Rdb, a place of Alface, in the diocefe of Stralburg. *p. Strafburg,* Rolbbanet, a place of Alface, in the bailiwick of Oberbronne. *p. Strafburg.* Rollampont, a village of Champagne, in the diocefe and election of JLangres, *p. Langres,* Rolle. I. A place of Burgundy, in the bailiwick of Nuits, *p. Nuits,* z. See *Redet* Rollencourt. See *Roilleccurt.* RAiepot, a place of Artois, in the diocefe and bailiwick of Hefdin. *Hjdin.* Rdleville, a viihge of Normandy, in the élection of Montivillieis. *p. S. Valéry.* Rollet, л fmall town of Picardy, in the election of Mondidicr. *p. Afontreuil,* Rom, a town of Poitou, on the Dive, in the diocefe and election of Poitiers, *p. Couché.* Romagnac, a village of Agénois, in the diocefe and election of Agen. *p. Agen.* Romagnat, a town of Auvergne, in the diocefe and election of Clermont, *p. Clermont.* Romagnat, or 5. *Sulpice-de-Romagnat,* a fmall town of Périgord, in the diocefe and election of Périgueux. / *Caßllon.* Romagne, a town of Bretagne, in the diocefe and receipt of Rennes. /, *Fougères.* Romagne, a town of Poitou, in the diocefe and election of P»itiers. /. *Tifauge.* Romagne,la. i.A town of Anjou,in the election of Montreuil. *p. Saumur.* 2. A village of Champagne, in the diocefe and election of Rheims, *p. Retbel.* 3. A commandery of Malta, in Champagne, *p. Chaumont.* Romagnieu, a village of Dauphiny4' in the diocefe and election of Vienne. *p. Bourgcin.* Romagny, a place of Alface, in the" bailiwick of Delle, *p. Hun'mgue.* Rcmaja, a fmall town of Périgord, in the diocefe and election of Périgueux, *p. Périgueux.* ' Rcmuigne, a village of Bazadois, in the election of Condom, *p. Bazas.* Romain. I. A fmall town of Périgord, in the diocefe and election of Périgueux. *p. S. Pardoux.* 2. A village of Champagne, in the diocefe and election of Rheims, *p. Fifmes.* 3. A village of Franche-Comte, in the bailiwick of Vcfoul. *p. Vejaul.* 4. A place of Merlin, in the diocefe and receipt of Metz. *p. Metz.* 5. A place of Franche-Comté, in the receipt of Dole. *p. Dole.* Romaine, a place of Champagne, in the elcéKon of Bar-fur-Aube. *p. Bar-fur-Aube.* Rmaiville, a village in the Ifle of France, in the diocefe and election of Paris, *p. Bendy.* Romanan, a village of Dombes, in the chatdlany of S. Trivier. *p. Belleville.* Romanay. I. A village of Burgundy, in the bailiwick of Avalon. /. *Saulieu.* 2. A parilh of Burgundy, in the diocefe and bailiwick of Mâcon. *p. Tournas.* Romambe, a river of Dauphiny, which runs into the Drac near Grenoble. Romanecbe. I. A« large parifli of Burgundy, in the dioccfc and bailiwick of Mâcon." *p. Mâcon.* 2. A place of Brefle, in the bailiwick of Bourg. *Bourg-en-BreJJe.* Romanct, a place of Burgundy, in the bailiwick of Avalon, *p. Avalon.* Romange, a place of Franche-Comté, in the bailiwick of Dole. *p. Dole.* Romaniarges, a village of Auvergne, in the diocefe and election of S. Flour. *p. S. Flour.* Romanil, a place of Provence, in the viguery of Tarafcon. *p. Avignon.* Romans. I. A town of Dauphiny, Jituatcd on the Ifere, in the diocefe of Vienne, and generality of Grenoble, the feat of an election &c. 4 leagues from Valence, 19 from Grenoble, 16 from Montelimart, 30 from Orange, 37 from Avignon, 31 from Lyons, and from Paris. *Bu reau depoße.* 2. A village of Poitou, in the election of S. Maixant.. *la Motte-Ste.-Heraye.* Romans & S. *George,* places of Brefle, in the bailiwick of Bourg, *p. Bourg-en BreJJi.* Romas, a village of Biarn, In the receipt of Pau. *p. Pau.* Remanieres, a village of Poitou, in the election of Niort, *p. Niort.* Romany, a village of Bretagne, in the diocefe and receipt of Rennes, *p Rennes.* Rombies, a place of Flanders, in the diocefe of Cambray. *p. Valenciennes.* Rombly, a place of Artois, in the bailiwick of Lillicrs. *p. Aire.* Rome, a fm.-'.l town of VcxinNormand, near Bezu.f. *Ecouy.* Rojneccurt. See *Azondange.* Romegoux-deFaucb, a village of Upper Languedoc, in the diocefe and receipt of Alby. *p. Alby.* Rtmemonl. See *Vilaine.* RmtB) a village of Normandy,in the election of Conches, *p. Evreux.* Romer.ault, a village of Burgundy in the bailiwick of Semur. *p. Semer»* Romenay, a town of Burgundy, in the diocefe and bailiwick of Macon. *p. Tournas.* Romtrée, a village of Fbndcrs, in the diocefe of Cambray, and the government of Charlemont. *p. Charlemont.* Romeries, a village of Flanders, in the diocefe of Cambray, and the. government of Quênoy. *p. Shinoy.* Romery. I. A village of Picardy, in the election of Quife. *p. Guife.* 2. See *Cormoyeux.* Rome/camps, a town of Picardy, in the diocefe and election of Amit-ns. *p. Aumale.* Romtftaing, a villagcof Condomois, in the diocefe and election of Condom, *p. Banas.* Romelte. 1. A village of Dauphiny, in the diocefe and election of Gap. *p. Gap.* 2. Aplace of Franche Comté, in the bailiwick of Lons-le-' Saunier, *p. Lons-lc-Saunier.* Romeyer, a village of Dauphiny, in the eleition of Montelimart. *p. Die.* Rcmiere & *Solelbac,* a village of Lower Languedoc, in the diocefe and receipt of Puy. *p. le Puy.* Romigny. I. A village of Champagne, in the diocefe and election of Rheims, *p. Rheims.* 2. A village of Picardy, in the diocefe and election of Soiftons. *p. Charly.* Romiguiere, la. 1. A village of Rouergue, in the election of Milhaud.. *Milbaud.* 2. A place of Lower Languedoc, in the diocefe and receipt of Puy. *p. le Puy.* Romiguieres, a place of Lower Languedoc, in the diocefe and receipt of Béziers. *p. Béliers.* Romillé, a village of Bretagne, in the diocefe and receipt of S. Malo. *p. Becherel.* Romilly. I. A townof Champagne, in the election of Nogent-fur-Seine. *p. JSt'ogent-Jur-*

Seine. 2. A village oí Normandy, in the election of Con-' ches. *p. Evreux.* 3. A village of
Seauce, in the election of Châteaudun. *p. Châeaudun.* Rmmatie, a foreft of 9013 arpents, in the jurifdiftion of Rouen.

Rommcis. See *Roumois. Romollts.* See *Roumoules.* Romont, a place of Picardy, in the elcftion ol Doulcns./. *Montrtuil-Jurtner.* — Romorantin, a considerable town of Bléfois, on the Saudre, the capital of Sologne, in the diocefe of Blois, and generality of Orleans; it has an election, bailiwick, &c. about 11 leagues from Blois, 15 from Amboife, 22 from Tours, and 53 from Paris. *Bureau de poße,* Romprey, a place of Burgundy, in the bailiwickof Châtillon. /.*C¿zfi//en.* Ronny, a village of Champagne, in the diocefe and election of Troyes. *p. Vandeuvre.* Roticamp, a village of Normandy, in the election of Vire. *p. Vire.* Ronce, la, a place of FrancheComté, in the bailiwick of Poligny. . *Salins.* Roncenay, le, a place of Normandy, in the election'of Conches. *p.Я-vreux.* Ronceray, a convent in Angers. Roncerotz, /es, a village of Normandy, in the diocefe and election of Li*beux.p. Lifieux.* Roncey, a fmall town of Normandy, in the diocefe and election of Coilranees, *p. Coutances.* Ronebamps, a village of FrancheComté, in the bailiwick of Vefoul. *p. Lure.* RonebauxA. A village of FrancheComté, in the diocefe and bailiwick of S. Claude, *p. Salins.* 2. A place of Franche-Comté, in the bailiwick of Quiñgey.f. *Befanf on.* R.ncberes. I. A village of Brie, in the election of Château-TMerry. *p. la Fere.* 2. A village of Gàtinois, in the election of Gien. *p. Gieh.* Ror.cberolles, a vilhgc of Normandy, in the diocefe and election ofRoutn. *p. NeufcbJtel.* Kaneberolles-tn-Bray, a fmall town ef Noi niaudy, in the iocefe and dec tion ef Rouen, *p. Eenuy.* Roncbeville. I. A village of N0» mandy, in the election of Pont-l'Eveque. *p. Bont-l' Eveque.* 2. See *S. Meßain.* Ronebin, a village of Flanders, in the fubdelegation of Lille, *p. Ldlt.* Roneboy, a village of Normandy, in the election of Neufchâtel. *p. Au male.*

Ronctj, a fmall town of Flanders, in the fubdelegation of Lille, *p. Lille.* Ronde, la, a fmall town of Poitou, in the election of Thouars. *p. la Cbateigneraye.* Rondeboeuf. See *Caßendet.* Rondebaye, la, a fmall town of Normandy, in the election of Codtanccs. *p. Coûtantes.* Rc-ndot, a wood containing 166 ar pents, in the jurifdiction of Challón. Ronejfe, a town of Angoumois, in the diocefe and election of Angoulême. *p. Angouleme.* Ronfeugeray, a village of Normandy, in the election of Falaifc. *p. Conde'-Jur-Noireau.* Ronge, la, a village of Perche, in the election of Mortagne. *p. Nogent-le-Rctrou.* Rongemontitr, a fmall town of Normandy, in the election of PontAudemer. *p. Boucaebard.* Rengieres. I. A village of Bourbonnois, in the election of Moulins. *p. Moulins.* 2. A village of Bourbonnois, in the election of Montlucon.. *Mmtheon* .3. A village.of Auvergne, in the diocefe and election of Clermont, *p. Clermont.* Ronnay. I. A village of Champagne, in the election of Bar-furAube. *p. Bar-fur-sfube.* 2. A villa¿e, in the election of Normandy, in the election of Falaife. *p. Falaife.* Ronnet, a village of Bourbonnois, in the election of Montluçon. *p. Montluçon.* Ror.no, a fmall town of Beaujolois, in the elcctiou of Villefranchc. *p. yillefranebt.* Reitjutrollesï. A village of Picardy, in the diocefe and elision Senlîs. *p. Clermont.* Ronquerolies, or *S. Andre-deRor.queroilesy* a village of Lower Languedoc, in the diocefe and receipt of Karbonne, *p. Narbanne.* Ron/at, le, a place of Bourbonnois, in the election o(Moulins, *p. Moulins.* Rcnfenac, a fown of Angoumois, in the diocefe and election of Angoulême. *p. Augouleme.* Ron-fiy, a fmall town of Picardy, in the election of Péronnc. *p. le Cátele t.* Ллоп/uelj a village of Dombes, in the chatellany of Chalamont. *p. Jiovrg-en-Brejfe,* Rontallon, a village of Lyonnois, in the diocefe and election of Lyons, *p. Ronûgnon,* a village of Béarn, in the receipt of Pau. *p. Pau.* Ronton, a village of Normandy, in the diocefe and election of Avranches. *p. Avranc&i.* Ronxoux, a village of Normandy, in the election of Alcnçon. /. *Mortagne.* Roebecqw, a fmall town of Artois, in the bailiwick of Lillkrs. *p. Betbune.* Roocourt-la-Coße, a village of Champagne, in the election of Chaumont. *p. Cbaumont,* Roppe, a village of Alface, in the Vailiwick of Delle, *p. Btffort.* Roppenbám, a village of Alface, in the bailiwick of Flcckenftein. p, *le Tort-Louis.* Roquageix, a. place of Lower Languedoc, in the diocefe and receipt of ßeziers. *p. Be'z'nrs.* Roquaincourt) a village of Norrr.andy, in the election of Caen. *p. Cain.* Rcquajfels, a phec of Lower Languedoc, in the diocefe and receipt of Béziers. *p. Éhlers.* Requería, i. A town of Languedoc, in the diocefe of Nîmes, *p. Nîmes.* 2. A fmall town of RouflUJon, in the diocefe and generality of Perpignan/*p. Perpignan* 3. A village of Normandy, in the election of Punt-l'Evcque. *p. L'tfieux,* 4. A village of Normandy, in the election of Pont-Audemer./. *Pont-Auderr.er.* 5. A village of Guiennc, in the diocde and ele¿tion of Bourdcaux. *p. Cadillac.* 6. A village of Armagnac, in the diocefe and election of Auch. *p. Caßelnau-de-Magr.ac.* 7. Л vilbge of Lower Languedoc, in the diocefe and receipt of Uzés.. *le Vtgan.* 8. A village of Lower Languedoc, in the diocefe and receipt of Montpellier, *p. Montpellier,* 9. A village of Ncbouzan, in the diocefe of Comminge». *p. S. Gaudens.* 10. A village of Normandy, in the election of Vire.. *Vire.* Rcqut-Aimier, la, a village of Lower Languedoc, in the diocefe and receipt of Montpellier, *p. Montpellier.* Roque-Bafoergue9 la, a village of Rouergue, in the diocefe and election of Rhodcz. *p. Rbodtz.* Roque-Baron, a village of Provence, in the vigueryof Hieres. *p.Biigr.oLcs.* Rcque-Bouiilac, la, a village of Rouergue, in the election of Villcfranche. *p. Figeac.* Rcque-Broue, la, a fmall town of Auvergne, in the election of Aurillac./. *Jlu¿ iliac.* Roquebrune. 1. A fmall town of Lower Languedoc, in the diocefe and receipt of Béziers. *p. Beziers,* 2. A village of Bazadois, in the election of Condom, *p. Condom.* 3. A village of Armagnac, in the diocefe and election of Auch. *p. Auch.* 4. A village of Provence, in the viguery of Draguignan. *p. Frejus.* 5. A place of Provence, in the diocefe of Digne, *p. Digne.* 6. A pariih in the diocefe of Embrun, *p.*

Embrun. Rque-Bru jane, la, a villrge of Provence, in the viguery of Erignollcs. *p. Br'ignoUcs. Roquecor,* a village of Agénois, in the diocefe and election of Agen./. *Agen. Roquecourbe.* I A village of Upper Languedoc, on the Agout, in the diocefe and receipt of Caflres./. *Cβrtt.* a. A place of Lower Languedoc, in the diocefe and receipt of Narbonne. *p. Narbonne. Roque-Lesiere,* a village of Rouergue, in the election of Milhaud. *p. Milhaud. Roque-d'Antarony lat* a village of Provence, in the diocefe and viguery of Aix.. *Pertuis. Roque-deSa9 /a,* a village of Lower Languedoc, in the diocefe and receipt of Narbonne. *p. Narbonne. Roque-d'Efcfapon, la,* a village of Provence, in the viguery of Dragui,$nan. *p. Draguignan. Roque-dyOlines, la,* a fmalltown of Upper Languedoc, in the diocefe and receipt of Mirepoix. *p. Mirepoix. Roque-Γ01meъ,* a town of Languedoc, in the diocefe of Caftrcs. *p. Caβrei. Roque-Dur,* a village of Lower Languedoc, in the diocefe and receipt of Aiais. *p. Sumefne. Roque-du-Travet,* a village ofUpper Languedoc, in the diocefe and receipt of Alby. *p. Alby. Roquefere,* a village of Lower Languedoc, in the diocefe and receipt of Carcaffbnne. *p. CarcaJJimie. Roqueferé.* See *Ejcrcuje. Roquefeull.* i. A fmall town of Upper Languedoc, in the diocefe and receipt of *Att. p. Limoux.* 2. A place of Provence, in the viguery of S. Maximin. *p. S. Maximin.* Roque-FirmacMjla, a" fmall town of Condomois, in the diocefe and election of Condom, *p. Condom. Roquefort,* i. A fmall town of Upper Languedoc, in the diocefe and receipt of Alet. *p. Limoux.* 2. A village of Rouergue, in the election of Milhaud. *p. MJbaud.* 3. A village of Normandy, in the election of Caudebec. *p. Fawville.* 4. A village of Provence, in the viguery of Aix. *p. Aubagne.* 5. A village of Armagnac, in the election of Lomagne. *f. Beaumontde-Lomagne.* 6. A village of Gafcony, in the diocefe and election of Comm Inges, *p. S. Gaudcr.s.* 7. A village of Armagnac, in the diocefe and elec tion of Auch./». *Auch.* 8. A village of Lower Languedoc, in the diocefe and receipt of Narbonne. *p. Narbonne,* 9. A foreft of 1648 arpents, in the jurifdiction of Quillan. *Roquefart llbdty* a village of Upper Languedoc, in the diocefe and receipt of Mirepoix. *p. Mirepoix. Roquefort-de-Marfan,* a town of Gafcony, on the Douze, in the receipt of Marfan, *p. Mont-de-Morfan. Roquefort-de-Turjany* a fmall town of Gafcony, in the election of Landes. *p. S. Sewer. Roquefure,* a village of Provence, in the diocefe and viguery of Apt. *p. Apt. Roquegaja, /a,* a fmall town of Périgord, in the diocefe and election of Sarlat. *p. Sarlat. Roque-Giro, la.* See *la Roche Giron. Roquelaure.* ï. A town of Armagnac, in the diocefe and election of Auch. *p. Auch.* 2. A village of Rouergue, in the election of Milhaud. *p, Rhodes. Roquemadour,* a town of Qnercy, in the election of Figeac. *p.-Peyrae. Roqutmamban, la,* a village of Condomois, in the diocefe and election of Condom, *p. Condom. RoquemareXy la.* See *Montaflrutq. Roqucmartine £f S. Pierre-de-Vence,* a village of Provence, in the viguery ofTarafcon. *p. Orgon. Roquemaur,* I. A town of Upper Languedoc, in the diocefe and receipt of Montauban, *p. Montauban.* 2. A place of Condomois, in the diocefe and election of Condom, *p. Condom. Roquemattre,* a town of Lower Languedoc, fituated on a rock near the Rhône, above 2 leagues from Avignon, *p. Bagnols. Roquemeyrahy la,* a fmall town of Périgord, in the diocefe and electiorr of Sarlat. *p. Bergerac, RojucmicQtu ty* a village oí Normandy, in the election of Caën. *p. Caen, Roquemont. 1.* A village of Picardy, in the election of Crefpy.*p.Crefpy.* 2. A village of Normandy, in" the diocefe and election of Rouen, *p. £. Saen. Roquenelle, la* See *Trefoil. Roquepertuis,* or 5. *Andre-de-Roquepertuis,* a village of Lower Languedoc, in the diocefe and receipt of Üzés. *p. Bagnols. Roquepine,* a village of Condomois, in the diocefe and election of Condom, *p. Bergerac. Roqucrolhs,* a village of Picardy, in the diocefe and election of Senlis. *p. Senlis. Roque-Roquaffèl, la,* a village of Upper Languedoc, in the diocefe and receipt of Alby, *p. Alby. Roques. 1.* A village of Gafcony, in the diocefe and election of Comminges. *p. Toulcufe.* z. A village of Kormandy, in the election of Bernay. *p. Bemay.* 3. A village of Armagnac, in the diocefe and election of Auch. *p. Auch,*,4, A Village of Rouergue, in the election of Villefranche, *p. VtlUfrancbe-de-Rùuergue. Roques-Fernere,* a village of Upper Languedoc, in the diocefe and receipt of Touloufe. *p. Alby,* Roques-Hautes, a place of Provence, in the diocefe and viguery of Aix./. *Aix. Roque-Ste.-Marguerite, la,z* vilbge of Rouergue, in the election of Milhaud.. *Milbaud. Roqueβcir,* a village of Artois, in the bailiwick of Aire. *p. Aire. Roquet,* a place of Dombes, in the chatellany of Trévoux./;. *V'ülcfranche. Roquetai/lade.* x. A village of Upper Languedoc, in the diccefe and receipt of Alet. *p. Limoux.* a. A village of Armagnac, in the diocefe and election of Auch./. *Aucb.* 3. A village of Rouergue, in the election of Milhaud. *p. Milbaud.* Roqueta Hade, or *S. Pey-de-Roquetaillade,* a village of Bazadois, in the diocefe cf Bazas, and election of Condom, *p. Rbodt%.* Roqu e-Timbaui, la, a (mall town of Agénois, in the diocefe and election of Agen. *p. Agen. Rùçue-ïeïrac, la* a vilbge of Quer cy, in the eleftion of Figeac. *p. F'tgeac. Roquette,* a village of Gafcony, in the diocefe and eleftion of Comminges. *p. Toulouje. Roquette, la* I. A village of Provence, in the diocefe and viguery of of Graffe. *p. Große, г.* A village of Normandy, in the eleftion of Andely. *p. Ecovy.* 3. A village of Provence, in the viguery of Barjols. *p. Cannes. Rouqueite-Cbanan, la,* a village of Provence, in the viguery of Entrevaux, *p. Caβellane. Rcuauetle-de-Marquercn, la,* a place of Agenois, in the diocefe and election of Agen. *p. Agen. Roquevatre,* a town of Provence, on the river Veaune, in the diocefe of Marfeillcs, and viguery of Aix, in the road from Aix to Toulon, 6 leagues from Marfeilles, 6 from Aix, and Ii from Toulon. *Bureau dépolie. Roqcvei onde,* a village of Lower Languedoc, in the diocefe and receipt of Béziers. *p. Bc'zurs. Roquevidal,* a village of upper Languedoc, in the diocefe and receipt of Lavaur. *p. Lavaur. Rojutbil/e, la,* a fmall town of Auvergne, in the eleftion of Aurillac. *p. Amillac. Roquexels,* a village of lower

Languedoc, in the diocefe and receipt of Béziers. *p. B 'ziers.* Roquler. See *Wambaye.* Roquigny.i. A fmalltown of Champagne, in the diocefe and eleftion of Rheims, *p. Rethel.* 2. A village of Artois, in the bailiwick of Bapaume. *p. Bapaume, Roqmgny & Montreu'tl,* a village of Picardy, in the eleftion of Guife. *p. Vrvini.'* Roquüle, la, a village of Agénois, in the diocefe and eleftion of Agen. *p. Agen.* Rorthéy, a place of Champagne, in the eleftion of Chaumont. *p. Chau mont.* Ros-Landr'uux, a village of Bretagne, in the diocefe anj receipt of Dol. *p. Dot.* Rts-Sur-Couefnon, a village of Bretagne, in diocefe and receipt of Dol. *p. Fontarfcn.* Rofantieres, a village of Auvergne, in the diocefe and election of Clermont, *p. CUrmont.* Rofay. I. A village of Normandy, in the election of Lions, *p. Etouy.* 2. *A* village of Normandy, in the election of Neufchâtel, *p. Neufchâtel.* 3. A village of Franche-Comté, in the bailiwick of Vefoul. *p. Vefoul.* 4. A village of Bcauce, in the election df Mantes *p. Mantes.* 5. See *Roxoy.* Rofay, ov *S. 'Georges-du-Rofay,* a town of Maine, in the diocefe and election of Mans. *p. le Mem.* Rofay,-DoudevUle, a place of Normandy, in the election of Anddy. *p. Gad/on.* Rofebeweir, a village of Alface, in the bailiwick of Ribauville. *p. Beffart, Rcfcof tr Rofcou,* a fea port town of Bretagne, about a league froniPoldc-Léon. *p. Moriaix.* Rofde, la, a fmall town ofAuvcrgne, in the diocefe and election of Cleriuont. *p. Clermont.* Rtfearrvel, a village of Bretagne, in the diocefe and receipt of Quimper.
jumper. Rofelies. See *VJlechaJfon.* RcfenvteUler, a village of Alface, in the bailiwick of DacTiftcin./. Meljhiim. Roferette. See *Ajfoux.* Rcfey, It, a place of Dombes, m the diocefe of Lyons, and chatcllany, of Ambericu. *p. Belleville.* Reßeirn, a city of Alface, fituatcd at tlit foot of a mountain on a fmall river, in the bailiwick of Dachftein, about 4 leagues from Stralburgh. /, *Mdßeims.* Roßer, or Roßeres, a fmall town cf Limoiin, in the diocefe and election cf Tulles, *p. Tulles.* Rßere, a place of Burgundy, in the bailiwick of Charollcs. *p. Dijon.* Rcjicre-S.-Ceoige, a fmall own of Limofin, in the diocefe and election f Limfcgcs. *p. Brives.* Roßerc-fur-la-Maufe, a village of Franche-Comté, in the bailiwick of Vefoul. *p. Vefoul.* Roßeres. I. A village of Limofin, in the election of Brives. *p. Brives.* 2. A place of Franche-Comté, in the bailiwick of Beaume. *p. Beaume.* 3. A priory, in th _ diocefe of Rheims. 4. See *Realeres.* Rßers. See *Roxiers.* Roßgr.ol. See *Liomer.* Roßey, a village of Burgundy, in the bailiwick of Nuits, *p. Nuits.* Rojnay, I. A fmall town of Berry, in the election of Blanc, *p. le Blanc.* 2. A village of Poitou, in the election of Fontenay. *p. Luçon.* 3. An ancient comté of Champagne, in the diocefe and election of Troyes. 4. See *Lcvigny.* Rojnokan, a village of Bretagne, in the diocefe and receipt of *Sjfmpcr. p. Landerneau.* Rofry. i. *A* fmall town of Bcauce, in the election of Mantes, *p. Mantes.* 2. A village in the diocefe and election of Paris, *p. Bor.dy.* Rofoy, I, A village of Champagne, in the diocefe and election of Langres, *p. Retbcl.* 2. A village of Champagne, Jn the diocefe and election of Sens. *p. Sens.* 3. See *Roxey.* Rofpez & Miniby, a village of Bretagne, in the diocefe and receipt of Treguier. *p. Guingamp.* Ro/pcrden, a town of Bretagne, iu the diocefe and receipt of Quimper; 5 leagues fram Quimper, 6 from Quimpcrlay, 22 from Vannes, 24 from Breft, ti from l'Orient, and 48 from Narircs. *Bureau de poße.* Rojfay, a town of Poitou, in the election of Loudun. *p. Lcudun.* Rojjáyrolies, a place of upper Languedoc, in the diocefe and receipt of Alby. *p. My.* Roß'e, a lake of Franche-Comté, at the bottom of Mont-Jura. Roffe, a village of Champagne, in the diocefe and election of Langres. *p. Langres.* Roßdden, a village of Alface, in the bailiwick of Ben eld. *p. Benfeld* dy, in the eleftionof Falaife. . FaUife, Rots, a village of Normandy, Î» the eleftion of Caê'n. *p. Caen.* Rottel/beim, aplace of Alface, in the bailiwick of Hagueeau./. Haguenau. Rottonayy a village of FranchcComte, in the bailiwick of Orgelet. *p. Lens-le-Saunier.* Rcuy a village of Anjou, in the eleftion of Saumur. *p. Saumur.* Rouaillant, a village of Bazadois, in the eleftion of Condom, *p. Баы.* Rovandiercy /я, a town of Anjou, in the diocefe and eleftion of Angers, *p. Mondîubkau* Rouanne. I. A village of Auvergne,, in the eleftion of Aurillac. *p. Aurillae.-1* See *Roanne.* Rouansy a place of Bretagne, in the diocefe and receipt of Nantes, *p. PortS.-Pere.* Rouaumeixy a village of Meflin, in the diocefe and receipt of Toul. *p-Toü/.* RoayrouXf a fmall town of upper Languedoc, in the diocefe and receipt of Caitres. *p. Caßres.* RmbaiXy a fmall town of Flanders, in the fubdelegation of Lille, *p. Lille.* Roube/ot, or *S. Pierre'de-Roubeloty* a village of Agénois, in the diocefe and election of Agen. *p. Agen.* Roubia, a village of lower Languedoc, in the diocefe and receipt of Narbonne. *p. Narbonne.* Roubiacy a village of lower Languedoc, in the diocefe and receipt of Uzés. *p. S. Ambrcix.* Roubiacy or *S. Mkhel-de-fRoubiaCy* a a place of Rouergue, in the eleftioa of Milhaud. *p. Milbaud.* Roubicbouxy a place of upper Lan- gucdoc, in the diojeîe and receipt of Mirepoix. *p. Mirepoix.* Roubellet, a village of upper Languedoc, in the diocefe and receipt *of Alet. p. Limcux.* RoubinCy la. See *Robine.* Roubion. î. A village of Venaifuoi in the judicature of Lille, *p Avignon.* г. Sec *Robiotu Stsuldfe.* See *Rovliebmfe.* Roubroueky a fmall town of Flanders, in the fubdciegation of Caffel. *p. Cafe!.* Rvucboufe, la, a village of Forez,/ in the election of S.Etienne, *p. S. Etienne.* Roucoarr, a village of Flanders, in the fubdciegation of Bouchain. *p. Quefnoy.* Raucous, a village of Rouergue, in the diocefe and election of Rhodcz. *p. Mi/baud.* Roucy, a town of Picardy, in the diocefe and election of Laon. *p. Fifmes.* Roudarefas, a village of Mnrche, in the election of Bourganeuf. *p. Bourganeuf.* Roudoubns, a village of Agénoïs, in the diocefe and election of Agen. *p. Agen.* Roue, a Village of Frajiche-Comté, in the bailiwick, of Quingey. *p BeJançon.* Reue, ¡a, a village of Bourbonnois, in the generality of Moulins, *p. Mou hns.* Rouecourt, a village of Champagne, in the election of Joinville./.oiMi/i7/f.* Rouede, a village of Gafcony, in the diocefe and election of Comminges. *p. Cafie/nau-dc-Ma-*

gnac. *Rouelle',* a village of Normandy, in the election of Domfront, *p. Domfront. Rouelles.* I. A village of Normandy, in the election of MontivilHeis, *p. le Havre, i.* A village of Burgunds, in the election of Chàtillon. *p. ChàtilUn. Rouen,* a very ancient and capital city of Normandy, on the borders of the-Seine, the fee of an archbiihop, who is the primate of Normandy; its commerce is very confîdcrablc in all forts of merchandize j it contains 36 parifhes, feveral hofpitals, and 60,000 inhabitants; 14 leagues from Dieppe, 29 from Abbeville, 35 from Alencon, 26 from Amiens, 28 from Argentan, It from Havre, and 33 from Paris. *Bureau de poße. Räuirgue,* a province about 30 leagues in length and 20 in breadth, bordered on the eaft and fouth bv Languedoc, on the weft by Quercy, and on the north by Auvergne; the land is not very fertile, but produces much wood, and mines of copper, iron, fulphur, vitriol, *Sec.* the principal rivers are the Tarn and the Lot. Rodez is the capital city. *Roue-jjé, Roueße' & Fontamt,* town of Maine, in the diocefe and election of Mans, *p Frefnay. Rouet,* a p'чee of lower Languedoc, in the diocefe and receipt of Montpellier, *p. Montpellier. Rouez,* a town of Maine, in the diocefe and election of Mans. *p. Frefnay. Rouffacb,* or *Rouffack,* or *Rußach,* a town of Alface, fituatcd on the river Rotbach, in the diocefe of Bale, the capital of Obermondat; about 10 leagues from Bale, 4. from Mulhaufen, 6 from Brifac, 20 from Strafburg, and about 120 from Paris. *Bureau de poße. Rcujfiac.* i. À town of Sa'mtonge, in the diocefe and election of Saintes. *p. la Grolle,* ft. A fmall town of Auvergne, in the election of Aurillac. *p. Aurillac.* 3. A village of Guienne, in the diocefe and election of Bourdeaux. *p.Blaye.* 4. A village of Bazadois, in the election of Condom.. *Bazas.* 5. A village of Angonmois, in the diocefe and election of Angoulême. *p.Angoulême.* 6. A village of upper Lan uedoc, in the diocefe and receipt of CarcaflTonne. *p. Carcaßonne.* 7. A village of upper Languedoc, in the diocefe and receipt of Tculoufe. *p. Tculoufe.* '8. A village of lower Languedoc, in the diocefe and receipt of bïarbonne. *p. Tou laufe.* 9, A village of Angoumois, in the election of Cognac, *p. Cognac.* 10. A village of Qiiercy, in the diocefe and election ot Cahors. *p. Cabors.* i if A village of Rouergue, in the election of Villefranche. *p. A/by. Rwßiac,* or *S. Martin-de-Roußae9* a village of Agenois, in the diocefe and election of Agen. *p. A&tn RouffignaCf* a village of Pcrigord, in the election of Sarlat. *Sttrlat. Roijßgnat & Lair,* a town of Rérigord, in the diocefe and election of Périgueux. *p. Perigueux. Roußigny,* a village of Normandy, in the diocefe and election of Avr;:nches. *f. Villedieu. Roußllac,* a village of Quercy, in the diocefe and election or Cahors. *p. Cabers. Roujßange,* a village of FrancheComte, in the bailiwick, of Dele . *Dole. Rcuffy,* a place of Champagne, in the diocefe and election of Chalons. *p. Ej ernay. Roufieu,* a village of Vivarais, in the diocefe and receipt of Viviers, *p. Vhiers. Rcugé & Soulevacbe,* a village of Bretagne, in the diocefe and receipt of Nantes. *p. Cbateaubriar.t. Rouge, la,* a village of Normandy, in the election of Mortagne. *p. Mortagne. Rovgeague,* a place of FrancheComté, in the bailiwick of Dole. *p. Dole. Rougcauy* a village of Blefois, in the election of Romorantin. *p. Ro moran tin. Rougefaix,* a village of Artois, in the bailiwick of Hefdin. *Hcfdm. Rougegoute,* a village of Alfacc, in the bailiwick cf BefFort. *p. Beffort. Rougemaifon, la,* a village of Picardy, in the diocefe and election of Bcauva's. *p. Beauvais. Rovgcmcnt.* i. A town of Bugey, irr the bailiwick of Belley, about 6 leagues from Châtillon-fur-Seine. *p. S. Ran bert.* 2. A vllbge of FrancheComté, in the bailiwick of Vefoul. *p. Vefoul.* 3-A village of Champagne, in the election of Tonnerre. *p. Aкеу-le-Franc.* 4. A village of Alface, in the bailiwick, of BefFort, *p. Btffort.* 5. See *Aran. Rtvgemonticr,* a imall town of Normand, in the election of PontAudemer. *p. Boucachard. Rcugemontof,* a place of Franche Comté, in the bailiwick of Vefoub *p. Veful. Roi gères,* a village of Berry, in the election of Châtre, *p. la Châtre. Rougeris,* a village of Picardy, in the diocefe and election of Laon. *p,_ Marie. Rcuges-Pierres,* a village of Normandy, in the election of Conehes *p. Neuf bourg. Rougeux,* a village of Cliamnagne. in the diocefe and election of Langres. *p. Lar.gres. Rongiez,* a village of Provence, in the viguery of S. Maxrmin. *p. S. Aiax.m n. Rovgnac.* I. A fmall town of Angoumbis, in the diocefe and election of Angoulême. *p. Angouleme.* 2, See *Rognac. Rcugr.at,* a town of Auvergne, in the election of Combrailles. *p. Chambón. Rougnes Gf les Nobles,* a village of Provence, in the diocefe and viguery of Aix. *p. Pertuis. Rougnon,* a place of Franche-Comté, in the bailiwick ofVefoul. *p. Vefoul. RougnonaSjZ* village of Provence, irr the viguery ofTarafcon. *p.Tarafcon. Rougon,* a village of Prove n:e, ilt the viguery of Mouftiers./». *Rim. Roubeyreut,* a village of Auvergne, in the election of IíToire. *p. iß'oire. Roujan,* a fmall town ¿f lower Languedoc, in the diocefe and receipt of Beziers. *p. Pizenas, Rcuil/ac.* I. A town of Angoumois, in the election of Cognac, *p. S. Cibardeaux.* 2. A village of Armagnac, in the election of J-omagne. /». *Left ou re. Rouillas,* a village of Périgord, in the election of Sarlat. *p. Bergerac. Rouillé,* a town of Poitou, in the diocefe and election of Poitiers, *p. Lußgnan. Rouillerot & la Planche,* a village of Champagne, in the diocefe and election of Troyes. /. *Troyes. Rcuill£t& Rochcyaud,* a fmall town of Angoumois, in the diocefe an, election of Angouleme. *p. Angmlm' RwHl'iers,* a town of Maine, in the diocefe and election of Mans. *p. Domfront. Rouillis, le,* a village of Beauce, in the election of Vendôme, *p. la Vil¿e-aux-C/ercs. Rouîllott)* a village of Maine, in the diocefc and election of Mans. *p. te Man¿. Rouilly,* a village of Brie, in the election of Provins, *p. Melun Rouilly, le.* See *Trefols. Rouilly-les-Saccy,* (if *Rouilly.-$ Loup,* villages of Champagne, in the. dioccfe and election of Troycs. *p. 7ryes. Roule, le.* I. A village of the-10c ©f France, in the diocefe and election of Taris, *p. Paris.* 2, A village of Normandy, in the election of i ions. *p. Eccuy. Rouiens,* a village of upper Languedoc, in the dio, efe and receipt oi CarcaiTonne. *p. Lmoux._ Roulhboije,* or *Robo'fe,* a village of Normandy, in the election of Chaumont. *p. Montes. Routlery.* See *Πο ital-le-Mercier, л Rouille, la,* a village of Flanders, in the government of Avefne. *p. Avefne.* RoulUurs, a village of Normandy, in the election of Vire. *p. Vire. Rwmagney.* I. A town of Normandy, in the election of Mortain. *p. Mortain.* 2. A place of Allace, in the bailiwick, of Bettort. *p. Beffort. Routnare,* a village of Normandy, in the diocefe and dc¿tion of Ruuen. *p. XeriAlie. Rouma-iicres,* a village of Angoumois, in the diocefe and election of Angoulème. *p. la Ruckcfoucault. Roumegoux.* I A town of Saintongc, in thedioccfe and election of Saintes. *p. Saintes-*2. A village of Auvergne, in the election oi Aui lilac. *p.Aurillac. Roumegoux & Tels,* a vilhge of upper Languedoc, in the dioccfe and receipt of Alby. *p. Ally.* RoumengouXf a village of upper Languedoc, in the diocefe and rcpeit of lircpaix. *p. MirepQix. Roumenil,* a figniory of Normandy, in the election of Arques, *p. p. ValUmont.* .

Riumeus, a village of upper Languedoc, in the diocefe and receipt of Toulouie. *p. Touhuje. Ruumieu, la,* a town of Condomois, in the diocefe and election of Condom, *p. Condom Ronmiliy. i. A* village of Normandy, in the dioc-fe and (lection of Rouen, *p Rouen.* 2. A village of Maine, in the election of ChâteaHdu-Loir. *p. Cbouau-du-Loir. Roam.is, le,* a fruitful country o"f Normandy, between the Seine and the Rillc. Quillebcuf is the capital. *Romnwles,* a village of Provence, in the vigucry of Mouftiers. *p. SiesC Rcun.ycs,* a village of Auvergne, in the election of Iíioire. *p. IjfÀrt. Ravor.,* a village of Dauphiny, ir» the diocefe and ele¿Vion *of* Valence. *p. Valence. Rouperoux Terrebaut,* a town of Maine, in the dioccfe and Rectum of Mans. *p. Bonmßable. R.upsrroux,* a village of Normandy, in the election of Alenton. *p. Sccx. RoupiyA* village of Picardy, in the election of S. Quentin, *p. S. Quentin. Rouquerte,* a village of Périgord, in the election of Sarlat. *p. Bergerac. Rouquette, la.* 1. A village of Périgord, in the diocefc and election of Péiigueux. *p. P/rigueux.* 2. A village of Roucrguc, in the election of Villefranche, *p. PriUe!rancbe-de-Rouerguí.* 3. A village of Ruuergue, in the diocefc and election of Rhodcz. *p Rhodes.* 4. A placent upper Languedoc, in the dioccfe and receipt of Montauban. *p. Cujhes. Rouquette-Bcrmcval,la,* a village of Rouergue, in the diocefc and election, of Rodez, *p. Rfadcz. Roure, /e, ¿3 la Mure,* a village of Forez, in the election of Montbvifon. *p. Muib₂'ɸn. Rçuret, le,* a place of Provence, in the diocefe and viguery of Grafle.. *Graß. Rou/aSf* a village of Dauphinyä m *RcuJTyques,* a village of upper Lin-*Rouvray. i. A* imall town of guedoc, in the diocefe and receipt of Normandy, in the election of NeufCarcañonne. *p. Carcaß'onne.* châtel. *p. Ntufibátel.* ». A place of *Routes,* a town of Normandy, in Burgundy, in the bailiwick.of, Beaune, the eleftion of Caudebec. *p. Fecamp, p. Beaune.* 3. A village of Burgun *Routier,* a village of upper Lan-dy, in the bailiwick of Avalon, *p.* guedoc, in the diocefe of Narbonne. *Avalon.* 4. A iigniory of Norp% *Lavaur,.* mandy, in the diocefe and eleftion of *Routot. i. A* market town ofNor-Evrcux. *p. Pont-de-fArcbe.* mandy, in the election of Pont-Au-*Rouvray,* or *S. Etienne-de-Rouvrayt* demer. *p.Pont-Audemer.* ». A mar-a fmall town of Normandy, in the ket town of Normandy, in the elec-eleftion of Rouen, *p. Rouen.* tion, of Montivilliers. *p.Harfieur., Rouvray ¿sf S.Florentin,* a village of *Routtier,* a village of Dauphiny, in Beauce, in the diocefe and eleftion of the diocefe and eleftion of Gap. *p. Chartres, p. Chartres. Mont-Dauphin, . Rouvray-S.-Denis,* a village of *Ronvaux,* a village of Mcflîn, in Beauce, in the eleftion of Dourdan. the diocefe and receipt of Verdun, *p. p. Angerville. Verdun. Rouvray-Ste.-CroiXfZ* village of Or *Rouvaux-la-Grange. See*Echenol. léannois, in the diocefe and eleftion *Rowuenac,* a village of upper Lan-of Orleans, *p. Artenay.* guedoc, in the diocefe and receipt of-*Rouvre.* 1. A village of Cham Alet. *p. Limoux.* Pagne, in the eleftion of Bar-fur *Rouver,* a priory in the diocefe of Aube. *p. Bar-fur-Auie.* ». A vi. Meaux. läge of Poitou, in the eleftion of *Rowverges,* a village of Auvergne,

Niort, *p. Niort.* 3. A village of in the eleftion of *AurWlac. p. Auri/lac.* Burgundy, in the diocefe and baili *Rowvero-,* a village of Normandy, wick of Dijon, *p Dijon.* in the eleftion of Vire. *p. Conde'-Jur-Rouvre-fous-Mjilly,* a village of *Noireau,* Burgundy, in the bailiwick of Arnay *Rouvroy,* a village of Champagne, le-Duc. *p. Pouilly.* in the eleftion of "Tonnerre, *p. Chai-Rouvrefitr-Auie,* a village of Cham I'tt., pagne, In the diocefe and eleftion of *RouveyrouXyt* town of Rouergue,in Langres. *p. Langres,* the eleftion of Villcfranche. *p. V'ult-RouVrel.* 1. A village of Picardy, *francbe-de-Rouergue.* in the eleftion of Mondiáicr./. *Mon Rou-vure, la.* 1. A village of lower *didier.* 2. See *Magny.* Languedoc, in the diocefe and receipt *Rouvres.* 1. A village of Beauce, of Mende. *p. Mende.* ». A village in the eleftion of Dreux, *p. Dreux.* of lower Languedoc, in the diocefe » A village of Normandy, in the and receipt of Uzés. *f. Uze's.* eleftion of Falaife. *p. Fa/aife.* 3. A *Rauvigay.* See *Prouvy.* village of Picardy, in the eleftion of *RouvSri, la,* (MPulcheridon, place of Crtpy. *p. la Ferte-Milon.* 4. A lower Languedoc, in the diocefe and village of Orléannois, in the eleftion receipt of Nîmes, *p. Aitmes.* of Pithiviers. *p. Pitbrviert. Rouville.* I. A village of Norman-*Rouvrts-les-Bois,* a fmall town of dv, in the eleftion of Caudebec. *p.* Berry, in the eleftion of Château *Lillebonr.c* ». A village of Picardy, roux. *p. Ltvroux.* in thecleftion of Crépy. *p. Ctipy.* 3. *Rouvroy. i.A* fmall town of Picar

A village of Orléannois, in the elecdy, in the eleftion of Péronne. *p.* tion of Pithiviers. *p. Etampes Pe'rmne.* ». A village of Picardy, *Rowiller,* a village of Picardy, in in the diocefe and eleftion 'of Laon. the eleftion of Clermont, *p. Compie'gne. p. Laon,* 3. A v'lage of Flanders, m the" fubdelegation of Douay. *p. Lille-*4. A village of Champagne, in the election of Joinville. *p. Rethel.* 5. A village of Picardy, in the election of S. Quentin, *p.Á Quentin.* 6. A village of Artois, in the bailiwick of Lens. *f. Lens.* ' *Rouvroy-en-Dormoy,* Ë? *Rcuvroyles-Rote%,* villages of Champagne, in tfcie diocefe and election of Rheims, *p. Rheims. Rouvroy-hs-Merles,* avillage of Picardy, in the election of Mondidier, *p. BreteuiL Roux, le Cap,* a cape or-promontory, on the coaft of Provence. *Roux-deCommkrsy* a village of Dauphiny, in the diocefe and election of Grenoble, *p. Grenoble. Rouxey la.* See *Ban-S.-Clement. Rouxiere, la petite,* a village of Bretagne, in the diocefe and receipt of Kantes. *p. Nantes. Rouxiers,* a place of Marche, in the election of Bourgaaeuf. *p. Bourgaeuf. Rouxmtml,* a figniory of Normandy, in the electioB of Caudebec. *p. Caudebec. Rouxons,* a village of Perche, in the election of Verqeuil.. *Mortagne. Rouy.* I. A fmall town of Nivernois, in the diocefe and election of Nevf rs. *p. Nevers.* 2. Sec *sjnigny. RcuyerCy* a place of Provence, in the diocefe and viguery of Aix. *p. A'tx. Rouyre,* a village of upper Languedoc, in the diocefe and receipt of Alby. *p. Alby. t Rouzaut.* See *Ffcffe. Rouzede,* a village *ni* Angoumois, in the diocefe and election of Angou9 ême. *p. Angoultme. Rouzieres.* 1. A village of Auvergne, in the election of Aurillac. *p. Auriliac.* "a. A village of upper, Languedoc, in the diocefe and receipt of Alby. *p. Alby. Rouxiers.* I. A fmall town of Touteine, in the diocefe and elect on of Tours, *p. Yours.* 2. A place of Marchçj in the election of Bourga aeuf. *p. Bourgareuf. Roussies,* a village of Flanders, it the government of Maubeuge. *p.ASaw beuge. Royal,* a village of Bretagne, in the diocefe of Rennes *p. Rennes. Royal-Lieu.* See *RoyauVieu. Royan,* a town of Saintonge, near the mouth of the Garonne, abouti leagues From Blaye. *p.Marennes. Royanez,* a fmall country of Dauphiny, part of the diocefe of Gap, about 6 leagues in length and 4 broad. *Rayât,* a fmall town of Auvergne, in the diocefe and election of Clermont.. *Clermont. Royaucourt,* a village of Picardy, in the diocefe and election of Laon. *p. Laon. Royaulieu,* a convent in the diocefe of Soiflons. *p. Compiegne. Royaumeix,* a village of Toulois, in the diocefe and receipt of Toul./.7W. *R&yaumont,* an abbey in the diocefe of Bcauvais. *p. Luprtbes. Royboijfy,* a village of Picardy, in the diocefe and election of Bcauvais. *p. Eeawvais. Royben,* a village of Dauphiny, in the election of Romans. *la-Cote-S.Adre. Roye.* i. A flxong town of Picardy, in the diocefe of Amiens, and election of Mondidier; the feat of a bailiwick, &c. it contains 3 pariihes, 2 hofpkals, &c. 10 leagues from Amiens, 7 from Perenne, ia from Bapaume, 18 from Arras, 15 from Senlis, 4 from Mondidier, and 27 from Paris. *Bureau depofie,* 2. A village of Franche-Comté, in the bailiwick of Vefoul. *p. Lure. Rye-S.-Nicolas,* a village of Picardy, ' in the election of Crêpy. *p. Crí/y. Roye-fur-la-MatVy* a village of Picardy, in the election of Mondidier. *p. Roye. Royer,* a parifh of Burgundy, in the diocefe and bailiwick of Challón, *p. Cbailon. Royere,* a village of Marche, in the lection of£ Bourganeuf. *p. Bourgantuf. Rcyree-hcrs-la-Roche,* a" village of Limofin, in the diocefe aud election of Limoges, *p. Limoges. Rcyerefres-S.-Leonard,* a viltage of Limofin, in the diocefe and election of Limoges, *p. S. Leonard. Roynac,* a village of Dauphiny, iu the election of Montelimart./. *Montclmart. Royon.* i. A village of Artois, in the bailiwick, of S. Pol. *p.Hefdin. 2.* See *Viejne. Rcyjeys,* a village of Forez, in the election of S. Etienne, *p. S. Etienne. Royville,* a village of Normandy, tn the election of Arques, *p. Dieppe. Roxan,* a village of Bazadois, in the election of Condom./. *Cafiillon. Romans,* a village of Dauphiny, in the diocefe and election ot Gap. *p. Cap. Rcxay.* I. A village of Champagne, in the election of Vitry. *p. Vitry.* 2. See *Rofay. Rcje,* a (ignioryxf Normandy, in the election of Andcly. *p. Etouy. Riae'-Preveß,* a village of Beauce, in the election cf Dreux, *p. Dreux. Roxel. 1.* A village of Normandy, in the election of Cam./ Caen. 2. *A* village of'Normandy, in the election of Valognts. *p. Valognet.* 3. A village of Picardy, in the election of Doulens. *p. Doukns. Rozel-S. Albin,* a village of Pieardy,,in the diocefe and election of SoiiTons. *p. Soißons.* Roxclieures, a village of Meffin, in the diocefe and election of Met'/.. *p. Luneville. Röxes,* a village of Armagnac, in the diocefe and election of Auch. *p. Condom. Rcxet,* a place of Franche-Comté, in the bailiwick of Dole *p. Lolt. Roxetle-Forret,* a village of Franche-Comté, in the bailiwick of Orgelet, *p. Lons-le-Saunier. Roxey,* a village of Burgundy, in the diocefe and bailiwick of Challón. *p. Cbalhn. Rouzier, le,* a fmall town of lower Languedoc, in the diocvlc and receipt of Mende. *p. Mende. Rozier.* See *Roßer. Roxiere,* a village of Champagne, in the election of Bar-fur-Aube. *p. Barfur-Aube. Roxiere, la.* I. A village of Normandy, in the election of Lions, *p. Ecouy.* 2. See *Roquigny. Rozicres.* I. A town of Picardy, ia the election of Mondidier. *p. Mondsdier.* 2. A village of Orléannois, in the election of Beaugency. *p. Orleans.* 3. A village of Picardy, in the diocefe and election of Soiflons. *p. SoifJons.* 4. A pariih of Burgundy, compofed of fcveral hamlets, in the bailiwick of Montcenis. *p. Autun.* 5. See *Roßeres. Raviers. J.* A village of Limofin, in the election of Brives. *p. Brves.* 2. A village of Forez, in the election of Montbrifon. *p. Montbrifon.* 3. A village of Forez, hi the election of Roanne, *p. Ríame.* 4. A village of Burgundy, in the bailiwick of Montcenis. *p. Autun.* 5. A place of Burgundy, in the diocefe and bailiwick of Dijon, *p. Dijon.* 6. A pariih of Touraine, in the diocefe of Tours, *p. Tours. Roziers, les,* a town of Anjou, in the diocefe and election of Angersj about 3 leagues from Beaufort, 10 from Flèche, and 8 from Angers. *Bureau depoße. Reviers & le Bac,* a village of Picardy, in the diocefe and" election of Laon./. *Laon. Rozoy.* i. A town of Brie, in the diocefe of Mtaux, and election of Paris, about 8 leagues from Menux, 5 from Coulomiers, and 12 from Paris. *Beaureau de 'poße.* 2. A village of Picardy, in the election of Clermont. *p. Clermet.* 3. A village of Gâtinois, in the election of Nemours, *p. Sens. Rozoy & Apremont,* 3 town of Picardy, in the diocefe and election of Laon. *p. Laon. Roxoy en Mulden,* a village of Picardy, in the election ofCrêpy. /. *Li£f. Roxoy.Gaßtbltd,* a village oí Bri», in the election of CUateauThicrry. /. *Cbф. Rozey-les-Aucby,* a village of Picardy, in the diocefe and election of Solfions, *p. Soifp.ns. Ruage,* a village of Nïvernois, in the election of Vezelay. p.*Corblgny. Rúan. j.* A village of Orléannois, in the diocefe and election of Orléans. *p. Arteray.* 2. A village of Beaucc, in the election of Châtcaudun. *p. Cbateaudun.* 3. A place of FrancheComté, in the bailiwick of Vcfoul. *p. fefoul. Ruau-de-LaJfc,* a large wood in the jurifdiftion of Vicrzon. *Ruaudln-en-BeTm,* a town of Maine, in the diocefc and election of Mans. *p. le Mans. RuhajJ'c)* a place of Dombes, in the chatellany of Beauregard, *p. Villefrancbe. Rubayy* or *Ríbay, le,* a town of Maine, in the diocefc and election of Mans. *Bureau de poße. Rubecourt,* a place of Champagne, in the receipt of Sedan, *p. Sedan, Rubelles,* a villageof Gârinois, in the election ofMelun. *p. Me fun. Rubetnpre,* a fmall town of Picardy, in the election of Doulens. *p, Amiens. Rubercil,* a village of Normandy, in the diocefe and election ofBayeux. *p. B ay eux. Rubercourt)* a village of Picardy, in the election of Mondidier. *p. Mittdidier. Rtfèermmtf* a village of Normandy, in the election of Bernay. *p.Bcrnay. Rulewillc,* a parifh of Normandy, in the diocefc of Coûtances. *p. Coutances. Rubigny,* a village of Champagne, in the diocefc and election of Rcthel. *p. Rabe/. Rubriment* Sec *Rubermont. Ruca,* a village of Bretagne, in the diocefe and receipt of S. Bricux. *p. Lamballe. Ruch,* a village of Bazadois, in the election of Condom, *p. Condom, Rucourt,* a village of Picardy, *ia* Vol.iu. the election of Compiégnc. *p. Vcrberie. Ru£fuerWet* a vilbge of Normandy, in the election of Caen./». *Caen. Rudciie,* aviltrgeof Qurcy, in the election ofFigcac. *p. Ftgeac. Ruderbach,* a place of Alface, in the bailiwick of Altkirch, *p. Altkirch. Rudicaßel,* a village of Normandy, in the eleétion of Caudebec. /. *Cuudebee. Rudlingt* Ê? *Ruß i off,* pi ace s of Meffin, in the diocefe and receipt of Metz. *p. Мая. Rue.* i. A town of Picardy, on the river Maye, in the election of Abbeville, about 2 leagues front S. Valéry, *p. Abbeville.* 2. A fmall river of Auvergne, that runs into th» Durdogne. *Rue, la,* a place of Marche, in the election of Gucrct. *p.Guerct,* Rue & Sagellot

j places of Provence, in the diocefc of JFréjus. *p. Frejus.* Rue-de-la-Croix,la, a villageof Burgundy, in the bailiwick of Avalon, *p. Ahtatoit,* Rue-de-Saws-Us-Marçuion, la, a village of Artois, in the diocefe and bailiwick of Arras, *p. Arras. Ruc-du-Fief,* a village,of Champagne, in the receipt of Vavicouleuri. *p. Void.* Rue-Prévet, /a, a village of Picardy, inthe election of Clermont, *p, Clermont.* Rue-S.-Pierre, la. X. A village of Picardy, in the election of Clermont. *p. Clermont.* 2. A village of Normandy, in the diocefe and election of Rouen, *p. Rouen. Rucil,* a village of Normandy, in the election of Verncuil. *p. Pot;t dc-V Arche. Rucilly,* a priory of Berry, in the diocefe of Bourges. *Ruel,* a town of the lile of France, in the diocefe and election of Paris. *p. Nanterre. Ruelle,* a fmall town of Angoumoi, in the diocefe andcJc£tioa of AUgOUfe lerne, *p. Angpultmt Rufleu,* a village of Valrmcv, in the generality of Dijon, *p. Bcliey. Rujjigné,* a village of Bretagne, in the diocefe and receipt of Nantes. *j. Châteaubiïant. Rujjigry,* a village of Poitou, in the diocefe and election of Poitiers. *p. Poitiers. Rufwveille,* a town of Normandy, in the election of Mortain. *p. Mortain.* Rugles, a market town of Normandy, in the election of Conches. *p. Г Aigle.* Rugny &1 Fouffry, a fmall town of Picard), in the diocefe and election of Soifions. *p. la Fere.* Rugny, a_village of Champagne, in the election of Tonnerre, *p. Tonmzzz. Riigy,* a village of Meflin, in the diocefe and receipt of Metz. *p. M tz. Ruicb,* a village of Artois, in the diocefe and bailiwick of Arras. /». *Arras.* Ruigny, a pariíh of Touraine, m the diocefe of Tours, *J. 'Tours.* Rullle'. i. A town of Anjou, in the election of Château-Gontier. *p. Cbateau-Gontiet.* 2. A town of Maine, in the diocefe and election of Mans. *p. Ic Mans.* 3 A town of Maine, in the diocefe and electm of Laval. *p. Lav-.il. Ruilie,* a fmall town of Rouergue, in the election of Villefranche. *f. Villejranche-de-Rouirgue. Ruilly.* i. A town of Beauce, in the election of Vendôme, *p. tuefboent.z.* A village of Normandy, in the election of Pont-de-l'Arche. *p. Pont-def Arcbe.* 3. A village of Champagne, in

the election of Rethcl. *p. Rethel. Ruines,* a village of Auvergne, in the diocefe and election of S. Flour. *p. S. Flour. Ruipeyroux,* a place of Beam, in th.: receipt of Morias, *p. Pau. Ruis,* a wood of Bretagne, in the jurïfdiction of Vannes. *Ruiffáuville.* i. A village of Ar toisj in the bailiwick of S. Pol. *p. Aras. 't.* An abby in the diocefe of Boulogne, *p. H ¡din. Rwjjotte,* a place of Burgundy, in the receipt of Avalon, *p. Avalon.* Rule, *fa,* a village of Gafcony, in the receipt of Bigorrc. *f. Tarbcs. Rullecourt)* a village of Artois, in the bailiwick of Arr?F. *p. Anas. Rdly.* i. A fmall town of Normandy, in the election of Vire. *p. Conde-Jur-Noire au.* 2. A v i l läge *t* ; f Picardy, in the diocefc and election of Senlis. *p. Sentis. Rul/y,* or *Rtiitly,* a village of Burgundy, in the d.occfe and bailiwick of Challón. *p.Chagny, Rumaucourt)* a village of Artois, in the diocefe and bailiwick of Arras. *p. Arrau* Rumegies, a village of Flanders, in the fubdekgation of S. Amand. *p. S. Amand. Rumiml.* i. A village of Picardy, in the diocefe and election of Amiens. *p. Amiens.* 2. A villageof Normandy, in the election of Pont-pEvêquc. *p. Poni-FEt Цие.* Rumerßelm, a village of AKace, in the bailiwick of Haguenau. *p. Hagaer.au. Runùgny. j.* A town of Champagne, in the diocefe and election of Rhcim.s. *p. Retbel.* 2. A town of Picardy,-in the diocefe and election of Amiens.. *Vervwt.* 3. A fmal! town of Picardy, in the diocefe and election of Noyon./1. *Noycn.* Rumily. i. A village of Picardy, in the generality of Amiens, *p. S. Omerf* 2. A village of Flanders, in the diocefeand fubdclegation of-Cambray. *p. Cambray.* 3. A foreft of-2919 arpents, in the jurisdiction of Troyes in Champagne. *Rummgbar.)* a village of Artois, in the diocefe and bailiwick of S. Omer. *p. S. Omer. Rumolive'dler,* a village of Alfacc, in the diocefe ofStraiburg. *p. Strafhurg.* Rum ont *y* a village of Gàtinoîs, in the election of Nemours, *p. Ne meurt.* doc, in the diocefe and receipt of Uzés. *p. Uze's. RuJJy.* I. A village of Normandy, in the diocefe and election of Bayeux. *p. Bayeux.* 2. Sec *Monhgny. Rufián,* a fmall country of Gafconv, on the confines of Bigorrc.

Rufirely a village of Provence, in the diocefe and vigucry of Apt. *p. Apt. Ri. njcty* a village of Picardy, in the diocefe and élection of SoifTons. *p. Charly. Rwvïgry,* a village of Champagne, in the diocefe and election of Troyes. *p. Troyes. Ruy.* i. A village of Picardy, in the election of Compiégne. *p. Verberie.* z. A village of Dauphiny, in the diocefe and election of Vienne. *p. Bourgo'w. Ruyaucourt,* a village of Artois, in the bailiwick of Bapaume. *p. Ba paume. Ruys,* apeninfulaof Bretagne, in the diocefe and receipt of Vannes. *Ruyfebeüre,* a fmall town of Flanders, in the fubdelegation of Cafièl. *p. Caß'ei. Ry,* a market-town of Normandy, in the diocefe and election of Rouen, *p. Ecouy. Rya,* a village of Franche-Comté, in the receipt of Dole. *p. Dole. Rye,* a village of Normandy, in the diocefe and election of Bayeux. *p. fiayeux,*

S A *βAACYj* a fmall town of Brie, in the diocefe and election of Meaux. *p. Ferte-fous-Jouare. Saales, л* village of Upper Alface, in the bailiwick of Ville, *p. Bale. Saane.* See *Saenne, Saare.* See *Sare. Saar Isms.* Sec *Sarlouts, Saas,* a place of Gafcony, in the election of Landes, *p. S. Sever. Sahadel,* i. A village of Quercy, in the diocefe and election of Cahors. *p, Cahors.* 2. A village of Quercy, in the diocefe of Cahors and election of Figcac. *p. Flgeac. Sabaillan,* a fmall village of Gafcony, in the diocefe and election of Comminges. *p. Lombez. Sa tale f* a fmall village of Navarre, in the receipt of Cize. *p. Pau, Sábalos,* a place of Gafcony, in the diocefe of Tarbesj and the receipt of Bigorrc. *p. Tarées. Sabaraty* a village of Foix, in the receipt of Foix. *p. Touloufe, SabaroSy* a village of Armagnac, in the diocefe of Auch. *p. Cafielnau-deMagnac. Sabazan,* a village of Armagnac, in the diocefe of Auch, and election of Armagnac, *p. Mont-de-Marfan. Sablé,* an ancient town of Maine, fituatc on the river Sarte, 29 leagues from Rennes, 26 from Tours,.« 13 from Mans, 10 from Laval, 10 from Angers, and 61 from Paris. *Bureau de pofie. Sablcneeaux.* Sec *Sabknceaux. Sables-d'Olonne, les,* a town on the fea-coart of Poitou, in the diocefe of Luc on, and generality of Poitiers, with a fmall port, admitting mips oí 150 tons. It is about 8 leagues from Luçon, and il from Rochelle. *Bureau de pofie. Sablety* a village of VenahTm, in the judicature of Carpentras. *p. Avignon. babl'wesy* a fmall town of Upper Languedoc, in the generality of Touloufc. *p. Gencuillac. Sablón,* a large village of Dauphiny, in the diocefe of Vienne, and election of Romans, *p. Romans.* 2. See *Habitans-du-Sablon. Sablcn, le,* a place of Poitou, in the election of Richelieu. *f, Richelieu. Sablonceaux,* a town of Saintonge, upon the Seudre, in the diocefe and election of Saintes, from which it і» 4 leagues diftant. *p. Saintes. Sablotvere,* a village of Brie, in the election of Coulomiers. *p. Rcbets. Sablonieres,* a village of Dauphiny in the election of Vienne, *p. Bourgcin9 Sablons,* or *les Sablons,* a village of Normandy, in the diocefc of Seez, and election of Argentan, *p. Argentan, Sabonneres,* a village of Gafcony, in the diocefe and ele¿tion of Comminges. *p. Sama tan. Sabrán,* a fmall village of Lower Languedoc, in the diocefc and receipt of Uzés. *p. Bagnols. Sabrée,* a village of Mefïïn, in the diocefe and receipt of Metz. *p. Mete. Sabres,* a village of Gafcony, in the election of Landes, *p. Tartas. Sacy* or *leSac,* a village of Normandy, in the election of Conches. *p. Notiarcourt. Sac7* or *les Sacsf* a place of Normandy, in the diocefc of Séez, and election of Falaife. *p. Falaije. Sace, orSaJJe,* a fmall river of Provence, which falls into the Durance above Sifteron.

Sac/. I. A town of Normandy, in the diocefe and elect ion of Avranches. *p. Pontorfon.* 2.. A town of Maine, in the diocefe of Mans, and election of Laval, *p. Laval. Saceu,* 2 viilage of Champagne,(in the diocefe and election of Troyes. *p. Trcyes. Sache,* a chatcllany of Touraine, in the diocefe of Tours, and election of Chinon. *p. Tcurs. Sacbin-lesPcrnes,* a place of Artois, in the bailiwick, of Saint-Pol. *p. Beth une. Sac by, 2* place of Mcffin, in the receipt of Carignan. *p. Sedan. Sacierge.* See *Sancierges. Sacias,* a town of Beauce, in the diocefe of Sens, and election of Etarapes. *p. Etampes. Saconin,* a village of Picardy, in the diocefc and election of SoiiTons. *p. Soijßns. Saconnex,* or *Saconnay,* a village of Valromey, in the bailiwick, of Gex. *p. Gex. Sacquenay,* a village of Champagne, in the dioccfe and election of Langres. *p. Selongey. Sacfuenn/iile,* a village of Norman'¿y, in the diocefe and election of

Evreux. *p. Evreux. Sacy.* i. Avillageof Champagne, in the diocefe and election of Rheims. *p. Rheims.* 2-A village of Champagne, in the diocefe of Langres, and election of Tonnerre, *p. Auxtrre.* 3. A village of Normandy, in the diocefe of Séez, and election of Falaife. *p. Vofiil/. Sacy-le-Grand,* a fmall town of Picardy, in the election of Clermont. *p. Clermont. Sacy-U-Pefit,* avillageof Picardy, in the election of Clermont, *p. Clermont. Sadeillan,* a village of Armagnac, in the election of Allante, *p. Mbrtmde. Sadulac,* a village of Pcrigord, in the diocefe and election of Sarlat. *p. Bergerac. Sadiac.* 1. A fmall town of Guienne, in the diocefe and election of Bourdeaux. *p. Bourdeaux.* 2. A fmall village of Bafadois, in the election of Condom. *r. Bafas, Sadirac-Haren,* a place of Beam, in the receipt of Morias, *p. Pau. Suùùllc:,* a fruall village of Nivcrnois, in the dîoccie and t-íceñon of Nevers. *p. Never. Sadourfiifi,* a village of Armagnar, in the election of Alt ¿rae. *p. CafleU nau-de-Magna c. Sadror,* a village of Limofin, in the election of Brjves. *p. Br'ntet. Saenne,* a town of Normandv, in the election of Arques, *p. Dieppe. SaennCy* or *Suone,* a river in Normandy, which rifes oppofitc Bourdainvjlle, and falls into the fea about a league from Longucil.

Safflsz, a fmall village of FrancheComté, in the bailiwick, of Poligny. *p. Salins. Sajfre,* a village oí Burgundy, in the b ü Hi wick of Scinurcn-Au;ois. *p. Vît eaux. Saffrc,* a village cf Bretagne, in the dioccfe and receipt of Nantes. *p. Nvzay. Sagdia-de-Belvcs,* a village of Férigord, in the diocefc and election of Sarlat. *p. Sarlat.* Forez, in the election of MontbrifoQ. *p. Monthrijon. Saiiban,* a village of Armagnac, in the diocefe and election of Oletoa. *p. Afontrejeau, Sai/batís,* a village of Guienne, in the diocefe and election of Bourdvaux. *p. Lib our ne. SaiûaCf* a village of Quercy, in the dioccfe and election of Motttauban. *p. Mjr.tauhan. Saii/agMiJjêt* a town of Rouflillon, in the vigucry of Cerdaigne. *p. M;nttouis, Saillan,* a village of Béarn, in the generality of Auch. *p. O'er ou. SMlans.* i. A town of Dauphiny, upon the Drome, in the dioccfe of Die, and election of Mont limait, *p. Creji.* 2. A fmall town of Auvergne, in'the election of Iffuîre. *p. If/aire* 3. A village of Auver ne, in the dioccfe and election of Clermont, *p. Clermont, SnilleraxSj* a town of Dauphinyj in the diocefe and election of Gap.

diocefe and generality of Auch./ *Pau. Sally.* I. A village of Champagne, in the receipt of joinville. *p. Joinville,* 2. A village of Mcffin, in the receipt of Carignan. *p. Sedan.* 3. A fmall village of Burgundy, in the diocefe and bailiwick of Macon, *p. Mácon* 4. A fmall village of Beauce, in the election of Mantos, *p. Manta.* 5. A place of Mcffin, in the diocefe and receipt of Metz. *p. Mttz. Suilly-su-BoU.* I. A village of Picardy, in the election of Péronne. *p. Albert.* 2. A place of Artois, in the dioccfe and receipt of Arras, *p Arias. Sai!ly-eit-Oflrevent,* a village ofArtois, in the diocefe and receipt of Arras, *p. Arrai. Sailly Lauret,* a village of Picardy, in the election of Doulcns. *t. Corbie. SàUy-lt-Sec.* I. A village of Pi-, cardy.'in the election of Doulens. *p. Doi'lcns.* 2. A village of Picardy, in the election of Abbeville-*p. Áabevillf. Saîlly-les-Cambray,* a village of Artois, in the diocefe and receipt of Arras, *p. Beîbune. Saiijy-Ies-Btwfes,* a village of Artois, in the bailiwick of Bcthune. *p. Bethunt. Sailly-SaUlhtt,* a village of Picardy, in the election of Péronnc. *p. Perenne. SainglUn cSf Wtïpe,* a village of Artois, in the receipt of Tens. *p. Lens. Sainntm'ûle,* a fm:¡ll town of Normandy, in the election of Montivillicrs. *p. S. Romain. Sains,* a viibgc of Flanders, in the generality of Maubcugc. *p At'tfnes. S-ins,* or *le Pair-Sains,* a village of Picardy, in the élection of Mo.ididier, *p. Mondidier. Sams & Peth-Hcwuins,* a place of Artois, in the bailiwick of S. Pol. *p. Anas. Salns-en-Let:s,* a place of Artois, in the bailiwick of Lens. *p. Lens. Sa¡ns-lesFr(ffinsy* a village of Artois, in the diocefe of Amiens, and bailiwick of S. Pol. *p. Heßin. Sai.ns-les-Marçcin,* a place of Flanders, in the diocefe and fubdelegation of Cambray. *p. Lille. Saint,* a village of Bretagne, in the diocefe and receipt of Quimper. *p. jumper. Sainteaux,* a village of Normandy, in the election of Caen. *p. Fa'aifi. SaintcgrJe,* a village of Picardy, in the diocefe and election of Amiens. *p. Amiens. Saintes,* a confiderable city, the capital of Saintonge, in the generality of Rochelle: it is fituated at the foot of a mountain, near the Charente, 32 leagues from Bourdeaux, 17 from Rochelle, i6f from Angoulême, 52 from Nantes, and 126 from Paris. *Bureau de poße. Saintois,* a village of Bretagne/ in the diocefe and receipt of Quimper. *p. Quimper. Saintonge,* a province of France, about 2.5 leagues long and 12 broad; bourded on the eart by Angoumois and Périgord, on the fouth by Gui enne, on the'weft by the fea, and orí the north by Poitou and Aunis: the air is mild, and the land is fertile in wheat, wine, and fruit; with good palUirage: this province, of which Saintes is the capital, is wstcrcd by the rivers Boutonne, and Charente, which divide it into north and fouth: it has a fénéchauíTée, which is a(Saintes,and threebiilivicks,Brouage, Rouffignac, and Champagnac: the horfes of this country are much efteemed; and fo is the fait, in which they carry on a confiderable traffic. *SaintroC)* a parí lb of Bourbonnois,in the election of G.mnat. . *S. Powcaift. Saint ry,* a village of the lile of France, in the diocefe and election of Paris, *p, CorUU. Saints.* I. A village of Picardy, iJi the diocefe and election of Amiens. *p. Amiens.* 2. A village of Brie, in the election of Coulomiers. *p. Farmcuticrs.* 3. A village of Bretagne, in the diocefe and receipt of *Xo.p.Dcl. Saints & Rkhaumon',* a town of Picardy, in the diocefe and election) of Laon. *p. Laon. Saints-en-Pnifaye,* a fmall town of Nivernois, in the election of Clamecy. *p. Clamecy, Saint-Aaron,* a village of Bretagne, in the diocefe and receipt of Brieux. *p. hambaUe. S. Abit,* a place of Beam, in the receipt of Pau. *p. Pau. S. Abraham,* a village of Bretagne, in the diocefe and election of S. *Malo, p. Ploermel. S. Abris,* a town of Quercy, "in the diocefe and élection of Cahors. *p. Caßelnau-de-Montr aitier. S--Ackatil-les-Amiens,* a village of Picardy, in the diocefe of Amiens, and election ofDoulens. *p. Amiens. S.-Acquelin* cУ *Commanderie-dc-Boffet,* a fmall town of Périgord, m the diocefe and election of Périgucux. *p. Perigucux. S-Acquien d"Hautejort, SecHautefort. S.-Adricn-de-Betify,* a priory oí Beauvifis. *S.-Aßaire-la-Mcntagne,* a village of Marche, in the election of Gueret. *p. TeuMhûn. S. Ajfcriar.d,* a town of Marche, in the election of Gueret. *p. Gueret. S.-Afrîquet* or *Ste.-Fiiquey* a town of Rouerguc, in the diocefe of Vabrcs and election of Milhaud; about 2 leagues from Vabres, 7 from Milhand, and *it* fiom Rhodcz. *Bureau de pifie. S. Afrique,* a village of Upper Languedoc, in the diocefe and receipt of Lavaur. *p Cafires.* 5-*Aguan,* a village of Dauphiny, in the diocefe ami election of Vienne. *p. Die. S. Agn'm,* a village of Dauphiny, in the diocefe and election of Vienne. *p. Vienne. S. Agny,* a village of Berry, in the election of Blanc, *p. le Blanc. S. Agon Hr.,* a village of Bourbonpois, in the election of Gannat. *p. ¡igue-Ptrje. S. Agrcve,* a town of Vivarais, in the diocefe and receipt of Viviers. *p. Vcrmux. S. Agrkolf* a village of LowerLangucdoc, in the receipt of Puy. *pMPuy. S.Algtian.* i. A town of Berry, iituated on the Cher, on the confines of Touraine; about 15 leagues from Tours, 9 from Amboife, 22 from Bourges, and 9 from Blois; in the diocefe of Bourges, and election of Romorpntin. *Bureau de poße.* 2. Л fmall town of Dauphiny, in the election of M jn tel i mart, *p-De.* 3. A priory in the election of Tonnerre. 4. A village of Normandy, in the election of Alençon. *p, Alençon.* 5, A village of Picardy, in the election of Château-Thierry, *p. ChateauThierry.* 6. A village of Champagne, in the diocefe and election of Rheims, *p. Doncbery.* 7. A village of Normandy, in the election of Eu. *p. Eu* 8. A village of Guienne, in the diocefe and election of Bourdeaux. *p. B laye.*

9. A village of Agcnois, in the diocefe and election of Agen. *p. ViHencwvcdAgen.* 10. A village of Briej in the election of Mon tercau. *p. Montereau.* II. A village of Burgundy, in the bailiwick of Bourbon-Lancy. *p. Bourban-Z»amy.* 12. A village of Auvergne, in the election of Combraülcs. *p. Chambón.* 13. A village of Upper Langudoc, in the diocefe and receipt of Lavaur. *p. Lavaur.* 14. A village of Bretagne, in the diocefe and receipt of Nantes, *p. Plantes,* 15. A village of Normandy, in the dtocefe and election of Rouen, *p. Rquiti.* 16. A village of Dauphiny, in tic election of Montclimart. *p. Montelbnart.* 17. A village of Périgord, in the diocefe and election of Sarlat. *p.Sarlat.* 18. A village of Bazadois, in the election of Condom, *p. Leêloure.* 19. A village of Armagnac, in the diocefe of Aire, and election of RivièreVerdun, *p. Grenade,* 20. A village of Burgundy, in the bailiwick of Avalon, *p. Avalon.* 2J. A fmall village of Bourbonnois, in the election of S. Amand. *p, S. Amand.* 22A village of Orléannoia, in the diocefe and election of Orléans, *p. Orleans.* 23. A place of Berry, in the diocefe and election of Bourges. *p. Eourges.* 24. A figniory of Normandy,in the election ofPont-Audemer. *p. Pcnt-Audemer, S. Aignart,* or *S.-Cbignan-de-IaCorn,* a town of Languedoc, in the receipt of Pons. *p. B esters. S.-Aigftan-de-VercorSy* a village of Dauphiny, in the diocefe of Vienne, and election of Romans, *p. Romans. S. Atgnatldts-Noyersf* a village of Berry, in the flection of S. Amand. " *p. Never s.*
S'. *Aignan-en-CrámtS)* a town of Anjou, in the election of ChàteauGonticr. *p. Château-Gontier. t S. Aignan-en-LcJJayj* a town of Maine, in the diocefe and election of Mans. *p. le Ribay. S. Aignan-le-Malherbe 9* a village of Normandy, in the election of Caen. *p. Caen. S. Aignan-jousBalon9* a town of Maine, in the diocefe and election of Mans. *p. le Mans. S. Aignan-Jur-Erre,* a village of

S A

Perche, in the election of Mortagne. *p. Nogent-le-Rotrou. S. Agnan-jur-Ry,* a village of Kormandy, in the d'iocefe and elcction of Rouen, *p. Reuen. S.*

Aignes, a village of Picardy, in the election of Crépy. *p. C'ê.y,* „ *S.Aigulin,* two towns of Saintonge, in thediocefe and election of Saintes, on either fide of ahe Dronne. *p. la Grolle. S. Alary,* i. A town of Quercy, in the election of Figeac. *p. Tigcac.* 2« A village of Rouergue, in the diocefe and election of Rhode?.. *p. Rb. dex.* 3. A fmall village of Gat cony, in the diocefe and election of Commingcs. *p. Toukuje. S. Albain,* a village of Burgundy, in the diocefe and receipt of Màcon. *p. Macon.* 5". *Allan.* I. A town of Lower Languedoc, in the diocefe and receipt of Mende. *p. Mende.* 2. A village of Bugey, in the diocefe and bailiwick of Bugey. *p. Bdlty.* 3. A village of Dauphiny, in the diocefe and election oí Vienne, *p. Bourgoin.* 4. A village of Bretagne, in the diocefe and receipt of Brienx. *p. Lamballe. r* 5. A fmall village of Forez, with three fprings of mineral water, in the diocèíe of Lyons, and election of Roanne, *p. Roanne.* 6. A fmall village of Dombcs, in the chatellany of ToiiTey. *p. Belleville, S. Alban & Vitr'ieuxy* a village of Dauphiny, in the diocefe and election of Vienne, *p. le Buis. S. Alban-de-Cafeíaze,* a village of Upper Languedoc, in the diocefe and receipt of Toulouic. *f. Toulcuf:, S. Alban-en-Mor.tagne,* a village of Lower Languedoc, in the diocefe and receipt of Viviers, *p. Viviers. S. Albanda,* a town of Vivarais, in the diocefe and receipt of Viviers. *p. Vtviers. S. Albert,* a village of Bazadois, in the election of Condom. /. *Bazas, S. Albin,* a village of Artois, in the diocefe and recept of Arras, *p. Arras. S. Ally-à"Aigutfmdcy л* village of Upper Languedoc, in the diocefe and receipt of Lavaur. /. *Caßres. S. Alky& S. Ptrdou,* a village of Agénois, in the diocefe and elect um of Agen. *p. Agen. S. Alefpijje,* a village of Beam, in the receipt of Morias, *p. Pau. S. Alexandre.* 1. A village of Lower Languedoc, in the diocefe and receipt of Uzés. *p. tide's.* 2. A village of Burgundy, in the diocefe and election of Challón, *p. Challen. S. Algy,* a village of Picardy, in the election of *Gu(c.p. Уезч/u. S. Alierwofity* a town of Normandy, about 3 leagues from *Dicppcp.Diepfe S. Adre.* Sec *Allire. S. Alivcs,* a fmall village of Burgundy, in

the receipt of Châtillon. *p. Châtillon. S. Allire & Mouton,* a town of Auvergne, in the diocefe and election of Clermont, *p. Clermont. S. Allire-p. es-la-Cbaije-DiCu,* a fmall town of Auvergne, in the election ofliíoire. *p. Ijjoire. S. Allire-prh-MontbciJßir,* a village of Auvergne, in the election of Iffoire. *p. Bri.ude. S. Allire-jous-Aureny* a village of Auvergne, in the election of IiToire. *p. Ißirc. S. Alilre-aux-Montagr.es.* 1. A village of Auvergne, in the election of Riom. *p. Riom.* 2. A village of Bourbonnois, in the election of Moulins, *p. Moulins. S. Attire-de-Valence,* a pnriih of Bourbonnois, in the election of Moul ns. *p. Moulins S. Alouefire,* a village of Bretagne, in the diocefe and receipt of Vannes. *p. Pont ivy.* 5Г *Ahydt-Wlgo, Josfer,* places of Agenois, in the diocefe and election of Agen. *p. Agen. S. Alvard,* a place of Auvergne, in the diocefe of Clermont, and election of Riom. *p. Riom. S.Alvere,* a.fmall town of Périgord, in the diocefe and election of Périgucux. *p. le Bugue. S. Amador,* a place of Normandy,

D S

in the diocefe and election ot Baytux. *p. Bcyeux. S. Amadou,* a village of Upper Languedoc-, in the diocefe and receipt of Mirepoix. *p. Aftrepcix. S. Amand.* i. A town of Bourbonliois, in the diocefe and generality of Bourges: it is ntuatcd on the river Cher, about 7 leagues from Bourges, and 9 from Moulins, on the confines of Berry. *Bureau de pofie 1.* A town of Flanders, on the Scarpe, in the diocefe of Tournay, and generality of Lille; containing about 7co houfes, and about 4C00 inhabitants; 10 leagues from Lille, 3 from VaK-nciennts,S fromDouay, 10 from Canibray, and 5 lromTournay: near it are mud baths and medicinal fprings, with a military hofpitaL *Bureau de pofie.* 3. A town of Gâtinois, in the election of Gien. *p. Newvy.* 4. A town of Auvergne, in the election of Ifífloire. *p. Jffiire.* 5. A town of Champagne, in the election of Vitry. *f. Vity. f.* A town of Poitou, in the election of Thouars. *p. ¥bcuars.* 7. A fmall town of Normandy, in the election of S. Lo. *p. S. Lo.* 8. A village of Bcauce, in the election of Vendôme, *p. Vendôme.* 9.

A village of Marche, in the election of Gucrct. *p. Auhujj'm.* 10. A village of Agenois, in the diocefe and election of Agen. *p. Agin.* II. A place of Bcauce, in the diocefe and election of Chartres, *p. JlÜers.* 12. A confiderable tract of land in the election of Poitiers.

S. Amand & la Bcylie, a fmall town of Pe'rigord, in the diocefe and election of Sarlat. *p. S.irlat. S. Amand-de-Coy,* a village of Pe rigord, in the diocefe and election of Sarlat. *p. TeraJJin. S. Amand-de-Roquepine,* a place of Per'gord, in the diocefe and election of SarJat./. Bergerac. *S.Anumd-dtsfiautes-'TcrrtSi* a village of Normandy, in the election of Pont-de-l Arche, *p. Neufécurg. S. Amavd-Jarkuààx,* a village of M«ichc3 in the election of Bourra neuf-*p. Eourganeuf.*

S. *Amans.* 1. A town of Auvergne, in the diocefe and election of Clermont, *p. Clermont,* 2. A town of Upper La"hgucdoc, in the diocefe and receipt of Lavaur. *p. Lavaur.* 3. A fmail town of Lower Languedoc, irr the diocefe and receipt of BerierSv *p. Beziers.* 4. A village of Agénois, in the diocefe and election of Agen. *p. Agen.* 5. A village of Lower Langui doc, in the diocefe and receipt of Mende. *p. Mer.de.* 6. A village of Upper Languedoc, in the diocefe and receipt of Min poix. *Pamiers.* 7. A village of Gafconv, in the diocefe and election of Commingcs./. *Montrcjeau.* 8. A village of Quercy, in the diocefe and election of Cahors. *p. Cabors.* 9. A village of Agenois, in the diocefe and election of Agen. *p. Agen. S. Aman s-de-Noire y* a town of" Angoumois, in the diocefe and eleo tion of Cognac, *p. Cognac. S. Amant.* I. A village of Armagnac, in the diocefe and electionof Auch. *p.Aucb.* 2. A village of Artois, in the bailiwick of Lens. *p. Lens. S. Amant-de-BoijJey* a town of Angoumois, in the election of Cognac, *p. Aigrc.*

S *Amant-déterrés,* a village of Agénois, in the diocefe and election, of Agen. *p. Agen. S. Amant-de-Tairac,* a fmall town of Agénois, in the diocefe and election of Agen. *p. Agen,* 5. *Armant-de-Termes,* л village of Lower Languedoc, in the diocefe aná receipt of Viviers, *p. Viviers.* ц *S. Amant-de-Ver g,* a fmall town, of Périgord, in the diocefe and election of Périgueux. *p. Pe'rigu.ux. S. Amant-le-Petit,* a place of Limofin, in the diocefe and election of Limoges, *p. Bourgareuf. S. Ajnant-Magnazeix.,* a village of Limofin, in the diocefe and election of Limoges, *p, Bcjßneu S. Amaran,* a village of Qcrcy, in the diocefe and election of Cabtfrs. *p. Peyrat.*

S A -*S. AmauJTet,* a village of Upper Languedoc, in the diocefe and receipt of Lavau. *p. Caßres. &Amireui¡,* a village of Burgundy,. in the diocefe and bailiwick of Challón, *p. Challón. S. Ambrcife,* or *Amhr$:xt* a town of Lower Languedoc, on the Ceze, in the diocefe and receipt of *Uzts;* about 7 leagues from Uz.cs, 10 from Bagnols, 4 from Alais, and n from Pont-S.-Efprit. *Bureau depoße. S. Ambrci/e-de-Bourgcs,* an abby in Bourges./». Bourges. *S. Ambroij'e-jur-Arnom,* a village of Berry, in the diocefe and election of IiToudun. *p. IJf.ütiun. S. Ambrúx.* See *Ambroife. S. Atnur.* i. A town of FrancheComté, in the bailiwick, of Orgelet. *p. Lons-le-Saunier.* 2. A village of Burgundy, in the diocefe and bailiwick of Mâcon. *p. Mácon, S.Anaßafe,* a village of Normandy, in the election of Argentan, *p. Argentan. S. Anaßazi,* a village of Lower Languedoc, in the diocefe and receipt of Uzés. *p. Usufs. S. Andelin* a village of Nivernois, in the election of Charité-fur-Loire. *p. Pcuilty. S. Andeol,* or *le-Bourg-S.-Andeof. j.* A town of Lower Languedoc, in the diocefe and receipt of Viviers, *p, Pierrelate.* 2. A village of Daiiphiny, in the diocefe and' election of Vienne, *p. Tain.* 3. A village of Dauphiny, in the election of Grenoble, *p. Grenoble. S. Andeoly & S. Etenney* villages of Dauphiny, in the election of Montelimart. *p. Montelimart. S. Ande&I-de-Ber,* a village of Lower Languedoc, in the diocefe and receipt of Viviers, *p. Viviers, S. Andeol-de-Fourcbades,* a village of Lower Languedoc, in the diocefe and receipt of Viviers, *p. Viviers. S. Aл deux & Perrière,* a village of Burgundy, in the bailiwick of Avalon, *p. Avalen,*

& *Andiol,* a village of Provence, in tfie viguery of Tarafcon. *p. Tü» rajcon, S Artdocke & Trecourt,* a village of Champagne, in the diocefe and election of Langres./. *Landre:. S. Andoel-le-Cbaftcly* a Cm all town of Forez, in the election of S. Etienne, *p. S Et.enne. S. Andre',* 1. A town of Lower Languedoc, in the diocefe and receipt of Lodeve. *p. Lodcve.* 2. A town of Champagne, in the diocefe and election of Trove-; *p. Troy es.* 3. A town of Fore, in the uioccfc and election of Roanne, *p. Roanne,* 4. A market-town oí Norman.!y, in the diocefe and election of Evreux. *p. NOnancourî.* 5. A town of Angoumo's, in the election of Cognac, *p. Cognac.* 6. A (mall town of Orléannois, in the diocefe and election of Orléans. *p. Orléans.* 7. A fmall town of Poitou, in the election of Thoiur. /. *Tbouars,* 8. A large village of Périgord, in the diocefe and election of Sarlat. *p. Sarlat.* 9. A village of Angoumois, in the diocefe and election of Angoulêmc. /. *Ar.goulcme.* 10. A village of Agenois, in the diocefe and election of Agen./. *Agen,* 11. A village of Nivernois, in the election of Vezelay. *p, Vezelay.* 12. A village of Rouiiillon, in the diocafe and viguery of Perpignan, *p. Perpignan.* 13. A village of Bazadois, in the eleion of Condom, *p. Bajas.* 14. A village of Burgundy, in the bailiwick of Laurent. *p.Loiiens* 15. A village of Auvergne, in the election of Riom, *p. Riom.* 16. A village of Bretagne, in the diocefe and receipt of Nantes, *p. Dinan.* 17. A village uf Provence, in the viguery of Caftellane, *p. CaßeUanc.* - 18. A village of Dauphiny, in the diocefe and election of Grenoble, *p. Grenoble.* 19. A village of Burgundy, in the bailiwick of Avalon, *p. Avalon.* 20. A village of Flanders, in the fubdekgation of Lille, *p. Lille* 2ï. A pariíh of Burgundy, in the diocefe and bailiwick of Autun. *p Autut.* 22. An abby in the diocfe *S. Andre-le-Dejert,* a town of Burgundy, in the diocefe and bailiwick of Mâcon. *p. Macon.* 5. *André-ie-Hauty* a convent in Vienne.

S. *Andre-le-Panoux,* a village of Burgundy, in the bailiwick, of B reffe. *p. Bùurg-en-Bre£e. S. Andrc-U-Puy,* a village of Forez, in the election of Monttffifon. *p. Mcntbrijbn.* 6. *Andre'-ks-Cler-*

mo/ityZn aoDy near Clermont, in Auvergne, *p. Clermont.* S. *Andre'-les-Gap,* a village of Dauphiny, in the diocefe and election of Gap. *p. Gap.* S. *André-prh-Villcncivuc-les-Ax ignon,* an abby, in the diocefe of Avignon. /. *Vdler.eu-ue-les-A'v'gnon.*

¿". *Andre'-fur-Ca'i'ty,* a village of Normandy, in the diocefe and election of Rouen, *p. le Bolebard,* S. *AndréjurMareu.ly* a village of Poitou, in the election of Fontenay. *p. Tiré.* S. *Andreas,* a town of Guien ne, in the diocefeandelcction of Bourdcaux. *p. Blaye.* S. *Andreau.* I. A village of Armagnac, in the diocefe ofComminges. *p. Montrejeau.* 2. A village of Armagnac, in the election of RivièreVerdun, *p. Grenade.* S. *Andrieu,* a village of Roucrguc, in the electb n of Vi lief ran che. *p. Villcfrancke-de-Rovergae.* S. *Ange.* T. A village of Perche, in the election of Verncuil. *p. Nonancourt.* 2. A priory, in the diocefe of Limoges.
S. *Angeau,* a villageof Angoumois, in the diocefe and election of Angoulême. *p. Angoulhne.* S. *Angel.* I. A fmall town of Limofín, in the election of Tulles, *p. Tulles.* 2. A village of Auvergne, in the election of Riom. *p. Riom.* 3. A village uf Péngord, in the diocefe and election of Périgueux. *p. Per'igueux.* 4. A village of Bourbonnois, in the election of Montluçon. *p. Mont lu con.* S. *Anges,* a village of Dauphiny, in the diocefe and election of Vienne. *p. Romans.* S. *Anne de Vɋpe,* a village of Normandy, in the election of Pont-deFArche. *Pont-de-FArche»* S. *Antelme,* a town of Auvergne in the election of lffoire. *p. JJ/oire,* S. *Antiot,* a place of Burgundy, in the bailiwick of Semur-en-Auxois. *p. Semur-en-Auxois.* S. *Antoine.* I. A town of Dauphiny, in the diocefe and election of Vienne *p.' S. Marcel lin.* 2. A village of Normandy, in the election of Montivilliers. *j. Lillebor.ne.* 3. A village of Armrgnac, in the election of" Lomagne. *p. Beaumont-de-Lomagne.* 4. A village of Franc he-Comté, in the bailiwick of Pontarlier. *p. Pontarlier.* 5. A village of Provence, in the viguery of Entrevaux. *p. Cafiellane,* S, *Antoine fif & Privat,,* a fmall town of Péngord, in the diocefe and (lection of Périgueux.. *PeYxgueux.*

S. *Antoine a"1' Auberoche,* a village of Périgord, in the diocefe and election of Périgueux. *p. Pe'rigucux.* S. *Antoinc-de Sommaire,* a village of Normandy, in the election of Verncuil. *p. /' Aigle.* S. *Am oim-dit-Rocher,* a village of Tourainc, in the diocefe and election of Tuiirs. *p. Tours.* St *Anto'me-h-.rs-Trenn:,* a place of Limofin, in the election of Brives. *p. Brwes.* S.*Antcnin. l.* A town of Rouergue, fituated on the Aveirou, on the frontiers of Quercy. *p. Vülejrancbe-deRouergue.* 2. A place of Quercy in the election of Villefranche. *p. Montauban.* 3. j. place of Provence, in the dioceie and viguery of Aix. *p. Aix.* 4. A place of Languedoc, in the diocefe and receipt of Alby. *p. Alby.* 5. A parifh of Provence, in the viguery ot Entrevaux. *p. Cafiellane.* S *Antoty* a village of Burgundy, in the bailiwick of Semur. *p. S mur.* S. *Aoufi,* a village of Berry, in the election of Iffoudun. *p. Ifjbudun.* S. *Apollinard.* I. A fmall town of Forez, in the election of S.Etienne. *p. S Etienne,* z. A village of Dauphiny, in the election of Romans, *p. Romans.* 3. A village of Dauphiny, in the dioccfe of Embrun, *p. Cap,* 4. A village of Dauphin y, in the election of Gap. *p. Embrun.* 5. A village of Beaujolois, in the election of Villefranche. *p. VUlefrancbe.* 6. A village of Lyonnais, in the dioccfe and election of Lyons, *p. Tarare.* 7. A village of Burgundy, in the dioccfe and bailiwick of Dijon, *p. Dijon.* S. *Aquilin-d¿-P'acy,* a village of Normandy, in the dioccfe and election of Evreux. *p. Bernay.* S.*Arblon.* a village of Anjou, in the diocefe and election of Angers., *p. Angers.* S. *Arcons,* a village of Auvergne, in the election of Brioude. *p. Brioude.* S. *Arcy,* a village of Dauphiny, in the dioccfe and election of Grenoble. *p. Grenoble.* S. *Arà'le,* a village of Gafcony, in the diocefe and election of Comminges. *p. Montrejeau.* S. *Armel,* a village of Bretagne, in the diocefe and receipt of Rennes, *f. V Orient.* S. *Arnacy* a place of Upper Languedoc, in the diocefe and receipt of Alet. *p. Limeux.* S. *Arnault,* a village of Agénoîs, in the diocefe and election of Agen. *f. Agen,* S. *Arnoul. i.* A town of Beaucc, in the election of Dourdan. *p. Dourdan.* 2. A village of

Picardy, in the diocefe and election of Beauvais. *p. Beauvais.* 3. A village of Normandy, in the election of Caudcbec. *p. Caudebec.* 4. A village of Beaucc, in the election of Vendôme. /. *Memoire.* 5. A village of Normandy, in the election of Argentan, *p. Argentan.* 6. A village of Normandy, in the election of Pont-rEvêqiR'. *p. Btnt-VEwque.* 7. *jA* foreft of 1684 arpents, in the jurifdiction of Dourdan. S. *Arnoul'-des-Bois,* a place of Bcmce, in the diocefe and election f Chartres, *p. Courv'lle.* S. *Arnoux,* a figniory of Norman dy, in the diocefe and election of Rouen, *p. Rouen.* S. *Arroman, i.* A village of Armagnac, in the election of Aftarac. *p. Mirande.z.* A village of Armagnac, in the diocefe of Auch. *p. Morande.* S. *Arramccg.* a village of Armagnac, in the election of Lomagne. *p.* S. *Nicbolas-de-la-Grai/e. SbAjprCy* a village of Périgord, in the diocefe and election of Périgueux. *p. Bourde'dles.* S. *Affaire & S. Brist* a town of Saintonge, in the diocefe and elect on of Saintes, *p. Yi.ïdebùurg.* S. *Niftier.* I. A town of Périgord, in the dioc.ic ahd election of Périgueux./». *Béiigueux-z.* A village of Agénois, in the diocefe and election of Agen. *p. Ste. Foy.* S. *Ava'dle,* a fmall town of Condomois, in the diocefe and election of Condom, *p. Condom.* S. *Avaugour-des-LandeS)* a village of Poitou, in the election of Sablesd'Olonne. *p. ks Sables.* S. *Auban. i.* A village of lower Languedoc, in the dioccfe and receipt of Uzés. *p. Mendc. z.* A village of Provence, in the viguery of Graife. *p. Graffe.* 3. A village of Dauphiny, in the election of Montelimart./». *le Buis.* S. *Auban-de-Samp%on,* a village of lower Languedoc, in the diocefe and receipt of Viviers, *p. Viviers.* S. *Auban-les-Die,* a village of Dauphiny, in the election of Montclimart. *p. Die.* S. *Aubert. s.* A village of Normandy, in the election of Falaife, *p. Falaife. z.* A village of Cambrefis, in the dioccfe and fubdelegation of Cambray. *p. Cambray.* S. *Aubin,* a town of Bourbonnoisj in the diocefe and election of Moulins, *p. Bourlon-PA' cbambault. z.* A fmall town of Normandy, in. the election of AlenSon./ *Alenpn.* 3. A fmall town of Normidy, in the election of Andcley. *p.Fcouy.* 4. A fmall tcwa ofGuicnne, in the dioccfe and election *ji BouidtWÄ. p.Bwdcaux* 5, A imall town of Bazadois, in the election of Condom, *p. Baz-t/s.* 6. A village of Normandy in the "election of Vire. *p. Villcduü.* 7. A village of Champagne, in the election of Nogent, *p. Nogtnt-fur-Stinë.* 8. Alliage of Picardy, in the diocefe and election of Amiens, *f. Amiens.* 9. A village of Picardy, in the dioccfe and election of Beauvaîs.. *Beavvais.* 10. A village of Picardy, in the diocefe and election of Soiflons. *p. Soijjbns.* il. A village of Picardy,m the election of Abbeville, *p. Abbeville, 22.* A village of Picardy, in the election of Clermont, *p. Clermont.* 13. A village of Normandv, in the election of Anddey. *f. Guillen.* 14. A village of Normandy, in the election of Pont-Audemcr *p. Pcr.t-Audcmer.* 15. A village of PicarJy, in the government *cf* Nfontreuil. *p. Montr euil-furÂïer.* 16. A village of Normandy, in the election of Montivilliers. *p. Honfleur,* 17. A village of Normandy in the election nf Caen. *p. Caen.* 18. A village of Burgundy, in the bailiwick of Beaunc. *p. Ccagny,* 19. A village of Bcauce, in the election of Montfort. *p. Monifort -V Amaury,* 2,0. A village of Berry in the election of IfToudun. *p. JjJ'oudun.* 21. A village of Poitou, in the election of Fontenay. *p. Fontcnay-ia-Comte.* 22. 'A village of Armagnac, in the diocefe and election of Auch. *p. Aucb.* 23. A village of Hainaut, m the government of Maubeuge. *p. Pbllitprviile.* 24. A village of FrancheComté, in the bailiwick of Dole. *p. Bole.* 25. A village of the Ifle of France, in the diocefe and election of Paris./. *JsleauJ-ble.* 26. A village of Normandy, in the diocefe and election of Evreux. *p. Evreux.* 27. A village of Burgundy, in the bailiwick of Bourbon-Lancy. *p. Bcurkon-Lar.cy.* 28. A village of Poitou, in the election ofLoudun. *p. Loudun.* 29. A place of Burgundy, in the bailiwick of Avalon, *p. Avalon.* 30. A place of Franche-Comté, in the bailiwick of Gray. *p. Gray.* 31. A parifhof Burgundy, in the bailiwick of Charolles. *p. Dijon.* 32. A foreti of 13728 arpents, in the jurifdiction of Rennes in Bretagne.

& *Aubin-Château-Neufy* a town of Champagne, in the election of Joigny. *p. Jo:gny.* _ 5. *Aubin-d?Aubigne,* a village of Bretagne, in the diocefe and receipt of Rennes, *p. Renr.es.* S. *Aubin-d"Aub'tgny,* a diftrict in the election of Maulton, in Poitou.
S. *AubLn-de-Barre,* a village of Normandy in the election of Conches. *p. Beaumor.t-lt-Roger.* 5 *Aub'tn-dt-CebbzaC)* a village of PJrigord, in the diocefe and election of Sarlat. *p. Sariat.* S. *AuMn-de-Gr p,* a village of Saintonge, in the election of S. Jcand'Angely. *p S. yean-d'Angely.* ¿. *Aubin-de-Gmr ande.* See *Gutrar.de.* S. *Aub'in-de-Lenquahy* a village of Périgord, in the dioccfe and election of Sarlnt. *p. Bergerac.* S. *Aulin-de-Logue,* a village of Normandy, in the diocefe and election of Coûtances. *p. S. ho.* 6 *Aubin-dt Rennes,* a village of Bretagne, in the diocefe and receipt of Rennes, *p. Rennes.* S. *Aubin-dcs-Bcis.* i. A village of Bcatice, in the dioccfe and election of Chartres./». *Courville.* 2. An abby in the diocefe of S. Brieux. *p. Lamballe.* S. *Aubn-d¿s-CbüttauXy* a village of Bretagne, in the diocefe and receipt of Nantes, *p. Chateaubrtant.* S. *Aulin-de-Seilon,* a fmall town of Normandy, in the diocefe and election of Lifieux.. *Lijteux.* Я *Aub'm-dcs-Grott,* a village of Perche, in the election of Mortagne. *p. BelUjme.* S. *Aubin des-fiayes,* a fmall town of Normandy, in the election of Conchen, *p. ¿ernay.* S. *Aubin-dés-Landes,* a village of Bretagne, in the diocefe and receipt of Rennes, *p. Vitre'. m*
¿'. *Aubin-des-Pieaux,* a village of S. *Aulin-fur-Cailly,* a figniory of Normandy, m the diocefe and ejection of Rouen. /. *le Bohbard.* 5. *Aubin-jur-Gailon,* a fmall town of Normandy,in the-election of Andcly. *p. Gahlen.* S. *Aub.n-fur-lton,* a village of Normandy, in the election of Verneuil. *p l'Aigle.* S. *Aubinfitr-la-mer, fur-Saer.ne,* villages of Normandv, in the election of Arques, *p. Dieppe.* S. *Aulin-fur-Ri.le,* a village of Normandy, in theelection of Bernay. *p. Bernay.* S. *Aubin-fur-Scye,* a village of Normandy, in the election of Arques, *p. Die/pe.* S. *Aubin-4'ergaßc,* a town of Normandy, in the election of Arranches.

p. Ste. James. S. *siuiin fur Tine,* a village of Champagne, in the election of Joig S. *Ave,* a village of Bretagne, in the diocefe and receipt of Vannes. *P. Vannes.* S. *Aventin.* i. A village of Armagnac, in the election of Rivière-Verdun, *p. Grenade.* 2. A place of Champagne, in the diocefe and election of Troyes. *p. Troyes.* S. *Auge-U-Vieil,* a village of Brie, in the election of Montercau. *p. Montereau.* S. *Augußin,* I. A town of Saintonge, in the diocefe and election of Saintes, *p. Ccxe-z.* 2. A fmall town of Brie, in the election of Coulomiers.*p. Coulcmiers.* 3. A fmall town of Limofin, in the election of Brives. *p. Tulles.* S. *Augußin-deч-Bois,* a village of Anjou, in the diocefe and election of Angers, *p. Ingrande.* S. *Augußin-de-Terouane,* an abby in the diocefe of S. Orner, *p. Aire,* S, *Augußinpres-Angers,* a fmall town of Anjou, in the diocefe and ekction of Angers, *p. Angers.* S *Arid,* a village of Agénois, in the diocefe and election of Agen. *p. Vi. Ienm ve-d1-s gcn.* ¿S. *Avid-de-Lede & de Souleignes* villages of Agénois, in the diocefe and election of Agen. *p. Agen.* S.*Avid-Rt'i;ure-dc-Mcntfctrand& S. A-uid-Seigneur,'* fmall towns of Périgord, in the diocefe and election of Sarlat. *p. Sar/at.* S.*Avis,* j. village of Saintonge, in the diocefe and election of Saintes. *f. Samtes.* 2. Sec *Habitans-du-CberetS--Avis.* S. *Afvis-de-Tarde, & S. Avis-!ePauvre,* villages of Marthe, in the election of Gucret. *p. Aithujjin.* S. *Avit.* i. A village of Auvergne, in the election of Riom. *p. Riom,* 2. m A village of Upper Languedoc, in the diocefe and receipt uf Lavaur. *p. Caflies.* 3. A village of Armagnac, in the election of Lomagnc. *p. Beaumont-de-i.cmagnc.* S. *Aviîty* a village of Dauphiny, in the dioccfe and election of Vienne. *p. Vienne.* S. *Aulaie.* i. A town of Angoumois, in the diocofe and election of Angoulême. *p. Barbrßcux. 2.* A fniall town of Périgord, in the diocefe and election of Périgueux. *p. Ste. Foy.* 3. A village of Guicnne, in the diocefe and election of Bourdcaux. *p. Bourdcaux.* S. *Au/a'tre.* 1. A fmall town of Limofin, in the election of Brives. *P. Brives.* 2. A village of Périgord, in the diocefe and election of Sarlat. *p. Sarlat.* S. *Aulais,* a village of Saintonge, in the dioccfe and election of Saintes. *p. Saintes.* S. *Aume/y,* a village of Condommois, in the di'ccfe and election of Condom, *p. Agen,* S.*Aunisy* ;f village of Armagnac, in the diocefe and election of Auch. *p. Auch,* S. *Aupericnty* a village of Marche, in the election of Gucret. *p. Aufraffen.* S. *Aure,* a village of Dauphiny, in the diocefe and election of Grenoble, *p. Grenoble.* S. *Aarence,* a vilbgc of Armagnac, in the election of AÜarac. *p. Moni* S. *Bernara-les-Bcis,* & *Bernardles-Toßez,* places of Champagne, in the diocefe and election of Langres. *p. Langres.* S. *Beroin-les-Gurgy,* a hamlet of Champagne, in the diocefe and election of Langres. *p. Langret.* S. *Beroïn-les-Moines,* a village of Burgundv, in the bailiwick of Châtilion, *p. Chât'xlhn-ur-Séne.* S. *Bcroh-furd'Heune,* a village of Burgundy, in the diocefe and bailiwick of Challón, *p. Challón.* S. *Beroïng,* a village of FrancheComté, in the bailiwick of Gray.4/. *Gray.* S. *Bertbenin.* 1. A town of Maine, about a league from Laval, *p. Laval.* 2. A town of Maine, in the election of Mayenne, *p. Mayenne.* S. *Bertin,* an abby in the city of S. Omer.

S. *Bertrand,* a city of Gafcony, fituatcd on the Garonne, in the generality of Auch; about 17 leagues from Auch, and 10 from Tarbesj the capital of Comminges, and reiidence of the biihojj. *p. Monirejeau,* S. *Beurey* a parilh of Burgundv, in the bailiwick of Semur. *p. Scmuren-Auxois.* S. *Bit-r-cn-Belin,* a town of M.-ine, in the diocefe and election of Alans. *p. Foultourte.* S. *Bla.je. i.* A village of Dauphiny, in the diocefe and election of Vienne, *p. Vienne.* 2. A village of Burgundy, in the dioceTc and bailiwick of Autun. *p. Autvn.* 3. A village of Dombcs, in the chateîlany of ToJITey. *p. Bellewille.* 4. A place and priory of Provence, in the vigueryof Draguignan. *p. Draguignan.* 5. A priory in the diocefe of Bourges. S. *B!a':fe,* ¿2? *Bl'ienjbach,* a village of Alface, in the diocefe of Straiburg. *p. Molßeim.* S. *Blancard.* 1. A village of Nebouzan, in the generality of Auch. *p. Tarbcs.* 2. A village of Armagnac, in the election of Aftarac. *p,, Mirande.* S. *Д/imentj* a (mail town of Picaráy, in the diocefe and election of Amiens./. *AbbeúÜle.* S. *BГm,* a priory in the diocefe of Toul, in Champagne. S. *Bob aire,* a village of Blefois, in in the diocefe and election of Blois. *p. Blois. IS. Boil,* a village of Burgundy, in Che bailiwick of Macon, *p. Challón.* S. *Bois.* I. A village f Bugey, in the diocefe and bailiwick, of Bellcy. *p. Be/ley.* 2. A village of Beam, in the receipt of Orthez. *p. Ortbez.* S. *Borner9* a fmall town of Normandy, in the eleitkm of Domfront. *p. Domfront.* S. *Bomert,* a village of Beauce, in the election of Châteaudun. *f. laFer té-Bernard.* S. *Bon* ££f. *Vilouretttj* a village of Champagne, in the diocefe and election of Troyes, *p. Vrflencce.* S. *Bonnet, i.* A town of Dauphiny, in the diocefe and election of Vienne, *p. Vallier.* 2. A town of Dauphiny, in the generality of Grenoble, *p. Gap,* 3. A town of Auvergne, in the eleélion of Riom. *p. Riem.* 4. A fmall town of Auvergne, in the diocefe and cleft-ion of S. Flour, *p.* S. *Flour.* 5. A village of Dauphiny, in the diocefe and election of Grenoble, *p. Grenoble.* 6. A village of Dauphiny, in the diocefe and election of Vienne, *p.* S. *Marctllin.* 7. A village of Bourbon nois, in the election of S. Amand. *p.* S. *Amar.d.* 8. A village of Bourbonnois, in the election of Moulins. *p. Moulins.* 9. A village of Burgundy, in the diocefe and bailiwick of Macon, *p. Macon, Jo.* A village of Languedoc, in the diocefe and receipt of Alais, *p. Anduve. h. Bonnet-à-Valou%e) & S. Bonnetle-Pairvrey* villages of Limofin, in the diocefe and election of Tulles, *p. Tulles.* S. *Bonnet-dc-B elle-Na-ve* a pariih *bl* Bourborinois, in the diocefe and election of Gannat. *p. Gannat.*

& *Bonnet-de-Crayy* a fmailtown of Forez, in the election of Montbrifon. *p. Monthriion.* 2. A fmall town of Auvergne, in the election of IiToire. *p. IßUre.* S. *Bonxct-Ie-Port-Diev,* a village of Limofin, in the di;cefe and election of Tulles, *p. A-riliac.* S. *Bwet-Outraillur,® S.Bon.MPrworth al,* fmall towns of Auvergne, in the diocefe andel.Étioa of Clermont, *p. Clermont.* S. *Bcnnct-près-SfHac,* a fmall town of Limofin, in the diocefe and election oí Limages, *f. Bdiac.* S. *Bonnet-jom-VieUUvignej* apariíh of Burgundy, in the bailiwick of Charolles. *p. la Paucavdiire.* S. *Bonnof. i.* A village of Nivernois, in the election of Charitéfur-Loire, *p. la Cba ite'-fur-L'Are. 1.* A village of Burgundy, in the bailiwick ot Auxonne, *p. Auxonne.* 3. A village of Burgundy, in the diocefe and bailiwick of Challón, *p. Chal/on.* S. *Bouife,* a village in Berry, in the diocefe and election of Bourges. *p. Sancerre.* S. *Brarxhi,* & S. *Brancbi-enMorvantj* villages of Burgundy, in the diocefe of Autun, and bailiw'ck of Avalon, *p. Avalon.* S. *Branches,* a town of Touraine, in the diocefe and election of Tours. *p. "Tours.* S. *Brandon,* a village of Burgundy, in the diocefe and bailiwick of Autun. *p. Autan.* S. *B/ es,* a vilhge of lower Languedoc, in the diocefe and receipt of Montpellier, *p. Montpellier.* S. *Brejq,* a place of Armagnac, in the diocefe and election of Auch. *p. Aucb..* S. *Breffjbn.* I. A village of lower Languedoc, in the diocefe and receipt of Alais, *p. U Vigan.* 2. A village of Franche-Compté, in the-baihwick of Vcfoul. *p. Lure.* 3. A village of Quercy, in the election of Figeac. *p. ligeac.* S. *Bre-vaw,* a village of Bretagne, in the diocefe and receipt of Mantes, *f. Pahnbceuf.* S. *Bra,* a village of lower Languedoc, in the diocefe and rccejpt of Uzts. *p. Uze's.* S. *Briuc,* a village of Bretagne, in the diocefe and receipt of S. Malo. *p.* S. *Malo.* S. *Bric. 1.* A town in the diocefe and election of Paris, *p. Ecauen.* 2. A town of Anjou, in the election of Flèche, *p. Sable.* 3. A fmall town of Limofin, in the diocefe and election of Limoges, *p.* S. *Janlen.* 4. A village of Normandy in the election of Domfront. /. *Domfrtnt.* 5. A village of Brie, in the election of Provins, *p. Provins.* 6. A village of Bretagne, in the diocefe and receipt of Rennes, *p. Ponrorjon.* 7. A village of Agénois, in the diocefe and election of Agen. *p. Agen.* 8. A figniory of Vexin-Franeois, in the election of Chaumont and Magny. *P. Magny.* S. *Brice* & *Couceltcs-les-Rbäms,* a village of Champagne, in the diocefe and election of Rheims, *p. Rheims,* S, *Bricen,* a chatellany of Berry, in the diocefe and generality of Bourg.я. *p. Bourges.* S. *Btieux-,* or 5. *Br'seuc,* a city of Normandy, near the fea, in the generality of Nantes, the fee of a bifhop, the chief place of a receipt, &c. 5 leagues from Lamballe, 26 from Rennes, 7 from Guingamp, 34 from Breit, 30 from l'Orient, 16 from Dinan, 45 from LavaJ, 54 from Nantes, 54 from Caen, 58 from Aleivon, 78 from Tours, 45 from Mayenne, 2nd 114 from Paris. *Bureau de pcfie. S. Br'uuc-de-Mauror.,* a village of Bretagne, in the diocefe and receipt of S. Malo. *p. Ploermd.*

S. *Br.euc-des-lffsj* a village of Bretagne, in the diocefe and receipt of S. Malo. *p. Be-berel. S. Bris.* i. A town of Burgundy, in the diocefe and election of Aux-»erre. *p. Auxerre.* 2. A town of Angoumois, in the election of Cognac, *p. Ctgnec.* 3. A village of

Bafsd Ms, in the election of Condom. *p. Bofas. S. BrjJJbn.* i. A village of Nivernois, in the election of Nivers. *p. Saul eu. 1.* A vilhge of Gàtinois, in the election of Gïen. *p. Gien.* 3. A village of Nivernöisr in th dioccfe and election of Nivcrs. *p. Nivers. S. Brix.* i. A fmall town oí Poitou, in the election of Niort, *p. Niort.* 2. A village of Normandy, in the elect on of Falaife. *f. Falaife. S. Brixs-pres-Azranches,* a village of Normandy, in the diocfe and' election of Avranch?s *p. Av.anches, S. Brcladre,* a village of Bretagne, *n* the diocefe and receipt of *DA. p. 'Del. S:e.-Barbe,* a village of Normandy, in the election of Andcly. *p. Pont FEvequc. Ute.-Barbe-en-Auge y* a town of Normandy, in the diocefe of1 Lifieux. *p. Ufizux. £te. Bar¿e-fur-Gaiihn,* a village of Normandy, in the election of Andejy. *p. Caillou. Ste-Baume, la,* a celebrated grctto of Provence, in which it is by fomc believed, that Mary Magdalene died; about 2 leagues from S. Maximin, and 5 from Marfeille. *p. S. Maxlmin. Ste.-Bazeille,* a town of Bazadois, in the election of Condom, *p. Marmande. Üte-Beuve-aux-Cbamp,* a village of Normandy, in the election of NeufChûtel. *p. Aumale. Ste-B ave-en-Rtvière,* a village of Normandy, in the election of Neufchâtcl. *p. Neufchdtel. Ste-Bexcnne,* a confiderable traft of land in Poitou. *Ste-Blandine.* 1. A village of Poitou, in the election of S. Maixant. *p. Niort.* 2. A village of Dauphiny, in the election of

Vienne, *p. la Tourdu-Pin. S te.-Brigitte,* a place of Upper Languedoc, in the diocefe of Lodéve. *p. L&deue.* 5. *Calais,* a town of Maine, on thc river Anille, about 6 leagues from
©F Normandy, in the election of Alençon. *p. Alençon. S. Cenery-pres-$ée%,* a village of Normandy, in the election of Alençon. *p. S (ex. S. Cenhz,* a village of Quercy, in the diocefe and election of Cahors. *p. Çetèors. $. Ceols,* a fmall town of Berry, about 5-leagues from Bourges. */. Bourges. S. Cere,* a town of Quercy, tutted on the river Bave./». *Cahors. S. Cernin,* i. A town of Rouergue, in the election of Milhaud. *p. Milbaud, %. /,* A fmall town of Auvergne, in the election of Aurillac. *p. Aurillac. 1,* A village of Agénois, in the diocefe and election of Agen. *p. Agen.* 4. A village of Quercy, in the diocefe and election of Cahors. *p. Cahors. S. Cernin-de-la-Barde-Viclf* a village of Agénois, in the diocefe and election of Agen. *p. Agen. S. Cemïn-de-ReUlat,* a village of Périgord, in the diocefe and election ©f Ptrigueux. *p. Perigueux. S. Germn-d'Eyß'et,* a fmall town of Agénois, in the diocefe and election of Agen. *p. Agen. S. Cerr.y-dela-Bard?,* a fmall town of Périgord, in the diocefe and election of Sarlat. *p. Sarlat S. Cervaixj* a village of Lower Languedoc, in the diocefe and receipt of Uzés. *p. Uze's. S. Cefatre,* a village of Provence, in the diocefe and viguery of GraiTe. *p. Große, S. Ceja':re-les-Arles,* a convent in one of the fauxbourgs of Aries, in Provence, *p. Aries. S. Ceßters,* a village of Limofin, in the diocefe and election of Tulles. *p. Tulles. S. Cczary,* a village of Provence, in the diocefe and viguery of GraiTe. *p. Graft. S. Ce-zert,* a village of Armagnac, in the election of Lomagnc. *pBeaumont-dc -Lomagne. S. GflKft* a village of Gafcony, in the diocefe and election of Comminges. *p. Montrcjeau. S. Chahraix,* a fmall town of Marche, in the election of (?ucret *p. Chcnerailles. S. Cbafre,* a town of Languedoc, in the diocefe and receipt ofPuv. *$ le Puy., S. Cha/rey,* a village of Dauphiny,. in the election of Gsp. *p. Briancon. S. Cbalard,* a priory in the diocefe of Limoges, *p. Limoges. S.Chamand.* 1. A

town of Limofin, in the diocefe'and election of Tulles. *p. Tulles. 1.* A fmall town of Auvergne, in the diocefe of S. Flour, *p. AurMlac. S. Chamas,* a village of Provence» in the viguery of Aix. *p. Salon. S. Chamaßy,* a fmall town of Périgord, in the diocefe and election of Sarlat. *p. Sarlat. S. Chamond,* or *Cbamont,* or *Cbau' motit,* a fmall city of Lyonnois, with a ftrong caftle; 3 leagues from S. Etienne, 6§ from S. Rambert, Il from Montbrifon, and 10 from Lyons. *Bureau de pcfle. S. Champs,* a village of Bugey, m the diocefe and bailiwick of Belley. *p. Belley. S. Chapte,* a village of Lower Laaguedoc, in the diocefe and recei Uzés. *p. XJx.es. S. Charles,* a town of Maine, in thfi election of Laval, *p. Laval. S. Charrier,* a itown of Berry, in the elect ion of Châtre, *p. la Chatre. S. Chartres,* a village of Poitou, in the election of Richelieu, *p. Air vault. S. Chef,* a town of Dauphiny, about 7 leagues from Vienne, *p. Bourgoin. S. Chely d'Apcher,* a town of Lower Languedoc, in the diocefe and receipt of Mende. *p. Mende. S. Chely-d'Eßain,* a village of Rouergue, in the diocefe and election of Rhodcz. *p. Rhodes. Si Chely-âe-Tam,* a village of Lower Languedoc, in the diocefe and receipt of Mende. *p. Mende. S. Cheron. I.* A fmall town of Beaux c, in the election of Dourdan, of S. Fhur. *p. S. Flour.* 6. A village of Poirou, in the election ofChâtelkrauf. *p.Cbdtclleraut.* 7. A vilbgt of Burgundy, in the diocefc and bailiwick of Challón, *p. la Pacaudiere.* 8. A village of Lwer Languedoc, in the diocifc and receipt of MenJe. *p. Mendt.* 9. A village of Normandy, in the eleétion of Argentan, *p. Argentan.* 10. A village of Normandy, in the election of Vcrneuil. */. Ver-, neuxl.* il. A village of Bléfois, in the election of Romorantin. *p. Romorantin.* 12. A village of Normandy, in the election of Mortain. *pt V.re.* 13. A village of Picardy, in the diocefe and election of Senlis. *p. SerJis.* 14. A village of Beauce, in the election of Châtcaudun. *p. Cbdteaudun.* 15. A village of Bourbonnois, in the election of Gannat. *p.Gannat. t¿.* A village of Bourbonnois,

in the election of S. Amand.
. *S. Amand.* 17. A vilhgc of Bourbonnois, in the election of Montluçon, *p. Montlucon.* 18, A village of Rouergue, in the election of Villefranche, *p. Villefrancbe-de-Rouergue,* 19. A village of Rouergue, in the election of Milhaud. *p. Milbaud. 20.* A village of Poitou, in the election of Confolans. *p. Confiions.* 21. A viUagcof Agénois, in the diocefe and election of Agen. *p. Lajptirc.* 22. A village of Marche, in the election of Gucret. *p. Gueret.* 23. A village of Dioiphiuy, in the diocefe and election *oVienn&.p.laCóteS.xAndre'.* 24. A village of Limofin, in the diocefe and election of Limoges, *p. Confolens.* 25. A village of Franche-Comté, in the bailiwick of Orgelet, *p. bons le Saunier.* 26. A village of Provence, in the diocefe and vigucry of Apt. *p. Apt.* 27. A village of Dauphiny, in the diocefe and election of Grenoble, *p. Grenoble.* 2S. A village of Dombes, in the chatellany of S. Trivers. *p-Belleville.* 29. A village of Champagne, in the election of Bar-fur-Aube. *p. Bar-jur-Aube.* 30. A village of Normandy, in the ehro tion of Fabife. *J. Falaije* ..

Guicnn?» in the diocefe and election *oí* Bourdeaux, *p. Bourdeaux.* S. Ciers-de-CanЦ'e. See *Canejfe.* S. Get s-de-la-Lande, a town of Guiennc, in the diocefe and election of lïourdeaux. *p. Blaye.* C. *Gçrs-du-'TaHLnt* a town of Sa'mt-tnge, in the diocefe and election of Saintes, *p. Saintes.* S. *C'ifreírpve,* l. A village of Nivernois-, in the diocefe and election of Nevéi s, *p. Nweru* 2. A place of Nivernois,. in tbc election of Château-СЫ non. *p. Decrze.* S *Cpoy,* a village of Auvergne, in the diocefe and election of S. Flour, *f. S. Flour, S. tir.* i. A town of Maine, in the diocefe and election of Mans. *p. it Mans.* 2. A town of Maine, in the election of Laval, *p. Lavai.* 3. A town of Anjou, in the election of Saumur. *p. Saumur.* 4. A town of Brie, in the diocefe and election of Meaux. *p. la-Fertc-fous-Jouare.* 6. A fmall town of Poitou, in the election 'of Confolens. *p. Confolens.* 7. A village of Perche, in the election of Mortagne. *p.* *BeUefme.* 8. A village of Beauce, in the election of Dourdan. *p. Duurdan.* 9. A village of Orléannois, in the diocefe and election of Orleans, *p. Orleans,* то. "A village of Gâtinois, in the diocefe and election of Etampes. *p. Etamfes.* 11. A village of Normandy, in the election of "Vulogncs. *p. Valognes.* 12. A fignio-ry of Vexin, iff cbe election of Chaumont and Magny. *p. Magny S. Ch;* or *S. Cirau-Val-dt-Galhe* a village of Beauce, in which is a celebrated convent for the daughters of nobility, *p. Versailles.* S. *Gr-de-Salerne,* a village of Normandy, in the election of B:rnay. *p. Brijne.* S. *Cir-de-Sarge,* a fmall town of Maine, in the election of Chutcaudu-Loir. *p. JVir,nt doubl eau.* S. *Cir-du-Gault,* a village of ToUraineí" in the diocefe and election of Tours, *p. Tours.* S. *C/air* fe? *Didier,* a village oí Dauphiny, in the generality of Grenoble, *p. Grenoble.* S. *Ctair* ¿3 S. *Jean-de-Monclar,,* Sec *Monclar.* S. *Clair-de-Hides,* a v i lb ge of Agénois, in the diocefe and election of Agen. *p. Agen.* S. *Ш₂-d'Herce.* See *Herd.* 8. *Clair-outrc-Haloufe,* a fmall town in Normandy, in the eleftion of Vire. *p. Conde'-fur-NoireaUw* S. *Clair-prh-Condrieux,* a village of Dauphiny, in the election of Vienne. *Vienne.* S. *Clair-yur-Epte,* a town of Vexin-Francois, m the eleftion of Chaumont and Magny. *f. le Tille.* S. *Clair-jur-les-Monts,* a vilUge of Normandy, in the election of Caudehec. *p. Tvett.* S. *Clamem,* a village of Quer cy, in the diocefe and election of Cahors. *p. Cahors.* 5. *Ciar.* i. A town of Armagnac, in the diocefe of Lectoure, and election of Lomagnc, about 3 leagues from Lectoure, 9 from Auch, and 8 from Condom. *Bureau de Poße.* %. A village of Armagnac, in the election of Rivière-Verdun./». *Grenade.* 3. A vilbge of Quercy, in the diocefe and election of Cahors *p. Peyrae.* S. *Claud,* a village of Angoumois, in the diocefe and election of Angouледае. *p. Angoulime.* TS. *Claude,* or 5. *Oyen,* a city of Franche-Comté, in the generality of Befancon, fituated between high mountains on the fmall river Ltfon; the fee of a biihop; it owes its origin to a celebrated abby, founded in the middle of the 5th century fo called from S. Claude, the Archbihop of Befançon. About 5 leagues from Clcrvaux, and 4 from Moyrans, 7 from Orgelet, 16 from Salins, 5 from Dotirtan, 24 from Befancon, and 6 from Geneva. *Bureau de poße.* S. *Claude,* i. a town of BîéfoiSj in the diocclc and election of Bloii, 3 5. *Crapaíy.* i. A town of Age'nois, in the diocefe and election of Agen. . *4'onnevns.* 2. A fmall town of Guicnne, in the diocefe and election of Bourdeaux. *p. Boutdemix.* 3. A village of Quercy, in the diocefe and election of Montauban. *p. RUritauban.* 4 A village of Rouergue, In the election of Milhaud. *p. Mdhaud.* 5. A village of Quercy, in the diocefe and election of Cahors. *p. Calors.* 6. A village of Agénois, in the diocefe and election of Agen. *p. Agen.* 7. A village of Condomois, in the diocefe and election of Condom, *p. Cbndom.* S. *Crapaxy-de-Lcrme,* a village of Agénois, in the diocefe and election of Agen. *p. Ae/t.* S. *Crcfpin & Siglieraz* fmall town of Dauphiny, in the election of G?p. *p. Gap.* $ *Crejpift.* 1. A town of Anion, in tne diocefe and elect on of Ar.gfrs. *p. Av.g-.ru z.* A village of Saintonge, in the election of S. Jean-cTAnge'y. *p. Ta.muy-Boutonne.* 3. A village of Périgord, in the diocefe and election of Sarlat. *p. Sur laW* 4. A village of Normandy, in the election of Arques, *f. Dieppe.* 5. A figniory of Normandy, in the election of Pont-TEvccjue. *p. Pont-PEicquc.* S. *Crejfui aux-Boh & Offrcn:ontt* a village of Picardy, in the diocefe and election of Soi fions, *p. Comfñegne.* S. *Crejpxn-d1 Auberochtj* a village of Périgord, in the diocefe and election of Périgueux. *p. Périgueux.*

& *Crefpin-de-Bourdcille,* a fmall town of Périgord, in the diocefe and election of Périgueux. *p. BourdeUle.* S. *Crefpin-en-Cbayet* an abby in the diocefe of Soifions. *p. Soißbns.* S. *Cric q-du-Gare y* a village of Gafcony, in the election of Landes. *p. Dax.* S. *Crig,* a village of Armagnac, in the diocefe and election of Auclu /. *Aucb,* S. *Crig* Êf *Marquevilh}* a village of Gafcony, in the election of Landes, *p. S. Sever.* S. *Oißoly* a village of Lower X-anguedoc,' in the ciiocefe and receipt of Alais, *p. sitáis.*

S. Cybard, an ancient ahby, in one of the fauxbourgs of Angoulème. *p. Angoulème. S. Cypñcn.* i. A town of Ptírigord, in the diocefe and election of Sarlat. *p. Sarlat.* 2. A village of Limofin, in the election of Brives. *p. Brlws.* 3. A village of Forez, in the election of Montbrifon. *p. Motitbi'tfon.* 4. A village oi Agénois, in the diocefe and élection of Agen. *p. Agen.* 5. A village of Roufiillon, in the diocefe and vjguery of Perpignan, *p. Perpignan.* 6. A village of Saintur.¿c, in the diocefe and election of Saintes, *p. Saintes.* 7. A village of Roucrgue, in the election of Vjllefraochc. *p. Pilitfranche-âe-K'Aiergue.* %. A village of Bourbonnois, in the election of Gannat. *p. Gannat.* 9. A village of Lyonnois, in the diocefe and election of Lyons, *p. Lyon. S. Cyr.* X. A fmall town of Poitou, in the diocefe and election of Poitiers, *p. Tbmare.* 2. See 5. Cir. *S. Cyre.* See *S. Cire. S. Cy rice,* a village of Dauphiny, in the diocefe and election of Gap. *p. Gap. S. Cyr'die-de-VaUtte,* a village of Agénois, in the diocefe and election of Agen. *p. Agen.* Sainte Camelle. 1. Á village of "Upper Languedoc, in the diocefe and receipt of Mirepoix. *p. Mlepoix.* 2. A place of Foix, in the generality of Rouffillon. *p. Foix.* Ste. Cathartne. I. A town of Agénois, in the diocefe and election of Agen.-*p. Agen,* 2. A town of Condomois, in the dioceie and election of Condom, *p. Condom.* 3. A village of Mcflin, in the diocefe and receipt of Metz. *p. Met».* 4. A. village of Dauphiny, in the ge neralíty of Grenoble, *p. Grenoble.* 5. A village of Provence, in the chatellany of Montmcrle. *p. Belleville.* Ste. *Cathetüne-ii-Rowvre,* a priory in the diocefe of So'iTons. *p. SviJJors. Sie. Catherine-dy Abfy,* a convent in the city of Abuy.
Sie. *Catbirine-d" Apt%* a convent in the city of Apt. *Ste. Catbirine-de-Coin* a priory of Berry, in the diocefe of Bourns, *p. Bourges. Ste. Catberir.e-de-T'terboisy* a town of Touraine, in the election of Chinon. *p. Ste. Allure. Sie. Catítr't:e-de-VAl:ergemeuty %* village ot Burgundy, in the bailiwick, of Món. *y. MCon. Sic Cathaiine-de-Lûvaly* 3 priory in the town of Laval, in Maine. Ste.

Cathjime-fur-Livtrie, a village of Fore?. , in the election of S. Etienne, *p. Chateliei. Ste. Cécile,* x. A tuwn of Poitou, in the election of Mauleon. /»» *Chantor.ay.* 2. A fmall town of Normandy in the election of Vire. *p. Valledku.* 3. A fmall town of Venaifiin, in the judicature of Valreas. *p. Valreas.* 4. A village of Agenois, in the diocefe and election of Agen. *p. Agen.* 5. A vilbge of Maine, in the election of Château-du-Loir. *p. Château-du-Loir.* 6. A village of Berry, in the dioceie of Bourges, *p. Rcmorantin.* 7. A village of Burgundy, in the dioceie and bailiwick of Mâcon. -*p.Macon. Ste. Cecile-d"Ar.dorge,* a village of Lower Languedoc, in the diocefe and receipt of Uzés. *p. Usus. Sie. Cc.-otte,* a village of Maine, ín the election of Château-du-Loir. *p. Montotre.* Ste. *Cbrißti.* A town of Armagnac, in the diocefe and election of Auch. *p. Auch.* 2. A village of Armagnac, in the diocefe and election of Auch. *p. Mont-de-Mar jan. Ste. Cbrißine.* 1. A vilbge of Bourbonnois, in the election of Rannat. *p. Gar.nat.* 2. A village of Poitou, in the election of Niort, /. *Ñiort.* 3. A village of Anjou, in the diocefe and election of Angers. *p. Angers. Ste. Ctaire,* a convent in the city of Vienne., See. *C3/'jmj & Funaubtrte,* places ef RouiTillon, in the diocefe an4 vigutry of Perpignan, *p. Pcrjiran. Stz. Colomb t. ï.* A town of Yore/, in the election of Roanne, *p. Vienne. . s.* A town uf Anjou, in the election of Fjèche. *p. la Fleche.* 3. A fmall town of upper Languedoc, in the ttiocefe and receipt of Mirepoix. *p. JUircfcix.* 4. A fmall town of Agé»ois, in the diocefe and election of Agen. *p. Agen.* 5. A village of Korcz, in the election of S. Etienne. *f. Si Etienne.* 6. A village of Agénois, in the diocefe-aud election of Agen. *p. Agen.* 7. A village of Normandy, in the election of Conihes. *p. Cr.nt!* 8. A village of Normandy, in the election of Valognes. *f. Valognes.* 9. A village of Normandy, in the election of Caudebec. *f. l'Aigle.* 10. A village of Gnienne, in the diocefe and election of Bouidcanx. *p. CaflUlon.* II. A village of Nivernais, in the election of Clamccy. *p. Clamery.* 12. A village of Nivernais, in the election of Vii.clay.

p. VixeUtjr. 13. A village «f Nivcrnois, in the election of Chariré-rur-Loire. *p. Cdje.* 14. A village of Brie, in the election of Provins, *p. Provins.* 15. A village of Beaujolais, in the election of Villffranche. *p. Villefrar.ckc.* 16. A village of Saintonge, in the diocefe and election of Saintes, *p. Saintes.* 17. A village of Berry, in the election of lifoudun. *p. JJJhudvn.* 18.
A village of Burgundy, in the bailiv'm к of Semur-en-Auxois. *p. Setnur-en-Auxcis.* 19. A village of Burgundy, in the bailiwick of Châtillon. *p. Cbitilloit-fitr-Snne.* ao. A village nf Angoumois, in the diocefe and election of Angoulêtne. *J. la Riïbefoucauit.* 21. A viljaje of Périgord, in the diocefe and efec tion of Perigucux. *p. la Linde,* zz. A village of Normandy, in the election of Pont-de-11 Arche, *p. F'ont-defA che.* 23. A village of Franche Comté, in the bailiwick of Pontarlier. *f. Pontarlier.* 24. A village of Quercy, in the election of Figeac. *p. Figeac.* 25. A village of Dauphiny, in the dioce.e and election of Gap. *f. Gup.* 26. A village of Dauphiny, in the generality of Grenoble, *p. GrcnoBlf. Zfi* A village of Bretagne, in the diocefe and r4-eipt of Nantes? *p. Chateaubr'mnt. Ste. Columbfy* or *Ste. Cohmbe-aM'wadeux,* a town of Armagnac, in the election of Loinagne. *p. Beaumcnt-de-Lomagne. Ste. Colombe-Ia-Petitey* a village of Normandy, in the election of Alearon, *p. Sfess. Ste. Coiombt-les-SettSf* an abby near Sens, in Champagne, *p. Sens. Ste Colombe-fur-Rilie,* a fmali town of Normandy, in the election of Alençon. *p. Cizay, Ste. Colomme,* a village of Béam, in the dio:cfe and fénéchaufiee of Olcron. *p. Oleron. Ste. Conforce & 2Marey-fc-Loutff* a village of Lyonnois, in the diocefe and eleñion of Lyons, *p. Ly.n. Ste. Coulombe,* a fmall town of Gafcony, in the election of Landes. *p. Dax.* % *Ste. Cotdombe-de-Montouroux,* a village of Lower Languedoc, in the diocefe and receipt of Mende. *p. Mende.* . *Ste. Croix,* i. A village of AI face, in the bailiwick of Enfiiheim, *p. Colmar.* 2. A town of Maine, in the diocefe and elect on of Mans. *p. h Mans.* 3. A fmall town of Normandy, in jhe election of S. Lo-*p. S. ho.* 4. A village of Normandy,

in the election of Lio is. *p. Bcouy.* 5. A village of Normandy» in the election of Montiviliicrs. *p. Harfieur.* 6. A village of Nurmandy, n the élection of Caën. *p. Câen.* 7-A village of Normandy, in the diocefe and election of Bayeux. *p. Bayeux.* 8. A village of Brefle, in the bailiwick of Bourg-en-BrciTe. *P» Bourg-en-Breße.* 9. A village of Burgundy, in the bailiwick of Challón, *p. Lovant.* 10. A village of Gafcony, m the election of Landes, *p. Tardas, il.* A village of Agénois, in the diocefe and election of Agen. *p. las Peyres.* I2-. A village of Gütinois, in the election of Nemours, *p. Nemours.* 13. A village of DauphVny, in the election *of* Mon tel ¡ mart. *p. Monte.'ima/t.* 14. A village of Provencer in the viguery of MoU fliers *p. Cafielîane.* 15. A village of Rouergue, in the election of Villefrarfthe, *p. Vi/leJranebe-de-Rouergue.* i6; An abby in the diocefe of Trcguier, in Bretagne, *p. Guingamp. Sie. Crcix c» Allifnans,* a village of Agénois in-the diocefe and election of Agen. *p.-Agen Sie. Croix C2f C'iiiaty* a village of Upper Languedoc, in the diocefe and receipt of Rieux, *p. Touhufe. S/e..Crcix & Fontanes.,* a village of bower Languedoc, in the diocefe and receipt of Montpellier.*p. Montpellier. Ste. Cr¿x-á-la-Haguc)* a village of Normandy, in the election, of Valognes. *p. Valognes. Ste. Crcix-a-TAwze,* a village of Provence, in the viguery of ForçaiCjuicr. *p. Forcalquier. Ste. Croix-en-Bcfcage,* a village of Normandy, in the election of Valögncs. *p. Vahgr.es. Ste. Crcix-d Angle,* an abby in the diocefe of Poitiers, *p. S. Savin. Ste. Croix-d Apt,* a-convent' in the city of Apt. *St. Cro'ix-de-Beimontcly* a village of Quercy, in the diocefe and election of C hors. *p. Cabors. Ste. Croix-de-Caderics,'* a village of Lower Ltnguedo-, in the diocefe and receipt of Alais, *p. AUis. Ste. Croix-de-Cormeille,* a village of Normandy, In the election of Muntivillicrs. *p. Pont-Andeme". Ste, Crcix-de-Joßeiirij* л village of diocefe and election of Bloïs. *p. Bloh.* 5. A village of Bugey, in the receipt of Bclley. *p. Amber'ieux.* 6. A village of Normandy in the election of Caudebec. *p. Fnuville.* 7. A village of Normandy, in the election of Domfront. /. *Domfront.* 8. A village of Normandy, in the election of Gifors. *p. Gifors.* 9. A village of Beauce, in the election of Châteaudun. *p Cbâteaudun.* 10. A village of Poitou, in the election of Niort, *p. Niort, и.* A village of Lower Languedoc, in the dioccfe and receipt of Mendc. *p. Mendt,* 12. A village of Lower Languedoc, in the diocefc and receipt of Uzés. *p. Usee's.* 13. A village of Angoumois, in the diocfe and election of Angoulcme. *p. Angouitme.* 14. A village of Quercy, in the dibce:"e and election of Cahors. *p. MuIIIac,* 15. A village of Brcfle, in the receipt of Bourg, *p. B:urgen-BrejJ'e.* 16. A village of Normandy, in the election of Falaife. *p. Falaife. i"f.* A village of Perche,, in the election of-Mortagne. *p. Mortagne.* 18. A chatellany of Berry, *p. Chateauroux.* lo» A place of Champagne, in the diocefe of Sens. *p. Sens, S. Denis-en-Francej* a town in the Ifle of France, îttuated on a fmail river in a very fertile plain. In an ancient abby, arc the tombs of the Kings of Fiance, of the firft and fécond race, and Come of th third. 2 leagues from Paris, in the road from Chantilly. *Bureau de pfle, S. Der.is-B(Jguerardf* a village of Normandy, in the election of PuntAuderner. *p. le Boultroude, S. Dens-Combarna%ani* a village of Bourbonnois, in the election oí Gannat. *pr Gannat. ß. uenis-iP Anjou y* a town eГ Anjou, in the election of ChatcauGontier. *p. Sable. S. Denis-d4iaieon* a village of Normandy, in the election of Arques, *p. Dieppe. S. Dtnh-de-LoiV - V,!lef* a place of Nwmandy, in the diLccie and eke tion of Rouen, *p. Rouen.* % 5". *Denis—de s-Bordes y* a village of Agénois, in the diocefe and election of Agen. *p. Agen. S. Denis-dc-Brcn,* a village of Dauphiny, in the generality of Grenoble, *p. Grenoble. S. Denis-de-Gaßines,* a town of Maine, in the election of Mayenne. *p. Mayenne. S. DennisчГHerkmrt,* a village of Normandy, in the election of Candebec. *p. Tvetot. S. Denis-de-Joubel,* a village of Berry, in the diocefe and generality of Bourges, *p. la Châtre. S. Denis dc-V Houme'e,* a village of Saintonge, in the diocefe and election of Saintes, *p.* Suintes. *S. Denis-de-la-Chera£êf* a village of Poitou, in the election of Sablcs-d- 01 o n n c. *p. Mon taigu, S. Denis-de-Paix,* a priory in Picardy, about 6 leagues from Amiens, *p. Amiens. S. Dcnis-dc-Palin,* a village of Berry, in the dioccfe and election of Bourges, *p. Bourges. S. Denis de-Pcw,* a vHhgc of Burgundy, in the diocefe and receipt of Autun. *p. Autun. S. Denis-de Caudray,* a village of Perche, in the election of"Mortagne, *p. la Ferte'-Bernard. S. Denis-des-Monts,* a village *of* Normandy, in the election of PontAudemer. *p. Pont-Audemer. S. Denis-des-Nivaux,* a fmall town of Límoíín, in the diocefc and election of Limoges, *p. Limoges. S. . Dcnis-des-Pu'u st* a village of Beauce, in the diocefe and election of Chartres, *p. Cour-ville. S. Dems-de-Vaux,* a village of Burgundy, in the diocefe and electioa of Challón, *p. Challón.*

¿'. *Denis-du-Behel nt,* a village of Normandy, in the election of Conches, *p. Evreux. S. Denis-du-Mame y* a tow n of Maine, in the election of Laval, *p. Lana!. S. Demt»du'Parcd,Orquei* a place ctfe and rXeipt of Nantes, *f.* tonge, in the diocefe and electiprt *JVantes.* 18. A village of Lower of Saintes *p.Jonfac.* Languedoc, in the diocefe and re-5. *Difant-du-Bois,* a village in the ceipt of Viviers, *f. Viviers.* 10. diocefe and election of Saintes, *p.*

BurgunJy, in the bai'iwick of Se-the bailiwick *oc* Delle, *p. Bcffcrr.* mur-en-Auxois. *p. Semur. & Dmier.* I. A city of Cham*S. Didkr-de-la-Tour, & S. Didier*-pagne, fituated on the Mame, in the *Je Mare,* villages of Da tphiny, in diocefe of Châlons, and election of the diocefe and election of Vienne. Vitry: it was formerly *iirongry p. Vienne.* fortified, and held out againft Charles *S. Didier-en-Billy,* a village of the V. with an array of 100,000 Bourbonnois, in the election of raen for fix weeks, and then furrcn.— Moulins, *p. S. Gerand.* dered on capitulation. 15 leagues *S. Du'ier-en-Bricnncis,* a town of from Chalons, 8 from Joinville, iS Burgundy, in the diocefe of Autun. from Chaumonr, 27 from Langrej, *p. la Puaudicrc.* 6 from Bar-le-Duc, 21 from Toul, X *Didicr-en-Vonjoi,* a village of 27 from Nancy,

34 from Luneville,. B'irgundy, in the election of Mou-37 from Sarrebourg, 53 from Straflins. *p. la PaljTc.* bur?, and 55 from Paris. Bureau *S. Didier-les-A/lier,* a village of *de Poße.* I. A vill ge of Marche, Lower Languedoc, in the diocefe in the election of Bonrganeuf. *p.* and receipt of Puy. *p. le Puy. Bourganeuf.* 3. A village of Dan's. *Didjer-la-Bc'u,* a village of phiny, in the election of Montelit'ranche-Comté, in the receipt of mart. *p. Montelbnart.* 4. A village Lons-le-Saunier. *p. Lons-lc-Siuiiier.* of Agénois, in the diocefe and elcc

S. *Didier-i'ur-Arrùvx,* a village of tion of Agen. *p. Tomeims.* Burgundy, in the diocefe and baili-5. *D'mtr-CbtncraiUes,* a village of vrkk of Autun. *p. sîuf.m.* Marche, in the election of Gueret.

5. *DiMer-ßus-Rivtri,,* a town of *p. Chene.aillcs.* Forez, in hc election oí S. Eiienne. S. *Diüer-les-Domaines,* a village of *p-S. Chôment.* Marche, in the election of Gueret. 5 DivJ a town of Bléfois; fimte *p Gueret.* on the fide of the Loire, in the dio-£ *Dole',* a village of Bretagne, in cefe and clcct'on of Blois; about 5 the diocefe and receipt of Nantes, leagues from Blois, 2 from Chsm-*p-I" Roche-Bernard.* bort, 9 from Ron)oran:in, and 10 5 *Dolus-?Hôpital,* a village of irom Orleans. *Bureau de Poße.* Quercy, in the election of Figeac. S *Die,* i r S. *Diez,* or 5. *Dity,* a *p-Peyrac.* town of Lorraine; 12 leagues from S. *Dornet,* a village of Marche, in Luneville, and 11 from Scheliftat. the election of Gueret. *p. Gueret.* Bureau de *Pße.* S. *Domincuc,* a village of BrctagS. *Diejy,* a fmali town of Au-ne, in the diocefe and receipt of S. Vergne, in the diocefe and election of Malo. *p. S. Malo.* Clermont, *p. Jfüre.* S. *Donan,* a village of Bretagne S. *Dünas,* a village cf Limofin, in the diocefe and receipt of S. Brittle diocefe and election of Tulles, eux. *p. S. B i.ux'. f. Tulles.* S. *Dontt,* a village of Dauphiny, o *Dhnijy,* a village of Lower in the e'ection of Romans, *p. Tain.* Languedoc, in the diocefe and re-& *Dona:Un,* a fmall town of Bre

A pbee of Bugcy, in the receipt of Belley. *p. Bellcy.* 20. A place of 5. *Doms,* a village of Guienne, in the diocefe and election of Bourdeaux. *p. Bwdcaux.*

S. *Donnât,* a fmall town of Auvergne, in the diocefe and elc¿tionof Clermont, *p. Clermont.* 2. A fmall town of Dauphiny, in the diocefe and election of Vienne, *f. Vienne,* S. *Dos,* a place of Beam, in the receipt of Sauvctcrre. *p. Oleron.* S. *Doua'tfo,* a priory in the diocefe of Sens. *p. Sena.* S. *Doulcbard,* or *Doucbard,* a village of Berry, in the diocefe and election of Bourges, *p. Bourges.* Sainte *Dcde,* a village of Armagac, in the election of RivièreVerdun, *p. Grenade.* Sainte *Eaux,* a village of Normandy, in the election of Caën. *p. Caen.* S. *Eble,* a village of Auvergne, in the election of Brioude. *p. Br'toitde.* S. *Ebremni-dt-Bonfojfc,* & S. *Ebrcmortdde-Somhly,* villages of Normandy, in the election of S Lo. *p. S. Lo.* S. *Ebremondfur-V Ofon,* a village of Normandy, in the dioceic and election of Ct/Citances. *p. Coûfances.* S. *Ebrmond-jur-O-.on,* a iigniory of Normandy, in the diocefe of Coútances. *p. Coûtantes.* S *EccolMle,* a village of Bcauce, in the election of Dourdan. *p. Dour dan.* S. *Egreve* Ê? 5. *Robert,* a village of Dauphinv, in the diocefe and election of Grenoble, *p. Grenoble.* S. *Elipb,* a fmall town of Bcauce, in the diocefe and eleition cf Chartres, *p. Champrond.* S. *Eiix.* i. A village of Upper Languedoc, in the diocefe and receipt of Rieux, *p. Totdoufe.* %. A village of Armagnac, in the election of Àrtarac. *p. Mirande.* 3. A village of Ncbouzan, in the diocefe of Comminges. *p. S. Gaudens.* S *Elix-d?Aßarac* a village of Armagnac, in the election of Aftajac. *p. Mirande.* S. *E/licr,* a iniall town of Maine, in the election of Mayenne, *f. Fougères.* 2. A fmall town of Normandy, in the election of Alençon. *Alenpn.* 3. A village of Anjou, in the election of Augers, *p. Angers.* 4. A village of Normandy, in the election of Conches, *p. Evreux.* S. *Eime,* a fort in Rou&Hon, ft. *Collioure.* S. *Efcy.* I. A village of Limofin, in the diocefe and election of Limoges, *p. Limoges.* 1. A village of Berry, in the diocefe and election of Bourges, *p. Bourges.* 3. A village of Auvergne, in the eleâton of Rbm. *p. Jjjiire.* 4. A village of Marche, in the election of Guerct. *p. Guère'.* 5. A village of Normandy, in the election of G i fors. *p. Offers.* 6. A village of Nivcrnois, in the diocefe and election of Nevers. *p. Ncvers.* 7. A village of BrtiTe, in the receipt of Bourg, *p. BcurgenBzþ.* S. *Eloy-a-V.rgultQ,* the name of a priory in Anjou.

S. *Elty-de-Gy,* a town of Berry, about 2 league from Bourges, *p. Bourses.* S. *Eloy-de-Fourgues,* a village of Normandy, in the election of PontAudemcr. *p. le ñoultroude.* S. *Eloy dü-TAint.* Sec *Mont-S.»* Eloy. S. *Eloy-Fontaine 1* an ancient abby in the diocefe oí Noy on, *f. Qbaurif.* S. *Emilian,* or *Emilien,* a town of Guienne, firuatcd near the Dordogne, about 6 leagues from Bourdcaux. *p. Liboume.* S. *Empuyfaye,* a fmall town of Nivcrnois, in the election of Clamccy. *p. Clcnucy.* S. *Bnogat,* a village of Bretagne, in the diocefe and receipt of S.M. ilo. *p. S. Malo.* S, *Ery,* a town of Normandy, in the election of Carentan. *p. Cu rentan.* S. *Epure,* a village of Meflin, in the diocefe and receipt of Metz. */». Metx.* 5". *Erblon,* a village of Bretagne, in the diocefe and receipt of Nantes. *p. Ancents.* S. *ErLry,* a fmall town of Guiennc, in the diocefe and election of Bourdcaux. *p. Bourdcaux.* S. *Ernte,* a fmall town of Poitou, in the diocefe and election of Laon. *f. Laon,* S, *Eroges,* a village of Gâtinois, in the election of Gien. *p. Glen.* S. *Efpain,* a town of Touraine, in the election of Chinon. *p. Stc. . Maure.* S. *Effrit.* I. A town of Gafconv, on the fide of the Nive,.oppofite to Bayonne, to which it is considered as a fauxbourg, and with which it is connected by a bridge called Pont-S.-Efprit. *p. Bayonne. 2.* See *Pont-S.-Efprit.* S. *Eßüuryf* a village of Augoumois, in the diocefe and election of Angoulême. */. la Rocbeftucuult.* S. *Eßcbin,* a village of Navarre, in the generality of Auch. *p. Bayonne.* S. *Eßepht,* I. A town of Angournois, in the election of Cognac. *p. Qhateannevf.* 2. A fmall town of Guiennc, in the election of Bourse iux. *p. Caßillc M?* 3. A pbte of Upper Languedoc, in the diocefe and receipt of Mirepoix. *p. M'trepoix.* S. *Eßeve.* 1. A village of Rouffillon, in the diocefe and viguery of Perpignan, *p. Perpignan.* 2. A village of Provence, in the diocefe and viguery of Digne, *p. Digne* 3. A village of Provence, in the diocefe of Fréjus, and viguery of Barjols. *p. Barjols,* 4. See *S. Etienne. ¿. Eflew* fï? *Janjon,* a village of Provence, in the diocefe and viguery of Aix. *p. Aix. S. Etienne, j.* A town of Normandy, in the election of Pont-Audemer. *p. Pcnt-Audemer.* 2. A fmall tow n of Normandy, in the election of Montivillicrs. *p. Harßeur.* 3. A fmall town of Agenois, in the diocefe and election of Agen. *p. Villencu-ved"Agen.* 4. A fmall town of Auvergne, ш the diocefe and election of S. Flour, *p. Ifjbire.* 5. A fmall town of Limoim, in the election of Tulles, *p. Tulles.* 6. A fmall town of Dauphiny, in the generality of Grenoble, *p. Die.* 7. A fmall town of Dauphiny, in the diocefe and election of Vienne, *p. la-Cste-S.-Andre.* 8. A village of Normandy, in the election of Andely. *p. Gaillon.* 9. A village of Agénois, in the diocefe and election of Agen. *p. Agen.* 10. A village of Picardy, in the-diocefe of Senlis, and ele¿tion of Crefpv. *p. Crejpy.* 11. A village of Burgundy, in the bailiwick of S. Laurens, *p. Challón.* 12. A village of Bourbonnois, in the election of Moulins./. *S. Gerand.* 13. A village of Angoumois, in the election of Cognac, *p. la Rocbefoucault.* 14. A village of Picardy, in the generality of Amiens. *p. Boulogne.* 15. A village of Navarre, in the diocefe of Bavonne. *p. Bayonne.* 16. A village of Dauphin v, in the diocefe and election of Grenoble, *p. Grenoble.* 17. A village of Perche, in the election of Mortagne. *p. Mortagne.* iS. A village of Rouergue, in the election of Milhaud. *p. Ste.Afrij ne.* i g. A village of Dombes, in the chatellany of Toiflèy. *p. BtllwUU.* 20. A place of Perche, in the election of Verneuil. *p. Verлеu!.* 2i. A place of Norman ay, in the election of Pont-l'Evêque. *p. Pont-VEvicjue.* 22. A place of Provence, in the diocefe and viguery of Aix.. *Aix.* ч' *S. Etitnneà-Arne,* a village of Champagne, in the election ot Bethel *p. Rljeims. S. Etknneau-TempUy* a village of Champagne, in the diocefe and election ot Chalons, *p. Cbálons. S. Etienne-Cantale,* a village of Auvergne, in the election of Aurillac. *p. AuriUac. S. Etienne-de-Blemar,* a town of Touraine, in the election of _ Araboife. *p. Amboije. S. Eutnnedc-Boulogne,* a village of Lower Languedoc, in the receipt of Viviers, *p, Auвcицu* & *Etienne-fur-Maßac,* a phee of Auvergne, in the election of Brioude. *p. Brioude. S. Etienne-fur-Rejfouxe,* a village of BrefTe, in the bailiwick of Bourg, *p. Bourg -en-BrefTe. S. Ettennefur-Sulppe,* a village of Champagne, in the diocefc and receipt of Rheims, *p. Retbel. S. EvarzeCf,* a village of Bretagne,, in the diocefe and receipt of Quiraper. *p. èfuimper. S. Eufraißte,* a village of Burgundy,, in the bailiwick of Semur-en-Auxoib. *p. Semur-en-Auxois. S'. Eugene., i.* A town of Saintonge, in the diocefe and election of Saintes, *p. Вяzbфeux.* 2. A village of Picardy, in the election of Château-Thierry, *p. Chat eau-Thierry,* 3. A village of Burgundy, in the bailiwick of Montcenis *p.Autwt.* 4. A village of Normandy, in the election of Argentan, *p. Argntan.* 5. A village of Normandy, in the diocefe and election of Avranches. *p. Aur¿ncbes.* 6. A village of Normandy, In tlie election of Pom%PEvequc. *Pont-l'EveoUe.* 7. A place of Burgundy, in the bailivick.of Charolles. *P. Dijon. S. Exfolie,* a village of Qjercy, in the. election of Fjgeiic. *p. Figeac. S. Eulalie-de-VArzat)* a village of R'ouergue, in the election of Milhaud., *p. Rbodez. S. Eulalie-eTOlt,* a village of Rouergue, in the eleition of Milhaud. *p. Milhaud. S. Eulieny* a village of Champagne, in the election of Vitry. *p. S. Dißer: S. Eunonty* a place of Anjou.

S. Eupkemie, a village of Dnuphiny, in the generality of Grenoble.. *Gap..*
S. Euphra'iße, a village of Champagne, in the diocefc and election of Rheims, *p. Rheims. S. Eure,* a wood of 40 arpents, in the jurifdiction of Troyes. *S. Evremont.* See *S. Ehremmd. S. Evroul,* a market t-wn of Normandy in the foreft of Quchc, about election of Agen. *p. Agen.* 3. A village of Lower Languedoc, in thé diocefe and receipt of Viviers, *p. lowers.* 4. A village of Lower Languedoc, in the d'ocefe and receipt of CarcaiTonne. *p. Carcaß.nne.* 5. A village of Dauphiny, in the generality of Grenoble./. *Grenoble.* 6. A village of Agénuis, in the diocefe and election of Agen./. *Agen.* 7. A village of Lower Languedoc, in the dircefe and receipt of *Uzés. p. Vtct. Ste. Eulalie & S. Hilaire,* a village of Dauphiny, in the diocefe and election of Valence, *p. Valence. Ste. Eulalie y* or *Gailleraud,* a village of Vivarais, in the receipt of Viviers. *p. Vwiert, Ste. EulaTtet-de-jLajfac,* 1. A commandery of Malta, in the election of Milhaud. *p. Mdhaud.* 2. A foreft oí 200 arpents, in the election of Milhaud. *Ste. EulatiedUzerebeSj i* village of Limofin, in the diocefe and election of Limoges, *p. Uxerckes. Ste. Euphemie.* 1. A village of Dauphiny, in the election of Montelimart. *p. le Buis.* 2. A village of Dombcs, in the chatellany of Villeneuve, *p. Bcurg-fn-Bieffè. Saint Fargeau. 1.* A town of Gâtinois, fituated on theriver Loing; about 5 leagues from Briare, 8 from Gien, 7 from Ch;.tillon fur Loing, and 12 from Auxcne. *Bureau de foße.* 2. A village of Gâtinois, in the election of Melun. *p. Melun. S. Farjcl,* a village of Nivernois, in the election of Montlucon. *p, Montlucon. S. Farcn-Iez-Mcauxj* an abby near the city of Mcavix. *p. Meaux. S. Faufl-Larún,* a village of Beam, in the receipt of Pau. *p. Pau. S. Faußc* a village of Berry, in the election uf IfiToudun. *p. lJjoudun, S. Félicien r* a fmall town qf Vivarais, in the diocefe and receipt of Viviers, *p. Tain. S. Fel'mdAmontt* a village of Rouflillon, in the diocefe and viguery of Perpignan./. *Perpignan.*

Ä *FeUu-d'Aval,* a fmall town of Rouflillon, in the diocefe and viguery of Perpignan, *p. Perpignan, S. Felix, i.* A town of Quercy, in the election of Figeac. *p. Figeac.* . A fmall town of Guicnne in the diocefe and election of Bourdeaux. *p. Caß'ilUn.* 3. A village of Roucrguc, in he election of Milhaud. *p. S. Afrique.* 4. A village of Lower Languedoc, in the diocefe and receipt f Lodeve. *p. Clermont-de-Lodfve.* 5. A village f Picardv, in the election of Clermont, *p. Clermont.* 6. A village of Quercv, in the diocefc and «Jccthrn of Cahors. *p. (labors.* 7. A village of Roueruc, *m* rhe election of Vilfcfranche. *p. RUdcx.* 8. A village of Jïoarbonnois, in the election of

Moulins, *p. S. Gerund,* 9. A priory in the diocefe of Valence, *p. Valence.* S. *Felix-Pourdeille,* a village of Péngord, in the diocefe and election of Périgueux.

S. *Felix-de-Lerasj* a place of Lower Languedoc, in the diocefe and receipt of Lodeve. *p. Lodeve.* S. *Fr/nr it Tweet,* a village of Rouergue, in the election of Villefranche, *p. Villefranche-de-Rouergue.* S. *Felixde-Pai/lieresf* a village of Lower Languedoc, in the receipt of Alais, *p. Alms.* S. *Felix-dt-V'illadeyS)* a fmall town of Pengord, in the diocefe and election of Périgueux-*p. Ptrigueux.*

S. *Ferjeux.* I. A fmall town of-Champagne, in the diocefe and election of Troyes. *p. Troyes.* 2. A village of Champagne, in the diocefe and election of Rheims, *p. Ret be/.* 3. A place of Franche-Comté, in the bailiwick of Vefoul. *f. Vejoul.* S. *Ferio/,* i. A village of Daupbioy, in the election of Montelimart. *p. Montelimart.* 2. A place of Languedoc, at the foot of Mont-Noire, where is a refervoir 1200 toifes long and 500 wide to fupply the canal of Languedoc. S. *FeriJ-des-Cetter,* a fmall town of Auvergne, in the election of Illoiie. *f. Iffoire.* S. *Ferjust* a village of Dauphîny, in the diocefc and election of Greno ble. *p. Grenoble.* S. *Ferme,* a village of Bafadois, in the election of Condom, *p. la Reelle,* S. *Ferre'dy* a v liage of Auvergne, in the elect'--n oi Brioudc. *p. Briowde.*

S. *Ferric/.* I. A village of Agénois, in the diocefe and election of Agen. *p. Agen.* 2. A village of Upper Languedoc, in the diocefe and receipt of Alct. *p. Limoux.* 3, A vÜ'age of Gafcony, in the diocefe and election of Commingcs. *p. Mon trejeav.* 4. A village of Duphiny, in the election of Montelimart. *p. Montelimart.* S. *Fe'rio!-yuß'm,* a town of Forez, with a bailiwick., in the election uf S. Etienne, *p. S. Etienne.* S. *Fiacre,* i. A village of Bretagne, in the diocefe and receipt of Nantes, *p. CbjJ'on.* 2. A priory in the diocefe of Meaux. *p. Meaux.* S. *Fiel,* a village of Bcauce, in the election of Guerct. *p. Gueret.* S. *Firmain,* a village of Beauce, in the election of Vendôme, *p. Yce déme.* S. *Firttàn.* I. A fmall town of Picardy, in the diocofe and electiofl of Senlis. *p. Sen/is.* 2. A village of of Gütinois, in the election of Giert. *p. Etampes.* 3. A village of Lower Languedoc, in the diocefe and receipt of Uzés. *p. Usee's.* 4. A village of Dauphiny, in the diocefe and election of Grenoble, *p. Grenob/e.* 5. A place of Bourg, in the bailiwick of Mont enis. *p. Autun.* S. *Frmin-de-Be:bocourt,* a v'llage of Picardy, in the election of Doulens. *p. Abbeville.* S. *Firm'.n-des-BoiSy* a village of Gätinois, in the election of Montargis. *p. Montargts.* S. *Flary,* a village of Chompngne, in the diocefe and election of Troyci. *p. les Yroies-Ma'ifons.* S. *Fhurant,* a village of Berry, in the diocefe and election of Bourses. *p. Bourges.*

'S. *Floccel,* a village of Picar Jy, in the election of Valogncs. *p. Carenfan.* S. *Florens.* t. A fmall town of Poitou, in the election of Fontcnay. *p. Tbire.* z. A village of Lower Languedoc, in the diocefe and receipt of Uzés. *p. U%es.* S. *Florent. Л.* A village of Gat'inois, in the election of Gicn. *p. Cien. %.* A village of Pojtou, in the election of Niort, *p. Niort.* S. *Florent-de-Paizet-te-J-.ly,* a village of Berry, in the election of Blanc, *p. Bourges.* S. *Florent-ic-Vieil,* a town of Anjou, *c:* the Loire, in the diocefe and elc&iun of Angers; about 3 leagues from Ingrande, 10 from Nantes, and 10 from Angers. *Bureau di pcfie.* S. *Florert-les-Saumiir,* a village of Anjou, in the election of Saumur. *p. Saumur.* S. *Florentin.* ï. A city of Champagne, íituated on the Arman fon, about 3 leagues frum Brignon, 13 from T royes, 7 from Auxerre, 10 from Sens, 7 from Joigny, 6 from Tonnerre, 28 from Fontainbieau, and 42 from Paris. *Bureau depoße.* 2. A village of Berry, in the election of IiToudim. *p. Vatan.* S. *Floret.* ï. A village of Auvergne, in the diocefe and election of Clermont, *p. Clermont.* 2. A mineral fpring in Auvergne. S, *F/ori,* a village of Artois, in the bailiwick of Lilkrs. *p. Betbulte.* S: *F/ciier,* a town of Tonraine, in 'the election of Loches, *p. Loches,* S, *Flour,* a-city of Auvergne, íituated on a mountain, in the generality of Riom; the fee of a bifnop; 22 leagues from Clermont-Ferrand, 9 from Brioudc, 45 from Roanne, 25 from Riom, 30 trorrt Gannat, 44 from Moulins, and 115 from Paris. *Bureau de p-fie.* S *Fiour-prh-Courpiere,* a village of Auvergne, in the diocefe and election of Clermont, *p. Briiude.* S. *Fofyuin,* a vilbge ol Aitois, in the diocefe and bailiwick of S. Omer *p. S. Omer.* S. *Forgeot,* a village of Burgundy, in the diocefe and bailiwick of Autun. *p. Autun.* S. *Forget,* a vilbge of the Ifle of France, in the diocefe and election of Paris, *p. Paris.* S. *Forgeu'd-(uз-Сblке, я* place of Burgundy, in the bailiwick of Macon, *p. Mácon.* S. *Forjeux,* a fmall town of Lyonnois, in the diocefe and receipt of Lyons, *p. Tarare.* S. *Fort.* i. A town of Saintonge, in the dioceic and election of Saintes. *p. Sa'ntes.* 2. A town of Angoumois, in the ebcYon of Cognac, *p. BarktTÛitix.* 3. A town of Anion, in the clrftion of ChAtcau-Gonticr. *P. Cb¿:eau-Gortier.* S. *Fort Êf Malaigne,* a village of Saintonge, in the election of Marennés. *p. Marennés.* 5. *Fcrtanade,* a town of Limonn, in the diocefe and election of Tulles. *p. Tul/cs.* S. *Fortunat,* a fmall town of Vivarais, in the receipt of Viviers. *p. U Voutte.* 5. *Fraguere,* a village of Normandy, in the election of Vire./». *Villeduu,* S. *FraigtiCy* a town of Saintongc, 'in the election of S. Jean-d'Angdy. *P. S. Jean-d Angely.* S. *Fraimbault,* a town partly in Normandy, and partly in Maine, *p. Mayenne.* S. *Fraimbauhde-Pricres,* a town of Maine, in the election of Mayenne. *p. Mayenne,* S. *Frajou,* a village of Armagnac, in the election of Rivière-Verdun. *p. Lombv%*

& *Francby-en-Arcbere,* a village of Nivernois, inth diocefe and election of Ncvcrs. *p. Nevers.* S, *Francby-les-Afnay,* a place of Nivernois, in the diocefe and election of Ncvcrs. *p. Nevers.* S. *Frarçcisy* a place of Meflin, in the diocefe and receipt of Metz. *Tbior.vL'le,*

S *Francois-dc-Salis,* a village of Tauphiny, in the diocefe and election of Grenoble, *p. Grenoble.* S. *Fregant* a village of Bretagne, in the diocefe and receipt of S. Polde-I.éon, *p. Morlaix.* S. *Frejoulj* a village of Limofin, in the eleftinn of Tulles, *p. Tu/in.* S. *Frtmond,* a fmall town of Nor. mandy, in the election of Montivilliers./. *Harfleur.* S. *Fremontj* a town of Normandy, in the election of S. Lo. *p. S. Lo. S.Fremy,* a village of Burgundy, in the dioccfe and receipt of Autun.

Autun. S. Freon. i. A town of Marche, in the election of Gucret. *p. Feuilletai.* 2. A village of Auvergne, in the election of Com braille, *p. Chambón.* S. *Frezal-dAlèugei,* a village of Lower Languedoc, in the diocefe and receipt of Monde, *p. Alais.* S. *Frcxsal-dt-Ventclon,* a village of Lower Longuedoc, in the diocefe and receipt of Mende. *p. Alais.* S. *Frkbcuxy* a place of Upper Lan. guedoc, in the diocefe and receipt of Carcaiïonnc. *p. Carcaffonne.* S. *Frogent,* a fmail town of Perche, in the election of Mortagne. *p. Mortagne.* S. *From-d'Al¿m¡s,* a fmall town of Périgord, in the diocefe and election of Périgueux. *p. Mußdan.* S. *Frcm-dc-Piûd'jux,* a village of Périgord, in the diocefe and élection of Périgueux. *p. Mußdan.* S. *Frond,* a fmall town of Angoumois, in the diocefe and election of Angoulême. *p. Villcfagnan.* S. *Front.* I. A town of Normandy, in the election öf Domfront. *p. Domfront, 2.* A village of Agé,nois, in the dioccfe aud election of Agen. *p. Iri!leneu-ve-d'Agen.* 3. A village of Agcnois, in the dioccfe and election of Agen. *p. la Re'olle.* S. *Frant-Sntrmquut c¿f Pontours,* a fmall town of Perigord, in the diosefc and election of Sarlat. *p:* Swint. ef Lower Languedoc, in the diocefe and (receipt of Mirepoix. *p. Aîirtpcix.* 10. A place of Burgundy, tn the bailiwick, of Semur-en-Äuxois. *p. Semur-e ff-Anxoh.* Ste.-*Fty-de-Belvez-,* a village of Péiïgord, in the diocefe and election of Sarlat. *p. Mirfat. Src.-Foy-de-¥erufaIem,* a place of Agenois, in the dioccfe and electron Öf Agen. *p. Agen.* Ste.*Foyde-Congua,* a final 1 town of Périgord, in the diocefe and election of Périgueux. *p. la Linde.* Ste.-*Foy-des-Vxgnes,* a village of Périgord, in'the diocefe and election of Périgueux. *p. Bergerac.* Ste.-*Friaue.* See л *Afrique. Saint Gafo-'iel,* I. A village of Provence, in the vigucfy of Tarafcon. *p% Tarafcon.* 2. A village of Normandy, in the election of Caën. *p. Caen.* S. *Gal,* a village of Auvergne, in the diocefe and election of Clermont. *p. Clermont.* S". *Gall,* an abby in the diocefe of CoiUancc«. *p. Coûtantes.* S. *Ga/mier,* a town of Forez., in the election of Montbrifon; about 7 leagues from Lyons, *p. S. Etienne.* S. *Gans,* a village of FrancheComté, in the bailiwick of Gray. *p. Befanden,* S. *GaJJten,* a village of Normandy, in the election of Pont-l'Evcque. *p. Honßeur.* S. *Gaubcurge,* a village of Normandy, "m the election of A lengón, *p. Cizay.* S. *Gaubeurge,* a place of Perche, in the ejection of Mortagne. *p. Mortagne.* (S. *Gaudenz,* a ' town of Gafcony, thc-capital of Nebouzan, fituated on the Garonne; about 3 leagues from Montrejeau, 3 from S. Bertrand, 10 from Rieux, 9from Lombes, and 16 from Auch. *Bureau de poße.* S. *Gaudent,* a village of Poitou, in the diocefe and election of Poitiers, *J. Cbaunay.* 'Gauderic, a village of Upper Languedoc,-in the diocefe and receipt of Mircpoix. *p. Mirejoix.*

& *Gau/t & les Cbtbrcs,* a town of Anjou, in the election of ChâteauGontier. *p. Cbateau-Gontier.* S. *Gautier,* a village of Berry, in the election of Châtre, *p. Armenian.*

S. *Gauzens,* a mall town ot Lower Languedoc, in the diocefe and receipt of Caftrcs *p. Caflres.* S. *Geal,* a village of Lower Languedoc, in the diocefe and receipt of Mende. *p. Mende.* S. *Geing,* a village of Gafcony, in the election of Landes, *p. Dax.* S. *Gelais,* a fmall town of Poitou, in the election of S. Maixant. л. *N.ort.* S. *GeKn-Je-Rat,* a village of Dauphiny, in the diocefe and election of Grenoble. /. *Moirans.* S. *Gely-Dufeje,* a village of Lower Languedoc, in the diocefe and receipt of Montpellier, *p. Montpellier.* S. *Gerne.,* a village of Condomois, in the diocefe and election of Condom, *p. Bajas.* S. *Gemia,* a fmall town of Limofin, in the diocefe and election of Limoges, *p. Limoges,* S.*Genard,* a village oí Poitou, in the election of S. Maixant. *p, la Motte-Stt.-Herajt.* S. *Gemtc,* a (mall town of Limofin, in the diocefe aud election of Limoges, *p. Limoges.* S. *Gcneix-Cbjmpencilks,* a village of Auvergne, in the diocefe and election of Clermont, *p. Clermont.* S. *Gmeix-les-Mouges,* a village of Auvergne, in the election of Riom. *p. Riom.* S. *Geneh-près-Germain,* a village of Auvergne, in the election of lifo! re. *p. Jßoire.* S. *Geneix-prcs-S.-Paur¡n,* a village of Auvergne, in the election of Brioude. *p. Brioude.* S. *Généreux,* a village of Poitou, m the election of Richelieu, *p. Loadas.* S. *Geneß.* I. A town of Poitou, in tin elcflion of ChateHeraot. *p. p. Ycфc.* 3. A fmall town of Dauphiny, in the diocefe and elec-I tion of Grenoble, *p. Grenoble,* 4.. A fmall village of Condomois, in the diocefe and election of Cufidom.. *p. Condom.* 5. A village of Dauphiny, in the election of Monttlimart. *p. Mumman.* 6. A village of Daup!;iny, in the election of Gap. *p. Gap.* 7. A place of Angoumois, in the diocefe and election of Angouléme. *p. Cognac.*

S. *Gm:is-au-MerIet* a village of Limoiin, in the diocefe and election of Tuiles, *p. 4'ulhi.* S. *Getih-de Caßulon,* a fmall town of Guienne, in the diocefe and election of Bourdeaux. *p. Cafiillcn.* S. *Gems-de-Fontàne,* a village of Rouffillon, in the viguery of Rouffi!lon. *p. Perpignan.* S. *Genis-de-GronfaC)* a village of Guienne, in the diocefe and election of Bourdeaux. *p. Libourne.* S. *Gems-dc-P taint-Selve,* an abby in the diocefe of Bourdeaux. *p. Bourdeaux.* S. *Gems-en-Bcnauge,* a village of Guienne, in the diocefe and election of Bourdeaux. *p. Bourdeaux.* S. *G ems-en-BI ay ey* a fmall town of Guienne, in the diocrfc aud election of Bourdeaux. *p. Blaye.* S. *Gems-V' Argcmitre,* a village of Lyonnois, in the diocefe and election of Lyons, *p. Lyon.* S. *Genis-Lava/,* a village of Lvonnois, in the diocefe and eleition of Lyons, *p. Lyon.* S. *G enis-lez-0 Hieres,* a village of Lyonnois, in the diocefe and election of Lyons, *p. Lyon.* S. *Genh-Notre-Dame,* a village of Dauphiny, in the diocefe and ektion of Gap. *p. Gap.* S. *Gemtour-de-Blanc.* See *Blanc.* S. *Gewiß,* a place of Brie, in the election of Provins, *p. Pro-vins.* S. *Gerou,* a fmall town of Berryf in the election of Chàteauroux. *p. CbatWon-jw-Indre.* S. *Gcmvil-fur-InJrey* a barony in the diocefe of Bourges.

5. *Gío'.re.* I. A town of Dauphiny, in the diocefc and clctftion of Vienne, *p. V'unne.* 2, A village of Champagne, in

the bailiwick, of Chaumont. *p. Chaumonî.*
S. *George,* i.'A town of Anjou, in the diocefe and t-lection of Anders. *f. Angers.* 2. A town of Normandy, in the election of Mortmain, *p. vrancLci.* 3. A town of Saintonge, in the election of Marennes. *p. Saintes.* 4. A town of Saintongc, in the election of S. Jcand'Angcly. *p. S. yean-d'Angcly.* 5. A town of Pciu-u, in the diocefe and election of Poitiers, *p Poitiers.* 6. A town of Touraine, in.the election of Amboife. *p. Amboije.* 7. A town of Maine, in the election of Laval. *f. Lava* 8. A fmalltown of Auvergne, in the diocefc and election of S. Flour. *p.S. Flour.* 9. A fmalltown of Marche, in the election of Gucret. *p. FeuiiUtitt.* 10. A fmall town of Dauphiny, in the diocefe and election of Vienne, *p. Bcurgo'w.* 11. A fmall town of Dauphiny, in the diocefe and election of Vienne, *p. Vienne.* 12. A village of Normandy, in the election of Caudebcc. *pm Caudebec.* 13. A village of Lower Languedoc, in the diocefe and receipt of Montpellier, *p. Montpellier.* 14. A village of Berry, in the election of Bianc *f. Bourges.* 15. A village in the diocefe and receipt of Viviers, *p. y. v'urs.* 16. A village of Burgundy, in the bailiwick of Challón, *p. Sewe.* 17, 18. Two villages in the diocefe and receipt of Auxerre. *p. Auxerre.* 19. A village of Flanders, in the diocefe of S. Orner, *p. Gravelines.* 20. A village in the diocefe and election of Condom, *p. Condom.* 21. A village of Berry, in the diocefe and election of Bourges, *p. h Blanc.* 22. A village of Dombcs, in the chatcllany of Chafelar. *p. Bourg-en-Brcjjc.* 23. A village of Pet'igord, in the diocefe and election of Perigueux. *p. Muffidan.* 24. A'vilbgc of Franche-Comté, in the bailiwick of Baume, *p. Lwy,* of Avalon, *p. Sie. Reine. S. Geo/gele$-Ncnains.* Sec *Villertm les-Moines. S. George-Nigremont,* a town of Marelu-, in the election of Gucret. *p. Í euilUtin. S. G corge-Out rl Allier f* a village of Auvergne, in the dioeefeand élection of Clermont, *p. Feu'ilictin. S. George-près-Seure,* a village of Burgundy, iu the bailiwick, of ChaiIon, *p. Seure. S. George-fus-Mouhny* a village of Berry, in the diocefe and election ef Bourges, *p. Bourges.. S. Gtorgc-jur-AmoIIy* a village of Berry, in the election of Uloudun. *p. JJJbudun. S. Gm'ge-fur-Cher,* a village of Touraine, in the diocefc and election of Tours, *p. Tours. S. Georgefur-Erv/9* a town of Maine, in the diocefe and election of Mans. *p. Mayenne. S. George-fur-Eure.* I. A village of Beaurc, in the diocc/c and election of Chatres, *p. Dreux %.* A village of Normandy, in the diocefe and election of Evreux. *p. Evreux. S. George-fur-Fontaine,* a village of Normandy, in the diocefe and election of Rouen, *p. le Bolehard. S. George-fur-la-Pree,* a village of Berry, in the election of Iflbudun.*p. IJJiudun. S. Gcorge-fur-Loire,* an sbby in the diocefe of Angers, *p. Angers. S Geojme,* a village of Champagne, in the diocefe and election of Langrcs. *p. Langres, S. Gérais,* a fmall town of Agénois,-in the diocefe and election of Agen. *p. Agen. S. G er andde-Vaux y* a town of Burgundy, in the election of Moulins. *p.Vartnnes. S. jGerand-le-Puyy* a town of Boar bonnois, in the diocefe of Clermont, and election of Moulins, in the road from Lyons to Moulins; 8 leagues from la Pacaudiere, 10 from Moulins, 34 from Lyons, and 8i¿ from Paris. *Bureau defeßt. S. Gcraad-de-Corps,* a village of Prrigord, in the diocefe and election ©f Périgueux. *p. Périgueux. 5. Gcraviy* a provoftfhip in the diocefe of Limoges, *p. Limoges»* 6. *Cermaln.* I. A town oí" Champagne, in the diocefe and election of Châlons. *p. Chdlcns. z.* A town of Inmoiin, in the dioccfe and election of Limoges, *p. Limoges.* 3. A town of Touraine, m the lection of Loches. *p. Lecbcs.* 4. A town of Anjou, in the election of Baugé. /. *Bauge.* 5. A town of Perche, in the election of Mortagne. *p. Mortagne.* 6. A fmaJl town of Marche, in the election of Gueret. *p. Gutret.* 7. A Cmall town of Upper Languedoc, in the dioccfe and receipt of Lavaur. ¿. *Caßres.* 3. A fmall town of Gâtinois, in the election » of Montargis. *p. Montai gh.* 9. A fmall town of Angoumois, in the dioccfe nd election of Angoulème. *p. Confolant.* 10. A fmall town of Périgord, in the dioccfe and election of Périgueux. *p. Vültntwve-d' Agen.* Л. A fmall town uf Berry, in the election ot Blanc, *p. Cbatilhn-jurlndre.* 12. A village of Dauphiny, in the diocefe and election of Vienne. *f. Vienne.* 13. A village of Gâtinois, in the election of Etampes. *p. "Etampes.* 14. A village of Brie, in the election of Coulomiers. *p. Cculomiers.* 15. A village of Keauce, in the election of Châteaudun. *p. Bonneval.* 16. A village of Normandy, in the election of Caen. *p. Слен.* 17. A village of Nivernois, in the election of Clamccy. *p. Clamety.* 18. A village of Champagne, in the generality of Chalons, *p. Void.* 19. A village of Poitou, in the diocefe and election of Poitiers, *p, Partenay.* 20. A village of Agénois, in the diocefe and election of Agen. *p. Agen.* 21. A village of Agénois, in the jurifdictionof Villercal. *p. Agen,* 22. A village of Armagnac, in the dioccfe and election of Auch. *p. Mom-Je-Marfan.* 23. A village of Maine, in the-diy

Vob. UK

ceΓe and election of Man.. *le Mans,* 24-A village of Qucrcy, in the diocefe and election of Cahors. *pm Peyrac.* 25. A village of Lower Languedoc, in the dioccfe and receipt of Viviers, *p. V'dleneuvt-de-Berg* 26. A village of Franche-Comté, in the bailiwick of Salins, *p. Lure.* 27. A village of Normandy, in the election of Pont-Audcmer. *p. PontAudemer.* 28. A village of NivernoiS in the diocefe and election or Nevcrs. *p. Decide.* 29. A village of Bazadois, in the election of Condom. *p. Bazas.* 30. A village of Agenoi% in the jurifdiction oí Montpcfat. *p. Villcncwve-d'Agen.* 31. A village of Dombes, in the chatcllany of Chatelar. *p. Bourg-en-BreJJ'e.* 32. A place of Picardy, in the election of Crépy. *p. Crépy.* 33. A place of Alfacc, in the election of Bcffort. *p+ Beffort.* 34. A place of Bretagne» in the dicccfc and receipt of Bricux. *p. Lamballe.* 35. A place ofLimofin, in the diocefe and election of Limoges, *p. Limoges. S. Germj'm-Us-Villagetf* a village of Normandy, in the election of Pont-Audemcr. *p. Pont-Audemcr. S. Gdmain-au-Mcnt-d'Ory* a Village of Lyonnois, in the dioccfe and election of Lyons, *p. Lyon. S. Geimain-Cberut,* a town of Au» vergne, in the elcition of Iuoire.

p. Ißire. 5'. *Gcrmatn-d?Amberieuxf* a fmall town of Burgundy, in the bailiwick of Bugey. *p. AmberUux*. *S. Germain-du-Auxure*, a town of Maine, in the election of Mayenne. *p. Laval*. *S. Germain-de-Berbieres*, a fmáll town of Périgñrd, in the dioocfc and election of Sari at. *p. Sarlat*. *S. (ermain-de-Calberte*, a final I town of Lower Languedoc, in the diocefe and receipt of Mende. *p. Nîmes*. *S, Germaln-dc-CuUeSy* a village of Burgundy, in the bailiwick of MÜ-' con. *p. Macen*., *S. G'ermoin-dc Dion*, a viUjgt ot Burgundy, in the bailiwick of Macon, *p. ¡a Pacaudiere*. *S. Germain-de-Frefray*, a village of Normandy, in the election of Evreux. *ft, Evreux*. *S. Germain-de-Gravois*. See *Gravais*. *S. Germain-de-Jouz*, a village of Burgundy, in the bailiwick of Bugcy. *p. Ñantua*. *S. G ermain-d Entrevaux*, a village of Burgundy, in the election of Moulins, *p. S. Pourçain*. *S. Germain-d'Eclor*, a village of Normandy, in the diocefc and election of Bayeux. *p. Bayeux*. *S. Germain-de-VEp'wajfe*, a fmall town of Burgundy, in the bailiwick of Semur-cn-Briennois. *p. Roanne*. *S. Germa.n-de-la-Campagne*. I. A village of Normandy, in the election of Carentan. *p. Carentan*. i. A fmall town of Normandy,in the diocefc and election of Lifieux. *p. Orbee*, *S. Germain-de-la-Celle*, a pariib of Berry, in the chatcllany of Lignitres. *f. Lignieres*. *S. Germatn-de-la-Garde*, a fmall town of Burgundy, in the election of Gannat. *p. Gannat*. *S. Germain-delaGrange*, a village of Beauce, in the election of Mmtfbrt. *p Montfort*. *S. Germam-de-lahleue* a village of Normandy, in the diocefe and election of Bayeux. *p. Bayeux*. *S. Gcrmain-de-haxis*, a place of Gâtinois, in the election of Melun. *p.Melun*. *S. Gertnain-de-Lbomc/. SctLbcmel. S. Germain-de-TIße*, a village of Bretagne, in the diocefe and receipt ef Nantes. *p. Nantes*. *S. Gtrmaxn-de-Matignon*, a village ©f Bretagne, in the diocele and receipt of Brieux. *p.hamballe*. *S. Gcrmain-de-Mdeon*, a village of Burgundy, in the receipt of Saulieu. *p. Sau/ieu. S. Germa'm-de-Prinçay*, a town of Poitou, in the election of Foatenay. *p. Gbantonay*.

S. Gctmam-dc-Rtve. I. A village of Burgundv, in the bailiwick of Charolies. *p. la Pacaudiere*. z. A village of Burgundy, in the bail: wick of Semur-en-Bricnnois. *p. Dijon*. *S. Germain-de-Salles*, a village of Burgundy, in the election of Gannat. *p. Gannat*. *S. G'erma'm-des-Angles*, a figniory of Normandy, in the diocefe and election of Evreux. *p. Evreux*.

S. Germain-de-Talvande, a fmall town of Normandy, in the election of Vire. *p. Vire*. *S. Germain-de-Tournebus*, a fmall town of Normandy, in the election of Valognes. *p. Valognes*. *S. Germain-de-Vareviile*, a place of Normandy, by thefea, in the diocefe of Coutances. *p. Carentan*. *S. Germa'm-des-Bois*, a village of Berry, in the diocefe and election of Bourges, *p. Bourges*. *S Germain-des-BorgneSf* a town of Limofin, in the eleótion of Brives. *p. Brives*. *S. Germain-des-Bms & Jugy-* 3. village of Burgundy, in the bailiwick of Macon, *p.* To *rr.us*. *S. Germuh-des-Cbamps*, a village of Burgundy, in the bailiwick of Avalon, *p. Avalon*. *S. Germain-des-Fßburs*, a village of Normandy, in the diocefe and election of Rouen, *p. Rouen*. *S. Germain-des-G rois*, a village of Perche, in the élection of Mortagne. *p. Rtmalwd*. *S. G ermain-des-Noyers*, a village of the Iflc of France, in the diocefe and election of Paris, *p. Lagny*. *S. Germain-des-ParrojJh*, a fmall town of Burgundy, in the bailiwick of Bugey. *p. Belley*. *S. Germaindes-Pre%*. I. A own of Anjou, in the diocefe and election of Angers, *p. Ingrade*. 2. A fmall town of Périgord, in the diocefe and election of Périgucux. *p. Pe'i igueux*. 3. A village of Tourainc, in the eleétiun of Chinon. *p. Chinen*. 4 A village of Bretagne, in the ¿iocei-cand receipt of S. Malo. *p. $. Malo*. 5. A place of Normandy, near Evreux. *p. Evreux*. 6. A place of Bretagne, in the diocefe of S. Malo. *p.* 5. *Malo*. *S. Germain-des-Veaux*, a village of Normandy, in the election of Valognes. *p. Vahgnes*. *S. Germaln-du-Bois*. 1. A village of Burgundy, in the bailiwick of S, Laurent, *p. Challón*. z. A village of Burgundy, in the diocefe and bailiwick of Challón. *p.Cballon*. *S. Germain-du-Corbis*, a village of Normandy, in the election of Alençon. *p. Alencon*. *S. Germàïn-du-Pajquier*, a village of Normandy, in the election of Pont-dc-TArche. *p. Pont-de-V Arche*. *S. Germain-du-Pwel*, a village of Bretagne, in the diocefe and receipt of Nantes, *p. Vitré*. *S. Germaïn-du-Plain*, a village of Burgundy, in the diocefe and bailiwick of Challón, *p. Challón*. *S. Germaii-du-Puiby* a fmall town of Guicnne, in the diocefe and election of Bourdeaux. *p. Libourne*. *S. Germa'm-du-Puy*, a village of Berry, in the diocefe and election of Bourges. *Bourges*. *S, Germaindu-Sendrey* a town of Sa'ntonge, in the diocefe and election of Saintes, *p. Saintes*. *S. Germa'in-cn-CopJais*, a village of Bretagne, in the diocefe and receipt of Nantes, *p. Nantes*. *S. Germain-en-C)Spin*, a village cf Burgundy, in the election of Gannat. *p. Gar.nat*. *S. G e main-en-Lay et* a town of the lile of Fran e, fituated by the Seine: it has a palace, in which Louis XIV. was born, and James II. of England died: the foreft contains 5914 arpents: 4 leagues from Verfailles, 4 from Pontoife, 5 from Melun, 9 from Mantes, 3 from Nanterrc, and » from Paris. *Bureau de poße»* *S. Germain-en-Malles*, a village of Bourbonnois, in the election of Gannar. *p. Gannat*. *S. Germain-en'Montj* a village of f Maine, în the élection of Mayenne, *p. Laval*. *S. Germain-le-LiSvre*, a village of Lim oft n, in the election of Tulles. *p. Tuiles*. *S. Germam-le-Rocheux* a village of Burgundy, in the bailiwick of Chatillon. *p. Cbatillon*, *S. Gcrmain-le-Vaffiury* a village of Normandy, in the election of Falaife. *p. Falaife*. *S. Germain-ie-Vkomtet* a village of Normandy, in the election of Carerstan, *p. Coûtâmes*. *S. Germain-le-Vxdy* a village of Normandy, in the election of Alenon. *p. Seem*. *S. Germa'm-les-Cbátres*, a village in the diocefe and election of Paris. *f. Arpajon*. *S. Germain-hs-PьuШy*, a village of Brie, in the diocefe an¿l election of Meaux. *p. Meaux*. *S. Germanlci-Rhodc%)* a convent near Rhode?, *p. Rhodess*. *S. Germait!-Ls-Saiadiy*, a village of Burgundy, in the bailiwick of Semuren-Aujois. *p. Mor.tbard*. *S. Germain-les-Verberey* a place of Picardy, in the election of Compiégny. *p. Vcrher'ie.* S. *Gertr.a'mprh-Durtaly* a village of Anjou, in the election of Flèche. *p. Durtal.* S. *Germain-près-Hermenty* a village of Auvergne, in the election of *Riem, p. Riom.* S. *Germain-près-Mentfaucon, a* town of Anjou, in the diocefe and election of Angers, *p. Angers.* S. *Germainfeus.-Meymont,* a town of Auvergne, in the diocefe and election of Clermont, *p. Clermont.* S. *Germain-fm-UjJin,* a village of Auvergne, in the election of Iflbire. *p. ifj'cire., ¿i. Germainc-jur-Airej* a village of Normandy, in the election of Conches. *p. Evreux. £ & Get main-fur-Ay,* a town of Normandy, in the election ot Carentan. *p. Coutancet.* S,*Gtitxam-fur-£reJJe.* I. A village of Lyonnois, in the diocefe and election of Lyons, *p Lyon.* 2. A village of Normandy, in the election of Ncufchâtel. *p. Aumale.* S. *Germain-fur-Ca'dly,* a village of Normandy, in the diocefe and election of Rouen, *p. le Bolehard.* S. *Germain-fur-Eauney* a village of Normandy, in the election of Neufchâtel. *p. Neufchâtel.* S. *Germuin-jur-Ecoly* a village of Gâtinois, in the election of Melun, *p. Melun,* S. *Germainmonty* a village of Champagne, in the diocefe and election of Rheims, *p. Retbel.* S. *Germer-de'Flayy* a town of Picardy, about 5 leagues from Beauvais. *p. Ecouy. 'S.Germiéy* a village of Armagnac, in the diocefe and election of Auch. *p. Gimont.* S.*Gerjn'er.* 1. A village of Poitou, in the diocefe and election of Poitiers. *p. Pcitiers.* 2. A village of Upper Languedoc, in the diocefe and receipt of Lavaur. *p. Caflres.* 3. A village of Upper Languedoc, in the diocefe and receipt of Touloufe. *p. Toulcujc.* S. *Geron,* a village of Auvergne, in the election of Brioudc. *p. Brhude.* S. *Getöns,* a village of Auvergne, in the election of Aurillac.*/'./r/./jí-,* S. *Gervais,* i. A town of Upper Languedoc, in the diocefe and receipt of Caftres. *p. βeziers. %.* A town of Burgundy, in the election of Gannat. *p. Montluçcn.* 3. A fmall town of Guienne, in the diocefe and election of Bourdcaux. *p. Bourdeaux.* 4. A fmall town of Poitou, in the election of Sables *¿""Obrine. p. les Sabhs.* 5. A village of Angoumois, in the diocefe and election ot Angouléme. *p. I'i:Ljjgn?n* 6. A village of Bazadois, in the election of Condom, *p. la Rc'Jle.* 7. A village of Poitou, in the élection nf Châtcllcrrmlt. *p. Cbdtellcrault. .* A village of Poitou, in the election of Coniolans. *p. Confolans.* 9. A village of Vcxin, in the election of Chaumont. *p. Magny.* 10. A vil-. läge of Bléfois, in the diocefe and election of Bbis. *p. Bloh.* n. A Village of Normandy, in the election ©f Magny. *p.Cbaumont.* ii. A village of Agénois, in the diocefe and election of Agen. *p. le Temple,.* 13. A village of Dauphiny, in the election of Montelimart. *p. Montelimart.* 14. A village of Dauphiny, in the diocefe and election of Grenoble./ '. *Grembles* 15. A place of Burgundy, in the diocefe and bailiwick of Challón, *p. Bcaune.* 16. A place of Burgundy, in the diocefe and bailiwick of Challón, *p. Cbal/on.* 17. A partih of Burgundy, in the bailiwick pf Montccnis, *Autun.* S. *Gervais-a-Cur el,* a village of Dauphiny, in the election of Montelimart. *p. Moirans.* S. *Gervais á-Mofífrac,* a village of Dauphinyj in the election of Montelimart. *p. Montelimart.* S. *Gervais-d'Ajnieres,* a village of Kormandy, in the diocefe and election of Lifieux. *p. LÀfuux.* S. *Gervais-en-Belin* a town of Maine, in the diocefe and election of Alans. */. le Mans.* S. *Gênais-Terre-Foraine,* a fmall town of Upper Languedoc, in the diocefe and receipt of Caftres. *p. Caβrei.* S. *Gervajy.* т. A village of Auvergne, in the election of IiToire. *p. Jjjch e.* 2. A village of Lower Languedoc, in the receipt of Nîmes, *p. Jaimes.* 3. A village of Bazadcis, in the election of Condom, *p. Condom.* S. *Gery,* a village of Quercy, in the diocefe and election oi Cahors. *p. figeac.* S. *Geyrat,* a village of Perigord, in the diocefe and election of Périgucux. *p. Pe'rig'-eux,* S, *Gbin,* a village of Flanders, in in the moderation of Lille, *p. la Bajje.* S. *Gilbert.* See *Neußms.* S. *Gildas,* an ancient abby in the diocefc of Bourges, *p. Chateauroux. Ü, GUjbudAurayt* a village of "Bretagne, in the diocefe and receipt of Nantes, *p. Reden.* S. *Gildas-de-RuySy* a village of Bretagne, in the diocefe and receipt of Nantes, *p. Vannes.* S. *Gildas-des-Bcisj* a town of Bretagne, in the diocefe and receipt of Nantes, *p. Pontcbâteau.* S. *Gilles,* i. A town of Lower Languedoc, fituatcd near the Rhône, in the diocefe of Aries, and receipt of luîmes; about 5 leagues from, Nîmes, 5 from Bcaueaire, and % from Montpellier. *Bureau de p'βt. Z.* A fmall town of Normandy» in the election of S. Lo. *p.* S. *Lo.* 3. A village of Normandy, in the eke tion of MontiviUicrs. -*¿.* S. *Romain.* 4. A village of Champagne, in the diocefe and election of Rheims, *p. Rheims* 5. A village of Normandy, in the election of Domfront, *p. Dom" front.* 6. A village of Normandy, in the election of Caudebec. *p. Caudebec.* 7. A village of Burgundy, in the bailiwick of Montccnis. f, *Cballun.* 8. A village of Burgundy, in the bailiwick of Montccnis. *p. Cbagny.* 9. A village of Bretagne, in the diocefe and receipt of Nantes. *p.* S. *Pcre-en-Retx,* 10. A village of Bretagne,, in the diocefe and re» ccipt of Vannes, *p. Vannes,* it. Л village of Bretagne, in the diocefe and receipt of Treguier. *p. Guingamp.*

Ä *Gilht 6f 6" Bris,* a village of Bretagne, in the diocefe and receipt of Nantes, *p. Nantes.* S. *Gil/es-de-Livet,* a figniorv of Normandy, in the election of Pont PEvéque. *p. Pont-PEwque.* S. *Gilles-de-Men/f* a village of Bretagne, in the diocefe and receipt of S. Brictix. *p.* S. *Brkux. & Gilles-dts-BotSy* a village of Anjou, in the diocefe and receipt of Angers, *p. Angers.* S. *Gilles-Pligeau,* a village of Bretagne, in the diocefe and election of Quimper. *p. Rennes.* S. *Gilles-Pemm rit,* a village of Bretagne, in the diocefe and receipt oi Treguier. *p. Guingamp.* S. *G'tlles-Jur-V'tCj* a fmall town of Poitou, in the election of Sablesi'Olonne; about 15 leagues from Luc on, and 20 from Nantes. *Bureau de peβe.* S. *Giníeys,* a village of Upper Languedoc, in the diocefe and receipt of Touloufe. *pf Tüuioufe.* S. *Gïrauj* a place of Dauphiny, in t the diocefe and election of Grenoble. *p. Grenoble.* S. *Giren, f.* A town of Armagnac, in the election of Comminges. *p.* S. *Gaudens.* 2. A fmall town of Guienne, in the diocefe and election of Bourdeaux. *p. Blaye.* 3.

A village of Bretagne, in the diocefe and receipt of Nantes, *p. Arxems.* ff. *Gima,* a town of Gafcony, fituated on the Salat, in the election of Comminges. *p. 'Touloufe, S. Girons-du-LamP)* a village of Gafcony, in the election of Landes. *p.* A *Sever. S. Girons-du-Leß,* a village of Gafcony, in the election of Landes. *p. Dax. S. Glrons-en-Chaloffe,* an abby in the diocefe of Aire, in Gafcony, *p. Mont-de-Marfan. S. Ghy,* a village of Périgord, in the diocefe and election of Périgucux. *p. PetigueuX. S. Glen,* a village of Bretagne, in the diocefe and receipt of Bricux. *p. Lamballc. S. Gleyrats,* a village of Périgord, in the diocefe and lection of Sarlat. *p. Bergerac. S. Go.* i. A village of Gafcony, in the election of Landes, *p. Mont-deMarfan.* 2. A village of Armagnac, in the diocefe and election of Auch. *p. Acb. S. Gebert.* I. A village of Picardy, in the diocefe and election of Laon. *p. Mark. 2.* A village of Brie, in the diocefe and election of Meaux. *p. Meaux. $, Gobin,* a fmall town of Picardy, in the election of Soiffons. *p. ¡a Fere. S. Gond,* a priory in the diocefe 4Í Troyes, *p. Sezanne. S. Gctidon. t.* A fmall town of GAtinois, in the election of Gien. *p. Gien.* 2 An abby in the diocefe of Agen. *p. Agen. S. Gondran,* ts" *S. G onlay*) villages of Bretagne, in the diocefe and receipt of S. Malo. *p. S. Malo. S. Gvnnery,* a village of Bretagne, in the diocefe and receipt of Vannes. *p. Pontivy.*

¿'. *Gorjon,* a village of FrancheComté, in the bailiwick, of Pontarlier. *p. Pontarlier. S. Goual,* or *Loccal-en-Hennebcn,* a village of Bretagne, in the diocefe and receipt of Vannes, *p. Henneben. S. Goual,* or *Locoal-en-Awvrayy* a village in the diocefe and receipt of Vannes, *p. Vannes. S. Gouennoy* a village of Bretagne, in the diocefe and receipt of S. Brieux. *p. S. Brieux. S, Gourgon.* I. A village of Touraine, in the diocefe and election of Tours, *p. Blots.* 2. A place of Bretagne, in the diocefe and receipt of Vannes, *p. Cannes. S. Guuillard,* a fmall town of Marche, in the election of Bourgancuf. *p. Bcurgantuf. S. Goutry,* a place of Bretagne, in the d'ocefe and receipt of Nantes, *p. Nantes. S. Gourt* Êf *Cbaßelguion,* a

fmall town of Auvergne, in the election of Riom. *p. Riom. S. Goufiant-tTAury,* a village of Bretagne, in the diocefe and receipt of Nantes, *p. Vannas. S. Gradouxj* a village of Bourbonnois, in the election of Evaux. *p. Chambón. S. Grat,* a village of Rouergue, in the election of Villcfranchc. *p. Vülefvi m bedc-Rwergue. S. Graden. 1.* A town of Poitou, in the election of Loudun. *p. Loudun.* 2. A fmall town of Normandy, in the election of Pont-TEvequc. *p. Honfieur.* 3. A village of Picardy, in the election of Doulens. *p Amicm.* 4. A village in the diocefe and election of Pans. *p. Montmorency, S. Gulßtou,* a village of Bretagne, 5. A village of NÍvernois inthe in the diocefe and receipt of Dol. *p.* diocefe and election of Nevers. *p. Dol. Ne-vers. ¿,-Gy,* a town of Orléannois, in

Â *Grave,* a village of Bretagne, the diocefe and election of Orléans, in the diocefe and receipt of Vannes, *p. Orleans. p. Redon. Sainte Gauèurge,* л village of Norms'. *Grégoire,* i. A village of Nor-mandy, in the eleítion of Alcnçon. mandy, in the election of Pont-Au-*p. Alencon.* denier, *p. Pont-Audemer.* 2. A vil-*Ste. Gerne.* I. A village of Bafa lage of Dauphiny, in the diocefe and dois, in the election of Condom, *p.* election of Vienne. *p.Vkr.ne.* 3. A *Cafiel-Jaloux, t.* A village of Con vîllage of Upper Languedoc, in the domois, in the diocefe and receipt of diocefe and receipt of Albv. *p. A.by.* Condom, *p. Marmande.* 3. A vil— 4. A village of Bretagne, in the läge of Armagnac, in the diocefe and diocefe and receipt of Nantes, *p.* election of Auch. *p. Auch. Rennes.* 5. A village of Rouergue, *Ste. Gemme. 1.* A town of Snin iri the election of Milhaud. *p. Mil*-tonge, in the diocefe and election of *baud.* 6. A place of Agénoïs, in the Saintes, *p. Saintes.* 2. A town of diocefe and election of Agen. *p.* Berry, in the diocefe and election of *Vilkr.cwve-a" Agen.* Bourges, *p. Saacerre.* 3. A village *S. Gñede,* a village of Armagnac, of Champagne, in the election of in the diocefe and election of Auch. Epernay. *p. Epernay.* 4. A village *f'. Auch.* of Poitou, in the election of Thou *S. Guayran,* a village of Agénois, ars. *p. Tbouars.* 5. A village

of in the diocefe and election of Agen. Upper Languedoc, in the diocefe and *f. Agen.* receipt of Alby. *p. Alky.* 6. A *S. Guen,* a village of Bretagne, place of Guienne, in the diocefe and in the diocefe and receipt of Quirn-ejection of Bourdeaux. *p. Blaye.* psr. *p. Quimper. Ste. Gemmc-le-Sablon,* a t»wn of *S. Gueuolay & Eeuzcc-Capcanal,* a Berry, in the election of Chateau and receipt of Qu'mpcr. *p. Shimfer. Ste, Gtv:me-prh-Segre'y& Ste. Gem S. Guillaume* a village of Dauphi-we-*tur-hoire,* towns of Anjou, in the ny, in the diocefe of Die. *p. Die.* di-icefe and election of Aggers, *p, S. Guillaume G? S. Ar.deo* a village Angers. of Qauphinv, in the diocefe and *Ste. Genevieve. I.* A town of Gâ election of Gren/ble. *p. Grenoble.* tinojs, in the election of Man targes.

S. GttiIbem-du-Deferty a town of *p. ClotHlon-Jur-Loire.* 2. A fnull Lower Languedoc, m the diocefe and town of Normandy, in the election receipt cf Lodevc. *p. Gignac.* of Neufchâtcl. *p. Ñeufcbátei.* 3. A *S. Guillen-Labrovjfcy* a fmall town village of Normandy, in the election of Vivarais, in the receipt of Viviers, of Andely. *p. Bellemare.* 4. A vil *p. Vtvlers,* läge of Normandy, in the election of *S. CuiranSy A* village of Lower Valognes. *p. Valognes.* 5. A village Languedoc, in the diocefe and receipt of Normandy, in the election of Ar of Lodeve. *p.GignJC.* ques. *p. Bonnlere.* 6. A village of *S. Guiraudy* a village of Armagnac, Mcffin, in the diocefe and receipt of in tlc election of Aftaiac, *p. Mi-*Verdun, *p. Pont-à-Mouffen.* 7. A rande. 'village of Picardy, in the diocefe *S. Guircbj* a village of Rouflillon, and election of Beauvais. *p. Beau* in-the diocefe and receipt uf Ftipig-*aa s.* Ran. *p. Perpignan.* in tbe tKocefe of Beauvars. *f. Бeaavah. Ste. Genevi'tedes-Bois,* a village of the lile of France, in the diocefe. and election of Parts, *p. Linas. Ste. Genevu've-lesGafny,* a village.of Normandv, in the election of Andelv. *p. Gail/on. Ste. Geoirtj* a convent in the city of Vienne.

Sie, Germaine, a village of Con(faeioiSj in the diocefe and election of Condom, *p. Co.-.dom. Ste. Gertrude,* i. A place of

Pitardy, in the diocefe of Boulogne, *p. Boulogne* 2. A figniory in the election of Caudebec. *p. Caudebec.* Ste. Gillette, a village of Quercy, in the diocefe and election of Cahors. *p. Cabers.* Ste. Girbdle, a village of Roucrgue, in the election of Villefranche, *Villefranche-tU-Rouergtte.* Ste. Goburge. See Ste. Gauburgt. Ste. Guiterie, a village of Agénoís, *i:* the diocefe and election of Agen. *.p. Agen.* S-wt Haan, a fniall town of Lower
Languedoc, in the diocefe and receipt of Puy. *p. le Puy.* Saint Hacn-le-Cka tri, & Saht Haonle-Fleux, villages of Forez, in the election of Roanne, *p. Roanr.c.* S. H J u Ids j a village of Brie, in the diocefe and election of Meaux. *p. la Ferte'-fousJouard.* S. Heart, a town of Fore/., in the election of Montbrifon. *p. S. Etienne.* S. Hean-en-Fontanexiy a village of Forez, in the election of Montbrifon. *f. M r.rhifin.* S. Hehn, a village of Bretagne, in the diocefe and receipt of Dol. *p. Vol.* S. Helle. I. Л village of Picardy, in the diocefe and election of Amiens. *p. Ahli'ville.* 2. A place of Burgundy,in the bailiwick of Semur. *Viteaux.* S. Hellier. i. Дп ifbnd and town on the coalt of Normandy, *p. Coûtâmes.* %. A village of Normandy, in the election ot Arques, *p. BelUmare* S. Heïiïcr-de-Rennes9 a village «f Bretagne, in the diocefe and receiptof Nantes, *p. Rennes.* S. Henry. Sec £ Añg. S. HeʒbleʒΠy a village of Bretagne in the diocefe and receipt of Nantes *p. Nantes.* S Herblon-de-la-Rouxiere, a villageof Bretagne, in the diocefe and re ccipt of Nantes, *p. Ancenis.* S. Herent, a village of Auvergne in the election of Isbirc. *p, Iffoire.* S. Heriey a town of Samtonge, *uı* the election of S. Jean-dc-d'Angely, *p. S. Jean-d'Angely.* S. Hermandj a fmall town of Poitou, in the election of Fontena,. P S. Herniny a village of Bretagne in the diocefe and receipt of Quirnper. *p. Carbaix.* S. Hidcuc, a village of Bretagne, in the diocefe and receipt of Dul. *ŭ, Dol.* S. Hiereme, a fmall town of Bugey, in the diocefe and receipt of Bcltcyp. *BJhy.* S. HVaire. I. A town of Orleannois, in the diocefe and election of Orléans, *p. Orleans.* 2. A town of Saintonge, in the election of S. Jean-d'Angely./. *Taille-*
bourg, 3. A town of Anjou, in the election of Saumur, *p. Saumur.* 4. A town of Agénoís, in the diocefe and election of Agen. *p. S. L'wvrade.* 5. Л town of Bourbon not s, in the election of Moulins, *p. Moulins.* 6. A fmall town of Lower Languedoc, in the-diocefe and receipt of Car.affonne. *p Carcajjo.me.* 7. A fmall town of Normandy, in the election of Falaife. *p, Falmfe.* 8. A fmall town of Berry, in the election of Blanc, *p. le Blanc.* 9. A village of A génois, in the dincele and election of Agen. *p. Agen.* 10. A village of Normandy, in the. election of Carentan. *p. Carentan,* 11. A village of Normandy, in the election of Alençori. *p. Alenc;n.* 12. A village of Poitou, in the election of Chatcllleraut. *p. Cbaunay,* 13. A village of Bafadois, in the election of
Condom, *p. Bazas.* 14. A village of Condomois, in the dioccfe and election of Condom, *p. la Reolle.* 15. A village of Gàtinois, in the election of Nemours, *p. Nemours.* 16. A village of Gàtinois, in the election of Montargis. *p. Cbdiillon» fur-Lbire.* 17. A village of Forez, in the election of Montbrifon. *p. Montbrifon.* 18. A village of Forez, in the election of Roanne, *p. Roanne.* 19. A village of Champagne, in the election of Nogent. *p. Nogcnt-furSeine.* 20. A village of Perche, in the election of Mortagne. *p. Mortagne.* 21 A village of Marche, in the election of Bourganeuf. *p. Bourganeuf.* 22. A village of Hainaut, in the dioccfe of Cambray. *p. Avefnes.* 23. A village of Flanders, in the dioccfe and fùbdclegation of Cambray. *p. Cambioy.* 24. A village of Limofin, in the election of Brives. *p. Brives.* 25. A village of Dauphiny, in the diocefe and election of Vienne, *p. Bourgo'm.* 26. A village of Dauphiny, in the diocefe and election of Grenoble, *p. Grenoble-*27. A village of Dauphiny, in the diocefe and election of Vienne, *p. Vienne.* 28. A village of Beauce, in the election of Dourdan. *p. Dourdcn.* 29. A village of Nivernois, in the elefrion of Château-Chinon. *p. De» cife.* 30. A village of MeiTin, in the diocefe and receipt of Verdun, *p. Verdun.* 31. A village of FrancheComté, in the bailiwick, of Vefoul. *f. Vefoul.* 32. A place of MeiTin, in the bailiwick
of Verdun, *p. Verdun.* 33. A place of FrancheComté, in the bailiwick of Baume. *p. Baume.* S. JÍUave-Bxerres ¿sf Bevscnccuil, a village of Burgundy, in the bailiwick of Challón, *p. JViámt.* S. Hiialre-au-¥empȷet a place of Champagne, in the diocefe and clcc tion tf Chalons. l/. *Chalons.* ' S. HUaire-aux-Montagnes & PuyGuillaume, a fmall town of Büurƀon no is, in the election of Gannat, *p. G'anna't.*
Bellay *p. Angers.* 2. A (mall town of Poitou, in the eleftion of Fontetenay. *p. Cbantonay.* 3. A village of Saintonge, in the diocefe and election of Saintes, *p. Samtes.* 4. A village of Bretagne, in the diocefe and receipt of Nantes, *p. Nantes.* S. Hilaire-du-Chaleon, a village in the diocefe and receipt of Nantes, *p. Nantes.* S. Hilaire-Ju-Hareouet, a markettown of Normandy, in the diocefe of Avranches, and eleftion of Mortain; about 7 leagues from Avranches, 7 from Mortain, 7 from Fougerts, and 14 from Dol. *Bureau depofie.* S. Hilaire-en-Awvergne, Êf S. Hilaire-pres-la-Rouay, villages of £ourbonnois, in the eleftion of Gannat. *f. Gannat.* S. Hilaire-en-Barbeßsux, a village of Saintonge, in the diocefe and election of Saintes, *p. Barheßcux.* S. Hilaire-en-Liniere, a town of Berry, in the eleftion of Ifloudun. *p. l.Jfoudun.* S. Hilaire-en-Montaigu, a fmall town of Poitou, ¡11 the eleftion of Mauleon. *p. Montaigu.* S. Hilaire Êf *Fontaine,* a village of Nivernois, in the eleftion of Nevers. *p. Decije.* S. Hilaire & Lauche, a village of Picardy, m the eleftion of Doulens. *p. Doulens,* S. Шале fif & Pancrace, a village of Dauphiny, in the diocefe and eleftion of Grenobje. *p. Grenoble.* S. Hilaire-Foijac, S. Hilaire-le-Luc, têf 5. Hilaiie-les-Cctirbes, villages of Liraofin, in the eleftion of Tulles. *f. Ttille.* S. Hi/ aire-la-Palu, a fmafl town of Poitou, in the. election of Niort. *p. Niort.* S. Hilmre-la-Gerard, a village of Normandy, in the eleftion of Aknjon. *p. Aiençon.* S. Hilaire-las-Tours, S. HilaireMagna% eix, villages of Limofin, in the diocefe and eleftion of Linones. *f. Limoges.* "Ƀ ceîpt of Quimper. *p. Quimper.* 5. A village of Normandy, m the election of Arques, *p. Bctlemare.* S. Hirore-de-Ro-

quefaiour, a priory in the chócele of Arx, in Provence.

S. *Hugal,* a town of Maine, *p. le Mans.* S. *Humbert,* a place of Mcflîn, in the diocefe and receipt of Metz. *p. Verdun.* S. *Huruge,* a pariih of Burgundy, in the diocefe-and receipt of Macon. *J. Mâcon.* S.*Hymethiere,* a village of FrancheComté, in the bailiwick of Orgelet. *J. Lons-le-Saunier.* S. *Hippoiite.* I. A town of Lower Languedoc, on the river Vidourle, in the diocefc and receipt of Alais; about 6 leagues from Alais, and 3 from Andufe. *Bureau de poße.* 2. A village of Saintonge, 3!enguc.s from Rochefort. 3. A town of Tourine, in the election of Loches, *p. Cbdtilhn-jur-Indre.* 4 A village of Auvergne, in the election of Riom. *p. MrÏQude.* 5. A village of Guicnne, in the diocefe and election of Bourreaux, *p. Bourdeaux.* 6. A village of Normandy, in the election of Argentan, *p. Lifieux.* 7. A village of RouiTilion, in the diocefe and viguery of Perpignan, *p. Perpignan* 8. A village of FrancheCom te, in the bailiwick, of Baume, *p. Baume.* 9. A village of Quercy, in the diocefe and election of Cahors. *p. Cakors.* 10. A village of Burgundy, in the diocefe and receipt of Mâcon. *p. Mâcon.* il. A village of Anjou, in the election of Montreuil-Bclhy. *p. Saumur.* 12. A place of Bazadois, in tht election of Condom, *p. Bazas.* S. *Hypotue* CSF *Fumel,* a fmall town of Agenois, in the diocefe and election of Agen. *p. Agen.* S. *Hypolite-de-Cantelou,* Ê? S. *Hyfohtedu-Bout-des-Fres,* places of Normandy, in the d ocele and election of Lifieux. *p. Lßeux.* S. *Hypolite-de-Cajcn.* See *Caten.* S. *HypoHte-de-Cbeuz-Je,* a village f Daupiuny, in the diotcie and eLction of Vienne, *p. Vienne.* S. *Hypoliie-Jur-leDoux,* a fmalî town of Franche-Comté, in the diocefe and receipt of Befançon. *p. Cierva/. Sainte-Heteine,* a village of Normandy, in the election of Caudebec. *p. Fecamp. Sainte-Helein:-de-la-Lar.de,* a village of Guicnne, in the diocefe and election of Bourdeaux. *Laurentde-Medoe.* Ste.*-Heleine-de-Leßeing,* a village of Guicnne, in the diocefe and election of Bourdeaux. *p. Bourdeaux.* Ste. *Helene, x.* A village of Lower Languedoc,

in the diocefe and receipt of Mcnde. *p. Montpellier,* 2. A viibge of Burgundy, in the diocefe and bailiwick of Challou. *p. Challón.* Ste. *Helie,* a place of Burgundy, in the bailiwick of Semur-enAuxois. *p. Scmur.* Ste. *Hermine,* a village of Poitou, in the election of Fontenay. *p. Tbire.* Ste. *Honorine.* 1. A town of Normandy, in the election of Vîre. *p. Conde'-fur-Noireau. %.* A village of Normandy, in the election of Caen. *p. Trouard.* 3. A fca-port of Normandy, on the coaft of Beffin.

Ste. *Honorine-de-Dury,* CS5 Ste. *Ho norine-des-Pertus,* fmall towns of Normandy, in the diocefe and election/of Bayeux. *p. Bayeux.* Ste. *Honorine-laGuillaume,* a town of Normandy, in the election of Falaife. *p. Falaife.* Ste. *Honorine-la-Pelitet* a village in the election *oí* Falaife. *p. Falaifa. Saint yac,* a town of Limofin, in the election of Brives. *p. Brives.* S. *Jacques, t.* A fmall town of Normandy, in the election of Domfront. *p. Domjront. 1.* A village oí Condomois, in the diocefe and election of Condom, *p. Condom.* 3. A village of Dauphiny, in the diocefa and election of Gap. *p. Gap* 4. A village of Provence, in the receipt of Bajreme. *p. Caßellane.* 5. A convent near Vitry-lc-François, in Champagne, *p. Fitry.* 6. A priory in the diocefe of Bourdeaux. S. *Jacques £f S. Cbrißopbe-de-Retx,* a place in the diocefe and election of Paris, *p. Paris.* S. *Jacques-d Жхегтот,* a village f Normandy, in the election of Arques, *p. Dieppe.* S. *Jacques-deCii(fony* à place of Bretagne, in the diocefe and receipt ef Nantes, *p. Nantes.* S. *Jacques-de-Dot,* an abby near the city of Puy. *p. le Pay.* S. *Jacques-de-la-Lande,* a village f Bretagne, in the receipt of Nantes. *p. Rep ties.* S. *Jacques-de-F Hermitage,* a priory in the diocefe of Sens. S.*Jacqes-dcMovrfortj* an abby in the diocefe of S. Malo. *p.* S. *Malo.* S. *Jacques-des-Arrhsy* a village of "Beaujolois, in the election of Villefranche. *p. V'xllefranche.* S. *Jacques-de-GueretSf* a village of Beauce, in the election of Vendôme. *p. Memoire.* S. *Jacques -dIUkres.* See *llitres.* S. *Jaeques-en-Tillay-,* a vilkige of Poitou, in the election of Fontenay. *f. Fontenay-le-Comte.* S. *Jacques-fur-*

Derncta!, a village uf Normandy, in the diocefe and election of Rouen, *p. Rotten.* S. *Jacut. 2,* A village oí Bretagne, in the diocefe and election of S. Bricux. *p. Redon.* 2. A village of Bretagne, in the diocefe and receipt cf Dol. *p. Doi S. Jügut)* a village of Bretagnc, in the diocefe and receipt of Vannes, *p.* S. *Malo.* S. *JàiL* I. A village of BourbonTtnis, in the election of Gannat. *p. Cannât,* a A village of Auvergne, in the diocefe and election of S. Flour. *p.* S. *Flour.* S. *Jaimes,* a village of Armngnac, in the election of *Aix?.r?x.p. Âî'rande.* S. *Jal)* a figmory in Limofin. *p. Ufirchs.* S. *James,* i. A town of Normandy, in the diocefe and election of Avrahches; about 4 leagues from Avranches', 9 from Mortain, 5 from Fougères, ïo from Dol, and 14 from Domfront. *Bureau de poße. %.* A place of Gafcony, in the receipt of Gabardan. *p. Dax.* S. *Jannet.* i. A village of Provence, in the viguery of Digne, *p. Riexi.* 2. A village of Provence, in the viguery of S. Paul. *p. Amibes.* S. *Jan-verin,* a place of Berry, in the diocefe of Bourges, *p. la Chatre.* S. *Janet,* an abby in Bretagne, *p. Dol.* S. *Jbars,* a town of Foix, in th« diocefe of Pamicrs.. *Pamiers.* S. *IbartSy* a fmall tow n of Limofin, in the election of Brives. *p. Ujcches. $. Jean.* I. A town of Tonraine, in the election of Loches, *p. Loches. %.* A village of Gafcony, in the diocefe and election of Comminges. *p. Montre'jeau.* 3. A village of Bafadois, in the election of-Condom, *p. Bajas.* 4, A village of Champagne, in the election of Nngent. *p. Ncgcntfur-Seine.* 5. A village of Perche, in the election of Vcrneuil. *p. Vers tteu'il.* 6. A village of Agénois, in the diocefe and election oí Agen, *p, le Temple.* 7. A village of Agénois, in the diocefe and election of Agen. *p. Agen.* S. A village of Bretagne, in the diocefe and receipt of S. Pol deLean. *p. Morlaix.* 9. A village of Dauphiny, in the diocefe and rcc ipt of Vienne, *p. Moirans,* S. *Jeetn-ct'Tiuflasy* a village-of LyonnoiSf in the diocefe and election of Lyons, *p.* S. *Chamont.* 5. *Jean-aux-Bûs.* I. A village of Champagne, in the diocefe and election of Rheims./'. *Reche/.* 2. A village of Picardy, in the election of Crêpy. *p. Com-*

pi'gne. S. Jean-Balmes, a place of Rouergite, in the election of Milhaud. *p. Ml baud. S, Jean-Battſse-de-ChSteau-gontitrt* a p-i-ry In Crûteau-Gontier. *& Jean-Bmacful)* a fmall towa of Champagne, in the díocefe and election of Troy es. *p. T'rcyes. S. Jean-Brevelaj)* a fmall town of Bretagne, in the diocefe and receipt of Vannes, *p. Vannes. S. "JeanCet¡renier,* a village of Lower Languedoc, in the diocefe and receipt of Viviers, *p. Viviers. S. yean-Ckambre,* a village of Vivarais, in the receipt of Viviers, *p. 'Vi'u'iers. S. yeanCcu!ortt* a village of Bretagne, in the diocefe and receipt of S. Malo. *p. S. Мак. S. jfean-Courbetorty* a place of Brie, in the election of Montereau. *p. Aiontercau. S. Jean-d1 Adamy* a village of Franche-Comté', in the bailiwick, of Baume, *p. Baume. S. Jean-dAâmł)* a village of Agénois, in the diocefe and election oí Agen. *p. Agev. S. Jean-d? Amiens,* an abby in the city of Amiens.

Л. *J'ean-dAngely,* an ancient city of Saintonge, fituatcd on the Boutonne, in the diocefe of Saintes, and generality of Rochelle, the feat of an election, &c. in the road from Saintes to Poitiers, 6 leagues from Saintes, 30 I rom Poitiers, 3S from Bourdeaux and no from Paris. *Bu' rcau de poſse. S. 'Jcan-dAngUy* a town of Saintonge, in the election of Marcnnes. *p. Roebcfort. S. y ean-d Angles,* a village of Armagnac, in the diocefe and election of Auch. *p. Auch. & Yean-d"" Aftot,* a village of Normandy, in the election of Montivilliers. *p. Harſscur. S. Jean-d'Ardiere,* a village of Beaujolois, in the election of Villefranche, *p. Belleville. S. ycan-d"Ama!on,* a village of Daiiphiny, in the diocefe and generally of Grenoble, *p. Grenoble. S. yean-d'l'Amafìej* a village of Roucrgue, in the election of Milfeaud. *p. Mvbaud.*

& yean-d'AuWj a convent in *p. Aun. iy.* 1. A fmall town of Orléannois, in the diocefe and election of Or'.éans. *p. 'Or/eans. S. yean-le-Comtal,* a village of Armagnac, in the diocefe and election of Aftarac. *p. Mirande. S. yean-le-Grandy* a village of Burgundy, in the diocefe and bailiwick of Autun. *p. Autun, S. y can-le-Thomas y* a village of Normandy, in the diocefe and election of Avranches. *p. Arranches. S+yean-le-Vieux.* I. A fmall town of Bugey, in the diocefe and bailiwick of Bellcy. *p. Nantua.* a. A fmall town of Galcony, in the diocefe and receipt of Bayonne. *p. Bayonne.* 3. A village of Dauphiny, in the diocefe and election of Grenoble. *Bureau de poſle.* 4. A village of Navarre, in the diocefe of Bayonne. *p. Pau. S. yean-hermy* a village of Upper Languedoc, in the diocefe and receipt of Touloufe. *p. Touloufe. S. ycan-les-deuxyumeauxy* a village of Brie, in the diocefe and election of JVJeaux. *p. Meaux. S. yean-lcs-Monges,* a village of Auvergne, in the diocefe and election of Clermont, e *Clermont. S. yean-ks-Brocourty* a place of Picardy, in the election of Abbeville. *p. Abbeville. S, yean-ks-SenSy* an abbey in the diocefe of Sens. *p. Sens. S. yean-Ligonre,* a fmall town of Lijnofin, in the diocefe and election' of Limoges, *p. Pierre-Bujpcre. S. yean-Pied-de-Porty* a fmall city of Navarre, fituatcd on the Nive at the foot of the Pyrenees; about a league from the Frontiers of Spain, 8 leagues from Brwonne, and 12 from Panjckme. *p. Pau., S. yean-Ponchar eſey* a village of Lower. Languedoc, in the diocefe and receipt of Viviers, *p. Anduve.. S. yean-Poittge.* 1. A v'llage of Armagnac, in the diocefe and election of Auch. *p. Auch.* a. A village of Beam, in the receipt of Morias f, *Pau. S. yean-pris-Gcnüve,* a village oſ election of Milhaud. *p. Milhaud. S. Ignan,* a village of Gafcony, Jjt the dioccfe and election of Comminges. *p. Monttejeav. S. Igtiat,* a fmail town of Auvergne, in the election of Riora. *p. Riem. S. Tgne,* a village of Rouergue, in the election of Villcfranche. *p. VtlUfranchc-de-Rcuerue. S. lgneuc,* a village of Bretagne, in the diocefe and receipt of S. Brieux. *p. S. Btieux. S. Ignyt* a place of Franche Comté) in the bailiwick of Vefoul. *p. Vefouh S. Igny-de-Roche,* a pariih of Burgundy, compofed of fix hamlets, ia the diocefe and bailiwick of Mùcoa. *p. Macon. S. Igny-de-Vert,* a parifli of Burgundy, in the receipt of Semui-eiv Briennois. /. *Belleville. S. Illide,* a fraall town of Au# vergne, in the election of AurilJac *p. Auriliac. S. Illier.* I. A village of Beaucc, in the election of Mantes, *p. Mantes.* 2. A village of Brie, in the election of Provins, *p. Provint. S. îU'ier-les-Bohj* a village of Normandy, in the diocefe and election, of Evreux. *p. Bcnnhre. S. Ilpizcj* a town of Auvergne, *r* the election of Brioude. *p. Brtoudt, S. Im-er,* a frr.all town of Dauphiny, in the dioccfe and generality oí Grenoble, *p. Grenoble. S. Images,* a village of Champagne, in the dioccfe and election of Rbihus. *p. Rheims.* 5. *Inlcvere* a village of Picardy, in thcgcncralitv of Amiens, *p. Calais. S. Jcda¡d,* a village of Forez, in the election of Roanne, *p. Roanne, S. Jcrdy,* a village of Roucrgue, in the election of Villcfranche. *p. Vilkfrarhc-dc-Rouergve. S.Jire,* a village of Normandy, in the election of Falaife. *p. 4'rcuard. S. Jores,* a vilbge of Normandy, in the election of Carentan, *p. Ca rentan. S. Joyj* a town of Upper Lan *S. Jubrïan,* a place of Champagne in the diocefe and election of Chalons *p. Chalons. S. Judoce,* a village of Bretagne, in the diocefe and receipt of Dol. *p. Diñan. S. bvery,* a village of Upper Languedoc, in the diocefe and receipt of Ally. *p. Ally.*

& Juin, a village of Condomoîs, in the diocefe and election of Condom, *p. Condom. £. Juive,* a village of Poitou, in the election of Fontenay. *p. Thire. S. Jtdes,* an abby in the diocefe of Beauvais. *p. Beawvais. S. Julia,* т. A village of Upper Languedoc, in the diocefe and receipt of Alet. *p. Limoux.* 2. A village of Upper Languedoc, in the diocefe and receipt of Touloufc, *p, Mvepoix. S. Julia-de-Grajcapoux.* See *Grajcafoux. S. Julien.* X. A town of Touraine, In the election of Amboife. *Amhúje.* 2. A fmall town of Armagnac, in the election of Comminges. *p. Pau.* 3. A village of FrancheComté, in the bailiwick pf Orgelet, *p. Lcns-k-Saumer.* 4. A vilbge of Poitou, in the diocefe and election of Poitiers.*Púñers,* 5. A village of A génois, in *tiz* diocefe and election of Agen. *p. Agen.* 6. A village of Gafcony, in the election of Landes. *p. Dax.* 7. A village of Guicnne, in the diocefe and election of Bourdeaux. *p. Baurdeuux.* 8. A village of Burgundy, in the diocefe

and bailiwick of Dijon, *p. Dijon.* 9. A village of Burgundy, in the bailiwick of Montccnis. *p. Autun.* 10. A village of Burgundy, in the diocefe and receipt of Macon.*p. Mâcon.* XX. A village of Upper Languedoc, in, the diocefe and receipt of Alby. *p. Toulouje.* 12. A village of Normandy, in the diocefe and election of Evreux. *p.. Bur eux.* 13. A village of Normandy, in the election of Falaife. *p. Falaife.* 14. A village of Beaujolots, in the election of vMlefranche. *p. VШranche.* 15. A village of Marche, in the election of Gueret. */. Cbcneraitfes.* 16. A village of Marche, in the election of Bourgancuf. *p. Bourganeuf.* 17. A village of Auvergne, in the ek&on of Corobrail.'cs. *p. Camben.* 18. A village of Meffin, in the diocefe and receipt of Metz. *p. Metz* 19. A village of FrancheComté, in the bailiwick of Gray. f. *Gray.* 20. A village of FrancheComté, in the bailiwick of Baume. *p. Baume,* 21. A village of Blefois, in the election of Rorr.orantin. *p. Romorar.t'tTi.* 22. A village of C011domois, in the diocefe and election of Condom, *p Condom.* 23. A village of Provence, in the dioccfc of Marfeille. */- Aix.* 24. A village of Provence, in the vi¿uery of Caítellane. */. Cajlellane.* 25. A village of Dauphiny, in the diocefe and election of Vienne, *p. Vienne,* 26. A village of Dauphiny, in the diocefe and election of Montelimart. /». *Montelimart. »*7. A village of Rouergue, in the election of Villefranche. *p. Rodez.* 28. A village of Gafcony, in the diocefe and election of Comminges. *p. Montrejeau.* 2.9. A place of Berry, in the diocefe and election of Bourges. *p. Bourges* 30. A parifh of Burgundy, in the diocefe and receipt of Challón, *p. Challón.* 31. The name of a chatellany in Berry. *BVreatfdepoße. 2.* A villageofMarch?, in the election oí Bourgancuf. *p. ßourganeuf.* S. Julien £f *Rafy,* a village of Burgundy, in the diocefe and bailiwick of Challón, *p. Challón,* S. Julien & S. Julen-àJa-Montagne, a village of Dauphiny, in the diocefe and élection of Grenoble, *p. Grenoble.* S. Julien fe? *Segur,* a village of.Limofin, in the election of Brives. *p. Br'wes.* S. Julien-d *Aß'c,* a village of Provence, in the viguery of Digne, *p. Joigne.* S. *Jufien-de-Bonlfagucl,* a village of Agénois, in the diocefe and election of Agen. *p. Agen.* S. *Julien-de-Bourdtilies,* a village of Perigord, in the diocefe and election of Périgueu. *p. BourdcMei.* S.*Jumen-¡e-Petit,* Ê? S.*Jumen-lesCombes,* villages of Liuiofin, in the diocefe and election of Limoges, *p. Limoges.* S. *Inicre,* or S. *George.* Sec & *George.* S. *Jure,* a village of Mefiin, in the diocefe and receipt of Metz., *p. Metz.* S. *Jurs fef les Nibtes,* a village of Provence, in the vigucry of Mouftiers. *p. Rient.* S. *Y tuf onf* a place of Provence, in the viguery of Digne, *p. Dirne.* S. *Juß.* т. A town of Picard?, in ti:C road from Amiens to Paris, in the diocefc of Beau vais, and election oc Mondidier; 4 leagues from Mondidicr, 8 from Roye, 4 from Clermont, 12 from Amiens, and 19 from Paris. *Bureau He pcfie.* 2. A town of Saintonge, in the election of Marennes. *p. Rockefort.* 3. A town of Rouergue, in the election of VÍlïefranchc. *p. Viilfranche-di-Rwerguc,* 4. A fmall town of Limoiin, in the diecefc and election of "Limoges, *p. Limoges.* 5. A fmall town of Brie, in the election of Sezanne, *p. Sezanne.* 6. A village of Brie, in the election of Rozoy. *p. Natigis.* 7. A village of Auvergne, in the diocefe and c.cction of S. Flour, *p. Brlcude.* 8 A village of Agénois, in the diocefc and election of Agen. *p. Agen.* "9. A village of Normandy, in the election of Andely. *p. Dieppe.* 10. A village of Normandy, in the election of Arques. *p. Gailhn.* 1 r. A village of Berry, in the diocefe and election of Bourges, *p. Bourges.* iz. A village of Louer Languedoc, m the diocefe and receipt of Montpellier, *p. MartvejoIs.* 13. A village of Oltabares. *p. Bayonne.* 14. A village of Bretagne, in the diocefe and receipt of Vannes, *p. Redon.* 15. A village of Dauphiny, in the diocefe and election *ai* Vienne, *p. Grenoble.* 16. A place f Burgundy, in the bailiwick of 5. *Ixery,* a town of Rouergue, in the election of Miihauld. *f.* S. *Af frifue.* Sainte-Jaile, a village of Dauphiny, in the election oí Montelimart. *p. le Buis.*

Äe. *James.* I. A village of the Ifle of France, in the dio:efe and election of Paris, *p. Verfalles* 2. A village ofBeauce, in the election of Van dôme. *p. Dreux.* 3. A village of Berry, in the election of Châteauroux. *p. Châteauroux.* Ste, *JamS-le-Rcbertt* a town of Maine, in the election of Mayenne. *p. Mayenne* Ste. *James-fur-Sartbe,* a town of Maine, in the diocefe and election of Mans. *p. Frcfn.iy,* Ste. *Jama-ViU-reui-e,* a village of Benucc, in the election of Châteaudun. *p. Châ:eaudun. Stc. Innocence,* a village of Périgord, in the-diocefe and election of Sartat. *p. Bergerac. Sie. Jtdie,* a village of Bugcy, in thé bailiwick, of B.llcy. *p. Ambcrieux.* Ste, *Julitte,* a town cf Touraine, in the elcilion of Loches, *p Loches. Saint Labouer,* a town of Gafcony, in the dioccfe and election of Landes, *p.* S. *Sei'er.* S. *Laelancin,* a village of Berry, in the election of Châteauroux. *p. Châteauroux.* S. *Lagicr.* т. A fraall town of Beaujolois, in the etetion of Villcfranche, f. *Betlennll.* 2. A village of Forez, in the election of Roanne. *p. Roanne.* 3. A village of Auvergne, in the election of Brioude. *p. Brioude.* S. *Lamain,* a village of FrancheComté, in the bailiwick, of Poligny. *p. Salins.* S. *Lambert.* 1. A fmall town of Normandy, in the election of Vire, *p. Omdf-jur'Noireau.* 1. A village of Champagne, in the election of Rethel. *Ret bel.* 3. A village of the Ifle of France, in the dioccfe and receipt of Yxnv.*p.Cfavreufi,* 4. A village of Normandy,in the election ofArgen*tzn.p. Argentan.* 5. A village of Provence, in the generality of Aix. *p. Apt.* 6. A place of Normandy, in the election of Bernay. *p. Chambrois.* S. *Lambert-de-la-PoUriey* a town of Anjou, in the dioccfe and election of Angers, *p. Saumur.* S. *Lambert-de-Leveesj* a town of Anjou, in the election of Saumur. *p. Saumur,* S. *Langn,* a village of Perche, in the election of Mortane. *p. Mortagne.* S. *Lanne,* a village of Armagnac, in thediocefe and election of Auch. *p. Mont-de-Marfan.* S. *Laon,* a town of Poitou, in ihe election of Loudun. *p. Loudun.* S. *La'jn-de-Roquep'me,* a village of Périgf-rd, in the diocefe and election of" Saiiat. *p. Sarlat.* S. *Lary.* i. A village of Armagnac, in the dioccfe and election of Auch. *p. Auch.* 2. A village of Armagnac, in the diocefe of Corrw mtnges. p. *Auch* 3. A village of Gafcony. in the dioccfe and election of Comminges. p. *M'.ntrejeau* 4. A village of Armagnac, in the election of Lomagnc./. *Beaumont-de-Loma¿ne.* S-*Latter,* a Village of Dauphiny, in the election of Romans p. *Romans.* S. *Laud,* a fmall town of Anjou, in the diocefe and election of Angers. p. *Angers.* S. *Launatt c,* a fmall village of Bretagne, in the diocefe and receipt of DoL p. *Dol.* S. *Laure.* 1. A village of Auvergne, in the election of Riom. p. *R om* 2. An abby in Hamaut, near Valenciennes, p. *Vafeneiennis.* S. *Laurent.* I. A town of Angoumoiî, in the election of Cognac. p. *Cognac.* 2. A town of Provence, in the viguery of S. Paul. p. *Antikes.* 3. A town of Normandy, in the election of Mortain. p. S. *"James.* 4. A village of Dauphiny, in the generality of Grenoble, p. *Cap.* 5. A village of Normandy, in the election of Montivilliers.. *llarßeur,* 6. A village of Angoumots, in tlie dioccfe and election of Angoulême. p. *Barbeßjux* 7. A village of GafLony, in the election of Landes. p. *Dax.* 8. A village of Marche, in the election of Gueret. p. *Gutret.* 9. A village of Berry, in the dioccfe and election of Bourges, p. *Vierjon.* 10. A village of Auvergne, in the election of Brioudc. p. *Brioude.* 1 1. A village of Meflin, in the diocefe of Metz. p. *Verdun.* 12. A village of Provence, in the viguery of Mouftie'rs. p, *Barjols.* 13, A village of Artois, in the diocefe and bailiwick of Arras, p. *Arras*-14. A village of Lower Languedoc, in the diocefe and receipt of Narbonne. p, *Narbonne.* 15. A village of Bafadois, in the election of Condom, p. *la Recife.* 16. A village of Condomois, in the diocefe and election of Condom, p. *Condom.* 17, and i3. Two viliages of Agcnois, in the diocefe and election of Agen. . *Agen* 19. A village of Agénois, in the diocefe and election of Aen. p. *Ptrt-Ste.-Alat ie.* 20. A village of Rouergue, in the election of Milhaud. p. *Milkaud.* ZI. A village of Gafcony, in the diccefe and eleit'on of Comminges. p. *Mentrejeau.* 22. A place of Beam, in the receipt of Morias, p. *Pau.* 23. Aplace ofTouraine, near Langeft. p. *Langejl.* 24. A parifh of Provence, p. *Aries.* 25. A figniory of Poitou, in the diocefe and election of Poitiers, p-*Poitiers.* 26. A foreft of 564 arpents, in thejurifdiction of Vierfon.

£ *Laurent-aux-Bohj* a priory in Picariy.

S. *Laurent-d Agny* a village of Lyonnois, in the diocefe and election of Lyons, p. *Lyon.* S. *Laurent-d? Andenay* a village of Burgundy, in the diocefe of Autun. p. *Cbaihn.* S.*Lauiet-TAubeterret* a town of Touraine, in the election of Chateau roux. p. *Preuilly.* S. *Laurent-dyAygou%ef* a fmall tova of Lower Languedoc, in the S. *Legier-de-Mawvieres,* a town of Berry, in the election of Blanc. p *le Blanc.* S. *Legier-près-Mille,* a village of Poitou, in the election of S. Maixant. p. *la Motte-Sie.-Heraye.* S. *Leon.* I. A village of Condómois, in the diocefe and election of Condom, p. *Condom,* ъ. A village of Guienne, in the diocefe and election of Bourdeaux. p. *Bourdeaux.* S. *Leon-de-CauJJidiere.* See *Cauffidiere.* S. *Leon-de-Grigno/s.* See *Grignols.* S. *Leonard,* or S. *Leonard-le-Noblctt* a city of Limoiin, fituated on the Vienne, on the confines of Marche; 6 leagues from Limoges, and 6 from Bourganeuf. *Bureau de foße.* S. *Leonard, i.* A fmall town of Normandy, in the election of Montiviiliers. p. *Fecamp, z.* A village of Normandy, in the election of Alençon. p. *Argentan.* 3. A village of Beauce, in the election of Chilteaudun. p. *Châteaudun.* 4. A village of Picardy1, in the diocefe and election of Senlis. p. *Senfis.* 5. A village of Anjou, in the diocefe and election of Angers, p. *Angers.* 6. A village of Armagnac, in the diocefe and election of Lomagne. p. S. *Ciar.* 7. A village of Picardy, near Boulogne, p. *Boulogne;*

¿. *Leonard-des-Bois,* a town of Maine, in the diocefe and election of Mans.. *Frefnay,* $. *Leonard-des-ChaumeSj* a village of Aunis, in the diocefe and election of Rochelle, p. *la Rochelle.* S. *Leonard-dcs-Fenteres,* an abby in the diocefe of Poitiers, p. *Thenars.* 8. *Leonard-des-Fougères,* a place of Bretagne, in the diocefe and receipt of-Dol. p. *Del.* S. *Leonard-du-Corbgny,* an abby of Nivernois, in the diocefe of Autun. p. *Corhtgny.* S. *Lconard-Morlemont,* a village of Picardy, in the election of Pcronne. p. *Pe'ronne.* i'. *Leons,* a town of RoiuTillon, in the election of Milhuud. p. *Milhaud.* i¿, *Leopard'm,* a village of Bourbon

Jmhs, in the election of Moulins, p. Ä *Pierre-le-Moutier.* S. *heu,* a town of Picardy, in the diocefc and election of Senlis. f. *Oed.* S. *Leu-Taverni,* a fmall town of the Ille of France, in the diocefe and election of Paris, p. *Franconville.* S. *Lezin & la Chapelle-RouJ'din,* a fmall town of Anjou, in the diocefe and election of Angers, p. S. *Florens* S. *UHerí,* a village of Bretagne, in the diocefe and receipt of S-Malo. p. S. *Malo.* S. *Lkbault,* a village of Champagne, in the diocefe ¿nd election of Troycs. p. *Dreyes.* S. *Lier.ard,* or *Leonard,* a place of Champagne, in the diocefe and clcctionVjf Rheims, p *Rheims.* S. *Liens,* a village of Bourbonnois, in the election of Moulins. ¿. *Moulins.* S. *Liez,* a village of Champagne, in the diocefe and election of Troycs. j. *Tnyes.* S. *Lieu. t.* A village of Burgundy, in rhe receipt of Charollcs. p. *Dijon, z.* See *Septfonds,* S. *Lieux,* i. A fmall town of Upp"r Languedoc, in the diocefe and receipt of Lavaur, f. *Lavaur.* l. A village of Upper Languedoc, in the diocefe and receipt of Alby. p. *Ally.* S. *XAgier -des-Bruyères.* See & *i¿ger-des-Bruyères* S. *Liguahe,* л fmall town of Poitou, in the election of Niort./1. *Niort.*

«S'. *Lin,* a village of Poitou, in the election of Niort, p. *Partenay.* S. *Liphardj* a village of Bretagne, in the diocefe and receipt of Nantes. p. *Guerande,* S, *Lis,* a town of Armagnac, in the diocefe of Aire, and-election of Rivière-Verdun. *Bureau de poße.* S. *Lhicr,* an ancient city of Guienne, thecapital of Conferans, Jituarcd on thcSalat, in the generality of Auch, it isa bifhop's fee; about 7 leagues from Pamicrs, 8 from S. Bertrand,-and 18 from Touloufe. p. *4'ouhuje.* S. *Lo,* a city of Normandy, filiated on the Vire; in the diocefe of

Coûtances, and generality ef Caen, the feat of a government, a bailiwick, election, Sec. 8 leagues fron# Bayeux, 15 from Caen, 7 from Coûtances, 18 from Cherburg, and 68 from Paris.

Bureau de fofle. S. Lo-dOurtnlle, a village of Normandy, in the election of Valogncs. *p. Coûtâmes S. Lcmer,* a village of Normandy, in the election of Alençon. *p U Meiler-au t. S. Lomer-de-BJoh,* an abby in the city of Blois.

5. *Lomer-L'mfint,* a village of. Bcauce, in the election Chartrei. *p.* Chartres. *S. Lorn & S. Jufi* a fmall town of Galcony, in the election of Land«. *p. S. Sever. S. Longis,* л town of Maine, tn the diocefe and election of Mans, *p, Beilefme. S. Lormelf* a place of Bretagne, in the diocefe and receipt of S. Bricux. *p. S. βruux. S. Lors,* л village of Poitou, in the election of Fontenay. *p. FonUnay-leComte. S. Lot,* a place of Picardy, in the election of Abbeville, *p. Abbeville.*
5. *Louand,* a fmall town of Touraine, in the election of Chinon. *p. Cblnon. S. Lcubt,* a village of Gafcony, in the diocefe and election of Com loinges. *p. Montre'jeau. S. Loubert,* a village of Bazadoîs, in the election of Condom, *p. Baxa.*
S. *Loubes,* a village of Guienne, in the diocefe and election of Bourdeaux. *p. Mont-de-.Marfan. S. Lovely* a village of Normandy, _ in the election of S. Lo. /. *$. Lo. S. Lo et'Pres-Authk,* a village of Normandy, in tlie election of Caen. *p. Cain. S. Louct-fur-tOJ'on,* a fmall town of Normandy, in the diocefc and election of Coûtances. *p. CoCtsnces. S. Lou t-for-Seulle,* л village 1-f Normandy, in the election of Caen. . *Caen.* G *S. Louet-fur-Seine,* a village ef Normandy, in the election ot" CoùÄnces. *p. Coûtances. S. Louis,* i. A village of Guienne, in the diocefe and election of Bourdeaux. *p. Mont lieu,* 2. A village of Périgord, in the diocefe and élection of Périgueux. *p. Mußdan.* 3. A village of Lower Languedoc, in the diocefe and receipt of Touloufe. *p. Liinoux.* 4. An abby near the town of Orléans, *p. Orleans. S. Louis-fur-Olm,* a figniory of Normandy, m the generality of Caën. *p. Coûtances. S. Loup.* i. A town of Anjou, in the election of Flèche, *p. Sable.* 2. A fmall town of Gâtinois, in the election of Nemours, *p. Boh-Commun.* 3. A village of Blie, in the election ©f Provins, *p. Provins.*
4. A village III Lyonnais, in the diocefe and election of Lyons, *p. Lynn.* 5. A village of Marche, in the election of Gueiet. *p. Cbcncraillcs.* 6. A village of Normandy, in the diocefe and election of Avranches. *p. Avranches.* 7. A village of Blefois, in the election of Romorantin. *p. Romorantin.* 8. A village of Upper Languedoc, in the diocefe and receipt of Touloufc. *p. Touloufe.* 9. A village of Bourbonnois, in the election of Moulins, *p. Varmnes.* то. A village of Condomois, in the diocefe and election of Condom./', *ijferac.* It. A village of Frarîche-Cor/ité, in the election of Dole. *p. Dole. 22.* A village-of Gafcony, in the diocefe and election ©f Comminges. *p. Montrerait.* 13. jA. village of Bourbonnois, in the election of S. Amand. *p. S-Amand.* 14. A village of Champagne, in the diocefe and election of Langrcs. *p. ÏAingres.* 15. A village of FrancheComté, in the bailiwick of Gray. *p. Gray.* 16. A village of Rouergue, in the el ¿tion of Villefranchc. *p. Vdlefranchc-de-Rouergue.* 17. A village of Dombes, in the chatcllany of ToivTei. *p. Belleville.* 18. A place of Normandy, in the election of Falaife, *p. Falaife.* 19. A figniory of Niver nois, in the diocefe and elecYiom o" Nevcrs. *p. Decife.* 20. A priory in Mai ne.
S. *Loup & les Cberolles,* a village of Bourbonnois, in the election, ofMoulins. *p. Mtml'ms.* S. *Loup-aux-Bois,* a village of Champagne, in the election of Rethel. *p. Launoy.* S. *Loup-dt-Buffigni,* a village of Champagne, in the diocefe and election of Troyes. *p. les Treis-Maifons.* S. *Loup-de-Fribous,* a figniory-of Normandy, in the election of PontTEvequc. *p. Liß.ux.* S. *Lwp-de-Garty* a town of Maine, in the diocefe and election of Mans» *p. May nne.* S. *Loup-de-Conûs,* a village of Gâtinois, in the election of Nemours. *p. Nemours.* S. *Lmp-dt-Maifiertif* a village of Burgundy, in the diocefe and bailiwick of Challón, *p. Be aune.* S. *L-Mf-de-Varennss,* a village of Burgundy, in the diocefe and bailiwick of Challón, *p. Challan.* S. *Loup-d'Ordon,* a village of Champagne, in the election of Joigny. *p. Joigny.* S. *L'MpenCkampagnet* a village of Champagne, in the election of Rethcl. *p. Bethel.* S. *Lcup-HorSj* a vilbgc of Normandy, in the diocefe and election of Bayeux.. *Bayeux.* S. *L:up-ks0rle'ans* a village of Orleannoifi, in the diocefe and election of Oi leans, *p. Orleans.* S. *LoKp-S.-Maguet,* a village of Bourbonnois, in the election of Gannat.. *Gannat.* S. *Loup-fur-Cher,* a place of Berry, in the diocefe of Beurges. *p. ißbudi.n..* S. *L-Mpvent,* a place of Champagne, in the election of Vitry. *p. tftry.* S. *LGuiha'm* a village of FrancheComté, in the bailiwick, of Poiignv. *p. Salins.* S. *Louvier,* a place of Touraine, near Leches, *p. Loches.*
Champagne, in the election of Vitry. *p. Vuy.* S. *L'mier-la-Populeuje,* a place of Champagne, in the election of Vitry. *p. Vitry.* S. *Lumine-dt-Couflaye,* a village of Bretagne, in the diocefe and receipt of Nantes, *p.* CHJJcn. S. *Lunaire,* a village of Bretagne, in the diocefe and receipt of S. Мак». /. 5. *Malo.* S. *Luperct,* a village of Beauce, in the diocefe and election of Chartres. *p Chartres.* S. *Lupicin,* a place of FrancheComté, in the diocefe and bailiwick of S. Claude, *p. S. Claude.* S. *Lupin,* a priory in the diocefe of Befancon, in Franche-Conité. S. *lye',* a fmall town of Orleaanois,4u- the diocf fe and election of Orleans, *p. OzЫam.* S, *Ly,ns,* a harplet in the diocefe of Senez,in Provence, *p. Caßellane.* S. *Lyons-fur-Ve-zcre,* a fmall town of Périgord, in the diocefe and elec tion of Sariat. *p. Satlat. Sair.te Leocadie,* a place of Rouffillon, in the vigucry of Scrdaignt. *p. Perpignan. Sie. Luxrade,* a village of Armagnac, in the election of Lomagne. *p. Beaumont-de-Lcmagne. Ste. Lit'iere,* a village of Champagne, in the election of Vitry. *p. Viry. t + Ste. L'. vrad 1.* A town of Agcn'oU, fi tua ted on the river Lot, in the diocefe and election of Agen; abouti leagues from Villcr.cuve-d Agen, 17 from Cahors, and 7 from Agen. *Bureau de foße.* 2. A village of Condomois, in the diocefe and election of Condom, *p. Condom. Stc. Lizaigne,* a village of Berry, in the election of IíToudtin.. *JJfiudun, Ste. Luce.* 1. A village of Guienne, in the diocefe and election of Bourdeaux. *p. B laye.* 2. A village of Dauphiny, in the diocefe and election of Grenoble, *p. Grenoble* 3 A village of Dauphiny, in the generality pf Grenoble, *p. Gap.* 4. A village

S. *Marnant,* a village of Dnuphïny, in the generality of Grenoble. *p. Grenoble.* (S. *MamelyZ* place of Beaujolois, in the election of Viliefranchc. *p. Bellt' mille,* S. *Mamert.* i. A village of Guienne, in the diocefe and election of Bourdeaux. *p. Bourdeaux.* Ђ. A village of Dauphiny, in the diocefe and election of Vienne, *p. tiédie.* 5. *Mamet.* I. A village of Lower Languedoc, in the diocefe and receipt of Uzés. *p. Uz/s.* 2. A village of Gafcony, in the diocefe and election of Commingeb. *p. Montrejcau.* S. *Mamme,* a village of Férigord, in the diocefe and election of Périgueux, *p. Mußdan.* Я *Mande,* a priory near Vincennes. *p. Vinccnnes.* S. *Manges,* a fmall town of Champagne, in the election of Sedan, *p. Sfdan.* S. *Mannev'teu,* a figniory of Normandy, in the election of Andely. *p. Gaïlkn.*

& *Manfuy-les-Toul,* an abby in the diocefe of Tout. *p. TouL* S. *Marrvieu.* i. A fmall town of Normandy, in the election of Vire. *f. Vire.* 2. A village of Normandy, in the election of Caen.. *Caen.* S. *Maquaire.* I. A town of Anjou, in the diocefe and election of Angers. *p. Angers, 2.* A fmall town of Poitou, in the election of Thouars. *p. Tbouars.* S. *Marc.* i. A fmall town of Aunis, in the diocefe and election of Rochelle, *p. Mauz/. 2.* A village of Auvergne, in the diocefe and election of S. Flour, *p. Flour.* 3. A village of Brie, in the diocefe and e!e¿tion of Meaux. *p. Dammartin.* 4. A villaxof Provence, in the diocefe and viguery of Aix. *p, Aix.* 5. A village of Quercy, in the diocefe and election of Montaubañ. *p. Montauban.* 6. A village of Marche, in the election of Gueret. *p. Gueiet.* 7. A village of Burgundy, in the bailiwick oí Châtilbu. /-. *CtatUlon,* 5. *Mare-Affranget,* л village-of Marche, in the election of Gueret, *p. Gueret.* S. *Alare-Aloulan,* a town of Marche, in the election of Gueret.. *Feuiiletin.*

¿'. *Marc-de-Frefne,* a village of Normandy, in the diocefe and election of Lifieux. / *Orbec.* S. *Marc-dc-Gra'tn.',* a market town of Normandy, in the election of Domfront, *p. Domfront.* S.. *Marc-dei-Vaux,* a village of Burgundy, in the diocefe and bailiwick of Challón,

p. Challón. S. *Marc-dc$-Pt;s* a village of Poitou, in the election of Fontenay. *p. Fontenay-le-Comte.* S. *Marc-Dou:lly9* a fmall town of Normandy, in the election of Vire. *p. Conde'-fur-Ncireau.* S. *Marc'de-BэeuШcи* I. A town of Marche, in the election of Gueret. *p. FeuilLiin.* a. A village of Auvergne, in the election of Combraillcs. *p. Chambón.* S. *Marc-le-Blane,* a village of Bretagne, in tne dioófefe and receipt of Nantes, *p. Renr.es.* S. *Marc-trh-Nuits,* a village of Burgundy, in the bailiwick of Semur-'.n-Auxois. *p. Nuits.* S. *Marc-fur-Couefnçrty* a viibge of Bretagne, in the diocefe and receipt of Nantes./». *Fougères.* S. *Marc-jur-Jjle,* a viibge of Bretagne, in the diocefe and receipt of Nantes, *p. Ancen'a.-S. Marcan,* a village of Bretagne, in the diocefe and receipt of Dol. *p. Dol.* Щ *Marceau,* a town ef Maine, in the diocefe and election of Mans, /. *Frtfnay.* S. *Mcrcel.* i. A town of Lower Languedoc, in the diocefe and receipt of Narbonne. *p. Narbonne.* 2. Д fmall town of Norman'Jy, in the election of Andely. *p. Gaillon.* 3. A village of Champagne, in the diocefe and election of Rheims, *p. Retbel.* 4. A village of Burgundv, in the diocefe and bailiwick of Challón-*f.* Challo. 5. A village of Vivarais, in the receipt of Viviers, *f.* S. *Peray.* 6, A village of Bourbonnais, in the election of Montlucon. *p. Montlucon,* 7. A village of Rouergue, in the flection of Villefr?. nche. *p. Villefrancke-dc-Rcuergue.* 8. A village of Gafcony, in the diocefe and election of Comminges. *p. Montrejeau.* 9. A village of Dauphiny, in the áiocefe and election of Grenoble, *p, ¡lourgán.* 10. A village of Bretagne, in the dioccfc and receipt of Vannes. *f. Vannes.* 11 A village of Quercy, in the diocefe and election of Cahors. *J. Cahcrs.* 11. A place of BrciTe, in ithc bailiwick of Bourg, *p. Bour-enBrfife.* 13. A place of Upper Languedoc, in the diocefe and receipt of Alby. *p. Toulcufe.* 14. A place of.Melfin, in the diocefe and receipt of Metz. *p. Mefx.* 15. A place of Provence, near Marfeille. *p. Marjdlle.* 16. A chatellany in the generality and election of Paris.

S Marcel-Conques j a village of Rouergue, in the election of Villeftanche. *p. Villefrancht-d-'Rcu.rrue.* S. *Marcel-dyArdeche,* a town of Lower Languedoc, in the diocefe and receipt of Viviers, *p. le Pont-S. Ifprit.* $. *Marcel-de-Car eyr et,* a village of X-ower Languedoc, in the diocefe and receipt of Uzés. *p. Bagno/s.* S. *Marcel-de-Fonfcuilloufe,* a fmall town of Lower Languedoc, in the áiocefe and receipt of Alais, *p.* S. *Jean-de-Gardonitigue.* S. *Marcel-cn-Montluton* a village «f Bourbonnois, in the election of Montlucon. *p. Montlucon.* ф S. *Marcel-en-Nercnde,* a village of Forez, in the election of Roanne, *p.* У. *Simpborien.* S. *Marcel-Efclaire,* a village of Beaujolois, in the élection of Villefranche, *p. Villefrancbe,* S. *Marcel-les-Annonay,* a village of Vivarais, in the diocefe and receipt of Viviers. *p»* Anncnay. S. *Marcel-les-Argenron y* a village Ђ£ Berry, witb a chatellany in the election of Châtre, *p. Argtnton.* S. *Afartel-les-Sauxets,* a village oí Dauphiny, in the election of Montclimart. *p. MonleUmart.* S. *M.irt-cl-fur-le-Mont,* a village of Champagne, in the election of Rethel. *p. Rule!.* S. *Marcelin,* a village of Burgundy, in the dmcefc and bailiwick of Macon, *p. Macon.* S. *MazczШn.* i. A town of Dauphinv, fituated in a fruitful country near the river Ifere, in the diocefe of. Vienne, and generality of Grenoble; 13 leagues from Grenoble, 6 from Romans, and Ю from Valence. *Bureau de poße.* 2. A town of Forez, in the eleftion of Montbrifon. *p. Monti ifor.* 3. A village of Dau» phiny, in the diocefe and election of Vienne, *p. Vienne.* 4. A village of Dauphiny, in the diocefe of Gap. *p. Gap.* S. *MarceHin-d'sfncette,* a fmall town of Dauphiny, in the diocefe and generality of Grenoble, *p. Grenoble.* S. *Marcellin-les-Vuijon,* a village of Dauphiny, in the election of Montelimart. *p. Nions.* S. *Marcery,* a village of Périgord» in the diocefe and eleition of Sarlat. *p. Bergerac.* S. *Maney,* a village of FrancheComte, in the receipt of VefouL *p. Vcjoul.* S. *Marcey-les-JuJJcy,* a priory iu the diocefe of Bciancon.

S. *Marcea.* I. A village of Normandy, in the election of Carcntan. *p. Carenan,* 2. A village of Normandy, in the election of Bayeux. *p. ifigM S. M.trcoutes-Ißesdef* iflands or the coaft of Normandy, one called the iile of Amont, the other the ill of Aval. *p. Coûtâmes.* S. Marcoude-t'Jße, a pariih of Normandy with a château, in the diocefe of Coûtances. *p. Coûtantes.* S. Marcj, a village of Piordf, ia the diocefe and election of Amicus. . *p. Amiens.* S. Mard, a viUage of Picatdy, ia the diocefe and election of SoiíTons. *f. Sojföns.* S. Mard-enCaudyt a village of Picardy, in the election of Mondidier *p. Roye.* S. Mard-let-RouJfy, & S. MardJur-les-Mont, villages of Champagne, in the diocefc and election of Châlons. *f. Chalons.* S, Murd-tes-Triots, a village of Picardy, in the election of Mondidier. *p. MondJier.* S. Mard-jur-Aure, a village of Champagne, in the election of Ste. 'Manéhould. *p. &e. Manéhould.* S. Mardes, a village of Normandy, in the election of ront-Audemcr. *p, Pont-Audcmtr* S. Mards, ◻ town of Champagne, m the diocefe and election of Troycs. *p. 'Trojes.* S. Marecby a fmall town of Agénois, in the diocefe and election of Agen. /. *Agen.* S. Marian, a village of Bourbonnois, in the election of S. Amand. *p. S. Amand.* S. Marian-a" Auxerre an abby în the city of Auxerre. S. Mariai) a fmall town of Guienne, in the diocefe and election of Bourdecux. *p. Bourdeaux.* S. Mais. I. A village of Normandy, in the election of Arques.. *Belhmare. z.* A village of Brie, in the election of Provins, *p. Provins.* 3. A village of Anjou, in the election of Bcaugé. *p. le Lude.* S. Mars-de-Coußayej a village of Bretagne, in the diocefe and receipt of Nantes, *p. Nafites.* S. Mars-de-la-Briere, a town of Maine, in the diocefe and election of Mans. *p. Conner/.* S. Mars-de-la-Ja'dk, a village of Bretagne, in the diocefe and r.ceipt of Nantes, *p. Anccms.* S. Man-du-Ccr, a village of Maine, iu the election of Çhâteau(fu-Loir. *p. Ctâieau-du-Lotr..* S. Mars-du-DeJert. 1. A fmall town of Maine, in thè diocefe and tlcftion of Mans. p. *le Mans.* a. A vi'lage of Bretagne, in the Jiocefe anj recc'pt of Nantes, *p. Nantes.* 8. Mars-en-Pubelliardt a village of Poitou, in the èlection of FontenaVi *p ¥ ontenay-le-Comte.* S. Mars-la-Lande9 a village of Poitou, in the election of Niort, *Niort'.* S. Mars-Jvr-Cclmcet, Êf ó *Marsfur-ta-Futaye,* towns of Maine, in the election of Mayenne, *p. Mayenne.* S. Marjal c9 Belpuigt a village of Rouffillon, in the diocefe ancVviguery of Perpignan, *p. Perpignan* S. Marfaud, a village of Saintonge, in the election of S. Jean-d'Ang'Iy. *p.* S. Jean-d" Angily.. S. Alarfaultj a village of Poitou,, in the election of Thouars. *p. la Chat (igné raye.* S. ?Marjolle a town of Poitou, in the election of Loudun. *p. Loudun.* S. Martial. I. A fmall town of Périgord, in the diocefe and election of Sarlat. *p. Sarlat.* 2. A fmall town of Lower Languedoc, in the diocefe and receipt of Viviers. /». *Pliers,* 3. A fmall town of Lower Languedoc in the dioccfe and receipt of Alais, *p. Sumejne.* 4. A fmall town of Agenois, in the diocefe and election of Agen. *p. Agen.* 5. A village of Angoumois, in the diocefe and election of Angoulemc. *p. Confolans.* 6. A village of Guicnne, in the diocefeand election oí Bourdeaux. *p.* S. *Macaire.* 7. A village of Auvergne,, in the diocefe and election of S. Flour, *p.* S. *Flour.* 8. A place of Upper Languedoc, in the diocefe of Alby, *p. Cajlres.* S. Mariial-d1 Antraigues, S. Martial-de-Gimelle, 6? S. Martial-leVxeuX) villages» of Limofm, in theelection of Tulles, *p. tulles.* S. MartiaUde-Courcrs, a figniory of Auvergne, in the Comte of Aurilhc. *p. Auiilhc.* S. Manhd-dc-R'.beyratj a fmall town of Párigord, in the diocefe antfc election of Périgueux. *p. Ribeyrat. $.* Martial-dc-ValcttSy a (malí town of Pétigord, in the diocefe GS *p. Melun.* 16. A village of Champagne, in the election of Nogent. *p. Ncgent-Jur-Seine.* 17. A village of Hainaut, in the government of Quènoy. *p. le ¿¡uénoy.* 18. A village of Alface, in the bailiwick of Ville, *p. Scbelefiat.* 19. A village of Poitou, in the election of Chatellerault. *p. Chatellerault.* 20. A village of Anjou, in the elcition of Baugé. *p. Bauge.* 21. A village of Périgord, in the diocefe and election of Périgueux, *p. Périgucux.* 22. A village of Marche, in the election of Bourgancuf. *p. Bturganeuf.* 23. A village of Gabardan, in tke diocefe of Dax. *p. Condom.* 24. A village of Gafcony, in the receipt of Bigorre. *p. Tarées.* 25. A village of Picardy, in the election of Abbeville, *p. Abbeville.* 26. A village of Armagnrc, in the election of Aftarac. *p, Mirr.dc.* 27. A village of Armagnac, in the diocefe and receipt of Auch. *p. Auch.* 2S. A village of Armagnac, in the election of Lomagnc./. *G' ifol/es.* 29. A village of Armagnac, in the election of RivièreVerdun. /'. *Grenade.* 30. A village of Dauphiny, in the diocefe and election of Vienne, *p. Vanne,* 31. A village of Bretagne, in the diocefe and receipt of Quimper. *p. Щи'трег.* 32. A village of Quercy, in the dioccfe and election oí" Montauban. *p. Montauban.* 33. A village of Bafadois, in flie election of Condom, *p. Вьъаг.* 34-A village of Dombes, in the chatellanv of Chalamont. *p. Rûurg-en-B-eJJè,* 35. A village of Navarre, in the diocefe of Bayonnc. *p. Pau.* 36. A village of Condomois, in the dioccfe and election of Condom, *p. Condom.* 37. A village of Picardy, in the generality of Amiens, *p. Bodogne,* 38. A village of Provence, in the vigucry of Seine. *p. Digne.* 39. A priory of Normandy,-in the election of Eu. *p. Eu.* 40. See *Hommes-dc-S.-Martin.* S. Marth) la ville, a village of Bretagne, in the dioccfe and receipt of Nantes. /. *Nantes,* S. Martin-à-la-R;vicré, a village óf Picardy, in the election of Guifc. /. *Güije.* S. Martin-au-Bф. I. A village of Normandy, in the election of Gifors. *p. Gifors. %.* A village of Normandy, in the election of Eu. *f. Aumale.* 3. A íigniory and priory in the election of Arques, *p. Dieppe.* S. Mart'tn-au-Tartre, a village of the ifle of France, in the diocefe and election of Paris, *p. Luzarcbes.* S. Martin-aux-Arbres, a village of Normandy, in the diocefe and election of Rouen, *p. Tervji/e.* S. Marùn-aux-Buy a village of Pkardy, in the election of Mondidier, *f* A 5". Martin-aux-Buneaux, a market town of Normandy, in the election of Caudebeo. *Fecamp.* S. Martln-aux-Champs y a village of Champagne, in the election of Vitry. *p. Vitry.* S. Martin-aux-Chefnes," an abby in the diocefe of Metz. "*p. Metz.* S. Martin-eux-jfnmea:-x-£T'Amiens, a convent in Amiens. S. Martín-Cantalea y a village of Auvergne, in the diocefe and eledtion of S. Flour, *p. & Flour.* S. Martin-*Chargnaty* a village of Marche, in the eleftion of Guerct. *p. Gueret.* S. *Martm-Choquel,* a village of Pioirdy, in the generality of Amiens. *p. Boulogne.* S. *Martin-a'Abaty* a fmall town of Otléannois, in the diocefe and election of Orleans, *p. Orleans.* S, *Martnd"Ablon,* a village of Dauphiny, in the diocefe and election of Vienne. *p. Vienne.* S. *Martin-d Agonnat,* a fmall town of Périgord, in the diocefe and election of Périgueux.. *Bergerie.* S. *Marûnd'Ahe,* a village of Dauphiny, in the diocefe and election of Grenoble, *p. Grenoble.* S. *Martin-dAlas, &? 5. AfartintfsJfry,* villages of Saintonge, jn the oWcfc and election of Saintes, *p, &:n;est* S. *Martin-eFAlbres,* a village of Condomois, in the diocefe and elec-' tion of Condom, *p. Condom.* S. *Martind Amblu,* a town of Champague, in the election of Epernay. *p. Epernay.* S. *Marûn-d Ampremont, Si Martin-a Allies,* villages of Agénois, in the diocefe and election of Agen. *p. Agen.* S. *Martin-d Ancette* a fmall town of Dauphiny, in the generality of Grenoble, *p. Grenoble.* S. *Martial'-d"Après,* a village of Normandv, in the election of Vcrneuil./. *VerneuiL* S. *Martin-tCArc,* a village of Lower Languedoc, in the diocefe and receipt of Viviers, *p. Viviers.* S. *Mart'm-d'Afmeres.* See *Ajnieres?* S. *Marûn-d'lAudonviHe,* a village of Normandy, in the generality of Caen. *p. Caen.* i S. *Martin-dAuxignjy* a village of Berry, in the diocefe and generality of Bourges, *p. Bourges.* S. *Martind'Eniraigucs,* a village of Poitou, in the election of Niort. *p. Niort.* S. *Mar tind'Eβraux,* a village of Forez, in the election of Roanne, *p. Roanne.* S. *Marthîd'ExidtuUy* a village of Périgord; in the diocefe and élection de Périgueux. *p. Cbabano'is.* S. *Martîn-dc-Barbas,* a village of Agénois, in the diocefe and election of Agen. *p. Agen.* S. *Marûn-de-Baudemor.t,* a village of Normandy, in the election of Gifors. *p. Gijors.* S. *Martïn-dc-Blagny,* a village ofl Normandy, in the diocefe and election of Baycux. *p. Buyeux.* S. *Martin-de-Binfcj'se,* a village of Normandy, in the election of S. Lo. *p. S Lo.* S. *Martin-deBirne,* a village of Agénois, in the diocefe and cleótioft of Agen. *p. Agen.* S. *MariindeB.afane,* a village of Provence, in the diocefe and viguery of Apt. *p. Apt.* and receipt of Viviers, *p. Vivien.* S. *Mazûn-dc-Veulhs,* a fmall town of Normandy, in the election of Arques, *p. Dieppe,* S. *Martin-dts-Aires,* an abby in diocefe of Troycs, in Champagne. *p. Troyes.* S. *Mart'm-iet-Altxbtt,* a village of Bourbonnois, in the election of Gannat. *p. Ganr.at.* S. *Mariin-des-Champs.* I. A village of Gâtinois, in the election of Gien. *p.* S. *Farjeau.* г. A village of Brie in the election of Coulomiers. *p. la Forte-Gaucher.* 3. A village of Brie, in the election of Provins, *p. Provins.* 4. A village of Normandy, in the diocefe and election of Avranches. *p. Arranches.* 5 village of Burgundy, in the diocefe and bailiwick of Challón, *p. Chalhti.* 6. A place of Normandy, in thé election of S. Lo. *p.* S. *Lo.* S. *Mart'm-des-Combes,* a village of PérigorèÇin the diocefe and election of Périgueux. *p. Pe'rigueux.* S. *Martm-des-Entre'es,* a village of Normandy, in the diocefe and election of Baveux, *p. Baycux.* S *Martin-des-Fontaines,* a village of Poitou, in the election of Fonte « nay. *p. Tbhe.* S. *Martindes-Laix,* a village of Bourbonnois, in the elusion of Moulins, *p. M Jim.* 5. *Martin-des-Lande,* a village of Normandy, in the election of Falaife. *p. FaLife.* S. *Man'm-dcS-Lauricres,* a village of Saintonge, in the election of Marrennes. *p. Maremtes.* S. *Martin-des-Monts,* a fmall town of Maine, in the diocefe and election of M ns. *p. la F¿rte'-Bernard.* S. *Ma: tin-des-Noyeri,* a fmall town of Poitou, in the election of Fonte-, nay. *p. la Ejffans.* S. *Martin-des-Pres.* I. A village of Perche, in the election Verncujl. *p. Verneuil.* 2. A place of Agénois, in the diocefe and election of Agen. *p. Agen.* S. *Martir.-des-Pu'tts,* a place of tion of Angoulème. *p. Villefagnan. Martin-du-Fouillouxy* a village of Poituu, in the diocefe and election of Poitiers, *p. Poitiers.* S *Martin-duFrifnCy* a village of Bugey, in the bailiwick of Belley. *p. Cet don.* A*Zirtin-duHonfi',* a village of Nivernois, in the eleétion of Charité, *p. Coj'ne.* S. *Martin-du-Lac,* a village of Burgun iy, in the baFliwick of Semur-en-Briennois. *p. la Pacaudiere.* S. *Martin-duManozzy* a village of Normandy, in the election of Montivilliers. *p. Havjicur,* S. *Martin-du-Mefnifty* a village of Normandy, in the election of Valognes. *p. Valognes.* S. *Martin-du-Mont.* I. A village of Burgundy, in the bailiwick of BrciTe. *p. Louans.* 2. A village of Burgundy, in the bailiwick of S. Laurent, *p.* §. *Seine.* 3. A village of Burgundy, in the bailiwick of Châtillon. *p. Châtillon.* S. *Martin-du-Parcy* a village of Normandy, in the election of PontAudemcr. *p. Pont-Audcmer.* S. *Manin-du-Pearsy* a vilhge of Beatice, in the election of Cháteaudun. *p. Bonneval.* S. *Martin-duPlcβs,* a vilhge of Normandy, in the diocefe and generality of Rouen, *p. Rouen.* S. *Martïn-du-Prc'y* a village of Nivernois, in the ehrition of Charité-furLoire, *p. Cofre.* S. *Murtin-du-Puy* a village of Bazadois, in the election of Condom, *p. Bazas.* S. *Martin-du-Tartre.* 1. A village of Champagne, in the diocefe and election of Sens. *p. Sens.* 2. A vilage of Burgundy, in the diocefe and receipt of Mâccn. *p. Mâccn.* 3. A village of Burgundy, in the diocefe of ChaUon. *p. Dijon.* S. *Murtin-en-ElayeSy* a village of Guienne, in the diocefe and election of Bourdcaux. *p. ffflaye.* S. *Martin-enBr e£'e,* a village' »f of Breflc, in the bailiwick of Bourg. *p. Bourg-cn-BreJfe.* S. *Martir.-Leβra,* a village of Foyez, in the election of Montbrifon. *Chamelles.* S. *Martin-k-Vi¿l,* i, A village of Normandy, in the election of Bernay. *p. GrandfWe.* 2. A village of Normandy, in the xlioeefc and election of Coùtances. *p. Coûtâmes.* S. *Martin-le-Vieux.* ï. A village of Upper Languedoc, in the dioccfe and receipt of CarcaíTonne. *p Cariajfonne.* 2. A village of Lirarfm, in the diocefe and election of Limoges, *p. Cbalus.* 3. A village of Xormandy, in the diocefe and election of Baveux, *p. Baycux. Martn-le-V'mcux,* a village of Dauphiny, in the dioccfe and election f Grenoble, *p. Grenoble.* S. *Martin-lesCoucbes,* a pariih of Burgundy, in the bailiwick of Monteenis. *p. Autun.* S. *Martin-les-Daudes,* a place of Champagne, in the diocefe and electinn of Troyes. *p. Treats.* S. *Martin-lesVinets,* a place of Champagne, in the diocefe and election of Chalons, *p. Cbalcns.* S. *Martin-Lezayre,* a village of Flanders, in the fubdelegation of Caifel. *p. CaJJel.* S. *Mzrtin-les-Boulogne,* a village of Picardy, in the generality of Amiens. *f. Boulogne,* S. *Martin-les-Faiaogney,* a village of Franche-Compté, in the bailiwick of Vefoul. *p. Lure,* S. *Martin-la-Langresy* a place of Champagne, in the diocefe and election of Langres. *p. Laigrcs.* S. *JIa2 tin-les-Troyes,* a town of Champagne, in the diocefe and ejection of Troyes. *p. Troyes.* S. *Martïn-t'Heureux',* a village of Champagne, in the dioccfe and election of Rheims, *p. Rkâm.* S. *Mavt'w-LQngueSue,* a village of Picardy, in the elect or. of Clermont. *f» Clermont,* 5. *Martin-tOrtbi",* a village of Kormandy, in the election of Neufchâtcl. *p. Neufcbatel.* S, *Mertin-frh-Hcvficttr,* г village S. *Martinet,* a village of Li raofin, in the diocefc of Limoges, *p. ttmoges,* S. *Marthry,* a town of Gafcony, iö the iHoccie and election of Com mhiges. *p. S Gaudeits.* S. *Mary,* a place of Auvergne, in the election of AuriHac. *p. Iffoire.* S. *Maryy* or S. *May,* a place of Provence, in the diocefc and viguery of Sifteron. *p. Sißeron.* S. *Mary-le-Groiy* a fmall town of Auvergne, in the diocefe aud election of S. Flour, *p. & Flour.* S. *МЛ2у-n-Pfain,* a fmall town of-Auvergne, in the election of Brioude. *p. Brhude.* St *MafmeSy* a village of Champagne, in the diocefc and election of: Rheims, *p. Rheims.* S. *Majry,* a fmall town of Angoumois, in the dincefe and election of Angotïlémc, *p. laRochefoucauh.* S. *Mathieu,* a town of Poitou, in the election of Confolans. *p. RccheCkouard.* S. *Mathur'm-de-Larehant,* a town of Gàtinois, in the election of Nemours, *p.* "*Beaufort.* S. *Maire,* a village of Quercy, in the diocefe and election of Cahofs. *f. Cahors.* S. *Maucety* a vtlage of Auvergne, in the election of Aurillac. *p. Aurillac.* S. *Maudan,* a village of Bretagne, în the diocefc and receipt of S. Brieux. *p.* S. *Brieux.* S. *Maude',* a village of Bretagne, in the diocefe and receipt of S. Malo. *p. Dinan.* S. *Maugand,* a village of Bretagne, in the diocefc and receipt of S, Malo. *p. S.Malo.* S. *Maü/vis,* a fmall town of Picardy, in the diocefe and election of Ami?ns. *p. Amiens,* S. *Maur.* i, A fmall town of Picardy, in the diocefe and election of Bcauva's. *p. Beawvais.* 2 A fmall town of Berry, in the election of Chatcauroux. *p. Châteaurcux.* 3. A village of Beauce, in the election of Châteaudun. *p. Bonntval.* 4. A village of Franche-Comté, in the bailaiwick of L' ns-le-Saunier. *p-Lonsle-Saunier.* 5. A village of Armagnac, in the election of Aiiarae. *p. Aiirande,* S. *Maur-de-Bejfe,* a village of Bourbon nois, in the election of Montluton. *p. Mcntiuan.* S. *Maur-d¿-Cbarocbe.* See *Cbarocbe.* . S *Maur-dez-Boh,* a village of Normandy, in thcelection of Vire. *p.Vire.* S. *Maur-des-Fo/fez,* a town or the Ifle of France, in the diocefe and election of Paris, *p. Vmcer.nes.* S. *Maur-j:.r-Loirey* a town of Anjou, in the election of Saumur. /. *let Roßers.* / , S. *Manràly* a village of Marche in the election of Bourgancuf. *p. Bourgatteuf.* S. *Maurice,* I. A fmall town of Normandy, in the election of Falaife. *p. Carentan.* 2. A fmall town of Bourbonnoi», in the election of Gannat. *p. Feuilletin.* 3. A fmall town of Auvergne, in the diocefe and election of S. Flour, *p. Riom.* 4. A village of Foret, in the election of Roanne. *p. Roanne.* 5. A village of Normandy, in the election of Valognes. *p. Valcgr.es.* 6. A village of Normandy, in the election of Caudebcc. *p. Caudebec.* 7. A village of Normandy, in the election of Verneuil. *p. VtmeuM.* 8. A village of N01 m.Vndy, in the diocefe and election cf Rouen, *p. Rouen.* 9. A. village of Normandy, in the election of Neufchattl. *p. Ñeufâdtel.* 10. A viliage of Burgundy, in the diocefe and bailiwick of Challón, *p. Challón.* il. A village of Burgundy, in the diocefc and bailiwick of Màcon. *p Mâcon. iz.* A village of Bugey, in the generality of Dijon, *p. Belley.* 13. A village of Forez, in the election of Montbrifon. *p.* S. *Etienne.* 14. A village of Perche, in theclection of Mortagne. *p. Cbamrond.* 15. A village of Beauce, in the election of Dourdan. *p. Dourdan.* 16. A village of Beauce, in the election ef ChateauJun. *p. Bonncval.* 17. A village of Berry, in the election of in rhe election ef Verneuil. *p. Fer neuiL* S. *Mcfm'm.* I. A town of Poitou, in the election of Thouars. /. *Paujjauge.* 2. A village of Champagne, în the diocefe and election of Troyes. *p. träfet,* S. *Meßmnde-Micyt* a fmall town of Orléannois, in the diocefe and cleft ion of Orléans, *p. Orleans.* S. *MeUàl,* a place of Normandy in the election of Conches, *p. £ю2 eux.* S. *Meury,* a village of Dauphin y» in the election of Grenoble, *p. Grenoble.* S. *Mexant,* a vilbge of Limofin, in the election of Brives. *p. Tulles.* S. *MextMj* a village of Touraine, in the election of Chinon. *p. Cb'tn:n.* S *Miymy,* a fmall town of Limofin, in the election of Brives. *p. Brives,.* S. *Mezard)* a vilbge of Condomois, in the election of Condom. *p+ ie Temple,* S. *Miardt* a village of Forez, in the clc¿tion of Monbrifon. *p. Montbnjon. Ü, Micaut,* a pariíli of Burgundy, compofed of feveral hamlets, in th diocefe of Challón. *p, Chullon.* S. *M-ekel, i.* A village of Touraine, in the election of Chinop. *p. Loches,* 2. A village of Normandy, in the election of Falaife. *p. Г Aigle,* 3. A village of Noimandy, in the election of Lions, *p. E-vrtux.* 4. A village of Normandy, in the election of Montivilliers. *p.* S. *R:mtàn,* 5, A vilbge-of Bazadois, *in* the election of Condom, *p. Baaas.* 6. A vilbge of Picardy, in the generality of Amiens, *p. Mcnti tuil-jurmer.* 7. A village of Ctînois, in the election of Montargts. *p. Ed s-Cowmzttt, %* , A village of Upper Laugueduc, in the diocefe and receipt of Rieux, *p. Tenleiife.* 9. A village of Lower Languedoc, in the diocefe and revxipt of Lodeve *p. Lodevt.* 10. A village cf Agénuia, in tht áioccíj and electîon of Agen, *p Valence d'Aven* II. A village of Périgord, in the diocefe and eleftion of Sarlat. ' *p. Sariat.* II. A village of Gafcony, in the eleftion of Landes, *p. Dax.* 13. A village of Berry, in the diocefe and election of Bourges, *p. Bourges.* 14. A village of' Champagne, in the diocefe and election of Langres. *p. Langres.* 15. A village of Poitou, in the eleftion of Confolatis. *p. Confoiam.* 16. A village of Dauphiny, in the diocefe and eleftion of Grenoble, *p. Gr&nobUs* 17. A village of Dauphiny, in the diocefe and eleftion of Vienne, *p. Vienne.* 18. A village of Dauphiny, in the dioce'e and eleftion of Gap. *p. Gap.* 19. A village of Rouifllon, in the eleftion 0/ Villefranche. *p. Rhodes,* 20. A village of Provence, in theviguery of Forcalquier. *p. Forcalquier.* 21. A village of Qucrcy,inthe diocefe and eleftion of Cahors. *p. Cabors.* 22. A village of Armagnac, in the eleftion of Aftarac. . *Mirande,* 23. A village of Navarre, in the diocefe of Bayonne. *p. Pau.* 24. A village of Guienne, injthe-diocefe and eleftion of Bourreaux, *p. Bourdeaux.* 25. A place of Upper Languedoc, in the diocefe and receipt of Touioufe. *p. Touloufe.* S-6. A place of Condomois, in the a'.ocefe and eleftion of Condom, *p. Condom.* 27. See *Mont-S. Michel. S. Mkhel-Chalon,* a village of Dauphiny, in the diocefe and eleftion of Vienne, *p. Vienne. S. Michel-d'A-ltcourt,* a village of Normandy, in the eleftion of Liens. *p. Ecoay. S. Michel-d AllJfecourt,* a place of Picardy, in the diocefe and eleftion of Beauvais. *p. Beawvah. S. Michel'-de-Boulogne,* a village of Lower Languedoc, In the diocefe and receipt of Viviers, *p. "Privai. S. Mtcktl-de-Cbabrïlhanaux.* Sec *Chabñthanaux.* iL *M'.cbel-de-Cbaliol,* a village of bauphlny, in the eleftion of Gap. *p. Gap.*

ëVigord, in the diocefe and election of Peri gueux, *p. Périgueux. S. Micbel-des-Loups,* a village of Normandy, in the diocefe and election of Avranches. *p. Grand-ville, S. Micbel-du-Bois.* i. A village of Anjou, in the diocefe and election of Angers, *p. Angeri.* z. A village of Touraine, in The election of. Loches, *p. Preu'dly. S. Michel-en-Beaumont,* a village of Dauphin y, in the diocefe and election of Grenoble, *p. Grenoble. S. Michel-en-Brenne,* a town of Touraine, on-the confines of Berry, in the election of Châteauroux. *p. Cbâteauroux. S. Mkbel-en-Grcve,* a village of Bretagne, in the diocefe and receipt of Treguicr. *p. Gumgamp. S. Micbel-en-Landiras,* a village of Guienne, in the diocefe and election of Bourdeaux./. *Liboume. S. Mkbel-en-C'Herm,* or *en Γ Ernte,* a village of Poitou, in the election of Fontcnay. *p. Lucen. S. Mxbel-en-V Hermitage,* a fmall town of Poitou, in the election of Fontenay. *p. Fontenay-le-Comie.* S. Michel-en-*Thieracbe,* a village of Picardy, in the election of Guife. *p. У er vim. S. Michel Ïa-Rvvière,* a fmall town of Périgord, in the diocefe and election of Périgueux. . *Liboume. S. Michel-Laurier e,* a village of Limoíin, in the diocefe and election of Limoges, *p. Limoges. S. Michel'-It-Cloud,* a fmall town of Poitou, in the election of Fontenay./. *F ont en ay-le-Comte. S. Michel-h-ance,* a village of XiOwer Languedoc, in the diocefe and receipt of Viviers, *p. Vwiers S. Rüchtl-Paladru,* a village of Dauphiny, in the diocefe and election of Vienne, *p. Vienne. S. Michel-prh-Gùng 'mpj л* village of Bretagne, in the di сек and receipt of Treguicr. *p Guwgamp. S. Micbci-lous-Ccndrieu,* a village of Forez, in the election of S. Etienne, *p. Yxnne. S. Michel-fur-Orge,* a village of the iíle of France, in the diocefe and election of Paris, *p. Linas. S. Mitre,* a village of Provence, in the viguery of Aix. *p. le Marùguesm S, Moard,* a town of Touraine, on the Loire, in the diocefe and election of Tours, *p. Tours. S. Molpb,* a village of Bretagne, in the diocefe and receipt of Nantes. *p. Guerande. S Mont.* See *Saramcn.* , *S. Montan,* a fmall town of Lower Languedoc, in the diocefe and receipt of Viviers, *p. Vtllcnewve-de-Berg. S. Mere,* a village of Champagne, in the election of Tonnerre *p. Aux erre. S. Morel сЭ Corbon,* a village of Champagne, in the election of Rcthel. *p. Ret bel. S. Muart,* a fmall town of Guienne, in the diocefe and election of Bourdeaux. *p. Bowdeaux. S. Mûris Ê? Montchenu,* a village of Dauphiny, in the election of Romans, *p. Romans. S. Muris-Monteymond,* a fmall town of Dauphiny, in the diocefe and election of Grenoble, *p. Grenoble. S. Muris-prh-Montbonoud,* a village of Dauphiny, in the diocefe and election of Grenoble, *p. Grenoble. S. Myon,* a villaje of Auvergne, in the election of Riom. *p. Riom.* Sainte Madelaine-de-Bournei, a village of Agenois, in the diocefe and election of Agen. *p. Agen.* Ste. *Madelaine-de-Châteaudun.* See *Cbâteaudun.* Ste. *Magnanee,* a village of Burgundy, in the bailiwick of Avalon. *p. Avalon.* Ste. *May.ure,* an abby in the diocefe of Bordeaux, *p. Bourdeaux.* Ste. *Mjndin 'a,* a (mail town" of Auvergne, in the diocefe and election of S. Flour, *p. S. Fl ur.* Ste. *Manckculd,* or *MerJbould,* an ancient and confub-rnble city of Cliampagne, the capital of Argonne, ftuated between two rocks on the river Aifnc; in the diocefe of Rheims and generally of Chalons; it has a governor, is the feat of a bailiwick, ele&îon, Sec. it was anciently very ftrong but the fortifications have been long dcmoliihed and furVered to decay; io leagues from Chalons, 18 from Vitry le François, 7 from Grandpre, 19 from Mczicrcs, i4from Mou zon, г o from Rheims, 33 from Soifïbns, 10 from Verdun, 25 from Metz, 24 from Longwy, 37 from Sarrelouis, 43 from Sarcbruck, 20 from Montmedy, 29 from Sedan, 56 from Liege, 29 from Thionville, 69 from Lille, 28 from Троуеь, 31 from Nancv, 38 from Lunevilk-, 49 frpm Sarrcbourg, 55 from Deux Ponts, 51 from Biche, 64 from Fort Louis, 74 from Landau, 82 from Spire, 68 from Stralburg, 75 from Befancon, 4 from Clermont-enArgonnc, and 48 from Paris. *Bureau de fofie..,* Ste. *Margueiite.* i. An ifland in the mediterranean on the coafl: of Provence, it has 3 forts. *p. Cannes* 2. A fmall town of Normandy, in the election of Couches, *p. Eurcux.* 3. A village of Normandy, in the election of Neufchatel. *p. Aumale.* 4. A village of Touraine, in the dioccfe and election of Tours, *p. Tours,* 5. A village of Normandy, in the diocefe;пвД election of Coùtances. *p. Cotbances,* 6. A village of Provence, in the viguery of Toulon, *p. Cannes.* 7. *A* place of Metfin, in the diocefe and receipt of Metz. *p. Meta. Sie. Marguerite-de-Viette,* a im ail town of Normandy, in the election of Falaifc. *p. Trouard.* Ste. *Marguerte-en-Ouche,* a village of Normandy, in the election of Bcrnay. *p. Cbambrois.* Ste. *Marguerite-fa-Figierc,* a village of Lower Languedoc, in the diocefe and receipt of Viviers, *p. Viviers.* Ste. *Mdrgmnte-fur-DuclerC)* a fmail t/wn of Normandy, in the election of Caudebec. *p. Caudebec.* Ste. *Marguerite-fui-Faufil/e,* a village of Notmandy, in the election *oí* Caudebec. *p. FaunUle,* Ste. *Marie.* 1. A town of th We of Ré, in the diocefe and election of Rochelle, *p.*

IjLeJU-Re'. 2. A town of Saintonge, in the diocefe and election of Saintes./'. *Suintes,* д. A village of Bretagne, in the diocefe and receipt of Nantes, *p. Nantes.* 4. A village of Auvergne, in the diocefe and election of S. Tplour. *p. Aurillaci* 5. A village of Burgundy, in the bailiwick of Arnay-le-Duc. *p. Dijon* 6. A village of Limofin, in the election of Tulles, *p. Tulles.* 7. À village of Armagnac, in the election of Rivière-Verdun, *p. Grenade.* 8. A village of Dauphiny, in the generality of Grenobí?. *p. Grenoble.* Ste Marie ö 5. *Remain,* a villageof Dauphiny, in the diocefe and election of Vienne, *p. Vienne.* Ste. Ma: ic & le-Pontde-Panyy a parilh of Burgundy, in the diocefe of Dijon, *p. Dijon.* Ste. M:rie-à-Pyy a village of Champagne, in the election of Rethci. *p. Rheims.* Ste, Лlл'.e-au Bofcy a village of Normandy, in the election of Montivilliers. *p. Fecamp,* Ste. *Marie-aux-Anglais,* a village of Normandv, in the elect.on 5f Falaifc. *p. Trouard.* Ste. *Mai.-aux-Bds,* an abby 'a the diocefe of Toul. *p. TouL* Ste. *Mirie-aux-Champs,* a village of Normandy, in the election of Caudebec. *p. Yvetot.* Ste. M'irii-aux-MtneSy or *Marhire,* a town of Alface, in the bailiwick of Ribauvillc. *p. Colmar.* Ste. *Marie-Biarotte,* a fmall town of Gafcony, in the election of Landos, *p. D¿x.* Ste. *Rlârie-Capel,* a village of Flanders, in the Cub delegation of Caüei.. *Caßel.* Ste *Marie-dy'Alois,* a village of Dauphiny, in the diocefe and election, of Grenoble. *j. Grenoble.* Ste. *Maric-dAudottvillet* a village, of Normandy, in the election of Valogncs. *p. Carentan.* StcAlarie-de-CbigKac. Se« *Cbignc.* Ste. Marit-dc-FlayoüeSy a pariíh f Nivernois, in the diocefe and election of Ncvers. *p. Ncvers.* Ste. *Mariedem-Maurees.* See *Maurern.* Ste. *Marie-des-Chamfsy* a village of Normandy, in the election of Gifors. /. ie *Txllc.* St. *Marie-de-Serresf* a place of Beam, in the receipt of Pau. *p. Pau.* Ste. *Marxe-des-Verg,* a village of Perigord, in the diocefe and eleftion of Périgucux. *p. Ptriguuix.* Ste. *Marie-de-Vaux,* a village of Poitou, in the election of Confolans. *f. Confolans.* Str. *Marle-du-Boh,* a town of Maine, in the diocefe and election of Mans. *p.* h *Mans.* Str. *Marie-du-Mnt.* i. A town of Normandy, m ar the fea, about 3 leagiies from Carentan, and 6 from Valognes. *p. Carentan.* 2. A village of Normandy, in the election of Vire. *p. Vire.* Ste. *Marie-du-Selj* a village of Périgord, in the dioccfe and deftion of Périgucux. *p. Per'gueux.* Ste. *Marie-du-Tno,* a priory in the diocefc of Mans. *p. It Mam.* Ste. *Marie-en-Cbamoy,* £f Ste. *Maric-en-Chaux,* villages of FrancheComté, in the bailiwick of Vcfoul. *f. Lure.* Ste. *Marie-la-Blanche,* a town of Burgundy, in the buüiwick of Bcaunc. *p. Beaune.* Ste. *Marie-ia-Mer,* a village of Routfiilon, in the dioccfe and viguery of Perpignan, *p. Perpignan.* Stc. *MarU-Ja-Rolerty* a village of Normandy, in the election of Argentan, *p. Argentan.* Ste. *Mttric-Laumonty* a town of Normandy, in the election of Vire. *p. yjre,* Ste. *Marie-Шle-Г Eau,* a village of Normandy, in the elcition oí Vire. *f. S. Lo.* Ste. *Marie-fucrçuej* a village of Artois, in the dio;cfe ami bailiwick, f S. Omer. *p. S. Omer.* Ste. *Marie-joui-Bcur#,* a village of

Vol. III.

Champagne, in rhceleftion of RctheU *p. Rheims.* S(e, *Marthe.* 1. A village of Normandy, in the election of Caudebcc. *p. Caudibec.* z. A viMage of Normandy, in thex election of Conches. *ft. En/reux.* 3. A village of Condomois, in the dioccfe and election of Condom, *p. Marmande.* 4. A village of Agénois, in the dioccfe and eleftion of Agen. *f. Ncvac.* Stt. *Maw.,* i. A town of Tourainc, in the dioccfe of "Jours, and eleftion of Chinon; about 7 leagues from Tours. *Bureau de feße z.* A village of Chnmpane, id the dioccfe and eleftion of Troycs. *p.* 'JVoy«. Ste. *Maxime,* apariih of Provence, in the viguery of Dr:..guignan. *p. Draguignan.* Ste.Mci'fc, a village of Gafcony, in the eleftion of Gabardan. *f.* M.titele-Mar fon. Ste. *Mdaigr.e,* a village-of Normandy, in the eleftion of PoBt-PEvêque. *p* Pont -Z1 *Evique,* Ste. *Mmcbould.* Sec Ste. *Alanebould.* Ste. *Mere.* I. A village of Condo. mots, in the dioccfe and eleftion of Condom, *p. Leil'jwe.* 2. A village of Armagnac, in the eleftion of Lomagnc. *p. BcavnKnt-dc-Lcmagre.* Stc. *Merc-Eglifc,* a market-town of Normandy; about 3 leagues from Carentan. *p. Caren'an.* Stc.Miftr.cs, a village of Bcauce, in the eleftion of Dourdan. *p. Dwdan.* Sie. *Mondarme,* a village of Périgord, in the diocefe and eleftion of Sarlat. *p. Sarlat.* Ste. *Montainc.* A village of Berry, in the dioccfe and eleftion of Bourges, *p. Auligny. Saint Nahord,* i. A vilbge of Champagne, in the diocefe and election ot Troves, *p. Arris fur-Aube.* z. A place of Alface, in the dtocefc of Straiburg. *p. Rcnúrimonf.* S. *blauf amy y л* village of UppT Languedoc, in the dioccfe and election of Montauban. *p. Montauban.* S. *Notaire,* i, Atcapoit-Wwn ot H Bretagne, near the mouth of the Loire; about lo leagues from Nantes, and 3 from Pairabceuf. *f.Guerar.de.* 2, A town of Siintonge, in the election of Marenncs. *f. F.ocbefort..* 3. A fmali town of Dauphiny, in, the generality of Grenoble, *p. Die.* 4. A village of Lower Languedoc, in the dioccfe rind receipt of Uzés. *p. Bagno's.* 5. A village of Lower Languedoc, in the dioccfe and receipt of Narhonne. *f. Narbcr.r.e.* 6. A village of Provence, in the dioccfe and receipt of Toulon, *p. OШ'юuHe.* 7. A village of Dauphiny, in the diocefe and elcótion of Grem-ble. *p. Grenoble.* 8. A village of Dauphiny, in the generality of Grenoble, *p. R.omans.* 9. A vilhige of Dauphiny, in the diocefe and election of Valence, *p. Romans.* 10. A village of Roufiillon, in the diocefc of Perpignan.*p. Perpignan,* il. A place of Lower Languedoc, in the diocefe and receipt of Montpellier, *p. hunel.* S. *Notaire ¿£f Rocbefourehat,* a village of Dauphiny, in the election of Montclimart. *p. Montclimart.* S. *Naxaire* fijf *Fontnugier,* avillage of Berry, in the election of Châtre. *f. la Chatre.* S. *Naxaxr e-de-Gar dure y* a place of Lower Languduc, in the diocefe and receipt of Nîmes, *p. Ntmes.* St. *Na-zaire-de-Ludtrex,* a fmall town of Lower Languedoc, in the diocefc and receipt of Béziers. *p.* S. *Nazarin-du-Corcoul,* a town of Saintongc, in thediucefe and election of Saintes, *p. Satmes.* S. *Naztre,* a village of Agénois, in the diocefc and election of Agen. *p. Mar-*

mande. i. Neclairet a fmall town of Auvergne, in the diocefe and election of Clermont, *p. Jffoire.* S. NexanSy a fmall town of Périgord, in the diocefe and election of Sarlat. *p. Bergerac.* S. Nicolas, i. A town of Armagnac in the eleilion of Riviere-Verdun. *GriJJolles.* 2. A town of Blé fois, in the dioccfe and election of Blois. *p. Bloh.* 3. A fmall town of Normandv, in the dioccfe and election of Coutances. *p. Ccûrances.* A village of Dauphiny. in the dioccfe and election of Vienne, *p. Gap.* 5. A village of Normandy, in the cleólion of Montvilliers. *p. Harfleur.* 6. A village of Normandy, in the election of AleiTcon. *p. Aknçon.* 7. A vi;lage of Bretagne, in the diocefc and receipt of Quimpcr. *p. Redon.* 8. A v illage of Artois, in the diocefe and bailiwick of S. Omer./». 5. *Omer.* 9. A village of Limofin, m the d;ocefe and election of Limoges. *p. Limoges.* 10 A village of Normandy, in the election of Caudebcf. *p. PAiglc.* 11. A priory in Compiégnc.

S. Nicolat-aux-Bois. 1. A village of Picardy, in the diocefc and election of Laon. *p. Creffy.* z. An abby fituatcd in the wood of Coucy in Picardy. S. Nuolas-d'Alicrmoatj a fmall town of Normandy, in the election of Arques, *p. Dieppe.* S. Nicotas-d'Arrouaife. Sec *Arrouaife.* S. Nicolas-Dattes, avillage of Normandy, in the eleétion of Conches. *p. Evreux.* S. Nicolas-de-Cbanre'ile-Ie-Cbateau See *Cbjnteile-le-Cbateau.* S. Nicolas-de-Joffelin. See *Jojfelin.* S. Nicolas-de-la-Chaume. See *Chaume,* S, Ni.olas-de-la-Haye. Sec *Haye.* S. Nicolas-de-la-Pree-fcus-Arcy, л village of Burgundy, in the bailiwick, of Bourbon-Lancy. *p. BourbcnLancy.* IS. Nicolas-de-la-Taille, a fmall own of Normandy, in the election of Montivilliers. *p. Lillebonne.* S. Nkolas-tie-Maulaunay, a village of Normnndy, in the dioccfe and election of Rouen, *p. Rouen.* S. Nicolas-de-P'mrepent. See *Pierrepont.* S. Nicolas -de-Regny, a fmall town of Picardy, in the diocefc and election of Amiens, *p. Amiens,* S. Nkoïas-de-Saumaire, a village of Normandy, in the election of Verneuil. *p. VAigle.* S. Nkolasde-Veullts, a village of Normandy, in the ejection of Arques, *p, Dieppe.* S. Nkolas-de-Voron,* a village of Dauphiny, in the diocefe and election of Grenoble, *p. Moirar.s.* S. NkJas-de-tieft, a village of Bourbonnois, in the election of Gannat. *p. la PaliJJè.* S. N.colas-des-B clsy a village of Normandy, in the diocefe and election of Avranches. *p. VilUdieu.* S. Nkclas-des-Lettics,* a village of Normandy, in the diocefe and elec tion of Lifieux. *p. Noyer-Menard.* S. Nkolas-des-Pre's,* an abby, in the diocefe of Laon. *p. Laon.* S. Nicolas-du-Bojc, a village of Normandy, in thfc election of Conches, *p. le Neuf bourg.* S. Nicoias-du-Bsjelw, a figniory of Normandy, in the election of Pont de l'Arche, *p. Pont de VArche.* S. Nkolas-du-Pont-Saint-Pierre, a village of Normandy, in the diocefe and election of Rouen, *p. Rouen.* S. Nicolas-du-. Verbots, a figniory of Normandy, in the diocefe and election of Rouen, *p. le Bolehard.* S. Nkolas-le-Moteux, a place of Touraine, near Chateau-Rcgnault. *p. Tours.* S. Nicolas-les-Angers, an" abby in one of the fauxbourgs of Angers, *p. Angers.* S. Nkolas-les-Argentan, the name of a priory, in the diocefe of Bourges. *p. Argentan.* S. Nkolas-le-Citeaux, a village of Burgundy, in the bailiwick of Nuits. *p. Nuits.* S. Nkolas-les-vUlenewve-le-Roy, a fmall town of Champagne, in the diocefe and election of Sens. *p. Villeneuve-fur-Yonne.* S. Ni-zier. i. A fmall town of Forez, In the diocefe of Roanne, *p. Roanne.* z. A fmall town of Forez, in the election of Montbrifon. *p. Montbrijon.* 3. Avil läge of Burgundy, in the diocefe and bailiwick of Autun. *p. Autan.* 4. A village of Dauphíny, in the diocrfe and election of Grenoble, *p. GrenxlU,* S. Nhier-a Azergue, a fmall town of Beaujolois, in the election of Villefranche, *p. Vtllefrancbe.* S. N'tzier-dHeuriage, a village of Dauph&y, in the diocefe and election of Grenoble, *p. Grenoble.* S. Nizkr-le-Boaebcux, a village of BreíTe, in the bailiwick of Bourg, *p. Bcurg-er.-Breff'e.* S. N'rzkr-le-DeJert, a place of B reffe, in the bailiwick of Bourg, *p. Bourg-en-Brejfe.* S. Nizier-jous-Cbarm-cyy a village of Burgundy, in the bailiwick of Mont cenis. *p. Dijon.* S. No!f a village of Bretagne, in the diocefe and receipt of Vannes, *p. Vannes.* S. Nom-de-Levy, fe? 5. Ncm-laBrcteche, fiefs in the diocefe and election of Paris, *p. Villepreux.* S e. Nadalaine, a village of Pérírigord, in the diocefe and election of Sarlat. *p. Sarlat,* Ste. Ncotnaye, a fmall town of Poitou, in thcclcction of S. Maixant *p. S. Ma'txant.* S. O'.ng, a village of Nivernois, in the diocefe and ekcti Jn of Nevers. /. *Nevers.* S. Olas & Bons, a village of Dan 1 phiny, in the diocefe and election of Vienne, *p. Vknne.* S. Olle & RaUlcttCOurty a village of Flanders, in the diocefe and fub-delclegation of Cambray. *p. Cambray.* S. Omer. i.Aílrong city of Artois, fituated in maríhy land, on the river Aa, the feeof a hifhop; it owes its origin to a celebrated abby of S« Bertin, founded about the year 65c. Bcfidcs the cathedral it has 6 pariihe?, general hofpital, an Englifh feminary, &c. 10 Leagues from Calaij, 26 from Ofteni, 12 from Dunkirk, 12 from Boulogne, 16 from Lille, 3S from Bruffels, 19 from Douay, 10 from Bethune, 17 from Arras, ij from Cambray, 3 g from Landreq, 59 from Avefnes, 54 from Givct, 75 from Liege, 46 from Laon, 28 from Péronne, 34 from S. Quentin, 135 from Strafburg, 66 from Chalons, 121$ from Dijon, 165J from Geneva, 166 from Lyons, èifrom Paris. *Bureau de Pofte.* 2. A village of Picardy in the diocefeand election f Bcauvais. *p. Beauvtàu 'j.* A village of Normandy, in the election of Falaife. *p. Falaije.* S. Omer-CaeUe, a village of Artois, in the dioccfe and bailiwick of S. Omer. *p. Arrat.* S. Onen, a village of Bretagne, in the diocefe and receipt of S. Malo. *f.* S. *Mulo.* S. Oradvvr. I. A village of Auvergne,in the election of Combrailles. *f. Chambón,* 2. A village of Marche, in the election of Gucrct. *p. Feuilletn.* S. Orens. i. A fmall town of Agénois, in the dioccfe and election of Agen. *p. Agen.* 2. A village of Condornois, in the diocefe and election of Condom. *p. Cond'.m.* 3. A village of Armagnac, in the dioccfe and elec¡on of Auch. *p. Gimont.* S. Orfe, a fmall town of Périgord, in the diocefe and election of Periuciix. *p. Uxercbei.* S. Oft. I. A "village of Armagnac, in theelectidn of Aftarac/. *M'uande.* i. A village of Armagnac, in the diocefe uf Comminges.

p. CnftelnaudeMagnat:. S. Ojv'm, a village of Normandy, in the diocefe and election of Avranches. *p. Avrarxba.* S. Ouanne, я village of Poitou, in the election of S. Maixant. *p. Niort.* S. Oucbard, a village of Bern', in the dioccfe and election of Bourges. *p Boi rges.* S. Oudras, a village of Dauphiny, in the diocefe and election of Vienne. *p. Vienne.* S. Ouen. 1. A town of Touraine, in the election of Amboife. *p. Amioife.* 2. A fmall town of Maine, in rhe election of Laval, *p. haual.* 3. A imaji town of the Hie of France, in the bailiwick of Auxerre. *p. Auxerre.* S. Pancrace. ї. A town of Dau phiny, in the generality of Grenoble. *p. Gap.* 2. A village of Dauphiny, in the diocefe and election of Grenoble, *p. Grenoble.* S. Pandelou, a village of Gafcony, in the election of Landes, *p. Dax.* S. Panialeen. I. A town of Limofin, in the election of Brives. *p. Briles.* 2. A vilbge of Limofm, in the election of Tulles, *p. Tulles.* 3. A village of Burgundy, in the diocefe and bailiwick of Autun. *p. Autun.* 4. A village of Quercy, in the diocefe and election of Cahors. *p. Cabors.* S. Panta/y. i. A vílbże of Provence, in the diocefe and vijucry of Apt. *p. Apt.* 2. A village of Périgord, in the diocefe and election of Péi igueux. *p. Périgueux.* S. Pantalyi'Exideuil, a village of Pcrigord, in the diocefe and election of Péiigneux. *p. Pér'igueux.* S. Papouly a city of Upper Languedoc, fituated on the Lembe, in the generality of Touloufe, the fee of bifhop fuffragan of Touloufe, about 3 leagues from Caftelnaudary, 8 from Carcaflonne, 13 from Touloufe, and 10 from Miiepoix. *Bureau de pofle.* S. Pardoi/x. I. A town of Poitou, in the election of Niort, *p. Niort.* 2. A town of Auvergne, in the diocefe and election of Clermont, *p. Chambón.* 3. A village of Limofm, in the election of Brives. *p. Brives.* 4. A village of Marche, in the election of Bourganeuf. *p. Bourganeuf.* 5. A vjllage of Saintonge, in theelection of S. Jean-d'Angely.. *S. JeandAngely,* 6. See S. Perdoux.
& Pavdoux-de-Gimel, S. PardcuxU-Vieuxt & S. Pardoux-la-Croxitle, villages of Limoiin, in thcelection of Tulles, *p. Tulles.* S. Pardoux-de-lA-Vill-te,* a village of B jurbonnois, in which is a fpring of mineral water, in the ele¿tion of Gannat. *p. Feuilletin.* S. Pardoux en-Luber%at3 & 5.
Par doux-en-Rançon) fmal! towrs of Limofin, in the diocefe and election of Limoges, *p. Limoges.* S, Pardoux-la-Manche, a village of Bcurbonnois, in the election of Montluyon. *p. Monluçon.* S. Pat deuxle-Ncvf. I. A village of Limofin, in the election of Tulles. *p. Tulles.* 2. A village of Marche, in the election of Gueret. *p. Aubvjjbn.* S. Pardoux-le-Pawvre, a village of Marche, in the election of Guerct. *f. Aubuffon.* 2. A village of Auvergne, in the election of Cumbrailks. *p Chamice.* PardoiiX-tes-Cords, a fmall town of Marche, in the election of Gueret. *P Cbenerailies.* S. Pard',uxJes-S.Cbamant, a place of Limofin, in the diocefe and ejection of Tulles, *p. Tulla,* S. Pardoux-fres-Ccc, a village of Auvergne, in the election of Combrailles. *p. Ckamhn.* S. PargohC) a fmall town of Lower Languedoc, in the diocefe and receipt of Bézicis. *p. Pe'жz.аь.* S. Paris-en-У.zy. See S. Parijeen-V'-ry. S. Parife,a vilbge of Bourbonnois, in the election of Moulins, *p. Moulins.* S. Pariée J c-Chai el y a fmall town of Nivcrnois, in the di cefe r.nd election of Nevera; here is a fpring of mineral waters, *p. Nevers.* S. Partfe-en-V'vy, a parifh of Nivcrnois, in the diocefe and election of Nevers. *p. Dectfe.* S. Parre-aux-Tertres, 5. Parreles-Vaudes, villages of Champagne, in the diocefe and election of Troyes. *p. Troyes.* S. Parten, a village of Rouerguc, in the election of Villefranche. *p. Figeac.* S. Paßour, a fmall town of Agénois, in the diocefe and election of Agen. *p. Villenewve-d'A¿tn.*
S. Pater, i. A town of Touraine, in the diocefe and election of Tours. *p. 'Jours.* 2. A town of Maine, in the diocefe and election of Mans. *p. Cha'eau-du-Lcir,* S. Patern?, aparimof Touraine, in the diocefe and generality of Tours. *p. Tours.* E. Paterrie-/esCbamps, a village of Bretagne, in the diocefe and receipt of Vannes *p. Vannes.* S. PatbuSy a village of Prie, in the diocefe and election of Meaux. *p. Dan: martin.* S. Patrice. I. A fmall town of Touraine, in the election of Chinon. *p. Tours.* 2. A village of Normandy, in the election of Falaife, *p. Domfront.* v S. Patrix, a village of Normandy, in the election of Carentan. /:-Carentan. S. Patrix-de-Clair, a barony of Normandy, in the generality of Caen. *p. Ccutances.* 5 Pau. t. A village of Armagnac, in the diocefe and election of Auch. *p. Auch.* 2. A place of Condoniois, in the diocefe and election of Condom. *p.Nerc.* S. Pьч/ace, a town of Maine, in the diocefe and election of Mans. *p. le Mans.* 6 Pav'w, a village of Normandy, in the election of Falaife. *p. Fa.'aije.* S. Pai'in-des-CbampSy a town i.f Maine, in the dioccie and election of Mans. *p. le Mans.* S. Paul. i. A fmall city of Provence, fituated on a fmall river, about a league from Vence, and 3 leagues from Antibes. *p. Ar.tibes.* 2. A town of Limofin, in the diocefe and election of Limoges. /. *Limoges.* 3. A town of Gafcony, in the election of Landes, *p. Vax* 4. A fmall town of Picaray, in the diocefe and election of Beauvais *p. Beawvais.* 6. A fmall town of Auvergne, in the diocefe and election of Flour./-. *Ficur.* 7, A village of Dauphiny, in the diocefe and ekction of Vienne, *p. Remans.* 8. A village of Dauphiny, in the generality of Grenoble. *p.Grenotlc.* 9. A village of Limofin, in the election of Tu'.les. *Tunes.* 10. A village of Angoumois, in the diocefe and dec tonge, in the diocefe and eleftion o Saintes, *p. Mau%e,* 2. A village of Saintonge, in the eleftion of S. Je-and'Angely. *p. $. Jcan-d4 Angely.* S. Phtlix-de-Reillaty a village of Perigord, in the diocefe and-eleftion of Périgueux. *p. Caß lkn,* S. Pbilbert j. A markef-town of Normandy, in the diocefe of Liiîeux. *p. Li/ieux.* 2. A fmall town of Anjou, in the eleftion of Baugé. *p. Bauge,* 3. A village of Poitou, in the diocefe and eleftion of Poitiers. *p. Roche-Serviere.* 4. A village of Anjou, in the diocefe and eleftion of Angers, *p. Angers.* 5. A village of Anjou, in the eleftion of Saumur. *p. Saumur.* 6. A village of Dauphiny, in the diocefe and eleftion of Vienne, *p. Vienne.* 7. A village of Normandy, in the eleftion ofFalaife, *p. Boucachard.* S. Pkilbert-de-Grand-Lieu, a village of Bretagne, in the diocefe and receipt of

Nantes, p. *Machecoul.* S. *PbUèert-des-Cbamps,* a fmall town.of Normandy, in the diocefe and eleftion of Lifieux. p. *Lifieux* S. *Pb'ilhtrt-àii-Pwtcharault,* a village of Poitou, in the eleftion of Fontenay. p.*Chantonay.* S. *Pbiliert-fur-B ify,* a village of Normand V, in the eleftion of Pont-Audemer. p. *Pont-Audtmcr.* S. *PfMbcri-jur-Riße,* a town of Normandy, in the eleftion of PontAudemer. p. *Pont-Audemer.* S. *Piar,* a town of Beauce, in thç diocefe and eleftion of Chartres. /, *Chartres.* S. *Piat-de-Sedin,* an ancient collégial church, in the town of Seclin, in Flanders.

S. *Pierejfe%* a village of Picardy, in the diocefe and eleftion of Soif fons. p. *Syjfons.* S. *Pierre,* i. A town of Lower Languedoc, in the diocefe and receipt of Viviers, p. *Viviers.* 2. A town of the Ifle of Oleron, in the election, of Marcnnes. p. *Marennes,* 3. A town of Anjou, in the elcftiea of Mon treuil-Bellay, p. *Stumor,* 4. A fmall town of Picardy, in the government of Caláis, p. *Calais.* 5. A fmall town of Limofin, in the tfiocefe and election of Limoges, p. *Limoges.* 6. A fmall town of Nurmandy, in the election of Movtain. p. *Mortain.* 7. A fmall town of Dauphiny, in the diocefe and election of Vienne, p. *Vunne.* %. A village of Normandy, in the d ocefe and elect.on of Coûtances. p. *Cu anees.* 9. A village of Alfacc, in the bailiwick of Benfeld. p. *Benfdd.* 10. A village of Bretagne, in the diocefe and receipt of S. Pol-dc-L:on. p. *Morld.x.* il. A village of Quercy, in the election of Figeac. p. *Montauhan.* 12. A village ef Dombes, in the chatellany of Villeneuve, p. *Bourgen-BrfJ'e.* 13. A place of Touraine, in thediocef-of Tours. p.*Tours.* 14 A priory in the town ot-Abbeville, in Picardy. 15. A figniory of Normandy, in the election of PontrEvcque. p. *Fauiñlle.* S. *Pierre,* or *le-Grand-S.-Píe-re,* a large village of Maine, in the diocefe and election of M;ms. p. *le Mans.* 8. Pierre & S. Martin-d'Argenforty G? S. *Pierre-de-Mearosy* villages of Dauphiny, in the diocefe and election of Gap p. *Gap.* S. *Pierre,* c¿f S. *Mкbel,* a village of Angoumols, in the diocefe and election of Angoulême. p. *Angou¡eme.* S. Pierre, Êf S. *Paul,* a village of Bretagne, in the diocefe and receipt of S. Malo. /. S. *Malo.* S. *Pierre,* or *ГJße-S.-Pierre,* an ifland of Provence. S. *Pierre,* or S. *Pcred Auxerre,* an abby in the city of Auxerre. S. *Pierre-à-Ar-ves,* a vi'lage of Champagne, in the diocefe and election of Rheims, p. *Rheims.* S. *Pierre-à-Cbamps,* a town of Anjou, in the election of Mont,reuil-Bcllay. p. *Saumur.* S' *Piere-à-Gouy,* a place of Picardy, in the diocefe and election of Amiens, p. *Amiens.* S. *Piere-AJtf,* or *dct-I/s,* a village

Périgord, in the diocefe and election Périgucux. p. *Pe ig: eux.* S. *Pier&-la-Feuille,* a village of Quercy, in thed'iuccle and election of Cahors. p. *Cubors.* S. *Pierre-la Mon'agne,* a village of Iaimofin, in the diocefe and election of Limo, es. p. *Raxe's* S. *Pierre-Lancer y* a village of Normandy, in the dioccfe and election of Avranchcs. p. *GrandwlU.* S. *Pierre-L-NoaiUei* a village of Forer, in the election of Roanne. /. *Roanne.* S. *P errc-la-Palluây* a village of Lyonnois, in the diocefe and election Lyons, p. *Lyon.* S. *Pir.c-La'v's,* a village of Normandy, in the ckcYion of Caudebec. p. *Fuu-i hie.* S. *'Pier re-le-Bois,* a pi ice of Berry, in the diocefe of Bourges, p. *Eowgts.* S. *Pierre-ie-Boß,* a village of Marche, in the election of Gueret. p. *Biurgjrcuf,* S. *Pttrre-le-Chatel.* i. A village of Auvergne, in the election of Riom. p. *Riem.* 2. A place of Limofin, in the election of Tuiles, p. *Tulles.* S. *î3.er re-le-Moûtier,* a town of NiVcrnoiSj in the diocefe and election of Nevers, the feat of a bailiwick, &c. It lies in the road from Moulins to Paris; 7 bagues from Moulins, 7 from Nevers, 5 t from Lyons, and 64 from Paris *Bureau de pofie.* S. *Pierre-/2-Petit,* & S. *Piereleyîgeff* villa.es of Normandy, in the election of Arques, p. S. *Valéry-enCaux.* ч S. *Pierre-le-Pteifj* a fmall town of Norma! dy in the election of Arques. p, S. *Valéry-en-Caux.* S. *Pi er it-le Vieux.* 1. A villaje of Lower Languedoc, in the diocefe and receipt of Mende. p. *Mende.* 2. A village of Burgundy, in the diocefe and bailiwick, of Mâcon p. *Mtkôa.* 3. A village of Poitou, in the election of Fontenay. p. *Fonienay.* S, *Pierre-le-Vîf-les-Scns,* an abby, near the city of Sens.

p. *Sens.* S. *Pierre-les-Bois,* a village of Bсггy» in the election of Iifoudun. p. *JJJoudun* S. *Pierre-lei-Meli fey,* a village of Franche-Comté A in the bailiwick of Vefoul. p. *Lure.* S. *Pïerre-Г Eßrier,* a village of Burgundy, in the bailiwick of Autun. p. *Autun.* S. *Pierre-Ics-Montßeur,* a place of Franche-Comté, in the br-.iliwick of Orgelet, p. *tom-le-Saunier.* S. *Pierre-let Selincourt,* a village of Picardy, in the diocefe and election of Amiens, p. *Arnum.* S. *Pierre-Pertuy,* a village of Rouffillon, in the receipt of Vclefpir. p. *Perpignan.* S. *Pierre-Roche,* a fmall town of Au-ergne, in the diocefe and election of Clermont, p. *Clermont.* S. *Pierre-Jur-Dh'C,* a market-town of Normandy, in thi election of Falaifc. p *Trouard.* 5 *Piare-fur-Vanxe,* a village of Champagne, in the election of Rettich p. *Retbcl.* S. *P.erremont,* a village of Champagne in the election of Ste. Manéhould. p. *Sedan.* S. *Piton,* a village of Hainaut, in the government of Quènoy. p. *U $uhoy.* S. *Pluifir,* a village of Bourbonnois, in the diocefe and election of Moulins, p. *Bourbon-VArckamkauh.* S. *Plancher,* a fmall town of Normandy, in the diocefe and election of Coûtances. p. *Coûtâmes.* S. *Plantaire,* a fmall town of Normandy, in the diocefe and election of Coûtances. p. *C: ut anees.* S. *Plantaircdeça-les-Bois,* a village of Marche, in the election of Gueret, p. *Gueret.* S. *Plaintaire-le-Clocher,* a place in the election of Gueret. p. *Gueret.* S. *Point.* I. A village of Burgundy, in the diocefe and bailiwick of Ma con. p *Macon.* 2. A village of Franche Compté, in the bailiwicjt of Pontarlier. p. *Pontarlier.* 6 *Poix y* a town of AnjoUj i n: election of Château-Gontîer. p. *Château-G ont ter.* S. *Pol.* See 5. *Paul.* S. *Polâe-Leon,* an ancient city of Bretagne, near the fea, in the generality of Nantes, the fee of a biíhop and capital of Léonois; 5 leagues from Morlaix, and 15 from BrefL p. *Moria: X.* S. *Pol-en-Blayez,* a fmall town of Guienne, in the diocefe and election of Bourdeaux. p. *Blaye.* S. *Pol-en-Botit)* a vilirge of Guieine in the diocefe and election of Bourdeaux. p. *Bourdeaux.* S. *PolgueSf* a village of Forez, in the election of Roanne, p,

Roanne. S. Polycarpe, a village of Upper Languedoc, in the receipt of Limoux. *p. Limoux. S. Pompain,* a fmall town of Poitou, in the election of Fontenay. *p. Niort. S. Pompen,* a fmall town of Périgord, in the diocefe and election of Sarht. *p. Sar'at.' S. Parce,* a convent near the town of Aubagne, in Provence, *p. Jluiagr.e. S. Poney,* a fmall town of Auvergne, in the diocefe and election of S. Flour, *p. S. Flour. S. Pons,* or *S. Pons-de-Lommières,* a city of Lower Languedoc, fituatcd on the river Jaur in the generality of Montpellier; the fee of a biihop; the place of a receipt, &c. about 8 leagues from Narbonne. *p. B?'z'¡ers. S. Pons,* i, A village of Lower Languedoc, in the di icele and receipt of Viviers, *p. Vdlenewve-de-Eerg. %.* A Tillage of Lower Languedoc, in the diocefe and receipt of Agde. *p, Agde.* 3. A village of Auvergne, in the election of Gannat. *p. Gannat. S. Pons-dela-Cbampagney* a village of Lower Languedoc, in the diocefe and receipt of Uzés, *p. XJx.cs. S. Porcbaire.* 1. A town of Saintonge, about 4 leagues from Saintes. *p. Saintes.* 2. A village of Poitou, in the election of Thouars.. *Brefuire. S. Porquier,* a tpwn of Upper Lant gicdoc, in the d ocefe and receipt o Montauban. *p. Montaubaii. S. Port,* a village of Gâtinois, in the election of Melun. *p. Melun. S. Pcßan,* a village of Bretagne, in the diocefe and receipt of S. Brieux. *p. Lamballe. S. Pot,* a village of Armagnac, in the diocefe and election of Auch. *p. Auch. S. P:uange,z* village ofChampngne, in the diocefe and election of Troyes. *p. Troyes. S. Pourçain,* a town of Auvergne, filiated on the Siouie, in the diocefe of Clermont, and election, of Gannat, in the road from Clermont-Ferrand to Paris; 6 leagues from Gannat, il from Riom, 14 from Clermont, 8 Irom Moulins, aüd 79 from Paris, *Bureau de poße.* A piece of fcu'pture. eccc homo, in the par i fh- church if much eiteemed.
S. P.urçain-ds-Malckercs, S. Pcwçcànfur-e,ßre villages of Bourbonnois, in the election of Moulins. *p. M-ulins S. Powquicr,* a wood of 1328 arpent in the juridiction of Touloufe, in Languedoc. *S. P/ayt-Ies-Privas,* a village of Lower Languedoc, in the diocefe and receipt of Viviers. *pPrivas. S. P/egax,* a village of Auvergne, in the election of Brioude. *p. Brioude» S. Prtjtcl,* a piriih of Berry, in the diocefe of Bourges, *p. la Chatre. S. Preß,* a town of Beaucc, in the diocefe and election of Chartres, *p. Chartres. S. Prcu l,* a town of Angoumois, in the election of Cognac, *p. Cognac. S. Prudc-Maruil,* a village of Périgord, in the diocefe and election of Périgueux. *p. Pe'rigueux. S. Prie-la-Feuille,* a town of Berry, in the election of Blanc, *p. le Blare. S. Prê-la-Marche,* a village of Berry, in the election of Châtre, *p, la Châtre. S. Priechf* a village ofLimçun, in *Reuergue.* 17. A village of Champagne, in the diocefe and election of Chalons, *p. Epernaj,* 18. A vil-. läge of Champagne, in the election of Vitry. *p. Fury.* 19. A village of Normandy, in the election of Arques, *p. Dieppe.* 20. A village of Maine, in the election of Chateau-du-Loir. *p. la Ferte'-Bernard.* 21. A place of Normandy, in the election of Falaife. *p. Falaife.* 22. A figniory of Anjou, in the election of Bcaugé. *p. Beauge. S. Quentin-aux-Mauges* a priory in Anjou.
S. Quentin, S. From, a village in the diocefe and election of Agen. *p. Agen. S. Quentin -de -Cbabanois.* See *Cbabanois. S. Quentin-des-Monts,* a village of Lower Languedoc, in the diocefe and receipt of Puy. *p. le Puy. S. Quentindes-Ißesy* a village of Normandy, in the election of Bernay. *p. Bernay. S. Quentin-des-Marais,* a village of Nivernois, in the election of Charité-fur-Loire, *p. Cojne. S. Quentin títs-Ptis,* a village of Picardy, in the diocefe and election of Beauvais. *p. E-cuy,* 2. A parifh of Touraine, in the diocefe of Tours. *p. tourx. S. Quentin-du-Feulllage* a priory in in the diocefe of Sens.
S. Quir.Hn-en-Γ Jße an abby in S. Quentin. *S. Quentin-en-Tcurmont,* a village of Picardy, in the ckction of Doulcns. *p. Abbeville. S. Quernin-U-Petit.* I. A village of Champagne, in the diocefe and election of Rheims, *p. Rheims,* 2, A village of Perche, in the election of Moitagne. *p. Reynialard. S. Quintin.* I. A fmall town of Lower Languedoc, in the diocefe and receipt of Uzés. *p. Uzes. %.* A village of Upper Languedoc, in the diocefe and receipt of Mirepoix. *p. Mircpúx. S. Quirin,* i. A village of MeiTin, in the diocefe and receipt of Nfetz *p. Sarebourg.* 2. The name of a chapel a fmall diftance from Noyon *Ste. Quitttrie,* a village of Agé— nois; in the diocefe and election ot Agen. *p. Agen. S. Rabkr,* a fmall town of Perigord, in the diocefe and election of/ Sarlat. *p. Montignac. S. Rambert.* 1. A town of Forez, fituated on the Loire, in the diocefe of Lyons j 4-§ leagues from Montb &ifon, and 3 from S. Etienne, *p. S. Etienne.* 2. A town between Valence and Lvons, il leagues from Valence, 9 from Vienne, and 16 from Lyons *S. Rambertde-Joux,* a fmall city of Bugey, in t-he diocefe of Lyons, and bailiwick of Belley; about 7 leagues from Belley, and 15 from Bourg-en-Breffe. *Bureau de foße. S. Raphael,* t. A village of Périgord, in the diocefe and election of Péigucux. *p. Pe'rigueux.* 2. A village of Provence, im the viguery of Draguignan. *p. Draguignan. S. Raphael 6sT Beire,* a village of Baindois, in the election of Condom. *p. Baseas. S. Reigle,* a town of Touraine, in the election of Amboife. *p. Amboife. S. Remcyfe,* a village of Lewcr Languedoc, in the diocefe and receipt of Viviers, *p. Pierrelatte. S. Retuhe,* a village of Auvergne, in the diocefe and election of S. Flour, *p. S. Flour. S. Rcmy.* i. A fmall city of Provence, fituated in a fertile plain, in the diocefe of Avignon, and viguery of Tarafcon; 4 leagues from Tarafcon, 16 from Aix, and 69 from Lyons, *p. Avignon.* 2. A town of Anjou, in theele¿tion of Saumur. *p. les Rcxieis.* 3. A village of Poitou, in the election of Châtelieiaut. *p. Cbâtelleraut.* 4. A fmall town of Péigord, in the diocefe and election of Périgucux. *p. Pe'rigueux.* 5. A fmall town of Lim fin, in the election of Tulles, *p.-Tulla.* 6. A villäge of Normandy, in the election of Falaife. *p. Talaife.* 7. A village of Poitou, in the election of Fontcnay. *p. S. Maixant.* 8. A village of Brie, in the election of Coulomiers. *p. Rebels.* 9. A village of Auvergne) in the dtocefe and election of S. Flour. *p. S. Flour.* 10. A village of the lile of France, in the diocefe and elec-

tion of Paris, *p. Chcvreuje.* II. A village of Bc.iucc, in the election of Montfort. *p. Mont fort.* 12. A village of Saintonge, in the diocefe and election of Saintes./ » *Saintes,* 13. A village of Forez, in the élection of Montbrifon. *p. Monibñjcn.* 14. A village of Rouergue, in the election of Villefranche, *p. Rheden.* 15. A village of Agenois, in the diocefe and election of Agen. *p. Tcnne.ms.* 16. A place of Brie, in the election of Sezanne, *p. Säumst.* 17. A place of Ereffe, in the bailiwick of Bourg, *p. Bcvrg-tn-Breß.* i S A forcft of 400 arpents, in the jurifdiction of Vaffi, in Champagne 19. A wood of 168 arpciità, in the jurifdiction of Chatelleraut. S. *Remy & AkUs,* a village of Burgundy, in the diocefe and bailiwick of Challen, *p. Challón.* S, *Rerry bl Blaifast* a village of Burgundy, in the bailiwick of Scmur-en-Auxois. *p. Semur,* S. *Remy* S. *Maikurny* a town of Anjou, in the diocefe and election of Angers, *p. Beaufort.*
S. *Rewy-aux-Bets.* 1. A village of Artois, in the bailiwick of S. Pol. *p. jSrraii.* 2. A priory near the town of Amiens, in Picardy, *pr Anient,* S. *Remy-aux-Nm¿itr,st* an abby in the diccefc of Soiffons. *p. VilletsGitteren.* S. *Remy-Cazclhy* a village of Franche-Comté, in the bailiwick of-Vefoul. *p. Vefoul.* S. *Remy-Ckaufsee,* £í S. *Reir.yMbaflc,* villages of Hainaut, in the government of Maubcugc. *p. M..ubeuge.* o. *Rcviy-âe-Bloty* a village of Boitrlonucis, in the election of Cannât *p. Cannai.* S. *Remy-de-Sille',* a fmall town of Maine, in the diocefe and election of Mans. *p. Yrejnay.* S. *Remy-dcs-Bois,* a town of Maine, in the diocefe and electiuii of Mans. *p. le Mans.* S. *Remy-des-Landes.* 1. A village of Normandy, in the election of Valognes. *p. Ccû'ances.* 1. A coavent in the dtocefe of Chartres.4 *p. Rambouillet.* S. *Remy-des-Mints* y a town of Maine, in the diocefe and election of Mans. *p. B II¡me.* S. *Rcmy-du-Aîont,* a place of Biefle, in the bailiwick of Bourg, *p. Bcurgen-BrefJ'e,* S. *Remy-du-Rlain.* 1. A town of Maii.e, in the diocefe and election of Mans. *p. Bcllfme.* 2. A village of Bretagne, in the diocefe and receipt of Nantes, *p. Nantes.* S. *Remy-en-Bouzemcnt,* village of Champagne, in the election of Vitry. *p. Vary.* S. *Remy-en-Champagnet* £f S *Remy-en-R.niireJ* villages of Normandy, in the election of Eu. *p. Eu.* S. *Rimy-en-Lcave,* a village of Picardy, in the election of Clermont.
t-S-7-ß S. *Rcmy-en-Mauge,* a town of Anjou, in the diocefe and election of Angers, *p. Angtrs.* S. *Remy-en-Rollar,* a village of BoLiibonnois, in the election of-Moulins. *p. Moulins.* S. *Rcmy-le-R eût y* a place of Champagne, in the election of Rethel. *p» Rtbcl.* S. *Retny-prh-Ckateau -Ccnttert* a town of Anjou, in the election of Chàtcau-Gontier. *p. Ckâteau-Contier.* S. *Remy-feus-Parlui/e,* a village of Champagne, in the diocefe and elec tion of Tioyes. *p. Troyes.* S. *Remy-fur-Jlu₂e,* a village of Beaucc, in the election of Vcrncuil. *p. Verneu'd.* S. *Remy-fur-Bujfy,* a village of Champagne, in the diocefe and election of Châlons. *p. Chatons.* S. *Remy-fur-Loire,* a priory ill the election uf Saumur, in Anjou, *p. Sat/Mjtr,* S. *Remy-fur-Tliers,* a fmall town of Auvergne, in the election of Riora. *Thiers.* S. *Renan,* a town of Bretagne, in the diocefe and receipt of S. Pol-dcLeon. *p. Breß.* S. *Rcnobert-de-Quingey,* a priory in the diocefe of BeTancon. *p. Bcfanfon.* S. *Requier,* a village of Normandy, in the election of Neufchátel. *p. Neufikatel.* S. *Reqiàxr & Pleins,* a fmall town of Normandy, in the election of Caudebec. *p. Fecamp.* S. *Remy-cFHericourt,* a village of Normandy, in the election of Caudebec. *p. Caudebcc.* S. *Rtflitui,* a village of Danphiny, in the election of Montelimari:, *p. Pierrelatte.* S. *Reverend,* a village of Poitou, iñ the election of Sables-d'Olonne. *p.* S. *Gilles.* 6. *Rtverien.* i. A village of Nivernois, in the diocefe and ilcction of Nevcvs. *p. Never.* 2. A place of Bo'-irbonnois, in the election of Mouli s. *p. Moul'ms.* 3. A priory mar S. *Sauge.* S. *R'uul,* a p'ace of Bretagne, in the diocfe and receipt of S. Bricux. *p. Lamlalle.* S. *Rigavd,* a village of Burgundy, in the diocefe and bailiwick, of Macon, *p. Macon.*
& *Rigower-des-Bois,* a village of Maine, in the diocefc and election of Wans. *p. Alston.* o *Rimay,* a village of Bcauce, in the election of Vendôme, *p. Mcntoire.* S. *Riqunr,* an ancient town of Pícardy, fituatcd on the Cardon, about ₴±, leagues frotn Abbeville, *p. Abbeville.* S. *Rirand,* a village of Fovcz, in the election or Roanne, *p. Roanr.e.* S. *Robert,* a village of Agenois, in the diocefc and election of Agen *p. Agen.*
& *Robert,* is S. *Egr/ve,* a village of Danphiny, in the diocefe and election of Grenoble. *p. Grenoble.* S, *Robert Maurice,* a fmull town of Limnfin, in the election of Brives. *p. Brives. IS. Rich,* a village of Touraine, in the diocefe and election of Tours, *p. 7 curs.* S, *Rogatim,* a town of Atinïs, in the diocefe and election of Rochelle. *p. la Rochelle.* S. *Romain.* I. A large village of Normandv, in the diocefe of Rouen, and election of MontivilHers. *Sureau de poße.* 2. A markec-town of Normandy, in the election of Mortain. *p. Mortain.* 3. A town of Poitou, in the election of Poitiers *p. Chaunay.* 4. A village of Poitou, in the election of Châtelerault. *p. les Ormes.* 5. A village of Agénois» in the diocefe and election of Agen. *p. Agen.* 6. A village of A¿éno:s, in the diocefe and election of Agen. *p. las Peires.* 7. A village of Auvergne, in the election of IfToirc. *p. IJJ'o'ire.* %. A village of Burgundy, in the bailiwick of Bcaune. *p. Macon.* 9. A village of Bléfois, in the election of Romorantin. *p. Romo antin.* 10. A village of Baz.idois, in the election of Condom, *t. Bazas.* II. A village ofPicardy, in the diocefe and election of Amiens, *p. Amiens.* 12. A village of Périgord, in the diocefe and election of Pc igueux. *p.* S. *Par doux.* 13. A vil-läge of Querev, in the election of Figeac. *p. Figeac* 14. A village of Dauphiny, in the diocefc and generality of Grenoble, *p. Grenoble,* ly. A collégial church in the dinccfe of Limoji s.
S. *Rcmain-d"Albon,* a vilbge o£ Dauphiny, in the diocefc and election of Vienne, *p.* S. *Valiicr.* S. *Rjmain-de-Blaic,* an abby in the diocefcof Bourdeaux, inGuienne. S. *Romm-de-Bonet, л* town of Saintonge, in the diocefc and election S *Romain-de-Çollelafc,* a market-S. *Romans,* a village of Dauphiny, town of Normandy, in thediocefe of in the diocefe and election of Valence.
K mien. *p.* S. *Remain. p.* 5. *Marccllin.*

S. R'.main-de-Cordeirrs, a village-S. Romans-de-Mille, a village of of Lower Langued ic, in the dioccfe Poitou, in the election of S. Maixant.
and receipt of Alais, *f Ala'u. p.S. Maixant*. S. Romnin-de-la-VaUtie. a fmall & Romans-des-Cbatnps, a village of town of Angoumois, in the diocefe Poitou, in the election of Niort, *p.* and election of Angoulêmc. /. X *Aiort. Cibardeaux.* S. Rome, a village of Languedoc,
S. Romain-de-Rocbt, a village of in the diocefe and receipt of Touloufe.

Franche-Comté, in the diocefe and *p. Touloufe.* bailiwick of S. Claude, *p. S. Claude.* S. *Romc-de-Cernm,* & *S. Rome* S. Romin-en-Cerviercs, a vilbge *de-Tarn* towns of Roucrguc, in the of Forez, in the election of Mont-election of Milhaud. *p Milbaud.* brifon. *p. Mj. nt!rijln.* S. Romme, a village of Périgord, in 5. Romain-cn-Fr:nfados, a fmall the diocefe and election of Sarlat. *p.* town of Guicnne, in the diocefe and S-Pardoux. election cf Rourdeaux. *p. Liboume.* S. Rompbaire, a fmall town of
S. Romain-cn-Gada, & S. Roma n-Normandy, in the election of S. Lo. les-Ateux, villages of Forez, in the /. *S. Lo.* election of S. Etienne, *p. S. Etienne.* S. Ratos, a village of Berry, in the *S. Romain-en-Giers,* a village of election of Ifloudun. *p. ljf.udun.* Lyonnois, in the diocefe and election & *Ruf,* an abby in the city of of Lyons, *p. S. Cbaumom.* Valence.

'--.... O r. Л:-. _..: ri _f тт.— of Fore/ ., in the election of S.Etienne, Languedoc, in the diocefe and receipt *p.* 5. *Chaumvrif.* oí Touloufe. *p. Grifolles.* S. Romain-la-Molie, a fmall town *Sie. Radegonde.* I. A town of of Forez, in the election of Roanne. Age'nois, in the diocefe and flection /. *Roanne.* of Agen. *p. Agen.* 2. A town of *S. Romam-Lcrmp,* & *S. Remain-*Saintonge, in the diocefe and eleñion *le-Deßrt,* villages of Vivarais, in of Saintes, *p. jfonjac.* 3. A village the receipt of Viviers, *p. Viviers* of Bazadois, in tlie election of Con S. Romain-le-Puy, a town of Fo-dum. *p. Bazas.* 4. A village in the rcz, in the election of Montbrifon. diocefe and election of Agen. *p. p. Montbrijon. VdUncwvc-eP Agen,* 5. A village of

& *Romain-fous-Gerdoin,* a parifh of Poitou, in the diocefe and election of Burgundv, in the bailiwick, of Cha-Poitiers, *p. Poitiers.* 6. A village of rolles, *p. Dijon.* Poitou, in the election of Themars, *p. S. Romain-fous-Verfigny,* a fmall *T'ouars.* 7. A vilbge of Auvergne, town of Burgundy in the bailiwick in the election of Combraillcs. of Chnrollcs. *p. Dijon. Chambón.* 8 A village of Rouergue, S. Roman, a village of Dauphiny, in the election of Milhaud. *p. Rhodes.* in the election of Montclimart. *p.* 9. A pariih of Burgundy, in the bai*Die.* liw'ck of Montcenis. *p. Aulun..* S. *Romar.-de-D'Jan,* a village of Ste. Radegonde, or *Cufay.* See CиLower Languedoc, in the diocefe and *fay.* receipt of Mende. *p. Mende. Sre. Radegonde de-Pe/ine,* a village 5. *Romar.-de-Mltgarde,* Êf & of Agénois, in the diucefe and elec *Roman-en-l'iennoi;,* ill. igcs of Vc-tun of Agen. *p. Agen.* naiffin, in the judicature of Carpen-*Sie. Radegomle-le-Rtjuep'me,* a.
fmal! town of Périgord, in the diocefe and election of Sarlat. *p. Sarlat. Sie. Radtgonde-des-Nojers,* a fmall town of Poitou, ¡B the election of Fontenay. *p. Luçon. Sie. Radejande-la-Vmeufi,* a village ef Poitou, in the election of Fontenay. *p. Fontenay. Sie. Radegcnde-près-Pont-Г Abbe',* a village of Saintonge, in the diocefe and election of Saintes, *p. Saintes. Sit. Rafir.e,* a village of Agénois, in the diocele and election of Agen. *p. Agen. St:. Reine* & *Afee,* a town of Burgundy, in the diocefe of Autun, and bailiwick of Semur-en-Auxois; about 4 leagues from Semur. *Bureau de-piße.* See *Alije. Sie. Rußine,* a village in the diocefe and reciipt of Metz. *p. Mens.* S. Sabaßien, a village of Lower Languedoc, in the diocele and receipt of Alais. *p.Anduje.* S. Saens. I. A large town of Normandy, in the diocefe of Rouen and election of Neufchàtel; about 3 leagues from Neufchàtel, and 8 from Rouen. *Bureau de poße.* 2. A river in Caux.
& *Sain'inCantale%,* a fmall town of Auvergne, in the election of Aurillac. *p. Aurillac.* S. *Saintin-de-Maurs,* a village of Auvergne, in the election oí Aurillac. *p. Aurillac.* & *Saire,* a fmall town of Normandy, in the election of Neufchà-

tel. *p.-Neufchátel.* S. Salomon, a village of Bretagne, in the diocefe and receiptof Vannes. *p. Vannes.* S. *Salvadou,* a village of Roucrgue, in the election of Villefranche. *p. Villefranche-de-Rouergue.* -S. *Salvadour,* a fmall town of Limofin, in the election of Brives. *p. tulles.* S. *Salve,* a village of Limofin, in the eleaion of Tulles, *p. Tulles.* S. *Salvy.* 1. A village of Agénois, in the diocefe and election of Agen. *f. JPortSii.-Atarie,* 2. A village in the diocefe and election of Rhode?. *p. Rhoden.* S. *Salvy-de-Carcajes.* See *Carcaves.* S. Sandoux, a town of Auvergne, in the diocefe and election of Clermont, *p. Clermont.* S. *Sarrfert. i* A town of Anjou, in the diocefe and election of Angers. *p. Angin.* 2. A town of Maine, in the diocefe and election of Mans. *p. Pre%-en-PaiL* 3. A village of Picardy, in the diocefe and election of Beauvais. *p. Beawvah.* 4. A village of Bretagne, in the diocefe and receipt of S. Brieivx. *p. D'tnan,* 5. A vilLgeof Normandy, in the election of Andely. *p. Caillon.* 6. A village of Normandv, "in the election of PontTEveque. *p. Pont-l'Evéque,* S. *San/çn-de-Bon-Fo///',* a village of Normandy, in the election of S. Lo. *p. S. Lo.* S. *Sanßn-de-lat-Ropte,* a vilbge of Normandy, in the election of PontAudemer. *p. Pont-Audenter.* S. *Sanfm-Jouxte-Lii'eTj* a place of Bretagne, in the diocefe and receipt of Dol. *p. Dol.'* 4' S. *Satin-fur-Rille* a village of Normandv» in the election of PontAudemer. *p. Pont-Audemer.* S, *Sapbsiln-d'OxoH-en-Soiai%ei* a town of Dauphiny, in the election of Vienne, *p. Vunne.* S. *Sardos, i.* A village of Agénois, in the diocefe and election of Agen. *p. Cierac.* 2. A village of Armagnac, in the election of Rivière-Verdun,*p. Gnßblla.* S. *Sam,* an abby, in the diocefe of Valence, in Dauphiny.

& *Satur,* a town of Rerry, in the diocefe and election of B urges-*p. Sancerre.* S. *Saturnin, i.* A town of Auvergne, in'the diocefe and election of Clermont. *p. Clermont.* 2. A town of Auvergne, in the diocefe and election of S. Flour. *p. S. Flour,* 3. A town in the diocefe and election of Mans./. *le Mamt* 4. A town of Anjou, in the diocele and election of Angers, *p. CbatetU' Cmtt'ier.* 5. A town of Angoumois, in the diocefe and ele&idhof Angoulémc. *p. Châteauncuf-en-Angoumùs.* 6. A village of Berry, in the election of ChAtrc. *p. la Châtre.* 7. A village of Poitou, in the diocefc and election of Poitiers, *p. Poitiers.* 8. A village of Lower Languedoc, in the diocefc and receipt of Lodevc. *p. Lotteve.* 9. A village of Brie, in the election of Scz.annr. *p. Se%annc.* 10. A place of Gafcony, in the cle6inn of Landes, *p. S. Sever.* 11. A pariih. in the diocefc of Angouleme.

5. *Saturnin-de-Coh art)* a village of t,owcr Languedoc, in the diocefc and receipt of Nîmes, *p. Mendt. S. Satuminde-/a-Motte-S.yeanf* a village: of Burgundy, in the diocefc and bailiwick of Autun. *p. la Pacaudiere. S. Saturnin-du-BoiSj* a fmall town o'f Aunis, in the diocefc and election of Rochelle, *p. Mause. S. San/aje,* a village of Dauphiny, Jп the election of Montelimart. *p. Montelimart. S. Sauby.* I. A vi'lage of Armagnac, in the diocefc and election of Auch. *p. Gimcnt.* 2. A village of Armagnac, in the election of Lomagne. *p. Beaumont-de-Lomagne. S. Savin, 1.* A fmall town of Guienne, in the diocefe and election of Bourdcaux. *p. Blaye.* 2. A fmall town of Dauphinvj in the diocefc and election of Vienne, *p. Bourgcin.* 3. A village of Poitou, in the diocefe and election of Poitiers. *Bureau de pvße.* 4. A village of Bigorre, in the generality of Auch. *p. Tarées.* 5. A place of Saintongc, in the election of S. Jcand'Angely. *p. S. Jeand,Angely. S. Savinieñ)* a town of Saintonge, about 3 leagues from Saintes, and 7 From S. Savin-du-Port. *S. Sav'nien,* or *San'irt-du-Por',* a town of Saintongc, in the diocefe of Saintes and election of S. Jean-d'Angely; about 5 leagues from S. JcancTAngely, and 4 from Saintes. *Bureau de j-oße. S. Sai-enien-les-vJUy* a village of Champagne, in the diocefe and election of Sens, *p. V.l.tnewve-jur-Tcnne. S. SaviJj* a village of Poitou, in, the diocefc and election of Poitiers, *f. Cbaunay.* S *Sauigt,* a town of Nivernois, in the diocefe and election of Nevers. *p. Nevers. S. Savournin,* or *Saturnin.* т. A fmall town of VenahTin, in the judi-

cature of Carpentras. *p. Avignon.* 2. A fmall town of Provence, in the diocefc and viguery of Apr. *p-Apt* 3. A v'liage of Provence, in the diocefe and viguery of Aix. *p. Aix. S. Saury* a village of Auvergne, in the election of Aurillac. *p. Aurillac. S. Sawvant.* I. A town of Poitou, in the diocefe and cUction of Poit'ers. *Lußgnan.* 2-A town of Saintonge, in the diocefe and election of Saintes, *p. TaiHebourg. S. Sawve.* г. A town of Auvergne, in the diocefe and election of Clermont, *p. Clermont.* %. A village of Hainaut, in the generality of Maubeugc. *p. Valenciennes. S. Sauver y* a park of 1800 arpents, in the jurifdiction of Poitiers. 5. *Saui/eur.* i. A fmall town of Normandy, in the election of Argentan, *p. Argentan.* 2. A fmall town of Nivernois, in the election of Clamecy. /». *Chmeey.* 3. A village of Picardy, in the election of Compicgne. *p. Comfi/gne.* 4. A village of Limofin, in the diocefe and election of Limoges, *p. L'moges.* 5, A village of Dauphiny, in the election of Romans, *p. Tain.* 6. A village of Dauphiny, in the diocefe and election of Vienne, *p. S. Marcellin.* 7. A village of Dauphiny, in the generality of Grenoble, *p. Grencble.* 8. A village of Dauphiny, in the generality of Grenoble, *p. Gre.oble.* 9. A village ofDauphiny, in thediocefe and election of Gap. *p. Gap.* 10. A village of Dauphiny, in the election of Montelimart. *p. le Buis.* и. A village of Picardy, in the election of Doulens. *p. Doultns.* 11. A village »f Auvergne, in the election of Iftoíre, *p. IßbWe,* 13. A village of Gâtinois, in the élection of Mclun. *p» Meîun.* 14. A village of FrancheComté, in the bailiwick of Vefoul.

Lure. 15. A village of Bafadoisj in the election of Condom, *p. Bazas.* 16. A village of Poitou, in the election of Thouars. *p. Brefvire.* 17. A village of Poitou, in the election of Châtellerault. *p. Châtellerault.* 13. A village of Burgundy, in the diocefe and receipt of Dijon, *p. Dipt.* 19. A village of Upper Languedoc, in rhc diocefe and receipt of "Touloufc. *p. touhuje. 2o.* A village of Champagne, in the election of Nogent. *p. Nogent.* 21. A village of Berry, in

the diocefe and election of Bourges. *p. Bourges. 22.* A village of Condommois, in the diocefe and election of Condom, *p. Mar mande,* 23. A village of Quercy, in the diocefe and election of Ca hors, *p. Cabors.* 24. A village of Burgundy, in the bailiwick of Auxonne. *p. Auxonne.* 25. A place of Gatinois, in the election of Montargis. *p. Bois-Conmun.* 26. A place of Angoumois, in the diocefe and election of Angoulémé. *pAngoulémé.* 27. A place of Bretagne, in the diocefe and receipt of Treguicr. *p. Gu'mgamp.* 28. A convent in the city of Marfcille. 29. A territory of picardy, in the election of Compiégne. *S. Sauveur-i?' Aniane.* See *Amane.-_ S. Sauveur-de-Bijacbe,* an abby in the diocefe of Bayonne. *p. Baycnne. S. Sauveur le Yeφun,* a fmall town of Fore?., in the election of S. Etienne, *p. S. Etienne. S. Sauveur-de-Bonßffe,* a village of Normandy, in the election of S. Lo. *p. S. Lo. S. Sauveur-de-CbauUeu. SccCbaulieu. S. Sauveur-de-Qer ans* a village of Périgord, in the diocefe and election of Pérrguçux. *p. la Linde. S. Sawfur-de-GiugiereSy* a village pf Lower Languedoc, in the diocefe *gueuse,* 4,. A village of Dauphiny, in the generality of Grenoble, *p. Die. S. Secondin.* I. A village of Poitou, ín the diocefe and election of Poitiers, *p. Cbaunay.* 2. A village of Bléfois, in the diocefe and election of Blois. *p. Blets. S. Segal,* a village of Bretagne, in the diocefe and receipt of Quimper, *f. jumper. S. Seigne,* a village of Nivernois, in the election of Nevers. *p. Desife. S. Seigne-cn-Bajcbe,* a village of Burgundy, in the bailiwick of Auxonne. *p. Auxonne. S. Seillac,* a Gmall town of Limofin, in the election of Brives. *p. jBrives. S. Seine,* a fmall town of Burgundy, in the diocefe of Langrcs, and bailiwick of Châtillon; 6 leagues from Dijon, It from Montbard, 13 from Chàtillon-fur-Seine, 29 from Troyes, a i from Tonnerre, and 60 from Paris. *Bureau de jofle. S. Seine-jur-Vmgeane,* a village of Burgundy, in the diocefe and bailivick of Dijon, *p. Dijon, S. Selve,* a fmall town of Guicnne, in the diocTefe and election of Bourdeaux. *p. Bourdeaux. S. Senat,* a village of Périgord, in the diocefe and election of Péngueux. *p. Perigueux. S. Semers-*

prez-Avrancbes, a village of Normandy, in the diocefe and election of Avranchcs. *p. Avranches.* S. *Senocb,* a town of Tourainc, in the election of Lorhes. *p. Locbds.* S. *Semu,* a village of Bretagne, in the diocefe and receipt of S. Malo. *f. S. Mato.* S. *Sepulchre,* an ancient abby in Cambray. S. *Sequelin,* a village of Bretagne, in the diocefe and receipt of S. Malo. ¿p. *S. Malo.* S. *Serain,* a convent in the diocefe of Rhodez. *p. Rhodez.* S. *Serge-let-Angers y* an ancient abby, in the dioccie of Angers, *p. Anrät.* Vat. IIb S. *Scríex,* a village of Lower Languedoc, in the diocefe and receipt of Montpellier, *p. Montpellier.* S. *Sernïn.* i. A village of Upper Languedoc, in the diocefe and receipt of MirepVix. *p. Limoux.* 2. A village of Lower Languedoc, in the diocefe and receipt of Viviers. *p. Aubenas.* 3. A village of Upper Languedoc, in the diocefe and receipt of Alby. *p. Alby.* 4. A village of Lower Languedoc, in the diocefe and receipt of Alais, *p. Alai:.* 5. A village of Burgundy, in the diocefe and bailiwick of Mâcon. *p. Масон.* 6. A place of Rouergue, in the election of Milhaud. *p.* S. *Afrique.* S. *Srnm-du-Boii)* a pariíh of Burgundy, in the bailiwick of Montcenis. *p. Dijon.* S. *Scmin-du-Plain.* 1. A village of Burgundy, in the bailiwick of Montccnis. *p. Dijon.* 2. A pariíh of Burgundv, in the diocefe and bailiwick of Autun. *p. Autun. $. Scrninhavaux л* a village of Limofin, in the election of Brives. *p. Bri ves.* S. *Servand,* a town of Bretagne, in the diocefe and receipt of S. Malo. *p.* S. *Mjio.* S. *Servant* a village of Bretagne, in the dioccie and receipt of Vannes. *p. Plot: met.* S. *Seve, л* village of Bazadois, m the election of Condom, *p. la Re'vlle.* S. *Sever.* I. A city of Gafcnni, fituated on the Adour, in the diocefe of Aire and election of Landes; about 7 leagues from Aire, and *mo* from-Dax. *Bureau de pr.ße.* 1. Л market-town of Normandy, 3 logues from Vire, 3 from Villedieu, and 16 from Caën. *p. Vire.* 3. A village of Rouifilbn, in thcelcction of Milhaud. *p.* S. *Affrique.* S. *Severde-R:ißjn,* a town of Armagnac, in the election of Aitarar; about 2 leagues from Tarbes. *p, Tarbcs.* S. *Severe,* a town of Sainronge, i« the diocefe and clectioti of bauitcs.' *p. Saintel.* S. *Severin,* i. A town of Angoumois, in the diocefe and election of An¿uul¿me. *p. Barbeßeux.* a. A village of Poitou, in the election of Ni «t. *p. Niort.* 3-A village of Angoumois, in the election of Соgлас, *p. Cognac.* 4. A village of Marche, in the election of Gueret. *p. AitbuJJ'n.* S. *Severin-de-Château-Landonj* an abby in the diocefe of Sens, *p, Cbauau-handon.* S. *Sverin-de-Puy-Mircl,* a town of A génois, in the diocefe and election of Agen. *p. Agen.* S. *Severin-cn-Bourg,* a village of Guienne, in the diocefe and election of Bourdeaux. *p. Catiras.* S. *Scwßt* a village of Dauphiny, in the election of Romans, *p.-Romans.* S. *Sevzïïj,* an abby in Touraine. S. *Sevittf* a village of Gafcony, in the receipt of Bigorre. *p. 'Taries.* S. *Sevire,* a foreft of 800 arpents, in the jurifdiction of Bayeux, in Nu riñan dy. S. *Severin Aurignac,* a town of Sain tange, in the diocefe and election of Saintes, *p. Saintes.* S. *Sexre,* a place of Dauphiny, in the diocefe and election of Vienne. *p. Vienne.* S. *Sibourr.eî & Bay et y* a village of AgénoU, in the diocefe and election of Agen. *p. Agen.* S. *Sidrowe,* a priory in the diocefe of Sens. S. *Siffrety* a village of Lower Languedoc, in the diocefe and receipt of Uzés. *p. Uze's.* S. *Sigijmond.* I. A town of Anjou, in the dlocefeand election of Angers. *p. Ingrar.de.* 2. A village of Poitou, in the election of Fontenay. *f. Niort.* 3. A village of Orleannois, in the election of Beaugency. *p. Oi lcans.* 4. A convent in Beam, in the diocefe oí Dax. *p. Orthe.* S. *Siivain.* i. A town of Anjou, in the diocefe and election of Angers. *p. Angers.* 2. A place of Normandy, in the ekcticn of Arques. /. S, *Valéry.* S. *S'Ivain-de-Baleroty* S.*Sil-vainfcus-Tlvu,* villages of Bourbonnois, in the élection of S. Amand. *p.* S. *Amand.* S. *Silvain-de-Bellegerdet* a village of Marche, in the election of Guerct. *p. Chêneailles.* S. *Suvain-des-Averdines,* a village of Berry, in the diocefe and election of Bourges, *p. Bourges.* S. *Silvain-Mon-tegUf* a village of Marche, in the election of Gueret. *p. Gueret.* S. *Silveßre.* I. A fmall town of Limofin, in the diocefe and election of Limoges, *p. Race's.* 2. A village of Vivarais, in the receipt of Viviers. *p. Vcmcux.* 3. A village of Bourbonnois, in the election of Gannat. *p. Aigueperß,* 4. A village of Agénois, in the diocefe and election of Agen. *p. Vilknewve-dAgen.* 5. A village of Normandy, in the election of Caudebec. *p. LUlebonne.* 6. A village of Bazadois, in the election of Condom, *p. Bazas.* S. *Silveß/e-de-Cormeillcf* a village of Normandy, in the election of Pont-Auderaer. *p. Pont-Audemer.* S. *Silvin.* I. A market-town of Normandy, in the election of Caën. *p. Caen.* 2. A village of Normandy, in the election of Arques, *p. Fecamp.* S. *Sim/on.* I. A fmall town of Dauphiny, in the diocefe and election of Vienne, *p. ¡a Cote* S. *Anar/,-%.* A village of Brie, in the election of Coulomiers. *p. Relets.* 3. A village of Normandy, in the election of Pont Audcmcr. *p. Pcnt-Audemer.* S. *Simeux,* a village of Angeumois, in the election of Cognac, *p. Cbâteaureuf-en-Angcumcis.* S. *Similien,* a village of Bretagne, in the diocefe and receipt of Nantes. *p. Nartes.* S. *Simon,* i. A town of Picardy, in the diocefe and election of Noyon. *p. Ham.* a. A town of Auvergne, in the diocefe and election of Aurillac. /. *Aufillac* 3. A village of Guienne, in the diocefe and election ot' Bourdeaux. *p. Blaye.* 4. A village of Angoumois, in the election of Cognac. *p. Cbateauneuf-en-Angoum mois.* 5. A village in the diocefe and election of Condom, *p. Nerac.* 6. A village of Quercy, in the election of Figeac. *p.rigcac.* St *Simon-de-Bordes,* a town of Saintonge, in the diocefe and cle¿lion ôf Saintes, *p. Montendre.* S. *Simpbrien.* See S. *Symp-borien.* S. *Slmphcr'm-le-Petit,* a village of Forez, in the election of Roanne, *p. Roanne.* S. *Sirac fif Liffert,* a village of Upper Languedoc, in the diocefe and receipt of Mircpnx. *p. Mepoix.* S. *Siran.* Sec S. *Cyran.* S. *Sire,* a village of Burgundy, in the diocefe and bailiwick of Macon. *p. Your mis.* S. *Sire-les-Colon,* a town of Burgundy, in the diocefe and bailiwick of Auxerre. *p. Auxerre,* S. *Sixte,* i. A village of Forez, in the ele¿tion of Roanne, *p. Roanne.* 2. A village of Agénois, in the diocefe and election of Agen. *p. lat Peyres.* S *Solain,* a village of Bretagne, in the diocefe and receipt of. Dol. *p, Dinan.* S. *Solve,* a village of Limoiin, in the election of Brives. *p. Uzerches. S.Sorlin,* j. A town of Bugey, in he bailiwick of Belley. *p. Amber'uux.* 2. A village of Dauphiny, in the diocefe and election of Vienne, *P. Vienne.* 3. A village of Burgundv, in the diocefe and bailiwick of Macon, *p. Mâcon.* 4. A village of Poitou, in the election of Sables-d'Olonne. *p. Luçon.* 5. A village of Lyonnois, in the diocefe and election of Lyons, *p. Lyon.* 6. A village "bf Beaujolois, in the election of Villefnmche. *p. Lyw.* S. *Soi lin-de-Sechaud,* a tow n of Saintonge, in the diocefe and eleélion of Saintes, *p. Jor. %ac.* S. *Sor lin'de-Vas,* a village of Dauphiny, in the diocefe and election of Vienne, *p. Vienne.* S. *Sorlirt jcus-Cofnac,* a town of Saintonge, in thediocefc and elcctioa of Saintes, *p. Saintes.* S. *Sórnin.* i, A town of Saintonge, in the election of Marennes. *p. Marennes* 2. A fmall town of Angoumois, in the diocefe and election of Angoulême. *p. la Rtcbcfsucau/t.* 3. A village of Bourbonnois, m the election of Montlucon. *p. Montlucon.* 4. A village of Auvergne, in the ele&ion of Combraillcs. *p. Chambón.* S. *Sorniu-la-Marche, & S. SorninMayna%cix,* villages of Limofin, in the diocefe and election of Limoges *p. Limoges.* S. *Sou/an,* a village of Gafcony, in the diocefe and election of Comminges. *p. Samatan.* S. *Soupht.* 1. A village of Champagne, in the election of Rcthd. *p, Retbei.* z. A village of Brie, in the diocefe and election of Meaux. *p. Dammartin.* S, *Souflet & S. Cr ¿pin,* a village of Flanders, in the diocefe and fubdelegation of Cambray. *p. Camhay.* S *SremorJ,* a p.iriih of Normandy, in the generality of Caën. *p. Cou taras.* S. *Still ac,* a village of Bretagne, in the diocefe and receipt of S. Malo. *p. S. Malo.* S. *Sulficc.* i. A town of Berry, m the election of Blanc, *p. le Blanc,* z. *A* town of Anjou, in the election of Châtcau-Gontier. *p. Châtcau-Gontur.* 3. A town of Normandy, in the election ofVerncuil. *p. Verneu.il.* 4. A village of Poitou, in the election of Maulcon. *p. Maulmn.* 5. A village of Poitou, in the election of Fontenay. *p. Fomer.ay le-Cmte.* 6. A village of Anjou, in the diocefe and election of Angers, *p. Ange/s* 7. A village of Fore?,, in the election of Montbrifon. *p. Montbnjon.* 8. A village of Fore/, in the election of Roanne, *p. Rcanne.* 9. A village of Picardy, in the diocefe and electîon of Beauvais. *p. Beauvats.* io. A village of Picardy, in the election of S. Quentin, *p. S. Quentin.* 1 11. A x'illage of Perche, in the election of Mortagne. *p. Mortagre.* iz. A village of Brie, in the election of Provins, *p. Provins.* 13. A village of Blé fois, in thediocefe and election of Blois. *p. Bloh.* 14. A village of Périgord, in the diocefe and election of Périfueux. *p. Pirigueux.* 15. A village of Périgord, in the diocefe and election of Sarlat. *p. Sarlat.* 16. A village of Normandy, in the election of Pont-Audemer. *p. pGnt-Audtmer.* ij. A village of Burgundy, in the bailiwick: of Challón, *p. ChaiIon.* л8. A village of Quercy, in the election of Figeac. *p. Gabon.* 19. A A village of Rouerguc, in the election of Villefranche. *p. ViHefrancht-deMouergue.* 20. A village of Burgundy, in the bailiwick of S. Laurent, *p. Lcuhans.* a i. A place of Franche-Comté, in the bailiwick of Vefoul. *p. Vefoul.* 22. An abby in the diocefe of Bclley. *p. Belly.* 23. A priory in Maine.

S. *Sulpke & rEnclave-de-M'tgrcn'bourg,* a village of Angoumois, in the election of Cognac, *p. C'grac.* S. *Sulpke Ô? S. Bau%el-de-Sonlas% & S. SuIpice-de-Boéy* villages of Agéswis, in the diocefe and election of Agfti-*p. Agen.* S. *Sulpke S. Gcurßtij* a village of Angoumois, in the diocefe and election of Angoulêmc. *p. Angoulême.* S. *Sulpke-de-Favkres,* a village in the diocefe and election of Paris, *p. Arpa j on.* S. *Sulpice-de-PAblaye,* a village with a convent, in the diocefe and receipt of Nantes. /. *Rennes.* S. *Sulpke-de-Pkrrepont,* a priory in the diocefe of Soiffons. & *Su-p'tce-de-Ri'valede,* a village of Agénois, in the diocefe and election /if Agen. *p. Viliencuvc-d'Agen.* S. *Sulpke-de-S.-Emlhn,* a fmall £own of Gúiennc, in th&d'occfe and.election of Bourdeaur. a. *Uloume, ê S. Sulpke-des-Landesj* a village oí Bretagne, in the diocefe and rsceipt of Nantes, *p. Ancenis.* S. *Sulpice-Feylet,* a village of Limofin, in the election of Tulles, *p. Tul¿es.* S. *Snlpice-grande-Pre'vQte'j* a village of Guienne, in the diocefe and election of Bourdeaux. *p. Bourdecux.* S. *Sulpice-bors-les-Enclavesf* a village of Périgord, in the diocefe and élection of Périgueux. *p. Périgueux.* S. *Sulpke-Laurieref* a village of Limofin, in the diocefe and'elcction of Limoges, *p. Razes.* S. *Sulpke-le-Cbaßelj* a fmall town of Nivcrnois, in the diocefe and election of Revers, *p. Nevers.* S. *Sùlfice-Ie-DouzcUj* a village of Marche, in the election of Gueret. *p. Abun.* S. *Sulpkc-le-Dunois,* & S. *SulpkeîeXjueretoh,* towns of Marche, in the élection of Gueret. *p. Gueret.* S. *Sulpke-les-CbartîpSy* a village in the election of Gueret. *p. Gueret.* S. *Sulpke-Lezadois,* a city of Upper Languedoc, fituated on the river Leze; about a leagues from Rieux, and 5 from Touloufe. *p. TcuJoufi.* S. *Sulpice prh-MornaCy* a town of Saintonge, inthe diocefe and election of Saintes, *p. Cozes.* S. *Sulpke-prhP ont-P Abbe',* a towa of Saintonge, in the diocefe and election, of Saintes, *p. Saintes* S. *Sulpîs,* a place of Brefle, in the bailiwick of Bourg, *f. Bourg-enBreffe.* S. *Sumiere-de-Rivedcl,* a village of Agénois, in the diocefe and election of Agen. *p. Agen.* S. *Suplexy* a place of Normandy in the election of Eu. *p. Eu.* S. *Suplix* ï, A village of Normandy, in the election of MontiviU Hers. *p. Dieppe.* z. A village of Normandy, in the diocefe and election of Baycux. *p. Bayeux.* S. *Suplix-de-Bellcngeville,* a village of Normandy, in the election of Arques, *p, Dkppe* 3 S. *Suflix-de-Fontaine,* a figniory of Normandy, in the diocefe and election of Rouen, *p. Rouen.* S. *Supl'tx-de-la-Pierret* a village of Normandy, in the diocefe and election of Rouen, *p. Rouen.* S. *Sympbor'nn.* i. A town of Maine, in the diocefe and election of Mans. *p. le Mam.* 2. A town of Saintonge, in the election of S. Jean-d'Angdy. *f. S. yean-cfAngely.* 3. A fmall town of Guienne, in the diocefe and election of Bourdeaux. *p. Bourdtaux.* 4. A village of Saintonge, in the election of Marennes. *p. Marennes.* 5. A village of Limofin, in the diocefe and election of Limoges, *p. Limoges*, 6. A village of Beauce, in the diocefe and election of Chai tres. y. *Chartres*. 7. A village of Normandy, in the election of Carcntan. *p. Carentan*. 8. A village of Normandy, in the election of Mortain. /. *Mortain*. 9. A village of Normandy, in the election of S. Lo. *p. S. Lo*. 10. A village of Normandy, in the election of Pont-Audcmer. *p. Pont-Audemcr.* 11. A village of Anjou, in the election of Baugé. *p. Baugé*. 12. A village of Lower Languedoc, in the diocefe and receipt of Viviers, *p. Mendt*. 13. A village of Buurb nnois, in the election of Moulins, *p. Moulins*. 14. A village of Burgundy, in the diocefe and bailiwick, of Mâcon. *p. Macon*. 15. A village of Burgundy, in the diocefe and bailiwick of Autun. *p. Au: un*. 16. A village of Burgundy, in the bailiwick, of Montcenis. *p. Dijon*. 17. A village of Berry, in the election of IfFoudim. *p. Iffovdun*. 18. A village of Berry, in the diocefe and election of Bourges, *p. Bourges*. 19. A village of Bretagne, in the diocefe and receipt oí Nantes, *p. Ren ties*. ao. A village of Poitou, in the election of Niort, *p. Niort*. 21. A village of Provence, in the vigucry of Siileron. *p.S'tßeroa*. 22. A place of Burgundy, in the bailiwick, of Auxonne, *p. Auxonne*. 23. A place of Burgudy, iu the bailiwick of

Burgundy, in the diocefe ánd receipt "%i Dijon, *p. Dijon. Stit Sc nc-lcs-Halles*, a village 'of Burgundy, in the diocefe and bailiwick of Dijon, *p, Dijon. Sre. Seionne. i*, A village of Perche, in the election ofMortagne. *p. Morsagne. Ste. Severe*, i. A town of Berry, in the diocefe of Bourges; about 3 leagues from Chârtrc, and 11 from. Ifloudun. *p. la Cbartrg*, 2. A village of Angoumois, in the election of Cognac, *p. Cognac'. Si/. Sertrutfy* a town of Saintonge, in rhc election and election ol Saintes. *f. Stntes. S te. Si e*, a village of Champagne, in the diocefe and election of 1 royes. *p. Troyes. Sie. Sc'.cnr. e*, vijfege of Blé ibis, in the diocefe and election of BloU. *p. S/eis. Sie. Sau/enge*, a town of Berry, on the river "ïevre, about 3 leagues from Bourges: it is fomctimes called S. Martin, *p. Bourges. Sie. Sou!et* a t wn of Auais, in the diocefe and election of Rochelle, *p. Ja Rochelle. Ste. Souline. t*. A village of Poitou, in the-diocefe and election of Poitiers, *p. Poitiers*, 2. A village of Sainton ge, in the diocefe of Saintes. /. *la Gnlle. Ste. Su%3ttne*. 1 A (mail city of Maine, in the diocefe and election of &l¿ns; about 9 leagues from Mans. *p. Mayer.n*. 2. A village of Normandy, in the election of JÏ. *ho. p. S. Lo*. . 3. A village of Normandy, in the election of Carrntan. *p. Carentan*. 4. A place of Beam, in the leceipt of Orrhez. *p Onbez. S. Taurin*. I. A village of Normandy, in the election of Pont-Audemer. *p. Evretix*. 2. A place of Picardy, in the election of Mond idler. *p. Mondid'ter. S. Tbe!ot* a village of Bretagne, in the diocefe and receipt of S. Bncux. *p. S. Brieux. S. Tbeçdore*, a priory, in the dio cefe of Grenoble. *S. Teny*, a pari (h of Normandy, in the diocefe de Coútances. *p Corentan. S. Theofray*, a village of Dauphiny, in the d.ocefc and election of Grenoble, *p. Grenoble. S. Terny*, a village of Provence, in the vigucry of Apt. *p. Apt. S. Thibault*, i. A fmall town of Picardv, in the diocefe and election of Amiens, *p. Anmale*. 2. A village of Champagne, in the diocefe and election of Troycs. *p. Troyes*, 3. A village of Picardy, in the diocefe and election of Sot (Tons, *p. Stiffens*. 4 A pariih of Burgundy, in the bailiwick of Semur-enAuxob. *p. Vit eaux*, 5. A priory in the diocefe of Chalons. S. *'Thibault-des-Boisj* a priory m the diocefe of Auxerre. *S. Thibault-des-Vgnet*, a village in the diocefe and election of Paris. /. *Lagny. S. Thibery*, a town of Languedoc, in the diocefe and receipt of Agde. *p. Pestenos, S. Thlebault*, a place of FrancheComté, in the bailiwick of Salins. *p. Salins. S. Thierry*, a village of Champagne, in the dio-cfe and elect.on of Rheims. *p. Rheims. S. Thiers-de-Saon*, an abby in the diocefe of Valence, *p. Valence. S. Thomas. X*. A village of Normandy, in the "election of S. Lo. *p, S. Lo*. 2. A village of Normandy, in the. election of Monttvilliers. *p. Harßeur*. 3. A village of Gafcony, in the diocefe and election of Comminges. *p.Lombex*. 4. A village of Dauphiny, in the d'ocefe and election of Valence, *p. Valence*. 5. A wood of 254 arpents, in the jurildiction of IOe-Jourdain. *S. Thomas-dt-B aillé)* a place of Bretagne, in the diocefe and receipt of Nantes, *p. Fougères. S. Themas-de-Cbandieu1* a fmall town of frauphiny, in the generality of Grenoble, *p. Grenoble*. ... *S. Tkomas-de-la-Cbaufsee*. See *Cbaufsee*. , 5. *Thomai-dc-Touques&imaW* town of Normandy, in the election of Pont-PEvêque. *p. Pиu-Г Eveque. S. Tkomas-du-Bois*, a village of Sa'mtonge, in the diocefe and election of Saintes, *p. Saintes. S. Tbomas-la-Garde*, a village of Forez, in the election of Montbrifon. *Monibr fon. S. Tbome*, a town of Lower Languedoc, in the receipt of Viviers, *p. Vtnjiers. S. Tkonan*, a village of Bretagne, in the diocefe and receipt of S. Polde-Léon. *p. Moriaix.' S. Tbual*, a village of Bretagne, in the diocefe and receipt of Du), *p. III. S. Tburkn*, a village of Normandy, in the election of Pont-Audemcr. *p. P or. L-Ax dem er. S. îburin*, a village of Forez, in the ckíticn of Roanne, *p. Roanne. S. Tiren*, an abby in the diocefe of Chartres, *p. Chartres. S. Tourban*, or *Urion Êf Tremenon*, a village of Bretagne, in the diocefe and receipt of Quimper. *p. Şu:n:per. S. Tratlj* a pariih of Bourbonnois, in the election of Gannat. *p. Gannat. S. Trailley* a village of Armagnac, in the election of Aftarac. *p. Nerac. S. Treßn*, a village of Bretagne, in the diocefe and receipt of Quimper. *f. Potuixy. S. Tne*, a village of Limofin, in the diocefe and election of Limoges. *p. Limoges. S. Trifay* a fmail town of Poitou, in the generality of Poitiers, *p. Lufort. S. Triton*, a village of Armagnac, in the election of Rivière-Verdun. *p. Grenade. S. Tri-vler*. i. A town of BrcíTe, about 3 leagues from Bourg, *p. Macon*. 2. A town of Dombes, in the diocefe of Lyons, *p. Belleville. S. Trojan*, i. A town of Saintongc, in the election of Marennes.

p. Blaye. 2. A village of Angoumois, in the election of Cognac, *p. Cognac. S. Tropes*, i. A town of Provence, about 4. leagues from Fréjus, and 12 from Toulon. /. *Fr/jut*. 2. A c ape of the cnaft of Provence 5. *Tubery*. Sec S. *Tbiiery. S. Tugdua'*, village of Bretagne, in the diocefe and receipt of Vannes. *p. Vannes &e. Tulle*, a village of Provence, in the viguery of Forcalquicr. *p. Mamfyue.* Ste. *Tbortttt,* a village of Berry, in the diocefe and election of Bourges, *p. Bourges.* Sie. *Terre,* a fmall town of Guiennne, in the diocefe and election of BoLirdeaux. *p. Bourdeaux.* S.Vcaß. I. A feapoit-town of Normandy, about 2 leagues from Barflcur. *p. Vahgvts.* 2. A village of Normandy, in tlx election of Caudebec. *p. Caudebtc.* 3. A village of Normandy, in the election of Pont-l'Evêque. *p. Ptnt-rEvrftii.* 4. A village ot Hainaut, in the dr.— cefc of Camoray. *p-Baiay* 5 A village of Flanders, in the diocefe and fubdelegation of Cambray. *p-Cambray.* 6. A village of Picard/t in the election of Clermont. *BcrbcrU.* 7. A village of Picardy, in the election of Doulens. *p. Doulens.* S. A village of Picardy, in the election, of Compiégnc. *p. Compiegrte.* 9. A village of Normandy, in the electionof Caen. *p. Ca'cn.* 10. A village of Normandy, in the election of Pont-l'Evêque. *p. Do/ule.* и. A place of Picardy, in the election of Doulens. *p. Amiens.* S. *Vaaß,* or S. *rVaß-de-Ma'euU,* an abby near Abbeville, *p. Abbiuil.e.* S. *Vcafl-d1Arras.* See *Arras.* S. *Vaafl-d'Equíqueville,* & S. *Vaaß-du-Val,* villages of Normandy, in the election of Arques, *p. Dieppe.* S. *Vaaß-fur-Mer,* a village of Picardy, in the election of Doiilcns. *p. Détiens.* S. *Vain* a village of Auvergne, in the election of líToirc *p. Jffolre.* S. *Vmft%* a village of San.tongc, in the election of S. Jean-d'Angely. *p. Samtes.* S, *Valentin,* i. A town of Gafcony, in the ЫеЛ1оп of RivièreVerdnn. *p. Grenade.* 2. A village of Berrv, in the ejection of liloudun. *p. JJjmiuM.* S. *Faferiettf* a village of Gatinois, in the election of Nemours, *p. Sers,* S. *Va/erieu,* a village of Poitou, in tr election of Fonteiiay. *p. FontenayU-Comte,* S. *Valeria,* a village of Burgundy, in the dfoccfe and bailiwick oí Challón, *p. Challen,* S *Valéry,* i. A town of Picardy, t the mouth of the Somme, in the d'occfe and election of Amiens; about *4 l¿;* leagues from Abbeville,and 5 *froth Jiu.* Bureau de pißt. 2. A village of Normandy, in ths election of Ncufchfitel. *p. Neufcbâtel.* 3. A village ot Normandy, in the election of Argues, *p. Anmale.* S. *Valéry-en-Cauxy* a large markettown and tcaport of Normandy, in the diocefe ot Rouen, and 1 lection of Arques; about 7 leagues from Dieppe and Fecamp, and 14 from RwUtn. *Bureau de pifie,* S. *Va levin fis? la* îW, a village of Burgundy, in the diocefe and bailiwick of Challón, *p. Challen.* S *Valier,* a village of Satntonge, in the diocefe and election of Saintes, *p. Sain i es.* S. *Vallery* i. A village of Normandy, in the election of Arques, *p. Fecamp. 1.* A village of Normandy, in the election of Montivilliers. *p. Uarßevr.* 3. A village of Normandy, in the election of Neufchâtcl. *p. Nwfchatel.* S. *Vallier, t.* A town of Dauphiny, in the road from Lyons to Valence; 8 leagues from Valence, 12 from Vienne, and 19 from Lyon's. *Bureau depoße.* 2. A village of Burgundy, in the bailiwick-of Charollcs. *p. Dijon.* 3. A village of Franche Compté, in the bailiwick of Gray, *p. Gray.* 4. A village of. Provence, in the diocefe and viguery of GralTe, *p. Große.* 5. A village of Champagne, in the diocefe and election of Langre. *p. Langre.* 6. A priory of Dauphiny. S. *Va/mer,* a priory of Boulogae. S. *VatidrUU.* I. A town of Normandy, near the Seine; about a league from Caudebec, and 5 from Rouen. *p.Caudebec.* 2. A village of Normandy, in the election of Alençon. *p. le Melleraut.* S. *Varendy* a town of Poitou, in the election of Thouars. *p. Tbouars.* S. *Vauberty* a place of FrancheCompte, in the bailiwick of Vefoul. *p. Vefoul.* S. *Vaury,* a town of Limofin, in the diocefe and election of Limoges. *p. Limoges.* S. *Venant,* a town of Artois, fituatcd on the Lis, in the diocefe and government of Arras; about 3 leagues from Aix, 4 from Bethune, 10 from Arras, and 7 from S. Orner. *Bureau de poße.* S. *Vénérant,* a village of Lower Languedoc, in the diocefe and receipt of Mende. *p. Mende.* S. *Venfûy* a town of Rouergue, in the election of Villcfranche. *p. Villefranche-de-Rouergue.* S. *VeralrtyZ* town of Nivernois, in the election of Charité, *p. Cofne.* S. *Veran.* I. A village of Rouergue, in the election of Milhauld. *p. Milbauld.* 2. A village of Dauphin y, in the election of Vienne, *p. MontDauphin.* S. *Veran-d?Ejparror.j* a village of Lower Languedoc, in the diocefe and receipt of Alais, *p. Alais.* S. *Verand.* i. A village of Lyonnois, in the diocefe and election of Lyons, *p. Lyon.* 2. A village of Burgundy, in the diocefe and bailiwick of Macon, *p. Macen.* S. *Veramy* a village of Burgundy, in the diocefe and receipt of Mâcon. *p. Mâcon.* S. *Vuerin-de-Gcnr.es.* See *Ger.nes.* 5. *Vtnre,* a fmall town of Límofin, in the election of Brives. *p. Brives.* S. *Vian,* a village of Bretagne, in the dioccfe ami receipt of Nantes, *p.* S. *Pere-en-Rets.* S.Vic. See *S.-Vie'.* S. *Vitl,* a village of Agénois, in the diocefe and election of Agen. *p. Villetieuve-d'Agin.* S. *Vieltur,* a town of Maine, in the diocefe and election of Mans, *p, le Mans.* S. *Vinar* i. A town of Beaujolois, in the election of Villefranche. *p. Villejr. nebe.* I. A fmall town of Bléfois, in the diocefe and election of Blois. *p. Bleu.* 3. A fmall town of Auvergne, in the diocefe and election of Clermont, *p. Ckrmont.* 4. A village of Auvergne, in the election of Aurillac *p.. Auril'ac.* 5. A village of Miirche, in the election of Guerct. /. *Gueret.* 6. A village of Agénois, in the diocefe and election ef Agen. *p. Agin.* 7. A village of Bourbonnois, in the election of Montlucon. *p. Montluçon.* 8. A village of Burgundy, in the bailiwick of Arnay-le-Duc. *p. Dijor..* 9. A village of Lower Languedoc, in the diocefe and receipt of Viviers, *p. Vivien.* 10. A village of Normandy, in the election of VerntuiJ. *p. VtrяeuИ-en-Percíe.* 11. A village of Rouerguc, in the election of Milhaud. *p. Milhaud.* 12. A village of Dauphiny, in the dioccfe and election of Vienne./1. *Tain.* 13. A village of Dnuphiny, in the generality of Grenoble, *p. Grenoble.* 14. A wood about a league and a half in circumference, in Caux in Normandv.

& *Viflor 6» Auuillars, л* village of Burgundy, in the bailiwick of Arnayle-Duc. *p. Dijon.* S. *Vi flor & Effumin,* a village of Forez, in the election of Montbrifon. *p. Mor.tbrifon.* S. *V.flor-de-Cmmeur,* a village of Normandy, in the election of Pont-l'Evêque. *p. Lijieux.* S, *ViSier-dt-Grmieres.* See *Gra vieres.* S. *Viilor-de-la-Cфе,* a village of Lower Languedoc, in the dioccfe and receipt of *Viés. f Bag-*

nols. S. *Viäor-de-Malcjp,* a village of Lower Languedoc, in the diocefe and receipt of Uzcs. /. *Ambroix.* S. *Vici'or-d"Epine,* a vHIageof Normandy, in the election of *Hevmy.p. Briofne.* S. *Viclor-dts-Monts,* a fmall town of Normandy, in the election of Vire. *p. Villedku.*

S. *Victor-en-Caux,* a town of Normandy, near the river Scie, about a league from Aufray, and 6 from Dieppe-, *p. Rouen.*

& *Viilor-la-Campagne,* л village of Normandy, in the diocsfe and election of Rouen, *p. Telltile.* S. *Vilfsr-j: ra-Maffiac,* a village of Auvergne, in the election of Brioude. *p. B' ioude.* S. *Visieret,* a place of Provence, in the diocefe and viguery of Aix. *p. U Martigues.* S. *Vielour.* I. A village of Auvergne, in the election of IfToire. *p. Ifflire. z.* A village of Limofin, in the election of Tulles, *p. Tulles.* 3. A village of Périgord, tn the dioeefo and election of Périgueux. *p. Cercles.* S. *V.ilurnien,* a town ot Poitou, in the election of Confolans. *p.* S. *Junten.* S. *Vidal,* a village of Lower Lan» guedoc, in the diocefe and receipt of Puy. *p. le Pay.*

¿'. *Vie.* I. A fmall town of Lire- fin, in the dioccfe and election of Limoges, *p. Limoges.* 2. A village cf Bourbonnais, in the election of bAmand. *p. S Arnaud.* S. *Vhor,* a village of Normandy, in the election of Montivillicrs. *p.* S. *Romain.* S. *Vigor-de-Mieux,* я village of Normandy, in the election ofFalaife. *p. Fa/ aife.* S *Vigor-de-Meferets,* a village of Normandy, in the election of Vire. *p. Conde'-itr-Noireau.* S. *Vigor-des-Monts,* a place of Nor mandy, in the diocefe of Coûtances. *p. Vire.*

S. *Vgor-te-Grand,* a fmall town of Normandy, in the diocefe and election of Bayeux. *p. Bayeux.* S. *Vtgor-fur-Eurc,* a village of Normandy, in the eleftion of Pontde-l'Arche. *p. Pont-de-l'yircbe.* S. *Pincent,* i. A fmall town of Auvergne, in the diocefe of S. Flour, *p.* S. *Fkur.* 2. A village of Upper Languedoc, in the diocefe and receipt ofToulouse. *p. Tailouje.* 3. A village of Normandy, in the eleftion of Montivillicrs. *p. la Rouge-Maijon.* 4 A village of Burgundy, in the bailiwick of S. Laurent, *p. Nuits.* 5. A village of Burgundy,

in the bailiwick of Autun. *p. Macon.* 6. A village of Agénois, in the diocefe and election of Agen. *p. Agen.* 7. A village of Bazadois, in the eleftion of Condom, *p. Condom.* 8. A village of Bretagne, in the dioceseand receipt of Vannes, *p. Redan.* 9. A village of Dauphiny, in the generality of Grenoble, *p. Grencble.* 10. A village cf Provence, in the diocefe and viguery of Siileron. *p. Sißeron.* 11. A village of Provence, in the viguery of Seine, *p. Sßeren.* la. A village of Quercy, in the diocefe and eleftion ofCahors. *p. Cabors.* 13. A village of Burgundy, in the bailiwick of Charolles. *p. Di/rn.* 14. A place of Agénois, in the diocefe and election of Agcm *p. Villeneuve-d' Agcc.* $. An abby, in the city of Senlis. 16. A barony of Poitou, in the election of S Maixant. *p. S M.ixant.* 17. A figniory of Normandy, in the dinctfe and eleftion of Évreux. *p. Vernon* S. *Vincent-anx-B. s,* an abby in the diocefe of Chartres, *p. Chateauneuf-en-Thi rierais.* S. *Vincent-d'AgaJJas,* S. *V.ncentde-Corps,* S. *Vh. cent-de-Sals,* S. *Vmcent-de-SatAgnac,* S. *Vincent-de-Sou"lier,* i£? *Я. Vtncenidt-Soujcmpecb,* villages of Agénois, in the diocefe and eleftion of Agen. *p. Agen.* S. *V'mitnt-de-Barrį,* a village pf Périgucux. *p.* S *Privat.* S. *Vincent-fur-Gram,* a final! town of Poitou, in the election of SablescГ O Ion ne *p. Luęcn.* S. *Vincent-fur-yard,* a village of Poitou, in the election of Sablcsd'Olonne. *p. Ies Sables.* S. *Vine,* or *Vime,* a figniory of Normandy, in the election of PontPEvêque. *p. Lifieux.* S. *Vmomer,* a village of Champagne, in the election of Tonnerre. *p. Tonnerre.* S. *Vity* a village of FrancheComté, in the bailiwick of Dole. *p. Voie.* S, *Vivant,* i. A village of Burgundy, in the bailiwick, of Nuits, *p. Nuits.* 2. A place of FrancheComté, in the bailiwick of Dole, *p. Dole.* 3. A wood of 187 arpents, in the jurifdiition of Touloufe.

S. *Vivien,* i. A village of Périgord, in the diocefe and election of Pcrigueux. *p. BourdeUle.* 1. A village of Guienne, in the diocefe and election of Bourdeaux. *p. VEfpare.* 3. A village of Aunis, in the diocefe and election of Rochelle, *f. la Rochelle,* 4. A village of Agénois, in the diocefe and election of Agen. *p.*

Villeneuve-d"'Agen. S. *Vivim-de-Cbampons, SctCbampons.* S. *Vivien-de-la-Vallee,* a town of Saintonge, in the diocefe and election of Saintes, *p. Rocbefcrt.* S. *VfAett-en-Efpare,* a village of Guienne, in the diocefe and election of Bourdeaux. *p. VEjpare.* S. *Vivien-tes-Sa'mtes,* a town of Saintonge, in the diocefe and election of Saintes, *p. Saintes.* S. *Ulpbacey* a town of Maine, in the diocefe and election of Mans. *p. la Ter té-Bernard.* S. *Ulricbj* a village of Alface, in the bailiwick óf Altkirch, *p. Benfell* S. *UniaC)* a village of Bretagne, in the diocefe and receipt of Dol *p. Dot.* S. *Voîr* a village of Bourbonnoîij in the eleftionof Moulins, *p. Moulins.* S. *Volufian-de-Fox,* an abby in the diocefe of Pamiers, in Foix, *p Foix* S. *Vougay,* a village of Bretagne, in thediocefc and receipt ofS.Pol-deLéon. *p. Morlaix.* S. *Vratn.* i. A village in the diocefe 3nd election of Paris, *p. Arpajeu.* 2. A villa0e of Nivernois, in the election of Charité-fur-Loire, *p. Cofne.* S. *Vrain-de-la-Cenfe,* a village of Champagne, in the election of Vitry, *p.* S. *Difier.* S. *Uran.* I. A village of Bretagne, in the diocefe and receipt of S. Bricuxp. S. *Bricux.* 2. A village of Dauphiny, in the generality of Grenoble. *p. Grenoble.* S. *Urbain,* i. A town of Champagne, about a league from Joinville. *p. JñnvUli.* 2. A village of Poitou, in the eleftion of Sablcsd'Olonne. *p. Beauvoir.* S. *Urcia,* a village of Normandy, in the diocefe and eleftion of Cofitance$-. *C'-u'ances.* S.*Urc.Je.* I. A fmall town of Auvergne, in the diocefe and eleftion of S. Flour, *p.* S. *Flour.* 2. A fmall town of Upper Languedoc, in the diocefe and receipt of Montauban*Montaubaru,* S. *Urciffi.* I. A village of Quercy, in the diocefe and election of Cahors. *p.Cabors.* 2. A village of Agénois, in the diocefe and eleftion of Agen. *p. Agen.* S. *Urgean,* a village of Guienne, in the diocefe and eleftion of Bourdeaux. *p. Bourdeaux.* S. *Ur::a!,* a village of Bretagne, in the diocefe and receipt of S. Malo. J *Mab.* S. *Uriel,* a village of Bretagne, in the diocefe and receipt of Dol. *p. Dol.* S. *Uricn,* л village of Normandy, in the ticftion of Pcnt-Aiucmer. *p. Boni-Лu de mer.*

S. *Urßn.* i. A priory in the diqccfe of

Mans. 2. An abby. Sec & *Symphorien*. 5. *TJrfindEfperony* a village of Normandy, in the election of Caen. *p. Caen*. S. *Vruge*, a village of Burgundy, in the bailiwick of S. Laurent, *p Louans*. S *Uruge-jur-Guye*, a village of Burgundy, in the diocefe and bailiV'ick of Challón, *p. Cbailon*. S. *Uruges,* a village of BurgiTndy, in the dioceíe and bailiwick, of ChalJon. *p. Cbailon*. S. *Ufage,a.* villnge of Champagne, in the election of Bar-fur-Aube. *p. £ar-fur-Aube*. S. *Uflrcy* a village of Poitou, in the election of Châtellerault. *p. Ctateller au h*. S. *Vjuges*, a village of Burgundy, 'in the bailiwick of Challón, *p. Lou am*. S. *Utia*, a village of Champagne, in the election of Vitry. *p. VtrylcTrançois*. S. *VulbaSy* a village of Burgundy, in the bailiwick of Bugey. *p. Belley*. S. *VuïmcT)* an abby in the diocefe of Boulogne, *p. Boulogne*. S. *Wutfile-B'itxy* a village of Artois, in the bailiwick of Hefdin. *p. Heidin*. S. *linage*, a v'l! ge of Burgundy, jn the receipt of Dijon-*p. Auxorr.e*. 5. *Uxe*, a village of Dauphiny, in the diocefe and election ofViennc. *p. Ste. Vauhwrg*. I. A village of Champagne, in the diocefe and election of Rheims, *p. Rethel*. 2. A rommandery of Malta, in the diocefe cf Rouen. Ste. *Venture*, a mountain of Provence, between Aix and S. Maximin.

¿ví. *Virgc*, a fniall town of Poitou, 3a the election of Thouars. *p. Tbouars*. Ste. *Vertus* a village of Champagne, in the election of Tonnerre. *f. N'.yers*. S*:e. Vt£ïo:re* a town of Agénois, in the diocefe and election of Agen, *f. Agen, Ète*. U& 6? *Pertus*, a village of Dauphiny, in the election of Romans. *p. Remans*. Ste *Walhourg*, or Ste. *Walpurgr,* an abby in the diocefe of Straiburg. *p. Straflwrg*. S. *Xandre*, a town of Aunis, in the diocefe and election of Rochelle. *p. la Rochelle*. S. *Vaguen*, a village of Gifcony, in the election of Landes, *p. Tartas*. S. *Tan*, a village of Burgundy, in the bailiwick of Semur-en-Briennois. *p. la Paucaudiere*. S. *Third*, a village of Péngoid, in the diocefe and election of Périgueux. *p. Uzerchis*. S. *YHe*, a village of FrancheComté, in the bailiwick of Dole. *p. Dole*. S. *Tdlee*, or Ste, *Eulal'ie*, a fmall town of Périgord, in the diocefe and election of Périgueux. *p, Pcr'tgueux*. S. *Ton,* a village of the Ifle of France, in the diocefe and election of Paris, *p. yfrpajan*. S. *Tone,* a village of Bourhonnois, in the ckction nf Gannat. *p. Gannat*. S. *Tors,* a village of Armagnac, in the diocefe and cí-.dtion of Auch. *p.* S. *Gaudens* S *Upoly*, a village of Limofin, ia the ikä on of Tulle», *p. TulUs*. S. *T eix*. See 5. Trier. S. *Tr.cx-jcus-Aixt*, a village of Limofin, in the diocefe and election of Limoges, *p. Livoger*. S. *Tr er-de-la-Fc: cbe*, a fmall city of Limofin, on the river lile, in the diocefe and election of Limoges. In its neighbourhood are mines of iron; about 7 leagues from Limofin, 12 from Brives, and 14 from Tulles. *Bureau de poße*. S. *Triers,* a village of Angoumoiî, in the diocefe and election of Anoulême. *p. Angbulime*, S. *Tr.eux,* a town of Limofinj in the election, of Tulles, *p. Tulles.'* S. *Tvo'me,* a village of Auvergne, in the election of Iii cire. *p. IJJôire*. S. *Tzam-cn-CaßiUon-de-Meüöe*, a village of Guienne, in the diocefe anJ eleéVion of Bourdeaux. *f. Bcurdetmx*. S. *Zachare, л* village of Provence, in the viguery of b. Maximin. *p.* S. *M.rximin*. *Sainville*, a large village of Benuce, in the diocefe and election of Chartres, *p. Angeiillc*. *Sam*. I. A village of Poitou, in the diocefe of Poitiers, and eleétion of Richelieu, *p. Richelieu*. 2. A fmall river of Nomiandy, which rifes in the foreft of Brix, and runs into the fea near Reville. 3. Sec *Serre*. *Saires,* a village of Normandy, in the diocefe of See;, and election of Argentan, *p. Dwnfroni*. *Saifenay*, a village of FrancheComté, in the diocefe of Befanron, and bail wick of Salins, *p. Salins*. *Saijeray*. See *Saixeray*. *Saifon,* a place of Provence, in the viguery of S. Maximin. *p.* S. *Msxipiin*. *Saißac*, a town of Lower Languedoc, in the diocefe and receipt of Carcaffonne. *p. Cafielnaudury*. *Sajan*, a village of Lower Armagnac, in the diocefe of Auch, and election of Aftarac. *p. Msandt*, *SaijJ'ival*, a village of Picardy, in the diocefe and election of Amiens. *p. Amiens*. *Saiffy-les-Scis*, a village of Nivernois, in the diocefe of Auxerre. *p. Auxerre*. *Saijy*, a parifh of Burgundy, compofed of many hamlets, in the diocefe and bailiwick of Autun. *p. Aufuñ*. *Suivre*, a town of Poitou, in the election of S. Maixant. *p.* S. *Maixant*. *Saix*. I. A town of Poitou, in the diocefe of Poitiers,-and election of Loudun. *p. Loudun*. 2. A village of BrefTe, in the dioccfe of Belley, and bailiwick of Bourg, *p. Bourg-enBrtjft*. 5. A V'Uagc of Dauphiny, in the dioccfe and eleition of Gap. *p. Gap*. 4. Aplace of Upper Languedoc, in the diocefe of Cuftres. *p. CaJJres*. *Saixery*, a fmall village of Burgim.

dy, in the diocefe of Autun, and bailiwick of Saulicu *p. Sat.lieu*. *Salabesy* a village of A énois, in the diocefe and eleci on of Agen. *p. Clerac*. *Saiagnac*. i. A town of L-mofin, in the diocefe and election of Limoges, *p. Limoges*. 2. A fmall town of Périgord, in the diocefe and election of Sailaf. *p. SarUt*. 3. A village of Limofin, in the dioccfe and election of Limoges *p. Uzerches*. *Salagcu, la*, a river of LanguedoCj which runs into the Lcrgue. *Salagozcs*, з village of Lower Languedoc, in the diocete and receipt of Ala s. *p. jftms*. '*Salagrljfon*, a place of Provence, in the viguery of Guillaume, *p. Caftellanne*, *Salmgmn,* a village of Dauphiny, in the dioccfe and election of Vienne. *p. Vienne*, *Salanuesy* or *Abondance Dieu*, à convent in Foix. *p. Toulouse*. *Salaje*, a village of Lower Languedoc, in the diocefe and receipt of Lodeve. *p. Clermont-de-Lodeve*. *Salat, le,* a river of Languedoc, which rifes in the Pyrenees and lofes' itfclf in the Garonn". *Salavas*, a village of Lower Languedoc, m the diocefe and receipt of Viviers, *p. ie Pcnt-S.-Efprit*. *Saldiert y* a foreft of 384 arpents, in the jurisdiction ofS. Pons. *Salaunes*, a village of Guienne, in the diocefe and election of Bourdeaux. *p. Bourdeaux Salaure*, a village of FrancheComte', in the bailiwick of Orgelet. *p. Loni-le-Saunier*. *Salbcgneres*, a foreft of 484 arpents, in the jurifdiction of S. Pons. *Salbertran*, or *Saltrbertran*, a vil läge of Dauphiny, in the generality of Grenoble, *p. Briancm*. *Salèris*, a town of Blefois, In the election of Romorantin. *p. Rqtkqrant'in*. *Salbrwveau*, a village of Ibz.adois,, in the election of Condom.*p. Csnd.m*. *Salces*. See *Salfis. Sale,* a place of Franche-

Comté, with a commandery of Malta. *Sslecbau,* a village of Gafcony, in the diocefe of Lefcar. *p. Montnjeau. Salekh,* a village of Gafcony, in the diocefe of Commiuges. *p. Toukufe. Saleilles,* a village of Rouergue, in the election of Milhaud. *p. 3MJbaud. Sahlies.* See *Salldles. Salenelle.* See *Sallenclle. Salemy,* a fmall town of Picardy, in the diocefe and election of Noyon. *f. Noyon. Sahmball,* a place of Alface, in the diocefe of Straiburg. *p. Strafburg. Saltón,* a village of Dauphiny, in the diocefe and election of Gap. *p. Gap. Salerans,* a vilhge of Dauphiny, in the diocefe and election of Gap. *p. Sißeron. Saleras,* a village of Dauphiny, in the diocefe and election of Gp. Л *Gap. Saternes,* a town of Provence, in the viguery of Draguignan. *p. Barjds. Salers,* a town of Auvergne, the feat of a bailiwick; fituated on a mountain, about 4. leagues from Mauriac, and 6 from A¡.;rillac, *p. Aurillac. Sales.* I. A fmall town of Guienne, in the diocefe and election of Bourdeaux. *p. Bourdeaux. 1.* A village of Upper Languedoc, in the diocefe and receipt of Mirepoix. *p. Mirepcix.* 3. A village of Upper Languedoc, in tbe diocefe and receipt of Alby. *p. Alby.* 4. A village of Beaujolois, in the election of Villefranche. *Villefrancbt. Sales & Tuurttes,* a village of Dauphiny, in the election of Montclimart. *p.fdontelimart. Sales-Mongifcard,* a place of Eéarn, in the receipt of Orthcz. *p. Qrtbe%. Salefcbes,* a village of Flanders, in the government of Qüefnoy. *p, le Çuefnoy. Saiejhult,* a village of Auvergne, in the election of Brioude. *p. Brioude. SaleJJc,* a fmall town of Marche, in the election of Gueret. /. *AubujJen. Salette,* a village ot Dauphiny, in the election of Montelimart. *p. Mnteftmcrt. Salette, la,* a village of Dauphiny, in the election of Grenoble, *p. Bourgoin. Salen ßf Sallouet,* a village of Picardy, in the diocefe and election of Amiens, *p. Amiens. Sale vin,* a village of Gafcony, in the diocefe and election of Comminges. *p. Montrejeau. Salexax,* a village of Lower Languedoc, in the diocefe and receipt of Uz.es. *p. Uxe's. Salexe,* a village of Dauphiny, in the diocefe and election of Vienne. *p. Vienne, Salgues,* a village of Quercy, in the election of Figeac. *p. Figeac. Salies,* er *Sallies,* a town of Beam, in the diocefe of Dax. *p. Oleran. Saltes,* i. A town of Gafcony, in the diocefe aod election of Comminges *p. S. Gaudcns.* 2. A village of Foix, in the diocefe of Paniicrs. *p. Yarafcon-en-Foix. Saliez,* a place of Upper Languedoc, in the diocefe and receipt ef Alby. *p. Toulcufe. Salignac.* i. A village of Saintonge, in the diocefe and election of Saintes, *p. Cognac.* 2. A fmall town of Guienne, in the diocefe and election of Bourdeaux. *p. Lilourne.* 3. A village of Auvergne, in the diocefe and elect ¡oh of S. Flour, *p, S. Flzur.* 4. A village of Provence, in the viguery of Siiteron. *p. Sißercn.* 5. A village of Dauphiny, in the diocefe and election of Gap. *p. Gap. Saligney,* a village of FrancheComté, in the bailiwick of Dole. *p. Dole. t'aligny,,* i, A town of BourbonBois, in the eleftion of Moulins, *p. Moulins.* 2. See *Salligny. Saligny-le-Vif,* a village of Berry, in the diocefe and eleftion of Bourges. *p. Bourges. Saligos,* a village of Gafcony, in the receipt of Bigorre. *p. barbes. Salindres,* a village of Lver Languedoc, in the diocefe and receipt of Vzés. *p. Alais. Salinelles,* a village of Lower Languedoc, in the diocefe and receipt of Nîmes, *p. Sommieres. Salinsf* a city of Franche-Comté, firuated on a fmall river, in a fertile valley, in the diocefe and generality pfBefançon; with a bailiwick, receipt, &c. io leagues from Befançon, 33 from Geneva, io from Pontarlier, 21 from Vefoul, II from Lonsle-Saunier, 8 from Dole, and loSj from Paris. *Bureau de foße. Salival,* a place of Merlin, in the diocefe and receipt of Metz. ». *Vu. Salive,* a town of Burgundy, in the bailiwick of Châtillon. ». *IJliirtille. Sallans,* a village of FrancheComté, in the bailiwick of Dole. ». *Dole. Sallartaine,* a town of Poitou, in the election of Sables-d'Olonnc. *p. Ies Sables. Sullas,* a village of Gàtinois, in the eleftion of Etampes. *p. Etampes. Sallau,* a place of Artois, m the bailiwick of Lens. *p. Lens. Salle, la.* i. A fmall town of Lower Languedoc, in the diocefe and receipt of Alais, *p. S. Wrppolite.* 2. A fmail town of Dauphiny, in the receipt of Briançon. *p. Brian$cn.* 3. A village of Burgundy, in the diocefe and receipt of Macon, *p. Macon.* 4. A village of Burgun Jy, in the diocefe and receipt of Cliallon. *p. Challón.* 5. A village of Burgundy, in the receipt of Semur-en-Briennois. *p. la Pacaudiere. Salle, la, & Chapelle-*iuiry, a village of Anjou, in the diocefe and eleftion of Angers, *p. Angers. Salle-en-Beaumont, la,* a village of Dauphiny, in the eleftion of Grenoble, *p. Grenoble. Salie-prh-Vibier, la,* a fmall town of An jou, in the diocefe and eleftion of Angers, *p. Angers, Sallebert,* a place of Guienne, in the diocefe and eleftion of Bourdeaux. *p. Bordeaux. Sallebeeuf,* a fmall town of Guienne, in the dioccf? and eleftion of Bourdeaux. *p. Bourdeaux. Sallego.* See *Rue. Sallegriffon.* See *Salagriffon. Salielles.* i. A village of Lower Languedoc, in the diocefe and receipt of Narbonne. *p. Narbonne.* 2. A village of Upper Languedoc, in the diocefe and receipt of Carcaflonne. *p. Carcaffonnt. SatlJies, les.* I. A fmall town of Lower Languedoc, in the diocefe and receipt of Viviers, *p. Vivien.* 2. A fmall town of Lower Languedoc, in the diocefe and receipt of Mende. *p, Mcnde. Sal'enelle,* a village of Normandy, in the eleftion of Caen, *p. Caen. Sallefadiez, la,* a village of Upper Languedoc, in the diocefe and receipt of Alby. *p. Alby. Sall:faieney* a village of Bonrbonnois, in the eleftion of Gannat. *p. Gannat. Saliepirujjon,* э place of Upper Languedoc, in the diocefe and receipt of Lavaur. *p. Laiaur. Salles.* I. A town of Auvergne, in the diocefe and eleftion of Clermont, *p. Clermont.* 2. A town of Aunis, in the diocefe and elc&ion of Rochelle. *la Rochelle.* 3. A town of Angoumois, in the eleftion of Cognac, *p. Cognac.* 4. A town of Saintonge, in the diocefe and eleftion of Saintes, *p. Saintes.* 5. A illage of Lower Languedoc, in the diocefe and receipt of Narbonne. *p. Narbonne.* 6. A village of Upp;j Languedoc, in the diocefe and receipt *o* Bieux. *p. 'Toulotife.* 7. A villag« of Armagnac, in the diocefe and eleftion of Auch. *p. Matures.* %. A village ofGafconv, in the diocefc and ckction of Comingcs. *p. Montréteau.* 9. A village of Provence, in the dlxefe of Die. *p. Vulreas.* 10. A village of Poitou, in the election of Niort, p, Awrf. if. A place of Acnois, in the dioccfe and election of Agen p. Agen. z. A village of Bourbonnais, in the election of Gannat. /. Gannat. Salles y les. X. A village of Marché, in the election of Gueret. p. Gueret. 2. A village of Poitou, in the election of Confuíaos, p. Con fol ans, Salle? Êf Touck'mbert, a fmall town of Anguiimois, in the diocefc and election of Angoulême. p. Angou¿eme. Salles ££ Pwget. a village of Rouergue, in the diocefe and election of Rhodez. p. Rhoacaz. Salles-a-Dour, a village of Gafcony, in the receipt of Bigorrc. puų Yarbes. Salles-Corntaux, a town of Rouergue, in the diocefe and election o£ Rhodez. Rhodez. Sal/es-Ccurùaties, a village of Rouergue, in the election of Vilkfranchc. p. Vil(francbe-de-Rouergue. Salhs-Cwvau, As, a fmall town of Rouergue, in the election of Milhaud. p. Milhaud. Sallei-de-Eadefd, & Salles-deBclves, villages of Périgord, in the diocefc and election of Sarlat. p. Sarlat. Salles-de-Cafi'dlon, a village of Guicnne, in the diocefe and election of Bourdcaux. p. Cafiillon. Salles-en-S.-Maixant, a village of Poitou, in the diocefc and election of Poitiers, p. S. Maixant. Salles-en-Touhnf a village of Poitou, in the diocefe and election of Poitiers, p. Poitiers. Saliettes, a village of Provence, in the vigucry of Mouitiers. p. Riem. SaH'tgny, a village of Champagne, in the dioccfe and election of Sens. p. Sens. Sailorly a village of Champagne, in the dioccfe and ckction of Troyes. p. Arcis-fur-Jhibe. Salmaifey a fmall town of Burgundy, in the bailiwick of Châtilion. p. S. Seine Salmeranges, a fmall town of Auvergne, in the diocefe and election of Clermont, p. Clermont Sulmiecby a town of Rouergue, in the diocefe and election of Rhodez. p. Rl dx. Sximon-vWe-la-Riviere, or le Leage, ¿2? Sal-monvUle-la-Sauvage t pariihes of Normandy, in the diocefe and election of Rouen, p. Rouen. Sülms, a village of Auvergne, in the diocefe and election of S. Flour. p. S. Flour. Sa/om'me, a village of Flanders in the fubdelegation of Lille, p. Lille. SaJon, a fmall city of Provence, fituated on a branch of the Durance, about 8 leagues from Aix, and 11 from Aries. Bureau de poße. Sahnet, a village of Provence, in the viguery of Seine, p. Digne. Salons, a place of Picardy, near Airaine. p. Abbeville. Salonfac, a village of Normandy, in the dioccfe and election of Coùtances. p. Coûtâmes. Salomay-fur-Guye, a village of Burgundy, in the diocefe and bailiwick of Macon, p. Mácon. Sals, a mineral fpring in Forez» about a league from Feurs. Sal/a, a village of Champagne, in the election of Ste. Manéhould. p. S:e. Manéhould. Saljen, a village of Gafcony, in the diocefe and election of Commingcs. p. Montrejeau. Salces, a town of Rouiullon, fituatcd between Narbonne and Perpignan; 4 leagues from Perpignan, and II from Narbonne. p. Perpignan. Salfes, les, a place of Lower Languedoc, in the diocfe and receipt of Uzés. p. Uze's. Salfogne, a village of Picardy, in the diocefe and election of SoiíTons. p. Soffins. Sahagnac, a town of Upper LanfueJoc, in the dioceíe and receipt of Alby. p. Alby. Sal-vagny, a village of Lyonnois, in the diocefc and election of Lyons. p. Lyon. Sal-vaignac, a village of Rouergue, in the election of Villefranche. p. Villefrancbe-de-Rcuergue. Salvanez, an abby in Rouergue. p. S. Afrique. Sálvela, & Salve-Majeur, fmall towns of Guienne, in the diocefe and election of Bourdeaux. p. Bourdtaux. Salveîat, la or Sauvetat, a town of Rouergue, in the election of Villefranche. p. Villefrancbe-de-Rouergue. Safoetatj or Sauvctat, iat a town of Agénois, in the diocefe and election of Agen, p. ïaRcollc. Satvetat, la. i. A village of Auvergne, in the election of Aurillac. p. Aurillac. 2. A village of Périgord, in the diocefe and election of Sarlat. p. Bergerac. 3. A village of Rouergue, in the election of Villefranche. p. Villefrancbe-de-Rouergue. 4-A village of Quercy, in the diocefe of Cahors. p. Colors. 5. A village of Upper Languedoc, m the diocefe and receipt of Alby p. Alby. 6. A place of Quercy, in the diocefe and election or Montauban. p. Montauban. 7. A place of Armagnac, in the election of Lomagne. p. Beautnont-de-Lomagne. Sawiac, a town of Quercy, in the diocefe and election of Cahors. p Peyac. Salmigmn, a village of Dauphiny, in the diocefe and election of Vienne, p. Vienne. SalunauXf a village of Forez., in the élection of Montbrifon. Mwikrifon. Salza, a place of Lower LangueJoe, in the diocefc and receipt of Narbonne. p. Narbonne. Salî&s-Hcwtaltz, a villagcof Lower Languedoc, in the diocefe and receipt of Mcnde. p. Mende. Samadet, a town of Gafcony, in the election of Landes, p. S. Sever, Saman, a village of Gafcony, in the diocefe and election of Corarainges. p. Touloufe. Samanty a village of BrefTc, in the bailiwick of Bourg, p. Bourg-tnБгф. ¡Samaran, a village of Armagnac, in the election of Aitarac. p. Mirande. Samatbany a town of Gafcony, 'Actuated on the river Save, in the diocefe and election of Commingcs; about 3 leagues from Lombez, and XI from Touloufc. Bureau de poße. Samaban. 1. A fmall town of Bazadois, in the election of Condom. p. Mar mande. 2. A village of Armagnac, in the election of Aftarac. p. Mxrande. Sambiny a village of Bléfois, in the diocefe and election of Blois. p. B'ois. Samblancay, or SamblancSy a town of Touraine, in the diocefe and election of Tours, p. Tours Samblanceaux. . A fort in tlx Ifle of Ré. 2. See Sablonceaux. SambouCy a village of Champagne, in the election of Tonnerre, p. Ancyr le-Franc. Sambrcj le, a river which rifes near Nouvion, in Picardy, and runs into the Meufe, at Namur. Sambuc, la, a village of Provence, in the diocefe and viguery of Aix. p. Aix. Sambuty a pariih in the diocefe of Embrun, p. Embrun. Samcont a village of Flanders, ill the fubuelcgation of S. Amand. p. S Amand. Samer, or Samer-aux-BoUy a town of Picardy, in the road from Boulogne to Montruil, 4 leagues from, Boulogne, and 5 from Montrcuil. p, Boulogne. Samerly, a place of Burgundy, In the receipt of Auxor.nc. p. Auxonnc. SameroKy a village of Brie, in the diocefe and election of Mcaux. p. bI Fe'/te-jous-Jouarc. Sames, a village of Gafcony, in the election »f Landes. pS. Siver. SamcJJe, a village of Normaii4y in the diocefe and election ofLiíieux. f. te Sap. Samïlly, a village of Champagne,

in the election of Chaumont./. *Chaumofit. Samifet,* a village ©f VrancheComte, in the diocefe and bailiwick of S. Claude, *p. S. Claude. Sammathan.* See *Samatban. Samogniet,* a village of Bugey, in the diocefe and bailiwick of Belley. *p. Beilcy. Sammreau,* a village of Gàtinois, in the election of Melun. *p. Fontainebleau. Samois,* a village of Gatinois, ïn the élection cf Melun. *p. Melun. Samonnac,* a village of Guicnne, in the diocefe and élection of Bourdcaux. *p. Bot/rdeaux. Samoucy Etrepois,* a village of Picardy, in the diocefe and élection of Laon. *p. Laon. Samouillan,* a village of#Gafcony, in the diocefe and election of Comminges. *p. Teukufe. Sampans,* a village of FrancheCompte, in the bailiwick of Dole *p. Dole. Sampigny,* a village of Burgundy, in the bailiwick of Beaune. *p. Autun. Sampzort,* a place of Lower Lan guedoc, in the diocefe and receipt of Viviers, *p. Viviers. Samfirts,* a village of Dauphiny, in the diocefe of Valence-*p. Grtnolle. Santya,* a place of Franche-Comté, 'in the diocefe and bailiwick of S. Claude, *p. S. Claude. San-MaJJonniere, le,* a place of Dombes, in the chatellany of Ambeneu, *p. Belte-viUe. Sanavons,* a village of Gafcony, in the diocefe and election of Comminges. *p. Montrcjeau. Sareergues,* a town of Eerry, in the election of Charité-fur-Loirc. *p. la Cbarite. Sar. cerre,* an ancient city of Berry, fttuated on a hill, on the confines of Nivernois, near the Loire, it has a bailiwick, Sec. about 8 leagues from
Bourges, and 13 from Nevers. *Bureau dtpefie. Sanccy.* i. A fmall-town of Burgundy, in the diocefe and bailiwick of. Mâcon. *p. Macon,* 2. A village of Champagne, in the diocefe and election of Troyes. *p. Troyes. Sar.chay-le-Bas,* Gf *Sancbay -leHaut,* villages of Normandy, in the election of Eu,, *p. Eu. . Sancbe-ville,* a fmall town of Beauce, in the election of Châteaudun. *f. Bonncval. Sanciat,* a place of Breffe, in the bailiwick of Bourg, *p. Bourg-mBreffe. Sanccins,* or *Xancmns,* a town of Berry, on the confines of Bourbonnob, about 6 leagues from Nevers. *p. Nevers. Suncourt.* I. A village of Normandy, in the election of Gifors. *p. It Tille.* 2. A place of Flanders, in the fubdelegation of Cambray. *p. Cambray, Sancy.* i, A village of Burgundy, in the bailiwick of Noyers, *p. Noyers.* 2. A village of Brie, in the diocefe and election of Meaux. *p. Meaux.* 3. A village of Picardy, in. the diocefe and election of Soiflons. *p. Soijjons.* 4. A place of Brie, in. the election of Provins, *p. Provins. Scmdarville,* a village of Beauce, in the diocefe and election of Chartres, *p. Jlliers. Sandier,* a fmall town of Auvergne, in the diocefe and election of Clermont, *p. Thiers. Sand'xllon,* a town of Orléannois, in the diocefeand election of Orléans. *p. Orléans. SandouvUlc,* a village of Normandy, in the election of Montivilliers. *p. Fecamp. Sandrens,* a village of Breite, in the bailiwick of Bourg, *p. Villefranche. Sndricourt,* a considerable tract of land of Vexiu-François, in the pa rifh of Amblainville. *p. Magny. Sandt,* a village of AH'ace, in the bailiwick of Benfeld. *p. Benfeld. Sarrgate,* a village of Picardy, in thr government of Calais, *p. Calais. Sangben,* a village of Picardy, in the government of Andres. *p.Andres. Satigutynet,* a village of Guienne, in the dioccfe and election of Bourckaux. *p. Bourdeaux. ¿unieres,* a village of Beaucc, in the election of Vendôme, *p. Vendóme Siimlhac.* i. A village of Lower Languedoc, in the diocefe and receipt of Viviers, *p. Viviers,* 2. A place ot Lower Languedoc, in the dioccfe and receipt of Uzés. *p. Uzes. Suniilat,* a village of Périgord, in the diocefe and ekction of Périgueux. *f. Pscr'igutux. Sanh fef MorUiv'iHlerSj* a village of Picardv, in the election of Mondidicr. P. /tiendraier, Sanixy & Narpoul.,* a village of Nivernois, in the diocefc and élection of Nevers. *p. Nevcrs. Sanleques.* a village of Picardy, in the generality of Amiens, *p. Boulogne. Sannat,* a village of Auvergne, in the election of Cwnbrailles. *p. Chambón Sinne.* Sec *баекne.* Hannegrand a village of Marche, in the election of Gucrct. *p. Gueret. 8агмегъШел* village of Normandy, in the election of Caen. *p. Caen. San/jais,* a fmall town in the life of France, in the diocelc and election of Paris, *p. FranccniAlle. Sanry-le$Vigy,* a
place of Mefl-n, in the dioccfe and receipt of Metz. *p. Ma. S#nry-fur-Nied,* avillage of Meffin, in the diocefc and receipt of Metí. *p. Metz. &ans,,* i. A village of Gafcnny, in the diocefe and election ot Comminges. *p. Montrejeau.* 2. Sec *Sem. Sanfa,* a place of Roufiiílon, in the vigucry of Confiana. *p. Viilejrant. bedeConßans. Sanj'an,* a village of Armagnac, in the election of Altarac. *p. Mirande. Sanfavt* a village of Saintonge, in the election of S. Jean-d'Angely.
S. Jean-dAne!y. Sanjettbcmare. 1. A villr.ge of Not.mandy, in the election of Wontivilliers. *p. Harfleur.* 2. A village of Normandy, in the election cf Neufchatel. *p. Fecamp. Sanßeim,* a village of Alfacc, in the bailiwick of Landfer. *p. Huningue. Sanßm,* a plave of Franche-Comté, in the bailiwick of Quingey. *p Befanpn. Sanfcns,* a place of Beam, in the receipt of Morias, *p. Pau. Satifuyercy* a fmall river of Normandy, in the diocefc de Coûtances. *Sar.Lms,* a village of Franche-Comté, in the b3iliwick of Dole. *p. Dole. Santeau,* a village of Orléannois, in the election oí Pithivicrs. *p. Pi' tbivicrs. Kamcnay)* a village of Bléfois, in the dioccfe and election of Blois. *p. Blots. Santenay-le-Haut,* a fmall town of Burgundy, in the receipt of Beaune. *p. Cbagny. Santenoge,* a village of Champagne, in the diocefe and election of Langree. *p. Langres. Santerre,* or *Santois,* a fmall and fruitful country of Picardy, fituated to the fouth of the Somme and Péronne. Mondidicr is the capital. *Santes,* a fmall town of Flanders, in the lubdelegation of Lille, *p. Lille. Scnteuil.* i. A village of Bcauce, in the dioccfe and election of Chartres. *p. Chartres.* 2. A village of VcxinFrançois, in the elc¿tion of Pontoife. *p. Pontoife. Santignyf* a village of Burgundy, in the bailiwickof Avalon, *p. Avalon. SantUly,* i. Avillage of Orléannois, in the diocefe and election of Orleans, *p. Artenay.* 2. A village of Burgundy, in the diocefe and receipt of Macon, *p. Macen,* 3. A place of Burgundv, in the bailiwick of Macon, *p. Challan. Sanrcche,* a place of Franche-Comité, in the bailiwick of Baume, *p. Baume, Santeffè,* a place of Burgundy,.in the baili-

wick of Beaune. *Staune, Saníour-Nourry,* aconfiderable tract of land, in the election of S. Florentin. *Satvvie.* See *Sa'mneville. Sarvuignts.* I. A village of Burgundy, in the bailiwick of Charolles. /». *jhitun. z.* A village of Burgundy, in the bailiwick of Avalon, *p. Avalon. Sanxay,* or *Sanxay,* a town of Poitou, in the election of Thouars, *p. I'bouars. Sanmais,* a vill gcof Bourbonnois, in the election of S. Amand. *p. S. Am and. Sanzcilks,* a village of Flanders, in the government of Maubeuge. *p. PHiippevilte. Saon.* i. A fmall town of Dauphiny, in the election of Montelimart. *p. Monttlîmart. z,* A village of Normandy, in the dioccfeand election of Bayeux. *p. Bayeux. Saône,* a large river, which riles in Mount Vofge, in Lorraine, and after paiïing through Burgundy, Franche-Comté, and Breffe, and receiving many other rivers in its courfe, joins ihe Rhône at Lyons. *Saoncs, lei deux,* a village of Franche-Comté, in the bailiwick of Befan ç on. *p. Bejanpn. Saontte,* a place of Armagnac, in the election of Lomagnc. *p. S. Ciar. Saomie, laf* a vilbge of Dauphiny, in the diocefe and election of Valence, *p. S. Marcellin. Saonnety* a village of Normandy, in the diocefe and election of Bayeux. *p. Bayeux. Sapt le,* a town of Normandy, in the diocefe and election of Lifieux; about 3 leagues from MontreuUrArgtllc, and 7 from Lifieux. *Bureaude poße. Sapandr/t* a village of Norma ndy, in the diocefe and election of Lifieux. *p. le Sap. Sapei-îVkq,* a village of Artois, ia the diocefe and bailiwick of S. Omer. *p. S. Omer. Sapey,* a village of Dauphiny, in the diocefe and election of Grenoble. *p. Gr¿nrjbU. Sapkourt,* a village of Champagne, in the diocefe and election of Rheims. *p. Rheims. Sapigneulles,* a place of Champagne, in the diocefe and election of Rheims. *p. Rheims. Sapignicourt,* a village of Champagne, in the eleélion of Vitry. *p. S. Dijier. Sapigny,* a village of Artois, in the bailiwick of Bapaume. *p. Bapaum:. Sapogne.* i. A village of Cham pagne, in the election of Rethel. *p. Donchíry.* 2. A village of Meflin, in the diocefe of Verdun, *p. Aletx. Saponay,* a village of Picardy, in the diocefe and election of Soiffons. *p. la Fere. Saponcour,* a place of FrancheComté, in the bailiwick of Vefoul. *p. yefiul. Sappoy,* a place of Franche-Comté, in the bailiwick ef Poligny. *p. Salins. Sapte,* a place of Upper Langue Joe. near the town of Carcaffo ne. *p. Carcajfinne. Saramon,* an abby in the diocefe of Auch, *p.fiimont. Sarance.* See *Sananas. Sarancolin.* See *SarrancoYm. Saranfac,* a village of Agénois, is the diocefe and election of Agen. *p. Agen. Sararan,* a place of Condomois, in the diocefe and election of Condom *p. Condom. Sarafquette,* a place of Navarre, in thi diocefe of Bayonae. *p. Bayerns. Sara-Zy* a place of Franche-Comté, in the bailiwick of Salins, *p. Salins. Sarce.* I. A village of Maine, in the election of Chateau-du-Loir. *p. le Lude. z.* A parifh of Touraine, in the diocefe of Tours, *p. Tours. Saneaux,* or *Scneaux,* a village of S A Normandy, in the election of Argentan, *p. Agentan. Sarcelles,* a fmall town of the lile of France, in the diocefc and election of Paris, *p. Ecwy, Sarcenas,* a place of Dauphiny, in the diocefe and election of Grenoble. *p. Grenoble. Sarcey.* i. A village of Lyonnois, in the diocefe and eleftion of Lyons, *p. Lyon.* 2. A village of Champagne, in the diocefe and election of Lan gres, *p. Lan fres. Sarácourt,* village of Champagne, in the election of Chaumont. *p, Cbaumont. Sarck,* the name of two lmall iflands on the coaft of Normandy. *Sarclay,* or *Sarcle',* a village of the "Ifle of France, in the diocefe and eleftion of Paris, *p. Versailles. Sarcos,* a village of Armagnac, in 4he eleftion of Aftarac. /. *Caßelnaue-Magnac. Sarcus-le-Grand,* or *Sercu,* a fmall town of Picardy, in the diocefc and eleftion of Amiens, *p. Beauvais. Sarcy-en-Tardenois,* a village of Champagne, in the diocefc and election of Rheims, *p. Rheims. Sardan.* i. A village of Marche, in the flection of Gucrct. *p. Gueret.* a. A place of Lower Languedoc, in the diocefe and receipt of Nîmes, *p. Sauve. Sardinya & Joncet,* a village of îtouflillon, in the viguery of Conüans. *p. Vllefrancbe-dtQonßans% SardolUs,* a village of Nivernois, *in the* diocefe and eleftion of Nevera. *p. Nev-* ers. *Sardón,* a village of Auvergne, in the election of Riom. *p. Riom. Sardreu,* a village of Dauphiny, in (the diocefe and election of Vienne. *p. la Côte-S.-Ancré. Sardy.* I. A village of Nivernois, in the diocefe and election of Nrver« *J. Nevers. z.* A place of Nivernois, in the election of ChâteauChinon. *p. Corbigny. Sare,* a river of Lorraine, which joins the Mofclle, about a league above Treves. *Sarebourg,* or *Sarbourg,* an ancient city of Meflin» on the frontier of Alface; fituated on the Sarc, in the diocefc and receipt of Metz; 7 leagues from Saverne, 16 from Straiburg, 27 from Landau, 36 from Spire, *zt* from Sceleftat,.26 from Colmar, 42 from Verdun, 52 from Ste. Manéhould, 20 from Nancy, 26 from Toul, 2Ê from Metz, 32 from Thionville, 18 from Deux Ponts, 41 from Bar-le-Duc, 62 from Châlons, and 102.from Paris. *Bureau7e peße, Sarelouis.* See *Sarlouis. Saren,* a town of Orléannois, in the diocefe and election of Orleans. *p. Vrleans. Sarenne,* or *Surenne,* a foreft of.2242 arpents, in the jurifdiftionof Boulogne, in Picardy. *Sarge',* a town of Maine, in the diocefe and election of Mans. /. *Montoire. Sargnacy* or *Saragnac,* a fmall town of Lower Languedoc, in the diocefe and receipt of Nîmes, *p. Nîmes. Sarjac,* a village of Périgord, in the diocefe and eleftion of Sailat. *p. Sarlat. Sarignyy* a village of Poitou, in the eleftion of Richelieu, *p. Rtcbelku. Sarincourt)* a village of Normandy, in the election of Pontoife. *p. Pontotfo, Sarlabous,* a place of Gafcony, in the receipt of Nebouzan./. *'Taries, Sarlañde,* a fmall town of Périgord, in the diocefe and election of Périgueus,"/». *S. Yiiex. Sarlaty* a confiderablc city of Périgord, the fee of a brlhop, with a bailiwick, eleftion, Sec. j 14 leagues from Périgueux, 15 from Bergerac, 5 from Souillac, and 8 from Terraffan. *Bureau de poße. SarUatj* a village of Périgord, in the diocefe and election of Périgueux. *p. Pengucux. Sarlouh,* or *Sarelouis,* a ftrong town of Merlin, Oik the river Sarc; 30 leagues from Straiburg, 17 from Bitche, II from Thionvillc, 34 from Stcnay, 42 from Sedan,-47 irora Mezieres, 69 from Liege, *it* from Metz, 28 from Verdun,

38 from Ste. Manéhould, 48 from Chalons, 6 from Sarebruck, 23 from Luneville, 24 from Phaliburg, 37 from Sceleftat, 42 from Colmar, 24 from Nancy, 25 from Bar-le-Duc, 91 from Lille, and 88 from Paris. *Bureau de poße. Sartnaye.* See *Sermaife, Sarmaxes*, a place of Upper Languedoc, in the diocefe and receipt of Alby./. *Alby. Sarmuj* a place of Franche-Comté, in the bailiwick of Lons-lc Saunier. *p. Lons-le-Saumer. Sarnignetj* a village of Gafcony, in the receipt of Bigorre./. *Tarées. Sarncy* a village of Picardy, in the diocefe and election of Amiens, *p. Saron. t.* A village of Brie, in the election of Sezanne, *p. Sezanne, z.* See *Sat ron. SarpmiHas*, a place of Armagnac, in the diocefe of Comminges. *p. Mcntrejeau. Sarpcurcux*, a place of Beam, in the receipt of Oithez. *p. Ortkex. Sarra, lay* a village of FrancheComté, in the bailiwick of Orgelet. *p. Lcns-ïe-Saunier. Sarracave,* a place of Gafcony, in the receipt of Nebouzan. *p. Mirande. Sarragacbies*, a place of Armagnac, in the diocefe and election of Auch. *p. Auch. SarragaiUolts*, a place of Armagnac, in the election of Aftarac. *p. Mir ande, $atrame?an*, a place of Gafcony, in the receipt of Nebouzan. *p. Mtrande. Sarran*, a town of Armagnac, in the election of Rivière-Verdun, *p. GriffblUs. Sarrances*, a place of Beam, in the receipt of Morias, *p. Pau. Sarrancoliny* or *Sarrancoulin*, a town of Arnmgnac, in the diocefe of Comminges. *p. Bagnercs. Barrant,* i. A town of Armagnac, in the election of Rivière-Verdun. /. *Grenade, z.* A village of Limofin, in the election of TulUs./. *tulles..r Sanante*, a place of Upper Languedoc, in the diocefe and receipt or Mirepoix./. *Mirepoîx. Sarras*, a village of Vivarais, "m the diocefe and receipt of Viviers, *p. Viviers. Sarraxat,* a fmal! town of Périgord, in the diocefe and election of Périgueux. *p. Creffenfac. Saraziet & Ba/azin*, a village of Gafcony, in the election of Landes. *p. S. Sever. Sarret* a town of Gafcony, in the diocefe and receipt of Bayonne. *p. S. Jean-de-Lutz. Sarremeianne*, a village of Lower Languedoc, in the diocefe and receipt of Viviers, *p. Viviers. Saney*, a village of Champagne, in the diocefe and election of Langres. *p. hangres. Sarrlacy* a village of Gafcony, in the receipt of Bigorre. *p. Tarées. Sarrians*, a fmall town of Venatfnn, in the judicature of Carpentras. *p. Orange. Sarrie7* a village of Burgundy, in the bailiwick of Semur-en-Briennois. *p. Noyers. Sarrígny-(es-Doye*, a village of Burgundy, in the bailiwick of Beaune. *p. Beaune. Sarrls,* a village of the Ifle of France, in tht diocefe and election of Paris *p. Lagny. Sarrogna,* a village of FrancheComté, in the bailiwick of Orgelet. *p. Lons-le-Saunier. Sarron.* i. A village of Limofin, in the election of Tulles, *p. TulUs.* 2. A village of Picardy, in the election of ClermoDt. *p. Scnlis, Sa/ruSf* a village of Auvergne, in the election of S. Flour, *p. S. FUur. Sany.* i. A village of Burgundy, in the bailiwick of Avalon, *p. Avalon.* 2. A country feat near Chalons, in Champagne, *p. Cbáhns. Hacs-Poterie,* a village of Hainaur, ïn the government of Avefne. *p. Avefne. Sars-fur-Ca?;cbcj* a place of Artobj in the bailiwick of S. Pol. *p. Arras. Sars-Varhncourtf* a village of Artois, in the bailiwick of Bapaumc. *p. B a paume. Sart, le.* t, A village of Flanders, in the fubdek-gation of Mcrvillc. *p. Landrecy.* 2. A fmall river of Normandy, which runs into the fea between Dieppe and Eu. *Sartj* a village of Gutenne, in the diocefe and election of Buurdeaux. *p. Scurdeaux. Sart-fwSerre, ley* a village of Picardy, in the diocefe and election of Laon. *p. la Fere. Sane,* a river of Maine, which lofes itfelf in the Mayenne, a little above Angers. *Sartes-Rû/ifreSy* a village of Flanders, in the fubdelegation of S. Amand. *p. S. simand. Sari!f/y)* a market-town of Normandy, in the diocefe and election of Avranches. *p. branches. Sarton.* i. A village of Artois, in the bailiwick of Lens. *p. Lens.* 2. A river of Normandy, which lofes itfelf in the Sartc, near the town of S. Célérin. *SartcuXy* a place of Provence, in the diocefe and viguery of Grafie. *p. Graß Sarzau* Êf Р/чкгсг, a town of Bretagne, in the diocefe and receipt of Vannes, *p. Vanr.es. Sarzay,* a village of Berry, in the election of Ift;udun. *p. laCbâtre. Sarze'y* a village of Touraine, in the election of Loches, *p.-Liebes. &tflcim*, a village of Alface, in the bailiwick of Enfiiheim. *p.Rouffacb. Saß.rges.* Sec *Sajperges. Sojos,* a village of Gafcony, in the receipt of Bigorrc. *p. Tarées. Sa/ffJgy,* a village of Burgundy, in the diocefe and bailiwick of Challón, *p.Challón. Sajjay,* a village of Blaifois, in the diocefe and election of Blois. *p. Blois Saßenage,* a fmall town of Dauphiny, in the diocefe and election of Grenoble, *p. Grenvlle Saßcnay,* a village of Burgundy, in the diocefe and bailiwick of Challón, *p. Challón. SaJJenbeim,* a village of Alface, in the diocefe of Straiburg. *p. Mulficim. Saffetot.* I. A fmall town of Normandy, in the election of Caudebec. *p. Fecamp.* 2. A village of Normandy, ¡n the election of Arques, *p. Dieppe. SaJJiville,* a village of Normandy, in the election of Caudebec. *p. Cany. Sajiy,* a place of Cnampagne, in the diocefe of Rheims, *p. Rheims. Saßezr* a figniory of Normandy, in the diocefe and election of Evreux. *p. Evreux. Saßierges.* j. A village of Berry, in the election of Blanc, *p. le Blanc.* 2. A village of Berry, in the election of Châteauroux. *p. Châteauroux. Sajftgmes,* a village of Flanders, in the government of Quefnoy. *p. Landrecy. Saß,* a place of Gafcony, in the receipt of Bigorre. *p. barbes. Satillieu,* a village of Vivarais, in the diocefe and receipt of Viviers, *p. Viviers. Sating,* a village of Nivernois, in the diocefe and election of Nevcrs. *p. Ncvers. Satcnay,* a village of Breffe, in the bailiwick of Bourg, *p. Bourg-enBzф. Satonnay,* a village of Burgundy, in the diocefe and receipt of Mâcon. *p. Mâcon. Satojft,* a village of Burgundy, in the bailiwick of Beaunc. *p. Beaune. Satwargues.* i. A village of Lower Languedoc, in the diocefe and receipt of Montpellier, *p. Lunel.* 2. See *Stiuteirargucs. Savarr.age,* a wood of 473 arpents, in the juridiction of Caltelnaudary. *ia-vary.* i. A town of Upper Languedoc, in the diocefe and receipt of S. Papoul. *p. Caßclnaudaiy.* 2. A village of Touraine, in the election of Loches, *p. I'JjUBoufkatd. Saves,* a village of Dauphiny, in the diocefe and election of Vienne. *p. Vienne. Savafft,* a fmall town of Dauphiny, in the election of Montcli-

mart. *p. Monielimart.* Saubalade. See Sauvatade. *Saubagnac S" la Tarte,* a village of Gafcony, in the election of Landes, *p. Agen.* Saubens, a village of Gafcony, in the diocefe and election of Coramingcs. *p. Toulouje.* Saubetat, a village of Béarn, in the receipt of Pau. *p. LeCioure. Saub'mont,* a village of Gafcony, in the diocefe and election of Coraminges.-. *Somatan.* Saubion, a village of Gafcony, in the election of Landes, *p. Bay.nne.* Saubole, a place of Béarn, in the receipt of Morias, *p. Pau.* Saubrigues, a village of Gafcony, in the election of Landes, *p. Bayenne.* Saubuje, a village of Gafcony, in the clef Hon of Landes, *p. Dax.* Sauçais, a fmall town of Guienne, in the diocefe and election of Bourdeaux. *p. Bourdeaux.* Saucede, a place of Beam, in the diocefe and receipt of Oleront *p. Oleron.* Saucelle, a village of Perche, in the election of Verncuil. *p. Verncuil.* Sauces-aux-B'ois, a vilhge of Champagn, in the election of Rcthel. *p. Rabel.* Saucct or *Saunet i & S. Marcel,* a town of Dauphiny, in the election of Montclimart. *p. Montcl mart.* Saucey, a fmall town of Normindy, in the diocefe and election of Coûtances. *p. Ccûtances.* Saucbtry, a village of Brie, in the election of Château-Thierry, *p. Cbátcau-Tbierry.* Saucbmx, & Щитеих, places of Artois, in the bailiwick of Hefdin. *p. Hefin.* Saucbty, a place of Artois, in the bailiwick of Lens. *p. Lens.* Satubty or *Saucbay,* a village »f Picard/, in the diocefe and election of Amiens, *p. Amiens* Saucby-Canefac, fif *Saucty-l'Eßre',* villages of Artois, in the diocefe and bailiwick of Arras, *p. Arras.* Saucia, a village of Franche-Comte, in the bailiwick of Orgelet, *p. Lonslc Saunier.* Sauccurt. I. A village of Champagne, in the election of Joinville. *p. Joinville.* 1. A village of Picardy, in the election of S. Quentin, *p. Cambray.* Saucy. I. A village of Champagne, in the election of Bar-fur-Aube. *p. Bar-Jur-Aube.* z. A place of Burgundy, in the diocefe and bailiwick of Dijon, *p. Dijon.* Saudebonne, an abby in the dioccfe of Olcron. *p. Pau.* Saudemont, л vilhge of Artois, i the diocefe and bailiwick of Arras. *p. Arras.* Saudoy, a village of Brie, in the election of Sezanne, *p. Sezanne.* Saudre, la, a river of Berry, which joins the Cher, between Celles and Chàtillon.

Saudre-la-Petite, a fmall river, which runs into the Saudre at Pierrette, in Cologne. *Saudron,* a village of Champagne, in the election of Joinville. *p. JoinoIIIe.* Save, a itver of Armagnac, that rifes near Bagneres, and falls into the Garonne, near Grenade. Savegnie, a village of Picardy, in the dioccfe and election of Beauvais. *p. Beauvais.* Sai'i'lles, a village of Angoumois, in the diocefe and election of Angoulême. *p. Villefagnan..* Save!. I. A village of Dauphiny, in the election of Montclimart. *p. Montclimart.* 2. A place of Dauphiny, in the diocefe and election of Grc» noble, *p. Grenoble.* Savelierts, a place of Rouerguc, in the election of Milhaud. *p. Milbaud.* Savenas, a village of Marche, in the election of Guerct. *p. Gueret.* Stvenay & Boue'e, a village of Bee tagne, in the diocefe and receipt ef Nantes. *Bureau de poße.* SavexierS) a town of Anjou, in the diocefe and election of Angers. *f. Angers,* Saven»es, a village of Auvergne, in the diocefe and election of Clermont, *p. Clermont.* Saverange, a village of Burgundy, in the bailiwick of Arnay-leDuc. *p. Dijon.* Saverdun, a town of Foix, fituated on the Ariege, in the diocefe of l'amieres and generality of Rouflillon; about 9 leagues from Foix, and il fromToulouie. *BurеЛ defffie.* Sauerei, a village of Gafcony, in the diocefe and election of Comminges. *f. Montrejeau, Sai/erne* or *Savernest* a town of Alface, fituated on the river Tour, in an agreeable and fertile country, in the diocefe of Stralburg; 3 leagues from Phaiiburg, 7 from Haguenau, äo from Landau, 29 from Spire, 6 from Molmeim, 9 from-Stralburg, 13 from Sceleltat, 18 from Colmar, ro from Luncvillc, 27 from Nancy» 7 from Sarebourg, 33 from Toul, 48 from Bar lc-Duc, 31 from Metz, 46Í from Verdun, 56 from Ste. Manéhould, 66£ from Chalons, 75 from Sedan, 102 from Liege, I2lj from Lille, and 107 from Pans, *Bureau de poße.* Saveuze, a village of Picard)» in the diocefe and election of Amiens. *p. Sim'ens,* Sauge-

lyfio¡ital, a village of Anjou, in the diocefe and election of Angers, *p. Saumur.* Saugccn, a village of Guienne, in the diocefe and election oí Bourdcaux, *p. Bcwdeaux.* Saugccty a placeof Franche-Comté, in the bailiwick of Orgelet, *p. Lens le-Saunier.* Sauges, a town of Anion, in the election ofFlcchç. *p. ¡a Fleche.* Saugcy, a village of Burgundy, in the bailiwick of Châtillon. *p. IJJ'urtille.*

Vofc. *III.* Saugieresy a village of Auvergne, in the election of Rionb *p. Riem.* Saugnaey a village of Gafcony, in the election of Landes, *p. Dax.* Saugues. I. A town of Lower, Languedoc, in the diocefe and receipt of Mende. *p. Mende.* 2. A town of Auvergne, in the election of Brioude. *p. Brïoude.* Saviac, a village of Armagnac, *in* the diocefe of Comminges, *p. Mon trejeau.* Saviangc. 1. A village of Burgundy, in the bailiwick of Charo)le. *p. Dijon.* 2. A parith of Burgundy, in the bailiwick of Charoiles. *p. Dijon.* Saujat. Sec *Sauljat.* Swines, a village of Champagne, in the diocefe and election of Trove. *p. Troyes.* Savlgnac. I. A town of Limofin, in the diocefe and election of Limoges, *p. Ufercbci.* 2. A tovfn of Guienne, in the diocefe and election of Bourdcaux. *p. L bourne.* 3. A village 'of Rouergue, in the election of Villcfranche. *p. Vi'tlejrambe-deBouergue.* 4. A village of Gafcony, in the diocefe and election of Comminges. *p. S. Gaudens.* 5. A village of Franche-Comté, in the bailiwick of Orgelet, *p. Lom-U-Saunier.* Stcvignac-Dehey-j a vilhge of Armagnac, in the election of RivièreVerdun, *p. Grenade.* Savigf:¿icde-Nonti on a village of Périgord, in the dioccie and election of Périgucux. *p. P/rigueux.* Sa-vigxargues, a village of Lower Languedoc, in the diocefe and receipt of Nimes. *p. Sommieres.* S.ii-';n,u-de'M:rtmoiit,& Sav'ignat les-Eg/ifes. towns of Périgord, in the diocefe and election of Périgueuxt *pu S. Pardt ux.* Savane'. 1. A town of Arjou, in the election of Baugé. *p. It Lude,* г A village of Burgundy, in the baîîiwick of Charoiles. *p. Dihn.* 3. A village of Anjou, in the uincefc a'nJ election of Angers, *p.* К *Ça'vigtu-VEvêueЛ* town of Maine, ín the aioccfe and election of Mans. . *U Mans. Sa vigne-Γ E vefea u/*, a v i liage of Poitou, in the diocefe and election of Poitiers, *p. Poitiers. Savigneux*, a village of Doro bes, in the chatellany of ' Ambeneu. *p. Belleville. Sav'gney-jur-Braye*, a village of Mans, in the ele ft i on of Chüteau-duIioir. *p. Chateau-du-Loir. Sattigmeuy* a village of Forez, in the election of Montbrifon.. *Moatbrijon. SaiAgny.* f. A town of Normandy, on the frontiers of Bretagne and Maine; about 8 leagues from Avranches. *p. S. HiUire. z.* A town of Champagne, in the election of Rethcl. *p. Rheims.* 3. A town of Beaucc, in the election of Vendôme. *p. Vendôme.* 4.. A town of Normandy, in the diocefe and election of Coôtance. *p. Coûtâmes.* 5. A town of Touraine, in the election of Chiflón, *p Chiron.* 6. A (mail town of Lyonnois, in the diocefe and election of Lyons, *p. Lyon.* 7. A village of Berry, in the diocefe and election of of Bourges, *p. Bourges.* 8. A village of Champagne, in the diocefe and election of Rheims, *p. Retbel.* 9, A village of Champagne, in the diocefe and election of Langrcs. *p. Langres.* 10. A village of G:tinois, in the election of Nemours, *p. Nemwrs.* H. A village of Gatinuis, in the election of Melun. *Melun. zz.* A place of Burgundy, in the diocefe and bailiwick of Macon, *p. Macon.* 15, A figniory in the generality of Paris, and election of fompiégne. *Siivigny ¿f Mei.uguty* a vlüagc of Burgundy, in the diocefe and receipt f MAcon. *p. Macon. Savigny & VauXf* a village of the IfTe oi France in the diocefe and election of Paris, *p. Longjumeau. Sanigny-en-C'wrayt* n fuwn of Poitou, in the ciocefe and election of Foitiers, *p Cbaunay. Saulctau*, a village of Burgundy, in Ae bailiwick of Arnay-le-Duc. *p. Dijon. Saulcey*, a village of Burgundy, in the bailiwick of Beaune. *p. Beaur.e. Saukourt.* Sec *Souccurt. Sauldcy.* See *Scuday. Saule*, a village of Burgundy, in the diocefe and bailiwick of Mficon. *p. Nuits. Saules*, a village of Franche-Comté, in the bailiwick of Ornans. *p. BeJançon. Saulet* a village of Bourbonnois, in the election of Moulins, *p. Míulins. Sauley.* I. A place of Burgundy, 'in the bailiwick of Semur-en-Auxois. *p. Semur. z.* A place of Burgundy, in the diocefe and bailiwick of Dijon. *p. IJurtille. Saulge'*, a town of Poitou, in the diocefe and election of Poitiers, *p. Poitiers. Saulge*, or *Sauge*, a village of Maine, in the diocefe and election of Mans. *p. le Mans. Savlgon*, a town of Angoumois, in the diocefe and election of Angoulèmc. *p. Avgoulème. Sauiiac*, a village of Qucrcy, in the election of Figeac, *p. Figeac. Sauliat*, a village of Bourbonnois, in the election of Montluçon. /. *Monthçon. Saulieu*, a city of Burgundy, in the diocefe of Autun, and receipt of Semur-en-Auxois, with a bailiwick, &c. in the road from Lyons to Auxcrre; 9 leagues from Autun, 7 from Arnay-le-Duc, 50$ from Lyons, and 6i£ from Paris. *Bureau de pofle. Saulles.* I. A village of Burgundy, in Ihe bailiwick of Arnay-le-Duc. *p. Dijon.* 2. A villageof Champagne, in the diocefe and election of Langres. *p. Langres.* 3. A place of Burgundy, in the bailiwick of Mâcon. *p. Mâcon. Sauhiere*, a village of Marche, in the election of Gueret. *p. Gueret. Saulnieres.* 1. A village of Bretagne, in the diocefe and receipt of *Saurr.anf.* I. A village of Venaifiin, in the judicature of Lille, *p. Awgim. z.* A village of Lower Languedoc, in the diocefe and receipt of Alais, *f. Alais. Saumanc & FHofphaltt*, a village of Provence, in the vigucry of *tor*calquier. *p. Forcalyuier. Saumarcbais*, a village of Beauce, in the election of Montfort. *f, Montftrt-i'Amaury. Saumejean*, a village of Condomois, in the diocefe and election of Condom, *p. Cafld-Jaloux. Seamtray*, a village of Beauce, in the election of Cliâteaudun. *p. Ilhers. Saumont, le*, a village of Armagac, in the election of Lomagne. *p. A'erac. Saummt-la-Poteiie*, a village of Normandy, in the election of Lions. *p. Ecouy. SuumcKta, le*, a village of Rouergtie, in the election of Milhaud. *p. Milbaud. Saumcry*, a village of Champagne, in the diocefe and election of Rheims. *p. Rheims. Saumur*, a city of Anjou, on the Loire, in the diocefe of Angers, and generality of Tours: it is the feat of a fenefchal. election.. &c.; the capital of Saumurois; about 3 leagues from MontrcuiUBellay, 13 from Angers, 7 from Loudun, 7 fiom Thouars, and 17 from Tours. *Bureau de poße. Saumurois*, a fmall country of Anjou, in the environs of Saumur, which is the capital. *Saunât*, a village of Auvergne, in the election of Riom. *p. Riom. Saunay*, a village oí Berry, in the election of Châteauroux. *p. Ckateaumtx. Saune.* I. A place of Burgundy, in the bailiwick of S. Laurent, *p. Challón.* 2. A place of Daupliinv, in the bailiwick of Buis. *p. Alor.ulimart.* , *Sauniere & la Barre*, a village of Burgundy, i;; the bailiwick of Dijon. *p. Challón. Sauniereiy* a village of Perche, in tbe-dection of Verneuil. *p. VernemL Saunotte*, a village of Burgundy, in the bailiwick of Saulieu./». *Sanur. Savoijy*, a town of Burgundy, in the bailiwick, of Semur-en-Auxois. *p. Mont ban. Savol/e, & Sa-vonge*, places of Burgundy, in the diocefe and bailiwick of Dijon, *p. Dijon. Swvongej* or *Savouge*, a village of Burgundy, in the bailiwick of Dijon. *p. Dijon. Savonures*, a town of Tourainc, in the diocefe and election of Tours. *p. Tours. Savons*, a place of Gafcony, in the receipt of Bigorre. *p. Tarbes. Saiou/s*, a village of Dauphiny, in the election of Briançon. *p. Brianfon. Sanscurnoñ)* a village of Dauphiny, in the diocefe an4 election ot Gap. *p. Gap. SwuoyeuXf* a village of Franche Comté, in the bailwick of Gray. *p. Cray. Sauquevitte*, a fmall town of Normandy, in the election of Arques./". *Dieppe. Sauqueuje*, a village of Picardy, in the diocefe and election of Bcauvaîs. *p. Beawuais. OauΓ)* or *Sorr, ja*, a river of A lfacc, which runs into the Rhine near Fortlouis. *Saurac-Venaxes*, a village of Auvergne, in the election of A ur iliac. *p. Aurillac. Sauraty* a Town of Foix, in the generality of RouiliUon. *p. Tarafconcn-Fcix. Scui'izy*, a village of Poitou, in the election of Kiort. *p. Partenay. Sai.ry)* or *Sany*, a village of Champagne, in the diocefe and eke tin of Chalons, *p. Cbâiom. Saufay.* ï. A village of Beauce, in the election of Dreux, *p Dreux, z.* A confidcrabie trnct of land in Poitou, in the election of Thouars. *¿itiujay*, or *Sauferon*, a fmall rive »

Alais, ïo from Nîmes, and 9 from Montpellier. *Burecu de frjte.* 2. See *induje y Gevaudan. Sauve, la*, or *Sauve-*

Afajeure, or *¡a Grande-Sauve,* an' abby in the dioccfe of Boiirdeaux. *p. la Reo!le. Sauve-Benite,* a convent in the dioct-fc of Puy. *p. S. Etienne. Sauvc-Cam,* an abby in the diocefe of A ix. *Sauve-Plafttade,* a village of Lower Languedoc, in the diocefe and receipt eí Viviers, *p. Vivien. Sauvelade,* or *NCtre-D&me-de-Sauvclade,* a place of Bcarn, in the receipt of Orthez. *p. Onbe%. Sauves,* a town of Poitou, in the election of Richelieu, *p. Mirebeau. Sauvetat, la.* 1. A town of Auvergne, in the diocefe and election of Clermont, *p, Iffoïre.* 2. A town of Périgord, in the diocefe and elect on of Périgueux. *p. Bergerac* 3. A village of Lower Languedoc, in the ëiocefe and receipt of Puy. *p. le Puy.* 4. A village of Armagnac, in the election of Lomagne. *p. LeEÎQurc ¿. §çc Safoét/?. Sauvetat-de-Caumont, la, Sauvetatde-Saveres, la,* towns of Agénois, in the diocefe and eleétion of Agen. *f. las Peyres. Sauvetat-de-Mopgcs, la, Sauvetat-de-Völlens, la,* villages of Agénois. *p. Agtn, Sauvcterre.* 1, A town of Gafcony, in the diocefe and election of Commignes. *p. Lombes.* 2. A town of Bazadois, in the election of Conlom. *p. la Reolle.* 3. A town of Rouergue, in the election of Villefrsnche. *p. Rbodex.* 4. A town of Beam, with a fénéchaufsée and receipt, fituated on the gave of Oleron, about 7 leagues from Pau. *p. Pau.* 5. A town of Agénois, in the dideefe and election of Agen. *p. VdleneuvedAgen.* 6. A village of Armagnac, in the diocefe and election of Auch. *p. Auch.* 7. A village of Upper Languedoc, in the diocefe and receipt of Caltres. *p. Cafires.'* 8. A village of Quercy, in the diocefe and election ofMontauban. *p. Montauban, Sauviac.* I. The name of two pa rtfhes in the election of Condom, *p. Bazas.* 2. A place of Armagnac in the election of Aftarac. *p. Mirar.de. Sauvian,* a village of Lower Languedoc, in the diocefe and receipt of Beziers. *p. Beziers. Sauviat.* I. A town of Marche, in the election of Gueret. *p. Gueret,* 2. A village of Auvergne, in the diocefe and election of Ciermont. *p, Clermont. Sauv'teret,* a village of Auvergne, in the diocefe and election of Ciermont. *p. Clermont, Sawvignac Êf Meîae,* a village of Saintonge, in the diocefe and election of Saintes, *p. Saintes. Sauv'ignargues & S. StUtme-dЩ catte,* a village of Lower Languedoc, in rhe diocefe and receipt of Nîmes. *p. Sommieres. Sauvigne,* a village of Angoumois, in the diocefe and election of Angoulême. *p, AngoulfMf, Sauv'gney-les-Angierey, & Sauvigaeylts-Pefrus,* villages of FrancheComté, in the bailiwick of Gray. *p. Gray, Sauv'gny.* I. A village of Meffin, in the diocefe and receipt of Toul. *p. Void.* 2, See *Sav'igny, Sauv'dle,* a village of Champagne, in the election of Rethel. *p. Rheims. SauvUler-Mongival,* a village of Picardy, in the election of Mondadier. *p. Mondidier. Sauvoir-fous-Zaciî,* a convent in the diocefe and near Laon. *p. Laort. Sauvoye,* a village of Champagne, in the generality of Chalons, *p. Void. Saux.* I. A village of the lile of France, in the diocefe and election of Paris, *p. Lonjumeau.* 2. A village of Bourbonnois, in the election of Montiuçon. *p. Шопйцоп..* 3.. A parifh of Burgundy, in the bailiwick oí Avalon, *f. Avalon. Saux-de-'Tourniac,* a village of Quercy, in the diocefe and election of Cahors. *p. Gabors. Sauxle-Îĵuc.* See *Saulx-Je+Dut. Saux-S.-Rertty,* a village of Champagne, in the diocefe and eleftion of Rheims, *p. Rheims. Sauxens,* л village of Armagne, in the eleftion of Lomagne. *p. BeaumoKt-de-Lomagne. Sauxilanges,* a town of Auvergne,, in the eleftion of Iflbire. *p. Iffbire. Savy.* i. A village of Picardy, in the eleftion of S. Quentin, *p, S, Quentin.* %. A village of Artois, in the diocefe and bailiwick of Arr«s. /. *Ai ras, Sauce-ay.* See *Sanzay. Sau%e Éf Gouvenceaux,* a village of Dauphiny, in the eleftion of Gap. *p.. Briancon. Saussens.* I. A place of Upper Languedoc, in the diocefe and receipt of CarcafTonnc. *p. Carcajjbnne.* 2. A place of Upper Languedoc, in the diocefe and receipt of Touloufe. /. *"Toukuje. Sauxet.* I. A village of Lower Languedoc, in the diocefe and receipt of Uzés. *p. Uzes.* 2. A village of Quercy, in the diocefe and ehftion of Cahors. *p. Cabors.* 3. A village of Bourbonnois, in the generality of Moulins, *p. Cannat.* 4. A place of Dauphiny, in the eleftion of Montelimart. *p. Mcntdimart. Sau% et-le-Froid,* a village of Auvergne, in the diocefe and eleftion of Clermont, *p. Clermont. Sauxits,* a village of Rouerguc, ïn the eleftion of Vi lie franc he. *p. V'dlefrancbe-de-Roaergue. Sauzy,* a village of Artois, in the diocefe and bailiwick of Arras, *p, jarras. Saxibourdon,* a village of Nivernois, in the diocefe and eleftion of Nevers. *p. Never. Say,* a village of Normandy, in theeleftionof Argentan.*p. Argtntcto. Sayn,* an itland on the coaft of Bretagne, in the diocefe and receipt of S. Pol-de-Léun. *p. Moriaix. SayncvUle,* a village of Normandy, ш the diocefe and eleftion of Rouen. *p. Rouen. Says,* a village of Upper Languedoc, iu the diocefe and receipt of Lavaur. *p. Lavaur. Sazay,* a parifh of Nivernois, in the diocefe and eleftion of Nevers. *p. Nevers, St%e,* a village of Lower Languedoc, in the diocefe and receipt of Uz.('s. *p. VxHer.cuve-d?' drtigmn. Sazeray,* a village of Berry, in the eleftion of Châtre, *p. la CbStre. Savent* a village ni Botiirbonnois, in the eîcftion of Moiith.u,on. *pA-fonthcon. Souille,* the name of a pari(h. in Tourainc. *p. Cbinon. Savi/ly,* a village of Poitou, in the eleftion of Richelieu, *p. Ricbclieu.* &awt) a village of Bretagne, in the diocefe and receipt of Quimper. *p. ИШтрег, Scatsaofieresy* a village of Rouerguc, ni the eleftion of Villefranchc. *p. VilUjrum bt-de-Rouergue. Scarpf,* a river of the Pais-Bas, which riles near Aubigny, in Artois» and puffing by Arras, Douay, and S. Amand, and feparating Flanders from Hainaut, joins the Efcaut near Mortaigne. *Scay,* a pi ce of Franche-Comté, in the bailiwick of Vefoul. *p. Vefiul. Sceaux.* I. A market-town of the I'fic of France, in the diocefe and eleftion of Paris, *p. Bourg'la-Reine.* 2. A village of Anjou, in the diocefe of Angers, *p. Angers. Sediert* a place of Flanders, with a bailiwick, about 2 leagues from Lille, *p. Lilie. Scelle,* lay a fmall town of Normandy, in the election of Vire. *p. Vire. Sce'le-Jom-Char.tc-Merle la.* a village of Champagne, in the diocefe and election or Troyes. *p. Troycs. Salles,* avillane of Normandy, in the eleftion of Bcrnay. *p. Bcrnay. S eyy* a village of Franche-Comté, in the bailiwick of

Befanion. *p. Befa ncoм. Sclans, 3* fmall town of Provence, in the viguery of Draguignan. *p. Draguignan. Sclapons,* a place of Provence, in the viguery of Draguignan. *p. Draguignan. Scorandon,* a village of Limofin, in the elcflion of Tulles, *f tulla. Scorbe'y* a village of Poitou, in the ekaion of Châtellerault. *p. Cbâtellcrauli. Scoubroucq-les-Cla'irmariβi,* a vil.lage of Artois, in the diocefe and bailiwick of S. Omer. *p. S. Omer. ScuwartxÍMcb.* See *Infcuivartmbacb. Scy,* a village of Meffin, in the diocefe and receipt of Metz. *p. Met. Scye,* a place of Franche-Comté, in the bailiwick of Vefoul. *p. Vefoul. Scyoror,* a fmall town of Périgord, in the diocefe and eleition of Sarlat. *p. Sarlat. Scyreuilj* a village of Périgord, in the diocefe and election of Sarlat. *p. Sarlat. Seailles,* a village of Armagnac, in ïhe diocefe and eleition of Auch. *p. Condom. Sedutres,* a village of Lower Languedoc, in the diocefe and receipt of Viviers, *p. vUlenewve-de-Berg. Seawvt-Benite.* See *Sauve-Bemte, Siawve-Majeure.* See *Sauve-Majture. Seaux,* X. A town of Maine, in the diocefe and eleition of Mans. *p. le Fertt-Bernard. a.* See *Sceaux. Scbecourt,* a village of Normandy, in the election of Conches, *p. Mvrmx. SekeviUe.* See *Sebville. SebU,* a village of Gafcony, in the eleition of Landes, *p. Pau. Sehncourt,* a fmall town of Picardy, in the eleâion of Guife. *p. S. ¡¿luentin. Sebourg* a village of Hainaut. in the generality of Maubeuge. *p. Valenciennes. 3eвuгШе,* a village of Orléannois, in the election of Pithiviers. *p. Pi-. tbiviers, Sebville,* or *SepewiHe,* a village of Normandy, in the election of Carentan. *p. Carentan. Secavfe,* a fmall town of Normandy, in the election of Domfront, *p. Domfront. Secenans,* a place of Franche-Comté, in the bailiwick of Vefoul. *p. Vefoul Secbe* tsf *Matbeflonty* a town of Anjou, in the diocefe and election of Angers, *p. Angers. Secbebriere,* a village of Orléannois, in the diocefe and election of Orléans. *p. Bois-Commun. Sccbcbains,* a village of Normandy, in the election of FaUife. *f. Faĵaife. Secbele,* a place of Picardy, in the election of Laon. *p. Compiegne. Secfin,* an ancient town of Flanders, in the fubdelegation of Lille; it has a collégial church, and a bailiwick, *p. Lil/e. SecondigrJ-en-Cetβine,* a town of Poitou, in the election of Niort-*p. Partenay. Secmdigne-ur-Cbĵfe* a town of Poitou, in tne election of Niort, *p. Niort. Secourt,* a village of Meffin, in the diocefe and receipt of Metz. *p. Met%. Secour vielle,* a fmall town of Gafcony, in the diocefe and ek&ion of Comminges. *p. Montrejeau. Secquebille-en-Bejfirty* a village of Normandy, in the election of Caen. *p. Càèn. Secy-fur-Saonet* the name of a barony in FrancheComté. *Siâaittac,* a village of Gafcony, irt the diocefe and eleition of Comminges. *p. Montrtjeau. Sedan,* a ftrong town of Champagne, fituated on the Meufe, on the frontitrs of Luxemburg, in the diocefe of Rheims, and generality oi Chalons; about 17 leagues from' Luxemburg, zj leagues from Lieg, 3 from Bouillon, 5 from-Maures, 4 from Mouron, 8 from Stcnay, 19 (rom Verdun, 34$ from Metí, 12 irom Rocroy, 18 from Chimay, 25 from Avefnes, 29 from Landrecy, 32 from Quefnoy, 36 from Valenciennes, 39 from S. Amand, 4.9 from Lille, 46 from Tournay, 20 from Giver, 24 from Dinanr, 17 from Mariemburg, 25 from PhiJippcville, 36 from Maubeuge, 40 from Mens, 51 from Bruffcls, 39 from Cambray, 45 from Douay, 48 from Arras, 74 from Calais, 68 from Dunkirk, 11 from Montmedy, zi from Longwy, 31 from Thionville, 41 from Nancy, 29 from Stc. Manéhould, 16 from Bar-le-Duc, and 61 from Paris. *Bureau de paβe. Sedera,* a village of Provence, in the viguery of Silieron. *p. le Buh. Sethe,* a village of Beam, in the receipt of Morias, *p. Pau. Sediere,* a place of Beam, in the receipt f Morias, *p. Pau. See,* a river of Normandy, which runs into the fea near Mont-S.Michel. *Sal, le,* a village of Bretagne, in the diocefe and receipt of Rennes. *f. Ritmt!. S 'cru,* a village of Champagne, in the election of Vitry. *p. Vitry. Sc'ex,* or *Six,* or *Sais,* a city of Normandy, fituated in a plcafnnt and fertile country, on the river Orne; in the generality and élection of Ale neon; the fee of a biihop; befides the cathedral, it has feveral pariih churches, a college, hofpital, &c. 5 leagues from Alcnçon, 5 from Argentan, ioj from Falaifc, 29Í from Caen, 23 from Evreux, from Rouen, 37 from Tours, 17 from Mans, and 46 from Paris. *Sureau depoβe. Scfotkh,* a village of Gätinois, in the elecVmn of Gien. *p. din. &forges,z* fmall town of Normandy, in the election of Domfront. *Dutnfront. Segala,* a village of Rouerguc, in the diocefc and eleition of Rhodcz. *p. Tculcufe, Sígalas,* a place of Gafcony, in the receipt of Bigorre. *p. Tarées. Sigalaffure, la,* a village of Auvergne, in the election of Aurillac. *p. Aurillac. Segarret,* a fmall town of Gafcony, in the election of Landes, *p. S. Sever. Seglan,* a village of Gafcony, in the receipt of Nebouzan. *p. S. Gaudens. Segltor.,* a village of Bretagne, in the diocefe and receipt of Vannes. *p. Pontivy. Segantac.* I. A town of Angoumois, in the election of Cognac, *p Cognac,* z. A village of Limoftn, in the election of Brivcs. *p. Brivcs.* 3. A village of Rouergue, in the diocefe and election of Milhaud. *p. Rhodtx.* 4. A village of Périgord, in the diocefe and election of Perigueux. *p. Sarlat. Segas,* i. A village of Armagnac, in the diocefc and election of Auch. *p, Condom.* 2. A village of Quercy, in the diocefe and election of Cahors. *p. Cahors. Segouffielle,* a village of Armagnac, in the election of Lomagne. *p. l'JJleJburdain. Stgaunbac,* a village of Armagnac, in the election of Lomagne. *p. Beaumont-dc-Lomagme. Segre'& la Madela'me,* a town of Anjou, on the Odon, in the diocefe and election of Angers, *p. ChâteauGantier. Segrie,* a town of Maine, in the diocefe and election of Mans. *p. lzɖay. Stgric-Fantaine,* a fmall town of Normandy, in the election of Argentan, *p. ¿%-gtntan. Segiùs,* a place of Burgundy, in the bailiwick of Nuits, *p. Nuits. Segry,* a village of Berry, in the bailiwick of Iiibudun. *p. JJJbudun. Segucir.s,* a village of Bazadois, in the election of Condom, *p. Cond-.m. Seguenville,* fií *Segucrville,* villages of Armagnac, in the election of L magne. *S. Ciar. Segur,* i. A town of Rouergue, in the diocefe and election of Rl.odez. *p. Rimiez.* %. A town of Auvergne, in the diocefe and election of S. Flour. *p. S. Flour,* 3. A viscounty of Limofrn, in the fénéchaufsce of Uzerc'aes. *Segur, le,* a village of Upper Languedoc, in the diocefe and receipt of Alby. *p. Alby. Segura,* a village of Upper Languedoc, in the diocefe and receipt of Mirepoix. *p. Mireptix, Segurety* a village of Venaiflin, in the judicature of Carpentras. *p. Avignon. Segusy* a village of Gafcony, in the receipt of Bigorre. *p. Tarbes, Segy.* i. A village of Bkfo s, in the election of Rumorantin. *p. S. Amand.* z. A village of Brie, in the diocefe and election of Meaux. *p. N ant cud fur-Marne. Stjalicres,* a village of Lower Languedoc, in the diocefe and receipt of Puy. *p. U Buy. $екbI,* a village of Anjou, in the diocefe of Angers, *p. la Flèche. Seicbeiles,* csf *Stiches,* villajrs of Armagnac, in the election of RivièreVerdun, *p. Grenade. SeicbieieSy les,* a place of Limofin, in the diocefe and election-of Limoges, *p. Limoges.. Sbgnalens,* a village of Upper Languedoc, in the diocefe and receipt of Mirepix. *p. Mirepoix. Seignelay,* a town of Burgundy,, fituatcd on a hill near the Yonne; about j. leagues from Joigny, and 2. from Auxerre. *p. Auxerre. Seigneur--dc-Curieres,* Êf *Se'gncurdel-Grot* places of Kouergue, in the diocefe and election of Rhodez. *p. RJndex, Seigneurs, les,* or *les Nobles-d' Albus,* a place of Provence, in the viguery of Caftellane. *p. Cajiellane. Seigmß'e,* a village of Gafcony, in the ckction of Landes, *p.. S. Sever. Scillae,* a village of Dauphiny, in the diocefe and election of Cap. *p. Montdauphin. SeiiLns,* a town of Provence, i ft the vigucry of Dragu'igrun. *p. Draguignan. Seillat,* a place of Bléfois, in the diocefe and election of Bluis. *p. B/ois. S We, la.* I. A river of Lorraine, which runs into the M o falle at Metz. 2. A fmall river of the Netherlands, which falls into theEfcaut, near Valenciennes. *Seilte,* a village of Poitou, in the election of Fontenay. *p. Fontcnay-ieComte. Seilltnard,* a village of Burgundy, in the bailiwick of S. Laurent, *p. Challon. Stilliers,* a village of Anjou, in the diocefe and election of Anders, *p. Angers. Seilion,* a village of Provence, in the vigucry of S. Maxiruiru *p. S. Maximin. Stillons,* a village of Breftc, in the receipt of Bourg,

p. Bourg-cn-Brfjh: Sane, la. 1. A very considerable river which rifes near Chanceaux in Burgundy, pafiès through Champagne, and bv the city of Pan-., ſeparates Vexin from Beauje, and empties itfcll into the fea at Havrede-Grace. 2. Sec *Scyne. Scintrand,* a place of Marche, in the cleétion of Bourgancui. *p. Bourgancuſ.* a town of Armagnac, in the election of Aftarac *p. Aucb. Sei/Jes,* a village ot Gafconv, in the diocefe and elcitiun of Cummings. *p. Toakufe. Seij/eniSy* c35 *Scijfins,* villages of Dau p'ûny, in the diocefe and élection of Grenoble, *p. Gr.mkle. Sclefiat.* Se«-*Scbäeßat. Selgues,* a village of Roucrgue, in the election of Vilicfranche. *p. Montauban. S.lignât,* a place and chart reu fe in the diocclc ot Lyons, *p. BourgenBzϕ. SJigne'yA* village of Poitou, in the cl.ct.on of Niort, *p. Niort, Seligncy,* a village of FrancheComré, in the bailiwick of Dole. *p. Vole. Sellncourt,* a town of Picardy, 7 leagues from Amiens, *p. Amiens.. S He.* 1. A village of FrancheComté, in the bailiwick of Vefoul. *f. Vejoul.* 2. A p.irilh of Champagne, in the dioccfe of Rheims, *p. Rheims.* 3. See *Celle. Selle, la.* 1. A town of Auvergne, in the election of Riom.. *Riem.* 2. A village of Gâtinois, in the election of Nemours, *p. Nemours.* 3. A village of Berry, in the election of Iffoudun. *p. JJfoudun.* 4. A village of Picardy, in the generality of Amiens. *p. Boulogne.* 5. A parifh of Burgundy, in the bailiwick, of Autun. *p. Лuxun. Selle-Cranoife, la,* a town of Anjou, in the election of Château-Gontier. *p. CbalIlu-Gontier. Selle.en-Cogles, la,* Êf *Cuerchoife, la,* villages of Bretagne, in the dio«efe and receipt of Rennes, *p. Rennes. Selle-enHarmoy, la,* a village of Gâtinois, in the election of Montargis. *p. Mcntargis. Selle-Guenant, la,* a town of Touraine, in the election of Loches, *p. FnuMly. Selle-les-Bordes, la,* a village of the lile of France, in the election of Paris. *p, Rambouillet. Selles-Ies-S.-Cloud, la,* a village of the lile of France, in the diocefe and election of Paris, *p. Verfalles. ScltеS-Cir, la,* a town of Champagne, in the ele¿üon of Joigny. *p, Jehny. &iie-S.Oùên, la,* a parifh of Touraine. *Selle-fitr-Loire, la,* я village

of Gâtinois, in the election of Gicn. *p. Gun. Selle-jur-Niévrc, la,* a village of Nivernois, in the election of Charitéfur-Loire. *p. la Charité. Selledron,* a parifh of Tcnraine, in the dioceie and election of Tours, *p. Sellen,* a village of Picardy, in the dioccfe and election of Soiffons, *p. Soiffons. Selles,* or *Celles,* a town of Berry, iituntcd on the conflux of the Saudrc and Cher; about 3 leagues from S. Aígnan, 5 from Romorantin, and 10 from Blüis. *p. S. dignan. Seíles.* i. A fmali town of Normandy, in the election of Pont-Audemer. *p. Pont-Audemer.* a. A village of Champagne, in the election of Rcthel. /. *Rheims. Selles-S.-Denis,* a town of Bléfois, in the election of Romorantin. *p. Romorantin. Selles-fur-Nam,* a village of Berrv, in the election of Iffoudun. *p. ij fiudurt. Selletes,* a town of Bléfois, in the diocefe and election of Blois. *p. Blots. Saliers,* I. A village of FrancheComté, in the bailiwick of Polignyp. *Silins.* 2. An abby in the diocefe of Troycs. *p. Nogent-fur-Seine. Selkonaz,,* a village of Bugey, in the diocefe and bailiwick of Beliey. *t. Beliey. Seine,* or *Selnne,* a fmali river of Norrmndy, which falls into the fea near Mont,-S.-Michel. *Sdottgey,* a town of Burgundy, on the Venelle, in the diocefe and bailiwick of Dijon; about 10 leagues from Langres, and 7 from Gray. *Bureau de pofie, Sehre-Sermejj'e,* a village of Burgund in the bailiwick, of Semuren-Briennois. *p. la Pacaudiere. Selsj* an abby in the diocefe of Straibtirg. *p. Straſburg. Seit,* a town of Alface, fituatcd on the Rhine, about 3 leagues from Haguenau. *p. Fort-Louis. Selt%bactjR* fmali river of Alfare, which falls into the Rhine, near Seltz. *Selva, la,* a place of RoufTilloiij in the diocefe and viguery of Perpignan. *p, Pcrftgnan. Sehe. la.* I. A town of Rouerpue,, in the diocefe and electioo of Rho'dct. *p. Rhtdez.* 2. A village of Picardy, in the diocefe and election of Laon. *p. Laott.* 3. A wood of 423 arpents, in the jurisdiction of Caftel na udary. *Se/ve,* or *Grand-Stlvc,* a convent in Armaguac. *Selune.* See *Seine, Semalenij* a town of Upper Languedoc, in the diocefe and receipt of X-avaur. *p. Lavaitr. Sema/l/j* a fmall town of Normandy, in the election of Alençon. *f. Alex con. Semarrey,* a village of Burgundy, in the bailiwick of Arnay-le-Duc. *p. Dijon. Semen)* a village of Poitou, in the diocefe and election of Poitiers. *p. Poitiers. Scmklancay.* See *Samblançay. Scmbleeay,* a village of Bléfois, in the e'ection of Romorantin. *p. Römerantin. Semeae,* a village of Gnfcony, in the receipt of Bigorre. *p. Tarbes. Semecour:* £í *Fercomoiin,* a village of Meflin, in the diocefe and receipt of Metz. *p. Metss. Semelay,* a village of Nivernois, in the diocefe and election of Nevers. *P. Nevers. Semcnne fijf Girard,* a village of Forez, in the election of Montbrifon. *p. S. Etienne. Semens & Semenjan,* villages of Guiennc, in the diocefe and election f Bourdcaux. /. *Bourdeaux. Sementron.* a village of Nivernois, in the election of Clamecy. *p. Clamecy.* . *Scmeries,* a village of Hainaut, in the receipr of Quefnov. *p. Avejnes. Semtrmcnilj* a village of Normandy, in the election of Neufchàtel. *p. Neufcbátel. Semerville.* 1. A village of Beauce, in the election of Châteaudun. *p, Châteaudun.* 2. A village of Normandy, in the election of Conches. *f, le Neufbourg. SemeJJ'auge,* a village of Burgundy, in the bailiwick of Nuits, *p. Nuits Setncuxe,* a village of Champagne, in the election of Rethel. *p. Mecieres. SemezieSf* a place of Armagnac, in the election of Afterac. *p. Morande. Semiqgony* a place of Beam, in the receipt of Morias, *p. Pau. Semide,* a village of Champagne, in the election of Rethel. *p. Retbei. Semigncn,* a village of Guienne, in the diocefe and election of Bourdeaux. *p. lAbourne, Semil/aCy* a village of Saintonge, in the diocefe and election of Saiates. *p. Yonxac. Sem.lly.* i. A pariíh of Champagne, in the bailiwick of Chaumont. *p. Chaumont.* a. A pîrifh of Ntrmandy, in the diocele of Coûtantes. *p. S. ho. Semoine,* a village of Champagne, in the diocefe and election of Troyes. *p. Arcis-far-Aube. Semondy* a place of Burgundy, in the bailiwick of Châtillon. *p. Cba tillen. Semons* Ê? *Lieu-D'teuy* a village of Dauphiny, in the diocefe and election of Vienne, *p. la Cote-S,-Andre. Semonßier,* a village of Burgundy, in the bailiwick of Châtil-

lon. *p Châtillon. SemoulinSy* a village of Normandy, in the election of Conches, *p. Evreux. Semoujfac,* a town of Saintonge in the diocefe and election of Saintes. *p.* "Jомеле. *Semouville,* a figniory of Normandy, in the diocefe of Coûtances. *p. Coûtâmes. Semonz-ies,* a place of Hainaut, in the government of Maubeuge. *p. A V fnes. Semoy,* a village of Orléannois, in tbe diocefe and election of Orléans *p. Orleans. Sempafiotis,* a villa-e of Gafcony, in the receipt of Bigorre. *p. Tarées. Scmpigny,* a village of Picardy, ш the diocefe and election of Noyen. /. *Noyen. Sempy,* я village of Picardy, in the Abbeville, *p. Aumale.* generality of Amiens, *p. MontrcviL Seras,* a village of Provence, irt *Semur.* I. A village of Maine, in the viguery of Taraicon. *p. Salmi.* the election of Château-du-L-.ir. *p. Senat,* a village of Bourbonnois, in ¿*f Firte'-Bcrnard.* 2. A prjory of 'he election of Gannat. *p. Gannat.* Berry, in the diocefe of Bourges. *Senaud,* a place of Franche-Comté, *Semur.en-Auxois,* a town of Bur-in the bailiwick, of Orgelet, *p.bom.* gundy, fituated on an eminence, near *le-Saunier.* the Armançon, in the diocefe of *Senault,* or *Ssnots,* a village of Autun and generality of Dijon, the Ve.iin-François, in the diocefe of chief place of a bailiwick, receipt, Rouen, *p. Meru.* &c. 4 leagues from Montbard, 6 *Setiaux & Pomarddle,* a village of from Siulieu, from Autun, 27 Upper Languedoc, in the diocefe and from Chalons, and 27. from Truyes. receipt of Caftres. *p. Caßrcs.* Bureau de pofie. *Senay,* a place of Franche-Comt«', *Semur en-Briennois,* a town of Bur-in the bailiwick, of Orgelet, *p. Lorn.* gundy, fituated in a fertile country *le-Saunier.* near the Loire, the feat of a bailiwick, *Senbas,* a village of Agénois, in the receipt, &c. about 3 leagues from, diocefe and: election of Agen. *pL* Roanne, *p. la Pacaudkre.* 'igen. *Scmifljc-en-Didonnc,* a town of *Sencerey,* a village of Burgundy, in Saintonge, in the diocefe and elec-the bailiwick, of Arnay-lc-Duc. *ft.* tion of Saintes, *p. Saintes. Dljvn. Semuy,* a village of Champagne, in *Scnd-as,* an abby in the diocefe of the election of Rethcl. *p. Reibet.* Nîmes, *p. Nîmes. Senailac*

& *Dormenac-Senaliac, Sene',* a village of Bretagne, in the places of Quercy,' jn the election of diocefe and receipt of Vannes, *p.* Figeac. *p. Figeac. Vannes. Scnàdïy,* a village of Burgundy, in. *Sene-Fontaine,* a village of Cham the bailiwick of Semur. *p. Munt-*pagne, in the election of Chaumont. hard. *p. Chaumont. Senan & Vougré,* a town of Cham-*Senecay,* a village of Berry," in the pagne, in the election of Joigny. *p.* diocefe and election of Bourges, *p.* 'Jo *tgvy. Sancerre. Senanque.* See *Sxnanque. Senecey.* I. A village of Burgundy, *Senans,* a place of Franche-Comté, in the diocefe:¡nd bailiwick of Main the bailiwick of Vefoul. *p. Vejoul. con. p. Macan.* 2. A place of Bur*Senante,* a town of Picardy, in the gundy, in the bailiwick of Auxonne. diocefe and elcftion of Bcauvais. *p. p. Auxonne.* 3. A place of Burgun*Beauvais.* dy, in the bailiwick of Dijon, *p. DiSenantes,* a village of Beaucc, in *pn.* 4. A place of Brefle, in the the election of Dreux, *p. Dreux.* diocefe of Challón, *p. Challón.* 5. A *Scnard,* a village of Champagne, parifli of Burgundy, in the bailiwick in the diocefe and election of Chalons, of Avalon, *p. Avalon, p. Ste. Manéhau/d. Senecey,* or *Sennecey,* a fmall town *Senargent,* a village of Franche-of Burgundy, in the diocefe and Comte, in the bailiwick of Baume, bailiwick of Challón, in the road *p. Baume.* from Dijon to МЛсоп; o§ leagues *Sinarpmt & Bernapre',* villages of from Mâcon, and 21J from Dijon. Picardy, in, the diocefe and election Bureau de pope. of Amiens, *p. Amiens. Senegas & Treviiy,* a town of Senegbem. See *Seningbem. Stnljac,* a town of Rouergue, in the diocefe of Villefranche. *p. Rhode, &mjon © Lmbernade,* places of Guienne, in the diocefe and election of Bourdeaux. *p. Bourdeaux. Senely,* a village of Orléannois, in the diocefe and election of Oilcans. *p. Orléans. Senengour,* a place of Limofin, in the election of Tulles, *p. Tullis. Senergues,* a fmall town of Rouergue, in the election of Villefranche. *p. Rbodess. Sentriac,* a place of Gafcony, in the receipt of Bigorre. *p. Tarbes.* S.

ne's. See *Sene».* Sencjf, a village of Upper Languedoc, in the diocefe and receipt of Mirepoix. *p. Mirepcix.* 1 *Senruieres,* a village of Tourainc, in the election of Loches, *p. Loebes.* Seneuy. *l,* a village of Lower Languedoc, in the diocefe and receipt of Рну. *p. le Buy,* Sencul, a village of Lower Languedoc, *p. le Buy.* Senevoy, a village of Champagne, in the election of Tunnerre. *p. Laignes.* Seneyzelles, a village of Agénois, in the diocefe and election of Agen. *p. Sinet,* a fmall and very ancient city of Provence, with a bifhop's fee, fituated in a barren country, between two mountains; about 5 leagues from Digne, 16 from Embrun, and 5 from Caltcllanc. *p. Caßellane.* Senczay, or *Sanely,* a village of Berry, in the diocefe and election of Bourges, *p. Bourges.* Senezergue, a place of Auvergne, in the election of Aurillac. *p. A¡rillac.* Senil, a place of Upper Languedoc, in the diocefe and receipt of Lavaur. *f. havaur.* Senille, a town of Poitou, in the ejection of Châtellcrault. /. *Cbátellerault.* &angten, a village of Artois, in the bailiwick of S. Orner, *p. S. Omer.* Sentis. I. An ancient city in the Ifle of France, the fee of a bifhop, under the archbifhop of Rheims, with a bailiwick, election, &c. it contains feveral parifhes, 2 leagues from Chantilly, 8 from Compiégne, 6 from Crépy, 10 from S. Denis, 17 from Vcrfaillcs, 9 from Meaux, 18 from Soiffons, 31 from Rheims, and il from Paris. *Bureau depoße.* 2. A village of Artois, in the bailiwick of S. Pol. *p. Aire.* Senlis-Ucdeau-oille, a fmall town of Picardy, in the election of Douions. *p. Albert.* Senlijfe, a village of the Ifle of France, in the diocefe and election of Paris, *p. Cbevreufe.* Senne. See *Saenne.* , Senneccy. See *Senecey.* Senneterre, a village of Vexin François, in the election of Mantes, *p. Mantes,* Senneviere, a village of Picardy, in the election of Crèpy. *p. Créfy.* Senncvieres, See *Senevieres.* Senneville, a village of Normandy, in the election of Caudebec. *p. Fecamp.* Semncbes, a town of Perche, in the election of Verneuil, with a foreft in its jurifdiction, 7 leagues in circumference, *p. Brefolles.* Sencnecur, a village of FrancheComté, in the bailiwick of Vefoul. *p. Vefoul.* Senonnt, a town of Anjou, in the diocefe and election of Angers, *p. Angers.* Senonne, or *Sencne,* an abby, in the diocefe of Toul. *p. Roan.* Senonois, a fmall country of Champagne, fituated by the fide of the Yonne, of which Sens is the capital. SencuWae, a town of Upper Languedoc, in the diocefe and receipt of Alby. *p. Alby.* Scnoville, a village of Normandy, in the election of Valognes. *p. Vahgr.es.* Sens. I. An ancient city of Champagne, fituated in a very fertile country, on the rivir Yonne, the fee of an archbifh мр; it is the chief place of a bailiwick, election, &c. and contains about 16 paridles, a general hofpital, &c. It is in the road from Paris to Lyons by Auxerre, 14 leagues from Auxerre, 2 5-from, Avalon, 16 from Troyes, 14 from Mehm, 15 from Fontainbleau, and 29 from Paris. *Bureau de poße.* 2. A town of Berry, about 8 leagues from Bourges, *p. Saneerre.* 3. A village of Bretagne, in the dioccfe and election of Rennes, *p. Rennes.* 4. A place of Burgundy, in the bailiwick of Challón, *p. Scure.* Sens (Sf *la Farge,* a village of Burgundy, in the diocefe and bailiwick of Challón, *p. Challan.* Senjat, a village of Bourbonnais, in the election of Moulins, *p. Moulins.* SenffaC'de-Marmtffe, a village of Auvergne, in the election of Aurillac. *p Aurillae.* Sentar-viUe, a village of Armagr.ac, in the diocefe and election of Auch. /. *Лкb.* Senten, a village of Gafcony, in the diocefe and election of CommingLS. /. *Touhufe.* Sentenac, a village of Gafcony, in the diocefe and election of Comminges. *p. Foix.* Senrer.y, a village of the Ifle of France, in the diocefe and election of Paris, *p. Paris.* Sentbein, a village of Alface, in the bailiwick of Bcffort. *p. Beffart.* SentVly, or *Centilly,* a village of Normandy, in the election of Argentan, *p. Дzgent an.* a place of Armagnac, in the election of Aftarnc. *p-Mir ande.* Sentranges, a town of Berry, in the diocefe and election of Bourges, *p. Bonny.* Stntzicb, a vilhge of Mcffin, in the diocefe and receipt of Metz. *p. Mem.* Scnuc, a fmall town of Champagne, in the election of Ste. Mané hould. *p. Ste. Manebubl.* Sepebes, a place of Lower Languedoc, in the diocefe and receipt of Men de. *p. Mer.de Sepeaur,* a village of Champagne, in the election of Joigny. *p. Joigny.* Sepety ie Cap, a cape on the coift of Provence, near Toulon. Sepfville. See *Seb-vil/e.* Sepmes, a town of Touraine, in the election of Chinon.. *Sie. Maure, Seporety* a town of Poitou, in the election of Poitiers. *Seppcis-/e-Bas,* & *Seppds-¡tHauf*9 places of Alface, in the bailiwick of Delle, *p. Ahkircb.* Sept-Fonds S. Chyme, a town of Quercy, in the diocefe and election of Mohrauban. *p. Muuauban.* Sept-For.ds, or 5". *Lieu,* a phce and abby in the diocefe of Auturt. *p. Moulins.* . *Sep:-Fontaines.* I. A village of Franche-Comté, in the bailiwick of Gray. *p. Gray. z.* A village of Plcardy, in the generality and election of SoiiTons. *p. Soiflom,* 3. A place and abby, in the diocefe of Langrcs. *p. Cbaumont.* Sept-Fontaine, от *Sept-Fcires,* a village of F ran che-Com té, in the bailiwick oí Omans, *p. Befanden.* Sept-Forges, a pariih of Champagne, in the diocefe of Rheims, *f. Rheims.* Spt-Fors, a vilhge of Brie, in te diocefe ami election of Meaux. *p. Meaux.* Sept-Freres, a fmall town of Normandy, in the election of Virç. *p. Vire.* Sept-Ißes, illes of Marche, on the coaft of Bretagne, about 7 leagues from Treguier. *Sept-Meuies,* a village of Normandy, irr the election of Arques, *p. Eu.* Sept-Mcr.cel& Mijoux, a town of Franche-Comté, in the diocefe and bailiwick of S. Claude, *p.* 5. *Claude.* Sept-Monts, a village of Picardy, in the diocefe and election of Soiffons. *p. S'JJbns.* Sept-Outrest a village of Picardy, in the election of Mondldier. *p. Mon éidier.* Sept-Saux,a village of Champagne, in the diocefe and election of Rheims. *p. Rheims.* Stpr-fans, a town of Normandy, in thé dincefe and election of Bayeux. *p. Baysux.* Srpt-Yoyn, or *S. Georges-des-SeptVcycs,* a town of Anjou, in the election of Saumur. *p. Saumur.* Sptemes-Oyßcrcs, a fmall town of Dauphiny, in the diocefe and election of Vienne, *p. Vienne.* Seelenvolle, a place of Picardy, in the election of Doulcns. *p. Dou.'ens.* Septs, a village of Armagnac, in the election of Rivière Verdun, *p. Grenade.* Scptiigny, a village of Toulois, in the diocefe and receipt of Toul. *ft. Void. Sepwet,* a fmall town of Poitou, in the diocefe and election of Poitiers. *p. Pci i:r. » £(i,éiif'* v"age of Flankers, m the fubd' legation of Lille, *p. Lille. Stqutbart,* a vilbge of Picardy, in the cleaion of S. Quentin. /. *S. Sfentin. Stqucflte, le,* a village of Upper Languedoc, in the diocefe and receipt of Alby. *p Alby. Scjueville,* or *Segiilleta-Campagne,* a pariffi of Normandy, in the election of Caën. *p. Trouard. Sera,* a village of Foix, in the generality of Rouffillon. *p. Tarafcon. tn-Foix. Straw,* or *Serin,* a river of Burgundy, which runs into the Yonne, between Auxcrre and Joigny. *Seraincourt,* a village of VexinFrancois, in the election of Mantes. *p. F.ordeau-de-Vigny. Stran,* a village of Upper Linguedoc, in the diocefe and receipt of Lavaur. *p. Lavaur. Scra-ncburt-lc-Petit,* a place of Picardy, in the election of S. Quentin. *p.. Noycn. Serons,* a village of Normandy, in the ckflion of Argentan, *f. Ar Serenen,* a village of Provence, in the dioetfe and viguery of Grafie. *p. Graßi. Serent,* a town of Bretagne, in the diocefe and receipt of Vannes, *p. Plotrmel. Serents,* a village of Normandy, in the eleftion ofGifors./. *Gifirs. Serents, om Serons,* a village of Vexin-Frnncois, in the elcition of Magny. *p. Magny. Sereroußaing,* a village of Gafcony, in the receipt of Bigorre. *p. Tarbes. Sereulles,* a place of Burgundy, in the diocefe and bailiwick of Challón. *f. Challón. Serez,* a village of Normandy, in the diocefe and eleftion of Evreux. *p. Dreux. Sereum,* a village of Dauphiny, in the diocefe and eleftion of Vienne. *p. Boutgoin. Sefs-de-Vain, les, Serfs-de-laSaltjfe, les, & Serfs-du-uarfier, Ies,* villares of Marche, in the ejsftjnp. *zl Gueret. p. Gtieret. Sergenon, & Sergenoz,* places of Frachc-Compté, in the bailiwick of Doll. *p. Doll. Sergines,* a town of Champagne, in the diocefe and eleftion of Sens. *p. Bray-fur-Seine. Sergmon,* a village of Champagne, in the diocefe and eleftion of Rheims. *p. Rheims.. Scrgny,* a place of Artois, in the bailiwick of Aire. *p. Aire. Sergtteux,* a fmall town of Champagne, in the diocefe and eleftion of Langres. *p. Lang; es. Strguigny.* See *Serquigny. Sergy,* a village of Ficardy, in the generality of Soiifons. *p. Pontáje. Stri,* or *S'jry,* a village of Picardy, in tlie diocefe and eleftion of Amiens. *p. Amiens. Serian,* a place of Armagnac, in the eleftion of Aftarac. *p. Mirande. Seriemrt,* a place of Champagne, in the eleftion of Rethel. *p. Rethel. Sériel,* a place of Picardy, in the erection of Doulens. *p. Doulens. Series,* a village of Auvergne,, in flic diocefe and eleftion of S. Flour *p. S. Flour. Serignac.* I. A town of Agenois, in the diocef and election of Agen, *p. Agen. 2.* A town of Bretagne, in the diocefe and receipt of Quimper. *p. Quimper.* 3. A village of Saintonge, in the diocefe and eleftion of Saintes, *p. Saintes.* 4. A village of Armagnac, in the election of Lomagne. *p. Beaumoutde Lrmagne.* e,. A place of Q-?rcy, in the diocefe 3nd election of Cahors. *p. VUlenewvect'Agen. Serlgnany* a town of Lower Languedoc, in the diocefe and receipt of Kéziers./. *Be'úers.* 2. A fmall town of Venaiffin, in the judicature of Carpentras. *p. Orange. Sfrign/y* town of Poitou, in the election of Fontenay. *p. Fontenay-leCompte. Serigny,* a villcge of Perche, in the election of Montagne. *Bellefme. &'UL:r z.* town of Limoßn, in the diocefe and election of Limoge? *p. Limoges. Serifly,* a village of Burgundy, in the bailiwick of Châtillon. /. *Cbâtillan. Serin,* See *Strain. Serincourty* a village of Champagne, in the diocefe and election of Rheims. *p. Rethel. Seringe £f Nrßt,* a village of Picardy, in the election of ChateauThierry, *p. la Fere. Seris,* a-village of Orléannoís, in. the election ot Bcaugcncy. *p. Bcau gency. Ser'tmn,* a village of Dauphiny, inthe diocefe and election of Vienne, *p. Vienne. Serizols,* a town of Upper Languedoc, in the diocefe and receipt of Rieux; *p. Toulonfe. Ser ley j* a village of Burgundy, in the diocefe and bailiwick of Challón. *p. Challón. Sermages-f* a village of Nivernois, in the diocefe and election of Nevers. *p. Nevéi s. Sermaimag-ny,* a village of Alface, in the bailiwick of Beffurt. *p. B effort. Sermaife.* i. A town of Champagne, on the river Saux, about 5 leagues from Vitry, and 3 from S. Pifier. *p. Vitry, z.* A town of Beauce, in the cleft ion of Dourdan./. *Dourdan.* 3. A village o,f Anjou? in the election of Baugé. *f. Bauge.* 4. A place of Picardy, in the diocefe and election of Noy On. *p. Noy-on, Senna'rfe's,* a town of Orléannois, in the election of Puhiviers. *p. Petbivi rs. S:rmai%y,* a vilbgc of Burgundy, in the bailiwick of Challón. *p.Chalion. Set mange,* a village of FrancheCompte, in the bailiwick of Dole. *p. Dele. Sermanjanntiy* a village of Marche, in the election of Gueret. *p. Ckene ra'tlles. Sermantißn,* a town of Auvergne, in the diocefe and election of Clermont, *p. Clermont. Sermentel,* a village of Normandy, in the diocefe and election of Bayeux. *f. Bayeux. Armeriez,?.* fтма" fnwn of Dauphiny, in the generality of Grenoble. *f. Grenoble. Sermerjhem,* a village of Alface, in the bailiwick of Bcnfeld. *p. Ben S rmeffè.* i. A village of Burgundy, in the bailiwick of Auxonne. *p. Auxùnne* 2. A village of Burgundy, in the bailiwick of Challón, *p. ChaiIon.* 3. A place of Burgundy, in the diocefe and bailiwick oí Macon, *p. Siure. Sermetj* a village of Agcnois, in the diocefe and election of Agen.. *le Temple. Sermie'resy* a town of Champagne, in thedioccfe and election of Rheims. *p. Rheims. Sermixelle,* a village of Burgundy, in the bailiwick of Avalon, *p. Ávakn. Sermoife,* a village of Pkrardy, in the diocefe and election of SuifTons. *p. Seifforts. Sermoje-Bourbonnoh SermotfeNivernçis,* places of Kivcruuis, in the diocefe and election of Ncveri. *p. Ntvers. Sermonne,* a village of Champagne, in the diocefe and election of Rheims. *p. Maura. Sermons c£? Taramam,* a town of Dauphiny, in the diocefe and cleéU.n of Vienne *p. tienne. Sermoye,* a village of Burgundv, in the bailiwick of Bourg-en-Brefle. *p. Tournus, Strmur,* a town of Auvergne, in the election of Combraillcs. *p. Cbamiem. Sernay,* a town of Alface, in the bailiwick of Thann, *p. Rouffacb. Seron,* a village of Gafcony, in the receipt of Bigorre. *p. Tarées. Serou, le,* afmall-riverofRouergue, that lofes itfelf in the Aveirou. *Serpaize,* a vitage of Dauphiny, in the generality of Grenoble.. *Vienne. Serpente, la,* a village of Upper Languedoc, in the diocefe and receipt of Alet. *p. Liiztuz.* Serpolieer, a village of Dombes, in the chatellany of Chalamont. *p. jBoitrg-en-BreJJe,* Serpoliere, ¡a, a place of Dorhbes, in the chatellany of Anberieu./. *Bellewille.* Serque, a place of Artois, in the diocefe and receipt of S. Omer. *p. S. Omer.* Sercjues, a village of Artois, in the diocefe and receipt of S. Omer. *p. S. Omer.* Serjueux, a village of Normandy, in the election of Neufchâtel. *p. NeufcbâteL* Serquigny, or *Sarçuigny*, a village of Normandy, in the election of Bernay. *p. Beaumont-le-Roger.* Serrain, le, a village of Touraine, in the diocefe and election of Tours, *p. Tours..* Serralcngue, a village of RoufliUon, in the diocefe and viguery of Perpignan, *p.Perpignan.* Se'rre, a town of Dauphiny, in the election of Romans, *p. S. Marcelim.* 2. A village in the diocefe and bailiwick of Btfancon. *p. Bejancon.* J, Servaux, a priory of Champagne, în the election of Tonnerre, *p. Tonnerre.* Serve, a village of Dauphiny, in the ckition of Romans, *p. Tarn.* Serve, la, a place of Burgundy, in the bailiwick of Beau ne. *p. Beaune.* Serve'y a village of Dombes, in" the chatellanyof *Lent. p. Biurg-en-Brrffe,* Serveiilas, a place of Foix, in the generality of Rouffillon. *p. Pamieri.* Serve!, a village of Bretagne, in the diocefe and receipt of Trcguicr. *p. Gbingamp.* Servelle. i. A villageof Burgundy, in the bailiwick of S. Laurent, *p. Challen, z.* A place of Burgundy, in the diocefe and bailiwick of Challón. *p. Challen.* Scrvennay, a vilhge of Picardy, in the diortfe and election of SoiíTons. /. *ta Fere.* Serverette, a village of Lower Languedoc, in the diocefe and receipt of Mende. *p. Marvejoes.* Servian i a town of Lower Languedoc, in the diocefe and receipt of Béziers./». *Perenal* Serviere, a town of Lower Languedoc, in the diocefe and receipt of Mende. *p. Marvejols.* Servieret. I. A village of Lower Languedoc, in the diocefe and receipt of Uzés. *p. Uzes.* 2. A village of Rouergue, in the diocefe and election of Rhodez. *p. Rhode.* 3. A place of Dauphinj, in the election of Gap./. *Briançon.* Serviez, a town of Upper Languedoc, in the diocefe and receipt of Caftrcs. /. *Caflret.* Servie%-en-Y at, a village of Upper Languedoc, in the diocefe and receipt of Carcaflonne. *p. Carcajjvnne.* Servignat, a place of Brefle, in the. bailiwick of Bourg.. *Bourg-cn-BreJfe.* Servlgny, a village of Normandy, in the diocefe and election of Coûtanccs. *p. Cùutanees.* Servigny-te-granâ & Servigny-hPe'it, hamlets of Burgundy, in the bailiwick of Challón, *p. Cbailon.* Scrv¡gny:l¿i-M.ontbo%in a place of Fr.mehe-Comté, in the bailiwick *of УсШ.p.Уфu/.* Servigny-les-Raville, & Servignyles-Ste-Barte, villages of Meflin, in the diocefe and receiptof *Maz. p.Met»* Servigry-les-Saulx, a village of Franche-Comté, in the bailiwick of Vefoul. *p. Lure.* Serviile. I. A village of Burgundy, in the diocefe and election of Challón, *p. Challen,* z. A figniory of Normandy, in the eleftion of Montivillicrs. *p. Fecamp.* Serviile, a village of Beauce, in the eleftion of Dreux, *p. Hcudan.* Servilly, a village of Bourbonnob, in the eleftion of Moulins, *p. la Palife.* Serbin, a village of FrancheComté, in the bailiwick of Baume. *p. Баùme.* Str-viv-le.Grand, a village of Artois, in the bailiwick of *Lens.p. Lens.* Servian & Soun,, a village of Champagne, in the diocefe and eleftion of Rheims *p. Rocroy.* Serv'iflas-de'Maurice, Êf Servijfasde-Solignac, villages of Lower Languedoc, in the diocefe and receipt of Puy. *p. le Pay.* Servales, a place of Upper Languedoc, in tlic diocefe and receipt of Mirepoix. *p. Mlrepoix.* Servan. I. A village of Normandy, in the diocefe and eleftion of Avranchcs. *p. Avrancbes.* 2. A village of Bretagne, in the diocefe and receipt of Rennes, *p. Rennes.* 3. A village of the Ifle of France, in the diocefe and eleftion of Paris, *p. Paris.* Servotte, a hamlet of Burgundy, in the recei Jpt of Auxonnc. *p. Auxonve.* Sery. I. A town of Champagne« in the diocefe and eleftion of Rheims. *p. Rethel.* 2. A village of Burgundy, in the diocefe and bailiwick of Auxcrrc. *p. Auxerre.* Sery £f *Magneval*, a village of Normandy, in the eleftion of Cré-' py. *p. Cripy.* Sery-aux-Pex, an abbv in the diocefe of Amiens, *p. Abbeville.* $ery-!es-Mamicrci,a village of P¡cardy, in the diocefe and election of Laon. *p. Laon.* Serzy, a village of Champagne, in, the diocefe and election of Rheims. *p. Fi/mes.* Scjcbaux, a village of Champagne, in the diocefe and election of Rheims. *p. Rheims.* Seferia, & *Scßgna,* places of Franche-Comté, in the bailiwick of Orgelet, *p. Lons-le-SaunLr.* -Scfattzbeim, a village of Aiface, in the bailiwick, of Kockerlberg. *p. Strafirurg.* Sejarges, a village of Champagne, in the election of Ste. Manéhould. *p. Ste. Manéhould.* SJeinbeim, a village of Aiface, in the diocefe of Stiafburg. *p. Hagucnau.* Stflj, a place of Burgundy, in the receipt of Gex. *p. Gex. Seßat,* a village of Guienne, in the diocefe and election of BourI ileaux. *p. Bourdcaux.* Scire. Sec *Cette.* Sevauz, a village of Pic; rdy, in the diocefe and election of Laon. *p. Laon.* Seube-tfOlcrm, la, a village of Beam, in the diocefe and receipt of Oleron. *p. Oleron.* Seucbey, a place of Champagne, in the diocefe and election of Langres. *p. Langres.* Scudre, a fmall river of Saintonge, which runs into the fea near Marenncs. Sene. I. A fmall town of the Ifle of France, fituated on the Seine, over which is a bridge of 21 arches; 3 leagues from Verfailles, and 3 from Paris. *Bureau de p'jße.* 2. A river of Normandy, in the diocefe of Coùtances. Scve-de-Cor, or *Seoc-de-Cor,* a wood of 904 arpents, in the jurifdièétion of Pamiers. Scmlinges, a village of Beaujolois, in the election of Villefranchc. *p. Roanne.* Se-venan, a place of Aiface, in the bailiwick of Beffort. *p. Beffort.* Siennes, or *Ccvenms,* a country and mountains of Lower Languedoc, in which are comprehended the diocefe of Alais, and part of Uzcs, Mende, and Viviers. Scverac. 1. A village of Bretagne, in the diocefe and receipt of Nantes. *p. Redon.* 2. A village of Roucrguc, in the diocefe and election of Rhodez. *p. Rbodcx.* Severac-le-Cbatcl, a town of Raucrgue, in the election of Milhaud. *p. Aft/baud.* Severac-V Egtife, a town of Rouergue, in the election of Milhaud. *p. Rhodez.* Seves. See *Séve.* Seveufc, a priory in the diocefe of Bcfancon. *Seveux,* 3 village of FrancheComté, in the bailiwick of Gray. *p. Cray.* Seugnc, a hamlet of Burgundy, in the diocefe and bailiwick of

Challón-. *p Challón.* Scugrty, a village of Picardy, in the diocefe and election of Senlis. *p. Senlls.* Scv'ignac. 1. A town of Bretagne, in the diocefe and receipt of S. Malo. *p. Brcon.* 2. A village of Beam, in the receipt of Morias, *p. Pau,* Sevignac ¿£? Mcyracq, places of Beam, in the diocefe and fénéchauffée of Oleron. *p. Oleran.* Scvignon, a village of Burgundy, in the bailiwick of Mâcon. *p. Mácon.* Sevigny. 1. A town of Champagne, in the diocefe and election of Rheims, *p. Reibel.* 2. A village of Normandy, in the election of Argentan, *p. Argentan.* Sevigny-la-Foreft, a villagr of Champagne, in the diocefe and election of Rheims, *p. Rethel.* Seuignyes, a village of Flanders, in the diocefe and fubdelegation of Cambray. *p. Cambray.* Seuil, a town of Champagne, in the election of Rethel. *p. Rethel.* SeuHlet, a village of Bourbonnois. in the election of Moulins, *p. S. C er and.* Sevïllyy an abby in Touraine. Scvingbcm, a village of Artois, in the diocefe and receipt of S. Omer. *p. S. Omer.* Sévis, a village of Normandy, in the election of Arques. *p. la Rougetnaifort.* S ule, a river of Normandy, which runs into the fea at Courfculie. Seuline, a brook which runs into the river Seule. Scully-les'lanwy, a village of Flanders, ιιι the lubdclegation of Lille. *p. Lille.* Seurf a village of Bléfoi», in the diocefe and election of Blois. *p. Blots.* Seuran, a village of the Iflc of France, in the diocefe and election of Paris, *p. Vonejfi.* Seudresy a village af Anjou, in the diocefe and election of Angers. *P. Cbateau-Gcntier.* Seure. See Seurre. Seuret or Sevre-Nantoife, a fmall river, which runs into the Loire, oppofite Nantes. Sevré) a fmall town of Normandy, in the election of Argentan, *p. Jl?gen tan.* Sturéy or Sevré-Niort oxfe9 a river öf Poitou, which pafles by Niort, and falls into the lea between Luçon and Rochelle. Szurey, a village of Burgundy, in the diocefe and bailiwick of Challón. *p. Challón.* Seuris, a village of Angoumois, in the diocefe and election of Angoulème. *p. Cbabanots* Sevrony a pariih of Champagne, in the diocefe of Rheims, *p. Rheims.* Seurrej or *Bellegarde,* a town of Burgundy, near the Saone, in the diocefe of Befançon,

and bailiwick of Auxonne; 3 leagues from Beaune, 15 from Autun, 8 from Dole, 19 from Befançon j and 5 from Paris. Bureau de P'fle. Seurresy a village of Saintonge, in the election of S. Jean-d'Angely. *p. S. Jean-dlAnge'y.* Sevryt a village of Nivcrnois, in the election of Charité-fur-Loire, *p. la Charité.* Seury, a village of Berry, in the election of Charité, *p. la Chante.* Seux, a village of Picardy, in the diocefe and election of Amiens, *p. Amiens.* Sevys, a village of Normandy, in the election of Arques, *f. Dieppe.* Sex-Fontaine, a village of Champagne, in the election of Chaumont. *p. Chaumont* Sexcelles, a village of Limofin, in the election of Tulles. . *Tulles.* Sy, a market-town of FrancheComté, fituatcd on the Saône, *p. Sejancon.* Seycballe, a village of Auvergne, in the diocefe and election of Clermont, *p. Clermont.* Seye, a river of Normandy, that runs into the fea near Dieppe. Seyne, a town of Provence, fituatei among the mountains, on the frontiers of Dauphiny; about 4 leagues from Embrun, *p. Digne.* Seyne, la, a town of Provea ce, in the diocefe and viuery of Toulon. *p. Toulon.* Seynes, a village of Lower Languedoc, in the diocefe and receipt of Uzés. *p. Uze's.* Syreffe, a place of Gafcony, in the election of Landes, *p. S. Sever.* Seyrcjle. See *Ceirtfle.* SeyJJ'el, a town of Burgundy, on the Rhône, by the confines of Bugey and Savoy; it is a government and chatellany; about 7 leagues from Bclley, and ιι from S. Claude. *Bureau de polle.* SeyJJuel, a place of Dauphiny, in the diocefe and election of Vienne. *Pienne.* Seyure, a village of Poitou, in the diocefe and election of Poitiers, *p. Pdtiers.* Seyx, a fmall town of Upper Languedoc, in the diocefe and receipt of Rieux, *p. Touloufe.* Sezanne, a city of Brie, on the confines of Champagne, the feat of a governor and bjiliwick, &c in tr« diocefe of T royes, and generality of Chalons; about il leagues from Troycs, lo from Chateau-Thierry, and r6 fromParis. *Bureau de ¡ofic.* Sanne, à fmsli rivcr'of Provence, which empties irfelf into the fea near the port of NapooleV Siarrcy, a village of Gafcriny, in the receipt of Bigorre. *p.*

Tarbes. Sibtvil, a village of Bretagne, in the diocefe and receipt of S. PoldeLéon. *p Mcrhix.* Sibiville-Sericourt, a place of Artois, in the bailiwick of S. Pol. *p. Arras.* Sebourri, a town of Gafcony, in the diocefe ar.d receipt of Bayonne. *p. S. Jttn-d:-Lutz.* Siecicu & S. Julien, places of Dauphiny, in the diocefe and election of Vienne, *p. Vienne.* Sichamp, a village of Nivernois, in the election of Charité-fur-Loire. /. *ffe-vers.* Sich', le cap, a cape on the coaít of Provence, not far from Toulon. Sidiailles. See *Cidialles.* Sidoine, la,, a village of Dombes, in the chatcllany of Trévoux. *j. Villefrancbe.* Sie, a river of Normandy, that runs into the Douve. S;c-en-Erigmn, la, an abby, in the diocefe of Poitiers, *p. la Cbatcigneray.* Steges, a village of Franche-Comté, in the diocefe and bailiwick of S. Claude, *p. S. Ckude.* Sieges, les, a village of Champagne, in tlK diocefe and election of Sens. *p. Sens.* SJly en-Rcyaute', a village of Burgundy, in the diocefe and bailiwick of Autun. *p. Autun.* Sienne. 1. A village of Burgundy, in the diocefe and bailiwick of-Challón, *p. CbalUv.* 2. A river of Normandy, whi h runs into the lea between Agon and Regncville. Sief, or Stecq, a village of Saintmge, in 'the election of S. Jeanф Angdy. *p. S. Jcan-cV Angtiy.* Stercnta, a village of Alface, in the bailiwick of Landfer. *p. Huningue.* Sterquc. See *Sáerck.* Sierville, a fmall town of Normandy, in the diocefe and election of Rouen, *p. Yerville.* Sieujat, a fmall town of Auvergne, in the diocefe and election of S. Flour, *p. S. Flaut,* Siems, or Sieve/ ,2 village of Dauphiny, in the diocefe and eleilion of Grenoble, *p. Grenoble.* Sieurae, a place of Upper Languedoc, in the diocefe and receipt of Alby. *p. Ally.* Scurey, a village of Normandy, in the election of Andely. *p. Gaillon.* Seje¡, les, a plací of Provence, in the diocefe and viguery of Digne. *p. Digne.* Siga/ as, a village of Agénois, in the diocefe and election of Agen, *p.fowmm.* Sgevun, the name of a fmall wood, in the juriMiction of S. Pons, in Languedoc. Sighy, a village of Orléannois, in the diocefe and election of Orléans. *p. Orleans.* Sgnac, a village of Gafcony, in the diocefe and élection of Comminges. *p. Montrejeau.* Sigjtan, a place in the Pyrenees, in which arc quarries of marble. Signes, a town of Provence, in the diocefe of Aix. *p. Ollioule.* Signeville, a village of Champagne, in the election of Chaumont. *p, Cbaumont.* Signy, a village of Meffin, in the1 diocefe of.Verdun, *p. Sedan.* Signy-PAbbaye, Êf *Signy-le-Petit)* towns of Champagne, in the diocefe and election of Rheims, *p, Retbel.* Signy-Signets, a village of Brie, in the election of Coulomicrs. *p. la Ferte'-jous-jfouare.* Sigoltzheim, a village of Alface, in the' bailiwick of Enfifhcim. *p. Colpur.* Slgottierj a village of Dauphiny, ia the diocefe and eleftion of Gap. /ч *Sißeron.* Sïgwgue, or *Sigougne,* a town of Angoumois, in the election of Cognac, *p. Cognac.* Sigouigrtac *S Gaßel,* a village of Agénois, in the diocefe and election öf Agen. *p. V'alence-d'Agen. Sigouigne',* a town of Touraine, in the diocefe and eleftion of Tours. *p. Tours.* Sigiale's, a village of Périgord, in the diocefe and eleftion of Sarlat. *p. £ergerac.* Stgounce, a village of Provcnce in the viguery of Forcalquicr. *p. Fortalqmer.* Sigoyer. I. A fmall town of Dauphiny, in the diocefe and eleftion of Gap. *p. Gep. X.* A village of Provence, in the viguery of Siftcion. *p. Sißeron.* Sigua-,. a fmall town of Foix, in the diocefe of Perpignan, *p. IaritJcon-en-Foix.* Sigy. i. A fmall town of Normandy, in the eleftion of Lions, *p. F-couy.* a. A village of Champagne, in the eleftion of Nogcnt-fur Seine. *p. Nogent.* Sigy-U-CbSteau, a village of Burgundy, in the diocefc and bailiwick of Challón, *p Cballm.* Sijan, a town of Lower Languedoc, in the diocefe and receipt of Narbonne. *p. Narbonne.* Silfiac & F emit, a village of Bretagne, in the diocefe and receipt of Vijines. *p. Fontruy.* kllacParccllc-Baffe, & Sillac-ParCtlle-Haute, fmall towns of Vivarais, in the receipt of Viviers, *p. V.viers.* Sllacs, a village of Poitou, in the diocefe and eleftion of Poitiers, *p. Poitiers.* Sillans, a village of Provence, in the viguery of Barjols. *p. Barjols.* Sillans, or *Silam,* a village of Dauphiny, in the eleftion of Romans, *p. la Côte-S.-Ar.dré.* Sillas, a village of Bazadois, in the eleftion of Condom, *p.*

Bozas. SiUe'-lc-GuiUaumt, a town of Vol. III.
Maine, in the diocefe and election of Mans. *p. Frefnay.* Siil/-le-Philippe, a town of Maine, in the diocefe and election of Mans. *p. Conner e.* Sllegny, a village of Meflin, in the diucefe and receipt of Metz. . *Metz.* SilUgut) a place of Navarre, in the receipt of S. Palais, *p. Pau.* SJleryt a village of Champagne, in the diocefe and election of Rheims, *Bureau de poße.* sUley. / A place of FrancheComte, in the bailiwick of Ornans. *p. Befaron.* 2. A place in the bailiwick, of Baume, *p. Baume.* 3/See Sill/. Silly. I. A village of Brie, in the diocefe and election of Meaux. *p. Dammart'n.* a. A village of Normandy, in the election of Argentan. *p. Argentar/.* 3. A village of Picardy, in the diocefe and election of Bcauvais. *p. Bsawvais.* Slty-la-Poterie, a town of Pícardv, in the diocefe and election of Soiil"u:u. *p. la Fenc-Milon.* Si'/y-Saulnoy, a place cf Mennig in the diocefc and receipt of Mct7. /. *Merz* Silly-fur-Wied, a village of Meflin, in the diocefe and receipt of Metz.
Mftz. Silvacanne. See *Sawve-Canne.* Silvanet. Sec *Salvam%.* SU'varouvrtj a village of Champagne, in the election of Bar-furAubc. *p. Chateautnllaine.* Sil've-Bénite. See *Sawve-Bimte.* Smacottbrej a village of Beam, in rhc receipt of Morias, *p. Pau. S* mordre. I. A fmall town of Bur-, gundy, in the diocefe and bailiwick tf Challón, *p. Challón, г.* A village of Breite, in the bailiwick of Bourg. *p. Bourg-en-Brejfe.* 3. A village of Dauplvny, in the diocefe and election of Vienne, *p. Bourgoin.* 4. A village of Dombes, in the chatellany of Montmcrlc. *p. Belleville.* Simard, a village of Burgundy, ш the bailiwick of S. Laurent, *p. íouhans.* Simtncotirty a village of Artois, in the diocefe and bailiwick of Arras.*p. Arras.* Simian, a village of. Provence, in the diocefe and vigucry of Apt. *p. Apt.* Simiane-lcs-Aix, a village of Provence, in the dioccfe and vigucry of Aix. *p. Aix.* Simon, le, a village of Poitou, in the election of Fontenay. *p. Tbire.* 1 Simorre, a town of Armagnac; about 2 leagues from Lombez, and 6 from Auch. *p. Lombcz.* Simple, a town

of Anjou, in the election of Château-Gontier. *p.Ckd tcau-Gontier.* S.n-le Noble, a village of Flanders, in the fubdelcgation of Douay. *p. Douay.* Sinanyr. e, an abby of Provence, in the dioccfe of CavaUlon. *p. Avignon.* Sinard, a village of Dauphiny, in the diocefe and election of Grenoble. *p. Grenoble.* ' Singlet, a fmall town of Auvergne, in the diocefc and election of Clermont, *p. Clermont.* Singîy-let-Omonty a village of Champagne, in the election of Rctfiel. *p.Launoy.* Sinwes-P lanes, a place *oT* Lower Languedoc, in the diocefe and receipt of Mcnde. *p. Mendt.* Smcfe, a fmall river of Normandy, that runs into the fea near Quineville. Sinâs, a place of Gafcony, in the receipt of Bigorre. *p. Tarées,.* Sintratf. See *S. Traft.* Sintres, a village of Vivarais, in the Hiocefe and receipt of Viviers, *p. Javiers.* Sion. i. A village of Armagnac, in the diocefe and election of Auch. *p. Auch. z.* A place of Bretagne, in the diocefe and receipt of Nantes. *p. J)erwf.* Sienne, la, a fmall'fiver of Gafcony. $Kfnti£-.taFcrget a village of Cham pagne, in the election of Chaumont" *p. Neufdatcau.* Slonniac, a village of Limofin, in the election of Brives. *p. BrVoes.* Siorat, a village of Bourbonnais, in the election of Gamut, *p. Algue* Siorat-de-Ribeyrat, a village of PerigorJ, in the diocefe and election of Pe'rigueux. *p. le Chabart.* Stoule. See *Schule.* Sirac, I. A village of Armagnac, in the election of AHaracГ *p. Auch.* 2. A place of Rouflillon, in the vigucry of Conilans. *p. Vilhfrancke-deConßans.* Siran, i A town of Lower Languedoc, in the dioccfe and receipt of S. Pons. *p. Beziers.* z. A fmall town of Auvergne, ¡n the election of Aurillac. *p. Auril/ac.* Svaucourt, a place of Artois, "ni the bailiwick of S. Pol. *p. Arras.* Sirch. SccScieri. Sireix, a place of Gafcony, in the receipt of Bigorre. *p. Tarbes.* Sereu'il, a village of Angoumois, in the diocefc and election of Angoulême. *p. Château neuf-en-Angoumois.*
Srw, a place of Beam, in the receipt of Pau. *p. Pau.* Srrox, a village of Franche-Comté, in the bailiwick of Puligny. *p, Safins.* Sirques. See *Sàerck.* Sirva/, a wood of 1653 arpente, in the jurifdic-

tion of Pamiers.
Siffontie, a" town of Picardy, in the diocefe and election of Laon. *p Laon. Sißy & Villers-le-Vert,* a village of Picardy, in the dioccfe and election of Laon. *p. S. Quentin. Siflercn,* an ancient and ftrong city of Provence, fituated at the foot of a rock, by the Durance; the fee of a biíhop; with a íenéchaufsée, vigucry, and receipt; about 8 leagues from Gap, 20 from Aix, and 16 from Embrun. *Bureau de pofle. Siflorff,* a place of Mcßin, in the di'jccfe and receipt of *Metz. p. Metx, Sitele, U,* a village of Gafcony, in *the* receipt of Bigorrc. *p. 'Tarbes. Sivam,* a wood of 141 arpents, in the jurifdiction of S. Pons, in Languedoc. *Skandiere, la,* a priory in the diocefe of Angoulêmc. *Sivens,* a foreft of 231 arpents, in the jurifdiction of Touloufe. *Sivergues,* a village of Provence, in the diocefe and viguery of Apt. *p. Apt, Swras,* a village of Foix, in the generality of Rouffillon. /. *Tarafeon «n-Foix, Sin/ray.* See *Cvray.*
Ät/ry, a village of Gâtinois, in the elcftion of Mclun. *p. U Cbatelet, Sivry-en-Montagne,* (3 *Sivry-Iesufrnay,* villages of Burgundy, in the bailiwick of Amay-lc-Duc *p. Dijon. S'tvry-la-Perche, & S'mry-ValSte.-Marie,* villages of Meffin, in the diocefe and receipt of Verdun. *p. Verdun, Swry-les-Bufancy,* a village of Champagne, in the election of Ste. Manéhoull. *p. Stenay. Sivry-fur-Ente,* a village of Champagne, in the election of Ste. Manéhould. *p. Ste. Manebould. Sivry-fur-Mcufe,* a fmall town of Meffin; 6 leagues from Stenay, and 5 from Verdun, *p. Verdun. Six-Fours,* a town of Provence, in the diocefe and viguery of Toulon, *p. Olñiule, Sixtz,* a village of Bretagne, in the diocefe and receipt of Vannes, *p. Redon. Sfaun & Locmrfar,* a fmall town of Bretagne, in the diocefe and receipt of S. Pol-de-Léon. *p. Landernau. Sixun,* a fmall iiland on the coaft of Bretagne; about 3 leagues from the continent. *Socoa,* a fmall feaport, between Bay on ne, and S. Jean-dc-Lutz, *p. Bayonne, Socrac,* a place of Gafcony, in the receipt of Bigorre. *p. Tarbes. So Jes,* a village of Gafcony, in the diocefe and election of Commingei. *p. Mwtrejeau.*

Soeix, a village of Beam, in the diocefe and receipt of Oleron. *p. Oleron, Soffme.* Sec *Souefme. Soeßricb,* a place of MciTin. in the diocefe and receipt of Metz. *p.. Metz. Soewvres,* a place of Picardy, in the diocefe and election of Amiens. *p. Amiens. Sogne, la,* a village of Normandy, in the diocefe and election of Evreux. *p. Evreux. Sognes,* a village of Champagne, in the diocefe and election of Sens. *p. Sens. S'jguenne,* a village of Normandy, in the election uf Bernay. *p. Bcrnay. Sohefme,* a village of Meflin, in the diocefe and receipt of Verdun. /». *Verdun. SoignoIUs.* X. A village of the Illc of France, in the diocefe and election of Paris, *p. Brie. 1,* A place or Normandy, in the election of Falaife. *p. Fa/aije. Scigny,* a place of Brie, in the election of Sezanne, *p. Sezanne, Soilly,* a place of Champagne, in the diocefe of Rheims, *p. Dormant, Soindre, я* village of Beauce, in the election of Mantes, *p Mantes» Sjing,* a village of Franche-Comté, in the receipt of Gray. *p. Cray. Soings,* a fmall town of Bléíois» in the diocefe and election of £к»9 *p. Blois. Soiran,* a place of Burgundy, in the dicccfe and bail.wick of Dijon. *p. Dijon. So'u an Gf Souffran,* a parifh of BurgunJy, in the bailiwick of Auxonne. *p. Auxonne. SoiJft. 'vaL* Sec *SaiJJêval, Sojfñr,* a village of Burgundy, in the kiiliwick of Auxonnc. *p. Aux onne. Soibnnoisf* a fmall country of Pi? cardv, of which Suilluiis is the capital.'.. L *2 Scßontt* an ancient, large, and liandfome city of the lile of France, iituated in a very fertile valley, on the river Aifnc; with a bifhopric, under the archbifhop of Rheims, an election, bailiwick, &c. it contains feveral pariihes; 8 leagues from Laon, 41 from Givet, 62 from Liege, 30 from Valenciennes, 44 from Bruflels, 32 from Möns, 28 from Maubeuge, 24 from Avcfnes, 23 from Landrccy, 26 from Cambray, 32 from Douay, 40 from Lille, 59 from Oftende, 13 from Rheims, 23 from Châlons, 58 from Metz, 33 from Ste. Manéhoiild, 43 from Verdun, 62 from Thionville, 59 from Dunkirk, 30 from Anas, 56 from Calais, 57 from Boulogne, and 25 from Paris. *Bureau de pofle. Scijy,* a villp. gc of Brie, in the diocefe and election

of Provins, *p. Provins. Soiy-aux-Boix,* a village of Brie, in the election of Sezanne.-/). *&turne. Soify-Malejbcrbes,* a village of Oileannois, in thedectionof Pifhiviers. *f. Pitbivicrs. Soify-jous-Montmorcncy,* a village of the Ifle of France, in the diocefc and election of Paris.p. *Montmorency. Soljy-fiir-beine,* a village of the Ifle of France, in the diocefc and election of Paris, *p. Paris. &¡x, i* village of Berry, in the diocefe and election of Bourges, *p. Bourges. Soix-PEgHfe,* a place of Bourbonnois, in the election of S. Amand. *f. S. Amand. Seize,* a village of Picardy, in the diocefe and election of Laon. *p. Lion. Soixy-fur-Ecole,* a village of Gàtinois, in the election of Melun. *p. CcrieU. Soiaiga,* a village of Auvergne, in the diocefe and election of S. Flour. *f. S. Flour. Sclaife* S? *S. Saphorin-d'Oxon,* 3 town of Dauphiny, n tbe diocefe of Lyons. *Crtntbie. Solaife,* a village of Dauphiny, in the diocefc and election of Vienne. *p. Vienne. Solan,* a village of Armagnac, in the diocefc of Comminges. *p. Montrejeau. Solarte,* a fmall river of Limoftn, which runs into the Correze, near Tulles. *Soleil bas,* a p'ace of Provence, in the vigucry of Caftellanc. *p. Caftellane. Soleis,* a village of Provence, in the viguery of Caftellanc. *p. Caftellane. J Soleme,* a town of Maine, on the river ¿forte, about a league from Sable, *p. Sablé. Solente,* a village of Picardy, in the election of Péronnc. *p. Roye. Soler, le,* a village of Roufllllon, in the diccefc and viguery of Perpignan. *p. Perpignan. SoleJ'mes,* a village of Hainaut, in the government of Quênoy. *p. Qut noy. Soigne,* a vilhge of Mcflin, in the dicccfe and receipt of Metz. *p. Yxe. Solidor,* a chateau near £. Malo. *p. S. Malo. So/iers,* a village of Normandy, in the election of Caën. *p. Trouard. Sùlîgnac.* i. A town of Lower Languedoc, in the diocefc and receipt of Puy. *p. le Puy.* 2. A fmall town of Guicnne, in the diocefe and election of Bourdeaux. *p. Cadillac.* 3. Sec *Stlcgnac» Solignat,* a village of Auvergne, in the election of Ifloire. *p. Iffoire, Suligny.* I. A town of Perche, in the election of Mortagnc. *p. Mortagrn.* 2. A village of Champagne, in the diocefc and election of Troyes. *p. Nogent-fur-Seine.* 3. A parifh of Normandy, in the election of Coûtantes *p. Caën. Silimieu,* a village of Dauphiny, in the gcneiallty of Grenoble, *p. Grenoble. SolJe, la,* a village of Gafcony, in the receipt of Gabardan. *p. Mirande. Шbl% S, Martin, lêf* a ptaoe of Pi cardy, in the dioccfe and election of Noyon. *p. Royon. Sollet,* a village of Bourbonnois, in the election of Moulins, *p. Thiers. Solognac,* or *Solignac,* a fmall town of Limonn, in the dioccfe and' election of Limoges. *p. Limoges. Sologne,* a province which makes part of the government of Orléannois, Bléfois, and Berry; about 25 leagues in length and 12 in breadth, Romartin is the capital. *Sc/ogny,* a village of Burgundy, in the diucefeand bailiwick of Macon. *f. Macon. Solóme',* a village of Poitou, in the election of Loudun. *p. Louâun. SJomiac,* a place of Armagnac, in the election of Rivière-Verdun, *p. Gimo ne. Solon,* a village of Limofin, in the diocefe and eleition of Limoges, *p. Pierre-Bueßre. Solon & CbSteau-Mißer,* a village of Périgord, in the dioccfe and election of Périgueux. *p. Pc'ñgueux. SoloH.la-Rue,* a village of Burgundy, in the dioccfe and bailiwick of Dijon, *p. Dijon. Solmges,* a village of Burgundy, in the bailiwick of Arnay-le-Duc. *p. Dijon. SJre-le-Cbâteau,* a town of Hainaut, 3 leagues from Maubcuge. *p. Avejncs. Solrtnes,* a place of Hainaut, in the government of Maubcuge. *p. Maubeuge. Soliere,* 3 village of Gjtinois, in the election of MontJiges. *p. Monarges. Solutrey,* a village of Burgundy, in the diocefe and bailiwick of Macon, *p. Mâcon. Sombacour le Bourg,* a fmall town of Franche-Comté, in the bailiwick of Pontarlicr. *p. Pontarher. Sombarrante,* a place of Navarre, in the receipt of S. Palais, *p. Pau. Somberncn,* a town of Burgundy, fituatcd on one of the highelt mountains in Provence, in the bailiwick ot Arnay-le-Duc. *p. Ste. Reine. Sombre,* a figniory of Normandy, in the generality of Amiens. *Boulogne. Sombrin,* a village of Artois, in the diocefe and bailiwick of Arias. *p. Arras. Sombrun,* a village of Armagnac, in the dioccfe and election of Auch. *p. Mirande. Scmcbampj* a fmall town of Eeauce, in the election of Dourdan. *p. Dourdan. S.mloire,* a town of Anjou, in the eleition of Montrcuil-Bellay. *p. Saumur. Sommain,* a village of Hainaut, in the government of Quênoy. *p. It Шu! o;. Sommain & R'.eulay,* a village of Flanders, in the fubdelegation of Bouchain. *p. Boucbain. Sommaire,* a fmall diftrict of Normandy, in the diocefe of Evreux, near l'Aigle. *Sommaijne,* a place of Champagne, in the diocefe and election of Châlons. *p. Sie. Mancbould. Sommancourt,* a vilbge of Champagne, in the ekction of Joinvillc. *Sommane.* See *Saumane. Sommant,* a village of Burgundy, in the dioccfe and bailiwick of Autun. *p. ¿éttun. Somme, la,* a river of Picardy, whcb paffes by S. Quentin, Per nne, Amiens, Abbeville, &c. into the fea between Crotoy and S. Valéry. *Somme-Fontaine,* a village of Champagne, in the dioccfe and eleition of Troyes. *p. Nogcttt-fur-Seine. Somme-Py,* a town oí Champagne, about 8 leagues from Rheims, *p. Rheims. Smme-Su'ppe,* a village of Champagne, in the diocefe and election of Rheims, *p. Rheims. Somme-Tourbe,* a village of Champagne, in the election of Ste. Manéhoiild./. *Ste. Manéhould, Somme-Ya/,* a village of Champagne, in the diocefe and election ot Trojes, *p. Trojes Smme-Vtßtj* a village of Champagne, m the diocefe and election of Chalons, *p. Cbalons. Simmeautn,* t? *Ssmmerame,* villages of Champagne, in the election of Stc. Manehould. *p. Src. Mneliculd. &mmtas,* a village of Sa'ntonge, in tiic diocfe and election of Saintes. *p. Mantendré. Sommer mer.!,* a villa, e of Champagne, in the election of Joinville. *p. JcintUU, Smmeron9* a village of Picardy, in the election ofGuife. *p. Vervins.* , *Sommeruieux,* a village of Normandy, in the dioccfe and election of Bay tux. *p. Eayeux. Sommery,* a vilh'ge of Normandy, in the ekction oí Lions, *p. Ecct/ y. Sotrm f.ni)* a village of Champagne, in the dioccfe and election of Chalons, *p. Arcis-fur-Aube. ¿fammetonne-le-Hayon,* a village of Metz, in the diocfe of Verdun. *p. Sedan. Sommettc,* a place of Picardy, in the dioccfe and election of Noy on. *p. Ham. Sommette,* lay a place of FrancheCompté, in the bailiwick of Baume. *p. Bume. SmnsvUkj* a village of Champagne, in the election of Joinville. *p. Jfoinvilte. Sommvoire* a town of Champagne, in the election of Joinville. *p. Joinville. Sommieres y* a town of Lower Languedoc, on the Vidourlc, in the diocefe and receipt of Nîmes, the feat of a viguery; about 6 leagues from Montpellier, 7 from Andufe, and 6 from Nîmes.. *Bureau de poße. Somment y* a village of Lower Languedoc, in the discefc and receipt of Lodeve. *p. hedeve. Sommoyrvre,* a village of Champagne, in the dioccfe and élection of Çhâlcns. /. *Sie. Manébould. Somogr.îeux,* a village of Mcflïn, In the ditcefe and receipt of Verdun. jT, *Verdur. Scmjßls,* a villaje of Champagne, in the élection oí Vitry. *p. Vu.y" Somptj* a village of Poitou, in the election of S. Maixant. *p. la MotteSte.-Heraye. Sompuis,* a village of Champagne, in the election of Vitry. /». '*Reibet. Scmquaijcy* a village of Champagne, in the election of Joigny. *p. Jùgny Scmvilliers* a confidcrable tract of country, in the election of Poitiers. *Son,* i. A village of Champagne, in the election of Rethel. *p. Ret bel,* a. An ancient château, in Donncaan, *p. Merit louts, Scncellesy* a fmall town of Anjou, in the diocefeand election of Angers. *p. Angers.* In this place are fprings of mineral waters. *Scncourt.* i. A village of Champagne, in the election of Chaumont. *p. Cbaumont. 2.* Aplace of Meifcn, in the diocefe and receipt of Toul. *p. Tfiul. SoKcyat* a village of Franche-Comté, in the bailiwick of Orgelet, *p. Lons-le-Saunier. Scndebois,* a place of Burgundy, in the diocefe and bailiwick of Challón. *p. Challón. Sandemarchf* a village of Aîfacc, in the diocefe of Bale. *p. Huningue. Sondcrfdorffj* a village of Alface, in the bailiwick of Fer cette, *p. Bcf firt. Sondoffen* c3? *Apperßwer* a village of Alface, in the diocefe of Bale. /,, *Colmar. Sengeofity* a village of Picardy, in the dioccfe and election of Bcauvais. *p. Beauvais. Songeons & Loueujcy* a village «f Normandy, in the election of Andely. *p. Ecouy. Songefony* a village of FrancheComté, in the bailiwick of Poligny. *p. Salins. SongkUy* a villageof Valromey, m the generality of Dijon, *p. Seyjfel.* Songny-aux-Moulinsy a village of Champagne, in the diocefeand election of Châlons. *p. Cbalons.* Songny-en-Lang/r,a v i 11 age o f C h a m pagnc,in rtie election *QÍVÁ-ty.p.Vttttp Soagyf* a village of Champagne/ in the electkm-oi Vttrv. *p. Jr,try. Scnnac.* j. A town of Saintonge, m the election of S. Tcan-d'Angcly, *p. S. Jean dAr.gely.* 2. A village of Qjcrcy, in the election of Figcac. *p. Flgeac.* Sotmay, a town of Touraine, in. the dioccfe and election of Tour. *p. /imloije.* Sonnes, a town of Maine, in the d'occfe and election of Mans. *p. le Mem. Sot.nevtiïe ¿¿f AmhlenMU,* a village of Angoumois, in the election of Cognac, *p. S. Cibardeaux.* SonnevMle ÖS? Mott-tignuC-, a vllfage of Angoumois, in the election of 'Cognac, *p. Cognac.* Son-riere: & la Barre, a village of Burgundy, in the diocefc and bailiwick of Challón, *p. Sture.* Sonnois, a fmall country of Maine, atout и leagues in length. Memers is the capital. *Scnrtoy,* a village of Dauphiny, in the dioccfe and election of Vienne, *p. Vier.ne.* Son/ay, or Sonxay, a town of Tourainc, in the diocefc and election of Tours, *p. Tcurs.* Scm, a village of Picardy, in the diocefe and election of Laon. *p. Laon..* Son-thonaz, a village of Bugey, in the bailiwick, of Fellcy.. *p. Beliey.* Sony, a place of Gnfcony, in the receipt of Big»rre. *p. Tarées.* Soor. See *Sour,* Soquarce, a place of Normandy, in the election of FaJaîfe. *p. Trcuard. Sor,* a fmall river of,languedöc, which falls into the Agout, 2 leagues below Cailres. *Sorar. s.* See *Sourans. Sor bay i* a village of Picardy, in the election of Guife, *p. Pernnns. iSorèey,* a Village of Meiïïn, in the dioccfe and receipt of Metz. *p. Metz,. Sortiere:,* a fmall town of Dauphiny, in the diocfe and election of Cbp. *É Gap.* Sorhkrs, a villrge of Bourbonnoïs, in the election of Moulins: *p. Moulins.* Sorbon, or *Sorbonne,* a village of Crump gne, in the diocefc and election of Rheims, celebrated for bcuig the native place of Robert Sorbon who founded the famous college of Sor-bonne at París, *p. Retbel.* Sorbs, a village of Lower Languedoe, in the dio-cefe and receipt of Lodeve. *p. LcHcvc.*

Sorchapoum, a village of Navarrey in the dioccfe of Bayonnç. *p. Pint.* Sony, a village of Champagne, in the election of Rcthel. *p. Retbel.* Scrde, or *Sorda,* a town of Gafcony, on the gave of Oleron, in the election of Landes, *p. Dax.* Sordun, a fmall town of Krie, in the election of Provins, *p. Provins.* Sor eau, a village of Champagne, in the electron of RetheL *Rakel.'* Sorel, i. A village of Bcauce, in the election of Dreux, *p. Dreux,* 2. A village of Picardy, in the generality of Amiens, *p. Boulogne.* 3. A village of Picardy, in the election of Péronne. *pr Perenne.* 4. A village of Picardy, in the election, of Ah'-beville. *p. Abbeville.* Screfe, Soreze, or *la Son-fcalade-deSo'-eze,* a town of Upper Languedoc, on the river Sor; about 2 leagues from S. Papoul, and 9 from Touloufe.*P, Caßdnaxtdary.* Sorget» г. A fmall town of Pertgord, in the diocefc and election of Périgueux. *p. Périgueux.* 2. A village of Anjou, in the diocefe and election of Angers, *p. Angers.* Sorgieu, a village ot Bugey, in the diocefe and bailiwick, of Beliey. *p. Bellcy.* Sorgue, or le *Pônt-deScrgue,a* town of Venai-flin, fituatcd on the Sorgue, about 2 leagues from Avignon, *p. Avignon.* S-jr-gue, a river of Venaiflin, which takes its fource from the famous fountain of Vauclufe, and empties itfeJf into the Rhône, after being dividid into two ft reams. *Sorguts,* a village of Anjou, in the diocefc and election of Angers.-*p, Angers.* Sorbouetttf a village of Navarre, in the dioctfe of Bay on ne. *p. Pau.* Soribes, a village of Provence, in the viguery of Sifteron, *p, Siflcron.* Scrigny, a town of Touraine, 2 leagues from Montbrifon, and 7 from. Tuurs. *p. Tours.* Scring-*Béushwûlf* a village of Picard)-, m the dioccfe and election of Amiens, *p. simiens.* Setteres,7«, a place of Marche, in the ele¿tion of Gucret. *p. Gtterct.* Sormery, a town of Champagne, in the election of Florentin, *p. Brine.* Sarcay. i. A village of Burgundy, in the bailiwick, of S. Laurent, *p. Lit/bans.* 2. A village of Burgundy, in the receipt of Challón, *p. Challen.* 3-A village of Franche-Comté, in the bailiwick of Gray. *p. Gray. Same,* a parifh of Chan pagnej in the dioccfe of Rheims, *p.*

Rheims. Sornboffcn, a place of Alface, in the diocefc of Spire, *p. Strafburg.* &wy, a village of Picardy, in the rltoccfe and election of Son'fons. *p. Sjj/'ons.* Scrp, a confiderable fountain, in the diocefeof Riez, in Provence. Scrquauwille, a village of Normandy, in the election of Montiviliers. *p. Vallcmont.* Sorre. a frnall town of Gafcony, in the election of Landes. /. *S. Sever.* Sorrt-lc-Cbâteau, a place of Hainau, 3 leagues from Ave-fr.es. Sorrus, a village of Picardy, in the government of Montreuil. *p. Moitreuil-fur-Mcr.* Sortes, a village of Gafcony, in the election of Landes, *p. Dax.* Sort-bofville,' or *Sorttyville-en-Beaumcntj* a town of Normandy, in the election of Valognes. *p. Valognes.* Sortbofvi/le-près-Valognes, a village of Normandy, in the election of Valognes. *p. Valognes.* Stfts-ett-Marme/ps, л village of Gafcony, in the ejection of Landes, *Dax.* Ses, a town of Lower Languedoc, in the dioccfe of Auch, and election of Aítauc. *p. Mirçndt Sc/foy,* a v'Ibge of Poitou, in the eleftion of Châtellerault. *f. Cbât-clhrault.* Svttcjfard, a village of FrancheComté, in the bailiwick of Lons-leSaunier. *p. Lom-te-Saunier.* Sotevod, a village of Valromev, in the generality of Dijon, *p. Seiffet Scrtevafi-jZ* town of Normandy, in the eleñion of Valognes. *p. Valognes.* SottewUe. i. A town of Normandy, in the eleñion of Rouen. /. *Reuen,* 2. A town of Normandy, in the election of Arques, *p. Dieppe.* 3. A village of Normandy, in the election of Valognes. *p. Valognes.* ScttevUle-Jaa-le-Val, a village of Normandy, in the eleñion of Pontde-ГArche, *p Pont-de-1'¿irebe.* Souairt, a frnall town of Champagne, in the diocefe and eleñion of Rheims, *p. Rheims.* Soval, a village of Upper Languedoc, in the diocefe and receipt of Lavaur. *p. Ttu'oufe.* Souarce, a viliage of Al-face, in the bailiwick of Beffort. *p. Bef-firt.* Souaßre, a frnall town of Artois, in the dioccfe and bailiwick of Arras. *p. Arras.* Soubaignan, a village of Armagnac, in the eleñion of Aftarac. *p. Mirande.* S:ubeyrat, a village of Lower Languedoc, in the diocefe and receipt of Montpellier, *p. le Vigan.* Scube%, a fr-nall town of Lower Languedoc, in the diocefe and receipt of Lodeve. *p. Lodeve.* Soubirac, a village of Bnzadois, in the eleñion of Condom, *p. Bazas.* Soubirane, la, a wood of too arpents, in the jurifdiftion of S. Pons, in Languedoc. *SwiiJ'e,* or *Soubize,* a town of Saintonge, in the diocefe of Saintes, and eleñion of Marennes; about *z* leagues from Brouages, and 6 from Rochelle. *Bureau de pofie.* Soubrau, a town of Saintonge, in the diocefe and eleñion of Saintes. *p. Joribac.* Soubrebofc, a village of Marche, in the election of Bourganeuf. *p. Aubußöri.* Soubrecas, a village of Limbfin, in the diocefe and election of Limoges, *p. L'moges.* Soubsla-Caufe, a village of Armagnac, in the diocefe and election of Auch. *p. Auch.* Souceyrac, a town of Quercy, in the election of Figeac. *p. Figeac,* Sauche la, a village of Lower Landoc, m the diocefe and receipt of Viviers, *p. Viviers.* Soucbct, or *Soucbez,* a illage of Artois, between Arras and Bethune, 3 leagues from Arras, and 4 from Bethune. *p. Lens.* Souäen-en-Jareß, a lmall town of Lyonnois, in the diocefe and clection of Lyons, *p. Lyon.* Soucil, a village of Upper Languedoc, in the diocefe and receipt of Alby. *p. Alby.* Scucirac, a place of Quercy, in the diocefe and election of Cahors. *p. Cators.* Soucis, a village of Agénois, in the diocefe and election of Agen. *p. Agen.* Saucy, a place of Picardy, in the diocefe and election of Soiiions. *p. SoiJJins.* Scucy Jouvancyf a village of Champagne, in the diocefe and election of Sens. *p. Sens.* Soudan, a village of Bretagne, in the diocefe and election of Nantes, *p. Cbateaubriant.* Soudât, a village of Périgord, in the diocefe and election of Périgucux. *p. Cbalus.* Souday, a town of Maine, in the election of Château-du-Loir. *p. Mondcubleau.* Soudeilles, a village of Limolin, in theeleflion of Tulles, *p. Tulles.* Soudennts, a village of Limofin in the election of Tulles, *p. Tulles.* Soudcy-Notre-Dame, Êf SoudeySte.-Croix, villages of Champagne, in the dioccfc and election of Châ Ions *p. CLálms.* Soudiac, a village of Guienne, ii the diocefe and election of Bourdeaux. *p. Bourdcaux.* Souifan, a village of Bugey, in the diocefe anct bailiwick of Belley. *p. Amber'itux.* Soudorgues, a fmall town of Lower Languedoc, in the diocefe and receipt of Alais, *p. Alais.* Soudro/ty a village of Champagne, in the diocefe and election of Chalons, *p. Chalons.* Souecb-de-Conférant, a place of Gaffcony, in the election of Cornmi nges. *p. TouLufe.* Souccb-de-Salies; a place of Gafcony, in the diocefe and election of Comminges. *p. M.ntrejeau.* SouencS, a fmall town of Perche, in the election of Mortagne. *p. Mortagne.* Sou/s Êf le Ptrit-Gard, a village of Picardy, in the diocefe and election of Amiens, *p. Amiens,* Souefme, a town of Berry, in the election of Romorantin. *p. AuLigty.* SoveZj a village of Gafcony, in the election of Bigorre. *p. Tarées.* Souez & Rcuvroy, places of Picardy, in the eleîtion of Abbeville. *p. Abbeville.* S'ujjknbem, a village of Alface, in the bailiwick of Haguenan. *p. Haguenan.* Soußraignat, a village of Périgord, in the diwrefe and eleîtion of Pé.igueux. *p. FeYigueux.* Souffrignjc, a place of Aflgoumois, in the diocefe and eK/iion of Angoulêmc. *p. Angculhne.* Saug/, i. A kOwn of Maine, in the election o£ Laval, *p. Laval.* 2. A fmall town of Maine, in the election of C'lutteau-du-Loir. *p. Cbateaudu-Lùh:* 3. A village of Berry, in the election of Chatoauroux. *p. L¿vraux.* 4 A village of Beaucc, 'in the election of Vendóme, *p. Montoire.* Souge'-h-Ganelon, a town of Mainei ïn the diocefe and election of Mans. *p. Frejnay.* ¡¿ougéaly a village of B etagnc, in the diocefc and receipt of Nantes, *p. Hennés.* Sougramc, a village of Upper Languedoc, in the dioceíc and receipt of Alct. *p. Limoux,* Sbugy, a village of Orléannoisj in the diocefe and election of Orléans. *p. Artenay.* Ssuçj-Varcnncs, a village of NÍvernois, in the dioccfe and election of Kevers. *p. Nevers.* Souiey, a vilhge of Burgundy, in the election of Semur-en-Auxois. *p. Semur.* Ssubitrs, a village of G.ltinois, in the election of Gien. *p. S. Farjeau.* Souhkb. I. A village of Picardy, in the election of Doulens. *p. Doutens.* 2. A village of Artois, in the bailiwick of S. Pol. *p. Arras.* Souillac, or *Soullac,* a town of Quere y, fituatcd ou the Breie, near the Dordogne, in the dioccfe of Cabors, and election of Figeac; 5 leaguts from Brives, and 17 from Ca bors. *Bureau depoße.* Saufflade, a village of Roucrguc, in the election of Villefranche. *p. VMefrancbe-dt-Rcutrguc.* SouWaguet. i. A village of Bouerguc, iy the diocefc and election of Rhodez, /. *Rbcd.x.* 2.. A village cf Quercy, in the election of Figéac. *p. Figcac.* «, *Souill/.* I. A town of Maine, in the diocefe and ekction of Mans. *p. le Mans.* 2. A village of Upper Languedoc, in the diocefe and receipt of S. Papou), *p. Caßelmudary.* Swilfy. i. A village of lirie, in the diocefe and election of Meaux. /. *Clayt.* 2. A hamkn of Burgundy, in the diocefe and bailiwick of Auxcrre *p.Auxerre.* Sovittet a parifli of Bourbonnais, in thegençrality- of Moulins.*p.Nevcrs,,* Souittes, a village of Bourbonnois, in the election of Gannat. *p. Gannat.* Siulac, a fmall town of Guicnne, in the diocefc and election of Bourreaux, *p. Bourdcaux.* Smlade, la, a place of Upper Langucdoc; in the diocefe and receipt of Touloufc. *p. Toulouse.* Soulagez, a village of Lover Languedoc, in the diocefe and receipt o£ Narbonne. *p. Narbonne.* Soulalncourt, a pariíh of Champagne, in the election of Joinville. *P. Joinville.* Sûulame, I, A town of Anjou, in the diocefe and election of Angers. *p. Angers.* 2. A town of Champagne, in the election of Bar-furAube. *p. Bar-fur-Aube.* Soulaire, a fmall town of Anjou, ia the diocefe and election of Angers, *p. Angers* boulange, a village of Champagne in the election of Vitry. *p. Vhry.* Soulangis, a place of Champagne,, in the election of Tonnerre, *p.Noy ers,* Soulangy. X. A village of Burgundy, in the bailiwick of Avalon» *p. Avalon.* 2- A pariíh of Nivernois, in the dioccfe of Nevers. *p. Nevers.* Soulans, a place of Gäfcony in the diocefe and election of Comminges. *p. Hfontrejeau.* Sculatg/s, a place of Rouergue, Irv the diocefe and election of Rhodez. *p. Rhodez.* Soulaurc-de-Biron, a place of Péri gord, in the diocefe and election of Sarlat. *p. Sarlat.* Soulçois, legres, aplace of Franches-Comté, in the bailiwick of Dole. *p. Dole.* Soule. i. A fmall country of Gafcxny, between Beam and Navarre, Maleon is thc capital. 2. A townof Normandy,, in the election of S. Lo. *p.S. La. Soule, la,* a river of Normandy,, which runs into the Sienne. *Soulengy,* a village of Normandy, in the election of Falaife. *p. Falaife, Soulenx,* a village of Gafcony, irt the election of Landes, *p. Dax. Soutes,* a village of Armagnac, in the election of Aftarac. *p. Mirande. Szdejme,* a town of Anjou, in the election of Flèche, *p. Sable. Soulbaneh)* a village of Upper Languedoc, in the diocefe and receipt of£ S. Pupoul *p. Caßelnaudary Souliac.* Sec *Souillac. Sovfieret,* a village of Champagne, in the dioeefe and election of Chalons, *p. Epernay. Soj Hers,* a town of Provence, in the viguery of Hieres.*foulen. Souligné-fcus-Balon,* âf *Soul i mnefous-Valoneyio-wrs* of Maine,in the dioeefe and election of Mans. *p. le Mans. Soulignennes,* a town of Saintonge, in the dioeefe andelection of Saintes. *p. Saintes. Soulitre",* a town of Maine, in the dioeefe and election of Mans. *p. Conner/.. Seulla & Celles,* a fmall town of Upper Languedoc, in the dioeefe and receipt of Mircpoix, *p. Mirepoix. Seullaire,* a village of Beauce, in the dioeefe and election of Châtres. *p. Chatres. Seullange,* a village of Anjou, in the elect km of Saumur. *p. Saumur. Stmllangh,* a village of Berry, in the dioeefe and election of Bourges. *p, Bcurves. Sou/fans,* a town of Poitou, in the election of Sablcs-d'Olonne. *p. Chalan. Souliers* a village of Gatinois,. in. the election of Melun./». *Brie. Soulommes,* a village of Beauce, in the election of Vendome.*p. Vendóme.. S'MhmmiS)* a village of Quercy, in the dioeefe and election of Cahors. *p_. Cahors.* Soulon, a village of Gafcony, in thereceipt of Bigorre. *p. Tarées. Soultxla-VIIIe,* a town of Alface, in the bailiwick of Rouftach./. *Rouffacb. Soultebacb,* a village of Alface, in rlie.bailiwick of Enfuhciro, *p. Rouf- fach. Soultssbacb-lc-BaS)* fis? *Soult%bacble-Haut,* villages of Alface, in the bailiwick of Thann, *p. Rouffacb, Scultzmaty* a fmall town of Alface, in the bailiwick of Routfath. *pf Rouffacb.* Soumanst a village of Bourbonnois, in the election of Evaux. *p. Cbambtn, Seumejmilf* a village of Norrcandy, in the election of Caudebcc./.Ca«fc£ff« *Ssumofon,* a place of Beam, in the receipt of Pau. *p. Pau. SoumontSy* a village of Normandy, in he election of FaiajXe. *p. Falaife. Soupa'v&Cy* a pariih of Bourbonnois, in the election of Moulins, *p. Moulins, Soupex,* a village of Upper Languedoc, in the dioeefe and receipt of 5. Papoul. *p. Caßlenauda/y. Soupir t* a village of Picardy, in the dioeefe and election of Laon. *p. Laon.* Soupliaurt*f* a village of Picardy, in the dioeefe and election of Amicus. *p. Aniens. Scup/es,* a village of Gfttinois, in the election of N Стонт, *p.* Nemours. *Souprofe,* or *Sotipr(JJet* a town *of* Gafconv, in the election of Landes. *p»* Tartas. *Sour,* a river of Alface, which runs into the Mott-rn. *Siurajdty* a village of Gafconv» in the dioeefe and election oí Bayonnc. *p. Bcyonne. Sou/ansy* a place of Franche-Comt e, in the bailiwick of Baume./1. *Baume,, Sourans-les-Corditr,* a place of FrancheComté,, in the bailiwick of Vefoul. *pj Vtjouh SturbetSy* a place of Armagnac, in the dioeefe and election of Auch. *Aucb.. Sourbourg,* a village of Alface, in the bailiwick of Haguenau. *p. Ihiguenan. Sourcelles,* a town of Anjou, on theLoire, in the dioeefe and election oí Angers, *p. Angers. Sourcbes,* a m. irquifate of. Maine, in the election of Mans. *p. Frejnay. Sowdtval.* I. A town oí Normandy, in the election of Mortain. *p. Mortain. z.* A illage of Normandy, in the dioeefe and election of Coûtances. *Coûtanca. Sourdofif* a village of Picardy, in the election of-Mondidícr. #. *Breteull. Swtst,* or *Soi eost.* See *Sorefe. Sour/arts,* a village of Maine, in theelection of Ctutteau-daLoir, *p.* Coä-, *nere'. Souribts.* See *Scribes Sournac &f Rocbefort,* a fmaîl town of Limofin, in the cleft i on of Tulles. *f. Tulles, Scurr.ia,* a village of Lower Languedoc, in the dioeefe and receipt of Akt. *p. Limoux. Scut mac,* a place of Auvergne, in the dioeefe and election of S. FJour. *p. S. Flour, Sours,* a town of Beauce, about a league from Chartres. *p. Chartres. Sourfac,* a town of Limofin, in the deft ion of Tulles.. *Tulles, Sourzat,* a town of Périgord, in the dioeefe and election of Périgueux. *f. Mußdan. Soujmassanner,* a place of Mcflïn, in the diocefe and receipt of Verdun, *p. Verdun. Soujmentrain,* a village of Champagne, in the election of S. Florentin, *p. S. Florentin. Soujmerlan,* a fmall river of Brie, which runs into the Marne, between "Hermans and Château-Thierry. *Soußnculins,* a town of Saintonge, in the diocefe and election of Saintes. /. *Mor.tcnd'C. Soujparfac,* a village of Marche, in the election of Gueret. *p. Gueret. Soufpierre,* a place of Dauphiny, in the election of Montelimart. *p. Mentd'imart. Soußac. 1.* A village of Guienne, hi the diocefe and erection of Bourreaux, *p. Bcurdcaux. 1.* A village of Bazadois, in the election of Condom, *p. Condom. 'S ujfenacy* a village of Upper Languedoc, in the diocefe and receipt of A!by. *p. At by. SaiJJènans,* a place of FrancheComté, in the bailiwick of Orgelet. *p. Lonr,-leSaunier. St ßey,* a village of Burgundy, in the bailiwick of Arnay-lc-Duc. *p, Scmur,* Soufnile, a village of Lower Languedoc in the diocefe and receipt of Alais, *p. Alais. Stußon,* a town of Gafcony, in the election or Landes, *p, Dax. Sau к raine, la. i.* A town of Li moíín. about a leagues from Limoges, *p. Arnac. 2.* A town of Marcne, in the election of Blanc, *p. к Shut. Souterr.on,* a town of Forez, in the election of Roanne.*p. Roanne. Soutiers y* a village of Poitou, in the election oí" Niort, *p. Partenay. Sowvans, я* village of FrancheComté, in the bailiwick of Dole, *p. Dole. Souvence-Moxt-Dcyen,* a barony of Perche, near Nogent. *f Nogcnt-lcRotrou. Sowvemy,* a village of Valromey, in the bailiwick of *Gcx.p. Gex. Scwvigne'. I.* A town of Anjou, in the election of Flèche, *p. le Lude.' z.* A town of Maine, in the diocefe and election of Man«, *p. Sable. 3.* A town of Tournine, in the diocefe and election of Tours, *p. Tours. Souvigny. t,* A town of Bourbopnoit, in the election of Moulins; 3 leagues from Moulins, in the raid to Limoges, and 4 from Bourbonl'Archambaud. *Bureau de piß e. z.* A town of Touraine, in the diocefe and election of Amboife. *p. Amboije. 3.* A town of Poitou, in the diocefe and cleétion of Richelieu, *p. Riebt lieu. 4.* A town of Oilcannois, in the diocefe and election of Orleans, *p. Lailly. Souvigny-le-Tbiont* a village of Bourbonnois, in the election of Moulins, *p. Moul'ms. Souviile.* I. A village of Dauphiny, in the diocefe and election of Grenoble, *p. Grenoble,* a. A village of Orltannois, ih the election of Pithiviers. *p. P.tb'vviers. Sovzay,* a town of Anjou, in the election of Saumur. *f. Saumur. ¿cuzy-la-Brkbe* v illage of Beauce, in the election of Dourdan. *p. Etrecy, Scuxy-F'Argentiere,* a villageof Lyonnois, in the diocefe and cleition of Lyons, *p. Lyon. Sox,* a village of Flanders, in the fubdelegation of Bcrgues. *p. Bergue:. Soyons,* a village of DaupMny, in the election of Montelimart. *p. Montelimart. SoyauXf* a village of Angcumoiîj in the diocefc and election of Anguléme. *p. AngQultntt. Soycaux,* a village of Gafcotiy» in the receipt of Bigorre. *p. Tarbes. Soye,* a village of Franche-Comté, in the bailiwick of Baume./». *Baume. Soyer,* a place of Brie, in the election of Sezanne, *p. Sezanne. Soyers,* a village of Champagne, in the diocefe and eleition of Langres. *p. B ourbonne. Soyons,* a fmall town of Vivarais, in the receipt of Viviers, *p. S.Perray. Soyria,* a place of Franche-Comté, in the bailiwick of Orgelet, *p. Lonsie-Saunier. Sozay.* I. A village of Nivernois, in the eleition of Clamecy. *p. Ciamtcy.* a. A pariih of Nivernois, in the diocefe and election of Nevers. *p. Nevers, Spa bbach,* a village of Alface, in the bailiwick of Wert. *p. Strafoourg, Sparron.* See *Efparron. Spay,'* a town of Maine, in the diocéíe and election of Mans. *p. ie Mans. Specbbach-le-Haut, & Specbbacble-Bas,* villages of Alface, in the bailiwick of Thann./. *Roiffacb. Spehet,* a village of Bretagne, in the diocefe and receipt of Quimper. *p. ¿luimper. Spenâamont,* a place of Artois, in the bailiwick of "Aire./. *Aire. Spendaval,* a place of Artois, in the bailiwick of Aire. . *Aire, S/oy.* i. A village of Champagne, in the eleition of Bar-fur-Aube. *p. Burfur-Aubc.* 2. A village of Burgundy, in the diocefe and bailiwick of Dijon. /. *ijjkrttlh. Spycker,* a village of Flanders, in the fubdelegation of Bergues./. *Bergues. Squifiex & Kmorocb,* a village of Bretagne, in the diocefe and receipt of Treguier. *p. Guingamp. Staß'elfelden,* a place oí Alface, in the bailiwick of Thann, *p. Roujfacb. Stains,* a fmall town of the lile of Prance, in the diocefc and election of Paris, *f. S. Denis. Stapel,* a fmall town of Flanders, in the fubdelegation of Caffel. *p.*

еда *Stattmart,* a place of Alface, in the diocefe of Stralburg. *p. Haeuenau Steenbeque,* a town of Flanders, in the fubdelegation of Caffel. *Caffel. Steen,* a village of Flanders, in the fubdelegation of Bergues. *p. Btrguts. Steersvarde,* or *Steinford,* a town of Flanders, in the fubdelegation of Caffel. *p. Caffel. Steige,* a village of Alface, in the bailiwick of Ville, *p. Stheleflat. Steimbacb,* a village of Alface, in the bailiwick, of Thann, *p. Scbeleßat. Steimburg,* a town of Alface, in the bailiwick of Saverne. *p. Saverne. Steirford.* See *Steenvcrde. Steinfultss,* a village of Alface, in the bailiwick of Ferrette./. *llwùngue. Stelle,* a priory in the diocefe of Fréjus.
Sienay, a town in the diocefe of Treves, on the banks of the Meufe, on the confines of Luxemburg; j leagues from Dun, n from Verdun, 2i from Ste. Manéhould,8 from Sedan, 16 from Metz, 13 from Mczieres, 20 from Rocroy, 26 from Chimay, 33 from Avefncs, 37 from Landrecy, 57 from Lille, 3 from Montmcdy, 23 from Thionvillc, 18 from Rcthcl, 27 from Rheims, and 64. from Paris. *Bureau de poße. Sternberg,* a place of Alface, in the bailiwick of Thann, *p. Rouffaeb. Stetten,* a village of Alface, in the bailiwick of Landfer. *p. Huningue. Steuil,* a village of Beauce, in the election of Mantes, *p. Mantes. Stigny,* a village of Champagne, in the eleition of Tonnerre, *p. Ancyle-Franc. Still,* a village of Alface, in the bailiwick of Multzig. *p. Mol/hém. Sti-val,* a village of Bretagne, in rf-.e diocefc and receipt of Vannes, *p. Cannes. Stomourt,* a village of Lorraine, in the diocefe and receipt of Metz. *p. Metz. Suèlaines,* a village of Tourainej ¡a the election of Amboife. *p. Arnbcife. Subies,* a place of Normandy, in the diocefe and election of Bayeux. *p. Bayeux Sub/igny.* I. A village of Berry, in the diocefe and election of Bourges, *p. Sancerre.* 2. A village of Champagne, in the diocefe and election of Sens. *p.*

Sens. Subrebojje, a village of Agénois, in the diocefe and election of Agen, *p. Tcnndms. Subtray-Mezkres,* a fmall town of Bury, in the election of Châteauroux, *p. Chateawoux. Suc ¿5 S:-u¡enac,* a village of Foix, in the generality of Rouíüilon. *Feix. Suce/,* a village of Bretagne, in the diocefe and receipt of Nantes, *p Nantes. Sucinio,* a chateau of Bretagne, *p Vannes, Sucos,* a place of Navarre, in the receipt uf S. Pahis./. *Pau. Sucy,* a village in the diocefe and election of Paris, *p. Mrle. Sud ray, le,* a town of Berry, about1: two leagues from Bourges, *p. Bourges.* a place of Provence, in the dicefe and.viguecry of Aix. *p. Aix-. Sliecb, le,* a place of Upper Languedoc, in the diocefe and receipt of Alby.. *p. Ally, Sutge,* a vilage of Roucrgue, in the election of Milhaud. *p. Mil- . baud.' Sut die,* a fmall town of Provence, in the diocefe and viguery of Digne. *p. Digne. Sueiíly,* a town of Touraine, in. the election of Chinon. *p. Chinon, Suefquun,* a village of Navarre, iiy, the diocefe of Bayonnc. *p. Pau. Suelte,* a place of Berry, where there is a mineral fpring... *Suey,* a place of Gatinois, in-the, election of Melon, *p. JMelun. Sugny,* a village of Champagne, in the election of Rethel. *Retbel. Suhaft,* a place of Navarre, in the receipt of S. Palais, *p-Pau. Suilly,* a village of Poitou, in the ejection of Richelieu, *p. R ebelten. Suilly-en-Duche,* a village of Burgundy, in the diocefe and bailiwick of Autun. *p. Autun. Suilly-en-Royauté,* a village of Burgundy, in the diocefe and bailiwick of Challón, *p. Challan. Sum,* a village of Burgundy, in the bailiwick of Charolles./". *Dijon. Suippey* a fmall river of Champagne, which falls into the Aifne, tween Neufchâtcl and Rouci. *Suippe-la-Longuej* a town of Champagne, about S leagues from Rheims. *p. Rheim. Suìze,* a river of Champagne, which lofes it.elf in the Marne, near Chaumont.. *Su'J/e-en-Dcmtrts, la,* a village of Dombesj infulated in BreiTe. *p. Bourg en-BrefJ'e. Sufay-le-Franc,* a vilbge of Champagne, in the election of Epernay. *p. Dormant. Sullie,* a village of Picardy, in the diocefe and election of Bcauvais. *p. Beawvah. Sullignaty.* a village of BreiTe, in the bailiwick of

Bclley. /. *Bcurg-enBreJ'e*. Suily. i. A village of Normandy, in the diocefe and'election of Baycux. *p Bayeux*. 2. See *Semlt'y*. *Su/ly-la-Capelle*, a village of Orléannois, in the diocefe and election of Orléans, *p. Orléans*. Sully-fur-Loire, a town of Gûtinois,. on the Loire, in the election of Gien, about 8 leagues from Orléans. *p. Gien*. Sully-Vcrgers, a town of Nivernoís, on the river Naon, in the election of Charité, *p. Corne*. Sul-ly s j a place of Normandy, in the election of Andcly. *p. Gaiílon*. Sulniac, a village of Bretagne, in trie diocefe and receipt of Vannes, *p. Vannes*. Suhz. I. A town of Alface, in the diocefe of Bale. *p. Wißlmlourg*. 2, A village of Alface, in the dio.efe of Straíburg. *p. 'Straßurg*. д. A village of Alface, in the bailiwick of Hachftein. *p. Mdjhàm*. Sult%bacb, a fountain of mineral waters, near Mun-fter. *Sultzerem*, a village of Alface, in the diocefe of Bale.. *Strafiourg*. Sumene, or *Sumcjne*, a town of Lower Languedoc, in the diocefe and receipt of Alais. *Bureau de poße*. Suntgaw, a very fertile country of Alface, comprehending the bailiwick of Ferette, Atnd-fer, Alkirch, Thann, and BerFort; bordered on the enft by the Rhine, and the Canton of Bale; on the fouth by Franche-Comté; ort the weft by Lorraine j and on the north by Upper Alface. Supt, a piace of Franche-Comté, in the bailiwick of Salins, *p. SnLns*. Sur-ba & *Bcnaty* л village of Foix, in the generality of Roufiillon. *p. Tarajcon-en-Púx*. *Sunatnpsf* a place of Picardy, in the election of Doulens. *p. Doulcni*. Sur-cieux-jur-S.-Bel,, a village of Lyonnois, in the diocefe and election" of Lyons, *p. Lyon.'* Surdon, a village of Normandy, inthe election of Alenron. *p. JVeuil/y*. Surdoux, a village of Limofin, in the diocefe and election of Limoges. *p. Limoges*. Sure, a town of Perche, in the election of Mortagnc. *p. Belhjme*. Sure-da, a village of Rouilillon, in the diocefe and viguery of Perpignan, *p. Perpignan*. Surejne, a town of the lile of France, in the diocefe and election of Paris, p, *Neuilly*. Sunvi/le, *t* village of Normandy, in the election of Valogncs. *p. Coutances*. Surey, a village of Normandy, in the election of Andcly. *p. Quillón*. Sur-font, a pariÛi of Baliigny, in the election of Chaumont. *p, Cbaumont*. Surgen, a village of Guienne, in the diocefe and election of Bourdtaux. *p. Bourdtaux*. Surgeresj a town of Aunis, about 6 leagues from Rochelle, *p. Rochefort*. Surgues, a village of Picardy, in the government of Ardres. *p. Ardres*. Sur-gy,â town of Nivernois, in the election of Clamecy. /. *Clamecy*. Surbaute, a place of Navarre, in the receipt of S. Palais, *p. Pau*. Suriette, a village of Champagne, in the dioccfe and election of Châlons. *p. Chalons*. Su/bu, a village of Dauphiny, in the diocefe and election of Vienne. *p. Bourgoin*. Surin, i. A village of Poitou, in the election of Niort, *p. Cbaunay*. 2. A village of Poitou, in the diocefe and election of Poitiers, *p. Partenay*. 3. A figniory of Berry. *p. Bourges*. Suris-le-Bм. See *Sury-le-Bois*. Surmonty a village of FrancheComté, in the bailiwick, of Baume. *p. Baume*. Suro'toy a village of Normandy, in the diocefe and election of Bayeux. *p. Bayeux*. SurtainviUe, a village of Normandy, in the election of Valognes. *p. Valogncz*. SurtawuiUe, a village of Normandy, in the election of Pont-deГ Arche, *p. Louviers*. Survie, a village of Normandy, in the election of Argentan, *p. Argentan*. Surville. i. A village of Normandy, in the election of Pont-dcPArche. *p. Pont-de-Vyîrxbe*. 2. A village of Normandy, in the election of Pont-1'Evèque. *p. Louviers*. Surv'Uliers, a village of Picardy, in the diocefe and election of Scnlis. /. *Sinlts*, Sury, a village of Champagne, in the election of Rethel. *p. Retbel*. Sury Vaux, a town of Berry, in the diocefe and election oí Bourges. *p. Bourges*. Sury-aux-Bols, a village cf Orléannois, in the diocefe and election of Orléans, *p. Drléans*. £ury-ès-Bois, a town of Berrv, in the dircefe and eleftion of Bourges. *p. Cofne*. Sury-le-Bcts, a fmall town of Forez, in the eleäion of Montbrifon. *p. Afontbrtjon*. Sury-le-Comtal, a town of Forez, in the eleäion of Montbrifon. *p. Montbñfm*. Sury-fitr-Zthr, a parifh of Berry, in the diocefe and eleftion of Bourges, *p. Newuy*. Surzur, a village of Bretagne, in the diocefe and receipt of Vannes. *p. Vannes*. Sus, a village of Beam, in the fénéchaufsée of Sauve-erre. *p. Oleran*. Sus-S.-Leger, a village of Artois, in the bailiwick of S. Pol. *p. Deviens*. Sufe, la, a town of Anjou, in the election of Flèche, *p. le Mans*. Sujm-ton, a place of Beam, in the fénéchaufsée of Sauveterre. *p. Pau*. Sußac, a town of Limofin, in the diocefe and eleftion of Limoges, *p. Limoges.'* Suffat, a fijniory of Bourbonnois, in the eleftion of Gannat. *p. S. Pouream*. Sußy, a place of Burgundy, in the bailiwick of Arnay-le-Dac. *p. Sauüuu*. SuJJteu, a village of Dauphiny, in the diocefe and election cf Vienne. *p. Vienne*. SufvU/e, a village of Dauphiny, in the eleftion of Grenoble, *p. Grenoble*. Suturieu, a village of Valromey, in the generality of Dijon, *f. Belley*. Suye, la, a considerable territory of Poitou, in the eleftion of Châtcllerault. Suxan, a place of Gafcony, in th« eleftion of Landes, *p. S. Sever,*. Suzange, a place of Meffin, in the diocefe and receipt of Metz. *p. Metz*. Suzanne, a village of Champagne, in the eleftion of Rethel. *p. Rubel*. Suzannecour, a village of Champagne, in the eleftion of Joinville, *p. Cbaumont*. Suxay, a village of Normandy, in the election of Andely. *p. Eccuy*. Suze,a place of Burgundy, in the bailiwick, of Arnay-le-Duc. *p. Dijon*. Suxe-en-Diois, a village of Dauphiny, the election of Montelimart. *p. Die*. Suooe-la-RouJfe, a fmall town of Normandy, in the élection of Montelimart. /. *Pierrclate*. Su-zeanne, a village of Picardy, in the election of Péronne. *p. Périme*. Suxemont, a parih of Champagne, in the election of Joinville. *p. S. Difier*. Suzon. I. A river of Burgundy, which joins the Ouche, near Dijon, a. A place in the ifland of Bellelfle. *p. Nauta*. Suzoti, le, a fmall river of Gafcony, which runs into the gave of Oleron. Suzoy, a village ot Picardy, in the diocefe and election of Noyon. *p. Noyon*. Stay &f Subacourt, a village of Picardy, in the diocefe and election of Laon. *p. Laon*. Sy, a village of Champagne, in the diocefe of Rheims, *p. Sedan*. Syan, a place of Franche-Comté, in the bailiwick, of Poligny. *p. Salins*. Sydeville, a village of Normandy, in the election of Valognes. *p. Valognes*. Symeiroh,'A village of

Périgord, in the diocefe and election of Sarlat. *p. Sarlat.*
T A *CT'AB AILLE,* a place of Beam, in the receipt of Sauveterre. *p. Pau.* Tabanac, a village of Guiennc, in the diocefe and election of Boui'dcaujc. *p. Bourdeaux.* Tate, the name of a mountain in Foix.
Tablier, le, a fmall town of Poitou, In the election of Sablcs-d'Olunne. *p. Luçon.*
Tabrc-EJclaignac, a village of Up per Languedoc, in the diocefe and receipt of Mirepoix. /. *Tarajcon-enFoix.* Tachoire, a village of Armagnac, in the election of Riviere-Verdun. *p. Grenade.* Tacoigné, a village of Beaucc, in the election of Muntfort. *p. Montfort.* Tadain, a village of Bretagne, in the diocefe and receipt of S. Malo. *p. S. Malo.* Tadcujfe & Oujjau, a village of Beam, in the receipt of Morias, *p. Pau.* Taginat-d'Agegonie, a place of Auvergne, in the fénéchauf- sée of Riom. *p. Riom.* Tagij/et, a village of Brcffe, in the bailiwick of Bourg, *p, Loukans.* Tagnés, a fmall town of Périgord» in the diocefe and election of Sarlat. *p. Sarlat.* Tagnon, a village of Champagne, in the election of Rethel. *p. Retbel.* Tagoltzbeim, & Tagßorff, village» of Alface, in the bailiwick of Alt» kirch. *p. AltHrcb.* Tahur, a village of Champagne, in the election of Ste. Manéhould. *pi Ste. Manébould.* Tajac, a village of Rouergue, in the diocefe and election of Rhodez. *p. Rbodex.* Tajan, a village of Ncbouzan, in the diocefe of Auch. *p. Caßelnau-deMagnac.* Taicbousàn, a village of Armagnac» in the diocefe and election of Auch. *p. Auch.* Taignevaux, a place of FrancheComte, in the bailiwick of Dole. *p. Dole.* Taillac. I. A village of Armagnac, in the election of Lomagne. *p. Beaumont-de-Lomagne.* z. See *Taillan.* Taillades, les, avillageof VenaiíTin» in the judicature of Lille, *p. Avignon.* Taillan, or *Taillac,* a village of Guiennc, in the diocefe and election of Bourdeaux. *p. Bourdeaux.* Ta'dlancmrtf a village of Clьіtт pagncj in the bailiwick of Chaumont. *p. Paid.* Taillande, a village of Auvergne, in the dioccfe and election uf Clermont, *p. Clermont.* Taillant, a village of Saintonge, in the election of S. Jcan-d'Angcly. *p. S. Savimat,* TaiHard, a cape on the coaft of Provence, in the gulf of Genoa. *TaUiatf* a village of Auvergne, in the election of Brioude. *p. Brkudt* Taille, la, a village of Anjoiij in the election of Saumur. *p. Ancenis.* Taille-de-Bourbon, a wood of iz2 arpents, in the jurifdiction of Moulins. *Tai/leavat,* a fmall town of Baza áois, in the election of Condom. *P. h RhUe.* Tailleboh, a village of Normandy, in the election of Falaife. *p. CondeJur- Noireau.* Taillebourg. I. A town of Saintonge, fituated on the Charente, in the dioccfe of Saintes, and election of S. Jean-d'Angely; about 3 leagues from Saintes, 6 from S. Jean-d'Angely, and 7 from Cognac. *Bureau depoße.* 2. A village of Condomoïs, in the dioccfe and election of Condom, *p. Condom.* 3. A village of Armagnac, îa the election of Rivière-Verdun, *p. Grenade.* Taillebourg'S.-Pcrdou de, a village of Agénois, in the dioccfe and election of Agen. *p. Marmande.* Tailkfcntaxne, a village of Plcardy, in the election of Crêpy, *p. VMlenCotcñts.* Taillemouûer, a village of Normandy, in the election of Chaum-jnt and Magny. *p. Magr.y.* Taillepied, a village of Normandy, in the election of Valognes. *p. Vqlogres.* Tailleville, a village of Normandy, in the election of Caen. *p. Caen.* Taillis, a village of Bretagnr, in the dioccfe and receipt oí Rennes, *p. Rennes.* Tailh, i. A village of Norman dy, in the election of NeufchAtcK / Aumalt. 2, A village of Burgundy, in the bailiwick of Beaune. *pBeau/.e.* TallJy-le-Hameau, a village of Champagne, in the election of Ste. Manéhould. *p. Stenay.* . Tain, a town of Dauphiny, fituated on the Rhône, oppolîte to Tournon, in the diocefe and election of Valence, between Valence and Vienne; 5 leagues from Valence, 6 from S. Rambert, 15 from Vienne 22 from Lyons, and H7a from Paris. *Bureau de peße.* Tainnay-le-Mouhir, a village of Champagne, in the dioccfe and election (if Rheims, *p. Rctkcl.* Tamnemarcy a village of Normandy, in the election of Montivilliers. *p. Fecamp.* Ta'-nsj a town of Saintonge, in the diocefe and election of Saintes. *p. Cozez.* Tahville, la, a village of Normandy, in the election of Gifors. *p. Gi¡ors.* Tairae, or *S. Girmabt-deTairact* avilhge of Agénois, in the diocefe and election of Agen. *p. las Peyras.* Taife, a place of Burgundy, in the diocefe and receipt of Màcon. *p. Macon Y&ißt* a priory irr Poittou,, in the election cfThouars. *TaiJJèy,* a village of Burgundy in the diocefe and bailiwick of Chaiıon, *p. Challón.* Taiftñeres. See *Tefnieres.* Taijml, a village of Picardy, in the diocefe and election of Amiens. *p. Amiens.* To'ßr, or *S. ATartin-de-TaiffaCy* a village of Upper Languedoc, in the dioccfe and receipt of Alet. *p. Gaillac.* TaIllly-le-Vieux, a fmall town of Champagne, in the diocefe and election of Rheims, *p. Retbel.* Taiffy Ê? Glimmt a village of Picardy, in the diocefe and election of Amiens, *p. Amiens.* Taix. i. A village of Nivcrnois ¡n rhe diocefe and deítion of Ncvcrs. /. *Deciase,* 2. A place" of Upper.Languedoc, in the diocefe and receipt of Alby. *p. Alby.* Tatze'-Aizee, a village of Angoumois, in the diocefe and election of Angoulêmc. *p. Angoultmc.* Taizy, a village of Champagne, in the diocefe and election of Rheims, *p. Retid.* Tulaijan, a village of Bazadois, in the election of Condom, *p. Condom.* Tal. my, a village of Limofin, in the election of Tuiles. /. *Tulles.* Talante, a fmall town of Guienne, in the diocefe and election of Bourreaux, *p. Bourdeaux.* Talancieu, a village of Vivarais, in the receipt of Viviers, *p. Viviers.* Talafts, a place of Franche-Comté, in the bailiwick of Vefoul. *p. Vtjoul,* Talanjac, ı village of Bretagne, in the diocefe and receipt of S. Malo. *p. S. Malo.* galantj a town of Burgundy, about half a league from Dijon, *p. Dijon.* Talafac, a place of Gafcony, in the receipt of Bigorre. *p. Tarbes.* Talaurejfe, a village of Gafcony, in the election of Landes, *p. S. Sever,* Talayran, a village of Lower Languedoc, in the diocefe and receipt of Narbbnne. *p. Narbonne,* Talcy, a village of Bit fois, in the diocefe and election of Blois. *p. Bcaugency,* Talehsat-le-Bas, a fmall town of Auvergne, in the diocefe and election of S. Flour, *p. Aurillac.* Talijficu, a village of Bugcy, in the diocefe and bailiwick oí Bellcy. *p. Btlley.* Talland. I. A village of Burgundyf in the diocefe and bailiwick of Challón, *p. Cballon,* 2. A village

of Burgundy, in the diocefe and bailiwick of Dijon, *p. Dijon.* *Tattangc,* a village of MeШ'п, in thediocefe and receipt of Metz, *p. Metis.* *Tallard,* a town of Dauphiny, in the diocefe and election of Gap. *p. Gap.* *Tallecy,* a village of Burgundy, in the bailiwick of Arnay-lc-Duc. *p. Dijon.* *Tallenay,* a village of FrancheComté, in the diocefe and bailiwick of Befanron. *p. Bфnon.* *Tal/er,* a village of Gafcony, in the election of Landes, *p. Dax.* *Tollet,* a village of Roufhllon, in the dicjeefe and viguery of Perpignan. *p. Perpignan, Tallevende,* a village of Normandy, in the election of Vire. *p. Vire.* *Talláis,* a village of Guienne, in the diocefe and election of Bour deaux. *p. Bourdeaux.* *Tallu, le,* a village of Poitou, in the election of Fontenay. *p. Poujfange.* *Talmas,* a town of Picardy, in the election of Doulcns, *p. Doulens.* *Talmay,* a town of Burgundy, in the diocefe and receipt of Dijon, *p, Auxonne.* *Talmont,* or *Tellement,* a town of Saintonge, with a fmall port; about 8 leagues from Saintes, *p. Marenner.* *Talmont,* a town of Poitou, about g leagues from Sables-d'Olonne. *p. les Sables.* *Talmonticr,* a village of Normandy, in the election of Chaumont and Magny. *p. Magry.* *Talcire,* a village of Provence, in the viguery of CafleUane. *p. Caßellane.* *Talonnay,* a village of Normandy, in the election oí Alençon. *p. le Meller out.* *Talur, le,* a village of Poitou, in the election of Niort, *p. Niort.* *Taluycrs,* a town of Fores, in the election of S. Etienne, *f. & Etienne.* *Tambach* cS? *Ne'whoffen,* a village of Alface, in thediocefe of Straibusg. *p. Strasbourg, Tamгney,* a village of Nivernais, in the diocefe and election of Never. *p. Nevers.* *Tamervdle,* a fmall town of Normandy, in the election of Valognes. *p. Valognes.* *Tañaron,* a village of Provence, in the diocefe and viguery of Digne, *p. Digne.* *Tanavelle,* a village of Auvergne, in the diocefe and election of S. Flour, *p. S. Flour.* *Tanay,* or *Tafnay,* a village of Burgundy, in the diocefe and bailiwick of Dijon. *p. Dijon.* *Tancar-ville,* a town of Normandy, fituatcd „n the Seine, between Caudebec and Haine, *p. Lillebonne.* *Tame,* a town of Lower Languedoc, in the diocefe and receipt of Puy. *p. le Pay.*

Tanein, a village of Dauphiny» in the diocefe and election of Grenoble, *p. GrenMt. Tancoign/,* a town of Anjou, in the election of Montreuil-Bellay. *p. Sашюnг.* *Tonern,* a village of Burgundy, in the diocefe and bailiwick of Macon, *p. Roanne.* *Tancrou,* a village of Brie, in the diocefe and election of Meaux. . *Щ. Tandu,* a village of Berry, in the election of Chateauroux. *p. Chateauroux.* *Taney,* a village of Dombes, in the chatellany of Trévoux, *p. Vdlefrancbe.* *Tangry,* a village of Artois, in the bailiwick of S. Hoi. *p. Betbune.* *Tames,* a village of Normandy, in the diocefe and election of AvrSuches. *p. Pontorfon.* *Tanlay.* I. A town of Burgundy, on the Armancon, in the bailiwick of Noyers, *p. Tonnerre,* 2. See *Hemery.* *Tannay.* I. A town of Nivernois, in the election of Clamecy. *p. C/amccy.* 2. A village of Nivernois, in the election of Ncvers. *p. Nevers.* *Tanné,* or *S. Aubin-ie-Tanné,* a village of Normandy, in the election of Bernay. *p. Bernay.* *Tannerre,* a village of Champagne, in the election of Joigny. *p. Jigny, Tannes.* See *Thann.* *Tanme're,* a village of Picardy, the diocefe and election of Soinons. *p. SñJJons.* *Tanme're, la,* a village of Burgundy, in the bailiwick of Montcenis. *p. Au un.* *Tanoucs,* a village of Normandy, in the election of Argentan, *p. Argentan.* *Tanfac,* a town of Saintonge, in the diocefe and election of Saintes. *p. Pons.* *Tanfcment,* a village of Normandy, in the election of Bernay. *p. Bernay, Tали, le,* a fmall town of Normandy, in the diocefe and election of Coûtances. *p. Coûtâmes.* *Tenus,* a village of Upper Languedoc, in the diocefe and receipt of Alby.. *Alby.* *Tanyot.* See *Tafniot. Taponas,* a village of Beaujolois, in the election of Villefranche. *p. Belleville.* *Taponnat,* a village of Angourois, in the diocefe and election of Angouléme. *p. la Rocbefoucault.* *Tarabel,* a village of Upper Languedoc, in the diocefe and receipt of Touloufe. *p. Touloufe.* *Taradel.* I. A village of Agénois, in the diocefe and election of Agen. *p. Vdleneuve-d'Agen.* 2. A village of Provence, in the viguery of Draguignan. *p. Dragulgnan. Tarando!,* a village of Dauphiny, in the diocefe of Sifteron. *p. Sfteron.* *Tarare.* I. A town

of Lyonnois, fituatcd at the foot of a mountain of the fame name, in the road from Lyons to Moulins; io leagues from Lyons, io from Roanne, 16 from Paucardiere, 34 from Moulins, and from Paris *Bureau de poße.* 2. A mountain of Lyonnois, between Tarare and S. Saphorin-de-Laye, *Tarafcon.* I. An ancient city of Provence, fituated by the Rhône, oppofite to Beaucaire; 20 leagues from Aix, 6 from Nîmes, 17$ from Montpellier, 6 from Remoulins, 28 from Marfeilles, 37 from Toulon, 61 fromAntibes, 69 from Nice, 65 from Lyons, and I8i from Paris. *Bureau de pcfie* 2. A town of Foix, in the diocefc of Pamiers, and generality of Rouflillon, about 4 leagues from Foix, 8 from Pamiers, and 7 from Mirepoix. *Bureau de pifie.* *Tarbes,* a city of Gafcony, fituated on the fide of the Adour, in the generality of Auch; it is the capital of Bigorre, the fee of a bifhop, the feat of a fencchal, &c. 15 leagues from Auch, 31 from Touloufe, 35 from Montauban, 68 from Bourdeaux, lOOy from Limoges, 50 from Cahors, and 193 from Paris. *Bureau de pofie.* *Tarcenay,* a village of FrancheComté, in the diocefe and bailiwick of Befançon. *p. Befançon.* *Tard-l'Abbaye,* a place of Burgundy, in the diocefe and bailiwick of Dijon, *p. Dijon.* *Tard-le-Bas,* & *Tard-le-Haut,* villages of Burgundy, in the diocefe and bailiwick of Dtjon. *p. Dijon.* *Tarde,* à village of Auvergne, in the eleftion of Combrailles. *p. Chambón.* *Tardenois,* a fmall country of Picardy, which makes part of Soif.fonois. *Tardes,* a village of Normandy, in the «leftion of Verneuil. *p. Ytr. neuil.* *Tardiere,* a fmall town of Poitou, in the eleftion of Fontenay. *p. Fontenay.* *Tardinghen,* a village of Picardy, in the generality of Amiens, *p. Boulogne.* *Tardoire,* or *Lardouere,* a river of Angoumois. *Tarentaigne,* 3 village of Normandy, in the eleftion of Vire. *p. Y,ге.* *Tergafont Êf Pelmaml,* places of Roufliilon, in the viguery of Ccrdagne. *p. Mont-Louis.* *Targe',* a village of Poitou, in the eleftion of Châtellerault. *p. Cbitellerault.* *Target,* a village of Bourbonnois, in the eleftion of Gannat. *p. Pourcoin.* *Targon,* a fmall town of Guienne, in the diocefe and eleftion of

Bourdeaux. *p. Libourne. Tarn,* a town of Limofin, in the diocefe and eleftion of Limoges, *p. Limoges. Tarn, le,* a confiderable river of Languedoc, which rifes in the mountain Lofere, and after receiving the Agout f/ils into the Garonne, near Moiflac.

Tamac, a village of Limofin, in the eleftion of Tulles, *p. Tulles. Tarnés,* a village of Guienne, in the diocefe and eleftion of Bourdeaux. *p. Bourdeaux. Tarnos,* a fmall town of Gafcony, in the eleftion of Landes, *p. Bayonne. Taron,* a village of Béarn, in the receipt of Morias, *p. Pau. Taronnc,* the name of a fmall river in Sologne. *Tarraube,* a town of Armagnac, in the eleftion of Lomagnc. *p. Lectoure. Tarre,* a village of Touraine, ia the diocefc and eleftion of Tours. *p. Tours. Tarjacq,* a village of Beam, in the receipt of Orther., *p. Orthtz. Tarjul,* a village of Burgundy, in the diocefe and bailiwick of Dijon, *p. Dijon. Tart.* Sec *Tard. Tártaras Sf la Combe,* a fmall town of Fore», in the eleftion of S, Etienne, *p. S. Etiatne. Tartaris, les,* a village of Marche, in the eleftion of Gueret. *p. Cueret. Tartarone,* a village of Lower Languedoc, in the diocefe and receipt of Mende. *p. Mende.* -*Tartes,* a town of Cafcony, fc tuated on a bill, near the Midon, in the diocefe of Dax, and eleilion of Landes; about 7 leagues from Dax. Ii from Bazas, 8 from Mont-deMarfnn, and 20 from Bayonne. *Bureau de/ße. Tartas,* or *S. Paul-de-Tart as,* a village of Lower Languedoc, in the diocefe and receipt of Viviers, *p. Vivien. Tartceourt,* a village of Franchea Comté, in the bailiwick, of Vefoul. *p. Vefoul. Tarticr,* a village of Picardy, in the diocefe and election of Soiffons. *p. Soiffons. Tarùgny,* a village of Picardy, in the election of Mondidier. *p. Verneutl. Tartonnt,* a village of Provence, in-the diocefe of Senez. *p. Caflellane. Tarfre, le. t.* A village of Burgundy, in the bailiwick, of Challón. *f. Loubans.* 2. A place of Beauce, in the election of Dreux, *p. Dreux. Tarty,* a village of Champagne, in the diocefe and election of Rheims. *p. Rocroy. Tafnay. X.* A p̈iriih of Nivernois, in the diocefe and election of Nevers. *p. Nevers.* л. See *Tanay. Tajn'wt,* a village of Burgundy, in the diocefe and bailiwick, of Dijon. *p. Dijon. Tafque,* a village of Armagnac, in the diocefe and election of Auch. *M'trande, Tajfe,* a town of Anjou, in the election of Fièche. *p. Malicorne. TaJJene & TaJJêniere,* villages of Franche-Comté, in the bailiwick of Dole, *p. Dole. Tajfille,* a town of Maine,, in the diocefe and election of Mans. *p. le Mans. Taßlly,* a village of Normandy, in the election of Falaife. *p. Faleife. TaJJtns,* a place of Lyonnois, in the diocefe and election of Lyons. *p. Iyon. Taßre, le,* a village of Angoumois, in the diocefe and election of Angoulcme, *p. Angoulcme. Tatlbou.* Sec *Jfle-de-Tatibou. Tadngbtm,* a village of Artois, In. the diocefe and bailiwick of S. Omer. *p. S. Omer. Tavant,* a village of Touraine, in the election of Chinon. *p. tßeBoucbard. Tavaux,* a village of FrancheComté, in the bailiwick of Dole. *p. Dole. Tavay-t'Aire,* a village of Franche-Comté, in the bailiwick of Baume, *p. Baume. Tave,* a fmall river of Lower Languedoc, which runs into the Cezc. *Tavtau Pont-Fei icourt,* a fmall town of Picardy, in the diocefe and election of Laon. *p. Laon. Tavels,* a village of Lower Languedoc, in the diocefe and receipt of Uzés. *p. Bagnols. Tavernay,* a village of Burgundy, in the diocefe and bailiwick of Au-, tun. *p. Autun. Taverne.au,* a village of Dombcs, in the chatellany of Montmcrle. *p. Belleville. Tavernes,* a village of Provens, in the vigucry of Barjols. *p. Barjols. Tavemy,* a town of the Iíle of France, in the diocefe and election of Parisf *p. Franconvillc. Tavers,* a fmall town of Orléannois, in the elcctipn of Beaugency. *p. Beaugency. Tavls,* a village of Bazadois, in the election of Condom, *p. Condom, Taugott-la-Ronde,* a town of A11nis, in the diocefe and election of Rochelle, *p. la Rochelle. Taulane,* a village of Provence, in the vigucry of Caitcllane. *p. Digne. Taulboc,* a place of Lower Languedoc, in the diocefe and receipt of Puy. *p. le Puy. Taule,* a village of Bretagne,4n the diocefe and receipt of S. Paul-dcLéon. *p. Morlaix. Taulignan,* a town of Dauphiny, in the election of Montelimart. *p. Montelimart. Tauiis Crouartgesy* places of Rouffillon, in the diocefe and viguery of Perpignan, *p. Perpignan. Taulle, lat* a village of Picardy, in the election of Mondidicr. *p. Tdondidier, Taumczy,* a fmall town of Gâtinois, in the election of Meiun. *p. Melim. Taumiers,* a town ef Bourbonnois, about 3 leagues from S. Amand. *p. S. Amand. Taupont,* a village of Bretagne, in the diocefe and receipt of S. Malo. *p. PhermeL Taw,* or *S. Martin-dc-Taurt* a village of Upper Languedoc, in the diocefe and receipt of Alby. /. *PJße-d'Alby. Taurt ¡a,* a village of Upper Languedoc, in the diocefe and receipt of Alby. *p. Alky, Taureau,* an ifland/fituated at the mouth of the river Moríais, off the coalt of Bretagne. *Tauriae. I. A* (mail town of Guicnne, in the diocefe 2nd election of Bourdcaux. *p. Blayt:* 2. A village of Lower Languedoc, in the diocefe and receipt of Montauban. *p. fifontauban.* 3. A village of Roucrgue, in the election uf Villefranche. *p. Rhede. Taurignan,* a village of Gafeony, jn the diocefe and election of Comminges. *p. Tatkufe. Taurigné,* a village of Toitraine, in the diix:efe and election of Tours. *Tours. Taurine,* a village of Roucrguc, jn the diocefe and election of Rhodes, *p. Rbodez. Taurinya,* a village of Rouflillon, Kl the viguery of Confians. *p. FH'éfranche-dt-Conßans. Tauris,* a village of Upper Languedoc, in the diocefe and receipt of CarcafTonnc. *p. Carcaßhnne. Tauron. I.* A finall town of Marche, in the election of Gucret. *p. jituM.* 2. A village of Marche, in the election of Bourganeuf. *Hour gancuf. Taujfac,* a village of Lower Languedoc,-in the diocefe and receipt of Béziers. *p. Béwers. Taufjac & Bourgety* a village of Vivarais, in the receipt of Viviers *p. Vrvxcrx. Tautavel,* a village of RpufliHon, in the diocefe and viguery of Perpignan, *p. Perpignan. Taure,* a fmall river of Normandy, which falls into the Vay, near Carentan. *Tawvfy* a town of Auvergne, in the diocefe and election of Clermont. *p. C/ermont. Tawvenay,* a village of Nivcrnois, in the election of Charité-fur-Loire. *p. Sam erre, Taux,* a village of Picardy, in the diocefe and election of Solfions *p» Soi/fcns. TûMxitrty* a village of Champagne, in the election of

Epernay.. *Epernay. Taxât,* a village of Bourbonnoîs, in the election of Gannat *p. S, Pair fain, Tayac.* I. A fmall town of Périgord, in the diocefe and election of Sarlat. *p. Sirlat. 2.* A village of Guicnne, in the diocefe and ciedtion of Bourdcaux. *p. L'iboume. Tayhojey* a village of Armagnac, in the diocefe and election of Auch. *p. Lcfioure. TasaUji* a village of Nivcrnois, in the election of Nevers. *p. Nevers, Ttaux-dts-Nobles,* a village of Armagnac, in the election of Aftarac. *p. Mirande. TechjA* river of Rouflillon, which rifes in the Pyrenees, and empties itfelf into the gulph of Lyons, a little below Eine *TtevUf* a village of Upper Languedoc, in the diocefe and receipt of Alby. *p. Alby.* Tigbem, a village of Flanders, in the fubdclegation of Bergucs. *p. Bergues. Tegra,* a village of Quercy in the eleftion of Figeac. *p. Figeai. Teigny,* a village of Nivernois, in the eleftion of Vezelay. *p. Ve%eUn. teil, le.* I. A town of Bourbonnoisi on the Allier; about 6 leagues from Moulins, *p. Pcurçain.* 2. A town of Bourbonnois, in the eleftion of Moulins, *p. Moulins.* 3. A village' of Perche, in the eleftion of Mortagne. *p. Verneuil-au-Perche.* 4. village of Bretagne, in the diocefe and receipt oí Rennes, *p. Rennes. Teil-Nolent, le,* a village of Normandy, in the eleftion of Bernay. *p. Bernay. Tcit-Rabicr, le,* a' village of Angoumois, in the diocefe and eleftion of Angoulême. *p. Angoulême. Teille',* i. A town of Maine, in the diocefe and eleftion of Mans. *p. Frejnay.* 2. A village of Bretagne, in the diocefe and receipt of Nantes. *p. Ancenis. Teiltet,* i. A village of Bourbonnois, in the eleftion of Gannat. *p. Cbambon.* 2. A village of Upper Languedoc, in the dioc. feand receipt of Miiepoix. *p. Alby.* 3. A village of Bourbonnois, in the eleftion of Muntlucon. *p. Chambón.* Teilleul, *le,* a town of Normandy, in the eleftion of Mortain. *p. Martain.* Teißiercs, a village of Rouergue, in the diocefe and eleftion of Rhodez. *p. Rhodes.* Teißem-de-Cortiel *& Tcißcres-lesBoulies,* villages of Auvergne, in the eleftion of Aurillac. *p. Aurillac.* Teißeu, a village of Quercy, iç the eleftion of Figeac. *p. Figeac.'* Teißbäe, a fmall town of Upper Languedoc, in the diocefe and receipt of Lavaur. *p. Lavaur. ui Ttix&Madaillac,* a village of Auvergne, in the diocefe and eleftion of Clermont, *p. Clement. Tel,* a village of Beaujolois, in the eleftion of Villefranche. *p. Villefranche. Telgruc,* a village of Bretagne, in the diocefe and receipt of Quimper. *p. Quimper. Telbeide,* a village of Auvergne, in the eleftion of Riom. *p. Riom. T'ligne',* a fmall town of Maine, in the diocefe and eleftion of Mans. *p. la Ferte'-Bernard.* Tellecey, a place of Burgundy, in the diocefe and bailiwick of Dijon. *p. Dijon.* Teilen, a village of Dauphiny, in the diocefe of Die. *p. Die. Tellieres,* a village of Normandy, in the eleftion of Alençon. *p. Alencon. Tel/oя, /e, я* village of Bourbonnois, in the eleftion of S. Amand. *p. S. Amand. Tclhr. e & Noyers,* a village of Champagne, in the eleftion of Sedan. *p. Sedan.* Templas, a village of Auvergne, in the eleftion of Combraillcs *p. Cbambon. Temple, le.* X. A village of Poitou, in the eleftion of Mauleon. *p. Maûleen.* 2. A village of Guienne, in the diocefe and eleftion of Bourdcairx. *p. Bordeaux.* 3. A village of Picardy, in the eleftion of Doulcns. *p. Montreuil. Temple-d'Ayen, le,* a village of Limofin, in the eleftion of Brives. *p. Briues. Tcmple-le-Carentoir,* a village of Bretagne, in the diocefe and receipt of Vannes, *p. Ploermel. Templc-de-la-Champinel, le,* a village of Maine, in the eleftion of Châtcaudu-Loire. *p. Mondoubleau.* Temple-dela-Maâelàne, *le, & Temple-Maupertuis, le,* villages of Bretagne, in the diocefe and recejpt of Nantes, *p. Nantes.* Temple-la-Cuyon, *le,* a village of Périgord, in the diocefe and eleftion of Périgueux. *p. P/rigueux.* Templemars-*Cbáttcllenie,* 6f *Teittplemars-Empire,* places of Flanders, in the fubdelegation of Lille, *p. LiHr.* Templeuve-en -*Doffence & Templeuve -en -Peuele* fmall towns of Flanders, in the fubdelegation of LiUc. *p. Lille. 1tmpIeux-le-Foße,* and Templeuxk-*Guirard,* villages of Picardy, in the cleftion of Péronne. *p. Pe'ronne.* Tcnac & *les Arenes,* a town of Saintonge, in the diocefe and cleftion of Saintes. *p. Saintes.* Tenaille, an abby of Saintonge. *p. Barbefieux.* Tenance-îes-Moulins, a village of Champagne, in theeleftion of Joinville. *p. Joinville.* Tenarre', a village of Burgundy, in the diocefe and bailiwick of Challón, *p. Chailon. Tenay,* a village of Bugey, in the diocefe and bailiwick of Belley. *p. S. Rambert.* Tencua, a village of FrancheComté, in the diocefe and bailiwick of S. Claude, *p. S. Claude.. Tendos,* a village of Normandy, in the diocefe and election of Rouen, *p. Fecamp. Tenecy,* a village of Franche-Comté, in the bailiwick of Gray. *p. Gray.* Tenerand, a town of Saintonge, in the ekftion of S. Jean-d'Angely. *p. S. Jean-d'Angely.* Tenpville, a town of Bourbonnois, in the eleftion of Moulins, *p. Moulin.* Teneur, a village of Artois, in the bailiwick of S. Pol. *p. Arras.* Tennelieret, a village of Champagne, in the diocefe and cleftion of Troves, *p. Troyes.* Tennequin, *la-GroJfe,* a village of Meffin, in the diocefe and receipt of Metz. *p. Metx.* Tenme, a town of Maine, in the diocefe and election of Mans. *p. le Mans. Tens,* a village of Condomois, in the diocefe and cleftion of Condom. *Condom.* TertnAlle, a fmall town of Normandy, in the election of Alencun. *f. Valiemont.* Terain, *le,* a river of Beavoifis, which joins theGife near Creil. Terain-le-Petit, a fmall river, which runs into the Terain, near

Vol.. III.

Milly.

Terajfon, a town of Périgord, *tm* the river Vézerc,-in the diocefe and eleftion of Sarlat, near the border of Limofin; about leagues from Brives,6 from Sarlat, and 10 from Périgucux. *Bureau depoße.* Tetce', a village of Poitou, in the. diocefe and eleftion of Poitiers, *p. Cbautngny.* Tercband, a vicomte of Maine. Tercia, a place of Franche-Comté, in the bailiwick of Lons-lc-Saunier. *p. Lons-le-SaunUr.* Ttrcillac, a village of Berry, m the eleftion of Iffoudun. *p. ÏJJoudun.* Terdegbem, a village of Flanders, in the fubdekgation of Caffcl. *p. Caffel.* Tcrgny, a village of Picardy, in the diocefe of Noyon. *p. la Fere.* Terjat, a village of Bourbonnois, in the eleftion of Montluçon. *p. Montluçon.* Terlon, a village of Hainaut, in the receipt of Maubeuge. *p.Avejnes.* Tcrment%, a fmall country of Languedoc, to the fouth of the diocefe of CarcaiTonne. *Termes.* 1. A fmall town of Champagne, in the eleftion of Ste. Manéhould. *p. Ste. Mane'bouid.* 2. A village of Ncbouzan, in the diocefe of Auch. *p. S. Gaudens.* 3. A village of Lower Languedoc, in the receiptof Narbonnc. *p. Narbonne.* 4. A village of Lower Languedoc, in the diocefe and receipt of Mcnde. *p. Mend;.* 5. A village of Armagnac, in the diocefe and cleftion of Auch. *p. Cußelncau-de-Magnac.* Terminier, a fmall town of Orléannois, in the diocefe and cleftiun of Orleans, *p. Artenay.* Ternabrial, a place of Marche, in tlic eleftion of Gucret. *p. Güera.* Ternar.d. 1. A village of Lvonnois, in the diocefe and cleftion of Lyons, *p. Lyon.* 2. A village of Nivcrnois, in the diocefe and election of Nevers. *p. Severs,* 3. A village of Forez, in t!t elcflion of Montbrifon. *p. Mantbrijbn.* lernant. I. A village of Saintonge, in Ac election of S. Jeand'Angely. *p. S. Jean-d"Angely.* 1. A village of Auvergne, in the dioccfe and election of Clermont, *p. Clermont.* 3. A village of Normandy, in the election of Bernay. *p. le Sap.* 4. A village of Burgundy, in the bailiwick of Nuits, *p. Nuits.* Temant. le, a fmall river of Tourame, which runs into the Loire. Ttrmit & Jttbat, 3 pnníh of Marche, in the election of Gueret. *p. Gueret.* Ternay. I. A town of Poitou, in the election of Loudun. *p. Loudun.* %. A fmall town of Dauphiny, in the dioccfe and elfcVii»n of Vienne. *p Bourgoin.* 3. A village of Beauce, in the election of Vendôme, *p. Montaire.* Ternes, ¡es, a fmall town of Auvergne, in the dioccfe and election of S. Flour, *p. Montlueott.* Ternuay, a village of FrancheComté, in the bailiwick of Vefoul. *f Vejoul.* Terny л village of Picardy, in the ¿iocefe and election of SoilTons. *p. boißons.* fcrouane, an ancient city of Artois, deltroved by the armies of the Emperor Charles V. in 1553. Terrade, la, a village of Armagnac, in the diocefe of Comminges. *p. Mont-de-Marfan.* Tenade-de-Maur, la, and Ttrrsde/ S Aulin, lat villages of Armagnac, in the dioccfe and election of Auch. *p. Auch.* Terramiml, a village of Artois, in the bailiwick of Lens. *p. Lens.* Terrans, a village oí Burgundy, in the bailiwick of Challón, *p. Seurre.* Tetrajjeja, a viMafe of Daupbiny, in the d'mccfe and election of Grenoble, *p Grenoble.* Tenajfon Sec Teraffon. Terrats, a village of Rouffillon, in the diocefe and viguery of Per pignan, *p. Perpignan.* Terr e-Clapiers, la, a village of Upper Languedoc, in the diocefe and receipt of Alby. *p. Aiby.* Terre-des-Cbapelets, ¿a, a town of Poitou, in the election of Fontenay. *p. Fontenay-le-Comte.* Terre-Éfijcópale, la, a fmall town of Lower Languedoc» in the dioccfe and receipt of Mende. *p. Mende.* Terre-Fondree, a place of Burgundy, in the bailiwick of Chàtillon. *f. Cbatillov.* Terre-Foraine-du-Pujof, la, a village of Lower Languedoc, in the diocefe nd receipt of BéViers. *p. Béúers.* Terre-Franche, la, a diftrict of Flanders, which comprehends the chatellanies of Bourbourg, Berg-S.Winoux, and Gravelines. Tcrre-Françotfe, la, a diftrict which makes about a fourth part of Perche. Terre-de-Labour, la. See Labour, Terrette, a river of Normandy, which rifes near Carantilly, and empties itfclf into the Taute. Terrieres, a village of Champagne, in the dioccfe and election of Rheims. *p. Rheims.* Terron-lnVendrejje, and Tenonfur-Aixne, villages of Champagne, in the election of Rethel. *p. Retbel* Terrou & S. Me'ard, a village of Quercy, in the election of Figeac. *Figeae,* Ter roux, S. "Julien-dû, a village of Maine, in the diocefe and ejection of Mans. *p. U Mans.* Terfac. X. A village of Bazadois, in the election of Condom, *p. Condom.* 2. A village of Upper Languedoc, in the diocefe and receipt of Alby. *p. A/by.* 3. A village of Armagnac, in the diocefe and election of Auch. *p. Aucb.* 4. A village of Gafcony, in the diocefe and ele¿tion of Comminges. *p. Touhuje.* Terfarme & Juflacy a village of Berry, in the election of Blanc. *f Montmor'illon.* Terfanntsf a village of Limofm, in thedioccfeand eleftion of Limoges. *p. Limoges.* Terfis, a village of Gafcony, in the election of Landes. *j. Dax.* Tertre, le, a place of Burgundy, in the bailiwick of Challón, *f. Challan.* Tertret-S.-Denis, a village of Beauce, in the eleftion of Mantes, *p. Mantes.* Tertry, a village of Picardy, in the election of Péronne. *p. Perenne.* Tertu, a place of Normandy, in the eleftion of Argentan, *p. Argentan.* Tervay, a village of Franche-Comté, in the bailiwick of Dole. *p. Dole.* Tefcou, a mull river of Querxy, which runs near Montauban. Tefnieres, a village of Hainaur, in the fubdclcgation of Landrccy. *p. Landrtcy.* Tejnieres, or Terniers-Surbon, a village of Hainaut, in the fubdelegatïon of Bavay. *p. Bauay.* TeJJancourt, a village of Beauce, in the election of Maníes, *p. Mtufaan.* Teje. X. A town of Maine, in the diocefe and election of Mans. *p. Pre%-en-Pal.* î. A fmall town of Normandy, in the eleftion ofDomfront. *p. Domfront.* TeJe'la-Forit9 a fmall town of Angoumois, in the diocefe and election of Angoulême. *p. Ar. goulême,* TeJJenbeim, a village of Alface, in the bailiwick of Landler. *p. Hnmngue.* TeJJ'on, a town of Saintonge, in the diocefe and eleftion of Saintes. *f. Samtes.* Tejjou.ille, a fmall town of Poitou, in the eleftion of Mauleon. *p. Chol lu.* Teffj. j. A market-town of (ormandy, in the eleftion of S. Lo. *p. S. Lo.* 2. A village of Normandy, iu the diocefe and eleftion of Baycux. *p. Bayevx.* Ttfte-dc-Can, an i (land, in the mediterranean, off the coaft of Provence. *Ttßel.* I. A village of Normandy, in the eleftion of Caen. *p. Саёк.* i. A village of Roue. guej in the elec tion of Villefranche. *p. Rbodez.* Tiy, a village of Fran che-Comté, in the bailiwick of Salins, *p. Salins.* Tet9 a river of Roufillllon, which empties itfelf into the gulph of Lyons. Tetegbtm, a village of Flanders, in the fubdelegation of Dunkirk, *p. Dunkerque.* Tetbieu, a village of Gafcony, in the eleftion of Landes, *p. Dax.* Tettviller, a v illagc of Alface, in the eleftion of Stralburgh. *p. Strafbou%.* ftvf, or S. Mariin & S. Juliende-Tev/,Z village of Berry, in the eleftion of Châtre, *p. la Châtre.* Teu/e, a village of Gufcony, ia the" receipt of Bigorre. *p. Tarées.* Teulet, a village of Upper Languedoc, in the diocefe and receipt of Alby. *p. Alby.* Teuneres, a village of Rouerguc, in the eleftion of Villefranche. *Vitlefrancbe-ds-Rouergue.* 1 Teulley-les-La'voficourtf a village of Franche-Comté, in the bailiwick of

Gray. *p. Gray.* Teulon, a village of Franche-Comté, in the generality of Befan on. *p. Befançcn4 Teure,* a village of Normandy, in the eleftion of Bernay. *p. Berr.ay.* Tcurey, a village of Burgundy, in the bailiwick of Challón, *p. Challan.* Teurlcy. See *Turlty.* TeurttvUlc-au-Bocage, a town of Normandy, in the eleftion of Va lognes. *p. Carente.* TeMÍematrici) a village of A génois, in the diocefe and election of Agen. *p. Agen.* Texan, a village of Limofin, in the diocefe and eleftinn of Limoges. *p. Limoges.* Tcythu, a village of Poitou, in the in the eleftion of S. Maixant. *p. S. Maixant.* Terrón, a village of Lower Languedoc, in the diocefe and receipt of Montpellier, *p. Montp.il'ur.* Teyßere:, a village of Dauphiny, in the election f Montelimart. *p. Ñiutt.* Ma Texane, a village of Dauphiny, in rhe election of Montelimart. /. 2¡4ofít¡imart, 7ган, a village of Provence, in the viguery of Sifteron. *p. Sißeron.* Tbaat9 a village of Brie, in the election of Sezanne, *p. Sezanne.* Tbain See *Tbein.* Tbairet a town of Aunís, in the diocefe and election of Rochelle. /. *Rocbefort.* Tbaize, a village of Lyonnoîs, in the diocefe and election of Lyons, *f. Lyon,* Tball, a village of Alface, in the bailiwick, of Marmoutier. *p. Saverne.* 'iban, a village of Normandy, in the election ot Caen. *p. Caen.* Thann, a town of Alface, on the borders of Sundgau, near the mountains of Vofge and Rang. *p. Rouffach.* Tbaraux, a village of Lower Languedoc, in the diocefe and receipt of Uzés. *p. XJxii.* Tbaroijiatt. *t.* A village of Burgundy, in the bailiwick, of Arnayle-Duc. *p. D'tjon. z.* A village of Burgundy, in the bailiwick of Avalon, *p. Avalon.* Tbaroty a village of Burgundy, in the bailiwick of Arnay-le-Duc. *p. Dijut.* Tbary, a place of Berry, in the charellany of Châtre. *Thau,* a pond fo called. See *Magutlotu.* Tbaumiers. Sec *Taumiers.* Tbebiran, a village of Nebonzan, in the diocefe of Auch. *p. S. Gaudens.* Tbe'de & *Caûavil,* a village of Nebouzan, in the diocefe of Auch. *p. S. Gaudens.* Tbedirac, a village of Quercy, in the diocefe and election of Cahors. *p. Gabors.* Tbeilj ley or 5. Georges-du-Tbeil, a town of Normandy, in the election of Pont-Audemer. *p. Pont-Audetner.* Theil, le. i. A fmall town of Normandy, in the election of Vire. *p. Vire.-ф.-A* fmall town of Normandy, in the election of Valognes. *p. Vahgnes* 3. A village of Normandy, in the election of Pont-l'Evéque. *p. Pont-PEveouc.* 4. A village of Normandy, in the diocefe and election of Coûtances. *p. Coûtâmes.* 5. A village of Champagne, in the diocefe and election of Sens, *p. Sens.* Titillât, a town of Blé fois, in the election of Romorantin. *p. Romorantin.* Theillement, a village of Normandy, in the election of Pont-Audemer. *p. le Boultroude.* TbeillboSf a village of Limoiin, in the election of Brivcs. *p. Bribes.* Tbein, a fmall town of Dauphiny» in the diocefiymd election of Vienne. *p. Vienne.* Tbeix, a" village of Bretagne, in the diocefe and receipt of Vannes. *p. Vannes.* Tbelay Fraceliere, a village of Burgundy,in the bailiwick of Serauren-Auxois. *p. la Pacaudiere. Tbe/isíS? ¡a Combej* a village of Forez, in the election of S. Etienne."/. 5. Etienne. Tbelocbe-enrBelinj a fmall town of Maine, in the election of Châteaudu-Loir. *p. la Ferté-Bernard.* Tbelucb, a village of Artois, in the bailiwick of Lens. *p. Ai'ras.* Tbcmiiourt, a village of Bcauce, in the election of Mantes, *p. Bordeau-de-Vigny.* Tbe'miett*e*S) and *Themines,* villages of Quercy, in the election of Figeac. *p. Figeac. Tbe'nac,* a fmall town of Périgord, in the diocefe and election of Sarlat. *p. Bergerac.* Tbenailfes, a village of Picardy, in the diocefe and election of Laon. *p. Vervins.* I'benan, a village of Dauphiny, in the diocefe and election of Grenoble. *p. Grenoble.* Tbenarrey a village of Burgundy, in the bailiwick of Challón, *p. Challen,* Tbenay. i. A town of Touraine, in the elcftion of Amboife. *p. Montrkhard. 2.* A village of Berry, in the election of Châtre, *p. Lignieres.* Tbene/le, a village of Picardy, in the élection of Guife. *p. Gmfe.* Theneron. See *Tañaron.* Tbenemly a village of Poitou, in the election of Richelieu, *p.! lßeBmtcbard.* Tbenicu, a village of Bléfois, in the election of Romorantin. *p. Rcmerantin.* Thenijfey, a village of Burgundy, in the bailiwick of Châtillon. *p. Ste. Reine.* Tiennes, a village of Picardy, in the election of Mondidicr. *p. Mondidier.* Themes tŁf Bertauccurt, a village of Picardy, in the diocefe and election of Amiens, *p. Simiens.* Tienen, a fmall town of Périgord, in the diocefe and election of Périgueux. *p. Montignac.* Tbenorgves, a village of Champagne, in the election of Ste. Manéhould. *p. Ste. Mane'bould.* Tbeol, or Ther, a fmall river of Berry, which falls into the Arnon, at Reuilly. Tteb'e, a cape of Provence, near Kapoule. Ther. See *Tbeol.* Therme, a village of Picardy, in the diocefe and election of Beauvais. *p. Beeiwva'is.* Thenn, le, a village of Qnercy, in the diocefe and elcftion ol Cahors. *f. Cabers.* Tbcrvlle, a village of Mcflin, in the diocee and receipt of Metz. *p. Metx.* Tbcjlers, a village of Upper Languedoc, in the diocefe and receipt of Mifepoix. *p. Mirepoix.* Tkejfannarie', la, a village of Upper Languedoc, in the diocefe and receipt of Alby. *p. Mby.* Tbeffat, a village of Burgundy, in the diocefe and receipt of Màcon. *p. Mácon.* Tbeuil, a place of Touraine, near Chinon.

Tbev'ille. I. A village of Normandy, in the election of Valognes, *p. Valognts.'* 2. See *Thewvllle.* Tbculllcy. See *Ttuilley.* Tbewey. See *Tcurey.* Tbeury, a village of Normandy, in the election of Verncuil. *p Ver neuxî,* Tbeus, a village of Dauphiny, in the.diocefe and election of Embrun. *p. Embrun.* Tbewvilte. i. A fmall town of Normandy, in the diocefe and election of CoCitanccs. *f. Coûtantes,* 2. A village of Beauce,in the diocefe anj election of Chartres, *p. Chartres.* Tbeui'ilte-aux-MciilktSj a village of Normandy, in the election of Caudebec. *p. Fecamp.* Tbeux, a village of Dauphiny, in the diocefe of Gap. Tbey £f Forans, a village of Franche-Comté, in the bailiwick of Vcfoul. VejouL Tbeyjj a village of Dauphiny, in the diocefe and election of Grenoble. *p. Grenoble.* ¥bt%a Sálele a village of Rouffillon, in the diocefe and viguery of Perpignan, *p. Perpignan.* Tbzac. i. A, town of Saintonge, in the diocefe and election of Saintes. *p. Saintes.* %'. A village of Agénois, in the diocefe and election of Agen. *p. A en.* Tbe%ant a town of Lower Languedoc, in the diocefe and receipt of Bézieis. *p. Béx'ters.* *Tbevan-en-Corbierey* a village of Lower Languedoc, in the diocefe and receipt of Narbonne. *p. Narbonne.* *Theley* a village of Béarn, in the receipt of Morias, *p. Pau.* *Tbeze'cy* a village of Bléfois, in the election of Romorantin. *p. Romcrant'm.* *Tbeziers,* a village of Lower Languedoc, in the diocefe and receipt of TJzés. *p. Uze's.* *Tbiais,* a village of the Ifle of France, in the diocefe and election of Paris, *p. Villejuifve.* *Tblany* a village of Hainauf, in the fubdelegation of Bouchain. *p. Valenciennes.* *TbiiiHcowt,* a place of Alface, in the bailiwick of Delle, *p. Beffort.* *YbungtS)* a village of Nivernois, in the diocefe and election of Nevers. *p. Deckst.* *Tblanъtlle-la-CbapelU,* a village of Meffin, in the dioceie and receipt of Metz, *p. Rjcti.* *Tbiaumont%* a village of M elfin, in the dtoceïe and receipt of Vcidun. *p. Vadun.* *Thiktrmenil,* or *TUermenil,* a viHage/ of Normandy, in the election *of* Arques, *p. TermiUe.* *Tbtbou.'ot,* an ancient chateau, be tween Fécamp and Havre-de-Grace. *Tbibou-villt.* a village of Normandy, in the election of Conches, *p. ChaumoKt.* *Tbiebwham,* a village of FrancheComte, in the bailiwick of Baume. *p. Baume.* *Tb'uffenthal,* a village of Alface, inthebailwick of Ville. *p.Scbeißat.* *Tbitjfrar.ty* a village of FrancheComte, in the bailiwick of Vefoul. *p. Vefcul.* *Thiel,* a town of Bourbonnois, in the election of Moulins, *p. M ulim.* *Thielley,* a place of Burgundy, in the bailiwick of Challón, *p. CbaL fan.* *Theimbront,* a fmall town of Picardy, in the generality of Amiens. *p. Boulogne.* *Tbienans,* a village of FrancheComté, in the bailiwick of Vefoul. *p. Vefoul.* *Tbienne,* a village of Flanders, in the fubdelegation of CaiTel. *p. Caf jel* *Tbiepval,* a village of Picardy, m the election of Péronne. *p. Albert.* *Tbieracbe.* See *Tieracbe.* *Thieneville.* See *Tierccville.* *Tbiern.* See *Thiers.* *Thiemat,* a village of Picardy, in the diocefe and election of Laon. *p. Laon.* *Thierry,* or *Chebery,* an abby in the diocefe of Rheims, *p. Sedan.* *Thiers,* or *Tbiern,* a city of Auvergne, near the Durotte, on the frontiers of Forez, in the diocefe of Clermont, and election of Riom; 9 leagues from Clermont, 12 from Rbm, 32 from Lyons, and 114 from Paris. *Bureau dt p'fie.* *Tbierville.* j. A village of Normandy, in the election of Pont-Audemer. *p. Vallmont.* 2. A village of Meffin, in the diocefe and receipt of Verdun, *p. Verdun* *Tbiffcourt,* a fmall town of Normandy, in the diocefe and election of Noy on. *p. Ny.n.* *Tbunñlle, i* village of Normandy, in the election of Falaife. *p. Trouard.* *Tbieulloy & fVacbim,* a village of Artois, in the election of S-Pol. /. *Arras.* *Tbieulloy Г'Abbaye,* and *Thuulloyla-Vill,* villages oí Picardy, in the dio.efe and election of Amiens-*p. Auma le.* *Tbicures,* a place of Picardy, in the election of DoiuY-ns. *p Doulens.* *Tbicux.* I. A village of Brie, in the diocefe and election of MeauÄ *p. Dammanin.* 2. A village of Picardy, in the election of Mondidier. *p. Mondidier* 3. A village of Picardy, in the election of Clermont. *p. Ámliac.* *Thierac,* a town of Auvergne, in the election of Auiillac. *p. Aiaiilac.* *TbIl.* i. A town of Gafcony, in the election of Landes, *p. S. Server, z.* A village of Champagne, in the election of Báriur-Aube. *p. Barfur-Aube.* 3. A village of Champagne, in the diocefe and election of Rheims, *p. Sedan.* 4. A village of Burgundy, in the generality of Dijon, *p. Dijon.* *Tb'il, le.* 1. A village of Normandy, in the election of Arques, *p. Bellemare.* 2. A village of Normandy, in the election of Oifors. *p. U TM Tbil, & la Maifon-Dicu,* a fmall tpwn of Burgundy, in the bailiwick of Semur-enAuxois. *SauHeu.* *Tbii,* and *hs-Vlhieresy* places of Burgundy, in the diocefe and bailiwick of Challón, *p. Chailm.* *Tbilen-Bray,* a village of Normandy, in the election, of Neufchâtel. *p. Niufchâul.* *Tbi/-Fontaine,* a village of Champagne, in the election of Bar-furAube. *p. Barjur-shtbe.* *TbiUla-Viihy* a village of Burgundy, in the bailiwick of Saulieu. *p. St'mur.* *Thit-fur-ArrouXf* a parifh of Burgundy, in the diocefe and bailiwick of Autun. *p. Autun.* *TbilUrs,* a village of Picardy, in the election of Mondidier. *p. Mondidier.* *Tbilleux,* a village of Champagne, in the election of Bar-fur-Aube. *p. Bar-fur-Aube.* *Tbiiiois,* a village of Champagne, in the diocecíand election of Rheims. *p. Rbeitm.* *Tbi/ioloy,* a village of Picardy, in the election of Mondidier. /. *Rye.* *TLi/lotf* a village of Burgundy, in the bailiwick, of Arnay-leDuc. *p. Dijon.* *Tbilon,* a place of Bourbonnois, in the fénéchauíTée of Moulins, *p. Moulins.* *Tbmery* a town of Perche, in the election of Verneuil. *p. Brefolles.* *c£bImezau*ц adiih ict of Perche, of which Chitteauneuf is the capital. *Tbimorry,* a village of Garinois, in the elcitlon of Montargís. *p. Montargis,* *Ybin-U-Monfiieri* a fmall town of Champagne, in the diocefe and election of Rheims, *p. RetbeL* *Thiolenty Uy* a village of Auvergne, in the election of Brioudc. *p. Brioude.* *Tbionne,* a village of Bourbonnois, In the election of Moulins, *p. Garennes.* *Tbionvtlle.* I. A ftrong town of Luxemburg, on the Mofelle, ceded to France by the treaty of the Pyrenees; about iz leagues from Treves, 4 leagues from Frifange, 10 from Longwy, 20 from Montmedy, 31 from Sedan, 36 from Mcziercs, 5S from Liege, "50 from Givet, 60 from Landrecy, 43 from Rocroy, 47 from Mariemburg, 56 from Avcfncs, 60 from Maubeuge, 64 from Möns, 75 from Bruflels, 67 from Valenciennes, 80 from LilJe, 99 from Dunkirk, 99 from Oiiend, 92 from Bruges, 70 from Cambray, 76 from Douay, 78 from Arras, 95 from S. Omer, X05 from Calais, 6o£ from Laon, 66 from S. Quentin, 49 from Rheims, 39 from Chalons, 29 from Ste. Manéhould, 19 from Verdun, 7 from Metz, 35 from Nancy, 51 from Scheleftat, 56 from Colmar, 42 from Fortlouii, 47 from Straiburj, 32 from Larebourg, and 79 from Paris. *Bureau de fofit.* 2. A village of Normandy, in the election of Caudcbec *p. Famnlle* 3. A village of Beauce, in the election of Dourd.ni. *p. Dourdan.* 4. A village of Beauce, in the election of Montfort. *p. Houdan.* *Tbire'y* a village of Poitou, in the diocefe of Lucon, and election of Fontenay-le-Comte; about 5 leagues from Luc on, and 6 from Chateigne ray. *Bunau de feße.* *Tbiro/i,* a fmall town of Beauce, in the diocefe and electiоn of Chartres, *p iUiers.* *Tbisy* a village of Champagne, in. the election of Rcthcl. *p. Rctbel.* *ctLijayi* a village of Touraine, in the election of Chinon. /. *Cbincn.* *Tbi'y,* a village of Burgundy, in the bailiwick of Arnay-le-Duc. *p, Dijon. Tbivars,* a village of Beauce, in the diocefe and election of Chartres. /. *Chartres. Tblwucbey* a village of Burgundy, in the bailiwick of S'-mur-en-Auxois. *p. Semur. Tb'wcckellesy* a village of Flanders, in the fubdelegation of Bouchain. /. *Conde. Tbiverny,* a place of Picardy, in the election of Clermont, *p. Creil. Tbolongeon,* a village of FrancheComté, in the bailiwick of Lons-leSaunier. *p. Lons-le-Saunier. Thomegat,* a v liage of Upper Languedoc, in the diocefe and receipt of Mirepoix. *p. Mirefoix. Tblm.zey.* I. A village of Burgundy, in the bailiwick of Saulieu. *p. Semur. z.* A village of Burgundy, in the bailiwick of Beaunc. *p. Beaune. Ibon,* a river of Poitou, which runs into the Thoue, at MontreuiiBellay. *Tbonat)* a village of Dauphiny, in the diocefe and election of Vienne. *p. Vienne. Tbongny-aux-Berufs,* a village of Champagne, in the diocefe and election of Chalons, *p. Chalons. Tlonnac,* a village of Périgord, in the diocefe and election of Sarlat. *p. Seriat. Tkom-.ance-les-'Jüir.ville,* a fmall town of Champagne, in the election of Joinviffe. *p. JoTwillc. Tktnv.lle.* I. A village of Normandy, in the election of Pont-Audemer. *p. Ptnt-Audemer.* a. A village of Lorraine-Fiançoife, in the diocefe and receipt of Metz, *pMetos. Tixny,* a village of Normandy, in the election of Andely. . *Ecouy. Tbor, le,* a town of Venaiflin, about 1 league fror» Lille, and 3 from Avignon, *p. Avignon. Tboramt-bajfe,* or *Toramenos-bajfe,* and *Tborame-baute,* villages of Provence, in the viguery of Colmar, *p. Digne. Thörey.* See *Torey. Tbore',* a fmall town of Beauce, in the election of Vendôme, *p. Vendóme. Tbtre'e,* a village of Anjou, in the election of Baugé. *p. la Flèche. Tboreille-le-beffent,* and *Thoreilleles-Arnay-le-Duc,* villages of Burgundy, in the bailiwick of Arnayle-Duc. *p. Dijon. Tbtrcne,* a parifh of Provence, in the diocefe of Vence, *p. Große. Thörey, t.* A village of Burgundy, in the bailiwick of Beaune. *p. JBcaune. z.* A village of Burgundy, in the bailiwick, of Montcenis. *p. Jîatun.* 3. A place of Burgundy, in the diocefe and bailiwick of Dijon. *p. Dijon.*

Tborey-lcs-Epoifes, a village of Burgundy, in the bailiwick of Semur-en-Auxois. *p. Semur. Tborey-fous-Charny,* a village of Burgundy, in the bailiwick of Sau lieu. *p. Semur. Tborigne'.* I. A town of Anjou, in the diocefe and election of Angers, *p. Angers.* 2. A fmall town of Poitou, in the election of Fontenay. *p. S. Maixant. Thorigny,* a town of Champagne, in the diocefe and eleilion of Sens. *p. Sent. Thoronet.* I. A village of Provence, in the diocefe and viguery of Aix. *p. Aix.* 2. A village of Provence, in the viguery of Draguignan. *p. Draguignan. Tborre,* a village of Champagne, in the election of Tonnerre, *p. Tonnerre. Thors,* î. A village of Saintonge, in the eleilion of S. Jean-d'Angcly. *p. Cognac.* 2. A vilbge of Champagne, in the election of BarfurAube. *p. Bar-Jut-Auhe. Tbory.* I. A village of Picardy, in the election of Mondidicr. *p. Aîondidier.* 2. A village of Burgundy, in the bailiwick of Avalon. *p. Avalon. Thcfmei,* a village of Normandy, in the diocefe and election of Evrcux. *p. Evreux. Thofny.* Sec *Tbony. Thcfny-Pontavaire,* a village of Picardy, in the diocefe and election of Laon. *p. Fjimei. Thcjie w Beauregard,* places of Burgundy, in the bailiwick of Semur-en-Auxois. *p. Stmur.. Thou. 1.* A town of Berry, in the diocefe and election of Bourges. *p. Samerre.* 2. A village of Gâti nois, in the election of Gien. *p. Bonny. Thou, le.* I. A town of Aunis, in the diocefe and election of Rochelle, *p. la Rochelle.* 2. A village of Brie, in the election of Sezanne. *p. Montmirel. Thou-Ste.-Croixj* a village of Bourbonnois, in the election of S. Amand. *p. S. Amand. Tbouarc,* a village of Bretagne, in the diocefe and receipt of Nantes. *p. Nantes. Tbcuars.* I. A village of Foix, in the generality of Roufhllon. *p. Foix.* 2. Sec *Touars. Tbouault,* a place of Nivcrnois, in the diocefe and election of Ncvers. *p. Nevers. Tboucy,* a town of Cannois, about 5 leagues from Auxerre. *p. Gien. Tboue,* a river of Poitou, that joins the Loire near S. Florent. *Thoueos,* a village of Nivernois, in the election of Clamecy. *Clamecy. Thoulis & Harrencourt,* a village of Picardy, in the diocefe and eleilion of Soiffons. *p. Soi-*

jJons. Tboulon. See *Toulon. Tbouloufe.* See *Touloufe. Tbour, le,* a village of Champagne, in the diocefe and election or Rheims. *p. Kctbel. Tbourailles,* a village of Beauce, in the election of Vendôme, *p. Montoire. Tbourette, la,* a village of Limofin, in the election of Tulles, *p. Tulles. Tboury,* a village of Orlcannois, in the election of Bcaugency. *p. Beaugcncy. Tboußbn,* a village of Gitinois, in the election of Mclun. *p. Melun. Tbrejor,* or *It Trcfor,* a convent in the diocefe of Rouen, *p. Magny. Tbubebert, le,* a village «f Normandy, in the election of Pont-Audemcr. *p. Boucachard. Ibuillcric, la,* a village of Bour. bonnois, in the election of S. Amand. *p. S. Amand.* M 5 *Tbuißignol, It,* a fmall town of Normandy, in the eleftion of Conches, *p. Elbtuf. Ihuiffinier, le.* i. A village of Normandy, in the eleftion of Pontde l'Arche, *p. Elbeuf.* 2. A village of Normandy, in the election of Pont-TEvêque. *p. Bo: ItrouJe. 7buify,* a village of Champagne, in the diocefc and eleftion of Rheims. *p. Rheims. tbuitanger,* a village of Normandy, in the election of Pont-deΓ Arche, *p. Elbeuf. Tbume'ries,* a village of Flanders, in the fubdelegation of Lille, *p. Lille. Tbun-VEvêque,* and *Thun S..Martin,* villages of Flanders, in the diocefc and fubdelegation of Cambray. *p. Cambray. Tburagueau,* a fmall town of Poiou, in the eleftion of Richelieu, *p. Mirebeau. 'Jburcey,* a village of Burgundy, in the bailiwick of Châtillon. *p. S. S:ine. Thure',* a fmall town of Poitou, in the eicftion of Châtelleraut. *p. Cbátelleraut. 'Thurms,* a village of Lyonnois, in the diocefe and eleftion of Lyons. *p. J.yon. Tburon,* a place of Franche-Comté, in the bailiwick of Lons-le-Saunier. *p. Lcns-le-Siiunier. Tkvry.* I. A town of Gâtinois, in the election of Gien. *p. G:en.* Γ. A fmall town of Normandy, in the election of Falaifc. *p. Falaije.* 3. A village of Burgundy, in the eleftion of Arnay-le-Duc. *p. Dijon. Tbuy,* a town of Rouffillon, in the diocefe and viguery of Perpignan. '*p. Perpignan. Tbuxutnguet,* a village of Armagnac, in tiic eleftion of Aftarac. *p. Alirar.de. Tbfd liment,* a village of Champagne, in the eleftion of Vitry. *p. r.i.y.*

'liberie, a town of Anjou, in the diùccie and eleftion ei Angers. *Angers, TibernAlU)* a market-town of Normandy, in the diocefe and ele&ion of Lificux. *p. L'ßeux. Tibie,* a village of Champagne, in the diocefe and ele¿tion of Chalons. *p. Câhns, I'.bhnlUr,* a village of Normandy, in the eleftion of Chaumont and Ma;ny. *p. Magny. Ticbeville,* a village of Normandy, in the diocefe and eleftion of Lifieux. *p. le Sap, Ticbty,* a village of Burgundy, in the bailiwick of Auxonne. *p. Seurrc, Tie'deuille,* a village of Normandy, in the eleftion of Arques, *p. ĻaHemont. Tie'racbe,* a fertile country in Picardy, watered by the Oife and the Serre; to the weft of Champagne, and the fouth of Hainaut. *Tieffrain,* a village of Champagne, in the eleftion of Bar-fur-Aube. *p. Vandewvrt, Tierceville,* a village of Normandy» in the diocefe and eleftion of Baycux. *p. Gifors. TiergennUe,* a village of Normandy, in the eleftion of Montivillicrs. *p. Valiemont. Tifrpicd,* a town of Normandy, in the diocefe and eleftion of Avranches. *p. Aurancbes, Tieijan, le,* a village ofBrctagne, in the diocefe and receipt of Nantes. *p. Rennes, Tiefte,* a village of Armagnac the d;ocefe and eleftion of Auch. *p. Aucb. Tiefares,* a villages of Artois, in the diocefe and government of Arras. *p. Doulens. Tittrcville,* a village of Normandy, in the eleftion of Montivillicrs. *p, Hafleur. iíffauges,* a town of Poitou, (ituatcd on tlie Sevrc-Nanroifc, on tbi confines of Anjou and Maine; about 11 leagues from Nantes, from Montaigne and 6 from Maujeon. *Bureau de pcfle. TigeauXj* » village of Brie, in the election of Rozoy. *p. Crccy. Tigery* a village of the Ifle of France, in the diocefe and election of Paris, *p. Corbeil. Tignac-de-ĽEwquc,* a village of Périgord, in the diocefe and election of Sarlat. *p. Sarlat. Tigne7* a town of Anjou, in the election ofSaumur. *p. Savmur. Tignemont,* a village of Mtflin, in the diocefe and receipt of Metz, *p. Metz. Tignet,* a place of Provence, in the vigucry of Graffc. *p. Große. Tignieu,* a village of Dauphiny, in the diocefe and election of Vienne. *p. Vienne. Tignontnlle,* a village of Beaucc, in the diocefe of Sens. *p. Sens.*

Tigny, a village of Orléannnis, in the diocefe and election of Orléans. *p. Orléans. Tigny-Coûter man,* a village of Pícardy, in the diocete and election of SoiiTons. *p. Soißons. T.gny-Nemfontj* a fmall town of Picardy, in the election of Doulens. *p. Doulens. T-gny-Noy elle,* a vilbge of Picardy, in the election of Abbeville. *p. Mofitt-eut I -fur-Mer. Til,* a village of Bazadois, in the election of Condom. *p. Bazas. T'dcbatel.* a town of Champagne, in the diocefe and election of Langres. *p ĻJurtile. T¡lby* a village of Armagnac, in the election of Lomagne. *p. Beaunwnt-de-Lomagne. Tilbas,* or *Tillac,* a village of Armagnac, in the election of Aitarac. *p. JИ-ande. Tälard,* a market-town of Picardy; about 5 leagues from Bcauvais. *p. Beauvais, Tillay,* a fmall town of the Ifle of France, in the diocefe and elect ion of Paris, *p. Magny. Titlay-le Gjud'tn,* a village of Orleannois, in the diocefe and elcdUon of Orléans, *p. Toury.* 4 7 *Ulay-le-PencuXy* and *Tillay-S.BtnCit,* villages of OrJéannuis, in the diocefe and election of Orleans. *p. Orléans. Tillay-NabanNavau,* a village »f Champagne, in the receipt of Ch.u teau-Regnault. *p. Tours. Tille, la,* a river of Burgundy, which runs into the Saône, about a league from Auxonne. *Tillé,* a village of Picardy, in the diocefc and election of Beauvais. *p, Beawvais,* Tilknay, a village of Burgundy, in the bailiwick of Auxonne. *p. Auxonne. Tillet.* i. A village of Gafcony, in the diocefe and election of Comminges. *p. TouJoufe. 2.* A village of Condomois, in the diocefe and election of Condom. *p.Condont. . Tilleul,* i. A village of Normandy, in the election of MontivUliers. *p. Domfront.* 2. A village of Normandy, in the diocefe of Lifieux. *p. Lifieux. Tilleul, le,* a village of Normandy, in the election of Falaife. *p. Trouard. Tilleul-Datne-Agnes, le,* a village of Normandy, in the election of &nchcs. *p. Evreux. Tilleul-cn-Oucbe, le,* a village of Normandy, in the election ©f Bcrnay. *P. Chambr.h. Tilleul'fol-Enj"ant, le,* a place of Normandy, in the election of Bernay. *p. Bernay. Tilleul-Lambert, le,* a village of Normandy,intheele¿tionof Conches. *p. le Neufbourg Tilleul-Lot on, le,* a village of

Normandy, in the election of Conches. *p. Beaumont-le-Roger. TdliereSjQt TillicrsjA* market-town of Normandy, fituated on çli Aure, between Nonancourt and Verneuil, in the diocefe of Evreux, and election of Conches; ahout 3 leagues from Nonancourt, 4 from Vemcuil, 7 from Evreux, and 10 from Chartres. *Bur.au de peße. Tilliers, a* town of Anjou, m the, diocefe and election of Angers. *pS, Florent.*

M 6 *TilHers,* or *Tillim, les,* a village of Normandy, in the election of Gicardy, in the election of Péronne. fors. *Sureau Je poße. p Pfanne. TilUloy,* a village of Picardy, in *Tines,* a village of Lower Lan the diocefe and election of Amiens, guedoc, m the diocefe and receipt of *f. Abbeville. Viviers, p. les Vans. Tillmbols,* a village of Meffin, in *Tmgry,* a village of Boulogne, in the diocefe and receipt of Verdun, the generality of Amiens, *p. Bow f. Verdun.* hgne. *Tillouxe.* I. A fmall town of Tou-*Tingy,* a village of Nivernois, in raine, in the diocefe and eleftion of the eleftion of Clamecy. *p. Clamecy.* Tours, *p. VIße-Boucbard.* 2. A *Tinquee,* a village of Artois, in village of Armagnac, in the election the diocefe and bailiwick of Arras, f Aftarac. *p. Bagneres. p. Arras. TiUoy.* i. A village of Picardy, *Tinquettes,* a place of Artois, in in the diocefe and election of Amiens, the diocefe and bailiwick of Arras. *p. Abbeville. Л.* A village of Cham-*p. Arras.* pagne, in the diocefe and election of *Tinqueux,* a place of Champagne, Châlons. *p. Chalons.* 3. A village in the diocefe and election of Rheims, of Flanders, in the fubdelegation of *p. Rheims.* Douay. *p. Douay.* 4. A village of *Tinteniac,* a village of Bretagne Flanders, in the fubdelegation of in the diocefe and receipt of S. Malo. Cambray. *p. Cambray. p. Becberel. Tilhy-la-Naßines,* and *Tilly-let-Thtry.* 1. A village of Burgundy, *Herma'ville,* places of Artois, in the in the diocefe and bailiwick of Di iiocefe and bailiwick of Arras, *p. jon. p. Dijon.* 2. A village of Bur *Arras.,* gundy, in the diocefe and bailiwick *Tilloy-lcs-Bapaume,* a village of Ar-of Autun. *p. Autun.* tois, in the bailiwick of Bapaume. *Tintury,* a village of Nivernois, *Bapaume. .-"* in the diocefe and election of Nevers.

Tilly. I. A village of Meffin, in *p. Decixe.* the diocefe and receipt of Verdun, *p. Tioiieres,* a village of Auvergne, *Verdun,* 2. A village of Beку, in in the election of Iffoire. *p. Ijfoirc.* the election of Blanc, *p. le Blanc.* 3. *Tir, le,* a river of Rouflillon, that

A village of Artois, in the bailiwick runs into the Valefpir.

of S. Pel. *p. Arras.* 4. A village of *Tirande,* a village of Auvergne,

Normandy, in the election of Ande-in the election of Riom. *p. Riom. y. p. Gaillon.* 5. A village of Nor-*Tiranges,* a village of Force, in mandy, in the eleftion of Caëri. *p.* the election of Montbrifon. *p. Mont Cai'n... brifon.* Tilly-Flins, a village of Beauce, *Tiremande,* a place of Artois, in in the election of Mantes. *p.* the bailiwick of Aire. *p. Aire. Mantes.*

Tirent, a village of Armagnac, in *Ti/ques,* л vilhge of Artois, in the the election of Rivière-Verdun, *p.* diocefe and receipt of S. Omer. *p. S. Gimont. Omer.* ' *Tirlaneourt.* See *Gtiifcard. Tiltre, le,* a village of Picardy, in *Tiron,* an abby in the diocefe of the eleftion of Abbeville, *p.* Abbe-Chartres, *p. No¿ent-le-Rotrou. bille. Tironeau,* a village of Maine, ia *Tincbebray,* market-town of Nor-the eleftion of Mans. *p. Bonneßabk.* mandy, with a bailiwick, in the *Tijac-de-Yronjac,* a village of Gui T:/e, a village of Franche-Comté, ¡n the diocefe and bailiwick of Besançon, *p. Bcfancm.*

Tiff?, a village of Champagne, in the election of Tonnerre, *p. Tonnerre.* Tiffomneres, a village of Auvergne, in the election of Riom. /. *Rkm. Tiffy,* a market-to.wn of Normandy, in the election of S. Lo. *p. & Lo. Titan,* or *Cabaros,* the той eaftern of the iflands called Hieres, in the Mediterranean.

Tivernon, a village of Orléannois, in the diocefe and election of Orléans. *p. Toury. Twet,* a fmall town of Champagne, in the diocefe and election of Langree. *p. Langres. Tinners,* a village of Auvergne, in the diocefe and election of S. Flour. *p. S. Flour. Trxac,* a village of Roucrgue, in the election of Villefranche. *p. Villefranche. Tizac-en-Carton,* a village of Guienne, the diocefe and election of Bourdeaux. *p. Libourne. Tizat,* or S. *A-uid-de-Tizat,* a village of Périgord, in the diocefe and election of Périgueux. *p. Périgueux. T-zay,* a village of Berry, in the election of Iffoudun. *p. Iffoudun. Tizón,* a pariih of Bourbonnois, in the election of Cannat. *Gantât.*

Toaxac, a village of Rouergue, in the diocefe and election of Rhodez. *p. Rhodez. Tocqueville.* I. A village of Normandy, in the election of Valognes. *p. Valognes. z.* A village of Normandy, in the election of Pont-Audemer. *p. Pont-Audemer.* 3. A village of Normandy, in the election of Eu. *p. Eu.* 4. A village of Normandy, in the election of Montiviljiers. *p. Fecamp.* Tocqueville-en-Caux, a village of Normandy, in the election of Arques. *p. Dieppe. Todure,* a village of Dauphiny, in the election of Romans, *p. Romans. Toge,* a village of Champagne, *in* the eleflion of Rethel. *p. Retbel. Toillon* 6? *Lent clot,* a village of Franche-Comté, in the bailiwick of Pontarlier. *p. Pontarlier. Tare & Contentor,* a fmall town of Maine, in the diocefe and election of Mans. *p. Bcllefmc.*

Toire', a town of Anjou,' in the election of Flèche, *p. la Flèche. Tairel,* a fmall town of Breffe, in the bailiwick of Bourg, *p. Bourg-enBreffe. Toirey,* a village of Burgundy, in the bailiwick of Chfitillon. *p. Châtilhn-jur-Seine.* Toirin & Roche, a village of Dauphiny, in the diocefe and election of Vienne, *p. la Tour-du-Pin. Toiry,* a village of Beauce, in the election of Montfort. *p. Mantes.*

Toiffei, or *Toiffey,* a town of Dombes, in the diocefe of Lyons, the chief place of a chatellany; about 6 leagues from Trévoux, *p. Belleville. Tolanjac,* a priory of Quercy, in the election of Villefranche. *p. Villefranche-de-Rouergue. Tolaon,* a village of Dauphiny, in the diocefe and election of Grenoble. *p. Grenoble. Tolebre, la,* a fmall river of Provence, which falls into the fea of Martigues. *Toletne,* a village of Bazadois, in the election of Condom, *p. Condom. Tollent,* a village of Artois, in the bailiwick of Hefdin. *p. He/din. Toilet,* or *Tbtillet,* a town of Berry, in the election of Blanc, *p. le Blanc. Tollevafi,* a town of Normandy, in the election of Valognes. *p. Valognes. T'jlligny,* a village of Champagne, in the election of Rethel. *p. Retbel. Tclcbrc.* See *T»lehre.*

Tclonet, a village of Provence, in the diocefe and vigucry of Aix. *p. Aix. Tombe) la,* a village of Brie, in the election of Montereau. *p. Montereau. Tombebauf,* a village of Agénois, in the diocefe and election of Agen. *p. Vdlenewue-d?'Agen. Tombela'ine,* a fmall ifland, or rock, on the coaft of Normandy, between Avranches and S. Malo. *Tongerlo,* an abby in the diocefe of Cambray. *p. Cambra. Tongue,* a fro all river which falls into the Eraut, at S. Thibery. *Tonnac,* a village of Upper Languedoc, in the diocefe and receipt oí Alby. *p. Alby. Tonnay-Bouuonne,* a town of Saintonge, ntuated on the river Boutonne, in the diocefe of Saintes, and election of S. Jean-d'Angely; about 4 leagues from S. Jean-d'Angely, 9 from Rochelle, 7 from Saintes, and 10 from Cognac. *Bureau de poße.* Tonnay-Cbarente, a town of Saintonge, on the Charente; about.4 leaguès from Ton nay-Boutonne, and 5 from Taillebourg. It has a fmall port. *Tonne & Tbll,* Tonnela-JLong, and *Tonne-les-Pre%,* villages of Luxemburg, in the diocefe of Metz. *p. Stenay. Tonnelle,* a village of Luxemburg. *p. Sedan. Tonneim,* or *Tonnûns,* a town of

Agénois,-. on the Garonne, in the diocefe and election of Agen, between Bourd'aux and Touloufej leagues from Bourdeaux, 29 from Montauban, and 41 from Touloufe. *Bureau de poße. Tonnencourt,* a village of Normandy, in the diocefe and election of Lifieux. *p. Lifieux. Tonnerre,* a town of Champagne, fituated on the Armançon, in the diocefe of Langres, and generality of Paris, in the road from Dijun to Paris; 13 k-agues from Montb;¡rd, 31 from Dijon, 13 from Joigny, 34 from Fontainbleau, and 4& from Paris, *Bureau de poße Tonnerrois,* a fmall country of Champagne, in the environs of Tonnerre, which is the capital.

Tonnetml, a village of Normandy, in the election of Pont-Audemer. *p. Pont-Audemer. Tonneville.* I. A village of Normandy, in the election of Arques-*p. Dieppe.* 2. A village of Normandy, in the election of Valognes. *p. Valognes.*

Tompmer'tes, a village of Agénois, in the diocefe and eleition of Agen. *p. Agen.* *Tonquedec Êf Mimby,* a village of Bretagne, in the diocefe and receipt of Treguier. *p. Guingamp.* *Tonzeau,* a village of Burgundy, in the bailiwick of Saulieu. *p. Saulieu.* *Tooft,* л village of Champagne, in the diocefe and election of Langres. *p. Langres.* *Toralfe,* a village of Franche-Comté, in the bailiwick of Quingey. *f» Befanden.* *Toranches,* a village of Forez, in the election of Montbrifon. *p. Mont brifon.* *Torarrty* a village of Rouflillon, in the viguery of Conflans. *p. Villefr anche-de-Conßans.* *Torce',* i. A town of Maine, in the election of Mayenne, *p. Mayenne.* 2. A village of Bretagne, in the diocefe and receipt of Rennes. *p. Rennes.* *Torcenay,* a village of Champagne, in the diocefe and election of Langres. *p. Langres.* *Tcrcbampy* a fmall town of Normandy, in the election of Domfronf. *p. Domfront.* *Torcbe'y* a village of Dauphiny, in the diocrfc and election of Vienne. *p. la Tour-du-Pin.* *Torcby,* a village of Artois, in the bailiwick of S. Pol. *pArras.* *Torcby,* or *Trjy,* a place of Normandy, in the election of Andcly. *p. Ga'illon.* *Tords,* a village of Champagne, in the diocefe and eleition of Troyts. *p. Aràs-fur-Aube.* *Torcyy* or *Tborcy* a pariih of Burgundy, in the diocefe and bailiwick of Dijon, *p. Dijon.* *Torcy-cк-Bne,* a town in the diocefe of Paris, *p. Lagry.* *Torcy-le-Gtar.d* i. A markettown of Normandy, in the election of Arques, *p. Beihmare. z.* A village of Champagne, in the election of Rethel. *p. Sedan.* *Torcy-ie-Petit,* a village of Nor1 mandy, in the election of Arques, *p. Be Ut mare.* *Torcy-ies-Epoiflè y-a.* village of Burgundy, in the bailiwick, of Scmuren-Auxois. *p. Ssmur.* *TorderaSy* a village of RouiTillon, in the dioccfe and viguery of Perpignan, *p. Perpignan.* *Tordouety* a ímall town of Normandy, in thediocefe and election of JLifieux. *p. Ufieux.* *Toreiiesf* a village of Upper Languedoc, in the diocefe and receipt of Alct. *p. Limoux.* *Torely* a fmall river of Languedoc, which lofes itfelf in the Agoot. *Torfou.* I. A town of Anjou, in the election of Montreuil-Bellav. *p. Saumur.* 2. A village oí the lile of France, in the diocefe and election of Paris, *p. Linas.* *Toi igné,* i. A town of Maine, in the diocefe and election of Mans. *p. Frefnay.* 2. A town of Anjou, in the election of Flèche, *p. Satie.* g. A fmall town of Poitou, in the election of S. Maixant. *p. Tbtre.* 4. A village of Saintongc, in the election of S. Jean-d'Anely. *p. S. Jeand'Angely.* 5, A village of Bretagne, in thediocefe and receipt of Rennes. jt. *Rennes.* *Tongnyy* a town of Normandy, near the river Vire, about 3 leagues from S. Lo, and 8 from Coútances. *p. S. Lo.* *Tomac,* a village of Lower Languedoc, in the diocefe and receipt of Alais, *p. Alais.* *Tornan.* See *Tcurnan.* *Tornefort.* See *"Joumefirt.* *Tomus.* 1. A village of Dombee, in the diocefe of Lyons, *p. Bowß-mBreJJ'e.* 2. See *Tournus.* *Toronet.* See *Tboronet.* *Torp,* a village of Normandy, in the election of Falaife. *p. Falaife.* *Torp, it.* I. A village of Normandy, in the election of Arques, *p. Terv'Me.* 2. A village of Normandy, in the election of Pont-Audemer. *p. Pont-Audemer.* *Torpes,* i. A village of burgundy, in the bailiwick, of Auxonne. *p. Auxonne.* 2. A village of Franche-Comté, in the bailiwick of Qmngey. *p. Befançon.* *Tofuefr.e,* a village of Normandy, in the ejection of Pont-l'Evêque. *p. Pont-l Ewque.* *Tornbren.* I. A village of Agev nois, in the diocefe and election of Agen. *p. Agen.* 2. A village of Condomois, in the diocefe and elec. tion of Condom, *p. Condom.* *TorredieSy* a village of Roufiillon, in the diocefe and viguery of Perpignan, *p. Perpignan.* *Torrent,* a place of Roufillon, in the viguery of Conflans. *p» VÜUJranche-de-Ccnßans. t . Tcnettes,* I. A village of Provence, in the viguery of Draguigna;:. *p. Draguxgnan.* 2. A village of Provence, in the viguery of S. Paul, *p. Antiits.* *Torrigny,* a village in the diocfe and election of Paris, *p. Lagry.* *To₂/ac,* a fmall town of Angoumois, in the diocefe and election of Angoulême. *p. Angouleme.* *Tor),ay-S.-Ange,* a village of Beauce, in the election of Dreux. *p. Dreux.* *Toß.* See *Toreby.* *Torie,ie-Tempief* a village of Guienne, in the diocefe and election of Bourdcau;:.. *p. Bcurdcaux.* *Trteleieỳ* a village of Auvergne, in the ejection of Riom. *p. Riqm.* *Torttfontainty* a village of Artois, in the bailiwick of Hefdm. *p. ILjdin.* *Tertevaî,* a village of Normandy, in the diocefe and ekftion of Bayeux. *p. Baytux.* *Tortexais.* a village of Bourbonnois, in the eleâion of Montluçon. *p. Moulins.* *Ttrtifambert,* a village of Normandy, in the eleftion of Argentan, *p. Argentan.* *Torv'ilRirs,* a village of Champagne, in the diocefe and eleâion of Troyes. *p» Troyes.* *Torxe,* a village of Saintonge, in the eleftion of S. Jean-d'Angely. *p. S. Jean-d'Atgely.* *Tofoues,* or *& Romande-Tofques,* a place of Lower Languedoc, in the diocefe and receipt of Mcnde. *p. Mende.* *Tofsl;* a village of Gaffcony, in the eleftion,of Landes, *p. Bayonne.* *Tofsiat,* a village of Breflc, in the bailiwick of Bourg. /. *Bourg-enBreffi.* *ToJJigny,* a village of Touraine, in the diocefe and eleftion of Tours. *p. bicha.* *Toflcs.* I. A village of Normandy, in the eleftion of Pont-de-1'Arche. *p. Pont-de-Γ Arche.* 2. A village of Normandy, in the eleftion of Falaife. *p. Dofule'.* 3. See *Toles.* *Tot,* a village of Normandy, in the diocefe and eleftion of Rouen. *p. Fecamp.* *Totes,* a market town of Normandy, in the eleftion of Arques, *p. ia Rouge-Maijon.* *Touar,* a village of Condomois, in the diocefe and eleftion of Condom, *p. Port-Ste.-Marie.* *Touaret,* a fmall river of Poitou, that runs into the Thoue. *Touarcê,* a town of Anjou, in the diocefe and eleftion of Angers, *p. singers.* *Touars,* or *Tbouars,* an ancient, city of Provence, ntuated ona hill, near the river Thoue, in the diocefe and generality of Poitiers; about 6 leagues from Loudun, 16 from Angers, 16 from Poitiers, and 20 from Ñiort. *Buicju depnfle.* *Touars,* or *Trtnard,* an abby in the diocefe of Bayeux. *p. Cain.* *Touberville,* a village of Norman dy, in the eleftion of Pont-Audemer. *p. Pont-Audcmer.* *Toucbay,* a village of Berry, in the eleftion of Ifloudun. *p. Lignleres.* *Touche,* a village of Burgundy, in the diocefe and bailiwick of Challón. *p. Challón.* *Touche, la,* a village of Dauphiny, in the eleftion of Montelimart. *p. Aiontelimart.* *Ttucbes & le Château-de-Montaigu,* a'fmall town of Burgundy, in the diocefe and bailiwick of Challón, *p. Challón.* *Touches, les,* a village of Bretagne, in the diocefe and receipt of

Nantes. *p. Nozay. Toucbes-de-Pe'rigne', le,* a town of Saintonge, in the eleftion of S. Jeand'Angely. *p. S. Jean-d" Angely. Teuchel,* a town of Normandy, in the eleftion of Vire. *p. fire. Touffailles,* a village of Quercy, in the diocefe and eleftion of Cahors. *p. Cahors. Toußers,* a village of Flanders, in the fubdelegation of Lille, *p. Lille. Toucy.* See *Tboucy. Toue, la.* See *Thoue. Touffrewllc.* I. A village of Normandy, in the diocefe and eleftion of Rouen, *p. le Bolehard.* 2. A village of Normandy, in the eleftion of Andely. *p. Gaillon.* 3. A village of Normandy, in the eleftion of Caen.' *p. LUlebonne. Touffremile* Й" *S. Leon,* a village of Normandy, in the eleftion of Eu. *p. Trouard. Touffreviliela-Cahle,* and *Touffriville-la-Corbeline,* fmall towns of Normandy, in the eleftion of Caudebec. *p. Caudebec. Touget,* a town of Armagnac, ia the diocefe and eleftion of Auch. *p. Gmont. l Touhaut,* a figniory of Nivernois,.' in the diocefe and eleftion of Nevers.' *p. Nevert. Touille,* a village, of Gafcony, ia the diocefe and eleftion of Comfninges. *p. Motareeau. TouШом.* t. A village of Burgundy, in the bailiwick of ScmurenAtixois. *p. Montbard.* 2. A village1 of Franche-Comté, in the bailiwick of Pontarlicr. *p. Pontariier. Тои/,* an ancient and confiderable city of Lorrain, the capital of Toulois, lituated on the Moftlle, in a fertile plain; it is a biihoprick, with a bailiwick and receipt; it has 4 paribus, 2 hofpitals, a feminary, &c.; 15 leagues from Metz, 2a from Thionville, 39 frcm Sedan, 20 from Verdun, 44 from Mczieres, 66 from Liege, 85 from Lille, 6 from Nancy, 22- from Ep:nal, 30 from S ar louis, 13 from Luneville, 26 from Sareb»jurg, 30 from Phalibourg, 33 frcm Saverne, 42 from Straiburg, 15 from Bar-Ie-Duc, 28 from Vitry-le-Franois, 36 from Chalons, 26 from Chaumont,27 fromLangres, 45 from Dijon, 36 from Seheleftat, 41 from Colmar, 40 from Vezoul, 38 from Lure, 46 from BefTort, 61 from Bâle, and 76 from Paris. *Bureau de peße. Toulant,* a vilbgc of Vivarais, in the receipt of Viviers, *p. S. Peray. Toulcy* a village of Gafcony, in the receipt of Bigorre. *p. 'Taries. Toulignan.* See *Tauligr.an. Tout-tieu,* a village of Dauphinv, in the diocefe and election of Gap. *f. Gap. Tculois,* a territory in Lorraine, of wh ch Toul is the capital.' 7w/m, or *Tkoulon.* i. An ancient and itrong city and feaport of Provence, a bifliopric under the archbiIhop of Aries; it has a good citadel, and a magnificççnt arfenal, with the beft harbour in France, and is advantageouily lituated on the Mediterranean fca; 35 leagues from Antibes, 43 from Nice, 17 from Aix, 36 fr«»m Avignon, 43 from Orange, 96 from Lyons, 160 from Dijon, and aio§ from Paris. *Bureau depoße.* 2. A village of Bourbonnois, in the election of Moulins, *p. Moulins.* 3. A. village of Champagne, in the ei'tilion of Chalons, *p. E¡ ernay.* import of Normandy, in the election of Poiit-TEveque, fituatcd at the mouth of the river Touques; about *l* leagues from Pont-PEveque, and 4 from Honflrur. *p. Pont-VEwque.* a. A river of Normandy, which paffes by Lificux, and runs into rhe fea near Touques; before it arrives at Lificux, it is called Lez.on. *Tovquette,* or *Tou%uey* a village of Normandy, in the diocefe and election of Lificux. *p. Noyers-Menard. Tcuquin,* a village of Brie, in the election of Rozoy. *p. Roxoy. Tour,* a village of Normandy, in the diocefe and election of Bay eux. *p. Дӥуеих. 4 cur, la»* i. A town of Gafcony, in the diocefe and election of Comminges. *p. Montrejeau.* a. A village of Auvergne, in the diocefe and election-of Clermont, *p. Clermont.* -3. A village of Upper Languedoc, in the diocefe and receipt of Rieux. *f. Toulcuße.* 4. A village of Marche, in the election of Gucret. *p. Chenerailles.* 5. A village of Champagne, in the diocefe and election of Rheims, *p. Rheims.* 6. A village of Dombes, in the diocefe of Lyons. Jt. *Belleville,* ч *Tour-Aglaxre, la, я* p!ace of Champagne, in the receipt of ChâteauRegn.iult. *p. Sedan. Tour, la,* or *S. Clair-de-la-Tour,* a village of Dauphiny, in the diocefe and election of Vienne, *p. Lyon. T'.ur-Blanche, la,* a village of Angoumois, in the diocefe and election of Angoulême. *p. Angwlêmc. Tour-d Aigués, la,* a village of Provence, in the diocefe of Aix. *p. fer ruis. Tour-Daniel la,* a village of Lower Languedoc, in the diocefe and receipt vr Puy. *p. le Puy. Tour-de-Bouc, la,* л fmall fort, built on a rock, at the mouth of the fea of Martigues, on the coaft of Provence, *p. le Martigues. Tour-dc-Cordouan, la.* See Cer*douan. Teur-d'EIne, la,* a village of RoufIUlon, in the diocefe and viguery of Perpignan, *p. Ptrpignan. Tour-de-France, la,* a frmll town of Lower Languedoc, in the diocefe and receipt of Alet. *p. Limoux. Tour-dû-Prey, la,* a village of Burgundy,' in the bailiwick of Ava'.cn. *p. Avalon. Tour-de-Roußlhn, la,* л village of RoufliUon; the tower is the remains of an ancient city nameà Rufcino. *p. Perpignan. Tour-de-Vêvre, laf* a chatellany ot Berry, in the Comté of Sancerre. *p. Sancerre. Tour-du-Lay, la,* a priory, in the diocefe of Beauvais. *Tour-du-Mcix, la,* a village of Franche-Comté, in the bailiwick of Orgelet, *p. Lons-le-Saunier. Tour-du-Pin, la.* I. A town of Dauphiny, in the diocefe and election of Vienne, fituated on a fmall river of the fame name; 4 leagues from Bourgoin, и from Chamberry, and 14 from Lvons. *Bureau de toße.* a. fmall river of Dauphiny, which runs into the Rhône. *Toar-Landiy, la,* a town of Anjou, in the election ot Montreuil-Bellay. *p. Angers. Tour-Maubourg,* a fmall town of Lower Languedoc, in the diocefe and receipt of Puy. *p. le Puy. Tour-S.-Gelin, la,* a village of Poitou, in the election of Richelieu, *pVIße-Bouchard. Tour-S.-Prix, la.* See *S. Prix. Tour-fans-Venin, la,* an ancietit town of Dauphiny, built upon a rock, about a league from Grenoble. *Tour-ia-Villc* a town of Normandy, in the election of Valognts. *p. Valogr.es. Touraitle.* I. A village of Champagne, in the election of Chaumont. *p. Ligny.* 2. A village of Gatinois, in the election of Nemours, *p. Nemours. Tourailles, les,* a village of Normandy, in the election of Falaife. *p, Folaife,. Touraine,* an agreeable and1 fertile province, bounded onthecaft by Orléannois, on the Couth by Berry and Potou, on the w eft by Anjou, and on the North by Maine about 24 leagues in length, and 12 in breadth; the river Loire runs through it, and d vides it into Higher and Lower Tourainc. Tours is the capital. *Touranne-i* a village of Dauphiny, in the diocefe and election of Grenoble, *p.Grenoble. Tourax-Vax cilles,* a (mail town of Lowei. Languedoc, in the diocefe and receipt of Mende, *p. Menée. Tourbe,* a fmall river of Champagne, which runs into the Aifne. *Tcurles,* a village of Lower Languedoc, in the diocefe and receipt of Béziers. *p. Betters. Tourcb,* a village of Bretagne, in the diocefe and receipt of Quimper. *J, ¿luimper. Tourciat,* a village of Auvergne, in the diocefe and election of Clermont, *p. Clermont. Teurcy.* See *Tourtcirae. Tourdan.* i. A village of Armagnac, in the election of Aftarac. *p. Afirande.* 2. A village of Dauphiny, in the diocefe and election of Vienne. *ff. Vienne. Toureil, le,* a town of Anjou, in the election of Saumur. *p. Saumur. Tlürallesf* a village of Lower Languedoc, in the receipt of Limoux. *p. Lim ux. TourcUe,la.* ï. A v'liage of Upper Languedoc, in the diocefe and receipt of CarcaiConne. *p. Carcaffonne.* 2« A village of Forez, in the election of Montbrifon. *p-Montbrif'M. Tomettes.* See *Torrettes. Tovrge-vllle,* a village of Normandy, in the election of Pont-l'Evêque. *p. Pont-l'Eveque. Tomiers,* a village of Angoumois, in rhe election of Cognac, *p. Cognac. Tourliac,* a village of.Agénois, in the diocefe and election of Agen. *p. V HI neuve-a Agen. Tourly,* a village of Normandy, 'n the election of Chaumont and a1 id Magny. *p. Chaumont. Tourmanßne,* a town of Anjou, in the election of Mon treuil-Bellay, *p. Cbcllet. Tourmente,* a river of Quercv, which falb into the Dordogne, at Floriac. *Tounmgmetj* a village of Flanders, in the fubdeiegation of Lille, *p. Lille. Tourmigny,* a place of Artois, in the bailiwick of Lens. *p. Lens. Tournan,* or *Tournons,* t. A market-town of Brie, in the diocefe of Meaux, and election of Rozoy; % leagues from Fontenay, and 9 from Paris. *Bureau de poße.* 2. A village of Gafcany, in the diocefe and election of Commingrs. *p. Mr.ntrejcau.* Tournons 62? *la GranrCj* a village of Franche-Comté, in the bailiwick of Vcfoul. *p. Vфul. Tourt;avauxt* a place of Champagne, in the receipt of ChâteauRegnault. *p. Rheims. Tournay. t.* A city of Auirrian Flanders, fituated on the Seheldt j the fee of a bifhop; it was taken by the French from the Dutch, after the battle of Fontenoy, in the year 1745, but ceded to the Auftrians in the year 1748, by the treaty of Aixla-Chapelle; it was once a very ftrong place, but was difmantled by the late Emperor Jofeph; it i» 6 leagues from Lille, 12 from Bruffels, 24 from Dunkirk, and 34 from Paris. *Bureau de pofle.* 2. A town of Armagnac, fituated on the Arroz, about 4 leagues from Tarbes. *p. Tarbes.* 3. A villageof Normandy, in the election of Argentan, *p. Argentan.* 4. A village of Burgundy, in the diocefe and bailiwick of Dijon. *p. Dijon. Tourne* a village of Champagne, in the election ofRcthel. *p. Messier es. Tourne la,* a fmall town of Guienne, in the diocefe and election of Bourdeaux. *p. Cadillac. Tournebouis,* a village of Upper Languedoc, in the diocefe and receipt of Alct. *p. Limoux. Tournebu,* a village of Normandy, IB the election of Falaife. *p. Fa iaife Tourneecupe,* a town of Armagnac, in the election of Lomagne, /. *S. Ciar. Tournedos.* I. A village of Normandy, in the election of Pont-del'Arche, *p. Pcnt-dc-PAche.* 2. A village of Normandy, in the diocefe and election of Evreux. *p. le Neuf' ¿mrg.* 3. A place of FrancheComté, in the bailiwick of Baume. *p. Baume, Tourneffeuillr,* a village of Upper Languedoc, in the diocefe and receipt of ToLilcufe. *p. Touloufe. Tourn:fortt* a place of Provence, in the diocefe and viguery of Digne, *p. Digne. Tournekem,* a fmall town of Artois, in the diocefe and bailiwick of S. Omer. *p. Ardres. Tournel, S. Jullen-de,* a village of Lower Languedoc, in the diocefe and receipt of Mende. *p. Mende. Tournemierretz*village of Auvergne, in the election of Aurillac. *p. Aw rillac. Tcurriemire,* a village of Rouergue, in the election of Milhaud. *p. S. Ajfrique. TourncvWe,* a village of Normandy, in the diocefe and election of Evreux. *p. F.vreux. Tourneur,* ict a fmall town of Normandy, in the election of Vire. *p. Vire. Tourmac.* I. A village of Auvergne, in the diocefe and election of S. Flour, *p. S. Flour,* 2 A village of Rouergue, in the election of Villefranche. *p. Vdlefrancbe-de-Rouergue. Tournieres,* a villa, e of Normandy, in the diocefe and election of Bayeux. / Щ «y *Tourmffant* a village of Lower Languedoc, in the diocefe and receipt of Narbonne. *p. Narbonne.* Toun:*oifst* a village of Orléannoîs, in the diocefe and election of Orléans. *p. Orleans. Tournm.* I. A town of Vivarais» fituated on a mountain near the Rhône, in the diocefe of Valence, and receipt of Viviers; about 5 leagues from Annonay, 15 from Aubenas, and 16 from Viviers. *Bureau de pofie.* 2. A town of Agénois, in the diocefe and election of Agen. *p. Agen.* 3. A town of Berry, in the election of Blanc, *p. le Blanc.* 4. A town of Touraine, in the election of Loches, *p. Preuilly.* 5. A place of Provence, in the viguery of Graffe. *p. Graß. Taurnon & Lias,* a village of Lower Languedoc» in the diocefe and receipt of Viviers, *p. Viviers. Tournousj* or *Tcurnoux.* X. A fmall town of Armagnac, in the election of Rivière-Verdun, *p. Grenade.* 2. A viliage of Armagnac, in the election of Aftarac. *p. Puydarieux. Tournoux,* or *Tornofct,* a parîfh of Dauphiny, in the diocefe of Embrun. *p. Embrun. Tournus,* an ancient town of Burgundy, fituate on the Saône, in a pleafant and fertile country, in the diocefe of Challón, and receipt of Mâcon, in the road from Lyons to Dijon; 5-J leagues from Macon, 6 from Challón, 23 from Dijon, 23I from Lns, and 97 from Paris. *Bureau dc pofie. Toumyy* a town of Normandy, about 2 leagues from Andely. . *U Tille'. Toaron,* i. A village of Liraoiirj, in the diocefe and election of Limoges, *p. Limoges.* 2. A village of Armagnac, in the diocefe and election of Auch. *p. Auch. Tourotte,* or *Terete,* a village of Picardy, in the diocefe and election of Soiflbns. *p. Ccmpiegne. Touroujelhj* a village of Lower Languedoc; in the diocefe and receipt of Narbonne. *p. Narbonnt. Tourouvre,* a town of Perche, in the diocefe and election ef Chartres. *p. Mortagne. Touraine,* a village of Vivarais, in the receipt of Viviers, *p. Viviers Tourret* or *la Touvre.* See *Towur'e- Tourrençuets,* a fmall town of A r magnac, in the diocefe and election

of Auch. *p. Auch.* '*Tourrens,* a village of Armagnac» in the dioccfe and election of Auch. *p. Aucb. Tourrettes,* л village of Dauphiny, in the election of Montelimart. *p. Montelmart. Tourry-en-Sejcur,* a place of Nivernois, in the diocefe and election of Nevera, *p. Nevers. Tourry-Ferrottes,* a village of Brie, in the election of Montereau. *p. Mcntereau. Tourry-fur-Aèron,* a village of Nivernois, in the diocefe and election of Nevers. *p. Never. Tours,* i. An ancient, large, and beautiful city, fituated between the rivers Loire and Cher, the fee of an archbifhop; it is fuppofed to contain 25,000 fouls; 20 leagues from Mans, 37rom Alençon, 67 from Rouen, z8 from Angers, 49 from Nantes, 39 from Laval, 58 from Rennes, 84 from S. Brieux, 75 from Vannes, 121 from Bicft, 37 from Chartres, 30 from Poitiers, 15 from Blots, 29 from Orleans, 59 from Angouléme, 67 from Saintes, 65J from Rochelle, 72 from Rochefort, 94 from Bourdeaux, 152 from Bayonne, 25 from Chateau roux, 55 from Limoges, 130 from Touloufc, 168 from Narbonnc, 183 from Perpignan, and 59 from Paris. *Bureau de poße.* 2. A town of Auvergne, in the diocefe and election of Clermont, *p.Clermont.* 3. A vilkge of Bléfois, in the dioccfe and election of Blots, *p. blols.* 4. A village of Picardy, in the diocefe and election of Amiens, *p. /fmens. Tours-de-Cabordes,* a village of Languedoc, in the diocefe and receipt of Carcaflunne. *p. Carcaßbnne. Tt-un-fur-Marne,* a fmall town of Champag-.e, in the election of Epcrnay. *p. ßpcj my. Tourter.ay,* a fmatl town of Poitou, in the ejection of Thouars. *p. ¿bcuars. cf6urteron-/aSabotterie,* a town of
Champagne, in the election of Rethcl. *p. Ret bel. Tourtes,* a village of Agénoîs, in the diocefe and election of Agen. *p. 4P Tourtirac,* a village of Guicnnc, in the diocefe and election of Bourdeaux. *p. Caß lion. Tourtoirac,* a fmall town of Périgord, in the diocefe and election of Périgueux. *p, Pe'rigueujt Tourtour,* a village of Provence, in the viguery of Draguignan. *p. Draru'ignan. Tourtcuzt,* a village of Lower' LanguedW, in the dioccfe and receipt of Rieux, *p.*

Touloufe. Turves, a village of Provence, in the viguery of S. Maximin. *p. S. Aijximin. Tour-vdle,* I. A fmall town of Normandy, in the election of Coûtants, *p. Ccûtances. %.* A village of Normandy, in the election of PontAudcmer. *p. Font-Audeir.tr.* 3. A village of Normandy, in the election of Caën *J. Caen.* 4. A village of Normandy, in the election of Pont тEvéque *p. Pont-тEvi'que.* 5. A village of Normandy, in the election of Valognes. *p. Carman.* 6. A villfgc of Normandy, in the election of Montivilliers. *p. Fecamp. TourvUlela'Cbampagne,* a fmall town of Nermandy, in the election of Pont-de-Г Arche, *p. Lcuviers. Tourvii'e-ia-Cbapeile,* a village of Normandy, in the election of Arques. *p. Fecamp. Toù rvt/Je-ta'Rivière,* a village of Normandy, in the election of Pontde-l'Arche. *p. Pont-de-ГArcbe. Tounville-fur-Arques,* a village of Normandy, in the election of Arques. *p. Dieppe. Tcuryt* a town of Orléannois» fitU2ted between Artcnay and Angn ville, in the road from Orléans to Paris; 8 leagues from Orléans, and 20 from Paris. *Bureau de p.ße. Toury-en-Séjour, j.* A village of BourbonnoiS, in the election of Moulins, *p. Moulins,* 2. A village of Nivernois, in the election of Ncvertf. *p. Deckse. Toary-fur-Abron, & la Celle-UslÁvenay,* a village of Nivernois, in the diocefe and election of Nevers. *f. Nevera Touiy-furAbron,* a pariíh of Bourbonnais, in the election of Moulins. *p. Moulins. Tourye,* a village of Bretagne, in the diocefe and receipt of Rennes. *p. Rennes. Tournât,* or *S. yul'iende-Tourzaty* avillage of Auvergne, in the election ef Aurillac. *p. Anrittet. Tourzet,* a village of Auvergne, in the diocefe and receipt of Clermont, *p. Clermont. Tous,* a village of Armagnac» in the diocefe and election of Auch. *p. Auch. Toujcane,* a fmall town of Perigord, in the diocefe and election of Périgueux. *p. P/rigueux. Tcufeilles, /as,* a village of Upper Languedoc, in the diocefe and receipt of Lavaur. *p. La-vaur. TouJJaints,* a village *of* Normandy, in the election of Montivilliers. *f. Fecamp. Toßamtsdl Angers,,* an abby in the city of Angers.

Tot-jpùnîs-dc-Rcnnes, a village of Bretagne, in the diocefe and receipt of Rennes, *p. Rennes. Toußaints-en-Г Jßc-de-Cbahns,* an abbv near Châlons. *p. Chalons. Toujjaints-Rcfcoff,* a village of Bretagne, in the diocefe and receipt of S. Pol-dc-Léon. *p. liennebond. Toußieu,* a village of Dombes, in the chatellany of Trévoux, *p. VilkJranche. Toußeux,* a village of Dauphiny, in the diocefe and election of Vienne. *p. Vienne. Toußut,* a place of the Ifle of France, in the diocefe and election of Paris, *p. Paris. T'jbßainvU/e,* a fmall town of Norm. nuiy, in the clc¿tion of PontAudemcr. *p. Pont-Aude mer. Tufiat,* a village uf Gafcony, in the receipt of Bigorre. *p. Tarées. Toußenanf* or *'Tou/enas,* a paiiíh of Burgundy, in the diocefe and bailiwick of Challón, *p. Challón. Toutens,* a village of Upper Languedoc, in the diocefe and rece pt of Touloufe. *p. yillefranchede-Lawra Toutigeac,* a village of Guieone, in the diocefe and election of ßourdeaux. *p. Bourdeaux. Touroulon,* a village of Bazadois, in the election of Condom. *p.Bazau Toutry,* a village of Burgundy, in the bailiwick of Semuren-Aoxois. *p. Semur. Touttancourt,* a village of Picardy, in the election of Doulens. *p. Vow lens. Tournerai,* a village of Angoumois, in the diocefe and election of Angoulêmc. *p. Ja Grolle. Towville,* a village of Normandy, in the election of Pont-Audemer. */. Bcucacbard. Tcwvois.* I. A village of Bretagne, in the diocefe and receipt of Nantes. *p.Macbaou.* 2. A château and Baronny of Maine, in the diocefe of Mans. *Touvre.* I. A village of Angoumois, in the diocefe and election of Angoulême. *p. Angoulême.* 2. A place of Saintonge, in the election of S. Jean-d'Angely. *p. $. Jean-d'Aigely.* 3. A fmall river which rifes from a rock, about 2 leagues from Angoulême, and runs into the Charente at Angoulême. *Touyouje,* a village of Condomois, in the diocefe and election of Condom, *p. Condom. Touzac.* i. A town of Angoumois, in the election of Cognac, *f. Cognac.* 2. A village of Quercy, in the diocefe of Cahors. *p. Cabrs. Toxigny,* a town of Touraine in the eleétion of Loches, *p. 'Tours. Tcyria,* a village of

Franche-Comté, in the bailiwick of Lons-le-Saunier. *p. Lom-le-Saunier.* *Trablin* a village of Dauphiny, in the diocefe and election *u* Vienne, *p. Vienne.* *Tracy, 2,* A village of Nivernois, m the election of Char i té-fu r-Loi re. *p. la Charit/,* z. A village of Normandy, in the election of Caën. /». *Слеш.* 3. A village of Normandy, in the diocefe and election of Bayeux. *p. Soyeux. Tracyle-Mont,* or *le Haut,* and *Tracy-le-Va I,* or *It Bas,* fmall towns of Picardy, in the diocefe and election of Noyon. *p. Compiégne. Trades,* a village of Beaujolois, in the election of Villefranche. /. *Villefranche. Tradet,* a place of Burgundy,, in the bailiwick, of Màcon. *p. Масол. Tragny,* a village of Meïïin, in the diocefe and receipt of Metz. *p. Vic. Trainay,* or *Traifnay,* a village of Kivernois, in the diocefe and election of Nevers. *p. Nertrt. Tralmu,* a fmall town of Orléannois, in the diocefe and election of Orleans, *p. Artenay. Traionve,* the name of a foreft in the jurifdiction of Sezanne. *Trait, le,* a village of Normandy, in the election of Caudebec. . *Сйиdtbec. Trait, le, ¿S? Сояиnсе,* a village of Dauphiny, in the eleiiion of Gap. *p. Cap.* Traitie-Fontaine, a village of Franche-Comté, in the receipt of Vefoul. *p Vtfcui.* -Tra. 'age, a village of Limofin, in which are mines of tin and lead. *p. Limoges. Tramm!* a village of Bretagne, in the diocefe and receipt of S. Brieux« *S. Britux. Tramaifagues,* a village of Gafcony, in the diocefe of Auch. *p. ii/ufe. Tramaye,* a village of Burgundy, in the diocefe and bailiwick. 01 Macon, *p. Mâcon,* Tramblay, a village of Burgundy, in the diocefe and receipt of Macon. *p. Macon.* Tramtcwrt, a village of Artois, in the bailiwick of S. Pol. *p. Htfdin.* Tramery, a village of Champagne, in the diocefe and election of Rheims. *p. Fifmes.* Trament -*Ему,* Tramont -*Laffus,* and *Tramont-Lajus,* places of Meflin, in the diocefe and receipt of Toul. *p. Toul. Tramoye,* a village of Breifc, in the bailiwick of Bourg./. *Bourg-enBreß. Trampd,* a village of Champagne, in the election of Chaumonr. *p. Jtiwville.* Trancault, a village of Champagne, in the diocefe and election of Troy es. *p. Nogent-fur-Seine.*

Tranche, la, a fmall fea port, on the coaft of Poitou, *p. Lucon. Trancóles,* a village of Dauphiny in the diocefe and election of Vienne, *p. Vienne.* Trancrátinvilfe, a village of Btauce, in the election of Dourdan, *p. Angerville.* Trantliere, la, a village of BrefTe, in the bailiwick of Bourg, *p. Bourg, tn-Brejfe.* Trange', a town of Mainé, in the diocefe and election of Mans. *p. le Mans.* Tranbrim, a village of Alface, in the diocefe of Straiburg *p Mol ßeim.* Trannes, a village of Champagne, in the election of Bar-fur-Aube, *p. Bar-fur-Aube. IranyucvWe,* a village of Touloufe, in the diocefe and election of Toul. *p. Toul.* Trans, i. A town of Maine, in the diocefe and c ection of Man, *p. Muyeme.* 2. A village of Bretagne, 4 lcag ics from Dul. *p. Nantes.* 3. A village of Provence, in which are iron mines, in the viguery of Dra guignan. *p. Druguignan.* 4. A village of Bretagne, in the diocefe and" receip; of Rennes, *p. DoJ.* Tranfault, a village of Berry, in the election of Ifloudun. *p. la Châtre. Tranßerts,* a village of Normandy, in the election of Lyons, *p. Ecotiy, Tranßy & Arouaife,* a fmall town of Artois, in the bailiwick of Bapaume. *p. Bapaume.* Trape, a village of Beauce, in the election of Montfort. *p. Montfort.* Trape, ¡a. I-A village of Upper Languedoc, in the diocefe and receipt of Rieux, *p. Toulcufe.* 2. A village of Périgord, in the diocefe and election of Sarlat. *p. Sarlat.* 3. A famous abby, fituated in the mountains of Perche, *p. Mortagne.* Trappt. See *Trape.* Trappet, a village of Ronergue, in the diocefe and election of Rhodes. *p. Rhodes.* Trajlay, a village of Picardy, in the election of Abbeville, *p. Abbeville.* Trafleque, a village of Auvergne, in the election of Riom. *p. Riem.* Traflon, a village of Champagne, in the diocefe and election of Rheims. *f. Rheims.* Traffanel, a village of Upper Languedoc, in the diocefe and receipt of Carcaffonne. *p. Careiffonne. Чгиг 'иц,* a place of Marche, in the election of Bourgancuf. *p. Bmrganeuf.* Travaille, a village of Normandy, in the election of Andcly. *p. Gail lon.* Traubach-lt Bas, and *Traubachie-Haut,* villages of Alface, in the bailiwick of Thann, *p. Rouf-*

fach. Travecy, a village of Picardy, in the diocefe and election of Noyon. *p. Noyon.* Travers, le, a village of Lower Languedoc, in the diocefe and receipt of.Viviers. *p. Gemuillac.* Traverses, a village of Armagnac, in the election of Aftarac. *p. Mtm-de-Marfan.* Traverjonne, a village of Poitou, in the dioceie and election of Poitiers. *p. Poitiers. Través,* a village of Franche-Comté, in the bailiwick of Vefoul. *p. Vefml.* Travet, lej a village of Upper Lau guedoc, in the diocefe and receipt oF Alby. *p. Alby. Travoifyw Grand-Champ,* aplace of Burgundy, in the "bailiwick of Beaunc. *p. B taunt.* Trauron, a place of Champagne, in the bailiwick of Chaumont. *p. Chaumont.* Trauffan, a town of Lower Languedoc, in the diocefe and receipt of Narbonnc. *p. Narbonne.* Tram, a village of Bazadois, in the election of Condom, *p. Bazas.* Tre'al, a village of Bretagne, in the diocefe and receipt of Quimper. *p. Pjotrmel.* Treason, a village of Bretagne, in the diocefe and receipt of Quimper. *p. Quimper.* Treawville, a village of Normandy, in the election of Valognes. *p. Иalognes.* Trtbai», a village of Quercy, in the diocefe and election of Cabors. *p. Cakeru* Treban. I. A village of Bourbon» nois, in the election of Moulins, *p. S. Pour caw.* z. A village of Upper Languedoc, in the diocefe and receipt of Alby. *p. Alby.* Trebes, a town of Upper Langue, doc, in the diocefe andreccipt of Alby. *p. Alby.* Trebedan, a village of Bretagne, in the diocefe and receipt of Dol. *p. Dinan.* Treberden, a village of Bretagne, in tlie diocefe and receipt of Treguier. *p. Guingamp.* Trebes, a town of Upper Languedoc, in thetdiocefc and receipt of S. Papoul. *p. Carcaffonne.* 71 ebief, a place of Franche-Comte, in the bailiwick of Salins, *p. Salins.* Trebien, a village of Upper Languedoc, in the diocefe and receipt of Alby. *p. Alby.* Trebens. I. A village of Upper Languedoc, in the diocefe and receipt of Touloufe. *p. Touloufe.* 2. A village of Gafcony, in the receipt of Bigorre. *p. Tarbts.* 3. A village of Armagnac, in the eleftion of Rivière-Verdun, *f. Bagneres.* Trebrlvan & *U Monßoir,* a village f Bretagne, in the diocefe and receipt of Quimpcr. *p.*

Carhaix. frebry, a village of Bretagne, in the diocefe and receipt of S. Brieux. *p. Lamballe. Tre'cbateau,* or *Tré-Château,* a town of Burgundy, about 4 leagues from Dijon; a part of the town is in Champagne. *p.JJfurtil. Trecbes,* a village of Lower Languedoc, in the diocefe and receipt of Puy. *p. le Puy. Treclun,* a village of Burgundy, in the diocefe and bailiwick of Dijon. *p, Auxonne. frecon,* a village of Champagne, in the diocefe and eleftion of Chalons. *p. Epernay. Trcdaniel,* a village of Bretagne, in the diocefe and receipt of S. Brieux. *p. S. Brieux. Tredareec,* a village of Bretagne, in the diocefe and receipt of Trcguicr. *p. Guingamp. Trediazy* a village of Bretagne, in the diocefe and receipt of S.Malo. *p. S. Malo. Tredrcx,* a village of Bretagne, in the diocefe and receipt of Treguier. *p. Guingamp. Treduder,* a village of Bretagne, in the diocefe and receipt of Treguier. *p, Vännes. Tredun,* a village of Burgundy, in the bailiwick of Auxonne. *p. Auxonne. Tre'et,* a village of Beauce, in the election of Vendôme, *p. Vendôme. Tref-les-Cbarlin,* a village of Bretagne, in the diocefe and receipt of Vannes, *p. Vannes. Trefjy,* a village of FrancheComté, in the bailiwick of Poligny. *p. Salins. Trefbabu,* a village of Bretagne, ra the diocefe and receipt of S. Polde-Léon. *p. S. Malo. Trefcaientec,* a village of Bretagne, in the diocefe and receipt of S. Polde-Léon. *p. Morlaix..* V.L. Ш. *Tze/ня,* a village of Picardy, in the election of S. Quentin, *p. S. Suentin. TrtSagat,* a village of Bretagne, in the diocefe and receipt of Quimper. *p. QiAmper. Treffleuc,* a village of Bretagne, in the diocc.e and receipt of Nantes, *p. Nantes. Treffonds,* or *Tresfonds,* 3 village of Bourbonnois, in the election of Montluron. *p. Montlucon. Treffen.* I. A town of Breffe, in the bailiwick of Bourg, *p. Bourg en-Breß'e.* 2. A place of Dauphiny, in the diocefe and clcftion of Grenoble, *p. ('renoble. TreJglofnou,* a village of Bretagne, in the diocefe and receipt of S. Polde-Léon. *p. Morlaix. Tr:ßaouenin,* a village of Breurie, in the diocefe and receipt of S. Polde-Léon. *p. Vannes. Treflean,* a village of Bretagne, in the diocefe and receipt of Vapnes. *p. Vannes. Treßev-,* a village of Bretagne, in the diocefe and receipt of S. Pol-deLeon, *p. Landernau. Trefnyvez,* a village of Bretagne, in the diocefe and receipt of S. Polde-Léon. *p. S. Malo. Trefols,* a village of Brie, in the eleftion of Sezanne, *p. la Ftrté' Gaucher. l'rejorefiy* a village of Normandy, in the clcftion of Neufchàtcl. *p. Neiifcbátel. Trffumel,* a village "f Bretagne, in the diocefe and receipt of S. Malo. *p. S. Malo. Tregafltl,* a village of Bretagne, in the diocefe and receipt of Treguier. *p. Guerande. Tregcncflre,* a village of Bretagne, in the diocefe and receipt of S. Brieux. *p. Lamballe. Tr.glanus,* a vilhge of Bretagne, in the diocefe and receipt of Treguier. *p. Guingamp. Tregny.* See *Treigny. fregón,* a fmall town of Bretagne, in tlie diocefe and receipt f S. Mil». N *f. S. Malo. Tregondtrn,* a village of Bretagne, in the diocefe and receipt of S. Polde-Léon. *p. S. Malo. 'Tregonneau,* a village of Bretagne, in the dio:efe and receipt of Treguier. *p. Gumgamp. Tregofl,* a village of Normandy, in the diocefc and election of Coûtances. *p. Coûtances. , Tregoumar,* and *Tregoumeur,* villages oí Bretagne, 'in the diocefe and receipt of S. Br leu, *p. S. Brieux. Trcgrom,* a village of Bretagne, in the diocefe and receipt of Treguicr. *Guingamp. Tregourez,* a village of Bretagne, in the diocefe and receipt of Quimper. *p. Lamballe. Treguedel,* a village of Bretagne, in the diocefe and receipt of S. Brieux. ¿. *S. Brieux. Tregumet,* a village of Bretagne, in the diocefe and receipt of Quimper. *p. Stamper. Tregueux,* a village of Bretagne, in the diocefe and receipt of S. Brieux. *f. S. Brieux. Treguier,* a feaport town of Normandy, in the generality of Nantes, the fee of a bifhop; about 9 leagues from S. Brieux, and 28 from Brefr. The Bretons call it *Landriguet. p. Çutngamp.* f *tregunCy* a village of Bretagne, in, the diocefe and receipt of Quimper. *f. Quimper. Trebonranteul,* a village of Bretagne, in the diocefe and receipt of S. Malo. *p. Rennes. Treignac,* a town of Limofin, between Tulles and Limoges, *p. Uzercbes. Treignat,* a village of Bourbonnois, in the election of Montluçon. *p, Montluçon. Trtigny.* I. A town of Gatinois, in the election of Gicn. *p. S. Far' jeau.* 7,. A place of Nivernois, in the election of Clamecy. *p. Cbâteaulandcn. Treilbes,* a place of Lower Languedoc, in the diocefe and receipt of Narbonne. *p. Narbonne. Treille,* a village of Gâtinois, i the election of Nemours, *p. Ntmourt. Trejoux,* a village of Quercy, la the diocefe and election ol Cahors. *p. Gaillac. s TreiXf* a village of Champagne, in the election of Chaumont. *p. Cbaumont. Tzeble-Sams,* a village of Normandy, in the election of Argentan *p Argentan. Trelazé,* a town of Anjou, in the diocefe and election of Angers, *p. Angers. Trelevcrn,* a village of Bretagne, in the diocefe and receipt of Treguier. *p. Landemeau. Treliaires,* a village of Bretagne, in the diocefe and receipt of Nantes, *p. Nantes. Treliffac,* a village of Perigord, in the diocefe and election of Périgueux, *p. Perigueux. Trellvaer,* a village of Bretagne, in the diocefe and receipt of Quimper. *p. Shàmpcr. Trelivan,* a village of Bretagne, in the diocefe and receipt of S. Malo. *p. Dinan. Treliy,* a town of Normandy, in the diocefe and election of Coûtances. *p. Coûtances. Treten, t.* A town of Brie, in the election of Chateau-Thierry, *p. Dormans. 1.* A village of Flanders, in the government of Maubeuge. *p. Avejnes. Tremauiñlle,* a village of Normandy, in the election of Montivilliers. *p. Fawville. Tremblade, la,* a handfome feaport-town of Saintonge, near the mouth of the Seudre. *p. Marennes. Tremblay.* X. A village of the Iilc of Fiance, in the diocefe and election of Paris, *p. Maintenon.* 2. A village of Bretagne, in the diocefe and receipt of Rennes, *p. Fow gtrcs.* 3. A place of Burgundy, in the bailiwick, of Bourbou-Lancy. *p. Bourbon-Lahcy,* pents noble *Trembloy, le,* a village of Franche Comté, in the bailiwick of Gray. *p. Cray. Trembly.* See *Tremblay. Tremtaut,* a village of Bretagne, in the diocefe and receipt c f Quimper. *p. Stumper. Tremebeue,* a village of Bretagne, in the diocefe and receipt of Dol. *p. Vol. Tremelloir,* a village of Bretagne, in the diocefe and receipt of S. Bricux. *p. S. Bricux. Tremenech,* a village of Bretagne, in the diocefe and receipt of S. Polde-Léon. *p. Morlaix. Tremery*, a village of Meflin, in the diocefe and receipt of Metz. *p. Met%. Tremejreve*, a village of Bretagne, in the diocefe and receipt of S. Malo. *p. S. Malo. Tremmen*, a village of Bretagne, in the diocefe and receipt of S. Bricux. *p. S. B i ieux. Trcmcvent*, a village of Bretagne, in the diocefe and receipt of Quimpcr. *p. ¿¡uimperle'. Tremeur*, a village of Bretagne, in the diocefe and receipt of S. Malo. *p. Bruns.*

Poligny. *p. Salins. Tremmel*, a village of Bretagne, 'in the diocefe and receipt of S. Male. *p. S. Malo. Tremomlle*. See *Trlmualle. TretmiaUt-Marchai*, and *Trematille-S-Loup*, fmall towns of Au vergne, in the diocefe and election of Clermont, *p. Clermont. _ Tremouilles,* a village of Rouergue, 111 the diocefe and eleftion of Rhodez. *p. Rhodes. Tremmlat*, a fmall town of Périgord, in the diocefe and elefti.n of Périgucux. *p. Pe'rigueux. Tremoullet*, a village of Upper Languedoc, in the diocefe and receipt of Mircpoix. *p. Mirepoix. Tremuzon*, a village of Bretagne, in the diocefe and receipt of S. Brieux. *p. S. Brieux. r Tremí!,* a village of Franche-Comte, in the bailiwick of Lons-lc-Saunier. *p. Lms-lc-&iunkr. Trenard.* See *Tenais. Traiey*, aplace of Burgundy, in the bailiwick of Arnay-le-Duc. . *Dijon. r Trenheim,* a village of Alface, in the bailiwick of Wefloifen. . *Miifieim. Trenuv,-* a village of Dauphiny, in the diocefe and election of Vienne. *f. Vienne. Treme, la,* a village of Guicnne, in the diocefe and election of Bourdeaux. *p. Bourdeaux. Trenquelcon,* a fmall town of Con¿omois, in the diocefe and election of Condom, *p. Condom. Treogal,* a village of Bretagne, in the diocefe and receipt of Quimper. *p. Suimper. Treon,* a town of Beauce, in the election of Dreux, *p. Dreux. Treon, le,* a village of Bretagne, in the diocefe and receipt of S. Pol-dc-Léon. *p. Landernau. Treouergal,* or *Tsefgoutfial,* a village of Bretagne, in the diocefe and receipt of S. Fol-de-Léon. *p. Moriaix. Trcoullre'& Penmareb,* a village of Bretagne, in the diocefe and receipt of Quiraper. *p. jumper. Trepail,* a village of Champagne, in the election of Epcrnay. *p.*

Epernay. Trepercl, a village of Normandy, in the election of Falaifc. *p. FaJmfe. Treport,* a market-town of Normandy, hy the fca, at the mouth of the Brcflc, with a fmall port; about *n* league from Eu, and 6 leagues from Dieppe, *p. Eu. Trepet,* a village of Franche-Comté, in the diocefe and bailiwick of Befanjon. *p. Befançon. Trefaignes,* a village of Bourbonnois, in the election of Moulins, *p. SdouTxns. Trefandans,* a village of FrancheComté, in the bailiwick of Vcfoul. *p. Vefiul. Trejame,* a village of Dauphiny, in the diocefe and election of Vienne. *p. Vanne. Trejauvaux,* a village of Meffin, in the diocefe and receipt of Verdun.

Verdun. *Trejbeu,* a village of Bretagne, in the diocefe and receipt of Kcnnes. *p. Remet. Trejcbenu,* a village of Dauphiny, in the election of Montelimart. *p. Montelimart. Trejcleoux,* a village of Dauphiny, in the diocefe and eleition of Gap. *p. Gap. Trefetl,* or *Tresse/,* a village of Bourbonnois, in the-election of Moulins, *p. Moulins. Tresfort,* a village of Dauphiny, in the eleition of Montelimart. *p. Montelimart. Treftgneau,* a village of Bretagne, in the diocefe and receipt of S. Brieux. *p. S. Br'ieux. TrcßUty,* a village ef FrancheComté, in the bailiwick of Vefoul. *p. Vejoü. Trefiou,* a fmall town of Auvergne, in the diocefe and election of Clermont, *p. Clermont. Trefmacucisav,* a village of Bretagne, in the diocefe and receipt of S. Pol-de-Léon. *p. Mrlaix. Trefmes,* a village of Brie; its prefent name is Gefvres. Sec *Gévrcs. Trrjncl,* a town of Champagne, in the diocefe and election of Sens. *p. Nogent-fur-Seine. Trefor, le.* Sec *Tbrejo-. Trcjporias,* a figniory of Marche, in the election of Guerct. *Trefpcux,* a village of Quercy, in the diocefe and election ot Cahors. *p. Cabors. Trefques,* a village of Lower Languedoc, in the diocefe and receipt of XJzcs. *p. Bagnols. Treffac,* a village of Lower Languedoc, in the diocefe and receipt of Puy. *p. le Buy. Trefiiints,* a village of Bretagne, in the diocefe and receipt of Dol. *p. Dol. Trejjan,* a village of Lower Languedoc, in the diocefe and receipt of Bezicrs. *p. PeKenas. Trijf'i,* a village of Bretagne, in the diocefe and

receipt of Dol. *p. Dol. Treffens,* a village of Condomois, in the diocefe and election of Condena. */. Condom. Trexanr. e,* a village of Dauphiny, in the diocefe and election of Grenoble, *p. Die. Trent Septurti* and *Trexe Ventz* fmall towns of Poitou, in the election ©f Maulcon. *p. Mauleon. Trezeian,* a fmall town of Bretagne, in the diocefe and receipt of Trcgutcr. *p. Guingamp. Tre%ellde%* a village of Bretagne, in the diocefe and receipt of S. Polie-Léon, *p. Mcrfaix. Trezeny,* a village of Bretagne, in the diocefe and receipt of Treguier, *p. Guingamp. Trezette,* a village of Forez, in the election of Roanne, *p. Roanne. Triae,* a village of An¿oumois, in the election of Cognac, *p. S. Cibardeuux. Tr'mdoux, le,* a place of LowerLauguedoc, in the diocefe and receipt ef Montpellier, *p. Montpellier. Ti'ruize,* a village of Poitou, in the election of Fontenay. *p. Luçon. Trianon,* a beautiful manfion, in 'the Dirk of Ycrfaülc; onnofite the Mcnagcry. *p. Vujadltu Tf iaucourt,* a fmall tjwn of Champagne, in the election of Ste. Manéiiould. *f. Ste. Mane'hould. Tt.ibecourt & Jumcncourt,* a village cf Picard/, in the diocefe and election of Laon. *p. Laon. Tiibebou)* a fmall town of Normandy, in the election of S. Lo. *p. S. Lo. Trkaßin,* or *Tricaßinois,* a fmall country of Dauphiny, in the environs of S. Paul-Trois-Châteaux, which is the capital. *Trkbâtel,* or *VilleCbatd%* a barrony of Champagne. *Trkbey,* a village of Champagne, in the election of S. Florentin, *p. Tonnerre. Tricot,* a town of Picardy, in the election of Mondidier. *p. MomlWur. Trie. I.* A town of Vexin-Njrinrmdy, about a league from OiCbrs. *p. Rouen.* 2. A fmall town of Armagnac, in the election of RiviéreYerJuft. *p. PujdarUttxb Trie/,* a town of Vexin-François, fitu.ited on the Seine, in the diocefe of Rouen, and election of-Paris; 6 leagues from Mantes, 17 from Evreux, 34fromLifieux,45 from Caen, 25 from Rouen, and S from Paris. *Bureau de poße. Tr'xenbacb,* a village of Alface, in the bailiwick of Ville, *p. Scbeltfat. Trieux. i.* A village of Dauphiny, in rhe diocefe and election of Vienne. *p. Vienne.* 2. A fmall river of Bretagne, which falls into the Manche, 3 leagues from Treguier. Tr'ty, a village of Burgundy, in the diocefe and bailiwick of Dijon. *p. Dijon.* Trigance, a village of Provence, in the viguery of Draguignan. *p. Dragmgnan.* Trigarou, a village of Bretagne, in the diocefe and receipt of S. Malo. *p. Dinan.* Trigny, a village of Champagne, in the diocefe and election of Rheims. *p. Rheims.* Tr'tgonnan, a village of Périgord, in юс alócete ano Cicuikmj «1 -crrgueux. *p. Perigueux,* Triguerre, a town of GAtinois, in the election of Montargis. *p. Mлntargis.* Tüilbardou, a village of Brie, in the diocefe.and election of Meaux. *Bureau de poße.* Tri/port, a village of Brie, in the diocefe and election of Meaux. /. *Meaux.* Trimbach, a village of Alface, in the bailiwick of Fleckenitein. . *Wiffcmbourg.* Trimer a village of Bretagne, in the diocefe and, receipt of S. Malo. *p. S. Malo.* Trimou'ilU, hj a town of Poitou, fituated on the river Bcnaife, near the province of Marche; about 12 leagues from Poitiers, *p. Montmorillon.* Tñnay, a village of Orléannois, in the diocefe and election of Orléans. *p. Arte nay.* Trnite't la, I. A village of Nor cardy, in the diocefe and receipt of Boulogne, *p. Boulogne.* Trots Paliitf a village of Angoumois, in the diocefe and election of Angoirieme. /. *Angculime.* Tr̀us-Pierres, les, a village of Normandy, in the election of Montivilliers. *p. S. Romain.* Trois-Pu'tts, a village of Champagne, in the diocefe and election of Rheims, *p. Rheims.* Trcifaor.t, a village of Normandy, in the election of Caen. *p. Caen,* Trcijne, a village of Picardy, in the diocefe and election of Soiflbns. /. *Sojffons.* Tro'jfereux, a village of Picardy, in the diocefe and election of Ecauvais. *p. Beauvais.* TrofJy, a town of Champagne, in the eleiticn of Epernay./». *Da mans.* Troifvevrts, a ligniory of Nivereois, in the diocefe and election of Nevers. *p Never.* Troif+it.'it, a vilbge of Flanders, in the diocefe and fubdelegation of Cambray. *p. Cambray.* Trohe, a place of Picardy, between Soiflbns and Compiégne. *p. Compeg ne.* ч Tnlimont, a village of Bretagne, in the diocefe and receipt of Quimpcr. *p. jumper.* Trcmarey, a village of FrancheComté, in the bailiwick of Gray. *p. Gray.* Trcmpy le, a village of Auvergne, in the election of Combraillcs. /. *Chambón.* Tronc, le, a village of Normandy, in the election of Conches, *p. Ei/reux.* Troncens, and *Tror. eens la Fittc,* villages of Armagnac, in the election of Aftarac./. *Mirande.* Tronche, la, a village of Limofin, in the diocefe and election of Tulles. *p. Tulles.* Trcnchet, a town of Maine, in the diocefe and election of Mans. *p. Stenay.* Tronchct, le an abby in the diocefe of Dol, in Bretagne, *p. Dinan.* Troncbey, a village of Burgundy, in the diocefe and bailiwick of Challón, *p. Challón.* Trcnchoy. i. A village of Champagne, in the election of Tonnerre. *p. Tonnere.* a. A village of Champagne, in the election of Langres. *p. Langres.* Tronchoy & Boula'wviïle, a village of Picardy, In the diocefe and elcftioa of Amiens, *p. Amiens.* Tronchy, a village of Burgundy, in the bailiwick of S. Laurent, *f. Chalhn.* Tronco's, and *la VerSere,* places of Burgundy, in the bailiwick of Avalon *p. Avalon.* Trorcy, or *S. Bonnet-de-Tгоксу,* a village of Bcaujolois, in the election of Villefran he. *p. Vxll franche.* Tronde, a village of Toulois, in the diocefe and receipt of TouK *p. Toul.* Tronga, i. A vilbge of Bourbonnois, in the election of Mouline. *p. Moulins.* 2. A figniory of Bourbonnois, in the election of Montluçon. *p. Chambón.* Tronqtàere, la, a village of Quercy, in the election of Figeac. *p. Figtac.* Tronquoy, le, or *Tronquay.* I. A town of Normandy, in the election of Lions, *p. Ecouy.* 2. A village of Picardy, in the election of Mondidier, *p. Mondidier.* Tnnfanges, a village of Nivernois, in the diocefe and election of Nevers. *p Nevers.* Tronfoy, or *S. Mart'm-de-Tronfy,* a village of Nivernois, in the election of Char i té-fur-Loi re. *p. la Cha' rite'.* TromMle, a village of Meffin, in the diocefe and receipt of Meti./ *Met%.* Trontonas, a village of Dauphiny» in the diocefe and election of Vienne. *p. Vienne.* Troc, a fmall town of Beauce, in the election of Vendôme, *p. Yen dome.* Trepes, a village of Burgundy, in the bailiwick of Challón, *p. Se&i* Troquevilkj or *TзесаиеъⅢeCваяй* town of Normandy, in the election of Pont-Audemer. *p. Audtmer.* Troßy-Breuil, a village of Picardy, in the diocefe and election of Soiffons. *p. Soißhnt.* Trotebec, a fmall river of Coûtantin. Trau, a foreft of 3160 arpents, in the jurifdiction of Caudebec. *Trouan-lc-Grand,* and *Trouan-hPetit,* villages of Champagne, in the election of Vitry. *p. Vitry.* Trouard, or *Trauart,* a market town of Normandy, fituated on the Meance, in the diocefe of Bayeux, and election of Caën; about 4 leagues from Caën. *Bureau de pofle.* Troubat, a village of Ncbouzan, in the diocefe of Auch. *p. MontreJean.* Troubleville, a village of Beauce, *m* the election of Châteaudun. *p. Cbateaudun.* Troucey. See *Trouffcy.* TrouJeville, a villageof Normandy, in the election of Caudebec. *p. tétamp.* Troues-Moniabe', ¡es, a village of the Ifle of France, in the diocefe and election of Paris, *p. Paru.* Trouham, a village of Burgundy, in the bailiwick. of S, Jean-de-Lofnc. *p. Auxcnne.* Troubaut, a village of Burgundy, in the bailiwick of Châtillon. *p. S. Seine.* Trouilles, a village of Rouflillon, in the diocefe and viguery of Perpignan, *p. Perpignan.* Trcville, or *Trois-Villis,* a place of Flanders, in the fubdclegation of Douay. *p. Douay.* Trouirn, a parifh of Provence, in the vigutry of Caflellane. *p. Caßtllant.* Troulbas, or £ *Andreol-de-Tnulhas,* a village of Lower Languedoc, in the diocefe and receipt of Uzés. /. *Alaii.* Troupiac, a village of Upper Langudoc, in the diocefe and receipt of Lavaur. *p. Lavavr.* TrouJfeauvilU, a village of Nor mandy, in the election of Pont-1' Evcque. *p. Dofule'.* Troujjencourt, a village of Picardy, in the election of Mondidier. *p. Mondidier.* Troujfey, a village of Toulois, in the diocefe and receipt of Toul. *p Void.* Trouvant, a village of FrancheComté, in the bailiwick of Vefoul. *p. Veßul.* Trouvât, le, a village of Dauphinv, in the diocefe and election of Grenoble, *p. Grenoble.* Trouville. I. A village of Normandy, in the election of Pontl'Eveque. *p. Pont-VEvtaue.* 2. A village of Normandy, in the election of Caudebec. *p. Famsillc.* Trouvilie-fur-Mer, a village of Normandy, in the election of PontAudemer. *p. Pont-Audemer.* Troye, a village of

Upper Languedoc, in the diocefe and receipt of Mirepoix. *p. Mirepoix.* Tioye¡, an ancient and large ci«y of Champagne, fituated on the Seine, in the generality of Chalons; it is a bilhoprick the feat of a governor, bailiwick, election, and contains 14 parifhes; 19 leagues from Chalons, 29$ from Rheims, 40 from Laon, 61 from Valenciennes, 60 from Cambray, 95 from Calais, 74 from Lille, 76 from Bruneis, 29 from Ste. Manchould, 39 from Verdun, 47 £ from Meziers, 51 from Sedan, 78 from Liege, 44 from Toul, 50 from, Nancy, 57 from Luneville, 86 from Strafburg, 29 *i* from Langrcs, 54$ from Lure, 71 from Altkirch, So from Bale, 80 from Sceleftat, 21 from Chaumont-en-Bafltgny,r6 from Sens, 3 5 f from Dijon, 69 from Arras, 66 from Douay, 60 from Cam bray, and 38 J from Paris. *Bureau de paßt.* Trucbere'e, la, a village of Burgundy, in the bailiwick of Challón. *p. Tournus.* Trucbterjheim, a village of Alface, in the bailiwick of Kockerlberj. *p. Strafiturgr* Truly, i A village of Nivernois, in the eleítion of Clamecy. *p. Clamecy.* 2. A village of Picardy, in the diocefe and eleítion of Laon. *p. Loon.* 3. A village of Picardy, in the diocefe and election of Soiffons. *f. Sjffns.* True, la, a village of Marche, in the election of Gueret. *Gucret.* Trueire, la, or Trieure, a fmall river which rifes in one of the mountains of Gevaudan. Trufiis-Rogent, a village of Picardy, in the diocefe and election of Amiens. *p. Amiens.* Trugny. I. A village of Champagne, in the eleítion of Rethd. *p. Rabel.* 2. A village of Burgundy, in the bailiwick of Challón, *p. Auxunne.* Trumas, a village of Dauphiny, in the eleítion of Montelimart. *p. Aïonteltmart.* Trulbas, a place of Lower Languedoc, in the diocefe and receipt of Narbonne. *p. Narbonne.* Trumilly, a village of Picardy, in the eleítion of Crêpy. *p. Crêpy.* Trun-fur-Dive, a market town of Normandy, the feat of a bailiwick, in the eleítion of Argentan, *p. Argentan.* Trungy, a village of Normandy, in the diocefe and eleítion of Bay*ap. Bayeux.* Truffy, a village of Champagne, in the eleítion of Tonnerre, *p. Auxtrre.* Trutemer, a village of Normandy, in the eleítion of Mortain. *p.*

Morta'm. Iruttimir, a fmall town of Normandy, in the eleítion of Vire. *p. Vire.* Truy, a village of Berry, in the diocefe and eleítion of Bourges. *Bourges,* Truye, a fmall town of Touraine, in the eleítion of Loches, *p. Loches.* Trye. See Trit. Tuberjon, a place of Boulonnois, in the generality of Amiens, *p. Amiens.* Tuhery. See *S. Tbibery.* Tubauf. I. A town of Maint, in the diocefe and eleítion of Mans. *p. le Mans.* 2. A village of Normandy, in the eleítion of Verneuil. *p. l' Aigle.* Tucban, a village of Lower Languedoc, in the diocefe and receipt of Narbonne. *p. Perpignan.* Tucby, a village of Hainaut, in the generality of Maubeuge. *p. Mм. beuge.* Tudelle, a village of Armagnac, in the diocefe and eleítion of Auch. *p. Aucb.* Tuellin, a village of Dauphiny, in the diocefe and elcflion of Vienne. *p. Bourgoin.* Tue's-de-Liar, and Tues Entre, valles, places of Roußillon, in the viguery of ConSans. *p. VilUfrancbedt-Confians.* Tueyts-Cbatenac, a fmall town of Lower Languedoc, in the diocefe and receipt of Viviers, *p. Viviers.* Tuffe, a town of Maine, in the diocefe and election of Mans £. *Ctnnerf.* Tugeras, a town of Saintonge, in the diocefe and eleítion of Saintes *p. Jorrzac.* Tugny. I. A village of Champagne, in the eleítion of Rethel. *p. ResbeL* 2. A village of Picardy, in the elrflion of S. Quentin, *p. Ham.* Tuilbac, a village of Guienne, in the diocefe and election of Bourdeaux. *p. Blaye.* Tuillerie, la,л village of FrancheComté, in the bailiwick of Dole. *p. Dole.* Tuillieres, a parilh of Champagne, in the generality of Châlons. *p. Langret.* Tuiffjc & Maiffac, a fmall town of Périgord, in the diocefe and election of Sarlar. *p. Sarlat,* Tu'ete. Sec Tulla. Tulins, or Tuy. lms, a town of Dauphiny, in the eleítion of Romans *p. S. Marcelbt.* Tulle, or Tulles, a city of Limofin, fituated in a mountainous country, at *bieU. f. lifetx.* Turley, a village of Burgundy, i« the bailiwick of Scmur-cn-Auxois*p. Montbard.* Turlunn, an ancient château of Avivcrgnc, near Billion. Tut ne, /?, a village of Picardy r in the diocefe and receipt of Boulogne, *p. Montreuil-fur-Mcr.* Turny, a fmall town of Champagne, in the election of Joigny. p, &

Florentin. Turpenay, an abby in rhe diocefe of Tours, in Touraine. *p. Chinon.* Turquan, a village of Anjou, in the election of Sauniur. *p. Saumur.* Turqu.ville, a village ofNormandy, in the election of Carontan. *p. Carentan.* Turritx, a village of Provence, ire the vigucry of Sifreron. *p. Sßeron.* Twfan, a country of Gafcony bordered on rhe eaft by Armagnac on the fouth by Beam, on the weft by Chaloffe, and on the north by Landes. Aifne and S. Sever arc the' principal tewns. *Turf.* See *Tbury.* Tuley, a' village of Champagne, in the diocefe of Toul. *p. Void.* Tutriers. See *Turriez.* Tuy, a place of Burgundy, in the receipt of Bigorre. *p. Tarbes.* Tuzie & Ja Croix, a village of Angoumois, in the diocefe and elee tion of Angouléme. *p. síngouléme.* Туzая. See *Tirón.*

V.

TfAAS, a town of Maine, in the diocefe of Mans, and election ef Fleche, *p. le Lude.* Vaafi, le, a fmall town of Normandy, in the election of Valognes *p. Valogr.es.* Vabre. I. A fmall town of Upper Languedoc, in the diocefe and receipt of Caftres. *p. Caßrei.* 2. A village of Rouergue, in the eleitiort of Milhaud. *p. Villefrancbe-de-Rou»rgue.* 3. A village of Lower Lan guedoc, in the diocefe and receipt of Alais, *p. S. Hypolite'.* 4. A village of Rouergue, in the diocefe and receipt of Rhode, *p. Rhedez.* Vabrts. i. A fmall city of Rouergue, on the river Dour Jan, in the generality of Montauban, and election of Milhaud; it is abifhoprick; about it leagues from Alby, and 12 from Rhodez. *Burtau de poße.* 2. A town of Auvergne, in the diocefe and eledtion of S. Flour, *p. S. Fleur.* Vairettes, a place of Lower Lan fuedoc, in the diocefe and receipt of 'uy. *p. le Puy.* Vairon, a village of Gevaudan, in the dioeefe and receipt of Mende. *f. Mende.* Vacagmlax, a place of Brefle, in the bailiwick of Bourg, *p. Bourg-en Breje.* Vacarais, a lake of Provence, in Camargue, between the two branches of the Rhône. Vaccin, a place of Toulois, in the diocefe and receipt of Toul. . *Геu/.* Vacinr.e, a fmall river of Bugey. Vacbf,-la, a village of Dauphiny, i» the diocefe and election of Valence, *p. Valence.* Vacberawville, a village of Merlin, in the diocefe and receipt of Verdun. *f,* Verdun. *Vacberes,* a village of Dauphiny, in the election of Montelimart. *p. Büurgoin. Vacberejfes,* a village of Beauce, in the election of.Dreux. *p. Mamtencn. VachereßeiIes-BaJes,* a village of Beauce, in the diocefe and cleition of Chartres, *p. Ma'mtenm. Vacherie, la.* I. A village of Normandy, in the dioeefe and elecftion of Evrcux. *p. Beaumont-le-Roger.* 2. A village of Normandy, in the election of Conches, *p. Evreux.* 3. A village of Dauphiny, in the eleftion ©f Montelimart. *p. Creß. Vacb-.eres.* I. A fmall town of Lower Languedoc, in the diocefe and receipt of Puy. *p.le Puy.* . A village of Provence, in the viguery of Forcalquier. *p, Forcalquier. Vacque* a village of Agénois, in the diocefe and eleAion of Agen. *p. Agen. Vacquereffè, lay* a place of Picardy, in the diocefe and election of Amiens. *p. Amiens. Vacqumty la.* x. A fmall town of Normandy, in the election of S. Lo. *p. S. Lo.* 2. A village of Picardy, in the diocefe and election of Amiens. *p. Amiens.* 3. A village of Picardy, in the election of Doulens. *p. DcuUns. Vuquerie-le-Beug,* and *Vac quirie-les-Hcfdin,* villages of Artois, in the bailiwick of Hefdin. *p. Hefdin Vacaucville,* and *Venayf* places of Meffin, in the diocefe and receipt of Metz. *p. Racn. Vacquitrtsy* a village of Lower Languedoc, in the diocefe and receipt of Nîmes, *p. Sommieres. VacquitKy* a fmall town of Upper Languedoc, in the diocefe and receipt of Touloufe. *p. Touloufe. Vaequingben,* a village of Picardy, in the government of Montreuil. *p. Montreuil-fi r-Mer. Vadancourty* a village of Picardy, in the election of Guife. *p. Albert. Vadans.* i. A village of FrancheComté, in the bailiwick of Gray. *p. Gray.* 2. A village of FrancheComté, in the bailiwick of Arboisp. *Salins. Vadclaincourt,* a village of Champagne, in the receipt of Sedan, /. *Sedan. Vadenay,* a village of Champagne, in the diocefe and election or Chalons, *p Chalons. Vadetot-fur-Beaumont,* a village of Normandy, in the election of Caudebec. *p. LilleBonne. Vzdivi/re,* a village of Champagne, rn the diocefe and election of Chalons, *p.*

Chalons. Vadrincourty a village of Cham« pagne, m the receipt of Sedan. *Vages,* a town of Maine, in the election of Laval. *p. Laval. Vageville,* a village of Marche, 'in the election of Gueret. *p. Gueret. Vagnas,* a village of Lower Languedoc, in the diocefe and receipt of Viviers, *p. V.viers. Vai/bauautse,* a village of Lower Languedoc, in the diocefe and receipt of Montpellier, *p. Montpellier. Vaillac,* a town of Quercy, in the dioccfe and election ot Cahors. *p. Cabers. Vaillan,* a town of Lower Languedoc, in the dioccfe and receipt of Béziers. *p. Be'xicrs. Vaillant,* a vill ge of Champagne, in the diocefe and election of Langres. *p. Langres. Vaillàlles,* a village of Agénois, in the diocefe and election of Agen. *p. Agen. Vailhurles,* a town of Roucrgue, in the election of Villefranchc. *p. Villefrancbe. Vastly.* I. A town of Picardy, in the dioccfe and election of Soiifjns. *p. Abbeville,* 2. A village of Berry, in the diocefe and election of Bourges. *p. Aubgny. Vaiily& Feugt,* a village of Champagne, in the diocefe and election of Troyes. *p Troyes. Voire, la,* a village of Burgundy, in the bailiwick of Avalon, *p. Avalen. Vaires.* I. A village of Gâtinois, in the elcétion of Etampcs. *p. Etanspes.* a. A place of the lile of France, in the diocefe and election of Paris. *p. Chelles. Vairon,* a fmall country of Tourainc. *Varrs-Suartiers,* a village of Poitou, in the election of Confolans. *p. Rocbecbouard. Vaifin,* an ancient city of Venaiffin, fituatcd on a mountain, near the Ouvefe, in the judicature of Carpentras; it is a bifliop's fee; it was formerly a very large city, and the capital of the Vocontiens, but at Jhxícm there are but little remains of its ancient fplcndour; about 5 lcagutl from Carpentras, and 8 from Orange. *p. Valreas. Vaiffie, la,* a convent in the dio» ccfe of Clermont, in Auvergne. *Vaijj'ac.* Sec *Honor. Weite,* a Tillage of Franche-Comté, in the bailiwick of Gray. *p. Gray. Vaivre,* a place of Franche-Comté, in the bailiwick of Dole. *p. Dole. Valvre-la-Baß'e, Vaivre Montoille, la,* and *Vaivre-lis-Aûlevilleri, la,* villages of Franche-Comté, in the bailiwick of Vefoul. *p. Ve foul. Val,* a village of Dauphiny, in the election of

Romans. /. *Bourgoin. Val, le.* I. A fmall town of Provence, in the viguery of Brignolcs. *p. Brignoles.* ». A place of Alface, in the bailiwick of Beffort. *p. Beffort.* 3. A place of Beauce, in the election of Dreux, *p. Dreux.* 4. An abby in the diocefe of Bayeux. 5. An abby in the diocefe of Bcauvais. 6. Sec *Notrc-Dame-du-Val. Val,* or & *Germain-du-Val,* a town of Anjou, in the election of Flèche. *p. la Flèche. Val-Benoîte.* See *Valbe'n'tte. Val-Bro-ffsire,* or *Val-Brcßerey* a convent in the diocefe of Vienne) in Dauphiny. *Val-Bakns,* a convent in the dioccfe of Langres. *p. Langres. Val-Cbaßel,* a village of Auvergne, in the election of Brioude. *p. Brioude. Val-Chre'iitn,* an abby in the diocefe of Soi Hons. *p. Coincy. Val-Clair.* See *Valclair. Val-CorMon, le,* & *Brionval,* л village of Normandy, m the election of Gifors. *p. Gifirs. Val-Croiffam.* I. A village of Burgundy, in the receipt of Châtillon. *p. Saulitu.* ». An abby in the diocefe of Die, in Dauphiny. *p. Die. VaJ-a Abbeville, le,* a place of Picardy, in the election of Abbeville. *p. Abbeville, Val-a Awoelle, le,* a village of Lower Languedoc, ill the diocefe and receipt of Viviers, *p. Vivhr Val-de-Bon-Moutier* a place of Meffin, in the diocefe and receipt of Metz. *p. Metz. Val-de-Cere,* or *Baxme,* /?, a difri5t of Cotentin, comprehending about 30 pariihes. *Val-de-la-.Fontaine,* a place of Champagne, in the election of Borfur-Aube. *p. Bur-fur-Aube. Val-de-la-liaye, le.* 1. A village of Normandy, in the diocefe and election of Rouen, *p. Rouen.* z. A village of Normandy, in the election of Neufchatel. *p. Caudebec. Val-de-Mcrry,* a village of Burgundy, in the bailiwick of Auxerre. *p. Auxerre. Val-de-ParadU, le.* See *EJpagnac. Val-des-Cbmx,* a fmall town of Burgundy, in the bskliwick of Chât ilion, *p. Б ourbonne. Val-de-Zcie.* See *Valdeßt% Val-dti-Ecolien,* a village of Champagne, in the election of Chaumont. *p.Cbaumont-en-BajJigxy. Val-dei-Maifom,* a place of Picardy, in the election of Doulcns. *p Doulem. Val-des-Vignei,* a priory in the diocefe of Langres, in Champagne. *p. Langres. Fal-de-Suzon,* a village of Burgundy, in the diocefe anil bailiwick of Dijon, *p. Di-*

jon. Val-de-VirC) le, an archdeaconry in Normandy. *Vdl-Dieu.* i. An abby in the diocefe of Rheims *p. Sedan. 2.* A priory in the diocefe of Troyes. *p. Trcyeu* 3 A chartreufe in the diocefe of Séez. *p. Mortagne-au-Percbe. Val-du-Re'h le,* a village of Normandy, in the election of Eu. *p. Eu. Val-dü-Tñl) le,* a village of Nor, mandy, in the election of Bcrnay. *Chambrais. Val-Flaunex,* a village of Lower Languedoc, in the diocefe and receipt of Montpellier, *p. S, Gilles .. ny. p, Magny.* 2. A village of the diocefe and receipt of Normandy, in the election of Gifors, *p. Gifors. Valdavid, te,* a village of Normandy, in the diocefe and election of Evrcux. *p. Evreux. Valdbacb,* a village of Alface, in the bailiwick of Altkirch, *p. Aitiircb. yjdebourg,* an abby of Alface, in the diocefe of Straiburg. *p. Strajbourg. Valdelaneonrt,* a village of Champagne, in the election of Chaumont. *p. Chaumont-en-BajJigny. Valdensy la,* a village of Dauphiny, in the diocefe and election of Grenoble, *p. Grenoble. tenn. YaBluno,* a village of Provence, in the diocefe and viguery of Grafle. *p. Grafle. Valbadon* a village of Normandy, in the diocefe and election of Baycux. *p. Bayeux. Valbelle,* a place of Provence, in the diocefe of Sittenm. *p. Sifieron. yalbe'noite,* a fmall town of Forez, in the election of S. Etienne, *p. S. Etienne. Valbomais,* a village of Dauphiny, in the diocefe and election of Grenoble. *Grcnçblt,* and receipt of Alby. *p. Alby. Valdcft, le,* or *Val-de-Scie,* a village of Normandy, in the eleâion of Valognes. *p. Valognes. Valdonné, S.-Etienne-de.* a village of Lower Languedoc, in the diocefe and receipt of Mcndc. *p. Mende. Valdonne,* a priory of nuns, in the diocefe of Chalons, in Champagne. *Valdoye,* a village of Alface, in the bailiwick of Beffort. *p. Begirt. Valdrome,* a village of Dauphiny, in the election of Montelimart. *p. Die. Va/duecb,* a lake of Provence, fituated in Crau. *Valdurer.aue,* a village of Upper Languedoc, in the diocefe arid receipt of Caftres. *p. Caßrcs. Valí!.* See *Vallct Valée-de-Carol.* See *Carol. Valcc-de-Mars.* See *Man. Valegue,* a village of Upper Languedoc, in the diocefe and receipt of Toulouiê. *p. Villtfrancbe-de-Lauragais. Veláns,* a village of Dombes, in the châtcllany of Montmerle. *p. Belleville, Valer.ce.* I. An ancient city of Dauphiny, the capital of Valentinois, fituated by the Rhône, in the generality of Grenoble; the fee of a bilhop; it lies between Lyons and Avignon; 12 leagues from Montelimart, 26 from Orange, 33 from Avignon, 52 from Aix, 91 from Antibes, 97 from Nice, 37 from Nîmes, 4S J-from Montpellier, 17 from Lyons, and 141 from Paris. *Bureau de poße.* 2. A town of Agénois, fituated near the Garonne; about 6 leagues from Agen. *Bureau de poße.* 3. A town of Armagnac, on the Blaife, in the diocefe and election of Auch; about 5 leagues from Auch. *p. Condom.* 4. A town of Lower Languedoc, in the diocefe and receipt of Alby; about 3 leagues from Alby. *. Alby.* 5. A village in the diocefe and receipt of Utes. *p. U-z/t.* 6. An abby in-the diocefe of Poitiers. *(. Coube, Valence'.* See *Valencey. Valencey,* a town of Bléfois, fituated on the river Nahon, in the dio cefe and eleftion of Blois. *p. Blois. Valencienne,* a village of Dombes, in the châtcllany of Toiffci. *p. Belle-ville. Valenciennes,* an ancient, ftrong, and large city of Flanders, the capital of Hainaut-Franrois, fituated on the Efcaut, in the diocefes of Cambray and Arras, and the generality of Maubeuge; 10 leagues fro-ra Douay, 8 from Maubeuge, 19 from Philippcville, 24 from Givet, 49 from Liege, 13 from Lille, 8 from Möns, 20 from BruiTels, 29 from S. Omer, 39 from Calais, 32 from Dunkirk, 42 from Oftend, 4 from Quefnoy, 7 from Landrecy, 11 from Avefncs, 24 from Rocroy, 31 from Mcziercs, 36 from Sedan, 44 from Stenay, 55 from Verdun, 7ɔ§ from Metí, I ioj from Stratburg, 22 from Laorr, 33 from Rheims. 43 from Châions, 53 from Stc. Manéhould, 64 from Bar-le Due, 92 from Epinal, 77 from Nancy, 157 from Lyons, 68 from Thionvillc, 14 from Arras, 8 from Cambray, 18 from Péronne, 14 from Bapaume, 25 from Amiens, and 51J from Paris, *Bureau de poße.* s *Valennes.* See *Vallerns. Valenjole,* a town of Provence, in the viguery of Mouitiers. *p. Manofque. Valentees,* 2 village of Armagnac, in the election of *Aftarac. p. Mirande. Valcntigny.* I, A village of Champagne, in the election of Bar-furAube. *p. Bar-jur-Aube.* 2. A placs of Berry, in the châtellany of AixDam-Gil'on. *Valentin,* a place of Franche-Comté, in1 the diocefe and bailiwick of of Bcfanon. *p. Befançon. Valentin, le,* a château of Dauphiny, fituated near the city of Valence, *p. Valence. Valentine,* a town of Upper Languedoc, m the diocefe and receipt of Commingcs. *f. S Gaudens. Valenûmxsy* a country of Dauphíny, by the Rhône, in the environs of Valence, which is the capital.

Valerargues, a village of Lower Languedoc, in the diocefe and receipt of Uzes. *p. Uzes. Valeraugue,* a village of Lower Languedoc, in the diocefe and receipt of Alais *p. Alois Valernes.* See *Válleme. Vaterre,* the name of a mineral fpring in Touraine. *Valéry.* See *Vdory. Vale/court,* a village of Picardy, in the election of Clermont-*p. S. Juß. Val'fville,* a village of Upper Languedoc, in the diocefe and receipt of Touloufe. *p. Touloufe. Valette, la.* i. A town of Angoumois, about 4 leagues from AngouJêmc. *p. Angcultme.* 2. A town of Provence, about a league from Toulon, *p. Tuulon.* 3. A village of Upper Languedoc, in the dicceCe and receipt of Touloufe, *p. Touloufe.* 4. A village of Upper Languedoc, in in the diocefe and receipt of Carcaffonni *p. Carcaffcnnt.* 5. A village of Lower Languedoc, in the diocefe and receipt of Lodeve. *p. Lodeve.* 6. A village of Bretagne, in the diocefe and receipt of Rennes, *p. Clifford* 7. A village of Dauphiny, in the diocefe and election of Grenoble, *p. Grenoble* 8. A village of Li mofin, in the diocefe and election of Tulles. /. *Tulles.* 9. See *Vallate. Valeuge-tEgUfe,* and *ValeugeleJiautf* towns of Auvergne, in the diocefe and election of S. Flour, *p. S. Flow. Valemlb,* a village of Péngord, in the diocefe and election of Périgueux, *p. Bourdálle. Valeure,* a vilbge of Burgundy, in the election of Barfur-Seine. *p, ßar-fur-Scinet Va/gorge,* a fmall town of Lower Languedoc, in the diocefe and receipt of Viviers, *p. Genomllac. Valbeim,* a village of Alface, in the bvtiwicjt of AJtkiich. *p.*

Altkirck. Valbeureux, le, a place of Picardy in the election of Doulens. *p. Dowlens, VaWuon,* a place of Artois, in the bailiwick of S. V(A. *p. Arras. Valiere,* a town of Marche, in the election of Cuerct. *p. Gutret, Valignat,* a village of Bourbonnois, in the election of Gannat. *p, Gannat. Vaiigry.* i. A village of Berry, in the diocefe and election of Bourges. *p. Mcntluçon.* 2. A village of Bourbonnois, in the election of MontiJçon. *p. Montluçon. Valiguieres,* a village of Lower Languedoc, in the diocefe and receipt of Uzes. *p. Bagnols. Val'mcourt,* a fmall town of Cambrefis, in the diocefe and fubdclegation of Cambray. *p. Cambray. Valpffrty,* a village of Dauphiny, in the diocefe and election of Grenoble, *p. Grenoble. Valjoine,* or *Vaugine,* a village of Provence, in the viguery of Apt. *p. Apt. Valjouan,* a village of Gâtinois, in the election of Melun. *p. Melun. Valjouas,* a village of Normandy in the diocefe and election of Coutanccs. *p. Coûtantes. Valfouze,* a fmall town of Auvergne,-in the diocefe and election of S. Flour, *p. S Flour. Vallage,* a fmall country of Champagne, in the environs of Bar-fur-Aube, which is the capital. *Vallaines,* a fmall town of Touraine, in the election of Châteaudu-Loir. *p. Momoire. Vallam-S.-George,* a village of Champagne, in the diocefe and election of Troy es. *p. Troycs. Vallajfe.* See *Vahee.. Vallauricy* a village of Dauphiny, in the election of Montelimart. *p. Aforttelimart. Valley,* a village of FrancheComté, in the bailiwick of G ra/. *p. Gray. Vallée, la,* an abby ia the dioceCe of Evreux. p, *Lvrtux-,* e *Valléi-de-Mcnienaifin.* Ser *Mz-¡tt-naif on. Vallée-du-7îlleul,atcrwn* of M nine, in the diocefc and election of Mans. *p. le Mans'. Vallée-d'Yonne.* See *Tome. Vallée-Foßne,* an ahby in the diocefe of Cambray. *p. Camhray. Vallée, Saittte.* Sec *Val-Ste-Crotx. Vallées, les.* See *Qitatre-Vallées. Valleßn,* a village of FrancheComté, in the bailiwick of Orgelet. *f. Lons-le-Sa¡n:er. Vallemagne,* town of Lower Languedoc, in the diocefe and receipt of Montpellier *p. Limpian. Vallemont.* I. A market-town of Normandy, fituated on a fmall river of the fame name, in the dioccfe of Rouen, and election oí Montivilliers; about 3 leagues from Fecamp, 7 from Caudebcc, and 15 from Rouen. *B:cau de; fie.* i. A village, in the election of Caudebec. *p. Caudchtc.* 3. A fmall river of Normandy, that runs into the fea between Havre and S. Valéry en-Caux. *Vallenay,* a village of Bourbonnoit, in the election of Amand. *p. S. ¿Smand. Valientes,* a village of Brie, in the election of Montereau. *p Mmtereatt. Vallengoujard,* a village of Vcxin, in the election of Pontoife./. *Pontoife. Vallenton,* a village of the Iflc of France, *p. Villeneuve-S.-Georges. Val.'epeUt,* a place of Champagne, in the diocefc and election of Langres. *p. Langres. Valleraye,* a village of Champagne, in the election of Joinville. *p. Vcjjy. Valiere,* a village of Bléfois, in the diocefe and election of Blois. *p. 3l:is.* '*Vallergues,* a village of Lower Languedoc, in the diocefe and receipt of Montpellier, *p. Montpellier. Válleme,* a village of Provence, inthevigucry ofSilteron. *p. Sificron Vallercy,* and *VaJeroy-le-See',* villages of Champagne, in the election of Langte. *p. Langte. Vaihrty* a town of Touraine, in the diocefe and election of Tours. There is a fpring of mineral waters in this town. p, *Langeß. Vallet.* I. A village of Saintonge, in the diocefe and election of Saintes. *p. Saintes. 1.* A tillage of Bretagne, in the diocefe and receipt of Nantes. *p. Nantes. Vállete h,* a pariih of Provence, in the diocefe of Vence, *p. Antibes. Vattetesj* a village of Agénois, in the diocefe and election of Agen. *p. Agen. Valleure,* a village of Burgundy, in the bail.wick of Bar-fur-Seine. *P. Bar-fur-Seine. VaL'ure,* a village of Meifin, in the dioccfe and receipt of Metz. *p. Metz. Valbert, la,* a duchy in Anjou. *Baujré, yallierts-lts-GrangS)* a town of Touraine, in the election of Amboife, *p, Tours Vaiiierguesy* a village of Limofin, in the election of Tulles-. *p. Tulles, Vallisrsy* a village of Champagne, in the election of Bar-fur-Aube. *p. Bar-fur-Aube. yallognes.* See *Vqjognes. Valhirey* an abby in the diocefe of Amiens, *p. Montreuil-fur-Mer. Vallons,* a village of Bourbonnois, in the el'-ftion of S. Amand. *p. S. Amand. Fallon,* a village of Bourbonnois, in the election of Montlucon. *p. Montlucon. . Wallonne,* and *Valloreilie,* villages of Franche-Comté, in the bailiwick, of Baurac. *p. Baume. Vallory,* avillage of Franche-Comté, in the diocefc and election of Sens. *p. Sens, Vallowje,* a pariih of FrancheComté, in the receipt of Briancon. *p. Brianççn. Valmagne.* Sec *Vallemagne. Valmanga,* a place of RouffiHon, in the viguery of Confient, *p. Perpignan. Vulmartr.b* or *S. Ge/rge-ie-V4¿* in the election of Montbrifon. /. *Montbrijon. Va/puifeauxj* a village of Gatinois, in the election of Etampcs. *p. Etampei. Vainas,* a town of Venaiffin, in the diocefe of Vaifon; about 3 leagues from Vaifon, and 6 from Pont-S.Efprit. *Bureau de pdpe. Valromei,* or *Valrcmey,* a fmall country of Bugey, comprehending no more than 18 pariihes. *Valrouße,* a village of Quercy, in the diocefe and election of Cahors. *p. Cabers. Valrusyley* a village of Auvergne, in the diocefe and election of S. Flour. *p. S. Flour. Vais.* I. A town of Vivarais, about 5 leagues from the Rhône, celebrated for its medical waters, *p. Vivien.* 2. A village of Lower Languedoc, in the diocefe and receipt of Puy. *p. le Puy.* 3. A village of Upper Languedoc, in the diocefe and-receipt of Mirepoix. *p. Mire poix. Va/ferres,* a village of Daupniny in rne Qioceie ana election oT Gap, *p. Gap. Valjcnney* a village of Lyonnois» in the diocefe and election of Lyons. *p. Lyon. Valjptr,* a valley of Rouffillon, furrounded by the Pyrenees, except towards the eaft; Prats-de-Moillo is the chief place. *Valtorety* or *S. Amand-de-Valtorety* a village of Upper Languedoc, in the diocefe and receipt of Caitrcs. *p, Caflres. Valvigneres Mercoyrats,* a village of Lower Languedoc, in the diocefe and receipt of.Viviers./». *Vivien. Valville, la,* fe? & *Laurent,* a village of Normandy, in the election of Verneuil. *p. Verneuil. Valvion, la,* a place of Picardy, in the election of Doulens. *p. Doultns. Vanague,* a valley of Languedoc. *Vavans,* a village of Dombes, in the chatcllany of Toiflei. *p. BelUv'.Ue. Vanault-le-Chat ti,* and *Vanault-ltsDamcs,* villages of Champagne, in the diocefe and election of Chalons. *p. Vary. Vancayf* a village of Poitou, in the diocefe and election of Poitiers, *p. Poitiers. Vançay S. Aoerùn,* a town of Touraine, in the diocefe and election of Tours, *p. Tours. Vanclans,* a village of FrancheComté, in the bailiwick, of Omans. /. *Befunden. Vanircc,* a village of Normandy, in the election of Port Audemer./. *Rouen. Vandtl,* a village of Bretagne, in the diocefe and receipt of Rennes. *p. Fougères. Vandelans,* a place of FrancheComté, in the bailiwick of Vefoul. *p. Vefoul. Vatidelc'ct la,* a village of Normandy, in the diocefe and election of Coûtances./. *Coûtantes. Vandelincourt,* a village of Picardy, jn the election of Compiégne. *p. Compifgtu. Vandtmauge,* a village of Champagne, in the election of Epernay. *p. Rbiims. Vandemffe.* I. A village of Nivernois, in the diocefe and cledtion of Nevers. *p. Decizt.* ». A village of Burgundy, the the bailiwick of Arnay-lc-Duc. *p. Dijon. Vandeneß'e-hs-Cbarollts,* aparilh of Burgundy, compofed of lèverai hamlets, in the bailiwick of Charolles. *p. Dijon. Vndeneße-fur-Arrcux,* a pariih of Burgundy, in the diocefe and receipt of Autun. *p. Antun. Vandes,* a village of Normandy, in the election of Alençon. *p. Se'ez. Vandcville,* a village of Flanders, in the fubdeiegation of Lille, *p. Lille. Vandeuvre.* I. A village of Berry, in the election of Châteauroux. *p. Châteauroux.* 2. See *Vandocuvre. Vanditres,* a village of Brie, in the elcaion of Château-Thierry./. *ScfJins, Vandtemre,* a town of Champagne, in the diocefe of Langrcs, and election of Bar-fur-Aube, in the road from Langrcs to Paris; 22 leagues from Langrcs, j% from Troyes, and 46 from Paris. *Bureau de poße. Vandoire,* a village of Périgord, in the diocefe and election of Périgueui. *p. Perigueux. banden,* a village of Auvergne, in the election of Riom. *p. Riem. Vandrangcs,* a village of Beaujolois, in the election of Villefranche. *p. S. 'Smpborien. Vandre* a town of Saintonge, in the election of S. Jean-d'Angely.*p. Tonnay-Boutonne. Var.dreJJi,* a village of Poitou, in the election of Mauleon. *p. Aiaulan. Vandy-le-Moul:ny* a fmall town of Champagne,in thcclcction of Rethel. *p. Retbcl. Vanges,* a village of Burgundy, in the bailiwick of Saulieu. *p. Sauiieu. Varday,* a village of Champagne, in the election of S. Florentin, *p. S. Florentin. Vanmoifc,* a vilbge of Picard, in the election of Crêpy. *p. Cripy. Vannaire,* a village of Burgundy, in the bailiwick of Challón, *p. Challón. Vanne.* I. A village of FrancheComté, in the bailiwick of Gray. *p. Gray.* 2. See *Weaune. Vannes,* or *Vennes.* 1. An ancient city of Bretagne, about a league from the fea, in the generality of Nantes, the fee of a biihop; 26 leagues from Nantes, 27 from Quimper, 46 § from Breft, 14 from l'Orient, 25 from Retines, 41 from S. Malo, 64 from Caën, 66 from Alcncon, 95 from Rouen, and '113 from Paris. *Bureau defoße.* 2. A village of Orleans, *p. Romvantin.* 3. A village of Champagne, in the diocefe and election of Troyes. *p. Tnyes.* 4. A river Champagne, which dil'charges itfclf into the Yonne at Sens. *Vannoz,* a village of FrancheComté, in the bailiwick of Poligay. *p. sMins. Var/le.* I. A village of Dau" phiny, in the diocefe and election of Grenoble, *p. Grenoble, z. A* fmall river which feperates France from Italy; it rifes in the Alps, paffci through the Comté of Nice, which it divides from Provence, and difcharges itfelf into the fea, about a league from Nice. *Varade,* or *Varada,* a town of Bretagne, fituatcd near the Loire, oppofite S. Florent-le-Vieux; Ii leagues from Nantes, 3 from Ancenis, 9' from Angers, and 81 from Paris. *Bureau de pofle. Varages,* a village of Provence, in the viguery of Barjols. *p. Bat-jo's. Varagne 6 MoncctiMle,* a village of Upper Langudoc, in the diocefe and receipt of S. Papoul. *p. Caßelnaudaty. Varaignes,* a fmall town of Périgord, in the diocefe and cleftion of Périgneux. *p. Pe'rigueux. Varambon,* a town of Breffe, in the receipt of Bourg.' *p. Bourg-enBreffe. Vaianges,* a village of Burgundy, in the diocefe and bailiwick of Dijon. *p. Dijon. Varanguebec,* a fmall town of Normandy, in the election of S. Lo. *p. Carentan. Varannes,* a village of Poitou, in the election of Richelieu, *p. Loudun. Varas,* or *S. PauI-de-Varas,* a town of Breffe, in the receipt of Bourg. *p. Bourg-en-BreJJ'e. Varavil/e,* a village of Normandy, in the eleftion of Caën. *p. Trouard. Varees,* a village of Dauphiny, in the diocefe and election of Grenoble, *p. Grenoble. Vardaix, la,* a village-of Dauphiny, in the election of Montelimart. *p. Montelimart. Vardes.* I. A village of Normandy, in, the eleftion of Gifors. *p. Ecmy.* 2. A marquifate of Nermandy, in the eleftion of Lions, *p. Ecouy. VareMle.* I. A village of Berry, in the election of Blanc, *p.* 5. *Bcnoit¿u-Sault.* 2. A village of Champagae, hi the diocefe and election of Sens. *p. Sens. Pareille $ la.* i. A village of Burgundy, in the bailiwick of Mácon. *p. la Pacaud. ere. z.* A village of Marche in the election of Gueret. *p, Gueret. VareilU-Laßhaux, ta,* a village of Marche, in the election of Bourganeuf. *p. Gueret. Pareilles, les,* a village of Armagnac, in the election of Rivière-Verdun, *p. Grifclles. Parembw.* See *Varamhon. Varen* a town of Roucrgue, in the election of Villefranche. *p. Pillefrantbe-de-Rouergue. Parame, la.* I. A village of Upper Languedoc, in the diocecand receipt of Touloute. *p. Touleufe.* 2. Aplace Lower Languedoc, in the dioccie and Receipt of Puy. *p. le Pьιy. ParcngeiñUe.* I. A fmall town f Normandy, in the election of Arques, *p. Dieppe.* 2. A village of Kormandy, in the dioccie and election of Rouen, *p. Caudebec. Parcngicn,* a wood of 393 arpents, in the jurisdiction of Valognes, in Normandy. *Varenguclec.* See *Parangucba. Parenne.* I. A village of Champagne, in the election of Tonnerre. *p. Tonnerre,* я. A village of Burgundy, in the diocefe and bailiwick of Challón. *pXhallon.* 3. A village of Burgundy, in the bailiwick of Bcaune. /. *Bcaune.* 4. A fief ofBeaujolois, in the pariih of Quincy. *Parenne, la.* I. A town of Anjou, in the diocefe and election of Angers, *p. Sablé.* 2. A village of Auvergne, in the diocefe and election of Clermont, *p. lßoire, Parenne-le-Grand* a fmall town of Burgundy, in the diocfe and bailiwick of Challón, *p. Challón. Parenne, S. Maur,* a place of the Ifle of France, in the diocefe and election of Paris, *p. Pimennes. Païenne* or *Parennes.* I. A town of Bourbonnois, on the confines» of Auvergne., utuated on au eminence near the Allier, in the diocefe ef Clermont, and election of

Moulins; 7 leagues from Moulins, и from Pacaudiere, 21 from Nevers, 17 from Roanne, and 78 from Paris. *Bureau depofie. Parennes.* I. A town of Anjou, in the election of Saumur. *p. Saumur.* a. A town of Touraine, in the election of Loches, *p. Loches.* 3. A fmall town of Champagne, in the dioccfe and election of Langres. *f. Langres.* 4. A fmaJl town of Berry, in the election of Chariré-fur-Loire, *p. la Châtre.* 5. A village of Bléfois, in the election of Romorantm. *fRomsrantin.* 6. A village of Gâtinois, in the election of Montargis, *p. Mor.targU.*-7. A village of Brie, in the election of Montcrcau. *p. Montereau.* 8, A village of Nivernoisj in the election of Charité, *p. la Charité'.* 9. Avillageof Auvergne, in the election of Brioude. *p. Brhude.* 10. A parim of Burgundy, in the dbcefe and bailiwick of M.îcon. *Macon,* il. A priory, in the diocefe of Mcnux, *Parennes, les,* a fmall country in Touraine, fituHtcd along the Loire. *Parennes & Hïeri/Шc,* a village of Picardy, in the election of Doulens. *p. Doulens. Parennes & Jarey,* a village of Ifie of France, in the diocefe an4 election of Paris, *p. Paris. Parennes Bout eau,* a town of Anjou, in the election of Chàtcau-Gontier. *p. Chat eau-Gentier. Partnncs-de-Reu.lion,* and *Varenr.esen-Briennois,* villages of Burgundy, in the diocefe of Autun. *p. la Pacaudiere. Varennes-les-Ncvcrs,* a village of Nivernais, in the diocefe andelection of Nevers. *p. Nevers. Parennes-P ont oije,* a village of Picardy, in the diocefe and election of Noyon. *p. Pontoife. Varemies-S. &uveur,* a village of Burgundy, in the bailiwick of ChaiIon, *p. L,ou.ms. Parennes-jeui-Deue* a village of î
Anjou, in the election of Saumur. *p. Saumur. Varcnnes-fcus-Monteenis,* a village of Burgundy, in the bailiwick, of Montcenis. *p. Antun. Vartnnes furte-Dottx,* a village of Burgundy, in the receipt of Anxonne. *p. Seure. Vartnnes-fur-cfejchesy* a village of Bourbonnais, in the election of Moulins, *p. la Paliß. Pares,* a village of Agénois, in the diocefe and election of Agén. *p. JÍgen. Varefia* and *Afniere9* places of Franche-Comté, in the bailiwick of Orgelet, *p.*

Lons-ie-Saunier. Varéis, a town of Limonnj in the «leítion of Brives. *f. Brives, Vareviilet* a fmall town of Normandy, in the election of Carcntan. *p. Carentan. Varey,* a village of Bugey, in the diocefe and bailiwick of Bcllcy. *p. j&nberieuXt Varhem,* a fmall town of Flanders, in the fubdelegation of Bergues. *p. Bogues. Parí/bes,* a town of Foix» in the generality uf Rouffilbn. *p. Pamiers. Varimonty* a place of Champagne, in the election of Ste. Manchould. *p. Ste. Manihculd. Varimpare,* or *Varimpré,* a village of Normandy, in the election of Eu. *p. Eu. Varifcourt,* a village of Picardy, in the diocefe and election of Laon. *p. Lao rt. VarivUle,* a convent in the diocefe of Beauvais. *p. Bcawvals. Varize,* a village of Beauce, in the election of Chäteaudun. *p. Bonneval, Varneccurty* a village of Champagne, in the election of Rcthel. *p. Rei-he/. VarnevUle-au-GreeXy* a village of Normandy, in the diocefe and elecJion of Rouen, *p. la Rouge-Matron. Varnieuy* a village of Auvergne, in the election of Riom. *p. Riom. Varnonfay,* a village of Champagne, in the election of Bar-fur
Aube. *f. Bar-fur-jéibe. VaroiSy* a place of Burgundy, *a* the diocefe and bailiwick of Dijon. *p. Dijon. VarowvUl-ty* a village of Normandy, in the election of Valognes. *p. Valognes. Varraxniy* a town of Anjou, in the election of Saumur. *p. Saumur. VarredeSf* a fmall town of Brief in the diocefe and election of Mcaux. *p. Meaux. Varry* a village of Normandy, in the election of Argentan, *p. Argen tan. Vars.* I. A town of Saintonge, in the election of S. Jean-d'Angcly. *p. S. Jcan-d Angcïy.* a. A village of Limofin, in the election of Brives. *p. Brives.* 3. A village of Dauphiny, in the diocefe and election of Gap. *p. Montelimart. Van-les-TeuUfyf* a village of Franche-Comté, in the bailiwick of Gray. *p. Gray. Yazz-anneSj* a village of Normandy, in the election of Arques, *p, Yerville. Varzay,* a town of Saintonge, in the diocefe and election of Saintes, *p. Saintes. Var%y,* a town of Nivernais, in the receipt of Clamecy. *p. Clamecy. Vafceuilj* a village of Normandy, Fn the diocefe and election of Rouen. *P Rouen. Vafrau.* See *PVafgau.*

Vaßon, a town of Anjou, in the election of Flèche, *p. la Flèche. VaßongueSy* a village of Normandy, in the election of Caen. /. *Caen Vajj'auj* a village of Picardy, in the diocefe and election of Soiftbns. *p. Soijfons Vaffe'y* a marquifate of Maine, *p, Frefnay. Vujjely* a village of Auvergne, in the diocefe and election of Clermont. *p. Clermont. Vaff'elayy* a village of Berry, in the diocefe and election of Bourges. *p, Bourges, VaJJelin,* a village of Dauphiny, *Vâiarty S. Laurent-de,* a village of Blé lois, in the election of Roui o rantin. *p. Romorantin. VatiervïNe,* a village of Normandy, in the election of Ncufclûtel. *pцj Neufcbátel. ydtifieu,* a village of Dauphiny, in the election of Romans, *p. Romans. Vaûméml.* I, A village of Normandy, in the election of Gifors. *p. Gijors.* 2. A village of Mcflin, in the diocefe of Toul. *p. Mete. Vatros,* a village of Lower Languedoc, in the diocefe and receipt of Béziers. *p. Biúers. Vatry* a village of Champagne, in the diocefc and election of Chalons, *p. Chalons. Vattecr'U,* a village of Normamtyr in the election of Caudebec. *p. Caudebec. Vattctot.* I. A village of Normandy, in the election of Montivilliers. *p. Harßeur.* 2. A village of Normandv, in the election of PontAudenicr. *p. Pont-Audemer. Vatteinlle.* 1. A town of Normandy, in the election of Pont-Audemer. *p. Pont-Audemer. %.* A fmall town of Normandy, in the election of Caudebec. *p. Caudebec.* 3. A village of Normandy, in the election of Andelv. *p. Ecouy. Vaubeccurtf* a comtéof Champagne, in the election of Ste. Manéhould.
Vaublanc, a vilhge of Bretagne, in the dioccfe and receipt uf S. Brieux. *p. Cbagny. Vaubon,* a village of Champagne, in the diocefe and election of Langres. *p. Langres. Vaubum,* a village of Picardy, in the diocefe and election of SohTons-. *p. Siißonu Vaucé.* i. A town of Maine, in the election of Mayenne, *p. Mayenne.* 2. A fmall town of Normandy, in the election of Domfront, *p. Domfront.* 3. A village of Burgundy, in the bailiwick of Avalon./. *Avalon. Vaucelasy* a village of Gâtinois, in the election of £umpts./. *Еыт/м,*

Vauceiïes. I. A fmall town of Flanders, in the diocefe and fubdelegation of Cainbray. *p. Cambray.* 2. *Vaudtrc,* a village of Champagne.

A village of Normandy, in the dio- in the eleition of Vitry. *p. Vitiy.* ccfe- and eleition of Bayeux. /'. BrtVfi/x'. *Vaucloit.* 1. A village of Kiver

J. A village of Picardy, in the dionois, in the election of Vezclay. *p.* cefe and eleöion of Laon. *p. Laar:, Vexɔlay.* 2. A place of Nivernois, 4- An abby, in the diocefe of Apt, in the eleition of Château-Chinon.

in Provence, *p. Apt. p. Deeife.* *Vaucbamp!.* 1. A village of Brie, *Vauc'ufc.* 1. A village of Vcnaiflin, in the cleiVion of Château-Thierry, in the diocefe of Cavaillon and judi *p. Mommrtl.* 2. A place of Franche-cature of Lille, the rcfidence of Pe Comté, in the diocefe and bailiwick trarch; and where the famoufe of Befançon. *p. Bcfanfon.* fountain of Vauclufe, forms a river *Vaucbaßs',* a town of Champagne, called Sorguc, at its 6rft appcarance.

in the diocefe and eleition of Troyes, *p. Avirntn.* 2 A village of Franche *p. Dreyes.* Comte, in the bailiwick of Bcaume. *Vaucbellc-les-Authie,* a village of *p. Bcaume.* 3. A place of Franche Picardy, in the eleition of Doulens. Comté, in the diocefe and bailiwick *f. Dtulens.* of S. Claude. /-. *S. Claude.* 4. A *Vaucbelles.* 1, A village of Picar-priory in the diocefe of Befançon. dy, in the election of Abbeville, *p.* *Vaudufatc,* a village of Franche *Abbeville.* 2. A village of Picardy, Comté, in the bailiwick of Baume, in the diocefe and eleition of Xovon. *p.* *Baume. p. Noyon.* 3. A village of Picardy, *Vaucmmur,* a village of Franche-, in the diocefe and eleition of Dou- Comté, in the bailiwick of Vefoul. lens. *p. Deviens. p. fefoul.* Vauchelles-le-Sl-*ntJjr.ay,* a villige of Norman Picardy, in the eleition of Doulens. dy, in the eleition of Caën. *p. Cain. p.* Doulens. *VaucouhiurSj* a town of Cham *VaucUmn.* I. A village of Bur-pagnc, firuated on a hill near the

£undy, in the bailiwick of Beaime. Mcufc, in the diocefe of Toul, and *p.* Beaune. 2. A place of Burgundy, generality of Châlons. *p V.ill.* dependant on the pnriih of Nolay, in *Vauaulmain,* a parifh of Bour thc bailiwick of Beaune. *p. Beaune.* bonnois, in the bailiwick of Mou *Vaucbomj'lllicrs,* a village of Cham-lins. *p. Moulins.* pagne, in the eleition of Bar-fm-*Vaucairt.* 1. A village of Meffin,

Aubc. *p. Vandceu-vre.* in the diocefe and receipt of McU.

Vaucboux, a village of Franche-*p. Metz.* 2. A place of Picardy, in Comté, in the bailiwick of VefouL the eleition of Péronnc. *p. Pcronne. p. Vejoul. Vasiawtois,* a village of Brie, in *Vaucbriùen.* 1. A fmall town of in the diocefe and eleition of Meauy. Anjou, in the eleition of Angers, *p.* Meaux. *p. Angus.* 2. Sec *Val-Cbre'tkn.* *Vaucretmnt,* a place of Meffin, in *Vauiienne.* J. A villageof Picardy, the diocefe and receipt of Metz. *p.* in the eleition of Cri-py. *p. CrCjy. Mttx.* 2. A village of Champagne, in the *VaucreJJbn,* a village of the Ifle eleition of Epernay. *p. Epernay.* of France, *p. Versailles. Vaudaire,z* village of Picardy, in *and-Lemct,* *le,* aplace of Marche, the diocefe and eleöion of Laon. *p.* in the election of Bourganeuf. *p. Lam, Bourganeuf. Vauclaujiy* a parifh of Provence, *VuudabUs.* See *loadable.* the jurifdiction of Alencon, in Normandy.

Vittdancourtf a village of Normandy, in the election of Gifors. *Gifors. Vaudangiertla,* a village of Marche, in the clcftion oí Bourganeuf. *p. Bourganeuf. Vaudationstle$ta* village of FrancheComté, in the bailiwick of Omans. *p. Befançon.* *Vaudebanicre,* a village of Burgundy, in the bailiwick, of Charollcs. *p. Dijon.* *VauJelr.ay, le,* a town of Po'tou, in the election of Thouars. *p. Tbcuars. Vaudeloges,* a village of Normandy, in the eleition of Argentan. /». *Trcuard. Vaudenefje,* a fma'l town of Burgundy, in the bailiwick, of Charollcs. *p. Dijon.* *Vaudes,* a village of Champagne, in the diocefe and election of Troves» *p. Troyes. Vaudejjon,* a village of Picardy, in the diocefe and election of Soiffons. *p. Soijjlns. Vaudev'uie,* a village of

Champagne, in the election of Chaumont. *p. Ep'tnal. Vaud.vin,* a village of Vivarais,in the diocefe and receipt of Viviers. *p. Anwnay. Vaude-vire,* a place of Normandy, near the town of Vire. *p. Vire. Vendeurs,* a town of Champagne, in the diocefe and election of Sens. /. *Sens. Vaudewvres,* a figniory of Champagne, in the election of Bar-iurAube. *Vaudey,* a village of FrancheComté, in the bailiwick of Gj,ay. *f. Gray. Vaudcûncwrt,* a village of Champagne, in the election of Rethcl. *p. Retbel. Vaudberlant,* a village of the Iflc f France, in the diocefe and election of París, *p. GcneJ/e. VaudUu.* See *Valdleu. Vaudttu, la4* a village of Auvergne. in the election of Brioude./». *Brkude. Vaudicu, le,* a village of Berry, in the election of Blanc, *p. le Blanc. Vaudpurjc,* a figniory of FrancheComté, in the bailiwick of Poligny. *p. Saüns, Vaudoncwr,* a place of FrancheCmté, in the bailiwick of Baume. *p. baume. Vaudoncourt,* a village of Meffin, in the diocefe and receipt of Verdun, *p. Verdun. Vaudey,* a village of Brie, in the election of Rozoy. *p. Rozoy. Vaudratn,* a village of Forez, in the election of Montbrifon. *p. Montbt* *ißn. Vaudrevange,* a village of Meífin, in the diocefe and receipt of Metz. *p. Sarlouis. Vaudreuil,le, or S. C:r-de-Vaudreuilt* a fmall town of Normandy, in the diocefe of Evreux, and election of Pont-de-l'Arche; 4. leagues from GaiUon, 6 from Evreux, 6 from Rouen, and 27 from Paris. *Bureau de pofte.* *Vaudre-ville. t.* A village of Normandy, in the election of V¿Iognes. *p. Carentan. 2.* A figniory of Normandy, in the election of Arques. *Vuudrey,* a village of FrancheComté, in the bailiwick of Dole. *p. Salins. Vaudñcourt. i.* A village of Normandy, in the election oí Eu. *p. Eu. 2.* A village of Artois, in the bailiwick of Bethun;. *p. Betbune. Vaudrimare,* a village of Normandy, in the dio:efc and election of Rouen, *p. Rouen. Vaudrimcnty* a village of Champagne, in the election of Bar-furAube. *p. Bar-jurAube. Vavdris-Mjnilj* a village of Normandy, in the election of S. *Lo. f. Coût anees. Vaudrn/iüerSf* a place of FrancheComté, in-the bailiwick of Baume. *p. Baumt. Vaujrey,* a place of

Alface, in the bailiw.ck of Dille, *p. Hun'mgue. Vaugencwr* a village of Franche Comté, in the bailiwick of Baurrfe. *p. Baume.*
Gauges. See *Vcj¿es.*
Vaugicn, a handiome château, near Chcvreufe. *p. Cbevreufe.*
Vaugir.oïs, a parim, of Burgundy, in the bailiwick oí Châtillon. *p. Mor. tbard.*
Vaugirard, a village of the lile of France, in the diocefe and election of Paris, *p. Paris. Vaugneray,* a fmall town'of Lyonnois, in the diocefe and election of Lyons, *p. Lyon. Vaugogne,* village of Champagne, in the election of Bar-fur-Aube. *¿. Bar-fur-Aibe. Vau-grain.* See *Valmagne. Vaugtineujey* a village of the Ifle of France, in the diocefe and election of Paris, *p. Arpajon.*
Vaugisy a place of Dauphiny, in the diocefe and election ot Vienne, jf. *Venne.*
Vaubalant & Limars, a village of the Ilk of France, in the diocefe and election of Paris, *p. Pans. Vaujalade9 la,* a place of Marche, in the election of Gueret. *p. Gutret. Vaujour,* a village of Anjou, in the election of Baugc. *p. le Lude. Vau-jour s £& Montauban,* a village of the Iíle of France, in the diocefe and election of Paris, *p. Ciaye. Vauladouce.* Sec *Yaux-la-Douce. Vauldry9* a fmall town of Normandy, in the election of Vire. *pt Pire. Vaulent,* a village of Dauphiny, in the election of Montelimart. *p. Monte limar r. Vaulrcnard,* a fmall town of Beaujolois, in the election of Ville-franche. *p. Villefranche. Vau1/e≥≥e≥* a village of Dauphiny, in the diocefe and election of Vienne. *p. Vienne. Vault, lat* a pariíh of Marche, in the election of Gueret. *p. Montluçon. Vault-de-Puh'de-Sacs,* a village of Burgundy, in the bailiwick of Novcrs. *p. Avalen. Vautuiùnt, u* An abby in the *VauriTty* a fmall town of Flanders, in the fuhdelegation of Lille, *p. Lille. Vaurh)* a village of Agénois, in the diocefe and election of Agen. *p. Vxllemuce-d' Agen. Vaurogne,* a village of FrancheComté, in the bailiwick of Vefoul. *p. Vefoul. Varoux,* a village of Picardy, in the diocefe and election of Bcauvais. *p. Beatevais. Vaurouy, /≥,* a village of Normady, in the election of Caudebec. *p. Caudebet. Vaury,* a village

of Limofin, in the diocefe and election oí Limuges. *p. Bcllac. Vaufry.* See *Volfcry. Vauβay* a town uf Poitou, in the diocefe and election of Poitiers, *p. Saufe. Vaujferoux,* a village of Poitou, in the diocefe and election of Poitiers, *p. Partenay. Vaujfy* a village of Normandy, in the election of Caën. *f. Caen. Vautebis,* a village of Poitou, in the diocefe and election of Poitiers. *p. Poitiers. Vauûerm'jfft,* a village of Alfncc, in the bailiwick, of Keffoit. *p. Before. Vau-tortt,* a town of Maine, in the flection of Mayenne, *p. Moyenne. Vawvenague,* a village of Provence, in the dioccfu and vigucry of-Aix. *p. Aix. Vavvertj* a town of Lower Languedoc, in the diocefe and receipt of Nîmes, *p. Tfimcs. Vawuille. i.* A village of Nor mandy, in the election of Valognes. *f. Valognes. z.* A village of Normandy, in the election of PontTKvcque. *p. Dofule.* 3. A village of Picardy, in the election of Péronne. *p. Pe'ronne. Vawviller:,z(m)* town of FrancheComté, in the bailiwick of Vefoul. *p. Vefoul. Vau-voy,* a village of Burgundy, in the diocefe and bailiwick of Challón *p. Challan.* Vau-vray, or 5. *Etienne tie V vray,* and *Vawvray,* or & *Pierrc-deVaui-ray,* villages of Normandy, in the etóion of Pont-de-Γ Arche, *p. Lcwvien. Vauvre-âc-Rh)* lay a figniory of Bourbonnnis, in the election of Gannat. *p. Gannat. Vauwyj* a village of Burgundy, in the bailiwick of AuXonne. *p. Auxonne. Vaux, i.* A town of Beaujolois, in the election of Ville-franche, *p. Villefrancbe.* 2. A town of Angoumois, in the election of Cognac, *p. U Rocbefoucault.* 3. A town of Sain-tonge, in the dioccfe and election of Saintes, *p. Coxex.* 4. A fmall town of Poitou, in the election of Châtelleraud. *p. Cbatdhraud.* 5. A fmall town of Ar-tois, in the bailiwick of Bapaume. *p. Ba-paume.* 6. A fmall town of Gatinois, in the election of Nemours, *p. Nemours.* 7. A village of Beauce, in the election of Mantes, *p. Mantes.* 8. A village of Provence, in the vigucry of Forcnlquier. *p. Forcalquicr.* 9. A village of Champagne, in the diocefe and election of Langres. *p. Retbcl. to.* A. village of Me-fiin, in the di», cefe and receipt of Metz. *p. Metz.* и. A village of Meiïin, in the

dioccfe and receipt of Verdun, *p. Verdun. x%.* A village of Picardy, in the diocefe and election of Amiens.. *Abb-wtlle,* 13. A village of Angoumois, in the diocefe and election of Angoulême. *p. Angoulême.* 14. A villageof Burgundy, in the diocefe and bailiwick of Dijon. *puɥ Dijon.* 15. A village of Burgundy, in the bailiwick of *Chfoon. p. Avalon.* i6. A villageof Franche-Comté, in the dioccfe and receipt of Befançon. *p. Bffançen.* 17. A village of Franche-Comté, in the bailiwick of" Poligny. *p. Salins.* 18. A village of Bourbonnois, in the election of S. Amand. */. S. Amand.* 19. A village of Picardy, in the election of S. Quentin, *p. S. Quentin.* 20. A village of Meffin, in the dioccfe and receipt of Toul. *p. Tout. 21.* A vil.
Vayresj a fmali town of Cuienne, in the diocefe and election of Bourdeaux. *p. Libaurne Vays, leSy* (what they alfo call Ones) the name given to the mouths of the rivers Vire, Our, and Aure, in Marche. *Vaxálles.* I. A village of Lower Laneuedoc, in the election of Brioude. *p. Brioudc. z* A viilagcof Auvergne, in the diocefe and receipt of Puy. *f. h Buy. Vazeih'es* &f *Jffarles,* a village of Lower Languedoc, in the dioceieand receipt of Viviers, *p. Viviers. Ya-zouy,* a village of Normandy, in the ele¿tion of Pont-l'Eveque. *p. Honβeur. Ubaye,* a fmall river of Provence, which loofes ibfelf in the Durance. *Ubaye-Sanci';ot* a village of Provence, in the viguery of Seine, *p. Seine. Uberaebj* a village of Alface, in the jurifdiction of Wingeriheim. *p. Hagucnau. Uberkiminen,* a village of Alface, in the bailiwick, of Thann, *p. Rouffach. Uberβrals,* a village *of* Alface, in the bailiwick of Altkirch, *p. Alt Hrebt Ubrayey* a village of Provence, in the viguery of CafteHane./». *Caβellane.*
Uceîj a village of Vivarais, in the receipt of Viviers, *p. Aubenas. Uchon,* a village of Burgundy, in the bailiwick of Montcenis. *p. Autun. Ve.* I. An ancient chateau of Picardy, fituated between Crèpy and Villers-Cotterets. *p. Crfyy.* 2. See *Vays. Veaucbe,* and *Veaucbcttey* villages of Forez, in the election of Mont-brifon. *p. Montbrifon. Veaunaty* a fmall town of Péri, gord, in the diocefe and election of Périgueux. *p. Pe'/igueux.*

Veaune, a river of Provence, that difcharges itfelf into the fea near Marfcilles. *VcüuuiSy* a village of Berry, ш the diocefe and election of Bourges. *p. Bourgs, Vcaujfiy* a pariih of Bourbonnois, in the election of Gannat. *p. Cannât. Vcawu'ille,* a place of Normandy, in the election of Caudcbec. *p. Iveu. Vcawville-fur-les-Eaons,* a village of Normandy, in the election of Caudebec. /1. *Ivctot. Vebre and Urs,* a (mail town of Foix, in the generality of Rouiiillon. *p. Tarafcon-en-Foix. Veirety* a town of Auvergne, in the diocefe and election of S. Flour. *p. S. Flour. Vebron,* a village of Lower Languedoc, in the diocefe and receipt of Mende. *p. Florae. Vecemonty* a village of Alface, in the bailiwick of Beffort. *p. Begirt. Vecoursy* a village of BreiTe, in the bailiwick of Bourg, *p. Bourg-enBɜʄ. yecquenÀÎle,zV'Agt* of Champagne, in the election of Joinville. *p. Joinmil lc. Vede,* a fmall river of Touraine, which falls into the Vienne near Chinon. *Vedie.* See *Vendee. Vedenes,* a village of Venaiffin, in the judicature of. Carpcntras. *p. Avignon. Vedllhon,* a place of Lower Languedoc, in the diocefe and receipt of Narbonne. *p. Nùrbonne. Vcdrenas,* a village of Marche, in the election of Gueret. *p. Gutret. Vedrenneiy* a village of Limofin, in the diocefe and election of Tulles. *p. Tulles. Vedrims-S.-Loup,* a village of Auvergne, in the diocefe and election of S. Flour, *p. Brtoude. Vedrimttes,* a village of Roucrgue, in the diocefe and election оі Rhodcz. *p. Rhode. Vedrinyans,* and *Cruellsy* place of Roufnllon, in the vigucry of Cerdsgne. *p. Perpignan. yefvres-fivt-ÇbâlariCÊ,* a village of Champagne, in the diocefe and election of Langrts.. *Langres. Vegre,* or *Vejgre,* a fmall river of Hurcpoix, which fails into the Eure, a little above Yvry. *VchaU)* a village of Lower Languedoc, in the diocefe and receipt of Nîmes, *p. Nîmes. Vehty & Pcnit-cy,* a village of Eurgundy, in the bailiwick of Arnaylc-Duc. *p. Dijon. Vebey ¿if Porcey,* a place in the bailiwick f Arnay-le-Duc. *p. Dijon. Vcbixy,* a village of Burgundy, in the diocefe and bailiwick of Macon, *p. Tcumis. Vtboy* a village of Meffin, in the diocefe and receipt of Metz, *p. Metz. Vàgnc* a town of Touraine, in the diucefe and election of Tours, *p. Tears. Vcignols,* a town of Limofin, in the eTection ot Brives. *p. Brives. Veigfcheid,* a village of Alface, in the bailiwick of Beffort.. *Beffort. Veillarmafayty* a village of Lower Languedoc, in the diocefe aпЭ receipt of Puy. *p. le Puy. VUlers,* a village of Brie, in the election of Provins, *p. Provins. Veille,* a river of Dombcs, that runs into the Sâone near Macon. *Veilles,* a village of Upper Langue. doc, in the diocefe and receipt 01 Lavnur. *p. Lavaur. Veiilcy, let* a village of FrancheComté, in the bailiwick of Poligny. *p. Salins. Vt.i'!y-fiusyÇntlgny%* a village of Burgundy, in the bailiwick of Beauce. *p. Beaune. Vexmbeys,* a village of Meffin, in thediocicle and receipt of Verdun, *p, Yeblun. Veimcrange,* a village of Mefiin, in the diocefe and receipt of Metz.. *p. Met%, Veines,* or *5. Georgesde-Venes,* a village of Agénois, in the diocefe and. election of Agen. *p. Sigen. Vcmterol.* See *Vtnterol. VeiraSy* a village of Lower Languedocj in the diocefe and receipt cf vU icr«. *p. Viviers. l'eißembourg.* See *Wtiffembcurg. Veix,* avill.igc ot Limofm, in the election of Tulles, *f. ЧMn. Veive,* a village of Lvnnnois, in the diocefe and election ti Lyons, *p. Lyon. Vekring, л* vilhge of Merlin, in the dioctfj and receipt of A'ctz. *p. Metí. Vdainet,* a village of Flanders, in the fubdelegation of Lille, *p. Lille. Vilaines 6? Romemont,* a village of Meffin, in the receipt of Vic. *f. Vic. Vclanet, la. I.* A fmall town of Upper Languedoc, in the diocefe and receipt of Mirepoix. *p. Mirepoix.* 2. A village of Upper Languedoc, in the diocefe and receipt of Rieux. *j. Toulcufe. Velanr. c-la-V.l!e,* and *Velanne-leXcis,* figniories in the diocefe of Rouen. *Velrj-s-Dompiene,* n village of Burgundy, in the bailiwick of Senior, *p. Semur. Velars-Ies-Potiilly,* a village of Burgundy, in the bailiwick of Arnaylc-Duc. *p. Dijon. Velars-fur-l' Oucte,* a village of Burgundy, in the diocefe and bailiwick of Dijon, *p. Dijen. Velaux,* a village of Provence, in the viguery of Aix. *p. le Mortigües. Velay, le,* a country of Lower Languedoc, bordered on the eaft by Vivarais, on the fouth by Gevaudan, on the welt by Auvergne, and on the north by Forez. This country is fertile, although the mountains are covered with fnow near fix months in the year; the principal commerce is in cattle. Le Pay is the capital. *Vclercn,* a village of Venaiflin, in the judicature of Lille, *p. Avignon. Vclefmr,* a village of Franche-Comté, in the bailiwick of Qmngey. *p. Befançcn. Velfring,* a place of Meffin, in the diocefe and receipt of Metz. *p. Met%. Vdie,* a village of Champagne, in the diocefe and receipt of Chulons. *p. Chalons. V. lkux, я* village of Lower Languedoc, in the diocefe and receipt of S. Pons. *p. Béziers. Veñr.es,* a fmall И'ч of Périgord, in the diocefe and election of Périgueux, *p. Sie. Fey. Vdie-Franche,* a pkee of FrancheComté, in the bailiwick of Gray. *p. Gray. Velle-h-Chaflel,* a village of Franche-Comté, in the bailiwick of Vefoul. *p. Vefoul. Velle-fous-Guerey,* or *5. Philibert,* a village of Burgundy, in the diocefe and bailiwick of Dijon, *p. Dijsn. Velle-jur-Amanee,* a village of Champagne, in the diocefe and election of Langres. *p. Langres. Vellecbes,* a village of Touraine, in the election of Chinon. *p. Chino». Vellefaux,* a village of FrancheComté, in the bailiwick of Vefoul. *p. Vefoul. Velleferrot,* a place of Franche Comté, in the bailiwick of Vefoul. *p. Vefoul. Vellefrey,* a village of FrancheComté, in the bailiwick of Gray. *p. Gray. Veilefrie £f Ste. Marie,* a village of Franche-Comté, in the bailiwick of Vefoul. /. *Vcßul. Velleilair,* a place of FrancheComté, in the bailiwick of Gray. *p. Gray. Vellemont,* a village of FrancheComté, in the bailiwick of Gray. *p. Gray. Vellcnne,* a village of Picardy, in the election of Beauvais. *p. Beauvais. Veïicnnes,* a village of Picardy, in the diocefe and election of Amiens. *p. Amiens. Vdlequmdry,* a village of FranchsComté, in the bailiwick of Vefoul *p. Vefoul. Vellerot-les-Verfel,* and *Vellera. les-Blcrcye,* villages of Franche; Comté, in the bailiwick of Baume. *p. Baume, Vellerot-S.-Pierre,* a villageof Burgundy, in the bailiwick of Arnayle-Duc. *p. Dijon. Velleroy-les-Boii, Velleroy-lesBellevauxt* and *Velleroy-Lorioi,* places of Franche-

Comté, in the bailiwick of Vefoul. *p. VefouL VeUes,* a village of Berry, in the election of Châtcauroux. *p. Châteauroux".* , *Vellejcol,* a place of Alface, in the bailiwick of Delle, *p. Humngue. Vellejme,* a village of FrancheComté, in the bailiwick of Gray. *p.. Gray.. JPellevantj* a village of FrancheComté, in the bailiwick of Baume. *p. Baume. Vellezon,* a village of-FrancheComté, in the bailiwick of Gray., *p. Gray. VelioreHleles-Fretignyj,* and *Velioreille-lis-Oifelaya* places of FrancheComté, in the bailiwick of Gray. *p. Gray. Velluire,* or *S. Jean-de-Velluire,,* a village uf Poitou, in the election of Fontenay. *p. Fontenay-le-Comte. Velluyt* a fmall: town of Normandy, in the election of S. Lo. *Vdoïgny,* a village of Burgandy, in the bailiwick of Semur. *p. Semur. Vdorcey,.* a village of FrancheComté, in the bailiwick of Vefou!. *p. VejouL Velus,* a village of Artois, in the bailiwick of Bapaume. *p. Bapaume. Vely,* a chatellany of Picardy,, in the diocefe of Suiflons» *Vcmars,* a village of the lile of France, in the diocefe and election of Paris, *p. Louvre. Vemue, la,* an abby in Berry. *Venables,* a village of Normandy, in the election of Andely. *p. bouviers. Venaijfih, le Comté,* a country bordered on the eaft and fouth by Provence, on the weft by the Rhone, which feparatcs it from Languedoc, and on the north by Dauphiny; it is divided into 3 judicatures, that of Lille, Carpentras, and Valreas; the land is fertile in corn and wine, and well watered by the Rhône, the Durance, the Sorgue, and the Ouvefe. Carpentras is the principal town. *Venanceau,* a fmalJ town of Poitou, in the election of Sables-d'Olonne« *p. Beaulieu. Venarrey,* a village of Burgundy, in the bailiwick of Semur. *p. Sie. Reine. Venas Êf Broffi,* a village of Bourbonnois, in the election of Montlujon. *p. Montluçon. Vmafjue,* an ancient town of Venailhn, liluated on a mountain near the river Nefque, about 2 leagues from, Carpentras, *p. Avignon. Vencay,* a fmall town of Maine, in. the election of Château-du-Loir. *p. Cbâteau-du-Loir.. Vence,* an ancient city of Provence,, in Ae generality of Aix, fituated on the frontiers of Piedmont,

the fee of a bilhopr; about 2 leagues, from Antibes, and 4 from Grafle. *p. Antibes. Vencby,* a village of Normandy, in. tho election of Arques, *p.. Dieppe Vindaint,* a village of Brcue, in. the bailiwick, of Bourg, *p. Biurgen-BreJji. Vcndahves,* a village of Rouergue, in the election of Milhaud. *p. Mdbaud. Vendargues,* a village of Lower Languedoc, in ttie diocefe and receipt of Montpellier, *p. Montpellier-, Vendat & Cougnat,* a village of Bourbonnois, in the election of Moulins, *p. Gannett.. Vendiiys,* a village of Guienne, in the diocefe and election of Bourdcaux.. *p. Jkwdeawe. Vendelic,* a village of Picardy, in the. election of S. Quentin, *p. S. Quentin. Vendeicigne,* a village of Poitou, in the diocefe andtlection of Eoitiers... *p. Poitiers. Vendemian,* a village of Low«. Languedoc, in the diocefe and receipt of Rézicrs. *p. Gignac. Vender.ejfe.* See *Vanâtneffe. VendtnbtiMy* a village of Alfacc, in the diocefe of Straíburg. *p. Strafbourg. Vendes,* a village of Normandv, in the election of Caen. *p. Bayeux. VendeuiL* t. A town of Picardy, in the diocfe and election of Noyon. *p. S. Quentin, 2.* A v il läge of Champagne, in the diocefe and election of Rheims, *p. Rheims. Vendeuli (& (bplyy* a village of Picardy, in the election of Mondidier. *Mondidier. Vendeuure,* i. A town of Champagne, in the diocefe and election of Troyes; about 3 leagues'from Barfur-Aube. *Bureau de pcjîe.* z. A town of Poitou, in the diocefe and election of Poitiers, *p. Poitiers. Verdeares,* a village of Normandy, in the election of Falaifc. *p. rcuard. Vendiere,* a vülap? of Champagne, in the vülap? of Epernay. *p. Monttnirel. Vtndome,* a city of Beauce, filiated on the Loire, in the diocefe of Blois, and generality of Orléans, the i'eat of a bailiwick, election, &c. 15 bagues from Tours, 10 from ChiW tcaudun, 22 from Chartres, and 44 from Paris. *Bureau de poße. VendCmois, le,* a country of Beauce, tordered on the eaft by Dunois, on ihe fouth by Tourainc, on the weft by Maine, and on the north by Perche j it is fertile in grain and 'fruit. *Vendu y* a place of Lower Languedoc, in the diocefe and receipt of jPuy. *p. leVuy. Vendrez,* i. A town of Lower Langue-

doc, in the diocefe and receipt of Béziers. *p. Béziers %.* A fmall fea port of Rouffittoo. *p. Coliioure. Vendreffe* fif *la Caffine,* a fmall town of Champagne, in the election of RetheL *p. Sedan. Vcndrijj'e,* a village of Picardy, in the diocefe and election of *Lion, p. Laon. Vendréis,* a fma'l town of Brie, in the diocefe and election ofMeaux. *p. Lky. Vendue-Afigmt, la,* a village of Champagne, in the diocefe and election of Troyes, *p. troyes. Fendues,* a wood of 70 arpents, in thejiirifdiétion of Troyes, in Champagne. *Vendvdle,* a village of Picardy, in the election of S. Quentin, *p. S, Quentin. Venccy,* a village of Orléannois, in the diocefe and election of Orléans, *p. Orleans. Vemffe,* a village of Bretagne, in the diocefe and receipt of Rennes. *p. Rennes. Ventges-aux-Bm,* a village of Hainaut, in the government of Landrecy. *p. Landrecy. Vencgies-fur-Efcaïllon,-z* village of Hainaut, in the government of Quènov. *p. Valenciennes. Venenan,* a village of Lower Languedoc, in the dioceie and receipt of Uzés. */. Uses. Venelle,* a fmall river of Burgundy. *Venelles,* a village of Provence-, in the dioccfc and viguery of Aix. *p. Aix. Venere,* a village of FrancheC iraré, in the bailiwick of Gray. *p. Gray. Venenlles,* a village of Picardy, in the election of Guife. *p. Guije. Venejme,* a village of Berry, in the election of Iifoudun. *p. Lignieres. Vtmflanvdle,* a village of Normandy, in the election of Arques. *p. S. Valery-en-Catix. Venefvifk,* a village of Normandy, in the election of Caudebcc. *p. Cany. Vtnetce,* a village of Picardy, *in* the election of Compiégne. *p. Cm pie'gne. Veneufe,* a village of Burgundy, in the diocefe and bailiwick of ChaN Ion. *f. Cial/te. YeneuxbI Vadon,* a village of Brie,., in the election-of Montereau. *p. Aienter eau. Veneyrieu,* a village of Dauphiny, in the diocefe and élection of Vienne. *f. Bourgo'm. Yeneъ & Chef culs,* a village of Lower Languedoc» in the diocefe and receipt of Caftres. *p. Caflres. Vengeons,* a town of Normandy, in the election of Mortain. *p. Vire. Yemeъ,* a town of Poitou, in the. election of Loudun. *p. Lou.un. Veniot,* a village of Nivernois, in the election of Vezelay.

p. Vt%elay. Venifc, a village of FrancheComté, in the bailiwick of Vefoul. /. Ш *J; en'ifl'ieu,* a village of Dauphiny, in the dioccfe and eleition of Vienne. *J. Vienne. Verify-Chaîlie',* a town of Champagne, in the election of Joigny. *p. ¿. Florentin. Venvzel,* a village of Picardy, in the dioccfe and election of Soiflons-. *P. Soijjisns. Venk'e,* a river of Normandy, which runs into the little harbour of Cingrtfville. *Vennans,* a place of FrancheComté, in the bailiwick, of Baimie. *p. Baume,* y *Venncgies-aux-Bcis.* See *Vcneg-.esaux-Bois. Vennes,* т. A place of FrancheComté, in the bailiwick of Omans. *p. Befançon.* 2, See *Vannes. Venoix,* a place of Normandy j in the election of Caen. *p. Caen. Venon.* i. A village of Normandy, in the eleition of Pont-de-ГArche. *p. bouviers,* 2. A village of Dauphiny, in the diecefe and election of Grenoble, *p. Grenoble. Venouffe,* a village of Champagne, in the election of S. Florentin, *p. S. Florentin. Venoy,* a village of Burgundy, in th dioccfe and bailiwick of Auxerre.. *p. Auxerre. Venjac,* a village of Guienne, in, the dioccfe and election of Bourdeaux. *p. Bourdeaux. Ventabrent* a fmall town of Provence, in the diocéfé and vigucry of Aix. *p. Aix. Ventadour,* л chateau in the dîocefe of Limoges, *p. Tulles. Vintation,* or *S. Maurlcc-de-Ventation,* a village of Lower Languedoc, in the diocefc and receipt of Uzes. *p. U%cs. Ventejoul,* a village of Limofin, in the diocefe and election of Tulles *p. Tulles. Vtntelay,* a village of Champagne, in the diocefe and election of Rheims. *p. Fiâtes. Vtntenacr* I. A village of Upper Languedoc; in the diocefe and receipt of Mirep'iix. *p. Mircpoix.* 2. A village of Upper Languedoc, in the dioccfe and receipt of CarcaiTonne. *p. CarcaJ'onne.* 3. A village of Lower Languedoc, in the diocefe and receipt of Narbonne. *p. Narionnt. Venterol, l.* A village of Provence, in the vigucry of SHtcron. *p. Sijierun.* 1. A place of Dauphiny, *in.* the election of Montelimart. *p. Montelmarir Vente.-d'Eaüy, lesy* a market-town of Nurmandy. in the election of Arques, *p. Udlemare. Vcntes-de-Bonrfes, les,* a fmall town of Normandy, in the election of Alençon.

p. le Meße-fur-Sarte. Venteuilf a fmall town of Champagne, in the election of Epsrnay. *p. Epemtjy. Venteuil & Bautcrejje,* a figniory of Bourbonnois, in the election of Gannat. *p. Gannat. Ventilhc,* a village of Upper Languedoc, in the dioccfe and receipt of Montauban. *p. Montauban. Venioux,-a* place of Burgundy, in the dioccfe and bailiwick, of Dijon. *p. DijM. f Ventowse,* a village of Sai.ntonge, in the election of S. Jean-d'-Angely. *p. S. "Jcan-d'-Angely. Venxaim,* a fmall town of Perigord, in the diocefe and election of Périgueux. *p. Pe'rigueux. Vwúeu,* a fmall town of Vivarais, in the diocefe and receipt of Viv'rers. *p. Viv'ers. Ver.* I. A fmall town of Normandy, in the diocefe and election f Coùtanccs. *p. Cou'.ancei.* 2. A imall town of Normandy, in the diocefe and election of Bayeux. *p. Baycux.* 3. A village of Picardy, in the diocefe and election of Senlis. *p. Dammartin. Veracieux,* a village of Dauphiny, in the election of Romans, *p. S. Marcellin. Veranges,* a fmall river of Languedoc, which runs into the pond of Thau. *Veranne,* a village of Forez, in the election of S. Etienne, f. *S. Etienne. Verargues,* a place of Lower Languedoc, in the diocefe and receipt of Montpellier, *p. Montpellier. Verber'ie,* a town of Picardy, fituated on the Qifc, in the diocefe of Senlis, and election of Compiégne; it has a fpring of mineral waters; about 4 leagues from Compiégne, 3' from Senlis, 7 from Dammarcin, and 13 from Par's. *Bureau de poße. Verhieße,* a village of Champagne, in the election of Chaumont. *p. Cbaumont-en-Bßtgny-. Verbcis,* or *S Nicclas-du-Verbvis,* a village of Normandy, in the d occfe and election of Rouen, *p. NcyersMlnard. Verhojc, le,* a village of Normandy, in the election of Caudebec. *p. Tvctcr. Vercamere, la,* a place of Quercy, in the diocefe and election of Cahors. *p. Cabors Vereay,* a village of Touraine, in the diotife and election of Tours. *p. Tours. Vercel,* a fmall town of FrancheComté, in the receipt of Ornans. *p.* Ше. *Vcrcbampt,* a-pacc of FrancheComté, in the bailiwick о£ Ycfoul. /i *VejtuL Verebt,* or *S. Piirrc-de-VeráeTroïs-Hameaux,* a town of Anjou,

in the election of Montreuil-Bellay. *p. Saumur. Verde',* or 5. *Juß-de-Verche',* a village of Anjou, in the election of Montrcuil-ЧеЦау. *p. Saumur. Vercheres,* a place of Lower Languedoc, in the diocefe and receipt of Puy. *p. le Puy. Verchin Maugrf,* a village f Hainaut, in the diocefe of Cambray. *p. Valenciennes. Verebiy,* a village of Burgundy,, in the bailiwick of Semur. *p. ViCeaux. VercUfeuil. T.* A place of Burgundy, in the diocefe and bailiwick of Mâcon. *p. Macon.* 2. A place of Burgundy, in the diocefe and receipt of Auxerre. *p. Macon. Vercbby,* a place of Burgundy, in the bailiwick of Semur-en-Auxois-*p.Semur-en-AuxoU. Vercbocq,* a village of Boulonnois, in the generality of Amiens, *p. shniens. Vercia,* a village of Franche-Comté, in tbe bailiwick of Lons-lc-Saunier. *p. Lons-lc-Säunier. Vercieu & Anclenoud,* a village of Dauphiny, in the diocefe and election of Vienne, *p. Baitrgom. Vcrrigmcs-Maquignyy* a village о£ Picardy, in the diocefe and election, of Laon. *p. la Fere. Verein,* a village of Dauphiny, in the diocefe and/ election of. Vienne» *p. Vienne Verclaufe & Clermont,* a village of Dauphiny, in the election of Montelimart. *p. Momelimart. Verccirаn,* a village of Dauphiny,. in the election of Montelinurt. . /« *Buii. Vcrcourt,* a parifli of Picardy, in the election of Abbeville, *p. Àbic tAilc. Verä-Efpargnat, le,* a place of. Marthe, in tie election of Gueret. *p. Gueret. Vtrdacbes,* a village of Provence», in the viguery of Seine, *p. Digne.* 3 *ferdalle,* a fmall town of Upper Languedoc, in the diocefeand receipt of Lavaur. *p. Caßres. Verdelot,* a fmall town of Brie, in the election of Château-Thierry. *p. la Ferte-Gaucbcr. Verderonne,* a village of Picardy, in the election of Clermont. *p. Clermont. Verdes,* a village of Beauce, fituated near a lake of the fame name, in the election of Châteaudun. /. *Châteaudun. Verdeja* a village of Brie, in the election of Sezanne, *p. Sezanne Verdezun & Laffa'zes,* a village of Lower Languedoc, in the diocefe and receipt of Mcndc. *p. Mer.de. Verdler,* the name of a vicomte in Limofin.. *p. Usserches. Verdier, le,* a town of Upper Languedoc, in the dio-

cefe and receipt of AI by. *p. Ally. Verdiere,* a village of Provence, in the viguery of Barjo's. *P. BarjoU Vcrdigny,* a village of Berry, in the diocefe and election of Buurges. *p. Bourges. Verfalle,* a town of Angoumois, ifl the election of Cognac, *p. Aigre. Verdúly,* a village of Brie, in the election of ChâteauThierry, *p. Ctá teau Thierry, Verdun.* I. A village of Périgordj in the diocefe and election of Sarlat. *p. Bergerac, z.* A village of Brie, in the election of ChâteauThierry, *p. Montmirel.* 3. A river cf Provence, that falls into the Durance, a little below Manofque.. *Verdonnay,.* a viHage of Burgundy, in the bailiwick, of Semur. *p.Montbard. Verdun,* i. An ancient and flrong city of Mcffin, fituated on the Mcufe, in the generality of Metz, the fee of a biihop; 15 leagues from Metz, X9 from Thionville, 23 from Frifange, 23 from Sarlouis, 40 from Sarebourg, ϕ from Saverne, 22 from Nancy, 29 from i-uneville, 67 from Landau, 75 from Spire, 55 from Siralburg, 52 from Schcleftat, 57 from Colmar, 10 from Montmedy, 14 from Longwy, 19 from Sedan, 46 from Liege, 24 from Mczieres, 31 tromRocrcy, 37 from Chimay, 44 from Avefnes, 55 from Valenciennes, 68 from Lille, 87 from Dunkirk, 48 from Maubeuge, 64 from BrufTcls, 58 from Cambray, 66 from Arras, 64 from Douay, 10 from Stc. Manéhould, 20 from Châlons, 30 from Rheirñs, 41 from Laon, 3 from Lan gres, 49 from Vcfoul, 57 from Dijon,. 104 from Lyons, and 6o£ from Paris. *Bureau de pcfie.* 2. A city of Burgundy, fituated at the conflux of the Doux and the Saône; about 7 leaguesfrom Challón, and 12 from Dijon, *p. Challón.* 3. A city of Arnngnac, the capital of RivièreVerdun, fituated on the Garonne, about 8 leagues from Touloufe. *p. Grenade.* 4. A village of Upper L:tngucdoc, in the diocefeand receipt of S. Papuul. *p. Caßelnaudary,* 5, A village of Rouergac, in the diocefe and election of Rhodez. *puȵ Ricdcz.* 6. See *Riviere-Verdun Verdun & S. Counat,* a fmall town of Foix, in the generality of Roufiillon. *pTarajeon-cnl'Jx. Verdun-S.-Prejet,* a fmall town of Lower Languedoc, in the diocefe and receipt of Mcnde.. *p. Mende. Verdunoisj* a fmall province of Lorraine, bordering on Champagne, of which Verdun is the capital. *Vcrduxan,* a village of Armagnac, in the diocefe and election of Auch. *P.. Condcm, Veré,* a fmall town of Poitou,, in the election of Sablesd'Olonne. *p, lei Sables, VerejneSy* a village of Auvergne,.in the diocefe and election of S. Flour, *p. S. Flour. Veret,* a village of Normandy,, in the diocefe and election of Bayeux. *p.Iftgny. _ Verets,* a tow.n of Touraine, fituated on the Cher, in the diocefe and election of Tours, *p. Tours» VenuXf* a village of FrancheCom .Че, io the bailiwick of Gray, *f. Gray. Verey,* a village of Burgundy, in the bailiwick, of Beaune. *p. Beaune. Vtrfatil.* i. A town of Upper Languedoc, in the diocefe and receipt of Toiuoufc. *p. Tiukuje.* %. A village of Roucrgue, in the election of Viilefranche. *p. Villejranche-de. Rauergue.* 3. A village of Lower Languedoc, in he diocefe and receipt of Utes« *p. Bagnoli. Vcrfomalnt,* a place of FrancheComté, in the bailiwick, of Gray. *'p. G ray. Ver gaville.* See *'"ergav'dl;. Vergeal,* a viiage of Bretagne, in the diocefe and receipt of Rennes, *p. Vitre'. Vergeas,* a village of Bourbonnais, in the election of Gannat. *p. Gannat, Verger,* or *Norre-Dame-duVerger,* a convent between Douay and Cambray, *p Camhray. Verger, le,* the name of a château in Anjou, *p la Flèche. Vergeron,* or *S. Hypo!ite-du-Vergeron,* a village of Aunis, in the diocefe and election of Rochelle, *p. Rockefort. Verges,* a place of Franche-Comté, in the bailiwick, of Lons-lc-Saunier. *P. Lens-le-Saunier. Vergeßbn,* a village of Burgundy, in the diocefe and bailiwick of Macon, *p. Macon. Vergeto,* л village of Normandy, in the eleilion of Montivilliers. *p. S. Romain. Vergezac,* a village of Lower Languedoc, in the diocefe and receipt of Puy. *p. le Pay. Vergebe,* a fmall town of Lower Languedoc, in the diocefe and receipt of Nîmes *p. Calvißon. Vergief le,* and *Vergier, k,* villages of Picardy, in the election of S. Quentin, *p. S. Quentin. Vergies le Fay,* a fmall town of Picardy, in the election of S. Quentin., *p. S. Quentin. Vergigny Arboujfeau,* a village of Champagne, in the election of Joigny. *p. S. Florentin. Vergifjèn,* a village of Burgundy, in the diocefe and receipt of Màcon. *p. Mácon. Verglus,* a village of Armagnec, in the diocefe and election oí Auch. *p. Auch. Vergnas, las,* a village of Li mofin, in the diocefe and election of Limoges, *p. Limoges. Vergne, la.* 1. A town of Saintongc, in the election of S. Jeand'Angely. *p S. Jean-d'Angely.* 2. A village of Agénois, in the diocefe and-election of Agen. *p. Agen.* 3. A village of Rouergue, in the election of Milhaud. *p. Mdbaud.* 4. Se *Verne. Vergne,* a village of Poitou, in the election of Niort,,/. *Nhrt. Vergnies,* a village of Hainaut, in the government of Maubeuge. *p. Maubeuge. Vergence* a village of Normandy, in the diocefe and election of Avranches. *p. Avranches. Vergongbon,* village of Auvergne, m the election of Iffoire, /. *Brioudc. Vergönne,* a town of Anjou, in the diocefe and election of Angers. *p. Angers. Vcrgons,* a village of Provence, in the viguery of Caftellane. *p. Caftellanc. Verdamme,* a village of Franche» Comte, in the bailiwick, of Baume. *p. Baume. Vtrguelliere,* a valley of Foix, by the Larger.
Vergy, a village of Burgundy, in the bailiwick of Nuits, *p. Nuits. Vet'ignon,* a village of Provence, in the viguery of Draguignan. *p. Barjolt. Verigny,* a village of Beaucc, in the diocefe and election of Chartres. *p. Chartres. Verineourt-la-Forge,* a village of Champagne, in the election of Chaumont. *p. Cbaumont-enBaJJigny. Verines,* a town of Aunts, in the diocefe and election of Rochelle, *p, la Rscbelle. Verjo/ay,* a village of Picardy, in the election of Abbeville, *p. Deutens. Vcrjony* a town of Brefie, in the. bailiwick, of Bourg, *p. Bourg-enBreffe. Verifety* a village of Burgundy, in the dio..efe and bailiwick of ivlàcon. *p. Louant. Verijfey,* a pariíh of Burgundy, in the bailiwick of Challón. /. *Challen. Verjus,* a village of Burgundy, in the bailiwick of S. Laurent, *p. Challan. Verlbac-de-Tefcou,* and *Verlbac-S.Jean-V Hôpital,* villages of Upper Languedoc, in the diocefc and receipt of Montauban. *p.Mmtauban. Verlieu,* a village of ïorez, in tht election of S. Eti-

enne, *p. S. Etienne.* Vtrün, a viilage of Champagne, 'in the election of Joigny. *Vi.lencuve-jur Yonne.* V.rimBun, a village of Bourbonnois, in the generality of Amiens, *p. Boulogne.* Verhiugj a village of Artois, in the receipt of S. Pol. *p. Arras.* Verio, an abby m the diocefc of Quimpcr, in Bretagne, *p. Stumper.* Vtr-ly, a village of Picardy, in the election of Guife. *p. Roye.* Vermandy a town of Picardy, in the election of S. Quentin; about 3 leagues fromS. Quentin, and 4 from Péronne. *p. S. ¡¿fuentiñ.* Vermandauvilier, a village of Picardy» in the election of Ретотпе. *p. Perenne.* Vermandois, a country of Picardy, bordered on the eaft by Thierache, on the fouth by Noyonnois, on the weft by Santerre, and on the north by Cambrefis; it is very fertile in grain and flax. S. Quentin is the capital..1 Vermantes, See *Vernantes.* Vermanton, a town of Burgundy, fituated on the river Eure, in the road between Dijon and Auxerre; 6 leagues from Avalon, 5 from Auicrre, 12 from Joigny, 19 from Sens, 29 from Dijon, and 47 from Paris. *Bureau d: poße.* V¿manes fef *Marijjcn,* a village of Artois» in the bailiwick of Lens. *p. la Bл/ e'e.* Vermeils, a village of Lower Languedoc, in the diocefe and receipt of Alais. /. *Alais.* Vtrmo'von, a village of Burgundy, in the bailiwick of Avalon, *p. Avalon.* VermonJans, a village of FrancheComtü, in the bailiwick or Baumc. *p. Baume,* Vertty a town of Anjou, in the diocefe and election of Angers, *p. Angers.* Vernadc, lay a village of Auvergne, in the election of Riom. *p. Riom.* Virnaj.ul-la-BouiJJÎ, a village of Foix, in the generality of Rouiflllon. *p. Foix.* Vemaißn, avillane of Lyonnoiç, in the diocefe and election of Lyon. *p. Ly:n.* Vtrmaneottrt, a village of Champagne, in the diocefe and election of Chalons, *p. Vury,* VettanttSy a market-town of Anjou, in the election of Ваш;е; about % leagues from Bourgueuil, and 3 from Sauraur. *p. B auge.* Vernaniots-, a viiage of FrancheComté, in the bailiwick of Lons-leSaunier. *p. L.m-le-Saunter.* Vernasy a village of Daupbiny, in the diocefe and election of Vienne, *p. Bourgoin.* Ver nay. I. A village of Bour bonnois, in the election

of S. Amind. *p. S. Amand.* 2. A village of Beaujolois, in the election of Villefranche. *p. Belleville.* Vernay, la, a village of FrancheComté, in the bailiwick of Befançon. *p. Befancon.* Vernay, or 5. Baul-de-Vcrnayy a fmall town of Normandy, in the diocefe and election of Baycux. *pл B ay eux.* Verne, i. A village of FraachcComté, in the bailiwick of Baume. *p. Baume,* 2, A place of Bretagne
in the diocefe and receipt of Rennes. *f. Rennes.* Verne, la, a charter-hou fe of Provence, in the diocefe of Toulon. *p. Toulon.* Verneguet, le, a village of Provence, in the viguery of Aix. *p. Lambejc.* Verneige, a village of Auvergne, in the election of Combrailles. *p. Chambón.* Verneil. I. A town of Anjou, in the eleaion of Flèche, *p. la Flèche.* a. A town of Anjou, in the election ef Baugé. *p. Baugé.* Vemàx, a village of Bourbonnois, in the election of Montluçon. *p. Montluçon.* Vernet, a village of Auvergne, in the election of Riom. *p. R':om.* Veinct, le, I. A village of Bourbonnois, in the election of Moulins. *p Gannat.* z. A village of Upper Languedoc, in the diocefe and receipt of Touloufe. *p. Touloufe.* 3. A village of Auvergne, m the election of Brioudc. *p. Br'wude.* 4. A village of Provence, in the viguery of Seine. *p Digne* Verntt 6? Caßel, a village of Rouffillorr, in the viguery of Conflans. *p. Perpignan.* Vei net-en-Auvergne, a village of Bourbonnois, in the election of Gannat. *p. Gannat.* Vernet-en-Bourbonnois, a parifh of Bourbonnois, in the election of Gannat. *p. Gannat.* Ver net-Soutira, a village of Rouerguc, in the election of Vi He franche,. *p. VUlefranche-de-Roucrgue.* VerneuiL I. A city of Normandy, lituated on the Aure, in the diocefe of Evrcux, and generality of Alcnçon; % leagues from Argentan» 23 from Falaife, 5 from Laigle, 24 from Rouen, 27 from Mans, 9 from Dreux, % from Alençon, 67-from Rennes, 12 from Evreux, and 295 from Paris. *Bureau de pofle.* 2.. A town-of Bourbonnois, in the election of Moulins, *p. & Aniand.* 3. A town of. Picardy, in the diocefe and election of Scnlis; about iz leagues from Paris, *p. Creil.* 4. A town of Limofin,

in the diocefe and election of Limoges. *p-Limoges.* 5. A town of Touraine, in the election of Loches, *p. Lochet.* 6. A town of Champagne, in the election of Epernay. *p. Dormant.* 7. A village of Beauce, in the election of Mantes, *p. Mantes.* 8. A village of Poitou, in the election of Richelieu, *p. ГIße-Bouchard.* 9. A village of Nivernors, in the diocefe and election of Nevers. *p. Dcc'ize.* 10. A village of Berry, in the election of Châtre, *p. Argentan,* ir. A village of Brie, in the election of Rozoy. *p. Guignes.* Verneu'u'-Cowtonne, and VemeuiLfur-Serre, Tillages of Picardy, in the diocefe and election of Laon. *p, Laon.* Vemeuil-le-Petit, a village of Meffin, in the jurifdiction of Monrmedy. *p. Stenay.* Vcrr.emUjur-Bois, a village of Berry, in the diocefe and election of Bourges. *p. Bourges.* Verncuje, a village of Normand», in the election of Bernay. *p. Montreuil-V ArgxlU,* Verney, a village of Forez, in the election of Roanne, *p. Roanne.* Vernie, a town of Maine, in the. election of Mans. *p. le Mans.* Vernier-Font aine y a village of Franche-Comté, tn the bailiwick, of Omans, *p. Befaacon.* Vernictt:, a fmall town of Maine in the election of Mans. *p. Frejnay.* Verniolle, a fmall town xí Foix,, in the generality of Roufllllon. *p Pamiers.* Vermox, a village of Daupbiny, in the diocefe and election of Vienne. *p. Bourgoin.* Verr.iß'on, a river of Orlcannois, which runs into the Loing, a little follow Montargis.
Vernives, a village of Auvergne,, in the diocefe and election of Clermont, *p. Clermont.* Vernix, a village of Korniandyr in the diocefe and eeftion oí Avranchcs. *p. Avran:Ks.* Vernois, a village of Burgundy, in the diocefe and bailiwick of Dijon, *p. Sekngey.* Vtrncis, les, a village of Bourbonnais, rn the eleftion of Moulins. *p. Moulins,* yerrniisfur-Is-Mar.ee, le, a vilbge of Franche-Comté, in the bailiwick f Vefoul. /. *Vef'. ul.* Veruo.'s, a village of Auvergne, in the diocefe and eleftion of S. Flour, *p. S. Ficur.* Vernon. I. A town of Poitou, in the diocefe and election of Poitiers. *p. Parttnay.* 2. A town of Touraine, in the diocefe and eleftion of Tours, *p. tours.* 3. A fmall town,»f Bléfois, in the elef-

tion of Romorantin. *p. Romorantin.* 4. A village of Poitou, in' the eleftion of S. Maixant. *p. S. Maixatst.* 5. A village of Poitou, in the diocefe and eleftion of Poitiers, *p. Poitiers.* 6. A village of Limofin, in the diocefe and eleftion of Limoges, *p. Limoges.* 7. The name of a priory in Anjou. *Vernon,* or *Vernon-fur-Seine,* a town of Normandy, fituated on the Seine, in the diocefe of Evrcux, and general ty of Reuen; 13 leagues from Rouen, and 20 from Paris. *Bureau depoße. Vernon 0 la Helle,* a fmall town of Gâtinois, in the eleftion of Mclun. *p. Montereau. Vernon' de-la-Roche-en-Breml,* a place of Burgundy, in the bailiwick of Semur-cn-Auxois. /. *SemurenAuxois. Verncn-Ies-Jyenfe,* a village of Lower Languedoc, in the diocefe and receipt of Viviers, *p. Viviers. Vernonnet,* a village of Normandy, in the eleftion of Andely. *p. Vernon. Vernoni'illiers,* a village of Champagne, in the eleftion of Bar-u.trAubc. *f. Bar-jur-Auhe. Vernofe,* a fmall town of Vivarais, in the receipt of Vivien, *p. Vhiers, Virr.ot,* a village of Burgundy, in the diocefe and bailiwick of Dijon, *p. IJJiirtll. Vernou.* See *Verncy. Vernouillet.* 1. A village of the Ifle of France, in the diocefe and eleftion of Paris, *p. Brie.* a. A village of Bcaucc, in the eleftion of Preux, *p. Dreux. Vernoux,* a village of Brefie, in the bailiwick of Bourg, *p. Leurg-enBreß. Verr.oux, la,* a town of Gafcony, in the diocefe and eleftion of Comminges. *p. Montrejeau. Verncux-en-Cbalencon,* a town ef Vivarais, in the diocefe of Vienne, and receipt of Viviers; about 7 leagues from Annonay, and 12 froçn Viviers. *Bureau de pójie. Vcrmux-en-Voccamt,* a town of Vivarais, in the receipt of Vivierj, *p. Viviers, Vzrwuís.* See *Vernoux. Vernoy.* i. A town of Touraine, in the eleftion of Amboife. *p. Tours,* a. A village of Gâtinoifj in the eleftion of Nemours. /. *ito motas.* 3. A village of Franche. Comté, in the bailiwick of Baume. *p. Baume.* 4. A place of Champagne, in the diocefe and eleftion of Sens, *p. Sens. Vcrnoy, le,* a village of Franche. Comté, in the bailiwick of Lons-le. Saunier, *p. Lons-le-Saunier. Vernugbeol,* a fmall town of Auvergne, in the eleftion of Riom. *p. Riom. Vermis,* and *Sems,* places of Burgundy, in the bailiwick of Beaune. *p. Ißiirtil. Vermißubre,* a fmall river of Lan. guedoc, which falls into the Orbe, pear Ceffcnon. *Virmiffi & Mer/as,* a village of Bourbonnois, in the eleftion of Gannat. *p. Gennat. Vernujè,* a village of Berry, in the eleftion of Montlucon. *p, Montlucon, Verny.* I. A village of Gex, ¡a the generality of Dijon, *f. Gex. 2.* A village oí McITin, in the diocefe and receipt of Metz. *p. Mit%.* 3. A baronv if Touraine. *Vtroilt & Ttlfy,* a village of Nori inanely? in the election of Caen. *p. Слеü. Vercn,* л village of Champagne, in the diocefe and election of Sens, *p. Sent. Vérone,* a village of Dauphiny, in the election of Montelimatt. *p. Monteïhmert. Verenget)* a village of Brie, in-the election of Provins. la *FerteCau-ter. Vcronr.es -les-Grandes,* and *Vertnnes-les-Peiit.es,* vi.lages of Burgundy, in the diocefe and bailiwick of Dijon, *p. Sakngey. Virai rure,* a parifh of Burgundy, compofed of fcvcval hamlets in the bailiwick of Charolles. *p. Dijon. Véreux* a place of Bourbonriois, in the election of S. Amand, *p. S, Amand. Verpel,* a village of Champagne, in the election of Ste. Manéhould. *f. Ste. Manéhould, Verpillerey* a village of Champagne, in the election of BarfurAubc. *p. Bar-jur-Aube. VerpHlieres,* a village of Picardy, in the election of Mondidier. *p. Hoye. Verquieres,* a parifh of Provence, in the viguery of Tarafcon. *p. Tarefcen, Усцип3* and *Verquineul,* villages of Artois, in the bailiwick of Bethune. *p. Be!lune, Verrayon,* a place of Provence, in the viguery oí C.iitellane.* /. *Cûjteïlane. Verre-le-Peüi,* a place of FrancheCnmté, in the diocefe and bailiwick, of Eefaruun. *p. Befançon. Verrerie, la,* a place of Bazadois, in the election of Condom, *p. Babas.* Verity, a village of Burgundy, in the bailiwick of Châtilkm. *p. Verrey-feus-Drte,* a place of Bargundy, in the bailiwick of Semur. *p. l'iteaux, Verry-fous-Salmalje,* a village of Burgundy, in the bailiwick of Châtillon. *p. CbailUJon-fur-Seine. Verreyrolles,* a place of Lower Languedoc, in the diocefe and receipt of Mcnde. *p. Mende. Verrie,* a fmall town of Anjou, in the election of Saumur. *p. Saumur. Verrie, la,* a fmall town of Poitou, in the election of Mauleon. *f. Aiauleon. Verrière,* a town of Angoumois, in the election of -Cognac, *p. Csgnac. Verrière, la.* 1. A village of Picardy, in the diocefe and election of Amiens, *p. Amiens.* 2. A place of Champagne, in the diocefe and election of Langres. *p. Langres Verriere-des-GroJbois, la,* a village of Franche-Comte, in the bailiwick, «f Ornans. *p. Bejançon. Verriere-jous-Glenne,* a village cf Burgundy, in the diocefe and bailiwick of Autun. *p. Autun. Verrières.* I. A fmall town of Perche, in the election of Mortagne. *p. Remallará, %.* A village of the Ifle of France, in the diocefe and election of Paris, *p. Bourg-laRétne.* 3. A village of Champagne, in the diocefe and election of Ttoycs. *p. Troyes.* 4. A village of Champagne, in the election of Rethel. *p. Ret bel.* 5. A village of Fore?, in the election of Montbrifon. *p. Mwtbrifon.* 6. A village of Forez, in the election of Roanne, *p. Roanne.* 7. A hamlet of Burgundy, in the bailiwick of Charolles. *p. Dijon. Verrieres-de-Joux,* a village of Fran.he-Comte, in the bailiwick of Ponrarlier. *p. Pontarlier. Verrieres-fous-RcuJfillon,* a village of Burgundy, in the bailiwick of Autun. *p. Autun, Verrières-fur-Aixne,* a fmall town of Champagne, in the election of Ste. Manéhould. *p. Ste. Alane'bcuM P'err'igny,* a village of Normandy, in the eleftion of Verneui). *p. Verneuil. Verrines.* I. A fmall town of Poitou, in the ekftion of S. Maixant. *p. S. Maixant.* 2. A village of Poitou, in the diocefe and election of Poitiers, *p. Peltiers.* 3. A vil3age of Picardy, in the election of, Crépy. *p. Crcfy. Verrón,* a town of Anjou, in the eleftion of Flèche. /. *la Flècbe. Verrón, le,* a fmall country in Tou raine. *Verrotte,* a pariíh of Touraine, in the diocefe and election of Tours. *p. leurs. Verrue,* a town of Poitou, in the election of Richelieu. *p. Mirebeau. Verruyes,* a fmajl town of Poitou, in the diocefe and election of Poitiers, *p. Parterty. Vers, i* A village of Beaujolois, in the eleftion of Villefranchc. *p. Villefrancbe.* 2. A village of Lower Languedoc, in the diocefe and receipt of Uzés. *p. Uze's.* 3. A village of Franche-Comté, in the bailiwick of Salins, *p. Sülms.* 4. A village of

Dauphiny, in the eleftion of Montelimart. *p. Monitlmart.* 5. Aparilh of Burgundy, in the bailiwick of Mâcon. *p. Tournus. Vers,* or ?. *Igny-de-Vers,* a village of Burgundy, in the bailiwick of Semur en-Briennois. *p. la Pacaudiere. Vers & Villes,* a village of Quercy, in the diocefe and election of Cahors. *p. Gabors. Vers & Heubecurt,* a village of Picardy, in the diocefe and election of Amiens, *p. Aniens. Vers-Jous-Corl'ie,* a village of Picardy, in the diocefe and eleftion of Amiens, *p. Corbie. Versfous-Seilfieres,* a village of Franche-Comté, in the bailiwick ot Poligny. *p. Salins. Versailles,* a town of the Ifle of France, in the diocefe and ekftion of Paris j it was in the firft century a fmall village, till Louis XIII. built a chateau for the convenience of bunting,-which Louib XIV. formed into a moil fupcrb palace at a vaft expence; the park is about *it* leagues in circumference, containing 7 or 8 villages, and many châteaus and pleafure-houfcs; 3 leagues from Séve, and 6 from Paris. *Bureau dt pcfie. VerfainviL'e,* a village of Normandy, in the election of b'alaife. *p. Faiaife. Verfaüeuy* a village of BreiTe, in the bailiwick of Bourg. *p. Bourgen-Breffe. FerjeïlUf* a village of Upper Languedoc, in the diocefe and receipt of CarcafTonne. *p. Carcajjhnne. Vrrfà'les'DeffôuSfà* village of Champagne, in the diocefe and election of Langres. *p. Langres. Verßgny%* a vilbge of Picardy, in the diocefe and election of Senlis. *p. Sen/is. Verjtl/ac,* a town of Berry, in the election of Blanc, *p. Arnac Verßne, la.* I. A fmall town of Picardy, in the diocefe and election ofBeauvais. *p. Beauvah.* 2. A village of Picardy, in the diocefe and election of SoiiTons. *p% Soffins. Verfoix,* or *Verjoy.* l. *A* village of Gex, in the generality of Dijon. *puɥ Ger.eve.* 2. A river of Сеж, which runs ir.to the lake of Geneva. *Iɜeɸn* a village of Normandy in the election of Caen. *p. Caen, Ver$oudy te,* a village of Dauphiny, in the diocefe and election of Grenoble, *p. Grenoble. Verjoy.* See *Vir fax. Vert. X.* A village of Beauce, in the election of Dreux, *p. Dreux,* 2, A village of Beauce, m the election of Chartres, *p. Chartres.* 3. A village of Beauce, in the election of Mantes, *p. Mantes.* 4. A village of Gafcony, in the election of Landes, *p. Dax. Vert, Uj* a river of Beam, which runs into the gave of Oleron. *Vert la Faroife,* a village ot Champagne, in the diocefe and election of Chalons, *p. CbShns. Vcrt-de-Biron, le,* a village of Périgord, in the diocefe and election of Sarbt. *p. ¡a binde. Verlli-Grand,* and *Vert-te-PetU,* villages of the lile of France, in the diocefe and election of Paris, *p. isumrcs. Vert-S.-Denis,* a village of Gâtinois, in the election of Melun. *p. Melun. Vertagen,* a town of Auvergne, in the Jiocefe and election of Clermont, *p. Clermont. Vertamhz,* a village of FrancheComté, in the bailiwick of Orgelet. *p. Lons-lc-Saunier. Vertamhe,* a village of Lower Languedoc, in the diocefe and receipt of Puy. *p. le Puy. Vertault,* a village of Champagne, in the election of Tonnerre, *p. Xaignes. Verteillat,* a fmall t»wn of Périgord, in the diocefe and election of Périgueux. *p. Périgueux. Verteuil,* a town of Agenois, in the diocefe and election of Agen. *p. Totmeims. Verteuil,* or *S. Mc'ard-àe-Verteuil,* a town of Angoumois, in the diocefe and election of Angoulême. *p. Villefagnan. Verteuilb,* a fmall town of Guienne, in the diocefe and election of Bourdeaux. *p. Blaye. Vertiere,* a village of FrancheComté, in the bailiwick of Dole. . *Dole. Vcrftllac,* a town of Marche, in the election of Gueret. *p, Arnac. Vtrfilly,* a village of Champagne, in the diocefe and election of Sens. *f. Bray-fur-Seine. Vertin-Vertigueule,* я village of Hninaut, in the government of Quênoy. *p. le Qucnoy. Verthms, les,* a place of Angoumois, in the diocefe and election of Angoulême. *p. Ajignuléme. Vertolaye,* a village of Auvergne, in the diocefe and cleitioH of Cler. mont. *p. JJJlire. Vemn,* a fmall town of Picardy, in the government of Montrcuil. *p. Mor. trcuU-Jur-M¿r. Vertan,* or 5. *Marfm-de-Verton,* a village of Berry, in the election of Châteauroux. *p. Châteauroux. Vertrieu-ile-la-Balme,* a village of Dauphiny, in the diocefe and election of Vienne, *p. Bourgoin. Virtuelle,* a village of Champagne, in the election of Epernay. *p. Epernay. Vertus,* a town of Champagne, about 6 leagues from Chalons, and 12 from Rheims, *p. Epernay. Vervan,* a village of Saintonge, in the election of S. Jean-d'Angely. *f. S. Jem-ttylngely. Vervans,* a village of Angoumois, in the election of Cognac, *p. Cognac. Vervillon,* a village of Beauce, m the election of Châteaudun. *p. Jitters. Vervins,* an ancient town of Picardy, fituated on an eminence, near the Serre, in the diocefe and election of Laon, between Laon and Mau beuge; 8 leagues from Laon, % from Avcfnes, 12 from Maubcuge, arm 41 from Paris. *Bureau de pojle. Verune, la,* a village of Lower Languedoc, in the diocefe and receipt of Puy. *p. le Puy. Verya,* a village of Franche-Comté, in the bailiwick of Orgelet, *f. Lons-le-Saunier. Veryeres,* a village of Limofin, in the diocefe and election of Tulles. *f. Tulles. Verxat,* a town of Limofin, in the diocefe and election of Limoges, *p. Limcges. Verme',* a village of Burgundy, in. the diocefe and bailiwick of Mâcon. *p. Macon, Veraxnay,* a fmall town of Champagne, in the diocefe and election of Rheims, *p. Rheims. Verzet,* a village of Champagne, in the election of Vitry. *p. Vttry. Vcrnillac,* a (mail town of *b.vts* Languedoc, in the dioccfc snd receipt of Puy. . *U Puy. Pertsofs9* a town of Rouergue, in the election of Milhaud. *p. S. Affr'ique. Venfyy* a final! town of Champagne, in the diocefe and election of Rheims, *p. Rheims. Verfatgms,* a village of Champagne, in the diocefe and election of Langres. *p. Langres. Pe/cJe,* a village of Franche-Comté, in the bailiwick of Orgelet, *p. Lons-le-Saunier. Vejdun,* a village of Berry, in the election of S. Amand. *p. S. Aman J. Уɸу* a village of Dauphiny, in the election of Montclimart. *p. Montelimart. VefipuuX)* a village of FrancheComte, in the bailiwick of Ornans. *p. Befar.çon. Ve/tgneux-fur-Coolle,* and *Vefigneux fur-Marne,* villages of Champagne, in-the diocefe and election of Chalons, *p. Chalons. Vcfigwt)* a village of Burgundy, in the bailiwick, of Arnay-le-Duc.

Vißnesy the name of a part of the fore It of S. Gumaiiv-cn-Laje, near Paris. *Vtfms,* a fraall town of Normanciv, in the election of Mortain. *p. b Hitaire. Vtße,* i. A river of Champagne, 'which joins the Aifnc at Vdly. 2. A river of BrcfTe, which difcharges itfelt into the Saône, by two mouths, oppofue Varcnnes. *Vtße & Caumonty* and *Veflud*, villages of Picardy, in the dtocefe and election ofLaon. *p. Latin. Veßy.* i A town of the Ifle of France, about 4 leagues from Soiffuns, and 8 from Rheims. *p. S'j'ijßbns.* 2. A village of Nr»jm;indy, in the election of Giiors. *p. Gifrs. VtßtSy* a fmall town of Maine, in the diocefe and election of Mans. *p. le Mans. Vefouly* or *Vezculy* a city of Franche-Comté, fituattd at the botum *Veuve y la,* a village of Champagne, in the diocefe and election of Chalons, *p. Chalons Vewvey,* a village of Burgundy, in the bailiwick of Beaune. *p. Beaune. Vuvrai. 'ie,* a pariih of Burgundy, in the bailiwick óf Arnay-le-Duc. *p. Dijon. ViuxauliS)* a village of Champagne, in the diocefe and election of Langrcs. *p. Langres. ftWj* a yillage of Franche-Comté, in the bailiwick of Lons-lc-Saunier. *p» Lons-le-Saumer: Vexin,* a country fituatcd along the river Epte, which divides it into two parts, one called *Vtx'.n-Frjr. cxs,* the other *Vexln-Normand. Vexin-Francois,* a part of Vexin, fituatcd to the eaft of the river Epte, which Separates it from Vexin-Normand; it joins Beauvoifes to the north, on the eaft it is bounded by the river Oife, and on the fouth by the Seine; the principal towns are Pont oife, Chaumont, and Magny. *Vtxitt-Normand)* a very fertile country, weft ward of the river Epte; G'lfors is the principal town. *Veynes,* a town of Dauphiny, in the diocefe and election of Gap. *p. Gap. V/yzac,* a town of Guicnne, in the dioccfe and election of Bourdeaux. *p. Bourdeaux. Veyrac ¿£? la Sudrie,* a town of Rouergue, in the diocefe and election of Rhodez. *p. Figeac. ', Veyrane-lj-Baßidet la,* a village of Lower Languedoc, in the diocefe and receipt of Viviers, *p. Viviers Veyrteres,* a village of Rouergue, in the election of Milhaud. *p. Milbaud, Veyrignac,* a village of Périgord, in the diocefe and election oí Sarlat, *p. Sarlat. s " VtyrintS)* i. A village of Pengörd, in the diocefe and election of Sarlat. *p. Sarlat.* 2. A village of Périgord, in the dioccfe and election of Périgueux, *p. PSñgUSHX. FfyjiitieU)*

я village of Dauphiny, *PuâU fef Montgaeon,* a village of Auvergne, in the election of Riom. *p. Riom. Viam,* a village of Liraofin, in the election of Tulles, *p. Uzercbes. Vian & Bujjurel,* a village of Franche-Comté, in the bailiwick of Baumc *p. Baume. Viane,* a town of Upper Languedoc, fituated on the Agout, about 6 leagues from Caftres, on the confines of Roucrgue. *p. Caßres. V. ange,* a village of Burgundy, in the diocefe and bailiwick of Autun. *p. Saulieu. Viant%y* an abby in the diocefe of Alby. *p. Alby. Viast* a village of Lower Languedoc, in the diocefe and receipt of Agde. *p. Agde. Viasr* or & *ApoWnard-de-Vtas,* a village of Lower Languedoc, in the diocefe and receipt of Viviers, *f. VtK'icrs. Viafpre-fe-Grandt* and *Viafpre-lePerity* villages of Champagne, in the diocefe and election of Troyes. *p. Arris-fur-Aube. Viauht,* a village of Champagne, in the diocefe and election of Lanjres. *p. Langres. Viaur, le,* a fmall river of Lower Languedoc, that runs into the Avci'rou. *ViazaCy* a village of Quercy, in the election of Figcac. *p. Cabers. Vdeufy* a village of Normandy, in the election of Arques, *p. Yernnlle. Vtbrae.* i.A village of Angoumois, jn the election of Cognac, *p. Cbâ teauneuf-en-Angoumois.* 2. A village of Saintonge, in the diocefe and election of Saintes, *p. Saintes. Vibrac,* or *S. Germain-de-VibraCy* a town of Saintonge, in the diocefe and election of Saintes, *p. Saintes, Vibrais,* a town of Maine, on the river Braye, in the election of Château-du-Loir. *p. Mond'jubleau. Vic.* A town of Meifio, fituated on the Seille; about 6 leagues from Nmcy, i-i from Marfan, and 15 from Mela. *Bureau de poße.* a. A towju eîeftionof Confolens. *p. Ccnfi/en. Vidalait,* a place of Gafconjr, iir Che receipt of Bigorre. *p. Taries. Vidauban,* a village of Provence, in the vigucry of Draguignan. *p. h Lue. Viday,* a village of Perche, in the eleftion of Mortagne, *p. le-Mcßefur-Sarte, VidecofviUe,* a village of Normandy, in the election of Vakgnes. *p. Ca rantan. VidcßnIaine,* a parifh of Normandy, in the diocefe of Coútanccs. *p. Coútanccs. Vidâtes,* a village of Gâtinois, in the election of Melun. *p. Etatnpes. Vider-*

brmn, a village of Alfacc, in the diocefe of Straiburg. *p. Strajhourg. Vtd'urle,* a fmall r'rvcr of Lower Languedoc. *VidwjUle,* a village of Normandy, in the diocefe and eleftion of Baycux. *p. S. Lo. Vidcune,* a village of Armagnac, in the diocefe and election of Aiuli. *p. Tarbes. Vie, la.* I. A river of Poitou, which runs into the fea. 2. A fmall river of Normandv, which runs into the Dive. *V'ucvurt,* a place of Burgundy, in the bailiwick of Montcenis. *p. Auiun. VtefviHe,* a village of Picardy, in the election of Doulens. *p. Devient. Viefviller,* a village of Picardy, in the diocefe and election of Amicus *j). Ham. Vic!,* or *S. Marlin-du-Vicl,* a town of Perche, in the eleftion of Mortagne. *p. Nogcnt-lc-Rotrcu. Veille.* See *Vtel/e. Helles,* a fmall town of Normandy, in the election of Conches, *p. Ji-vreux. Viel-Capet,* a village of Armagnac, in the diocefc and eleftion of Autfl. *p. Autb. Viel-Cbâleaa,* a fmall town of Bourbonnois, in the eleftion of S. Amand. *p. S. Sbnar.d. Viil-Châtel,* 3 village of Burgundy, o *Viclle-Rue, la,* a village of Nor. mandy, in the diocefe and election of Rouen, *p. Rouen. Vielle-jous-Biran,* a village of Gafcony, in the receipt of Gabardan, *p. Aiont-de-Marfan. Vidle-Touloufe,* a village of Cpp:r Languedoc, in the diocefe and receipt of Touleufc. *p. Toulouse. Vidle-Vigne,* a village of Poitou, iti the election of Mauleon. *p. Mankos. Vidle-Vigne fif S.Andre',* a village of Bretagne, in the dioccfe and receipt of Nantes, *p. Ancenis. Vielle-Vignetfi* village of Armagnac, in thediocefeof Commi-tges. *p. Mмtrejeau. Vùile-Ville.* I. A village of Poitou, in the diocefe and election of Poitiers, *p. Poitiers.* 2. A place of Champagne, in the election of Rethel. *p. Retbd. Viellenave.,* 1. A village of Gafcony, in the election of Landes, *p. Dax.* 2. A place of Gafcony, in the receipt of Bigorre.*p. Tarbes.* 3. A place of Beam, in the receipt of Pau. *p. Pau. Viellevic,* a village of Auvergne, in the election of Aurillac. *p. Aurillac. Viellivigne.* See *Vidlc-Vigne. VidleviHe.* See *Vidle-Vil/e. Vielles-Ejpcces,* a village of Au» vergne, in the dioccfe and election of S. Flour, *p. S. Flour. Vidles-Maifons,* a village of Gâtinois, in the election of Montargis. *p. Montargis. Vidley,* a village of Franche-Comté, in the diocefe and bailiwick of Befançon../. *Befanccn. Vi-Uey-S.-Etienm,* a village of Mefftn, in the diocefe and receipt of TouU *p* ТЫ. *Vietlwerge* 6? *SmJJons, u* fmall town of Burgundy,, in the bailiwick of Aujonne. *p. Auxonne. Viellj,* a v.llage of Flanders, in the diocefe and fubdclegation of Cambray, *p. I8ndrety. V.elmetifon,* a place of Brie, in the election of Provins, *p. Previas. PieJiMncir, /e.* See *VteUMmw. Vielmoultn.* Sec *VielMoul'm. Vielmur,* a town of Lower Languсйос, in the diocefe and receipt of Caftres. *p. Caβres. Vitl'uicj* a village of Périgord, in the dioccfe and election of Sarlat. *p. Striae, Viemoiw,* a village of Picardy, in the election of Compiégne. *p. Comfiegne. Piennay,* a vilhge of Poitou, in the diocefe and election of Poitiers. Jb. *Poitiers. Vur.r.t.* I. Aconfidcrable city of Dauphiny, the capital of Viennois, fituatcd on lie banks of the Rhone, in the road from Lyons to Avignon: It is the fee of an archbiíhop, beftdes the metropolitan, it has 3 collegiate churches, a feminary, a college, &c. 7 leagues from Lyons, 20 from Valence, 34 from Orange, 41 from Avignon, 60 from Aix, 105 from Nice, 73 from Marfcilles, 57 from Nimcs, 68$ from Montpellier, and 122$ from Paris. *Bureau de poβe.* 2. A town of Champagne, fituatcd on the Aifne, about 2 leagues from Ste. Manehould, and 8 from Verdun, *p. Ste. Manehould.* 3. A village of Normandy, in the diocсfe of Rouen, *p Bannière.* 4. A village of Normandy, in the diocсfe and elecVion of Baveux, *p. Bayeux.* 5. A village of Blefois, in the diocefe and election of Blois. *p. Blots. Vienne, la,* a confiderable river which rifes on the confines of Limniin and Marche, and run into the Loire at Cande in Touraine. *Viennes,* a village of Qré.mnoís, in the dioccfe and elc/tion of leans. *p. Orleans. Vienmjt,* a country of Dauphiny, in the environs of Vienne, which is the capital. *Viens,* a Tillage of Provence, in the diocefe and vigucry of Apt, *pц Apt. Vier & Lttgcs,* a village of Gafcony, in the rectint o,t Bígorrc, *p. Tartes. Viemtè,* a fmall town of Picardy, in the diocefe and election of Senhs. *p. Senlis. Vierjatj* a village of Auvergne, in the election of CombraiHes. *p.Chamion. Vierfcbcimbeim,* a village of Alface, in the diocefe of Straiburg. *p. Strafbcurg. Vicvvilh.* i. A village of Normandy, *in* the dioceſe and election of Bayeux. *p. Bayeux.* 2. Aillage of Beauce, in the-election of Dourdans. *f. Angerville. Vier%m,* or *Vierfon,* a city of Berry, fituated in a fertile plain on the Cher, i a the diocefe and election of Bourges, in the road between Orleans and Limoges; 22 leagues from Orleans, 13 from Cháteauroux, 41 from Limogesj and 50 from Paris. *Bureau de pofle. Vterxy VaucaβiUe,* a village of Picardy, in the diocefe and election of Soiflons. *p. Solβcns. Viejcourt,* a phce of Burgundy, in the diocefe and receipt of Autun. *p. Autun. VieJfotXy* a town of Normandy, in the election of Vire. *p. Vire. Viefverges,* a village of Burgundy, in the bailiwick of Auxonne. *p. Auxcttne. Vt'efvignes,* a village of Burgundy, in the diocefe and bailiwick, of Dijon. *p. Dijon. V.efville, a* village of Champagne, in the bailiwick of ChaumontcnBafligny. *p. Caumont. 'V'ujiy,* a village of Burgundy in the bailiwick of Arnay-lc-Duc. /. *Dijon,* I *Viett,* a fmall town of Valromey, in the generality of Dijon, *p. Belley. Vieudixenaie,* a fmall town of Bugey, in the bailiwick of Bellcy. /, *Belly. Via/fuy* a village of Beauce, i the election of Cháteaudun. *p. Ck¿. teaudun. Vif-vigne,* a village of Burgundy, in the diocefe and bailiwick of Dijon, *p. Djon.* in the fubdclegation of Bouchain. *p. Conde'. Vieux-¥errette,* a village of Alface, in the bailiwick of Ferrette. *p II umngue. Vcux-Fume',* a village of Normandy, in the election of Falaife.*p. Trouard. Vieux-hs-Avaux,* and *Vieux-lesManre,* villages of Champagne, in the diocefe and election of Rheims. *p. Rheims. Vieux-Maijons,* a village of Brifj in the election of Cháteau-Thierry. *p. Montmirel. Vieux-Marcbe', le,* a village of Bretagne, in the diocefe and receipt of Treguier. *p. Gmngamp. Vieux-Mareuil,* a town of Périgord, in the diocefe and election of Pcrigueux. *p. Perigueux. Vieux-Me'nil & Meniβart,* and *Vieux Rang,* villages of Hainault, in the government of Maubeuge. *p. Mjubeuge. Vieux-Pont.* I. A fmall town of Normandy, in the election of Falaife. *p. Trouard. z.* A priory in the diocefe of Sens. *p. Sens. Vieux-Port, le,* a village of Normandy, in the election of Pont-Audemer. *p. Ullebonne. Vuux Thann,* a village of Alface, in the bailiwick of Thann.*p. Rouf, fach. Vieux-iAlle, la.* See *Vtcvil/e. Vieuxvy,* a village of Bcauce, in the dioccfc and election of Chartres. *p. Chartres, Viey,* a village of Gafcony, in the receipt of Bigorre. *p. Tarbes. Vezia%,* a village of Bugey, in the bj.'liwicV of Belley. *p. Beiley. Vif,* a village of Dauphiny, in the diocefe and election of Grenoble, *p. Grenoble. Viffort,* a village of Brie, in the election of Cháteau-Thierry .*p. Chewy. Vigan, le.* I. A town of Lower Languedoc, in the diocefe and receipt of Alais: about 3 leagues from S. Hypolite, and 6 from Alais. *Bureau de pifie, z.* A town of Quen y, iA the Jiocefe and election oí Cahors. *p. Peyrac. Vgard-fes-Verdun, z* wood of 1168 arpents, in the jurifdiction of Touloufe, in Languedoc. *Vigarcn,* a village of Armagnac, in the election of Lomagne. *p. Beauntont-de-Lomagne. Vige,* a village of Marche, in the in the election of Bourganeuf. *p. Hourgansuf. Vigean, ¿e,* a town of Poitou, in the election of Confolans. *p. Conflans. Vigente,* i. A town of Auvergne, in the diocefe and election of S. Flour, *p. S. Flour.* 2. A town of Limofm, in the diocefe and election of Limoges, *p. Limoges. Vtgeois, le,* a town of Limofin, in the election of Brives. *p. Uzcrcbes. Vigeon.* See *Уzpя. Viger,* a village of Gafcony, in the receipt of Bigorre./. *Tarées. Vigeñlle,* a village of Marche, in the election of Gueret. *p. Cbenerailles. V'tglam.* 1. A village of Orlcannois, in the diocefe and election of Orleans, *p. Orleans.* 2. A village of Blèfois in the election of Romorantin. *p. Ramorantm VignaCj le.* i. A town of Rouerguc, in the election of vUlefranche. *p Figeac.* 2. A village of Armagnac, in the elefübn of Lomagne. *p. Beaumont-He-Lomagne. Vtgnac-U-Haut,* a village of GuU enne, m the diocefe and election of Bourdeaux. *p Marmanàe. VignacourJy* a town of Picardy, in the election of Douions, *p. Douieris VignaltSy* a village of Normandy, in-the election of Falaife.

p. Falaife. Vignauxy a village of Armagnac, in the diocefe and election of Auch. *f. Mont-de-Marfan. Vignay-Courtilles,* a place of the Ifle of France, in the diocefe and election of Paris. *Vtgncgoul.* See *Vigmogpu. Viçncmcnt)* a village of Picardy, 141.lb; election of Compicgne. *p. Ccmtlegnc..' Vignens, I(j* a village of PicarJv, in the cle¿tion of Crêpy. /. *Crity." Vignes,* i. A village of Burgui.uv, in the bailiwick of Avalon, *p. Skalen. 1.* A village of Béarn, in the receipt of Moris, *p. Pan.* 3. A place of Champagne, in the election of Chaumont./. *Nogcnt-Çur-Se.ne. Vignes, Vàlles* Êf *Vurefort,* a village of Lower Languedoc, in ti.e diocefe and receipt of ¡N»rbonne, *p. $farl,onney Vignes & Lcm/'un,* a village of Condomois, in the diocefe and election of Condom, *p. Condom. Vignejyy* a place of Brie, in the diocefe and election of Mcaux. *p. Meaux. VignetSy* a village of Champagne, in the diocefe and election of Troyes. *p. Trcyes. VtgnetteSy* ¿Vi, a fort in the bay of Toulon. *Vigneu,* a village of Bretagne in the diocefe and receipt of Nantes. *p. Nantes. Vigneullcy* a village of MefTin, in the diocefe and receipt of Metz» *p Metis. Vigneux.* i. A village of Picardy, in the diocefe and election of Laon. *p. Laon.* 2,, A village of Luxembourg-François, in the diocefe of Treves, *p. Stenay.* 3. A village of Dauphiny, in the diocefe and election of Vienne j&. *Vienne. Vignlogouy* or *Bonlieu,* a convent in the diocefe of Montpellier, *p. Montpellier. Vignccy* a village of Bretagne, in the diocefe and receipt of Rennes, *p. Rennes. Vignolley* a village of Burgundy,, in the bailiwick of Beaune. *p. Beaune. Vignolles.* I. A village of Bazadois, in the election of Condom, *p. Baxas.* 2. A village of Saintonge, in the diocefe and eleition of Saintes *p. Samtes. Vignon-les-Vúlages,* a fmall town of Berry, in the diocefe and election, of Bourges, *p. Vierwti, Vtenor. et. l.* A fmall town, of Guicnne, in thedtocefe and election of Bourdcaux. *p. Ccßillon.* 2. A village of Auvergne, in the diocefe and election of S. Flour. *p. S. Fleur.* y£nmy,i д town of Champagne, on the Marne, ibout 3 leagues from Chaumont. *p. ydtwiile, Vigncu-jous-lcs-Aix,* a fmall town of Berry, in the diocefe and election of Bourses, *p. Bourges fogr:o. Xj* a village of Bnurboflnois, in the election of Montluçon. *f. AUntluccn. Vigny,* i. A village of Beauce, in. the election of Dreux, *p. Dreux.* 2. A village of Bcauce, in the election of Mantes, *p. Mantes.* 3. A village of Meffin, in the diocefe and receipt of Metz. *p. Metz.* 4. A pnriih of Burgundy, compofed of feveral hamJets, in the bailiwick of Charolles. *f. Dijon. . V¿goult* a place of Uppcf Languedoc, in the diocefe and receipt of Touloufe. *p. Toulcufe. Vigiuiant* or *Vigolant,* a village of Berry, in the election of Châtre. *p. la Chatte. Vigoureux,* a placé of Auvergne, in the election of Aurillac.. *AurUlac. flgouxj* a village of Berry, in the election of Châtre, *p. la Châtre. Vigy* a village of Mcflin, in the diocefcand receipt of Metz. *p. Metz. Vbiers,* a town of Anjou, in the diocefe of Angers, and election of Montreuil-Bellay; about 6 leagues from Montreuil-Bellay, and 8 from Angers, *p. Angers. Vijon,* a villrge of Berry, in the election of Châtre.. *la Châtre. Vilaine,* or 5. *George-de-Vilaine-laJubee'* a town of Maine, in the diocefe and election of Mans. *p.le Mans. Vilaine, le,* a river of Bretagne, which rifee in Maine, and difthargeà itfelf into the fea, oppofite the I fie of Majn. *Vilaine-en-Duefmoir,* a fmaJl town of Burgundy, in the bailiwick of Chf.tillon. *p. Sre. Reine. VИa.ne-la-Carelle,* ajjd *Vilaine-It Gomáis,* towns of Maine, in the diocefe and election of Mans. *p. U Mans. VVaine-lesPrévôts,* a fmall town of Burgundy, in the bailiwick of Semur.. *Clamccy. VUamblin,* a village of Orléannois, in the diocefe and election of Orléans, *p. Châteaudun, Vilamees,* a village of Bretagne, in thediocc c and receipt of Rennes. *p. Faulerer. Vtlamolaca,* a village of Rouflillon, in the diocefe and viguery of Perpignan, *p. Perpignan. Vüarceaux,* a château of VexinFrancois, in the parifli of Chaufiy; about 2. leagues from Magny. *p. Magny. VJard-Cbeorieres,* a village of Daupliiny, in the election of Romans, *p. Romans. Vilaroja,* a place of RouiuHon, in the diocefe and viucry of Perpignan*p. Perpignan. Vilbaudcn,* a village of Normandy, in the election of S. Lo. *p. Argentan. Vilbernier,* a town of Anjou, in the election of Saumur. *p. Saumur. Vilbert,* a village of Brie, in the, election of Rozoy. *p. R'ozcy. Vikbicn,* a fmall town ot Normandy, in thcelcction of Mortain. *p, Mortain. Vtfcbiron,* a village of Marche, in the election of Gueret. *p. Gueret. Vilde'-deBidon,* and *Vildé-de-laMarine,* villages of Bretagne, in the diocefe and receipt of Pol. *p. Dot. Vilde-Gu inguahm,* a v i l läge of Bretagne, m the diocefe and receipt of S.Malo. *p. S. Malo. Vdentroh,* a fmall town of Berry, in the election of Châteauroux. *p. Châteauroux. VilejoHer,* a village of Dombes, inthechatallany of ToiiTcy.*p. Belleville. Vilefpy,* a village of Upper Languedoc, in the diocefe and receipt of S. Pupoul. *p. Caßdnaudary. Vilctte, la,* a village of Normandy, in the election of Vire. *p. Cifldv Jur-Nc'irtau. Vilgagnt,* a village of Brie, in the election of Rozoy. *p. Rowy. Vi/ixac,* a fmali town of Guicnne, in. the diocefe and election of Bourdcaux. *p. Ëcurdeaux, Villades'fortsj la,* a place of Lower Languedoc, in the diocefe and receipt of Xarbonne./». *Narlcnne. V¡Íla-$.-Аляс]эсу /a,* a place of Lower Languedoc, in the receipt of Limoux. *p. Хлиих, VillaUny* a village of Berry, in the diocefe and election of Bourges. *p. Bourges Vilhcerf-U-Grand)* a village of Champagne, in the diocefe and election of Troyes. *p. troyes. VJlacum,* a place of Lower Languedoc, in the diocefe and receipt of JLodeve. *p. Lodevc. Villad'w,* a village of Champagne, in the diocefe and election of Troyes. *P. Troyes. VHlafons,* a village of FrancheComté, in the bailiwick of Vefoul. *f. Vefiul. Vidage, Ut* a village of Normandy, in the election of Mortain. *p. Mortam. Village-des-Bair.s,* a place of Rouffillon, celebrated for its hot fprings. *Village-Neufy le,* a village of Alface, in the bailiwick of Landfcr. *p. Huningue. Villages-d? Jimbert,* a fmall town of Auvergne, in the election of Ifloirc. *p. ÏJoire. Vdlages-de-Ia-Rocbette,* a village of Auvergne, in the election of Brioudc *p. Brioudc Villagei-dcla-Varer-e,* and *V,U lages-dc-S.-Germain,* villages of Auvergne, in the election of lifoire. *p. IJcire. Vdlages-de-S.*

-Eutropbe-les, a town of Saintonge, in the diocefe and election of Saintes, p. Saintes. Vtlldges-de-Vrvontu, /«, a fmall town of Poitou, in the diocefe and election of Poitiers, p. Vpvtfttu. Villages-dû-Pas-du-Brcuil, lei, a Village of Saintonge, in the diocefe Vdlardi, or & Aiil-de-Vdlards, a village of Périgordj in the diocefe and election of Périgueux. p. Pe t igutux. Vd/aref, a village of Poitou, in the diocefe and election of Poitiers. p. Cbaunay. Vdlartiy le, a place of Lower Languedoc, in the diocefe and receipt of Men de. p. Moide. VtUarel-Cahardis, les, a village of Lower Languedoc, in the diocefe and receipt of CarcafTonnc. p. Carcafjonne. Vdlaret-Cbcvaledles, a place of Lower Languedoc, in the diocefe and receipt of Mende. p. Mende. Villargeat, a village of FrancheComté, in the bailiwick of Vcfoul. /. Vefoul. Vdlargcaux. a place of Burgundy, in the diocefe and bailiwick of Challón, p. Challan. Villargeois, a village of Burgundy, in the bailiwick of Saulieu. pt Sauft eu. Villarmoufe-en-Morvant, and VU larnoux, villages of BurgunJy, in the bailiwick of Avalon, p. Avalon. Villars. I. A fmall town of Marche, in the election of Gueret. p. Gueret. 2. A village of Provence, in the diocefe and viguery of Apt. p.-dpt. 3. A Mliage of Saintonge, in the diocefe and election of Saintes. p. TailUbcurg. 4.. A village of An goumois, in the election of Cognac» p. Cognac. 5. A village of Forez, in the election of Roanne, p. Roanne 6. A village of Gâtinois, in the election of Melun. p. Me'un. 7. A village of Burgundy, in the diocefe and bailiwick of Challón, p. Challo», 8. A village of Forez, in the election if S. Etienne, p. S. Eiirrine. Villar i t les. ï. A village of Franche-Comté, in the bailiwick of Salins, p. Salins, z-. A v i liage of Lower Languedoc, in the diocefe and reciipt of Puy. p-le Puy. Vtllars-Domjierre, aplace of Bur Villecreme & Cerçay, a village in the diocefe and election of Paris, f, Uriel V¡llecro%et a fraall town of Provence, in the viguery of Draguignan. f. Barjois. ydUdagr.e, a town of Lower Languedoc, in the diocefe and receipt of Narbonne. p. Narbonne. yüledevrcy, a village of the lile of France, in the diocefe

and election of Paris, p. S.vc. Vdlcdemange, a fmall town of Champagne, in the diocefe and election of Rheims, p. Sezanne. Villcdieu. I. A market-town of Kormandy, in the diocefe of Coiil anees, and election of Vire; about t leagues from Avranches, 7 from Vire, and 7 from Coûtantes. Bureen de peße. ъ A town of Beauce, in the election of Vendôme, p. Véndeme. 3. A town of Tourair.e, near Neuvy. p. tours. 4. A fmall town of Auvergne, in tlie diocefe and receipt of S. Flour, p. S Fleur, 5. A fmall town of Berry, in the election of Chateauroux. p Chateauroux. 6. A fmall town of Maine, in the diocefe of Mans. p. le Mam. 7. A village of Champagne, in the flection of Tonnerre p. JIncy-leFranc. 8. A village of Normandy, in the election of Neufchatel. p, ïfeuftbâtel. 9. A village of FrancUc-Comté, in the bailiwick of Rontarlier. p. Portar lier. 10. A village jf Franche-Comté, in the bailiwick ef Ornans, p. Befançon. II. A village of Bléfois, in the election of Remorar.tin. p. Rcmorar.tin. 12. A place of Languedoc, in therreceipt of Limoux-f. Limoi.x. 13. A place mí Provence» in the viguery of Mou'Aicrs. J. Cajiellane. 14. An abby in the diocefe of Dax. Dax. Vtlledku, la. 1. A fraall town of "Dpper Languedoc, in the diocefe and receipt of Montauban. p. Montauban. z, A fmall town of Lower Languedoc, in the diocefe and receipt of Viviers, p Viilencwve-deBtrg. 3. A village of Poitou, in the diocefe and election of Poitiers. p. Poitiers. 4. A village of Marche, in the election of Guerct. p. FtusIletin. 5. A village of Lower Languedoc, in the diocefe and receipt of Men de. p. Mende. ViUedxeu-cC JIunay, la, a fmall town of Poitou, in the election of Niort, p. Niort. ViUedieu-en-Fontemyy ta, a village of Franche-Comté, in the bailiwick of Vefoul. p. Vefottl. Wledieu-le-Buillcul, a village of Normandy, in the election of Argentan, p. Argentan. Vdledomam, a town of Touraine, in the election of Loches, p. Cbâtilhr.-fur-Indre. vUledoßne a town of Touraine, in the election of Amboife. p. «л'штoift. VtlltdtmX) a village of Aunis, in the diocefe and election of Rochelle. p. la Rochelle. VilkdubcTt-y a village of Languedoc, in

the diocefe and receipt of Carca (Tonne, p. Carcaßinne. yU/efagruaif a town of Angoumois, in the diocefe and election of Angoulémc. Bureau de poße. Villejargeau £s? la Villotte, a village of Burgundy, in the diocefe and bailiwick of Auxerre. p. Auxcrre. Villefarlay, a village of FrancheComté, in the bailiwick of Arbois. P Salins. Villefawvre, a village of Limofm, in the diocefe and election of Limoges, p. Limoges. Vittefcrry, a village of Burgundy, in the bailiwick of Semur. p. Semur. Villtßourey a village of Languedoc» in the diocefe and receipt of Carcafionne. p. Carcajjbnne. Vu'lefolles, a fraall town of Champagne, iir the diocefe and election oí Sens. p. Vdltnfuve-fur-Tor.ne. yiilcfolletj a village of Poitou, in the election of Niort, p. Niort. yUlefortf a town of Lower Languedoc, in the dipcefe and receipt yf Uzés. p. Gtn.uïkç, Y,lief ranche, or Villefranche-enBcaujJ-As, a city of Beaujolois, of which it is the capital, fituated on the Morgón, in the dioccfc and generality of Lyons, between Lyons and Mâcon; 7 leagues fr-im Lyons, 9 from Mâcon» and 116 from Paris. Bureau dpofic. Villefrarxbe, or Vdlefranche-duConfiant, a ftrong city of Rouiullon, the capital of Confiant; fituatcd between two mountains on the river Tet, in the diocefe of Perpignan; about 10 leagues to the weit of Perpignan. Bureau de poße. VúUfrancbe, or VilkfancbedeRoutrgue, a city of Roucrgue, fituated on the Aveirou, in the dioccfc of Rhodcz, and generality of Montauban j 22 fcagucs from Cahors, 167 from Paris, and about 12 from Rhodes. Bureau de poße. Vdlefrancbe. J. A town of Upper Languedoc, in the diocefe and receipt of Alby. p Ally.. 2. A town of Bourbonoois, about 4 leagues from Montluçon p. AÍMtiufcñ, 3. A town of Périgord, 5 leagues frum Sarlat. p. Vdlenewve'tt Agen. 4. A village of Champagne, in the election of Joigny. p. Jolgny. 5. A village of Bléfois, in the election of Romorantin. p. Romcnantia. 6. A village of Dauphiny, in the election of Montclimart. p. Mentelimart. Villefrancbe, or 5. Capraifi-d "¡liefranche, a village of Périgord, tn the diocefe and election of Sarlat. p. Sie. Foy. Vdleftan-

che, la, a town of Champagne, about a league from Stcnay, and 5 from Verdun, *p. Stenay.* *Vùlefranche-de-Lauraguats*, a town of Upper Languedoc, in the diocefe and receipt of Touloufe, in the road between Touloufe and Carcaffonnc; 7 leagues from Touloufe,. 13 from CarcaiTonne, 28 from Narbonne,. 43 from Perpignan, 73 from Bourdeaux, and 178 from Pari. *Bureau de pifie.* *VUUfranchede-Loncbapt*, a town f Périgord, in the (Uoccic and elec
cy, in the diocefe and election of Montauban. *p. Montauhan.* *Vdlemagve.* 1. A village of Upper Ijtnguedoc, in the dioccfe and receipt of S. Papoul. *p. Caße/ttaudarj*, 2. A village of Lower Languedoc, in the diocefe and receipt of Béiiers. *p. Briers.* *Vilicmagnet* or *S. Atnns-de-Vdltm.igne*, a town of Upper Languedoc, in the diocefe and receipt of Caftrcs. */. Caßris.* *VilUmagnty* or *ViUevehaCy* a town of Lower Languedoc, in the diocefe and receipt of Agde. *p. Agde.* *Villemaitij* a village of Poitou, in the election of Niort, *p. Villcjag nan.* *Vìllcmanâevr*, a village of Gâtinois, in the election of Montargis. *p Mentarais*, *Vulemar.ocbe*, a village of Champagne, in the diocefe and election of Sens. *p. P ont-jur-Tonкe.* *yjiemarrly*, a village of Bcauce, in the election of Vendôme. *p + Vtndîme..* *vWtmarcchaïy* a fmall town of Gatinois, in the election of Nemours. */. Nemours*, *Pi/Iemereui/y* a village of Brie, in the diocefe and election of Meaux. *p. Mtaux.* *ViHemart'w*, a village of Bazadois, in the election of Condom, *p. Cafittlon.* *Vdlemaur* See *Vdlcmort.* *Vilhmbray*, a village of Picardy, in the diocefe and election of Beauvais. *p. Eeawvait.* *yillcmenfroyy* a village of FrancheComté, in the election of Vcfoul. *p. Lure*, *Vdlemcnfe*, a priory of Beaucc, in. the diocefe of Chartres.
Vdlemer, a village of Champagne in the election of Joigny. *p. Jcigity.* *Villemereuil*, a village of Champagne, in the diocefe and erection of Troyes. *p. Troyes.* *Villemcrt*) a place of Brie, in the election of Montcrcau. *p. Mcnte rCMb* Comminges. *p. Montrejeau.* 5. A village of Auvergne, in the election of Ifloirc. *p.Ißhire.* 6. A village of Beau ce,, in the election of Mantes. *p. Mantes.* 7.

A village of Condomois, in the diocfe and election of Condom, *p. Condom.* 8. A village of Upper Languedoc, in the diocefc and receipt of Alby. *p. Atby..* 9. A village of Upper Languedoc, in the dtoccfe and receipt of Lavaur. *p. Lavaur.* 10. A village of Anjou, in the díoceié and election o/ Angers, *p. Jngrarde.* n. A village of Bourbonnois, in the election of Moulins, *p. Moulins.* 12. A village ofPicardy, in the diocefc and election ofSenlis. *p. Sentis.* 13. A village of Picardy, in the election of Crêpy. *p. Cripy..* 14. A village of Franche-Comté, in rhe bailiwick of Vefoul. *p. Vefoul.* 15. A. village of Burgundy, in the bailiwick of BarШГ-Seine. *p Barfur-Seine.* 16. A village of Burgundy, in the bailiwick of Chajlon. *p. Seure..* 17. A village of Burgundy, in the diocefe and bailiwick of Challón, *p. Cballon.* 18. A village of Franche-Comté, in the bailiwick of Lons-le-Saunier. *p. tons-U-Saunier.* 19. A village of Provence,, in the viguery of Forçaiquier. *p. Forcalquier* 20. A-village of Franche-Comté, in the bailiwick, of Salins. *Salins..* ZI. A village of Franche-Comté, in the bailiwick of Arbois. *p. Befancon.* ал. A village of Armagnac, in the election of Aiiarsc. *p. Mirande-.* 23. A village of Provence, in the viguery of S. Paul, *p. Antihes.* 24.. A village of Brette, in the bailiwick of Bourg. *p. Bourg-cn-BriJf'e.* 25. An abby in the diocefe of Nantes, *p. Nantes.* 26. A priory in the diocefc of Rho-. dez.
Villeneuve, or *VMeneuve-les-Be'aiers*, or *Villeneuve-la-Cr emade*, a town of Lower Languedoc, in the dioeefc and receipt of Bcz-iers. *f_. B/sziers.* *Villeneuve*, or *Vdleneuve-d"Agftiùij* a town of Agénois, fituatcd од *V.Hera's*, 3 fmall town of Forez, in the election of Roanne.. *p. Roanne.* *Villetbzn*, a town of Bléfois, in the dio.efe and election of Blois. *p. Blols.* *Vllereau.* I. A village of Orleannois, in the diocefe and election of Orléans, *p. Or I fan t.* *1.* A village of Orléannois, in the election of Pithiviers. *p. Pitbiviers.* *Vtllereau Csf Hcriign'* «, a village of Hainaut, in the government of Quênoy. *p. le Quénoy.* *Villerecogr.edc*, *S. Martial-de*, a village of Saintonge, in the election of Saintes, *p.*

Saintes. *Villereglan*, a place of Languedoc, in the receipt of Limoux. *p. Limcux.* *Villercs.* I. A fmall town of Armagnac, in the election of RivièreVerdun, *p. Grenade*, i. A village of Armagnac, in the diocefc and election of Auch. *p. Aucb.* *VtHtrtt*, a village of Picardy, in the election of S. Quentin, *p. & Quentin.* *Vi/terets*, a village of Champagne, in the diocefe and election of Troycs. *p. Vtry.* *Vtliercverfure*, a fmall towri of Breffc, in the bailiwick of Bourg. *p. Btmrg-en-Brejfe.* *Villern*, a village of Normandy, in the election of Andcly. *p. Ecьıy.* *Villerborjf, le*, a place of Meffin, in the diocefc and receipt of Metz. *p. Met-..* *Ville, maias*, a village of Lower Languedoc, in the diocefc and receipt oí Pùy. *p. le Puy.* *Vtlltrmea*, a vii.lage of Orlcannois, in the election of Bcaugcncy. *p. Mmn.* *Villerch*, я village of Picardy, in the diocefc and election of Amiens. *p. Amiens.* *Vi/leronjir*, a village of Ecauce, in the election of Vcndùmc. *p. Véndeme.* *XUIerat*, a village of the lib of France, in the diocefe and election of I. л V *p. Louvres.* *VJlcrot*, a place of Burgundy, in the bailiwick of Avalon, *f. Avalon.* *Villerey.* i. A village of Meflin, in the diocefe and receipt of Tout. *p. Viiid. 2.* A village of Picaidy, in the election of Abbeville, *p. Aurr.ale.* 3. A village of Champagne, in the diocefe and election of Sens. *p. Sens.* 4. A village of Champagne, in the bailiwick of Vi try. *p. Vttry.* 5. A château of the Ifle of France, in the diocefe of Paris, *p. Corbeil.* *Villtrfol*, a village of Hainaur, in thi government of Quênuy. *p. le Sl¿iney.* *Villers.* i. A village of Normandy, in preelection of Pont-1'Evéque. *f. Pom. ГEve'que.* 1. A village of Franche-Comté, in the bailiwick of Vefoul. *p. Lure.* 3. A village of Berry, in the elect i-n of Châteauroux, *p. Châlcauroux.* 4. A village of Meflin, in the diocefe of Treves. *p. Mem.* 5. A marquifate of Brie, in the election of Provins, *p. Coultmiers.* 6. A lake near the town of Linieret, in Berry; about 8 leagues in circumference.
Villers, or *Villers-en-Buage*, a market-town of Normandy, in the election of Caen. *p. Cain.* *fillers & Camp/art*, a village of Picardy, in the diocefe and elec-

tion of Amiens, *p. Amiens. Filters,* or S. *Remy-de-Villers-Coterlr,* a convent in the diocefe of Scnlis. *p. Villers-Colterits. Villcrs-Allirand,* a fmall town of Champagne,in the diocefe and election of Rheim«;, *p. Rheims. Villert.au-lertre,* a village of Flanders, in the fubdelegation of Bouchain. *p. Boucbain. Villersau-Treau,* a village of Flanders, in the fubdelegation of Çambray. *p. Cambray. Villcrs-aux-Bois.* т. A village of Champagne, in the election of JoinVÜÍe. *p. fpernay. z..* A village of Artois, in the bailiwick of Lens. *p. Arras. Villers-aux.Clines,* a village of Champagne, in the election of Joinvillc. *p. Bar-fur-Aube. Villeri-aux-Erables,* a village of Picardy, in the election of Mondidier. *p. Amiens. Villers-auxNarufs,* a village of Cliampagne, in the diocefe and election of Rheims, *p. Rheims. Villcrs-Bain & Serre',* a village of Burgundy, in the bailiwick of Avalon, *p. Avalon. Villers-Bocage,* a village of Picardy, in the election of Doulens. *p. Amiens. Villers-Boulin,* a marquifate of Artois, in the government of Arras. *f. Arras. Villers-Bouton,* a village of Franche-Comté, in the bailiwick of Vefoul. *p. Vefoul. Villirs-Bretcnneux,* a village o. Picardy, in the diocefe and election of Amiens, *p. Corbie. Villers-Bufon,* a village of Franche-Comté, in the diocefe and bailiwick of Befançon. *f. B.fanfon. VU 1er i-Brulin, Villers. Cagnî-. court,* and *Villers.Caftel,* villages of Artois, in the diocefe and bailiwick of Arras, *p. Arras. Vjllers-Car.ivet,* a village of Nor« mandy, in the election of Falaife. *f. Falaife. Villers-Cauchies,* a village'of Flanders, in the fubdelegation of Bouchain. *p. Bouchain. Villers-Cernay,* a fmall town of Champagne, in the receipt of Sedan. *p. Sedan. vUlers-Chemins,* a village of Franchc-Comté,in the bailiwick of Gray. *p. Befartpn. Vi/ lers-Chicf,* a village of Franche-Comté, in the bailiwick oí Baume, *p. Baume. Villers-Cciieiêts, a,* town of Picardy, in the diocefe of Senlis, and election of Crêpy; it is fituated iu the foreft of Retz, 8 leagues from Compiégnc, 14 from Mcaux, aj gundy, in the bailiwick, of Avalon. *p. Au.iloi:. Vdhrs-U-Helhn,* a village of Pi-, c.irdy, in the diocefe and

eleñion of Saifions. *p. So'tßhns. VJ.'ersles-Blanmont,* a place of FrancheComté, in the bailiwick of Baume, *p. Baume. ViHen-les-Biis,* a village of Franche-Comté, in the bailiwick of Dole. *p. Dole. Villen-lc-Scc.* I. A village of Picardy, in the diocefe and election of Laon. *p. Laon.* 2. A village of Franche-Comté, in the bailiwick of Vefoul. *p. Vefoul.* 3. A place of FrancheComté, in the bailiwick, of Baume, *p. Baume. Villers-le-Secq,* 3 village of Nivernois, in the election of Clamecy. *p. Clamecy. Villen-les-Guife,* a village of Picardy, in the elcilion of Guife. *p. Guife. Villen-les-Momei,* or *Vil/ers-S. Georges,* an abby in the diocefe of ScnllS. *p. Villers-C'Jtterets. Villers-les-Nonaim,* a fmall town of Burgundy, in the bailiwick of Avalon, *p. Avalon. Villenle-lOutneury* a village of Champagne, in the diocefe and election of Rheims, *p. Reibet. Villers-les-Rigaux,* a village of Brie, in the diocefe and election of Meaux. *p. Lift. Villen-les-Roye,* a village of Picardy, *in* the eltflion of Mondidieri *p. Roye. Vtllen-Г Hôpital,* a village of Artois, in the bailiwick of Hefdin. *p. Doulens. Villen-Lame,* a village of Meffin, in the diocefe and receipt of Metz. *p. Metx. Villen-Mantel,* or *Mar.tclle,* » village of Normandy, in the election of Andely. *p. Gaillon. vMcri-Marmtry,* and *Villen. Mcurtry,* villages of Champagne, in the diocefe and eleition of Rheims. *p. Rheims. ViiUrs-Mmßrt,* a village ofSurdy, in the dioccfe and election of Noyon. *p. Nejen. Villefpfas,* a place of Upper Languedoc, tn the dioccfe and receipt of S. Papoul. *p. Cüßc/nkudary. Villetaneujsy* a village of the lile of France, *p. Paris. Villetarte,* fay a village of Normandy, in the election of ChaumodC *p. Cbaumont. VxlUtaudy* a village of FrancheComté, in the election of Orgelet. *p. Lons-le-Sdumer. Vilhtdle,* a village of Lower Languedoc, in the diocefe and receipt of Montpellier, *p. Montpellier. y.Uetelley* fay a village of Lower Languedoc, in the diocefe and receipt of Viviers, *p. VtvitrS, Vilktbieny,* a village of Cham ?igne, in the diocefe and election of ens. *p. Sens. Ville'.oureySy* a fmall town of Périgord, in the diocefe and election of

Périgueux. *p. la Chalard. m VHIetritouhy* a village of Lower Languedoc, in the dioccfe and receipt of Carcaflonne. *p. Carcañonne. Villetrun,* a village of Beauce, ill the election of Vendôme, *p. Vendant?.* -ч *VilUtte.* i. A village of Beauce, in the election of Mantes, *p. Mantes.* 2. A village.of Franche-Comté, in the bailiwick of Arbois. *p. Salins,* 3. A villane of Champagne, in the diocefe and election of T royes. *p. Doncbcry.* 4. A village of Franche-Comté, in the LailFv/ick of Dole. *p. Dole.* 5. A village of Champagne, in the election of Rethel. *p. Retbcl.* 6. A village of Dombcs, in the chatellnny of Chitelar. *p. Bourg-cnBiße.* 7. Л pince of Dombcs, in the chateíhny of Beauregard, *p. Vi/ Ufranche.* 8. A place of Breite, in the bailiwick of ßourg. *f. Bourg-en-BreJJê. Villette-de-Lcye,* and *Villette-dtKicbemonty* viibges of Breffe, in the bailiwick of Bourg, *p. Bourg-cnBzß. 'vMette-CttCtlomberet,* a village of *Viltiers-laGrange,* a village Burgundy, in the bailiwick of Noye rs. *p. Noyers. Villiers-le-Bajelc,* and *vUUers-leSeej,* villages of the Ille of France, in the diocefe and deftion of Paris. *p. Para. Pl/liersle-Bois,* and *fiüiers-Pcrtras,* villages of Champagne, in the eleftion of Tonnerre, *p. Tonnerre. Villar s-It-Ccmte, VilliersletPautons,* and *Vili.ers-Ncnain,* places of Burgundy, in the bailiwick of Avalon, *p. Àvalon. y¡¡l'ier¡-le-S«.* I. A village of Champagne, in the diocefe and election of Chalons, *p. Vitty.* 2. A village in the eleftion of Chaumont. *p. Cbnmont-tn-Bajjigry.* 3. A village of Nermandy, in the diocefe and eleftion of Bayeux. *p. Bayeux. Villiers-le-Matieu,* a village of Bcaucc, in the eleftion of Mantes. *p. Mantes. vUliert—Us-Herbiffa,* a village of Champagne, in the diocefe and election of Troyes. *p. Troyes. ViUiers-les-Apreiy,* a village of Champagne, in the diocefe and election of Langres. *p. Langres. Vdlitrs-Us-Hauts,* a fmall town of Burgundy, in the bailiwick of Avalon, *p. Noyers. Fi/liers-lesPofs,* a village of Burgundy, in the diocefe and bailiwick of Dijon, *p. Dijon. Villitrs-Montfort,* a village of Burgundy, in the bailiwick of Scmur-en-Auxois. *p.*

Smur-cn-JTuxois. Villiers-S.-Bartkelemi, a fmall town of Picardy, in the diocefe and eleftion of Beauvais. *p. Bcau-vais. Wfiert-S.-Benoît,* a village of Champagne, in the eleftion oi'Joigny. *p. Joigny. VilliersS-Framtcurt,* and *VtlViers-fms-S.-Lo,* villages of Picardy, in the dioccfe and eleftion of Scnlis. *p. Sen/is. VtlHers-S.-Paul,* a fma!! town of Picardy, in the dioceft and eleftio« of Scnlis. *p. Senlis. VilHers-S.-Scpukbre,* a priory in the diocefe of Béarnais, *p. Белuvan. Milliers-fous-Coudun,* a village of Picardy, in the election of Compiégne. *p. Compiégne: Villiers-fous-Praßin,* a village of Champagne, in the election of Barfur-Aube. *p. Bar-fur-Auie. fdliers-fur-Ecal/es,* a village of Normandy, in the diocefe and election of Rouen, *p. Rouen. Villitrs-fur-Foucarmont,* a village of Normandy, in the cUction of Neufch?tel. *p. Neufcbatel. VJliers-ur-Marne.* I. A village of the lile of France, in the diocefe and election of Paris, *p. Cbelles.* 2. A village of Champagne, in the election of Chaumont. *p. Cbaumont-cnBaßgny. ViUiers-fur-Orge,* a village of the Ifle of France, in the diocefe and election of Paris, *p. Linas. Filliers-fur-Port,* я village of Normandy, in the diocefe and election of Baycux. *p. B ay eux. Vdliers-fur-Suixe,* a village of Burgundy, in the bailiwick of ChâtilJon. *p. Cbâtillon. VUliers-jur-Tolkn,* a fmall town of Champagne, *im* the élection of Joig 11У *f-УЧ'У Vlitten-Vineux,* a village of Champagne, in the election of Tonnerre. *p. S. Florentin. Vdlxbe,* a parifh in Touraine.
V,llime'& Party, a village of Picardy, in the diocefe and election of Soiffons. *p. la Fere. Villon.* I. A fmall town of Champagne, in the election of Tonnerre. *Tcnnerre.* 2. A village of Donates, in the chatcllany of Villeneuve. *p. Bourg-cn-BreJje. Vilhneur,* a village of Angoumois, in the diocefe and election of AngouJême. *p. la Rscbefoucault. Vilkrfanges,* a fmall town of Auvergne, in the election of Rtom. *p. Riem. Vilkfc,* a village of Provence, in the viguery of Siftcron. *p.Siflersn. Vilktte.* i. A vUlage-ofBurgundy, in the diocefe and receipt of A uxerre. *p. Auxerre.* 2. A village of Burgundy, in the bailiwick of Châtil-

lon. *p. Cbitilkn-fur-Sme.* 3. A place of Champagne, in the election of Vitry. *p. Vitry-le-Francois. ViUotte-prh-S-Seine,* a village of Burgundy, in the bailiwick of Chátillon. *p. S. Seine. Villuis,* a village of Champagne, in tht election of Nogent. *p. Nogent. Villurlin* Ê? *Njrlois,* я village of Burgundy, in the bailiwick of Avalon, *p. A-val.n. Villy.* I. A village of Normandy, in the election of Caën. *p. Caen, z.* A village of Normandy, in the élection of Eu. /. *Eu.* 3. A village of Normandy, in the election of Falaifc. *p. Falaije.* 4. A village of Burgundy, in the bailiwick of Scmur. *p. Scmur.* 5. A village of Champagne, in the election of S. Florentin, *p. S. Florentin. Villy-le-BruU,* and *Г,1Гуг1e-Mou/tier,* villages of Burgundy, in the bailiwick of Nuits, *p. Nuits. VUly.le-Mare'cbal,* я village of Champagne, in the diocefe and election of Troyes. *p. Troyes. Vikry,* я village of FrancheComte, in the bailiwick of Vcfoul. *Vejoul. Viijpirg,* a village of Mcffin, in the diocefe and receipt of Metz. *p. Metz. Vilvoca,* я village of Gatinois, in the election of Nemours, *p. Nemours. Vimarcc,* a town of Maine, in the diocefe and election of Mans. *p. Frefnay. Vimenety* я village of Roucrgue, in the election of Milhaud. *p. Milbaud. Vmeu,* or *Vbneux,* a country of Picardy, of which S. Valéry is the capital. *Vimonßier.* See *Vimoutier. Vimont.* i. A village of Normandy, in the elcâioR of Caën. *p. Trnrâ. %,* A figniory of Normandy, in the election of Lions. *Vimoryy* a town of Gâtinois, in the election of Montargis. *p. Moritargis. Vunmttxer,* a market-town of Normandy, fituated on the river Vie; 6 leagues frorn Argentan, 9 from Lifieux, and 16 from Alençon. *f, Argentan. Vhnpelle,* a village of Champagne, in the election of Nogent. *f. Brayfur-Se!ne. Vmy,* or *Neuville.* See *Neuville. Vinadhre, la,* a place of Limolin, in the election of Tulles. *p. Uzcrcbes. Finante,* a village of Brie, in the dioccfe and election of Mcaux. *p. Meaux. ViTwjfëtt,* a village of Lower Languedoc, m the receipt of Limoux. *p. Nar bonne. Vinax,* a village.of Poitou, in the election of Niort. /. *Niort. Vinay.* i. A village of Champagne, ia the election of Epcrnay. *p. Epernay.* 2. A village of Daupbiny, in

the election of Romans, *f. S. Marcelin. Vm¿x,* a convent in the dioccfe of See/. , *p. Sttat, Vinca,* a town of Rouflillon, in the vigucry of Conflans. *p. Perpignan. Vincdle,* a vilbge of FranchcCnmté, in the bailiwick, of Lons-leSaunier. *p. L'. r.i-h'-Saunier. VinftUeu* t. A village of Burgundy, in the bailiwick of Chalons, *p. Louans.* 2. A village of Burgundy, in the dioccfe and bailiwick of Aux erre. *p. Auxerrt.* 3. A village of Champagne, in the election of Ep-rnay. *p. Dcrmans»* 4. A village of Burgundy, in the dioccfe and bailiwick of Challón, *p. Challón. Vincclotte,* a village of Champagne, in the election of Tonnerre, *p. Auxerrc Vintennes,* an ancient royal palacr, in the lile of France; 2 leagues from Taris, in the road to Mcáux. *Bu zeлu de poße. Vincent,* a village of FrancheComte, in the bailiwick, of Potigny. *p. Salins. Vincy-Manœuvre, г* village of Bric, in the diocefc and election of Meaux. *p. Lijy. Vincy Reuil, la, & Magny,* 2 village of Picardy, in thediocefe ani election of Laon. *p. Laon. Vinduy.* i. A village of Burgundy, in the bailiwick of Scmur-cnBricnnois. *p. Semur.* 2. A village ot Burgundy, in the bailiwick of Clurolles. *p. Dijon.* 3. A village of Brie, in the election of Sezanne, *p. S zjnne. Vmdille,* a village ci Angoumois, in the dioccfe and election of Angoulême. *p. Angoulêne. Vxnarac,* a vilbge of Upper Languedoc, in the dioccfe and receipt of Albv. *p. Alhy. Vine m:, mite,* a village of Normandy, in the election of Caudcbec. *p. Caudebtc. Vkctv,* a village of Champagne, in the dioccfe and election oí Chitons, *p. Chalons. VintuM,* i. A town of Blclois, in the dioccfe and election of Blois. *p. Bio's.* 2. A village of Berry, in the election of Châteauroux-*p. Château oux. Vineup,* a village of Poitou, in the election of Funtcnay. *p. Tbire. lr,ne:.fe, la,* a village of Burgundy, in the dioccfe and bailiwick of Micon, *p. Mâcw. Vitunsac,* a village of Lower Languedoc, i« the dioccfe and receipt of Viviers, *p. Aubcnas. Vir.genr. c, л* fmall river of Champagne. *Vwgrau,* a village of Rouffillor» in the dioccfe and vigucry of Perpignan, *p. Perpignan. Vmgrcl,* a village of Picardv, in the dioccfe and election of Süiifonb. *p.*

Soiß'om. Vinbanaps, a village of Normandy, in the election of Alençon. *p. Alençon, Vxriy-S.-Jean-Qoulpb*, a vilbge »f Brie, in the eleftion of ChâteauThierry, *p. Chateau-Thierry. Virmcufs*, a town of Champagne, in the eleftion of Nogent. *p. Villejsewve-la-Guyard. Vmo*, a village of Rouerguc, in the diocefc and eleftion of Rhodes. *f. Rhodes. Vinois*, a village of Forez, in the eleftion of Montbrifon. *p. Montbrijon. Yuan.1.* A village of Provence, in the viguery of Barjols. *p. Aix. %.* A village of Berry, in the diocefe and eleftion of Bourges. *p. Sancerre. Vim*, a village of Provence, in the viguery of Brignoles. *p. Brignoles. Vfnjohres*, a village of Dauphiny, in the eleftion of Montelimart. *p. Nions. Vintrou, le*, a village of Upper Languedoc, in the diocefc and receipt of Caftres. *p. Cajirts. Vimselle, la*, a village of Rouergue, in the eleftion of Villcfranche. *p. Vtllefranehe-de-Rouergue. Viradles*. I. A village of Burgundy, in the diocefe and bailiwick of M3con. *p. Mâcon.* 2. A village f Auvergne, in the eleftion of Biom. *p. Riom. VioUen-Laval*, and *VwI-le-Foreas*, towns of Lower LangTiedoc, in the diocefe and receipt of Montpellier. *f. Montpellier. Vu aine*. I. A village of Artois, m the bailiwick of Lens. /. *la Bajee*, г. A village of Picardy, in the diocefe and eleftion of Soiflbns. *f. Soiffons. Vidange & S. Clement*, a place of Meflin, in the diocefe and receipt of Metz. *p. Metse.. Violette, la*, a village of Champagne, in the eleftion of Joigny. *p. Jo':gr,y. Violey-Montipcn*, and *Violey-Villette*, villages of Forez, in the eleftion of Roanne, *p. Roanne. Violles*, a village of Armagnac, in the diocefe and eleftion of Auch. *p. Auch. Van.* I. A town of Anjou, in -the eleaion of Flèche, *p. Sah!/, v* A fmall town of Vivarais, in the diocefe and receipt of Viviers, *p. Tain. Vion Êf Hamencourt*, a place of Picardy, in the election of Abbeville. *p. Abbeville. yionville*, a village of Meflin, in the diocefe and receipt of Metz. *p. S. Nicolasen-Lorraine. Viplaix*, a village of Bourbonnois, in the election of Montîuçoiv *p. AÎorttluçcn. V.ra* I, A village of Lower Languedoc, in the diocefe and receipt of Alct. *p. Lmoux.* z. A village of Upper Languedoc, in the diocefe and receipt of M repoix. *p. Mirepuîx. Viracy* a village of Guienne, in the diocefe and election of Bourdcaiix. *p. Ba%a%. PtraciesoCordeS)* a village of Upper Languedoc, in the diocefe and receipt of Alby. *p. Alby. Virandrw'iUe*, a village of Normandy, in the election of Valognes. *f. Vahgnei. Virargues*, a village of Auvergne, in the diocefe and election of S. Flour, *p. S. Flour. Vire.* i. A town of Normandy, fituated on the river Vire, in the diocefe of Baveux and generality of Caen; 13 leagues from Cae'n, 26 from Rennes, 3 from S. Sever, 6 from Villedieu, 13 from Grandville, 11 from Avranches, 20 from Dol, 26 from S. Malo, 40 from S. Brieux, 43 fr»m Rouen, and 66 from Paris, *B u r eau de paß e.* 2. A r i v er of Lower Languedoc, which paiTcs by Vire, Tcffy. S. Lo, &c. and falls into the Manche, at *Vcz-S.-Clement*. 3. A town of Normandy, in the election of Mortain. *p. S. Htlahe.* 4. A village of Qucrcy, in the diocefc and election of Cahors *p. Villenewve-d" Agen. Thirty* a town of Anjou, in the election of Flèche, *p. Sable'. VireauXf* a village of Champagne, in the election of Тогшсrre. /». *Aflcy-lt-Yranc. Vtrclade*, a fmall town of Guiennc, in the diocefe and election of Bourreaux, *p. Cadillac, Virthuf-prh-le-Pa'vUlon*, a village of Champagne, in the diuccfe and election of T royes, *p. troyes. Virement*, a village of FrancheComté, in the bailiwick of Orgelet. *p. L',nt-le-Sauner. Vueville*, a village of Normandy, in the election of Montivillicrs. *p. Coûtances, Vr¿ux-U-VaUerantly* a village of Hainautj in the government of Charlemont. *p. ÇkarUmont. Virey.* i. A village of Burgundy, in the diocefe and bailiwick of Challón, *p. Challón.* 2. A village of Burgundy, in thé diocefe and bailiwick of Macon, *p. Maon.* 3. A village of Franche-Comté, in the bailiwick of Cray.'/». *Gray, Virey-JouS'Bar*, a village of Champagne, in the election of Bar-furAube. *p. Bar-fur-Aube. Virginité) la*, a..onvent, in the diocefe of Mans. *p. Vendôme, Virginy*, a village of Champagne, in the election of Ste. Manéhould. *f, Ste. Mane'bould. Viri.* i. A village of FrancheComté, in the diocefe and bailiwick of S. Claude. /. 5. *Claude,* 2. See *Vry.* ч *Viry & Cbatilkn*, a village of the lib of France, in the diocefe and election of Paris, *p. Lwjumeaut Viriat*, a village of BrelTc, in the bailiwick of Bourg, *p. Bsurg-en Breß. Virice/les*, a village of Forez, in the election of Montbrifon. *p. Mentir ijon. Virieu*, a town of Forez, in the election of S. Etienne, *p. S. Etienne. Viricu-le-Grand*, and *Vtrieu-lePetie*, towns of Bugey, in the diocefe of Belley. *p. Belley, Virievxy* a fmall town of Dauph'my, in the diocefe and election of Vienne, *p. S. Cbamtnt, VifigmcU)* a village of Forcz in the election of Montbrifon. *p. Mont brifon. Vuigmn*, a village of Bugey, in the bailiwick of Belley. *p. Belley. ViríuiUe*, a village of Dauphiny» in the election of Romans, *p. la Cot e-S.-Andre'. Virltt*, a village of Auvergne, in the election of Combrailles. *p. Cham' bon, tlrlet & la Communantelle*, a fmall town of Auvergne, in the election of Riom. *p. Плот., Viroßay*, a village in the diocefe and election of Paris, *p. Verfalles. Virolet & Maßion*, a village of Saintunge, in the diocefe and election of Saintes, *p. Cezez. Vtron*, a village of Beam, in the receipt of Orthez. *p. Ortbcz. Vironchaux*, a village of Picardy, in the election of Abbeville, *p. Abbeville. Virone*, a fmall river of Normandy, which falls into the Dattée. *Virfac*, a village of Guienne, in the diocefe and election of Bourdeaux. *p. Bourdeaux. Virfcn*, a village of Aunis, in the dWefe and election of Rochelle, *p. Maufë. Virville*, a village of Normandy, in the election of S. Lo. *p. S. Lo. Viry.* I. A parifh of Burgundy, compofed of feveral hamlets, in the bailiwick of Charollcs. *p. Djm.* 2. See *V,rl Viry-Noreuil*, a fmall town of Picardy, in the election of Noyon. *p. Noyon. Vis & Marcß*, and *V:s-fur-Autbie*, villages of Picardy, in the election of Abbeville, *p. Abbeville. , Vis-en-Arlois*, a village of Artois, in the diocefe and bailiwick of Arras. *p. Arras. Vis-fur-Aifne*, a town of Picardy, in the diocefe and election of Soiffons. *p. Soiffons. Vifcin*, a town of Venaiffin, in the judicature of Carpcntras. *p. Valreas. Vifecbe*, a village of Bretagne, ia in the diocefe anil receipt of Rennes. *Vitri. Vfets*, a village of Gafcony, in the Tec-

cipt of Bigorre. *p. Tarta. Viferry,* a village of Burgundy, in the bailiwick of Semur. *p Semur. Vifgearde,* a place of FrancheComté, in the bailiwick of Dole. *p. Ode. V.ßgneul,* or *Vißgnol,* an ab'y in the diocefe of Amiens, *p. Arnum. Vißis,* a village of Alfacc, in the bailiwick of Fcrrette. *p. llumngme. Vijmt,* a village of Picardy, in the election of Abbeville, *p. Abheiille. Viernes & Andecourt,* a village of Picardy, in the diocefe and election f Amiens, *p. Amiens. Vtfencourt,* a village ef FrancheComté, in the bailiwick of Vefoul. *f. Lure. Vßjuer,* a village of Gafcony, in the receipt of Bigorre. *p. Bagneres. Viß'ac,* a village of Auvergne, in the election of Brioude. *p. Brioude. Vife,* a village of Mcffin, in the iicccfe and receipt of Metz. *p. Metz. Viß'ec,* a village of Lower Languedoc, in the diocefe and receipt of Alais, *p. Alais, Vijfcr.a,,* a villaje of FrancheComté, in the bailiwick of Dole. *p. Vole. VJ';s,* a village of Gafcony, in the receipt of Bigorre. *f. Tarées. Vjfire, It,* a fmall river of Lower Languedoc. *Vitaiville,* a village of Mcffin, in the diocefe and receipt of Verdun. *p. Verdun. Vttalirr.e,* or *S. Martial-de-VUaleine,* a village of Saintonge, in the diocefe and election of Saintes, *p. Saintes. Vitien.* See *Vittcaux. Vierte,* a village of Upper Languedoc, in the diocefe and receipt of Lava nr. *p. La-vaur. Vttermnt,* a village of Picardy, in the election of Péronne. *p. Peronne. Vnfleurs.* See *Vittefliurs. Vubarel,* a village of Franche-Comté, in the bailiwick of Baume. *f. Baume. Vitcmcoutt,* a village of Mcffin, ta the diocefe and receipt of Metz. *p. Metz. Vitet,* and *Vttotel,* villages of Normandy, in the election of Conches. *p. le Ñeufbcurg.. Vitouard,* a brook of Normandy, which runs into the fea near Délivrandc.
Vitia-lc-Dognon, a village of Limofin, in the diocefe and election of Limoges, *p. Limoges. Vitrac.* I. A fmall town of Périgord, in the diocefe and election of Sarlat. *p. Sarlat. z.* A fmall town of Auvergne, in the election of Aurillac. *p. Auriliae.* 3. A village of Agénois, in the diocefe and election of Agen. *f. Agen.* 4. A village of Auvergne, in the election of Riom. *p. Aiguc-Pirfe. Vitrât,* a village of Limofin, in the diocefe and election of Tulles, *p. Tulles. Vitray.* I. A fmall town of Touraine, in the election of Loches, *p. Loches.* 2. A village of Beauec, in the election of Chátcaudun. *p. Bcnneval.* 3. A village of Bourbonnois, in the election of Montlueon. *p. Aîontluçan. V. tray-fcus-BrefoUis,* a village of Perche, in the election of Verneuil. *p. Brcfetles. Vitrty-feus-l'Aigle,* a village of Normandy, in the election of Verreuil. *p. l'Aigle. Vitre'.* 1. A city of Bretagne, fituated on the Vilaine, in the diocefe and receipt of Rennes; 9 leagues from Laval, 10 fr.m Rennes, 31 from Alençon, 17 from Mayenne, 26 from S. Malo, 38 from Nantes, 46 from l'Orient, 785 from Brcfr, 36 from Vannes, 45 trom Tours, and. 78 from Paris *Bureau de ptfit,* 2. A village of Poitou, in the election of S. Maixant. *p. S. Maixant. Vitreux,* a village of FrancheComté, in the bailiwick of Dole. *p. Cray.* from Lure, 65 from Bcffurt, 79 from Bale, 18 from Rheims, 28 J from Laon, and 48 from Paris. *Bureau de fojic. Vttry-Jur-Loire,* a village cf Burgundy, in the bailiwick of Bourbon-? Lancy. *p. Bourbon-Lamy. Vury-ßir-StiHt)* a town in the diocefe and election of Paris, *p. Vtilejuifve. Vitteaux,* a town of Burgundy, fituated in a mountainous country on the Brainc, in the diocefe of Autun, and bailiwick of Semur-en-Auxois; 10 leagues frem Dijon, 12 from Avalon, 23 from Auxcrre, and 37 from Taris. *Bureau de fuße. Vmeßeurs,* 0« *V tßeur,* a markettown of Normandy, fituatcd on the river Paluel; about 2 leagues from S. Valéry, *p. Fecamp. Vivaifi,* a village of Picardy, in the diocefe and election of Laon. *p. Laon. Viva!, le,* a village of Rouergue, in the diocefe and election of Rhodcz. *p. Rhoden. Vivans-en-Forez,* and *Vivans-enLycnnois,* villages of Forez, in the election of Roanne, *p. Roanne. Vivant.* i. A village of Burgundy, in the bailiwick of Charolles. *p. Dijcn.* 2. A village of Burgundy, in the bailiwick of Semur-en-Auxois. *p. Semur-en-Auxois Vivarais,* a fmall province of Lower Languedoc, bordered on the eaft by the Rhône, which feparatis it from Dauphiny, on the fuuth by tlx diocefe of (Jzés, on the well by Vclay snd Gevaiidun, ami on the north by Lyonnois; it is about 26 leagues in length, and 15 broad. Viviers is the capital. *Viturols,* a town of Auvergne, in the eleñion of Iflbirc. *p. lJjbire. Vives.* I. A village of Rouergue, in the election of Villefranche. *p. Villefrancbe-de-Rouergue.* 2. A fmall town of Armagnac, in the election of Lomagne. *p. S. Ciar. V. ves,* a place e'f Rouffillon, in in the dicccfc and viguery of Per pignan. *p. Petpignan. Vivey,* a village of Champagne, in the diocefe and eleftion of Langrcs. *p. Langres. Viveyrols,* or *5. Martial-de-Viveyrols,* a town of Périgord, in the Jiocefe and eleflion of Périgueux. *p. Périgueux. Vivier, le.* t. A village of Lower Languedoc, in the diocefe and receipt of AJet. *p. Limoux.* 2. A village of Bretagne, in the diocefe and receipt of Dol. /. *Dal. Vivier,* or *& Mart'w-du-Vivier,* a village of Normandy, m. the diocefe and eleflion of Rouen, *p. Rouen. Vivier-Jcurfault, le,* a village of Angoumois, in the diocefe and election of Angoulême. *p. Atgre. Vwiers.* I. An ancient city of Lower Languedoc, the capital of Vivarais, by the Rhone, the fee of a bilhop; about 5 leagues from Pont.-S.-Efprit, and 12 from Valence. *Bureau de poße.* 2. A town of Maine, in the diocefe and election of Mans. *p. Frcfney.* 3. A fmall town of Champagne, in the tkftion of Tonnerre, *f. Tcnner/e.* 4. A village of. Burgundy, in the bailiwick of Bar-fur-Seine, *p. BarJur-Seine.* 5. A village of Upper Languedoc, in the diocefe and receipt of Touloufe. *p. Touhufe.* 6. A village of Languedoc, in the diocefe and receipt of Mirepoix. *p. Mirefoix.* 7. A village of Forez, in the election of Montbrifon. *p. Montbrijoru* 8. A village of Champagne, in the eleftion of Rcthel. *p. Sedan.* 9. A village of Artois, in the bailiwick of Aire. *p. Aire.* 10. A place of Bourbonnois, in the election of S. Amand. *p. S. Amand. Viviers, le,* a convent in the diocefe of Arras, *p. Arras. ' Viviers-la-Montagne,* a town of Upper Languedoc, in the diocefe and receipt of Lavaur. *p. Cafires. Vtville,* a village of Angoumois, in the eleftion of Cognac, *p. Barbejieux. Vivam,* a town of Maine, in the diocefe and eleftion of Mans. *f. Frefnay. Vivone,* or *Vivonne,* a

town of Poitou, fituated on the Clain, in the diocefe and eleftion of Poitiers; 6 leagues from Poitiers, 23 from A11-goulème, and 95 from Paris. *Bureau de fcfie. Vivy,* a town of Anjou, in the eleftion of Saumur. *p. Saumur. Vix,* a town of Poitou, in the eleftion of Fontenay. *p. Marans. Vizille,* a chateau of Dauphiny, in the eleftion of Grenoble, *p, Gren'Me. Ukange,* a village of Menin, in the diocefe and receipt of Met, *p. Met«. Ulcol,* a village of Poitou, in the eleftion of Themars, *p. Tboturs. Ulecbincbove,* a village of Flanders, in the fubdelegation of Bailleu l. *p. Bailleuil. Vlly,* or *Huilly,* a village of Burgundy, in the diocefe and bailiwick of Challón, *p. Challón. Ully-S.-Georges,* a town of Picardy, in the diocefe and eleftion of Beauvais. *p. Clermont. Vlmaye,* an abby in the diocefe of Agde. *p. Agde. Ulmer,* a village of Lower Languedoc, in the diocefe and receipt of Puy. *p. le Buy. Ulmes-S.-Florent, les,* a village of Anjou, in the eleftion of Saumur. *p. Saumur. Ulmey,* a place of Champagne, in the eleftion of Vitry-le-Francois. *p. Vitry-le-Francois. Umpau,* a village of Beauce, in the diocefe and eleftion of Chartres. *p. Chartres, Un,* a town of Normandy, in the eleftion of Arques, *p. Dieppe. Uncent & S. Amand,* a village of Foix, in the generality of Rouihllon. *p. Foix. Urxey,* a village of Burgundy, in the bailiwick of Semur. *p. Semur. Uncbair,* a village of Champagne, in the diocefe and eleftion of Rheims. *p. Fijmes. Undefontaine,* a village of Normandy, in the election of Vire. *f. Vire. Ungerßiem,* a village of Alface, in the bailiwick of Bofweiller. *p. Rouffacb. Vnienville,* a village of Champagne, in the eleftion of Bar-fur-Aube. *p. Bar-fur-Лике. Unieu,* a fmall town of Forez, in the election of S. Etienne, *p. S. Etienne. Unry,* a place of Champagn«, in the diocefe and eleâion of Rheims. *p. Rheims. Unvers,* a town of Beauce, in the election of Chütcaudun. *p. litters. Uny-S.-Georges,* a village of Picardy, in the election of Clermont. *p. Clermont. Voiles,* a village of Franche-Comté, in the bailiwick of Orgelet, *p. Lons-le-Saunier. Voccance,* a fmall town of Vivarais, in the receipt of Viviers, *p. Дпг.onay. Voclas,* a village

of Lower Languedoc, in the diocefe and receipt of Béziers. *p. Be'ziers. Vodable,* a town of Auvergne, in the election of IfToire. *p. Iffoire. Vogeltzbeim,* a village of Alface, in the diocefe of Bale. *p. Rouffacb. Vogna,* a village of Franche-Comté, in the bailiwick of Orgelet, *p. Lons-le-Saunier. Vogtlinpoffen,* a village of Alface, in the bailiwick of Enfifheim. *p. Rouffacb. Vogué,* a village of Lower Languedoc, in the diocefe and receipt of Viviers, *p. Villeneuve-de-Berg. Void,* a market-town of Toulois, near the Meufe; 16 leagues from Verdun, 0/§ from Neufchâteau, б from Touli Iï from Nancy, 30 from Chalons, and 70$ from Paris. *Bureau de peße. Voignarue,* a village of Normandy, in the election of Eu. *p. Eu. Voigny,* a village of Champagne, in the election of Bar-fur-Aube. *p. Bar-fur-Aubt. Voilecampte,* a village of Champagne, in the eleftion of Joinvilk. *p. Vaffy. Voilemont,* a village of Champagne, in the election of Ste. Manénould. *p. Ste. Maneoould. Voillans,* a village of FrancheComté, in the bailiwick of Baume. *p. Baume. Vomebaut,* a village of Mpffin, in the diocefe and receipt of Metz. *p. Max. Voing,* a village of Auvergne, in the election of Riom. *p. Riom. Vo.vße & le Breuit,* a Tillage of Brie, in the election of Rozoy. *p. Roxoy. Voipreux,* a place of Champagne, in the diocefe and election of Chalons, *p. Epernay. Voire,* a river of Champagne, which runs into the Aube, a little below Chalette. *Voires,* a village of Franche-Comté, in the bailiwick of Ornans. *p, Befançon. Voiron,* a town of Dauphiny, in the diocefe and election of Grenoble, *p. Moirans. Voife,* a village of Beance, in the diocefe and election of Chartres, *p. Chartres. Voifemn,* a village of Gâtinois, in the election of Melun. *p. Melun, Voijey,* a village of Franche-Comté, in the bailiwick of Vefoul. *p. VeJoui. Voißnes.* I. A fmall town of Champagne, in the diocefe and election ot Sens. *p. Sens.* a. A village of Champagne, in the diocefe and election of Langres. *p. Langrcs.* 3. An abby in the diocefe of Orleans. *p. Melun. Voißns,* a fmall town of Lower Languedoc, in the diocefe and receipt of Carcaifonne. *p. Carcaffonnt. Voißns & ¡es Hameaux,*

a village in the diocefe and election of Paris. *p. Megúx. Vqjay,* a village of Saintonge, in the election of S. Jean-d'Angely. *p. S. Jean-d'Angely. Vcβv'ercs,* a (mail town of Auvergne, in the election of Iffoirc. *p. Jffárc. Vojl,* a village of Marche, in the election of Gueret. *p. Gueret. Vcu,* a town of Tourainc, in the election of Loches, *p. Lo¡k.!. Vojtirces,* a village uf Brie, in the elcttion of Sezanne, *p. &ъanг.c. VoucLcy,* a place oi RurgunJy, in the bailiwick, of Beaunc. *p. Beaunc. Vcuaenne,* a place of Champagne, in the diocefe and election ot Chalons, *p. Chalons. Vudenay-lt-Ciateau,* a parifh of Burgundy, composed oi feveral hamlets, in the diocefe and bailiwick of Ailtlin. *p. Au;:.!:. Voudenay-1'Eglife,* a village of Burgundy, in the bailiwick of Arnay-le-Duc. */. Auuin. Vovc, /a,* an ancient chateau in Perche, *Voue,* a village of Aunis, in the dioccfc and election of Rochelle, *p. la Rochelle. Vouccourt,* a village of Champagne, in the election of Chaumont. *p. Cbaumont-cn-Bajj.gny. Vouel,* a village of Picardy, in the dioccfc and election of Noyon. *p. JNoycn. Voues,* a town of Bcauce, in the dioccfc and election of Chartres, *p. Chartres. Vauejcrcville,* a village of Normandy, in the election of Punt-A udemer. *p. Pont-Audtmer. Vouet,* a village of Berry, in the election of Blanc, *p. le Blanc. Vougeot,* a village of Burgundy, in the bailiwick of Nuits, *p. Nuits. Vougland,* a village of FianchcCorate, in the diocefe and bailiwick of S. Claude, *p. S. Claude. VougU,* a town of Poitou, in the diocefe and election of Poitiers, *p. Poitiers. Vougrey,* a village of Champagne, in the election of Bar-fur-Aube. *p. Bar-fur Seine. Vcbuarte,* a village of Angoumois, in the election of Cognac, *p. Agre, Vouhc,* a village of Poitou, in the election of Niort, *p. Ri.uje. Vcithcnans,* a village ot FrauchcComte, in the bailiwi.k of Vcfuul. *p. Vejad. VouLct,* a village of Marcl.e, in the election of Gueret. *p. S.Bcnoudu-Sault. Voui/lc.* I. A town of Poitou, in the election of Niort, *p. Marans.* 2. A fmall town or Poito.;, in the ejection of Fontcnay. *p. A.rwult.* 3. A fmall town of Poitou, in the diocefe and election of Poitiers, *p.*

Poitiers. Vouillon-Prieurc, à village of Berry, in the election of Iffoudun. *p. IJ'audun. Vouilly,* a village of Normandy, in the diucctrnnd election of Baycux. *p. Baycux. Voulaine,* a wood of 92 arpents in the jurildiction of Challón, in Burgundy.
Vculaine.les-Trir.plicrs, a village of Burgundy, in the bailiwick of Chutillon. *p. ChâtilUn-jur-Scine. Voulejme,* a fmall town of Poitou, in the diocefe and election of Poitiers, *p. Cbaunay. Voulgezac,* a village of Angoumois, in the diocefe and election of Angoulêmc. *p. Angculêmt. Voulgezac,* a village of Angoumois, in the election of Cognac, *p. Cognac. Voulgy,* a fmalltown of Bcaujolois, in the election of ViUcfranche. *p. Vilefranche. youlhon,* a village of Angoumois, in the diocefe and election of Angouléme. *p. Angoulcme. Voullangis,* or *S. Martin-de-Voullangis,* a lmall town of Brie, in the diocefe and election of Meaux. *p. Cray. Voulu,* a priory, in the diocefe of Sens. *p. Sens. Voulon,* a village of Poitou, in the diocefe and election of Poitiers, *p, Couhe'. Voulons,* a village of Limofin, in the d oct fe and cklUun of Lijuogcs *p. le Dorât. Vmtixac,* a town ef Limofin, in the eleftion of Brives. *p. Br'tves. Vautré,* a town of Maine, in the diocefe and eleftion of *Mans. p. Mayenne. Viutrtin,* a village of Aunis, in the eleftion of Rochelle, *p. ¡a Rockefirt. Voutte, la.* I.A town of Auvergne, in the eleftion of Brioude. *p. Aurillac.* 2. A town of Lower Languedec, in the diocefe and receipt of S. Pons. *p. Beziers. Vouttegon,* a town of Poitou, in the diocefe and eleftion of Poitiers. *p. Tbouars. Vou-vant,* a tewn of Poitou, in the eleftion of Fontenay. *p. Fontenay-hComte. Vottvautes,* or5. *Jutien-de-Vowvantes,* a village of Bretagne, in the diocefe and receipt of Nantes, *p. Nantes. Vmrve'ix,* a village of Marche, in the eleftion of Bourganeuf. *p. Bourganeuf. Vcterray.* I. A town of Touraine, on the CX--ÍC, in the diocefe and election of Tours, *p. Tours,* a. A town of Maine, in the diocefe of Mans. *p. la Ferté-Bernard.* 3. A village of Maine, in the diocefe and eleftion of Mans. *p. Connere.* 4. A village of Bugey, in the bailiwick of Bclley. *p.*

Belly. Уоия, a town of Brie, in the election of Montcreau. *p. Montereau. Vcw &alllesy* a fmall town of Poitouj in the eleftion of Richelieu, *p. Airvault. Vouzeau,* a fmall town of Angoumois, in the diocefe and eleftion of Angoulême. *p. Angtultme. Vcuneron,* a town of Berry, about 3 leagues from Mclun. *p. Vterfon.* Voïrzie, la, a river of Brie, which runs into the Seine, near Bray. *Vewûeres,* a town of Champagne, in the eleftion ofRethel. *p. Retbel. Vouzon,* a town of Orléannois, in the diocefe and eleftion of Orléans. *p. Orléans. Vouxy,* a town of Champagne, on the Aime; about 8 leagues from Se dan. and IO from Rheim?. *p. Rtthel. Voyde, le,* a town of Anjou, in the eleftion of Montreuil-Bellay. *p. Saumur. Voye, la,* an abby in the diocefe of Vannes, *p. Vannes. Voyenne.* I. A village of Picardy, in the diocefe and election of Noyon. *p. Ham.* 2. A village of Picardy, in the diocefe and cicftion of Laon. *p. Laon. Vozelles.* I. A village of Marche, in the eleftion of Gueret. *p. Guertt.* 2. A parifh of Bourbonnois, in the election of Gannat. *p. Gsnnat. Ufaix,* a fmall town of Dauphiny, in the diocefe and election of Gap. *p. &ßeron. Upie,* a fmall town of D uphiny, in the diocefe and cicftion of Valence, *p. Valence. Upio,* a village of Provence, in the diocefe and viguery of Graffe. *p. Graß. Ur, Fiery,* and *Brangol,* places of Rouflillon, in the viguery of Cerdagne. *p. Perpignan. Uraigne,* a village of Picardy, in the eleftion of Péronne. *p. Amiens. U/ainvi/le,* a village of Champagne, in the eleftion of Vitry. *p. r'à-e Urancourt,* a village of Artois, in the bailiwick of Bapaume. *p. Bapaume. Urajville,* a village of Normandy, in the eleftion of Valognes. *p. Vahges. Uraux,* a village of Champagne, in the diocefe and eleftion of Châlons. *p. Chalons. Urayi'Ule,* a village of Normandy, in the eleftion of Pont-dcl'Arche. *p. Liuviers. Urbach,* or *Fouday,* a place of Alface, in the diocefe of Strafburg. *p. Strajbourg. Urbanía,* a village of Rouflillon, in the viguery of Confient, *p. Perpignan. Urbeis,* a village of Alfacc, in the bailiwick of Ville, *p. Rouffach. Urban,* or *Dourbcn,* a convent in tlie diocefe of Gap, in Dauphiny.

Urce!, a village of Picardy, in ffta diocefe and eleftion of Laon. *p. Laon, Urcerey,* a place of Alface, in the bailiwick of Beffort. *p. Bcffirt. Ureters,* a village of Berry, in the eleftion of Chatre, *p. la Châtre. Ureignes,* a village of Picardy, in the diocefe and eleftion of Amiens. *p. Amiens. Urdacbe,* an abby, in the diocefe of Bayonne. *p. Bayonne. Urdens,* a fmall town of Armagnac, in the eleftion of Rivière-Verdun. *p. Lctloure. Urde's,* a place of Beam, in the fénéchauflee of Pau. *p. Pau. Urdus,* a village of Beam, in the diocefe and fénéchauflee of Oleron. *f. Oleron. Ure,* a village of Lower Languedoc, in the d:ocefe and receipt of Mendc. *p. Florae. Urecour,* a village of FrancheComté, in the bailiwick of Vefoul. *Vejoul. Uregny,* a village of Picardy, in the diocefe and eleftion of Soiflbns. *p. Soifföns. Urtly,* a village of Picardy, in the eleftion of Mondidier. *p. Mondid-cr. Uremy,* a village of Meflin, in the diocefe and receipt of Metz. *p. Metz. Uretot, le,* a fmall town of Normandy, in the eleftion of Valognes. *p. Vahgnes. Uretm,* a village of Bretagne, in the diocefe and receipt of Nantes, *p, Nantes. Urey,* a village of Burgundy, in the diocefe and bailiwick of Dijon. *p. Dijon. Urgons,* a town of Gafcony, in the eleftion of Landes, *p. S. Sever. Vrgoß'e,* a village of Armagnac, in the diocefe and eleftion of Auch. *p. Mont-deMarjan. Uriage,* a village of Dauphiny, in the diocefe and eleftion of Grenoble. *p. Grenoble. Uriat Sä Joze,* a fmall town of Auvergne, in the eleftion of Riom. *p. Rkm. Urigtemcvze,* a village of Champagne, in the election of Rcthcl./. Rett!. *Vrigny,* i. A fmall town of Orléannui, in the election of Hithtvicrs. *p. Ptibiv'icrs.* %. A village of Champagne, in the diocefc and election el Rheims./. *Rheims.* 3. Avillane of Normand.-, in the election of Argentan, *p. Urgenten. Ur'iz,* a village of Bretagne, "m the diocciе and receipt of Nantes, *p. Anceris. Urizy,* a fmall town of Champagne, in the election of Rethel. /. *Ret bel Vrmaib,* a vilhge of Aîface, in the bailiwick of *Mxtzg.p. ¡itrJbcurg. Urciowty* a village ot Picardy, in tíic diocciе and election of Bcauvais. *f. Beauvais. Vrci'y* a village of Champagne, in the diocefe and election ot Chalons. *p. V.try. Urotiy* and *Samenecurfy* village of Picardy, in the government of Montrcu:!. *p. Abbeville. Ur'fi.* i. A village of Berry, in the diocefc and election of Bourges. *p. Bourges.* 2. A place of Etarn, in the receipt of Morias, *p. Pau. xJrouy* a village of Normandy, in the election of Argentan, *p. Argentan. Utphe,* or *S. Marcel-dUrpbe'y* a fmall town of Forez, in the election of Roanne, *p. Roanne. UrrevtlUj* a village of Champagne, in the election of Barfur-Aube. *p, Bar-jur-Aube, Urritue,* a village of Navarre, in the diocefe of Bayonnc. *p. Bayotme. UrrcncbauXj* a village of Picardy, in the election of Doulcns. *p.Dwkns. Urjcbenbeim,* a village ot Alface, in the bailiwick of Marckolíheíin. *U'fit,* a village of Bourbonnois, in the election of Montluçon. *p. Ment façon. Urßnei® YeHяy,* a village of the Ifle of France, in the diocefc and election of Paris. *Baris. ü(yt* a village of Burgundy, in *xJJjiî,* i. A town of Limoiîn; about 2 leagues from ChûreaudeVentadour, /. *Tulles.* 2. A town of Auvergne, in the diocefe and election or S. Flour, *p. S. Flour.* 3. A village of Quercy, in the diocefe and election of Cahors. *p. Cabors. Vß'tl & Lux,* a village of Bourbonnois, in the election of Gannat. *p. Gar.nat. Ufeldun,* a village of Quercy, in the dioccfv-and election of Cahors. *p. Souillac. Ußon.* i. A town of Auvergne; about 4 leagues from Brioude. *p. Jffoire,* 2. A town of Forez, in the election of Montbrifon. *p Mombrifon.* 3. A town of Poitou, in the diocefe and election of Poitiers, *p. Cbaunay. UJly.* т. A fmall town of Brie, in the diocefe and election of Meaux. *p. laFerte'-Gaucber. %.* A village of Normandy, in the election of Falaife. /. *Falaife.* 3. A village of Burgundy, in the bailiwick, of Avalon, *p. Jüvalor.. Ußaritz £f yalzcuy* a town of Gai cony, in the diocefe and receipt ©f Bayonne. *p. Bcyonne. Ufiou,* a towja of Gafcony, in the diocefe and election of Comminges, *p. Mcnirejeau. Uttencbim,* a village of Alfa ce, in the diocefe of Stralburg. *p. Benfeld. Uttenkoffen,* a village of Alface, in the bailiwick of Nidcrbroan. *p. Strajbourg. Utfweiller,* a

village of Alface. in the bailiwick of Bouxviller./. *Saverne. xJtxiat,* a village of Navarre, in the diocefe of Bayonne. *p. Pau, Vuarûgvy,* я place of Champagne, in the dioccicand election of Rheims. *p. Mexicres. Vuen-Beauccupy* a place of Artois, in the diocefe and receipt of S. Omer. *p. S. Omer. Уuец* a village of Champagne, in the diocefe and election of Rheims. *p. Rheims, VmllafatiS)* a fmall town ©f Franche Comté, in the bailiwick of Vcfoul. *f. Lure. Vyvn.* See *Vion. Uxain,* a village of Béarn, in the receipt of Morias, *p. Pau. Uisan.* i. A village of Condomois, in the diocefe and election of Condom, *p. Condom, m..* A village of Beam, in the receipt of Morias, *p. Pau. Uayt fe,* a village of ßourbonnois, in the election of S. Amand. *p. S. jfmand. Uzeib-desOuISs,* a village of Quercy, in the diocefe and election of Cahors. *p. Cabors. Vtttgtf* a country of Lower Languedoc, of which Uzés is the capital; it is watered by the Rhone, the Serre, and the Gardon.

Uxel, a town of Bretagne,-with a bailiwick; about 6 leagues from S. Brieux. *p. Lamballe. U%ercbesy* an ancient town of Limofin, built on a rock near the Vefere, in the diocefe of Limoges, and election of Brives; o-§ leagues from Brives, 15 from Limoges, 35 from Cahors, 50 from Montauban, 62 from Touloufe, *f* from Tulles, zi£ from Aurillac,and lo$$ from Paris. *Bureau de poße. Uzen,* a village of Lower Languedoc, in the diocefe and receipt of Viviers, *p. Aubenai, Uze'si* a city of Lower Languedoc, in the generality of Montpellier, the capital of Uzege, the fee of a bifhop, fuffrav. an ofNarboraie; about 6 leagues from Nîmes, 7 from Bcaucairc, 7 from Bagnols, 8 from Avignon, 9 from Andufe, and 7 from Alais. *Bureau de poße. Uzet,* a town of Saintonge, in the diocefe and election of Saintes, *p. Saintes. Uxets,* a town of Bazadois, in the election of Condom, *p. Bazas. Uzos,* a village of Béarn» in the receipt of Pau. *p. Pau, U%uraty* a place of Limofin, in the diocefe and election of Limoges. *p. Limogts, Uzy,* a village of Burgundy, ia the bailiwick of Avalon, *f. Avalon.*

W.

TIMABAN, or *Waben & Greffiers,* a town of Picardy, in the élection of Abbeville, *p. Montreuil-fur-mer. Wacon,* a village of Meflin, in the diocefe and receipt of Toul. *p. Toŭ/. lVacourt,* a place of Picardy, in the eleition of Abbeville, *f. Abbeville. Wadencourt,* a place of Picardy, in the eleition of Péronne. *p. Péronne. ffadimont,* a villageof Champagne, in the diocefe and eleitien of Rheims. *f. Rubel. Wadoriville,* a village of Meflin, in the diocefe and receipt of Verdun. *p. Virdun. jVadringbent,* a village of Artois, in the diocefe an4 receipt of S. Omer. *p. S. Omer. Wagnon,* a village «f Champagne, in the elcaion of Rcthel. *pr.Rabcl. Wagnonlieu,* a place of Artois, in the diocefe and bailiwick of Arras. *p. Arras. Wagnomnlle,* a place of Artois, in the bailiwick of Lens. *p. Lens. Wabanier,* a village of Flanders, in the fubdelcgation of Lille, *p. Lille.* WM *& Siuatre-Vaux,* a village of Artois, in the bailiwick of Hefdin *p. He/dm. Wailly,* a village of Picardy, in tlie diocefe and eleition of Amiens, *p. Abbeville. jVailly-le-Hercbeu,* a place of Picardy, in the eleition of Péronne. *p. Péronne. Walbacb,* a village of Alface, in the bailiwick of Ribauville./'. *Altkirch. Waldclw'ßeim,* a village of Alface, in the bailiwick of Saverne. *p. Sa. verne. Walenbeim,* a place of Alface, in the bailiwick of Haguenau. *p. HaWittnau. Walff,* a village of Alface, in the diocefe of Stralburg. *p. Benfeld. Willdbach,* a village of Alface, in the bailiwick of Fenctte. *f. Шпцuu Wallefn,* 2 village ef FrancheComté, in the diocefe and bailiwick of S. Claude./. 5. *Claude. Waller)* a village of Haînaut, in the government of M au beuge, *p. Valenciennes. Waiters & Hej-ta;ng,* a village of Flanders, in the iubdelegation of Bouchain.# *Boucbain, Wallfebeidf* a village of Alfacc, in the diocefe of Strafburg. *f. Saverne. Vallyi* a village of Picardy, in the election of Abbeville, *p. Abbeville, Waljcappei-i* a village of Flanders, in the fubdelcgation of Cafifcl. *p. Caf fii. Waltenbcim,* a village of Alfacc, in the bailiwick of Laudier, *p. Huninque. WulierJbaA,* a village of Alface, in the diocefe of Strafburg. *p. Ssrafàcurg, Walrighßin,* a village of Alface, in the bailiwick of

Ferrette. *p. Alitireb. Walmstl,* a place of Picardy, in the election of Péronne. *p. Peronne. Wambaye* Êf *Roquier,* a village of Flanders, in the iubdelegation of Caffel. *p. Cambray. Wambe',* a village of Picardy, in the diocefe and election of Beauvais. *p. Beauvais. Wambrecbits,* a town of Flanders, in the iubdelegation of Lille, *p. Lille. Wancourt,* and *Wande.'wurt,* villages of Artois, in the bailiwick of Arras, *p. Arras. Wandigny,* a village of Flanders, in the fubdclegation of Bouchain. *p. Boucbain. Wane/,* a village of Picardy, in the election of Abbeville, *p. Abbeville. Wangen,* a town of Alface; about half a league from Wefthotfcn, and 3 leagues from Straiburg. *p. Mo/ßotim. Wam%cnau, la,* a town of Alfacc, the chief place of a bailiwick. *p. Stra/bourg. Warcj,* a village of Meffin, in the diocefe andreceiptofVerdun.. *Vcrdun. Warde,le,* a village of Flanders, in the iubdelegation of Douay. *p. Viuay. WarfufS,* a village of Picardy, ia the diocefe and election of Amiens. *p. Corbie. Wargnies,* a village of Pkardy, in the election of Doulcns. *p. Doulens, Wargomculin,* a village of Champagne, in the election of See. Manéhould. *p. Sie. Manehould. Warinfroy,* a village of Picardy, ia the election of Crêpy. *Cre/y. Warlainy,* a village of Flanders, in the fubdelcgation of Douay. *p. Douay. Warlincourt,* a place of A: tois, in the bailiwick of Lens. *p. Lens. Warloy-Bâillon,* a fmall town of Picardy, in the election of Doulens. *p. Doulcns. Warluis,* a village of Picardy, in the diocefe and election of Beauvais. *p Beauvais. Warlus.* I. A village of Picardy, in the diocefe andclection of Amiens. *p. Aniens.* 2. A place of Artois, in the diocefe and bailiwick of Arras. *p. Arras. Warlwtel,* a village' of Artois, in the diocefe and bailiwick of Arras. *p. Arras. Warneton,* a town of Flanders, on the Lys; about 3 leagues fromYpres, and 3 from Lille, *p. Lille. Warniller,* a village of Picardy, in the election of Mondidicr. *p. Mondidicr. Warq-les-Majons,* a village of Champagne, in the election of Rethcl. *p. Rethel. Warquehal,* a town of Flanders, in the fubdclegation of *VxWt.p.liUt. Warquies,* a village of Picardy, in the election of Mondidier..AiW/Vfcr. *Warti,* a town of Picardy, in the election of Clermont, *p, Clermont-enBeau-votßs. Wartigny,* a fmall town of Picardy, in the election of Guife. *p. Guije. Wajdone's,* a village of Artois, in the bailiwick of S. Pol.-*p. Arras. Wafgau,* or *Wajgovj,* a considerable country of Alface, which reaches from Wciffembourg to Saverne. *Wafnes-au-Bacq,* a village of Flanders, in the fubdclegation of Bou the bailiwick of Hefdin. *p. Hefdn. JVaurans.* I. A village of Artoisr in the bailiwick of Aire. *p. Aire.* 2. A village of Artois, in the bailiwick of S. Pol. *p. Arras. Wavrecbain,* a village of Flanders, in the fubdelegation of Bouchain. *p. Boucbain. Waurille,* a village of Meflin, in the diocefc of Treves, *p. Sttnay. Waux,* a village of Artois, in the bailiwick of Hefdin. *p. Hefdin. WaxemmeS)* a village of Flanders, in thcfubdelcgationof Douay .*p. Douay. Ifuz'eres,* a village of Flanders, in the fubdelegation of Douay. A. *Douay. Waxigny,* a fmall town of Champagne, in the dioccfe and election of Rheims, *p. Rbcims. Weaume.* See *IVeaune. iVeaune,* a fmall river ot Provence, which runs into the Mediterranean near Marfeille. *rfeckeljbcim,* a village of Alface, in the bailiwick of Ribauville. *p. Colmar. IVediben,* a village of Boulonnois, in thegenerality of Amiens.*p. Amiens. fVe'e,* a village of Nivernois, in the diocefe and election of Nevers. *p. Nevers. ff eiller.* I. A village ef Alface, in the bailiwick of Gebveiller. *p. Rouffacb.* a. A village of Alface, in the bailiwick of Altkirch, *p. Altkirch. Jftinburg.* I. A village of Alface, in the bailiwick of Baar.*p.Straßourg. z.* A village of Alface, in the bailiwick of Oberbronnc. *p. Haguenau. IVeiJfembourg,* or *Croat -Fifabourg,* an ancient town of Ah'ace, in thedioccfeof Spire; about 5 leagues from Landau. *Bureau de ptße. fViiúficim,* a village of Alface, in the bailiwick of Benfeld. *p. Benfeld. IVemarjcafel,* a village of Flanders, in the fubdelegation of Caffcl.f. *CaJJU. JVcndin.* I. A village of Artois, in the bailiwick of Lens. *p. Lens.* 2. A village of Artois, in the bailiwick of Bcthune. *p. Betbune. TYenouemm,* a village of Artois, W I in the election of Abbeville, *p. Abbeville. Wiberpeim,* a village of Alface, in in the J.occfe of Stralburg. *p. S:raJbsurg. Wicbcrßem,* a village of Alface, in the bailiwick of Bouxviller. *p. Saverne. Widefcntair.e,* a village of Normandy, in the election ef S. Lo. *p. Careman Widdert,* a village of Boulonnois, in the generality of Amiens, *p. Amiens. Widcnon,* a village of Boulonnois, in the generality of Amiens, *p. Boulogne. Widenjcblen,* a village of Alface, in the bailiwick of Enfifheim. *p. Rouffach. Widerenbeim,* a village of Alface, in the diocefe of Strafburg. *p. Strasbourg. Witl-le-Montitr,* a figniory of Boulonnois, in the generality ot Amiens. *Wiencourt & TEjuippe',* a village cf Picardy, in the diocefe and election of Amiens, *p. S. Suentin. Wier-aux-Bois,* a village of Boulonnois, in the generality of Amiens. *p. Boulogne. Wiere* fef *Orefmieux,* a place of Artois, in the bailiwick of Lens.f. *Lens. Wieie-Effrey,* a village of Boulonnois, in the generality of Amiens. *p. Бо-.logne. W.etrer.es,* a village of Artois, in the bailiwick of Aire. *p. Aire. Wuifs, les,* a village of Normandy, in the election of Caudebec. *p.Caudebi-c. Wigr.ebics,* a fmall town of Hninaut, in the government of Avefncs *p. Avefnes. Wign.ccurt,* 3 village of Champagne, in the election of Rethel. *p, Reibel. Wildcrfbacb,* a plnce of AlГ3ce, in the diocefe of Stralburg. *p.Strafliourg. Willecourt,* a village of Picardy, in the election of Péronne. *p. PSronne. Willem,* a village of Flanders, in *IVitre-aux-Bms,* я village of Boulonnois, in the generality of Amiens. *p. Amiens. rVurcban,* a place of Boulonnois, in the generality of Amiens, *f. Boulogne. Wuxtry & Burigny,* a fmall town of Champagne, in the diocefe and election ofUhcims. *p. Rbcims. Wmtnht'im,* a vilbge of Alface, in tbe bailiwick of Thann, *p. Rouffacb. ffo/ffrangtzen,* a village of Alface, in the diocefc of Bale. *p. Strajbourg. Wolffrjdorfs,* a village of Alface, in the bailiwick of Thann, *p. Rmffacb. firo!ßfltim,* a village of Alface, in the bailiwick of Vcrfthoften. *p. MolJbeim. Wollenbe'm,* a place of Alface, in the bailiwicK of Bouxvillcr. *p. Saverne. WoUJehwciller,* a village of Alface, in the bailiwick of

Ferrette. *p.Hunlngue. JVolftbeim,* a place of Alface, in the diocefe of Stralburg. *p. Mo:ßxim. Wolßieim,* a village of Alface, in the bailiwick of Wcrtfhoffcn. /. *MJjhcim. Wolxbeim,* a village of Alface, in the bailiwick of Hacftcin. *p MolJbeim. Wortb,* a place of Alfare, in the diocefe of Stralburg. *p. Strttjbcurg. Woucnbeim,* a village of Alface, in the bailiwick of Roufi'aeh. *p.Rouffacb. fVraque-Moulin,* a village or Picardy, in the election of Mondidier. *p. Mondidier. Wrdacbe.* See *Urdacbe. JVrelinguikem,* a fmall town of Flanders, in the fubdelegation of Lille, *p. Lille.* Writ, a village of Flanders, in the fubdelegation of Douay. *p. Douay. Wmcourt & Ijengrtmcl,* a fmall town of Picardy, in the diocefe and election of Amiens, *p. Amern. WmJ/inbeim,* a village of Alface, in the diocefe of Stralburg. *p. Моlвкm. IVu. ra, л* village of Flanders, in the fubdelegation of Lille, *p. Lille.* Wuldtr, a village of Flanders, in the fubdelegation of Bergues. *p. Bergan. ffultverd'wgbe,* a village of Flanders, in the fubdelegation of CaffeL *p. Ceffil.* Wut. I. A village of Champagne, in the election of Tonmirc. *p. Tonnerre,* ». A village of VexinFran ois, in the election of Pontoife. *p. Pcnioijc. IVußbauJen,* a village of Alface, in the bailiwick of Kockerfberg. *p. Strafiiow g. H'y.* i. Ä village of Kormandy, in the election of Chaumont. *p. Magny.* i. A village of Hainaut, in the generality of Maubcugc. *p. Valenciennes.* 4. See *Vy.*
X.
X'MHTES. Sec *Samtes.*
Xaintonge. See *Saintonge.*
Xuintray, a village of Poitou, 'in the" election of Niort, *p. Niort.* Xamhis, a village of Angoumois, in the election of Cognac, *p. Cognac. Xancoins.* See *Sancoins. Xanflon,* a villige of Poitou, in the election of Fontenay.. *Fontenayle-Comte. Xandci-ille,* a village of Saintonge, in the diocefc and election of Saintes. *p. Barbefieux. Xamey,* a village of Mcffin, in thr bailiwick of Vic. *p. Vic. Xavieres я* place of Picardy, in the election of Doulens. *p. Amiens.* Xelaincourt, a place of Mcffin, in the diocefe and receipt of Metz, *f. Metz. Xertigny,* a place of Lorraine; 4 leagues from Apinal, and 3 from Plombières. *Xcullty, я* village of Meffin, in the diocefc and receipt of *Toul.p.Toul. Xocourt,* a village of Mcflin, in the diocefc and receipt of Metz. *p. Mets. Xouagjange,* a village of Mcffin, in the diocefe and receipt of Meti. *p. Metz. Xauffe,* er *Vmjjc,* aplace of Meffin, *Xurtj* a village of Meflin» in the diocefe and receipt of Metz. *f. Ук.*
Y.
Y, a village of Picard/, in the election of Péronne. *p. Pe'rotine. Yanvllle,* a village of Normandy, in the diocefe and election of Rouen. *p. Rouen. Yanecurt,* a place of Picardy, in the diocefe and election of Noyon. *p. Perenne, Tauccurt,* a village of Picardy, in the election of Douiens. *p» Doulcns. Yburgcs,* a place of Provence, in the vigucry of Forcalquier. *p. ForcaЦuгeе. Tcqucbteuf,* a village of Normandy, in the diocefe and election of Rouen, *p. Raten. Ycbies & Guignes,* a fmall town ©f Gatinois, in the election of Melun. *p. Guignes,* Te/ on, a village of Normandy, in the diocefe and election of Rouen. *p. Dieppe. Yenville,* a town of Orléannois, in the election of Pithivicrs; about I league from Toury, and 9 from Orleans, *p. Toury. Yeres.* See *Hieres. Yermemmj'tihy* a village of Bcauce, in the diocefe and elect.on of Chartres, *p. Chartres. fere,* a river of Normandy, whirh rifes in Caux, and runs into the fea about a league from Eu. *Yerre,* a river of Brie, which runs into the Seine at VillencuvcS.-Georges. *Yerres y* a village of the Ifle of France, in the diocefe and election of Paris, *p. Villeneuve-S.-G earges. Yervilhy* a village of Normandy, ín the diocefe and election of Rouen. *Bureau de pofie. Yefme & ÂV/wavillageof Beauce,* in the diocefe and election of Chartres, *p. Maintenon. Yeut iif.e-d* a fmall ifbnd, about a league in length, near the coaft of Toit ou. *YeurCj* a town of Beauce, in the election of Châteaudun./. *Hfiers. Yevre,* a river of Berry. *Yevre & Courcelle,* a village of Champagne, in the election of Barfur-Aube, *p. Bar-fur-Aube. Yeurc-la-Vilky* a village of Orléannois, in the election of Pithiviers. *p. Bue. Yeure-le-Chátel,* a town of Orléannois, in the election of Pithiviers. *p. Pitbl-viers. Yffendie,* a village of Bretagne, in the diocefe and receipt or S. Malo. *p. S. Malo. YjßniaCi* a village of Bretagne, ¡n the diocefe and receipt of S. Bricux. *p. S. Bricux. Yfsties,* a village of Bretagne,:n the diocefe and receipt oí S. Malo. *p. S. Mah. Yguereinde,* a fmall town of Forez, in the election of Roanne, *p. Rcani.e. Ymarey* a village of Normandy, i n the diocefe and election of Rouen. *p. Rouen. Ymeray,* a village of Beauce, in the diocefe and election of Chartres. *p. Chartres, YmonvlUe-ia-Grande,* a village of Beauce, in the diocefe anij election of Chartres, *p. Chartres. Yneuily* a place of Berry, in the chatellany ,f S. Julien. *Ynosy* n place ot Lower Languedoc, in the diocefe and receipt of Mendc. *p. Meble.* Yollety a village of Auvergne, in the clecti-'П of A urillac. *p. ¿Ét/гШас. Ycny* a village of Dombes, in the diocefe of Lyons, *p. Bourg-en-ErejJ'e. Yon& 'Cer'verieUy* a village of Bugcy, in the bailiwick of Bcllcy. *p. Bdley.* Yon, *Igy* a fmall river of Poitou. *Yoneoy* a village of Champagne, in the diocefe and election of Rheims. *p. Rheims. Yonne,* a river which rifes in the mountains of Burgundy, and puffing by Crevant, Auxerre, Joigny, and Sens, and receiving fome other rivers in its courfe, falls into the Seine at Montereau, in Champagne. *Youjct* a village of Lower Lan guedoc, in the diocefc and receipt of Uzes: it has a mineral fpring. *Youx ¿S? Ladoux,* a village of Auvergne, in the election of Riom. *p. Riom. Youx-la-Boulle,* a village of Bourbonnois, in the election of Gannat. *p. G annate Yprcvitlc,* a village of Normandy, in the election of Montivilliers. *p. Fe.amp,* Yquelon, a village of Normandy, in the diocefe and election of Coutanccs. *p. Coût anees. Trais,* a village of Poitou, in the diocefe and election of Poitiers. *p. J&r-vauh. Yrodvur,* a village of Bretagne, in the diocefe and receipt of S. Malo. *p. Bechen/. YruA¿, S. Purre-d,* a village of Gnf ony, in the diocefe and receipt of Bayonne. *p. Bcyonne.* YwUlac, a vilbge of Bretagne, in the diocefe and receipt of Quimper. *p. Quimper.* Ys-S.-Martiti'd, a village of Berry, in the diocefe and election of Bourges. *p. Bourges,* Yfeures, a town of Tournine, in the (lection of Loches, *p.*

Loches. Yjneauville, a village of Normandy, in the diocefe and election of Rouen. *p. Rouen. Yßar.don*, a fmall town of Limofin, in the election of Brives. *p. B rives. Yffät & la Tourelle*, a village of Auvergne, in the election of Riom. *p. Ri'jm. Yß'cngeaux*. See *Jßgnaux. Yß'oudun*. See *Ißaudun. Yßiire*. See *Jffoire. Yirac*, a fmall town of Auvergne, in the election of Aurillac./../ 4«n//i?r. *Yttre*, a village of Picardy, in the eleition of Péronnc. *p. Bapaume. Yveenquej* a village of Normandy, in the election of Caudebec. *Yerville. Yvernau/ t*. See *Ivernault. Yverfay*, a village of Poitou, in the diocefc and election of Poitiers. *p. Poitiers, Yvesj* a ilhgc of Aunis, in the diocefc and elc¿tion of Rochelle, *p. Rocht fort. Y-vctaux, les*, a village of Normandy, in the election of Falaifc. *p. Argentan. Yvetct*. i. A town of Normandy, in the diocefc of Rouen, and election of Caudcbcc; 10 leagues from Pont-Audemer, 27 from Caen, 12 from Havre, 8£ from Rouen, 8 from Fecamp, and 41 from Paris. *Bureau de foße*. 1. A village of Normandy, in the election of Valognes *p.Valognes. Yvcvotc*, a village of Normandv, in the election of Valognes. *p. Va bgne. Yvias*, a village of Bretagne, in the diocefe and receipt of S. Bricu. *p. S. Brieux. Yvicrs*, a town of Saintonge, in the diocefe and election of Saintes. *p. Saintes. Yvignac*, a village of Bretagne, in the diocefc and receipt of S. Malo. *p. Braoa. Yvil/e*, a village of Normandy, in the election of Conches, *p. Ic Neuf bourg. YvUle-fur-Seine*, a village of Normandy, in the election of PontAudemer. *p. Boucacbard. Yvoix*. See *Car'gnan. Yvory*, a village of Franche-Comté, in the bailiwick, of Salins, *p. Salins. Yvoy*, a vilbge of Orleannois, in the election of Bcaugency. *p. TaHiy. Yitoy-U-Pre'*. See *Ivoi-Ie-Pre'. Y-vracy* a village of Guienne, in the diocefe and election of Bourdcaux. *p. Bourdcaux. Yurac-en-Ambares*, a village of Guicnne, in the diocefe and election of Bourdeaux. *p. Libourne. Yvré'tEvêque*, a town of Maine, in the diocefe and election of Mans. *p. le Mans. Y'ure-le-PoU'm*, a town of Anjouf in the election of Flèche, *p. Foultow te. Yvry*. T. A village of Bourgundy,

in the d-occÊB and receipt of Metz, *p. Metz*. the diocefe of Strafburg, *p.&rafbntrg*. *Zülßesm*, a village of Alface, in the bailiwick of Altknch. *p. Jilt, klrcb*. *Zimmcrfoe'm*, a village of Alface, in the bailiwiok of Landfer. *f. Hunmgue*. *Z'immerbacb*, a village of Alface, in the bailiwick of Ribauviile. *f, Colmar*. *Zlitxel*, a fmall river of Alface that runs into the Sour, a little below Stimbourg. *Zoafrt*, a village of Picardy, in the government of Ardres. *p. Calais*. *Zdeux, ¡es*, a village of Picardy, in the generality of Amiens, *p. Bmlogve*. *Zornkoff*, a village of Alface, in the diocefe of Straiburg. *p.Straßyourg*. *Zotheux*, a village of Picardy, in the generality of Amiens, *p. Montreuil*. *Zcuffcnne*, a village of Meifm, in the diocefe and receipt of Metfc. *p. Metz*. *Zudanßue*, a village of Artois, in the diocefe and bailiwick of S. Omer. *p. S. Omer*. *Zuderotte*, a village of Flanders, in the fubdelegation of Dunkirk, *p.. Dunlerque*. *Zudquerqtte*, a village of Artois, in the diocefe and bailiwick of Arras. *p. Arras*. *Zuidberquin*, a village of Flanders, in the fubdelegation of Caffel. *p. Caffel*. *Zuidj-eVne*, a village of Flanders, in the fubdelegation of Caffel. *p. Caffel*. *Zurdes*, an ancient chateau of Provence, belonging to the biftiop of Siftcron. *p. Sj/teron*. *Zutzetidwff*, a village of Alface, in the diocefe of Straiburg. *p. Stray bcitrg*. *Zuythoulck*, a fmall town of Flanders, in the fubdelegation of Baillcul, *p. BmlltuL* 1 и LORRAIN, MESSIN, TOULOIS, And VERDUNOIS, HOT MENTIONED IN THE GAZETTEER. *day*, 8 leagues SSW. from Thionville.

Omelment, 2¿ leagues N. from Vaudemont.
Or.ry, 3J leagues SSE. from Metz.
Ormes, 5 leagues S. from Nancy.
Ortntpivlllcr, 5 leagues N. from Bitche.
Orgcvaux, 4 leagues S. from Metz.
Orne, 3 leagues NNE. from Verdun.
Ottciueyler, 4J leagues N. from Sarbruck.
Ou/trancour, 5 leagues SSW. from Mirecour.
Oußrelar, 3j leagues NW. from Sarbruck.
P.
P.igney, 3 leagues W. from Toul. *pagny*, *г* leagues N. from Pont-àMouffon.
Paigney, 5 leagues SSW. from Toul.
Parfinru, 9 leagues SSW. from Thionville. *Paroye*, 3 leagues NE. from Luneville. *Pajfervant*, 11 leagues S. from Mirecour. *Pattern*, 1 league NW. from Sarrelouis. *Perlt*, 4$ leagues NNE. from Thionville. *Perte*, 2 leagues SSE. from Metz. *Pettelange*, 3 leagues SW. from Sarguemines. *Piccbcn*, 3 leagues S. from Blamont. *Pierre.Pence*, 3 leagues S. from Blamont.
PUrrefitte, 4 leagues W. from. S. Mihel.
Pierrefirt, 2$ leagues SW. from Pont-à-Mouffon.
Pierrefmt, 6§ leagues W. from Thionville.
Plaine, river, rifes near Raon-fur Plaine, and runs into the Meurte, near Raon-l'Eftape.
Plateville, ij leagues WNW. from Metz.,
Plombieret, 7 leagues S. from Ep'uial.
Pcmpey, 4 leagues S. from Pont-à-MoulTbn.
Pent, 2 leagues SE. from Remiremont.
5 *Avoid, i* leagues SW. from Sarbruck. i.
Aman, 5J leagues SE. from BarJe-Duc. 6
Balmm, 5 leagues S. from Mirecour.
S. *Germain*, 3 leagues SW. from Toul.
   S. *Germain*, 4J leagues SW. from Luneville. 5. *Germain*, *z%* leagues W. from
   Metz.
S. *Пои*, 3 leagues KKW. from Barle Duc.
S. *Martin*, 2 leagues W. from Blamont.
S. *Mengt*, 4 leagues SW. from Mirecour.

S. Mibel, on the Meufe, 8 leagues NE. from Bar-le-Duc, 17 SE. from Metz, 6 N. from Void, 8 S. from Verdun, 14 W. from Nancy, and 68 J E. from Paris. 5. *Nicolas,* 25 leagues SSE. from Nancv. & *Pierremont;* 3 leagues SW from Thionville. S. *Vincent,* 4 leagues E. from Toul. *S. Sauveur,* 5 leagues SSW. from

Sarbourg. *S. Thieiaut,* 5 leagues S. from Neauf cbûteau.

5. *Thomas,* 4 leagues NW. from Clermont-en-Argonne. *Sie. Margaret,* 1 league E. from S. Die. *Saiff'eray,* 3 leagues S. from Pont-à-Mouübn.

Salins, river, joins the Seille at Salonne. *Saint,* 7 leagues S. from Sarbourg. *Sulonne,* i league S. from ChâteauSalins. *Sal/burg,* on the Sare, ¿ league SE. from Sar-Albe. *Sampigny,* 2 leagues S. from S. Mi hel. *Sar-Albe,* on the Sare, 3$ leagues S. from Sarguemines, and 8 N. from Sarbourg.

Sarhruck, on the Sare, 6 leagues SE. from Sarrelouis, and 26 NNW. from Stralburj. *Sarech,* 1 league N. from Sarbourg. *Sarfeline,* 2 leagues NE. from Sarrelouis. *Sarguemines,* or *Zar-Guemine,* on the Sare, 6 leagues W., from DeuxPonts, 8 W. from Bitche, and 19 E. from Merz. *Sar-Infemin,* i league S. from Sarguemines. f *Samay,* 2 leagues N. from Bar-IeDuc. *Sartverden,* on the Sare, 6 leagues W. from Bitch, and 6 S. from Sarguemines. *Sau/cy,* 2 leagues S. from S. Die. *Sauljures,* 5 leagues S. from Toul. *Saulxures,* 6 leagues E. from Remiremonf. *Schawenbourg,* 5 leagues NNE from Sarrelouis. *Sekmalenlbal,* 2 leagues S. from Bitche. *Scborlach,* i¿ leagues N. from Bitche. *Sei¡rnev:l/e,* 3 leagues N. from Bar-leDuc. *Selgincour,* 4 leagues S. from Toul. *Seile,* 3- leagues S. from Blamont. *Senoncour,* 3 leagues SSW. from Verdun. *Sermn,* 5 leagues NNW. from Clermont-en-Argonne. *Serrieres, ₂* leagues SE. from Pontà-Mouflon. *Seieey-aux-Bois,* 3J leagues WNW. from Nancy. *Sierjperg,* 2 leagues NW. from Sarrelouis. *Siliigny,* 4 leagues S. from Metz. *Sa try,* 3 lergaes E. from S. Mihel. *Sionvlller,* I league NNE.from Luneville. *Sirfliiff,* at the conflux of the Nid and the Sare, 3 leagues NW. from Sarrelouis. *Sorneville,* 4J leagues E. from Nancy. *Soulefmes,* 3 leagues SW. from Verdun. *Spitzbergen,* 2j leagues NE. from S. Die. *Stcinbach,* 5 leagues SSE. fora Bitche. *Steinville,* 3 leagues S. from Bar-leDuc. *Sturtzelbrun,* ij leagues E. fron» Bitche.